ROUTLEDGE HANDBOOK OF SPORT COMMUNICATION

The *Routledge Handbook of Sport Communication* is the only book to offer a fully comprehensive and in-depth survey of the contemporary discipline of sport communication. It explores communication within, through, and for sport in all its theoretical, conceptual, cultural, behavioral, practical, and managerial aspects, tracing the contours of this expansive, transdisciplinary, and international discipline and demonstrating that there are few aspects of contemporary sport that don't rely on effective communication.

Including contributions from leading sport media and communication scholars and professionals from around the world, the book examines new media, traditional (print, broadcast, and screen) media, sociological themes in communication in sport, and management issues, at every level, from the interpersonal to communication within and between sport organizations and global institutions. Taking stock of current research, new ideas, and key issues, this book is an essential reference for any advanced student, researcher, or practitioner with an interest in sport communication, sport business, sport management, sport marketing, communication theory, journalism, or media studies.

Paul M. Pedersen is Professor of Sport Management at Indiana University, USA, and founding editor of the *International Journal of Sport Communication.*

ROUTLEDGE HANDBOOK OF SPORT COMMUNICATION

Paul M. Pedersen

LONDON AND NEW YORK

First published in paperback 2015
First published 2013
by Routledge
2 Park Square, Milton Park, Abingdon, Oxon OX14 4RN

and by Routledge
711 Third Avenue, New York, NY 10017

Routledge is an imprint of the Taylor & Francis Group, an informa business

British Library Cataloguing in Publication Data
A catalogue record for this book is available from the British Library

Library of Congress Cataloging in Publication Data
Routledge handbook of sport communication / edited by Paul Pedersen.
p. cm.
1. Communication in sports--Handbooks, manuals, etc. I. Pedersen, Paul Mark.
GV567.5.R68 2013
796.06'9--dc23
2012036637

ISBN: 978-0-415-51819-2 (hbk)
ISBN: 978-1-138-91695-1 (pbk)
ISBN: 978-0-203-12348-5 (ebk)

Typeset in Bembo
by FiSH Books, London.

Printed and bound by CPI Group (UK) Ltd, Croydon, CR0 4YY

CONTENTS

FIGURES

TABLES

CONTRIBUTORS

Andrew Baerg, PhD, *University of Houston-Victoria, USA*
Barbara Barnett, PhD, *University of Kansas, USA*
Frederick L. Battenfield, PhD, *North Greenville University, USA*
Alina Bernstein, PhD, *College of Management, Israel*
Christoph Bertling, PhD, *German Sport University Cologne, Germany*
Andrew C. Billings, PhD, *University of Alabama, USA*
Valérie Bonnet, PhD, *University of Toulouse 3, France*
Trygve B. Broch, PhD candidate, *Norwegian School of Sport Sciences, Norway*
Natalie Brown, *University of Alabama, USA*
Bryan Butler, PhD, *University of Houston, USA*
Beth A. Cianfrone, PhD, *Georgia State University, USA*
Galen Clavio, PhD, *Indiana University, USA*
Ian Cunningham, PhD candidate, *Charles Sturt University, Australia*
Stephen W. Dittmore, PhD, *University of Arkansas, USA*
Andrea N. Eagleman, PhD, *Massey University, New Zealand*
Tiffany E. Fields, JD, *University of Arkansas, USA*
John A. Fortunato, PhD, *Fordham University, USA*
Kirsten Frandsen, PhD, *Aarhus University, Denmark*
Marion E. Hambrick, PhD, *University of Louisville, USA*
Marie Hardin, PhD, *The Pennsylvania State University, USA*
Robin L. Hardin, PhD, *University of Tennessee, USA*
John Harris, PhD, *Glasgow Caledonian University, Scotland*
John S. Hill, PhD, *University of Alabama, USA*
Maria Hopwood, *University of Northampton, England*
Thomas Horky, PhD, *Macromedia University, Germany*
Sharon Hutton, PhD, *University of Tennessee, USA*
Holger Ihle, PhD, *German Sport University Cologne, Germany*
Jeffrey W. Kassing, PhD, *Arizona State University, USA*
Edward (Ted) M. Kian, PhD, *Oklahoma State University, USA*

Daekyung Kim, PhD, *Idaho State University, USA*
Kihan Kim, PhD, *Seoul National University, Korea*
Yu Kyoum Kim, PhD, *Florida State University, USA*
Elsa Kristiansen, PhD, *Norwegian School of Sport Sciences, Norway*
Dae Hee Kwak, PhD, *University of Michigan, USA*
Jacquie L'Etang, PhD, *Queen Margaret University, Scotland*
Guy Lochard, PhD, *University of Paris 3, France*
Adam Love, PhD *Mississippi State University, USA*
Tywan G. Martin, PhD *University of Miami, USA*
Joel G. Maxcy, PhD, *Temple University, USA*
Erin McNary, PhD, *Fontbonne University, USA*
Lindsey J. Meân, PhD, *Arizona State University, USA*
Joe Moore, PhD, *University of Central Missouri, USA*
Matthew Nicholson, PhD, *La Trobe University, Australia*
Jörg-Uwe Nieland, PhD, *German Sport University Cologne, Germany*
Joshua R. Pate, PhD, *James Madison University, USA*
Ann Pegoraro, PhD, *Laurentian University, Canada*
Lauren Reichart Smith, PhD, *Auburn University, USA*
David Rowe, PhD, *University of Western Sydney, Australia*
Brody J. Ruihley, PhD, *University of Cincinnati, USA*
Jimmy Sanderson, PhD, *Clemson University, USA*
Thomas Schierl, PhD, *German Sport University Cologne, Germany*
Hans J. Scholl, PhD, *University of Washington, USA*
Brad Schultz, PhD, *University of Mississippi, USA*
Mary Lou Sheffer, PhD, *University of Southern Mississippi, USA*
Merryn Sherwood, PhD candidate, *La Trobe University, Australia*
Peter Simmons, DComm, *Charles Sturt University, Australia*
James Skinner, PhD, *Griffith University, Australia*
Barbara Stelzner, PhD, *Macromedia University, Germany*
G. Clayton (Clay) Stoldt, EdD, *Wichita State University, USA*
Rasmus K. Storm, PhD candidate, *Danish Institute for Sports Sciences, Denmark*
Ilan Tamir, PhD, *Bar-Ilan University, Israel*
Jianjun Tang, PhD, *Shanghai University of Sport, China*
John Vincent, PhD, *University of Alabama, USA*
Travis Vogan, PhD, *University of Iowa, USA*
Ulrik Wagner, PhD, *University of Southern Denmark, Denmark*
Patrick Walsh, PhD, *Indiana University, USA*
Richard D. Waters, PhD, *University of San Francisco, USA*
Wei Wei, PhD, *Chengdu Sport University, China*
Lawrence A. Wenner, PhD, *Loyola Marymount University, USA*
Erin Whiteside, PhD, *University of Tennessee, USA*
Antonio S. Williams, PhD, *Indiana University, USA*
Sang Keon Yoo, PhD candidate, *Indiana University, USA*
Lira Yun, *Seoul National University, Korea*
Matthew H. Zimmerman, PhD candidate, *Ball State University, USA*

INTRODUCTION

Paul M. Pedersen

Sport has become one of the leading economic industries around the globe, with products and services ranging from golf instruction and cricket ball production to World Cup soccer entertainment and amateur volleyball participation. Through active participation, mediated and spectatorial consumption, commercial production and promotion, and overall involvement, sport is a major institution in societies throughout the world; from baseball in Japan to rugby in Australia, and from ice hockey in Canada to soccer in Brazil. In my classroom lectures and previous published work, I have postulated that the key facilitator of sport, not only as an economic force and pervasive sociological and cultural presence, but also as an influential commercial institution, is sport communication (Pedersen, 2013). This claim is still made because the communication aspect of the sport industry affects everyone and everything in the field. While the most obvious way in which communication influences the sport industry is through the media (such as newspaper sports sections, sports television and radio broadcasts, sports websites and social media platforms, and sports magazines), it also impacts interpersonal interactions, sport event settings, organizational functions, and any other areas of the sport industry in which communicative activity takes place. In an attempt to reflect communication's wide-ranging influence and ubiquitous presence in the sport industry, the *Routledge Handbook of Sport Communication* is an academic compilation of topics and authors representing a broad view of sport communication.

In addition to the handbook's international relevance, cutting-edge analyses, leading scholar contributors, up-to-date chapters, and topical blending of theory and practice – this expansive perspective of sport communication is one of the collection's unique and appealing features. Having a published assemblage of sport communication related articles or chapters is not novel in and of itself. That's because, in sport communication and tangential fields, there have been several notable edited volumes; however, for the most part, such collections have been typically fixated on the mediated aspects of sport communication. Examples include Wenner's groundbreaking *Media, Sports and Society* (1989) and *MediaSport* (1998) as well as more recent edited volumes such as Bernstein and Blain's (2003) *Sport, Media, Culture: Global and Local Dimension*, Rowe's (2004) *Critical Readings: Sport, Culture and the Media*, Raney and Bryant's (2006) *Handbook of Sports and Media*, Hundley and Billings' (2010) *Examining Identity in Sports Media*, and Billings' (2011) *Sports Media: Transformation, Integration, Consumption*. Thus, one of the key features of the *Routledge Handbook of Sport Communication* is that, while it also has chapters on mass media, the handbook is quite broad in its approach with only one (Section II) of its five sections devoted exclusively to what is considered the traditional sport mass media. Another related feature is the handbook's cutting-edge approach with another part (Section III) containing chapters specifically focused on emerging and niche media platforms used in the sport industry. Overall, the handbook's fifty chapters are divided into five, ten-chapter sections. Sport communication theories, concepts, and research methodologies are covered in the opening section, followed by the aforementioned mass media section containing chapters on the print sport media (Chapter 11 and Chapter 17), sport documentaries (Chapter 13), sports broadcasting (Chapter 14, Chapter 16, and Chapter 19), sports media reporting and personnel (Chapter 12 and Chapter 15), and even sport fitness (Chapter 20). The third section focuses on new and social media, while the fourth section is a collection of chapters related to sociological issues in sport communication. The business and management aspects of sport communication constitute the handbook's final section.

With these five sections containing chapters affiliated with the theoretical, cultural, behavioral, mediated, conceptual, practical, managerial, and sociological aspects of sport communication, the *Routledge Handbook of Sport Communication* is expansive, examining a wide array of sport communication topics and giving readers an idea of the complexity and breadth of communication in the sport industry. Such a varied collection of scholarship is a testament to the growth, influence, and diversity of sport communication research in particular, and its place in the academy overall. It is not in the too distant past that if a professor took a broad view of the field and wanted to teach sport communication, the suggested route would be to use a collection of journal articles and popular press stories as required reading materials in an assembled course packet for undergraduate and graduate classes. However, over the past few years there has been impressive growth in sport communication textbooks and the body of literature in this area overall. For instance, the overall field is examined in *Strategic Sport Communication* (Pedersen, Miloch, and Laucella, 2007). As expected, though, most textbooks do not go as deep into the various subjects as they are explored in the chapters of this handbook. While some of the other sport communication textbooks and critical or cultural analyses go into some depth with their various subjects, they would not be considered broad in their approach, as they have typically concentrated on niche areas of the field such as public/media relations (for example, Hopwood, Skinner, and Kitchin, 2010; Stoldt, Dittmore, and Branvold, 2012), economics (for example, Jeanrenaud and Késenne, 2006), sports reporting and journalism (for example, Andrews, 2005; Boyle, 2006; Gisondi, 2011; Steen, 2008), and sports media (for example, Boyle and Haynes, 2009; Hutchins and Rowe, 2012; Nicholson, 2007; Rowe, 2011), to list just a few.

While many of the preceding published tomes have focused on one specific aspect or segment of sport communication, the *Routledge Handbook of Sport Communication* casts a purposive wide net and thus examines the field from a variety of paradigms and through multiple disciplinary, theoretical, and practical lenses. Such an all-encompassing approach is in line with a conceptual view of the field – illustrated in the Strategic Sport Communication Model (SSCM). My colleagues and I first released the SSCM just a few years ago in *Strategic Sport Communication* (2007). This conceptualization "illustrates the uniqueness of sport communication" and "is built on the elements of theory (i.e., communication genres), context (that is, levels and segmentation), and the communication process" (Pedersen, *et al.*, 2007, p. 85). The SSCM includes both the communication process and the main categories of sport communication. This includes components related to personal communication (such as communicative interactions between individuals), organizational communication (for example, communication within and between sport entities), the mass media, and ancillary services and support such as advertising, public relations, and crisis communication. We noted that "Every activity and career in sport communication as well as every attribute and aspect of sport communication fits into either the process or a component of this model" (Pedersen, *et al.*, 2007, p. 86). Affiliated with this broad conceptualization of sport communication is the related definition, as detailed by Pedersen, Laucella, Miloch, and Fielding (2009). Here we note that:

> to truly recognize the broad scope of the discipline, a more complex definition is most appropriate. Sport communication is a process by which people in sport, in a sport setting, or through a sport endeavor, share symbols as they create meaning through interaction.
>
> *(p. 430)*

Therefore, this *Handbook* – using the aforementioned definition and conceptualization as a framework – takes an expansive look at the field of sport communication, a field that includes psychological and behavioral aspects (for example, Chapter 18 and Chapter 44) and economic ramifications (for example, Chapter 19 and Chapter 47) and everything ranging from organizational (for example, Chapter 3 and Chapter 29), gendered (for example, Chapter 10 and Chapter 32), and interpersonal (for example, Chapter 34 and Chapter 46) communication in sport all the way to the theoretical (Section I), sociological (Section IV), and managerial (Section V) issues affiliated with sport communication.

While sport communication used to be relegated to the margins of scholarly and pedagogical pursuits, the expansiveness of a publication such as the *Routledge Handbook of Sport Communication* is evidence of the field's diversity and increasing relevance. There are numerous other illustrations of how sport communication is becoming more mainstream and accepted in the academy. One example of this phenomenon involves sport communication programmatic development and course offerings. Entire undergraduate and graduate degrees in sport communication as well as a variety of undergraduate, master's, and doctoral courses (for example, sport public and media relations, sport communication, sport media studies) across numerous programs and disciplines are now available for interested students. Another example of sport communication's increased presence in the academy is the increasing number of scholarly outlets. For instance, the current handbook's wide view of sport communication is in line with the mission of the *International Journal of Sport Communication* (IJSC), a journal that is now in its sixth year of publication. As the IJSC was being formulated, I crafted the publication's mission statement to read that the IJSC, "is to provide a platform for academics and practitioners to disseminate research and information on the unique aspects and divergent activities associated with any communication in sport, through sport, or in a sport setting." A similar purpose could be applied to the current *Handbook*, which, as noted in the paragraphs above, is a collection of scholarship with direct and tangential affiliations with sport communication. In addition to the IJSC, there are two other journals solely dedicated to sport communication or a segment of the field. One is the more mass-media focused outlet called the *Journal of Sports Media*, which released its first issue back in 2006. The JSM was founded by Brad Schultz, who is also a contributor (Chapter 14) to the current *Handbook*. The other academic journal is the more broad-based scholarly publication *Communication and Sport*

(C&S), which just started in 2013. The inaugural editor of C&S is Lawrence A. Wenner, one of the contributors to the current *Handbook* (Chapter 41). Also contributing chapters to the *Handbook* are the journal's three associate editors, Marie Hardin (Chapter 15 and Chapter 24), Andrew Billings (Chapter 16), and David Rowe (Chapter 17).

Other examples of this burgeoning and diverse field of study include the growing number of scholars whose entire lines of research involve unique aspects of sport communication. The 74 contributors to this handbook are just a few of the hundreds of sport communication academics publishing in the journals noted above and in numerous other sport and non-sport journals which are open to sport communication-related research (for example, *Communication Research*, *Soccer and Society*, *Journal of Broadcasting and Electronic Media*, *Sport Marketing Quarterly*, *International Review for the Sociology of Sport*, *New Media and Society*, *International Journal of Sports Marketing and Sponsorship*, *Public Relations Review*, *European Sport Management Quarterly*, *Journal of Computer-Mediated Communication*, *International Journal of Sport Finance*, *Media Culture and Society*, *Journal of Sports Economics*, *Electronic Journal of Communication*, *Sport Management Review*, *Newspaper Research Journal*, *Sociology of Sport Journal*, *Journal of Sport and Social Issues*, and *Sport, Business and Management*). In fact, some of the journals (such as the *Journal of Sport Management* and the *International Journal of Sport Management and Marketing*) have devoted entire issues to sport communication topics. In addition to the journal research that is increasingly published in this area, as noted earlier in this introduction, there has been a rise in the number of textbooks (see, for example, Billings, Butterworth, and Turman, 2012; Reinardy and Wanta, 2009; Schultz, Caskey, and Esherick, 2010) devoted to sport communication. Furthermore, entire academic international gatherings (for example, the Summit on Communication and Sport and China's Academic Conference of Sport Communication) and session tracks or content areas at conferences are devoted to sport communication (for instance, for the past few years, there is typically a sport communication thematic session at the annual conference of the North American Society for Sport Management). The rise of sport communication interest and research is also evidenced in academic association activity. For instance, in recent years sport communication related groups have formed within professional associations such as the Broadcast Education Association (BEA Sports Division) and the Association for Education in Journalism and Mass Communication (AEJMC Sports Communication Interest Group). In fact, an entire professional academic organization is now devoted to sport communication with the arrival of the International Association for Communication and Sport (IACS).

Thus, over the past few years, an extensive overall interest and body of knowledge have emerged in sport communication. Given the growing number of scholars, textbooks, programs, courses, articles, journals, interdisciplinary activities, conference sessions, and research lines noted in the paragraphs above, it is time to take stock of the progress in this area through the publication of this expansive, transdisciplinary, and international *Routledge Handbook of Sport Communication*. While some of the research published in this area has been somewhat disconnected because it has focused on particular subjects (such as public relations, media coverage patterns, economic issues, and sociological influences), this *Handbook* helps to connect international scholars from a variety of disciplines and brings examples of their research and writings under one umbrella. Illustrating the global breadth of this multidisciplinary field of study, this *Handbook* is a collection of international contributors and content from a wide variety of disciplines – and sport-related sub-disciplines – including communication studies, management, telecommunications, marketing, psychology, gender studies, advertising, public relations, cultural studies, critical studies, history, journalism, sociology, and media studies. The 74 contributors range from internationally known sport communication researchers to emerging scholarly stars in their fields making their contributions from educational institutions located throughout the world. In addition to the USA, the chapter contributions come from Norway, Germany, China, Israel, England, Australia, Canada, South Korea, Denmark, New Zealand, France, and Scotland.

The wide-ranging and timely contributions of the handbook's international scholars will be of benefit to sport communication researchers, professors, students, and practitioners. By helping to map the territory and nature of sport communication scholarship in the second decade of the twenty-first century, the *Routledge Handbook of Sport Communication* is a timely and relevant compilation of this quickly emerging (and already flourishing) area of scholarly inquiry. The 50 chapters of this handbook examine the varied aspects of communication in and through sport and provide an academic overview of theories, perspectives, practices, personnel, and approaches affiliated with sport communication.

References

Andrews, P. (2005). *Sports journalism: A practical introduction.* Thousand Oaks, CA: Sage.

Bernstein, A., and Blain, N. (2003). *Sport, media, culture: Global and local dimension.* London: Fran Cass.

Billings, A. C. (Ed.). (2011). *Sports media: Transformation, integration, consumption.* New York: Routledge.

Billings, A. C., Butterworth, M. L., and Turman, P. D. (2012). *Communication and sport: Surveying the field.* Thousand Oaks, CA: Sage.

Boyle, R. (2006). *Sports journalism: Context and issues.* Thousand Oaks, CA: Sage.

Boyle, R. and Haynes, R. (2009). *Power play: Sport, the media, and popular culture* (2nd ed.). Edinburgh: Edinburgh University Press.

Brookes, R. (2002). *Representing sport.* London: Arnold.

Gisondi, J. (2011). *Field guide to covering sports.* Washington, DC: CQ.

Hopwood, M., Skinner, J., and Kitchin, P. (2010). *Sport public relations and communication.* Oxford: Butterworth-Heinemann.

Hundley, H. L., and Billings, A. C. (Eds.). (2010). *Examining identity in sports media.* Thousand Oaks, CA: Sage.

Hutchins, B., and Rowe, D. (2012). *Sport beyond television: The internet, digital media and the rise of networked media sport.* London: Routledge.

Jeanrenaud, C., and Késenne, S. (Eds.). (2006). *The economics of sport and the media.* Cheltenham, UK: Edward Elgar.

Nicholson, M. (2007). *Sport and the media: Managing the nexus.* Burlington, MA: Elsevier.

Pedersen, P. M. (2013). Reflections on communication and sport: On strategic communication and management. *Communication & Sport*, 1 (1) Online before print. DOI: 10.1177/2167479512466655.

Pedersen, P. M., Laucella, P., Miloch, K., and Fielding, L. (2009). The juxtaposition of sport and communication: Defining the field of sport communication. In J. Nauright and S. Pope (Eds.), *The new sport management reader* (pp. 429–44). Morgantown, WV: Fitness Information Technology.

Pedersen, P. M., Miloch, K. S., and Laucella, P. C. (2007). *Strategic sport communication.* Champaign, IL: Human Kinetics.

Raney, A. A., and Bryant, J. (Eds.). (2006). *Handbook for sports and media.* Mahwah, NJ: Lawrence Erlbaum.

Reinardy, S., and Wanta, W. (2009). *The essentials of sports reporting and writing.* London: Routledge.

Rowe, D. (Ed.). (2004). *Critical readings: Sport, culture and the media.* Berkshire, UK: Open University.

Rowe, D. (2011). *Global media sport: Flows, forms and futures.* London and New York: Bloomsbury.

Schultz, B., Caskey, P. H., and Esherick, C. (2010). *Media relations in sport* (3rd ed.). Morgantown, WV: Fitness Information Technology.

Steen, R. (2008). *Sports journalism: A multimedia primer.* London: Routledge.
Stoldt, G. C., Dittmore, S. W., and Branvold, S. E. (2012). *Sport public relations: Managing stakeholder communication* (2nd ed.). Champaign, IL: Human Kinetics.
Wenner, L. A. (Ed.). (1989). *Media, sports and society*. London: Sage.
Wenner, L. A. (Ed.). (1998). *MediaSport.* New York: Routledge.

SECTION I

Theoretical and conceptual aspects of sport communication

1

COMMUNICATION THEORIES AND SPORT STUDIES

Sang Keon Yoo, Lauren Reichart Smith, and Daekyung Kim

Until the 1980s, there had been a dearth of scholarly inquiry in the field of sport communication. Considering the vitality of sport communication and the existence of sport and communication studies for several decades, this seems incomprehensible. While sport is one of the most extensive and popular subjects, compared with other areas (such as sociology, anthropology), it has caught the attention of communication researchers relatively late. When early works exploring the relationship between sport and media appeared in academic publications, scholars questioned the need for understanding and inquiry of the field. Nevertheless, it is acknowledged that academic accomplishments in the field have exploded in the last two decades. After the initial works of particular scholars (for example, Lawrence A. Wenner's 1989 edited work, *Media, Sports and Society*), research has proliferated and sport communication as an academic discipline is showing remarkable scholarly potential. The crossroad where sport meets communication is a promising platform for both communication and sport scholars (Billings, Butterworth, and Turman, 2012; Bryant and Holt, 2006; Kennedy and Hills, 2009; Nicholson, 2007).

Research in sport communication continues to flourish as sport continues to have a global impact. The future of sport communication research should ground itself in theoretical and practical perspectives. Neglecting the study of mediated sport would be like ignoring the importance of "the role of the church in the Middle Ages" (Real, 1998, p. 15). Given the current state of sport communication study, the following questions should be raised: how are communication theories applied in sport communication study; how can communication theories contribute to the expansion of sport communication study; and what contributions can sport communication offer as an academic discipline? The following sections of this chapter provide some overview materials and insights that sport communication scholars can then use to more fully address these queries without the word restrictions affiliated with a handbook chapter.

Theory and Research in Sport Communication

A theory, defined as "a statement that predicts or explains how certain phenomena are related to one another" (Rosenberry and Vicker, 2009, p. 5), comprises an abstract set of ideas that helps understand or explain events observed in the world (Miller, 2005). Applying the theory in different circumstances allows the identification of key concepts and their relationship to each other. In communication, West and Turner (2007) noted individuals work in a social process using symbols to establish and interpret meaning. A communication theory allows the understanding of how symbols and signals are both produced and processed, as well as their effect (Chaffee and Berger, 1987). The primary purpose of a communication theory is to explain, predict, and control a certain communication phenomena. Looking specifically at sport communication, Pedersen, Miloch, and Laucella (2007) identified the basic elements of a communication theory in sport, a sport setting, or a sport endeavor. As sport and the media become increasingly interconnected, understanding their relationship becomes critical. For sport communication scholars, a theory allows the investigation of the relationship between sport and the media. Communication theories can be used to understand and explain the empirical sets of observations occurring in the sporting world.

As the mediated and commercialized sport culture has become an integral part of social life in contemporary society, research in sport communication has drawn special attention from scholars. In order to better explain mediated sport inquiry, Wenner (1989) suggested a transactional model comprising four elements, which include society, production, mediated content, and audience experience with content. Possible key research agendas in sport communication study subsume three major categories: production of sport texts, content of sport texts, and audience consuming sport texts (Kinkema and Harris, 1998; Wenner, 1989). In terms of the production of sports texts, it is important to recognize the process by which the content of mediated sport is being produced in society. With the understanding of a symbiotic relationship between sport and the media, it is of particular importance to understand how sport organizations interact with the media organizations in a political and economic context (Berke, 2011; Kinkema and Harris, 1998). In this process of mediated sport production, there are questions – such as what kind of role can sports journalists play or what kind of journalistic skills do they need to learn – which should be answered (Kinkema and Harris, 1992; Murray, Mcguire, Ketterer, and Sowell, 2011). Following production, the next category involves the content of sports.

As sport programs recreate an athletic event in a mediated reality, it is worthwhile to understand the social and cultural influences of mediated sport content (for instance, the values and ideology present in mediated sport programs). For example, as important techniques to form the mediated sport content, storytelling or narrative in television sport coverage could raise significant issues related to socialization, and the formation of values and norms (Kinkema and Harris, 1998; Mercurio and Filak, 2010; Wenner, 1989). Also, such narratives in sport media programs exhibit stereotyped characters of gender and race in the media, which, in turn, help viewers to cultivate social or cultural values and ideology (Kinkema and Harris, 1992; Van Sterkenburg, Knoppers, and De Leeuw, 2010). The cultivation theory, which will be examined in more detail below, found in media effect research can be a useful framework to examine the cultural influence of the mediated sport content on people's attitudes and perceptions.

The last major category involves the consumption of sport texts by audiences. Relatively little attention has been given to how audiences consume and interpret the content of mediated sport, even though it is very important to examine both media content and audiences' experience of mediated sport (Kinkema and Harris, 1992). Based on the social and psychological framework in traditional media research, past studies have found that people enjoyed watching sports violence on television (Bryant, 1989; Gunter, 2006) and also identified motives for viewing television sport programs (Clark, Apostolopoulou, and Gladden, 2009; Gantz, 1981; Kang, Lee, and Lee, 2010; Sargent, 2003) and online fantasy sports (Farquhar and Meeds, 2007). Studies along this line can be based on the uses and gratification approach (examined in more detail in the pages below), which often serves as a theoretical foundation in examining audience experiences with mediated sport.

Communication theories and sport studies

This section of the chapter first provides an analysis of the theories most often used in communication research and is then followed by an examination of the theories most often used in sport communication. Regarding theories in mass communication studies, one of the attempts to examine what theories are most frequently used was conducted by Bryant and Miron (2004). They examined 1,806 articles in the top three scholarly journals (*Journalism and Mass Communication Quarterly*, *Journal of Communication*, and *Journal of Broadcasting and Electronic Media*) from 1956 through 2000. According to their findings, 26 theories were cited most often in mass communication research and the three most frequently used were agenda-setting theory, uses and gratification theory, and cultivation theory. In the same study, the scholars also attempted to find which theories were most frequently used in six journals from 2001 through 2004. In this section, framing theory was used the most, followed by agenda-setting, cultivation, mediation models/theories, third-person effects, uses and gratifications, social cognitive/learning, and selective exposure.

Kamhawi and Weaver (2003) also examined mass communication research trends found in ten major mass communication journals over a different period (1980–1999) and reached similar conclusions as Bryant and Miron (2004). Their analysis found agenda-setting, uses and gratifications, cultivation, and diffusion of innovations to be used most frequently. In sport communication research, it should be noted that the theories examined and applied in the following pages mainly deal with media effects, even though many theories in communication study are classified in diverse areas, such as interpersonal communication, group and public communication, mass communication, and cultural context. While the following subsections are not an exhaustive list and evaluation of the theories, they do provide an overview of some of the commonly used theories and conceptual frameworks in sport communication research. Much sport communication research focuses on motivation for consumption and the effects of that consumption. Thus, media effects theories become increasingly popular as theoretical groundings for research. As avenues for sport consumption continue to grow, it is not unfounded to believe media effects theories will retain their popularity in the field of sport communication research.

Agenda setting

The roots of agenda setting began with Lippmann's (1922) *Public Opinion* and the idea that the mass media connected the events occurring in the world to the images in people's minds. Formally developed by McCombs and Shaw (1972), the theory posits that the media have power in their ability to define and shape the discussion of public events. In other words, the media do not tell people what to think, they tell people what to think about (Cohen, 1963). Rogers, Dearing, and Bregman (1993) contend that agenda setting offers an alternative to the search for direct media effect on attitude and overt behavior change. Over the last few decades, agenda-setting theory has contributed to the understanding of the media effects, especially regarding the salience of issues and attributes.

In the field of sport communication study, agenda-setting theory is used to explain how the media's agenda affects the public's attitudes and behaviors and makes them fans of certain sports (for example, Angelini and Billings, 2010; Fortunato, 2008; Zeng, Go, and Kolmer, 2011). McCombs (2005) asserts that the sports media agenda is defined by sports news and sports broadcasts. Sport organizations such as the National Basketball Association (NBA) and the National Football League (NFL) need the media to promote themselves as a sporting product because each sport competes for media attention. Lack of attention by the media can lead to a lack of exposure. The public perceive sport organizations by how frequently media cover sports and how attractively media present them. Thus, the strategy of sport organizations is crucial to what the fans think about sport *per se* and how they think about sport's attributes. For example, Fortunato (2000) demonstrates how the NBA continuously assisted media in selecting content and framing representations of basketball with public relations strategies. In this process, the NBA becomes a gatekeeper of selection and framed media contents. Fortunato concludes that the media should not be considered as the sole agenda-setting power because of the importance of content providers in the agenda-setting process.

Uses and gratifications

Uses and gratifications theory focuses not on the message portrayed by media but on the media user. From the perspective of this theory, individuals use media actively to achieve their own goals. Individuals who know what they want and how they can gratify themselves are active and goal oriented. Katz, Blumler, and Gurevitch (1974) propose that individuals actively use media to generate their specific gratifications. The basic assumptions of the uses and gratification theory are that:

> the audience is active and its media use is goal oriented; the initiative in linking need gratification to a specific medium choice rests with the audience member; the media compete with other sources for need satisfaction; people have enough self-awareness of their media use, interests, and motives to be able to provide researchers with an accurate picture of that use; value judgments of media content can only be assessed by the audience.
>
> *(West and Turner, 2007, p. 428)*

The primary questions ask why individuals choose certain media and what they get out of their media use (Miller, 2005). This theory underlines individuals' various motives and attitudes related to media use and highlights the fact that levels of media consumption vary by individual or group. The uses and gratifications theory has been used to study a variety of topics in sport communication study, such as television sports viewing (Gantz, 1981; Gantz and Wenner, 1995) and fantasy sports (Clavio and Kian, 2010; Dwyer and Kim, 2011; Farquhar and Meeds, 2007; Kim and Ross, 2006; Woo, An, and Cho, 2008). In examining fan motivations for fantasy sport participation, for example, Ruihley and Hardin (2011) noted fanship, competition, and social sport as the top three motivators for participating in fantasy sports. Farquhar and Meeds also attempted to classify the types of online fantasy sports users and identify their motivations. Casual players, skilled players, and isolationist thrill-seekers appeared as the three most common types of online fantasy sports users and two major motivations were arousal and surveillance.

Framing

Framing theory refers to the active process involving the selection of certain aspects of an issue by the media and its effects on the understanding of a message by media consumers. Entman (1993) noted that the process of framing selects certain elements of a perceived reality and makes them more relevant in some form of communication. Framing theory seems similar to agenda-setting theory in that it deals with the interpretation of media consumers, but there is a body of literature which examines framing theory as a field of study; where agenda setting tells us what issues are important, framing helps us understand the issues (Littlejohn and Foss, 2011).

In sport communication study, there is a body of literature conducted from the framing perspective (for example, Mastro, Blecha, and Seate, 2011; Parker and Fink, 2008; Zaharopoulos, 2007). For instance, Eagleman (2011) employs framing theory to discover what differences existed in the media frames used to describe Major League Baseball (MLB) athletes of differing race and nationality. In Eagleman's analysis of *Sports Illustrated* and *ESPN The Magazine*, the stereotypical media frames are maintained based on race and nationalities in both magazines and frames depict athletes differently by nationalities in portrayals of the same race.

Cultivation

Griffin (2003) argues that cultivation is one of the most overused theories of mass communication. The theory proposes that our views on reality are cultivated by television, which serves to create basic sets of beliefs. Cultivation is the consequence of cumulative and long-term exposure to messages repetitively rather than by exposure to particular content. Cultivation theory focuses on television's influence on the construction of our beliefs about reality. Signorielli and Morgan (2009) note that researchers focus more on the longitudinal effects of television, rather than the effects of a single program, issue, or interpretation of a message.

Two primary concepts of cultivation theory are *mainstreaming* and *resonance*. Mainstreaming means that heavy viewers tend to be similar in their viewpoints across groups; resonance occurs more strongly among a certain group. Regarding the application of cultivation theory to sport communication, television provides many sports programs which embrace violent content. Based on the assumption of this theory, a researcher may conclude heavy viewers of television sports containing violent content (for example, ice hockey players' fighting in the rink, Mixed Martial Arts events) would see the television portrayals of sports as a perception of actual reality (Atkins, 2002; Westerman and Tamborini, 2010).

Disposition-based theories

In examining why people enjoy different types of media content, disposition-based theories have been used across different areas of media including comedy, drama, tragedy, violence, and sports. Disposition-based theories of enjoyment explain why we like what we like. The theoretical framework hypothesizes that the enjoyment of media content is a function of viewers' affective dispositions towards media characters and the outcomes the characters face

(Zillmann and Cantor, 1976). Bryant and Raney (2000) identified five factors for the spectators' enjoyment of sports on electronic screens: Viewers' affective relationships to the players or teams involved in the contest; the favorableness of the outcome of the contest to the spectator; the amount of conflict and drama inherent in the contest or added to the sporting event by the sports casting or production team; the amount of suspense the contest has and how that suspense is resolved; the degree of novelty, riskiness, and effectiveness of play.

Sports and sport contests are a popular form of entertainment, and people find enjoyment in watching sporting contests of all types. Enjoyment is more about a team or player loyalty than about the display of skills by an athlete. The disposition theory of sports spectatorship states maximum enjoyment is reached when a favored team or athlete defeats an intensely disliked rival (Zillmann, Bryant, and Sapolsky, 1989). Studies have found that broadcast commentary has had an effect on viewer enjoyment (Bryant and Raney, 2000; Reichart Smith, 2012). In yet another example, Raney (2010) analyzed the role that morality has begun to play in our enjoyment and consumption of mediated sports.

Self-categorization and social identity theories

Two theories that can be seen as working closely together, having several similar principles go by the titles *self-categorization* and *social identity*. Self-categorization theory states that people view themselves as both individuals and as part of a group, and group memberships are important in the development of self-identity (Turner, Hogg, Oakes, Reicher, and Wetherell, 1987). Studies of self-categorization theory find that people sometimes view themselves as individuals, and at other times they perceive themselves as part of a group (Turner, *et al.*, 1987). Self-categorization theory proposed the idea of an in-group and an out-group; people align themselves with group members they feel they share similarities with, either in behaviors, thoughts, or attitudes (Turner and Reynolds, 2001). Perceived group memberships play a role in the formation of self-identity. Ruihley and Billings (2012) found that, within motivations for fantasy sport play, motivations of the genders appeared to be similar (similar behaviors), even though motivation levels were different (different behaviors), representing an interesting split in self-categorization between the genders. Other recent studies (such as Patridge, Wann, and Elison, 2010) have examined the relationship between team identification and the connection of styles of coping with shame.

Social identity theory states that individuals group themselves and others into various categories to make sense of the social world and their place within it (Tajfel and Turner, 1979). Placing themselves into groups of people with similar characteristics (in-group), and other people with different characteristics into different groups (out-groups) allows individuals to improve their self-esteem by finding people with whom they share similarities (Sartore and Cunningham, 2009). Sports research that focuses on social identity theory has brought us the phenomena of "BIRGing" (basking in reflected glow) and "CORFing" (cutting off reflected failure) as different ways that fans associate and identify themselves with teams, victories, and defeats (Wann, Hamlet, Wilson, and Hodges, 1995; Ware and Kowalski, 2012). Additional research on social identity theory has studied the notion of fans and team identification; Voci (2006) noted that fans categorized themselves into in-groups and out-groups. Fans believe themselves to be part of a group even when they are not active in an organized group (Reysen and Branscombe, 2010).

Hegemonic theory

Hegemonic theory (Gramsci, 1971; Sage, 1998) and, more specifically, hegemonic masculinity (Duncan and Brummett, 1993; Eagleman, Pedersen, and Wharton, 2009; Kian, Mondello, and Vincent, 2009; Pedersen, 2002) are widely used theories when studying and comparing genders in the context of sport. Hegemonic masculinity posits that cultural norms guarantee males the dominant position in society over women, encouraging traits such as aggressiveness, drive, ambition, self-reliance, and strength in males while discouraging them in females (Connell, 2005). Hegemonic masculinity has been used in studies to explain discrepancies in media portrayals between the genders. By continually ignoring and marginalizing female athletes in the media, such an action creates the illusion that females are nonexistent in the sporting world, supporting the notions of hegemonic masculinity (Gee and Leberman, 2011; Hardin, Dodd, and Lauffer, 2006; Kane and Greendorfer, 1994; Whisenant, Pedersen, and Clavio, 2010).

New possibilities in sport communication study

There is little doubt that journalism is facing tremendous challenges in the new ecology of digital media. The history of media development demonstrates that technological innovation in information and communication has brought transformative changes to journalism. Technological change affects the industry from job duties, industry structure and organization, and the relationship between the media and publics (Pavlik, 2000). King (2010) argues that news media organizations took advantage of the unique aspects of the newly emerging technologies, thereby creating a new type of journalism form and practice. Social networking sites provide new and elaborate ways to help people make connections and perform activities using technologies; furthermore on these sites, users are encouraged to engage and participate in the process of news production and distribution (Royal, 2010). Consumers are increasingly following news on Facebook and Twitter through computers, smartphones, and tablets (Pew Research Center, 2012).

As news experiences are more likely to be portal, personalized, and participatory (Purcell, Rainie, Mitchell, Rosensteil, and Olmstead, 2010), social networking sites will become an integral part of the digital news experience on the basis of daily news consumption. More importantly, how news audiences are engaged in the collaborative community of online news raises a set of important issues regarding the new type of online journalism and business model (Hermida, 2010). In terms of sport communication research, a recent study examined the desired job skills of sports journalists in the age of convergence journalism and found four key factors: broadcasting skills, editing skills, reporting skills, and sports knowledge (Murray, *et al.*, 2011). More importantly, the rise of social media such as Facebook and Twitter provides scholars with a new opportunity to investigate the different pattern of news distribution and consumption. Schultz and Sheffer (2011) found that social media became a more important platform in which people obtain and consume sport news and information.

Others also examined how sports journalists are adopting social media as a new tool for reporting and interaction with audiences (Reed, 2011; Schultz and Sheffer, 2010). Journalists used Twitter to find news sources or stories and tried to promote their stories through mutual interaction with audiences (fans). Based on the findings, Reed concluded that "there is a place for Twitter in the newsroom, whether it is a headline service for breaking news or a promotion for journalists work on other media" (Reed, 2011, p. 58). Given that the most unique aspect of social media is to enhance the greater potential for news audiences to engage and participate in the journalistic process, more attention should be paid to how sports news audiences (fans) are contributing to sports news reporting, as well as interacting with other users to build a community within the social media environment.

How sports fans consume sport content is also an area that should not be overlooked. As technology continues to expand, the various effects of technology on the viewing audiences should be examined; fans today can actively inform themselves about sports teams and players without ever turning on a television or watching a game. How does participation in fantasy chat boards affect enjoyment of mediated sporting events? Additionally, the ideas of fragmentation and the community of sport are areas deserving of investigation. Is technology pushing audiences to increased levels of fragmentation? What is the effect of that fragmentation on the community of sport? Such questions should be answered by sport communication scholars in the coming years.

Conclusions

The study of sport communication is beneficial for the study of both communication and sport. It must be pursued to find an underlying and abstract scheme of thoughts in a sports setting using the lens of communication theory. Simultaneously, it is not enough to simply seek the application of communication theories to explain sporting phenomena. Seminal research that incites wide discussion and shifts the way scholars think should be pursed in succession (DeFleur, 1998). Certainly, as Kennedy and Hills (2009) point out, the study of the sport–media relationship should go far beyond a reciprocal relationship. Furthermore, sport communication overall is in need of theories that can explain sport-specific phenomena (Pedersen, Laucella, Miloch, and Fielding, 2007). Thus, the application of communication theories is vital in fostering the understanding of sport and media.

Sport can be a distinctive field which provides new perspectives for scholars in sport communication. Sporting events have become some of the biggest events worldwide. Sport has been described as *unscripted*, *dramatic*, and even, *spiritual*. It contains political, sociological, cultural, and economical aspects. Because of these distinguishing features, the study of sport communication may produce unique perspectives and different approaches. Theory must look behind the scenes. It must go beyond mere spectacles and see through to the underlying meaning of phenomena. Historically, new theories in communication study have been discovered through the observation of political campaigns, television shows, and the process and effects of mass communication. While these are still effective areas for discovery, at the same time finding new theories based on sport as a new research arena is also possible. Sport could provide valuable means for sport communication researchers to expand the extent of their research area. It is acknowledged that sport research is still in its infancy, and the avenues for sport research continue to grow at an accelerated pace. Inquiry into sporting phenomena is expected to yield new theories that can be applicable beyond communication and sport.

References

Angelini, J., and Billings, A. C. (2010). An agenda that sets the frames: Gender, language, and NBC's Americanized Olympic telecast. *Journal of Language and Social Psychology*, 29 (3), 363–85.

Atkins, M. (2002). Fifty million viewers can't be wrong: professional wrestling, sports-entertainment, and mimesis. *Sociology of Sport Journal*, 19 (1), 47–66.

Berke, L. (2011). The future of media professional in sports organizations. *International Journal on Media Management*, 13 (3), 215–18.

Billings, A. C., Butterworth, M. L., and Turman, P. D. (2012). *Communication and sport: Surveying the field*. Thousand Oaks, CA: Sage.

Bryant, J. (1989). Viewers' enjoyment of televised sports violence. In L. A. Wenner (Ed.), *Media, sports and society* (pp. 270–89). Newbury Park, CA: Sage.

Bryant, J., and Holt, A. M. (2006). A historical overview of sports and media in the United States. In A. A. Raney and J. Bryant (Eds.), *Handbook of sports and media* (pp. 21–43). Hillsdale, NJ: Lawrence Erlbaum.

Bryant, J., and Miron, D. (2004). Theory and research in mass communication. *Journal of Communication*, 54 (4), 662–704.

Bryant, J., and Raney, A. A. (2000). Sports on the screen. In D. Zillmann and P. Vorderer (Eds.), *Media entertainment: The psychology of its appeal* (pp. 153–74). Mahwah, NJ: Lawrence Erlbaum.

Chaffee, S. H., and Berger, C. R. (1987). The study of communication as a science. In C. R. Berger, C. R., and Chaffee, S. H. (Eds.), *Handbook of communication science* (pp. 15–19). Newbury Park, CA: Sage.

Clark, J. S., Apostolopoulou, A., and Gladden, J. M. (2009). Real women watch football: Gender differences in the consumption of the NFL Super Bowl broadcast. *Journal of Promotion Management*, 15 (1/2), 165–83.

Clavio, G., and Kian, E. T. M. (2010). Uses and gratifications of a retired female athlete's Twitter followers. *International Journal of Sport Communication*, 3, 485–500.

Cohen, B. C. (1963). *The press and foreign policy*. Princeton, NJ: Princeton University.

Connell, R. W. (2005). *Masculinities*. (2nd ed.). Berkeley and Los Angeles: University of California Press.

DeFleur, M. L. (1998). Where have all the milestones gone? The decline of significant research on the process and effects of mass communication. *Mass Communication and Society*, 1 (1/2), 85–98.

Duncan, M. C., and Brummett, B. (1993). Liberal and radical sources of female empowerment in sport media. *Sociology of Sport Journal*, 10 (1), 57–72.

Dwyer, B., and Kim, Y. (2011). For love or money: Developing and validating a motivational scale for fantasy football participation. *Journal of Sport Management*, 25 (1), 70–83.

Eagleman, A. N. (2011). Stereotypes of race and nationality: A qualitative analysis of sport magazine coverage of MLB players. *Journal of Sport Management*, 25, 156–68.

Eagleman, A. N., Pedersen, P. M., and Wharton, R. (2009). The coverage of gender in *ESPN The Magazine*: An examination of articles and photographs. *International Journal of Sport Management*, 10 (2), 226–42.

Entman, R. M. (1993). Framing: Towards clarification of a fractured paradigm. *Journal of Communication*, 43, 51–8.

Farquhar, L., and Meeds, R. (2007). Types of fantasy sports users and their motivations. *Journal of Computer-Mediated Communication*, 12 (4), 1208–28.

Fortunato, J. A. (2000). Public relations strategies for creating mass media content: A case study of the National Basketball Association. *Public Relation Review*, 26 (4), 481–97.

Fortunato, J. A. (2008). The NFL programming schedule: A study of agenda-setting, *Journal of Sports Media*, 3 (1), 27–49.

Gantz, W. (1981). An exploration of viewing motives and behaviors associated with television sports. *Journal of Broadcasting*, 25, 263–75.

Gantz, W., and Wenner, L. A. (1995). Fanship and the television sport viewing experience. *Sociology of Sport Journal*, 12 (1), 56–74.

Gee, B. L., and Leberman, S. I. (2011). Sports media decision making in France: How they choose what we get to see and read. *International Journal of Sport Communication*, 4, 321–43.

Gramsci, A. (1971). *Selections from the prison notebooks*. New York: International.
Griffin, E. (2003). *A first look at communication theory* (5th ed.). New York: McGraw-Hill.
Gunter, B. (2006). Sport, violence, and the media. In A. A. Raney and J. Bryant (Eds.), *Handbook of sports and media* (pp. 353–64). Hillsdale, NJ: Lawrence Erlbaum.
Hardin, M., Dodd, J. E., and Lauffer, K. (2006). Passing it on: The reinforcement of male hegemony in sports journalism textbooks. *Mass Communication and Society*, 9 (4), 429–46.
Hermida, A. (2010). Twittering the news: The emergence of ambient journalism. *Journalism Practice*, 4 (3), 297–308.
Kamhawi, R., and Weaver, D. (2003). Mass communication research trends from 1980 to 1999. *Journalism and Mass Communication Quarterly*, 80 (1), 7–27.
Kane, M. J., and Greendorfer, S. L. (1994). The media's role in accommodating and resisting stereotyped images of women in sport. In P. J. Creedon (Ed.), *Women, media, and sport* (pp. 3–27). Thousand Oaks, CA: Sage.
Kang, S., Lee, S., and Lee, S. (2010). Student athletes' sports–program viewing: Motives and preferences. *International Journal of Sport Communication*, 3, 355–70.
Katz, E., Blumler, J., and Gurevitch, M. (1974). Utilization of mass communication by the individual. In J. G. Blumler and E. Katz (Eds.), *The uses of mass communications: Current perspectives on gratifications research* (pp. 19–32). Beverly Hills, CA: Sage.
Kennedy, E., and Hills L. (2009). *Sport, media and society*. New York: Berg.
Kian, E. T. M., Mondello, M., and Vincent, J. (2009). ESPN–The women's sport network? A content analysis of internet coverage of March Madness. *Journal of Broadcasting and Electronic Media*, 53 (3), 477–95.
Kim, Y., and Ross, S. D. (2006). An exploration of motives in sport video gaming. *International Journal of Sports Marketing and Sponsorship*, 8, 34–46.
King, E. (2010). *Free for all: Internet's transformation of journalism*. Evanston, IL: Northwestern University Press.
Kinkema, K. M., and Harris, J. C. (1992). Sport and the mass media. *Exercise and Sport Sciences Reviews*, 20, 127–59.
Kinkema, K. M., and Harris, J. C. (1998). MediaSport studies: Key research and emerging issues. In L. A. Wenner (Ed.), *MediaSport* (pp. 27–54). New York: Routledge.
Lippmann, W. (1922). *Public opinion*. New York: Harcourt Brace.
Littlejohn, S. W., and Foss K. A. (2011). *Theories of human communication* (10th ed.). Long Grove, IL: Waveland.
Mastro, D. E., Blecha, E., and Seate, A. (2011). Characterizations of criminal athletes: A systematic examination of sports news depictions of race and crime. *Journal of Broadcasting and Electronic Media*, 55 (4), 526–42.
McCombs, M. E. (2005). A look at agenda-setting: Past, present and future. *Journalism Studies*, 6 (4), 543–57.
McCombs, M. E., and Shaw, D. L. (1972). The agenda-setting function of mass media. *Public Opinion Quarterly*, 36, 176–87.
Mercurio, E., and Filak, V. (2010). Roughing the passer: The framing of black and white quarterbacks prior to the NFL draft. *Howard Journal of Communication*, 21 (1), 56–71.
Miller, K. (2005). *Communication theories: Perspectives, processes, and contexts* (2nd ed.). New York: McGraw-Hill.
Murray, R., Mcguire, J., Ketterer, S., and Sowell, M. (2011). Flipping the field: The next generation of newspaper sports journalists. *Journal of Sports Media*, 6 (2), 65–88.
Nicholson, M. (2007). *Sport and the media: Managing the nexus*. Burlington, MA: Elsevier.
Parker, H., and Fink, J. (2008). The effect of sport commentator framing on viewer attitudes. *Sex Roles*, 58 (1/2), 116–26.
Patridge, J. A., Wann, D. L, and Elison, J. (2010). Understanding college sport fans' experiences of and attempts to cope with shame. *Journal of Sport Behavior*, 33 (2), 160–75.
Pavlik, J. (2000). The impact of technology on journalism. *Journalism Studies*, 1 (2), 229–37.

Pedersen, P. M. (2002). Investigating interscholastic equity on the sports page: A content analysis of high school athletics newspaper articles. *Sociology of Sport Journal*, 19, 419–32.

Pedersen, P. M., Laucella, P. C., Miloch, K. S., and Fielding, L. W. (2007). The juxtaposition of sport and communication: Defining the field of sport communication. *International Journal of Sport Management and Marketing*, 2 (3), 193–207.

Pedersen, P. M., Miloch, K. S., and Laucella, P. C. (2007). *Strategic sport communication*. Champaign, IL: Human Kinetics.

Pew Research Center. (2012). *The state of the news media 2012: An annual report on American journalism*. Washington DC: Pew Research Center, March 19. Retrieved from http://stateofthemedia.org/.

Purcell, K., Rainie, L., Mitchell, A., Rosensteil, T., and Olmstead, K. (2010). *Understanding the participatory news consumer*. Pew Internet and American Life Project. Washington DC: Pew Research Center, March 1. Retrieved from http://www.pewinternet.org/Reports/2010/Online-News.aspx.

Raney, A. A. (2010). Media sports and viewer morality. In A. C. Billings (Ed.), *Sports media: Transformation, integration, consumption* (pp. 77–93). New York: Routledge.

Real, M. R. (1998). MediaSport: Technology and he commodification of postmodern sport. In L. A. Wenner (Ed.), *MediaSport* (pp. 14–26). New York: Routledge.

Reed, S. (2011). Sports journalists' use of social media and its effects on professionalism. *Journal of Sports Media*, 6 (2), 43–64.

Reichart Smith, L. (2012). Winning isn't everything: The effect of nationalism bias on enjoyment of a mediated sporting event. *International Journal of Sport Communication*, 5, 176–92.

Reysen, S., and Branscombe, N. (2010). Fanship and fandom: Comparison between sport and non-sport fans. *Journal of Sport Behavior*, 33 (2), 176–93.

Rogers, E. M., Dearing, J. W., and Bregman, D. (1993). The anatomy of agenda-setting research. *Journal of Communication*, 43 (2), 68–84.

Rosenberry, J., and Vicker, L. A. (2009). *Applied mass communication theory*. Boston: Pearson Education.

Royal, C. (2010). Social media and news as user experience. In M. E. McCombs, A. W. Hinsley, K. Kaufhold, and S. C. Lewis (Eds.), *The future of news: An agenda of perspectives* (pp. 107–18). San Diego: Cognella.

Ruihley, B. J., and Billings, A. C. (2012). Infiltrating the boys' club: Motivations for women's fantasy sport participation. *International Review for the Sociology of Sport*. 47 (4) Online before print. DOI: 10.1177/1012690212443440.

Ruihley, B. J., and Hardin, R. L. (2011). Beyond touchdowns, homeruns, and three-pointers: An examination of fantasy sport participation motivation. *International Journal of Sport Management and Marketing*, 10 (3/4), 232–56.

Sage, G. H. (1998). *Power and ideology in American sport: A critical perspective* (2nd ed.). Champaign, IL: Human Kinetics.

Sargent, S. L. (2003). Enjoyment of televised sporting events: Evidence of a gender gap. *Communication Research Reports*, 20 (2), 182–88.

Sartore, M. L., and Cunningham, G. B. (2009). The lesbian stigma in the sport context: Implications for women of every sexual orientation. *Quest*, 61, 289–305.

Schultz, B., and Sheffer, M. L. (2010). An exploratory study of how Twitter is affecting sports journalism. *International Journal of Sport Communication*, 3, 226–39.

Schultz, B., and Sheffer, M. L. (2011). Factors influencing sports consumption in the era of new media. *Web Journal of Mass Communication Research*, 37 (October). Retrieved from http://www.scripps.ohiou.edu/wjmcr/vol37.

Signorielli, N., and Morgan, M. (2009). Cultivation analysis: Research and practice. In D. W. Stacks and M. B. Salwen (Eds.), *An integrated approach to communication theory and research* (pp. 106–21). New York: Routledge.

Tajfel, H., and Turner, J. C. (1979). An integrative theory of intergroup conflict. In S. Worchel and W. G. Austin (Eds.), *The social psychology of intergroup relations* (pp. 33–48). Monterey, CA: Brooks-Cole.

Turner, J. C., and Reynolds, K. J. (2001). The social identity in intergroup relations: Theories, themes, and controversies. In R. Brown and S. Gaertner (Eds.), *Blackwell handbook of social psychology: Intergroup processes* (pp. 133–52). Malden, MA: Blackwell.

Turner, J. C., Hogg, M. A., Oakes, P. J., Reicher, S. D., and Wetherell, M. S. (1987). *Rediscovering the social group: A self-categorization theory*. Oxford: Blackwell.

Van Sterkenburg, J., Knoppers, A., and De Leeuw, S. (2010) Race, ethnicity, and content analysis of the sports media: A critical reflection. *Media, Culture and Society*, 32 (5), 819–39.

Voci, A. (2006). Relevance of social categories, depersonalization and group processes: Two field studies of self-categorization theory. *European Journal of Social Psychology*, 36 (1), 73–90.

Wann, D. L., Hamlet, M. A., Wilson, T. M., and Hodges, J. A. (1995). Basking in reflected glory, cutting off reflected failure, and cutting off future failure: The importance of group identification. *Social Behavior and Personality*, 23, 377–88.

Ware, A., and Kowalski, G.S. (2012). Sex identification and the love of sports: BIRGing and CORFing among sport fans. *Journal of Sport Behavior*, 35 (2), 223–37.

Wenner, L. A. (1989). Media, sports, and society: The research agenda. In L. A. Wenner, (Ed.), *Media, sports and society* (pp. 13–48). Newbury Park, CA: Sage.

West, R., and Turner, L. H. (2007). *Introducing communication theory: Analysis and application* (3rd ed.). New York: McGraw-Hill.

Westerman, D., and Tamborini, R. (2010). Scriptedness and televised sports: Violent consumption and viewer enjoyment. *Journal of Language and Social Psychology*, 29 (3), 321–37.

Whisenant, W. A., Pedersen, P. M., and Clavio, G. (2010). Analyzing ethics in the administration of interscholastic sports: Three key gender-related ethical dilemmas faced by educational leaders. *Educational Management Administration and Leadership*, 38 (1), 107–18.

Woo, C. W., An, S., and Cho, S. H. (2008). Sports PR in message boards on Major League Baseball websites. *Public Relations Review*, 34 (2), 169–75.

Zaharopoulos, T. (2007). The news framing of the 2004 Olympic Games. *Mass Communication and Society*, 10 (2), 235–49.

Zeng, G., Go, F., and Kolmer, C. (2011). The impact of international TV media coverage of the Beijing Olympics 2008 on China's media image formation: a media content analysis perspective. *International Journal of Sports Marketing and Sponsorship*, 12, 319–36.

Zillmann, D., and Cantor, J. (1976). Affective responses to the emotions of a protagonist. *Journal of Experimental Social Psychology*, 13, 155–65.

Zillmann, D., Bryant, J., and Sapolsky, B. S. (1989). Enjoyment from sports spectatorship. In J. H. Goldstein (Ed.), *Sports, games, and play: Social and psychological viewpoints* (2nd ed., pp. 241–78). Hillsdale, NJ: Lawrence Erlbaum Associates.

2

IN A DIFFERENT GAME?

Reflections on sports in the media as seen from a play and game perspective

Kirsten Frandsen

The Internet, other new distribution technologies, and the advent of various mobile devices and social media have led to a proliferation in mediated sports communication. It is, therefore, a good time to ask some more foundational questions regarding the nature of this communication. Is there a specific reason why people who are engaged with sports seize the new opportunities provided by these developments and at the same time continue to use the traditional media? And how do we, if at all possible, conceive of the communicative role of media and media professionals when media pervade every aspect of everyday life – including people's engagement with sport – and the media users, sports organizations, and individual athletes become "producers"? These are just a few of the very big questions that arise with the emergent mediascape, where audiences to a growing degree are multitasking when using media, and established media outlets, sports organizations, and new entrants on the market for sports communication are trying to gain, keep, or regain foothold.

In such a situation, where the whole field of communication is undergoing perceptible change, researchers may pursue different directions to gain understandings of the developments. Turning to new theories, new methods, or new empirical territories and phenomena is a likely and no doubt appropriate strategy pursued by many. But this chapter will look at the developments from a different perspective: through the lens of both "not so old" and "old" theoretical understandings and discussions about sport as a play and game phenomenon. The aim of the chapter is to present some basic reflections on what makes sports fascinating as seen from the perspective of sport as a playful, participatory experience. Also, how this in combination with an aesthetic perspective on sports may be instrumental in developing a more solid ontological understanding of the role of mediated communication in relation to sports.

Open-ended texts and motivated, active audiences

To take up a play and game perspective on mediated sport communication is not a new approach. In fact, this has informed much empirical, quantitative audience research rooted in communication studies, which, from a psychological perspective, has considered the uncertainty and the win-or-lose structure of sports games as being an essential feature in mediated sport content – the reason for the distinct types of emotional and cognitive connections that can be made with the sport media audience. This research has resulted in a robust and well-documented picture of the television sports viewer as a highly motivated media user who is watching sports for many reasons, but in particular seems to seek emotional eustress and suspense when watching games live, and in general appears more vested in this activity than fans of other genres of programming (Gantz, 2011; Raney, 2004). This chapter illustrates the fact that a combined play and game perspective can also offer a more nuanced understanding of the constituents in sport communication. The argument is that the play and game components of mediated sports communication facilitate the audiences' distinct participatory attitudes.

Research has emphasized repeatedly that the behavior of media sport audiences is distinct from the behavior of other audiences; in particular, audiences appear to be more actively involved both emotionally and cognitively when consuming media sport. Whereas communication scholars seem most inclined to refer to individual motivational aspects when seeking explanations for this particular behavior, Whannel (1998) and Real (2011) have considered the status and role of text, which they feel is important for an explanation. In a general discussion of the sport media audience, Whannel states that, "just as the texts are more open-ended, so is the audience a more active one, more involved with the process of offering or producing alternative interpretations of the action. With sport, to a greater extent than in news and current affairs, feeling, emotion and the affective dimension are an important part of the experience" (Whannel, 1998, p. 226). Unfortunately, Whannel does not elaborate on his notion of the text and it remains unclear whether this "open-ended" nature in the texts can be attributed to their particular way of representing sport by using certain types of symbolic representational forms or if it can be ascribed to specific characteristics of sports. Real argues along similar lines, but he is a bit more clear on this issue as he focuses on sports on television. He denominates sports programs as "polysemic" texts (Whannel, 1998, p. 25), and explains this using audiovisual theory, arguing that television's symbolic form automatically leaves room for the media consumer to "fill gaps" and make more subjective interpretations, thereby being rewarded with a feeling of agency by taking control of the viewing experience (Whannel, 1998, p. 31).

The idea behind this chapter is that this "open-ended" or "polysemic" nature of texts to some extent reflects the symbolic forms of the medium in question. But such an explanation of the relationship between sport and media is only partial. In the case of sports, media are dealing with an external social activity – a social institution, which is a communicative form in itself with its own inherent logics (Rothenbuhler, 2009) and aesthetic structures that also influence media production and consumption.

So, the argument is that, when it comes to sport communication, the audience's involvement is a reflection of the nature of the matter that the communicative texts are dealing with. The audience's engagement and the media and communication practices in relation to sports are both influenced by the technological specificities of the medium used and the organizational needs that inform the specific media practices, as well as by the specificities inherent in sports' status as a realm of its own outside the media. This is a realm with distinctive characteristics that in the following will be unfolded by a play and game philosophical view on sports and mediated forms of sports communication.

Experience of play in two orders

One of the major contributions on play and games comes from the anthropologist, Roger Caillois, whose work has inspired several scholars that have refined or expanded some of his ideas in relation to sports. Caillois' work did not address sport in particular; indeed, it was developed when sports were very different to today. Therefore, some caution must be taken when using the theory if the perspective of analysis is sports sociology and the focus is on the experiences of sports as seen from a professional athlete's point of view or the intention is to define sport as such (Meier, 1981). If, however, the aim is to understand central elements in the behavior, enjoyments, and engagement undertaken by the fans and the media audience, Caillois' contribution holds considerable explanatory power. In many respects, the fans' and media audiences' engagement in communication about sports is a playful activity – no matter how serious, commodified, or professionalized the world of sports has become. The fans and audiences enjoy indulging themselves in sporting experiences – at a distance – and, when it takes place through media, their experiences in some cases seem to take their own direction. They take agency in their own construction of an experience. However, as noted by Wenner and Gantz (1998):

> because much of this identification is held at a distance, sports spectating is often constructed as a 'no lose' situation and can contribute mightily to self-esteem (Branscombe and Wann, 1991). Evidence shows that many 'bask' in 'reflected glory' when 'we win' but disassociate from failure as 'they lose' (Sloan 1989).
>
> *(Wenner and Gantz, 1998, p. 235)*

Therefore, when using Caillois' contribution as a focal point for reflecting on how mediated sports communication is influenced by play, we may talk about the experiences of the immediate player and the spectator/audience as two orders of experience. They are grounded in the same type of fascination, namely that of play, and yet they are somewhat different. But, as we shall see below, the spectator/audience for sports is an inscribed part of a communicative act that fulfills a distinct social role by providing these receivers with human activities set into scene. Just like someone who is looking at an artwork plays an active and autonomous role, as he or she sort of "completes the object by viewing it" (Feezell, 2006, p. 6).

Play with a paradoxical relation to reality

The aim of Caillois' 1958 book, *Les jeux et les hommes*, translated in 1961 as *Man, Play and Games* (Caillois 2001), was to develop further the Dutch theoretician Johan Huizinga's play concept from 1933. He did so by providing a typology of games, which demonstrates how play is a very diversified field with important social and cultural functions. Play and games are thus seen as closely connected with common basic characteristics.

First of all, Huizinga and Caillois share a basic conception of play and games as activities taking place outside or as somehow separated from everyday life. This is one of the most disputed but also intriguing aspects of their theory. They see play as "a free activity" standing quite consciously outside "ordinary" life, as something "not serious", but at the same time something that absorbs the player intensely and utterly" (Caillois, 2001, p. 4, quoting Huizinga). The idea is that when people are engaging in playful activities they set themselves apart from the logics, necessities, and norms governing their everyday life and a central part of the pleasures linked to play activities derive exactly from this.

Ideally, the game must be performed on a voluntarily basis and the only goal of the activity must be the activity itself. Engagement is intrinsically motivated and the meaning of the activity is performing the activity in itself – nothing more. It is exactly this combination of purposelessness and freedom from the responsibilities and routines of ordinary life that make up the basics for getting an enjoyable experience – both by players and perhaps in particular by media audiences, for whom the act of choosing to consume sport in the media in itself marks this shift (Frandsen, 2010; Vorderer, Steen, and Chan, 2006). Mistakenly, this can be seen as a compensatory activity or escape from reality – but it is not, as it has its own clearly defined goal.

Caillois points out that those professionals who make a living on the field or on the track are participating in a different game; they are workers not players. But this does not necessarily mean that their engagement is not associated with enjoyment: "How many times have we heard even the professional athlete say that he was forced to give up the game because it was no longer 'fun'?" (Feezell, 2006, p. 14). Even for those players whose participation is also motivated by external factors like salaries, a certain element of joyfulness is perceived to be absolutely pivotal for continued engagement. No matter the competitive pressures and unpleasant experiences of tensions and physical exhaustion sport is still a human activity grounded in a world of play as long as the player, according to Feezell, "affirms, embraces, or identifies with the activity" (Feezell, 2006, p. 22).

Play is separated from the rest of life by way of rules that set the premises for participation and by its attachment to a demarcated time and place (Caillois, 2001). Even though play is a pleasurable activity and seems unserious, Caillois makes an important point when emphasizing that every player must be loyal to the rules that govern the play – no matter if they are formally explicated like in sports or dealt with more implicitly like in children's role playing activities where an "as-if" performs the same functions as rules (Caillois, 2001, p. 8). From this perspective, playing is a very serious matter, as one individual's violation of the "rules" potentially obstructs or spoils the enjoyment of the rest. Questioning or breaking the rules is not only detrimental for those actively playing, but also for those engaging with play at a distance as spectators or media users. In the case of sports, where sharing the experience with others and thus augmenting the experiential outcome is widespread, this is particularly valid. Watching and communicating with others, either on a face-to-face or mediated basis, is preferably done among persons that not only respect the rules, but also share the same level of knowledge and approaches to that particular sport (Frandsen, 2010).

Although play in general is governed by more or less explicit and regulating rules, most playing still calls for some degree of improvisation from the players: "The game consists of the need to find or continue at once to find a response *which is free within the limits set by the rules.*" (Caillois, 2001, p. 8). Much of the pleasure related to play – and not the least sports – originates from this margin. It leaves considerable room for the individual to perform according to his or her personal style or personality, and in particular it leaves very much open when the game involves several individuals who can perform together or against each other. The need for improvisation gives play an element of uncertainty, as no one knows the exact course of actions and events. Consequently, engagement with play activities involves a risk for all concerned. A condition which for instance the media in the case of sports are seeking to minimize by aesthetic refinements, by adding meaning and suspense to pre-game shows and by buying rights collectively (Stiehler, 2003), and which the dedicated fan can overcome by having a particular strong commitment that makes every type of action potentially meaningful.

In many ways, this element of improvisation explains why individuality and personality attract a lot of attention in sport communication and it also sheds light on our understanding of sports as a realm of its own. The playing individuals have a unique double status as both real persons and at the same time as performers of a role. Their attraction lies in this nexus between role and personality, but still the personal performance is restricted by the limits set by the rules, and only certain aspects of a player's personality may be unfolded or perceived as relevant. Therefore, players tend to become stereotypes in the communication around the activity performed, and communication about other dimensions in a player's personality or life situation may not please the core of the audience, which may react with indifference or even strong resistance to information that violates their play-oriented experiential contract with the phenomenon at hand (Frandsen, 2008). But still, seen from the perspective of the player, the play is played "for real" and is not unreal at all. As long as the player identifies with the activity and thus takes part in a free activity, he or she also expresses some sense of "real" or "true" self (Feezell, 2006, p. 28).

When television viewers are asked why they prefer to watch sports transmissions instead of other entertainment genres, they often refer to sports as a separate world – but still real. For instance, as one 62-year-old male sports viewer explains, "This is real life. I think sport is good entertainment. And it is with real people participating and doing their best every day in order to entertain – among other things. I find that unique." As media content, sport distinguishes itself by having such a particular relation to reality, and this is key for the audience. Sport is part of reality and at the same time it is a world of its own, it is both real and unreal (Feezell, 2006; Frandsen, 2010; Stiehler, 2003), and, in combination with the uncertainty of the game, this provides it with "a unique flavor" (Wenner and Gantz, 1989, p. 242). Stiehler has emphasized that sports' status as a world of its own does not prevent it from having close connections with other cultural and societal domains like economics, science, and politics. But sports' particular "doubling of reality" (a translation of *realitätsverdoppelung* in Stiehler, p. 162) also facilitates a rich field of possible meanings nurturing manifold interpretations of the games. The fact that the activities are taking place in real life, that the players are playing themselves, and that there is a constant need for improvisation by individuals is key to understanding this specific status of sports and the very active attitude and role performed by sports media users.

Games of competition – and recognition

As already mentioned, Caillois suggests a differentiation of our understanding of play by a typology comprising of four different types of games. He calls one of these the old Greek word, *Agon*, thus emphasizing that what these games have in common is a shared focus on contest and competition. The social principle behind games of *Agon* is one of recognition of a winner and of superiority. The players have specific skills and the "point of the game is for each player to have his superiority in a given area recognized" (Callois, 2001, p. 15). To ensure that the winner is actually superior and deserves social recognition, there is a strong focus on establishing equality for all players. This is provided by the rules in sports, which are constitutive, explicated in much detail, and seek to establish a somehow artificial but also ideal situation, namely one of equality – and therefore, provide the activities with both uncertainty and clarity.

What is special about sports is that the competitions are bodily performances in more or less special settings, the sports venues, which to varying degrees mark a symbolic boundary between the game and the surrounding society, and are designed to accommodate an audience. This type of play is thus not just expected to be of intrinsic experiential value for the player – but also to have an outward aspect of being an exhibition. The competitions are expected to have experiential value (Caillois, 2001) for the enjoyment of spectators, who participate in a different way, namely by way of identification, which allows them to get a different but nevertheless very involving experience of playing. And they are not just there for their own enjoyments' sake. The spectators are important inscribed partners in the event seen as a communicative act, as they sanction the principle of social recognition as a basic constituent in sports as play.

This aspect of sport as play reaches far beyond the activities and people present at the sports venues. First, there are the people sharing their sporting experiences with like-minded peers both in front of television screens, in social media, and when meeting face-to-face, and when involved in this they can be regarded as participants in communicative actions where the same basic principle of social recognition of skill is at stake. As Feezell notes, "It matters how we talk about sports" (Feezell, 2006, p. 17). Exchanging and performing viewpoints and interpretations of the actions are communicative acts where people are performing competency within a particular game, and these acts are associated with pleasure and most valued if they take place with what is regarded as "knowledgeable others." Second, the role of media – and in particular the role of traditional mass media – is among other things social in nature as well. Birrell has very briefly touched upon this in an analysis of sports as ritual embodying moral values of the community:

> The salience of the incidents recounted here is evidenced by the very fact that they were reported by the mass media for the benefit of those who were not fortunate enough to witness the demonstrations in person. Publication of such deeds serves as *institutionalized recognition.*
>
> *(Birrell, 1981, p. 373)*

The role of mass media has been one of sanctioning the basic principle of the sports game – that of social recognition of skill – not just for spectators and fans but also a broader public, and thus sanctioning that this particular type of play activity relates to the world outside, despite its separateness. Historically, this distinctive role has got its own expression and development in the design of the sports venues and events, allocating the press a privileged position and view on the actions taking place from a press box, and access to the players in locker rooms, press conference rooms, or "mixed zones."

Aesthetic perspectives on sports and sport communication

Whereas Caillois only very briefly touches upon the involvement of spectators and audiences, and mainly conceives of it as a matter of identification and social recognition, Feezell persistently argues that the experience of the active player/the athlete and the spectators is not identical but must differ in certain respects. Like Whannel (1998) and Real (2011), he points to the aesthetic dimension as key in understanding that the enjoyments of those not actively playing are about much more than just emotional experiences of suspense and uncertainty:

"Consider the notion that one of the significant elements in the fan's love for watching games like baseball, football, and basketball has something to do with the way in which sports structures experience and represents it to us" (Feezell, 2006, p. 33). His observation is purely philosophical, but there is a vast body of empirical evidence demonstrating how audience profiles for different kinds of mediated sports content vary in correlation with gender, age, specific interests, and culture.

Unlike Whannel and Real, Feezell follows up on this with a more fundamental argument about aesthetics as an important unique human source for getting experiences of enjoyment and pleasure. In this argument, he is very much in line with the anthropologist Ellen Dissanayake (1995) who, from a functional and biological perspective, has argued that aesthetic practice in general fulfills a fundamental art specific function for us as humans and therefore is basically experienced as "playful" and associated with joy. Seen from this perspective, sports are to be considered a specific type of symbolic activity where we as humans engage in something which is important for us, and therefore has been taken through a process of "making special" (Dissanayake, 1995, p. 39), and, as such, they have taken the form of highly structured and stylized representations of human, bodily activities. Sports have been taken outside the daily and mundane, and become extra-ordinary and non-utilitarian in a strict materialistic sense (Dissanayake, 1995). Engagement with aesthetics is from this perspective seen as a particular meaningful practice; it is a pleasurable process exactly because it involves both meaning-making and imagination both in the shaping of the form and the reception of it by a spectator.

According to Feezell (2006), sports games are aesthetic representations, where basic human experiences are given a certain form, and thus they are experienced in a different way. The experience of everyday life is one of contingency, a stream without a clear beginning or a result. But aesthetic practice intensifies, emphasizes, and points out certain elements, links certain moments in a narrative structure in the case of sports, and thus an aesthetic representation like a sports game is experienced by the spectator with pleasure, as it differs from ordinary life – it has been "made special" and separated from ordinary experiences. As Feezell notes, "experiences of sport and in sport, like the experiences associated with reading books, listening to music, going to movies, and so on, can be seen as attempts to replace aesthetically impoverished ordinary experiences with experiences that have aesthetic quality" (Feezell, 2006, p. 41). The experiential quality for those who watch sports or consume sports via the media lies in this kind of aesthetic involvement with meaning-making processes; the sports games are aesthetic representations in themselves, and these are represented in varying ways via mediation. Accordingly, it becomes even more important to bring attention to the aesthetic practice as a strong source of enjoyment when we are dealing with mediated forms of sport communication – no matter who loses or wins. Mediation of sports is aesthetic form-giving of sport of another order, which involves its own systems of interpretations and meaning-making processes with both the producers and with the audiences.

But, both for the spectators and the media audience, part of the enjoyment associated with sports has to be explained by this basic experience of pleasure in aesthetic practice. In particular, one aspect of the aesthetic structure in sports, namely its narrative structure, is important with regard to this. A sports game distinguishes itself by having a clear beginning and ending, and thus every game is offering a story-like experience and has a completely transparent meaning: Ending up with a result and a winner (Feezell, 2006; Stiehler, 2003). But Feezell elaborates further on this, arguing that the spectators and media audiences that are "participating" in the structure of such a story are experiencing it as extremely pleasurable, as narratives are basic vehicles for us to make sense of life in general. Feezell's argument is, that we simply have a basic need for experiencing that life has "some shape, pattern, or end" (Feezell, 2006, p. 45) and we understand ourselves, and the actions of others, through the form of narratives with moments linked together in a temporal structure. The actions taking place in a sports game offer us an alluring opportunity for engaging in an intrinsically valued experience of meaning-making in a broader sense. Feezell explains:

> We may experience our life or parts of our lives as essentially storyless. And when we do, it is natural for us to seek out new stories, or return to areas of experience that offer the meaningful possibilities of a story. I can think of no area in modern life (except for watching television, I suppose) that offers more possibilities for storylike experiences than sports.
>
> *(Feezell, 2006, pp. 43–4)*

The aesthetic structure in sports varies in terms of time, space, and participants/antagonists, and thus offers very different frameworks for interpretations and meaning-making – by the audience and by the media. Some of us seem to have a particular preference for road bicycle racing, others for baseball or figure skating – perhaps because what we are also looking for when enjoying sports is an aesthetic structure, that holds the greatest potentials for us to experience certain aspects of ourselves, of our lived life, and not the least our dreams about the "good life." Moral orientations play a role in audiences' choices regarding sports media content and their subsequent enjoyment (Frandsen, 2010; Raney, 2011). According to the aesthetic perspective on sport communication just outlined, this kind of relationship is established in a complex interplay between the aesthetic structure of the particular sports, the aesthetic structure of the media coverage, and the particular expectations and dispositions of the individuals constituting the audience.

Summing up, the two outlined perspectives on sports (play/game and aesthetic) seem to meet as they are both "intrinsically satisfying" (Feezell, 2006, p. 45), and, together, they seem to make up a particularly valid framework for understanding people's engagement with mediated sports. Engagement in both play and game activities and aesthetic practice is associated with pleasure and is based on a common mechanism, where human activities are "made special" and insulated from our everyday, mundane activities and experiences. This perspective applies, in particular, to mediated sport communication, as the media's representations involve an additional level of "making special", which, together with the separation in time and/or space from the actions performed by the players, seems to establish the experience of the media consumer or media user as different from that of the players. No matter how much the world of sports is pervaded by logics from other societal domains, mediation implies an aesthetic mechanism that tends to constitute it as a particular – and therefore playful – zone for the audience.

References

Birrell, S. (1981). Sport as ritual: Interpretations from Dürkheim to Goffman. *Social Forces*, 60 (2), 354–76.

Branscombe, N. R., and Wann, D. L. (1991). The positive social and self-concept consequences of sports team identification. *Journal of Sport and Social Issues*, 15, 115–27.

Caillois, R. (2001). *Man, play and games*. Translated by Mayer Barash. Urbana: University of Illinois Press.
Dissanayake, E. (1995). *Homo aestheticus. Where art comes from and why*. Seattle: University of Washington Press.
Feezell, R. (2006). *Sport, play and ethical reflection*. Urbana: University of Illinois Press.
Frandsen, K. (2008). Sports viewing – a theoretical approach. *International Journal of Sport Communication*, 1, 67–77.
Frandsen. K. (2010). Watching handball transmissions. Experiences of autonomy, competency and relatedness. *Nordicom Review*, 31 (1), 53–68.
Gantz, W. (2011). Keeping score: Reflections and suggestions for scholarship in sports and media. In A. C. Billings (Ed.), *Sports media: Transformation, integration, consumption* (pp. 7–18). New York: Routledge.
Meier, K.V. (1981). On the inadequacies of sociological definitions of sport. *International Review for the Sociology of Sport*, 16 (2), 79–102.
Raney, A. A. (2004). Motives for using sport in the media: Motivational aspects of sport reception processes. In H. Schramm (Ed.), *Die Rezeption des Sports* (pp. 49–74). Köln: Herbert Von Halem Verlag.
Raney, A. A. (2011). Fair Ball? Exploring the relationship between media sports and viewer morality. In A. C. Billings (Ed.), *Sports media: Transformation, integration, consumption* (pp. 77–93). New York: Routledge.
Real, M. (2011). Theorizing the sports–television dream marriage: Why sports fit television so well. In A. C. Billings (Ed.), *Sports media: Transformation, integration, consumption* (pp. 19–39). New York: Routledge.
Rothenbuhler, E. W. (2009). Continuities: Communicative form and institutionalization. In K. Lundby (Ed.), *Mediatization: Concept, changes, consequences* (pp. 277–92). New York: Peter Lang.
Sloan, L. R. (1989). The motives of sports fans. In J. H. Goldstein (Ed.), Sports, games, and play: Social and psychological viewpoints (2nd ed., pp. 175–240). Hillsdale, NJ: Erlbaum.
Stiehler, H-J. (2003). Riskante Spiele: Unterhaltung und Unterhaltungserleben im Mediensport. In W. Früh and H-J. Stiehler (Eds.), *Theorie der Unterhaltung. Ein interdisziplinärer Diskurs* (pp. 160–81). Köln: Herbert Von Halem Verlag.
Vorderer, P., Steen, F.F., and Chan, E. (2006). Motivation. In J. Bryant and P. Vorderer (Eds.), *Psychology of entertainment* (pp. 3–18). Mahwah, NJ: Lawrence Erlbaum.
Wenner, L. A., and Gantz, W. (1989). The audience experience with sports on television. In L. A. Wenner (Ed.), *Media, sports and society* (pp. 241–69). Newbury Park, CA: Sage.
Wenner, L. A., and Gantz, W. (1998). Watching sports on television: Audience experience, gender, fanship, and marriage. In L. A. Wenner (Ed.), *MediaSport* (pp. 233–51). London, New York: Routledge.
Whannel, G. (1998). Reading the sports media audience. In L. A. Wenner (Ed.), *MediaSport* (pp. 221–32). London, New York: Routledge.

3

GENDER IN THE WORKPLACE

Using a post-structural approach to theorize diversity in sports media organizations

Erin Whiteside

In its 2009 pre-Super Bowl coverage, the *Washington Post* published a somewhat provocative story about the advancements – or lack thereof – among women in sports broadcasting. The story acknowledged that more women than ever were involved in covering sports – including high-profile events like the Super Bowl – but had bumped into what the author termed a "glass – or 'grass' ceiling" when it comes to moving into the broadcasting booth (Farhi, 2009, para. 3). On record, several prominent female broadcasters praised the changes in attitude by media companies and male bosses and noted the advancements that women had made in sports media. Indeed, many broadcasts of major men's sports feature women as part of the reporting team – often working as sideline reporters where they stand near the action, providing color and background via short stories throughout the event. Furthermore, some women, including the likes of Erin Andrews and Andrea Kremer, are routinely part of the biggest sporting events of the year and have built successful and visible careers. But off the record, women spoke more candidly about the challenges they face in earning respect and opportunities on the job. One comment in particular proved telling. "'This is the most misogynist part of society,' [said] one, wary of offending her bosses. 'It's the last bastion of acceptable sexism'" (Farhi, 2009, para 9).

Indeed, few women have moved beyond the sideline role in major men's sports broadcasting. Furthermore, the play-by-play booth – where announcers explain the action and in many ways embody an authoritative figure in relation to the audience – remains a nearly exclusive male domain. More generally, women as a group constitute a small fraction of sports media professionals and an even smaller part of those working in leadership and management positions (see, for example, Lapchick, Moss, Russell, and Scearce, 2011; Whiteside and Hardin, 2010). The lack of gender diversity in this industry has been an ongoing concern for scholars, feminists, and industry groups alike. To address these issues, various groups have emerged to provide networking and help to women in the business; other industry organizations such as the Associated Press Sports Editors (APSE) have implemented ongoing internship, mentorship and scholarship programs aimed at cultivating a more diverse workforce and creating important opportunities for those who have traditionally been left on the outside of inner circles.

Scholars have similarly focused on these issues. Much work addressing gender in the sports media workplace has been underpinned by feminism, a perspective that fundamentally views society as structured around gender in ways that are inherently problematic for women. In light of the growing research and attention directed toward women's opportunities and experiences in sports media, this chapter reviews how gender diversity has been theorized and conceptualized. In doing so, it addresses the value various feminist orientations have provided in helping to understand the persistent lack of diversity – even while industry leaders work to rectify the problem. The chapter concludes by arguing that scholars draw from the arc of research in sports sociology, which has turned to a post-structuralist approach in considering similar issues in sports organizations and practices.

Shedding light on a problem

As women began to move into sport communication professions, an early body of work emerged that described their experiences and documented their minority status. For example, Neupauer's (1998) study of women in sports information used long interviews to highlight some of the challenges that female sports information directors faced at that time. His study touched on experiences of bias and women's generally pessimistic outlook toward balancing work and family. Several follow-up studies provided additional insight into where women stood within sports information. Stoldt, Miller, and Comfort (2000) used a survey to note that male sports information directors were often older than their female counterparts, generally earned higher salaries, dominated in manager positions, and were also more likely to report aspiring to such roles. An ongoing longitudinal analysis of women in sports has shown that the lack of women in leadership roles in sports information has declined over time; the most recent edition showed that 9.8 percent of all sports information directors were women, down from 13.1 percent in 1994. That gender disparity is amplified at more prestigious athletic departments; only 3.1 percent of head sports information directors at the Division I level are women, compared with 10.7 percent at the Division II level and 14.3 percent at Division III institutions (Acosta and Carpenter, 2010). Scholars have produced similar descriptive studies about the state of women in sports journalism. In a survey of sports departments, Hardin and Whiteside (2006) found that women made up just 12 percent of all sports reporters. The Institute for Diversity and Ethics in Sport has begun producing an ongoing tally of female sports journalists and editors among APSE-member newspapers (Lapchick, *et al.*, 2011), as well.

This early (and ongoing) work has provided a critically important assessment measure against the industry's efforts to improve diversity and create hiring opportunities for women. The data also provide a guard against letting calls for change exist without a quantitative check. Although descriptive data are necessary and important, they are limited in that such data do not explain why these disparities exist. As attention to women's status in sports media careers began to amplify, scholars have turned to critical theory, including that which draws from feminism, in moving beyond describing women's status and toward providing an explanation for their continued marginalization and subordination. The next part of this chapter reviews feminist theory and its application to women's status within the sport communication workforce.

Feminisms

Although feminist thought is often referred to as a singular type of inquiry, it may be more useful to think of it in the plural form as feminisms (Birrell, 2000; Scraton and Flintoff, 2002). Feminist thought has evolved throughout history. It has branched out and become influenced by other theoretical areas; it is thus difficult to partition feminists into neat categories. Despite feminist thought's inherent theoretical diversity, all feminisms are generally grounded in the belief that women are systematically oppressed and that oppression should be challenged (Ramazanoglu and Holland, 2002). Hall (2002, p. 12) calls feminism a "fundamentally political concept" and, thus, feminists are ultimately concerned with activism and societal change. The concept of oppression implies the existence of power and indeed, as noted by Ramazanoglu and Holland (p. 5), "feminism, therefore, entails some theory of power relations." Feminists have drawn from varying perspectives in their work of conceptualizing power; these assumptions are critically important as they provide a subsequent roadmap for how sports media's lack of gender diversity can be understood, and, importantly, addressed.

Liberal feminism

In their article on the lack of women in sports journalism, Hardin and Whiteside (2006, p. 48) urge newspaper sports departments to "intensify their efforts to recruit, hire and promote women." This assertion is underpinned by a liberal feminist perspective toward change in that there is a focus on advocating for equal opportunity; in this way, the goal is to level the playing field, so to speak, in terms of access and opportunity. Indeed, many liberal feminists advocate for equality and essentially same-ness with men (Tong, 1998). Many gender equity laws, such as equal pay laws or anti-discrimination legislation reflect a liberal feminist perspective in which, according to Tong, the goal is to enable "women to compete equally with men" (p. 33).

Perhaps the most obvious manifestation of liberal feminism in sports is Title IX; the law, which celebrated its fortieth anniversary in 2012, mandates that government-funded institutions provide equitable funding and opportunity to their male and female athletes. This piece of legislation has been credited with the surge in sports participation rates among girls and women and is considered one of the most important pieces of legislation challenging women's subordination in recent history (Suggs, 2005). For all the benefits Title IX has provided, however, it does not challenge the ideology related to sport and gender that naturalizes women's inclusion as illogical. Other types of feminist theories have helped expose how such ideology functions to guard against women's intrusion into (male) sporting spaces, despite the existence of anti-discrimination laws or industry programs aimed at providing opportunities to women. Most notably, radical feminism has provided a lens through which to understand these ongoing issues.

Radical feminism

Radical feminism advanced the women's movement by directing attention to how ideology functions as a justification for women's oppression; in opposition to liberal feminists – where the goal is gender equality – radical feminists argue that such "sameness" is based on male-defined norms and that true liberation will only come through a challenge to the supremacy of all things male and masculine (Tong, 1998, p. 47). In doing so, many radical feminists advocate for the celebration of the feminine and a re-articulation of what should be valued in a society. Going further, many radical feminists argue that femininity and "women" in general can bring a tangible improvement to society through an essentially feminine perspective. For instance, girls' and women's sports receive little media coverage and it has been speculated that if more women served as media gatekeepers, more and better coverage of girls and women's sports would see daylight (see, for example, Cramer, 1994). Limited research has suggested that women may bring a different perspective to covering women's sports. For instance, a content analysis by Kian and Hardin (2009) found that female reporters tend to use fewer stereotypical frames of female athletes in coverage compared with that produced by men. Other research has shown how the inclusion of women may lead to liberating content. A content analysis of Title IX coverage found that women use fewer war metaphor references, which may fundamentally change how the public views the law (Hardin, *et al.*, 2007). As numerous scholars have argued, Title IX has often been characterized as a "battle of the sexes" which works rhetorically to position the law as anti-male. Indeed, radical feminists have long indicted media content for promoting an ideology that upholds male superiority in sporting spaces and suggests a kind of ambivalence toward women's sports in a period where girls and women are routinely encouraged to participate and be all they can be (Heywood and Dworkin, 2003).

Through their examination of ideology, radical feminists turned a critical eye toward the institutions of gender and sexuality. Although there are differences among radical feminists, they generally see heterosexuality as problematic in marginalizing the experiences and opportunities for gay and transgender individuals and contributing to a culture that allows men's dominance over women to continue (Tong, 1998). Furthermore, radical feminists have urged individuals to reflect critically on how social structures – including the workplace – are organized around ideology that normalizes men's superior status; they thus work toward challenging such ideology and questioning taken-for-granted norms about gender. In sports, radical feminists have indicted the institutional practices and media content and organizational norms as fundamentally oppressive to women. For instance, despite exponential growth in participation, girls' and women's sports are still only marginally covered by the media (for example, Duncan, 2006). When female athletes do receive coverage, they are often featured off the field, where their femininity can be enhanced at the expense of their athleticism. Indeed, what is often termed the feminization of female athletes is a common trope among researchers (for example, Buysse and Embser-Herbert, 2004).

Sports media scholars have applied these ideas in thinking about improving opportunities for women in sports media professions. In particular, Hardin and Shain (2006) and Hardin, Shain, and Poniatowski (2008) have used a radical feminist orientation to illustrate the limitations of liberal feminist initiatives in changing workplace cultures. As Hardin and Shain note, more women than ever are hired in sports media careers – fulfilling the goal of liberal feminists, who advocate for equality of opportunity. But once they enter that space, "women are socialized into a newsroom that emphasizes their inferiority in relation to sports" (Hardin and Shain, 2006, p. 335). Everbach (2008) indicts workplace norms in her study, which found no differences in the amount of women's sports content produced by sports departments headed by women compared with those headed by men. As she writes, "instead of bringing a distinctly female standpoint to the sports sections they edited, the female editors at these newspapers appeared to reflect the prevailing norms and values established by male sports journalists" (Everbach, 2008, p. 64). Whiteside and Hardin (2011) similarly turned their attention to commonsense norms when they critiqued the norms of capitalism as problematic for women in sports information. As they note, ideologies that dictate that the ideal worker be available at all times and give their utmost allegiance to their careers are problematic for women, given that they are generally responsible for childcare responsibilities within the family.

Other research has criticized the institution of sports media for fostering a culture in which women's exclusion is justified. Whisenant and Mullane (2007) conducted an audit study of hiring practices at athletic institutions and found that athletic directors tended to hire sports information directors who match their own physical characteristics (white and male); this practice of homologous reproduction guards against challenges to men's control. Ideology also functions as a justification for decisions that systematically disenfranchise women. For example, when women do secure jobs in sports information, they are more likely to work with women's sports compared with their male counterparts; in a space in which women's sports are considered low value, these types of sporting assignments may lead women off the path of career growth and promotion (Whiteside and Hardin, 2010). In sports journalism, women have similarly reported feeling contained by norms that dictate they are better suited to cover women's sports (Smucker, Whisenant, and Pedersen, 2003). As Everbach (2008) notes, survival in sports media may depend on the adoption of dominant norms by women – even when they work to women's own detriment. Indeed, survey research shows that female sports information directors generally hold women's sports in low regard and do not believe that more women working in the profession would impact how women's sports are promoted at their institutions (Whiteside and Hardin, 2012). In reflecting on these attitudinal statements, the authors note that acceptance of norms that place a low value on women's sports ultimately "undermines the power of women in the profession" (Whiteside and Hardin, 2012, p. 64).

Shifting directions

The existing body of research has developed to provide an increasingly sophisticated picture of women's struggles to overcome oppression in sports media spaces. Fundamental to the research described above is a critique of the institution; more specifically, scholars have criticized the sports media workplace as governed by ideology that disenfranchises women and provides the logic for their marginalization. Consistent with liberal and radical feminist perspectives on power, such research assumes that women will only find liberation once discriminatory barriers and problematic ideology are eradicated. Although such research has been instrumental in casting a light toward ongoing systemic biases, post-structuralists have argued that, in general, such analyses leave various identity categories intact, which they see as fundamentally problematic. Furthermore, they question the way that power has been conceptualized, and instead offer new ways for thinking about how women might engage with power relations. This next section includes a review of post-structuralist theory and how it has been applied to sports studies.

Post-structuralist theory

In general, post-structuralists are concerned with categories, labels, and our overall way of knowing; they question the concept of truths and turn a critical eye toward how we come to understand things such as "good" or "bad" and "true" or "false" (Tong, 1998, p. 195). Thus, as noted by Tong, post-structuralists can also be termed as "anti-essentialists" (p. 195) in that they question the idea that everyone has a natural self, and that there exist natural truths that we can understand and articulate. At issue from this perspective is the way that subjectivities are constituted through discursive frameworks and how the self comes to be understood as a product of dominant discourses. In doing so, language is thus "reconceived as the primary means through which our consciousness is structured," implying an inseparable relationship between knowledge and power (Birrell, 2000, p. 68). Language then becomes less about personal expression ("As a woman, I bring a unique perspective") and more of a means through which identity is constituted and meaning is negotiated. This process is what Foucault (1995) calls the power struggle against subjectification and that which ties an individual to him/herself and becomes known to others. For post-structuralists, these "socially and historically produced identities endanger us, make us vulnerable, and close us off from possibilities" (McWhorter, 1999, p. xix).

Sports scholars have been heavily influenced by Foucault in this regard and his early work on sexuality offers an example of the process of subjectification. The Victorian age is often considered one of sexual purity, where church leaders outlawed what they described as deviant sexual behavior. Foucault (1990) argues that the censorship of images and judicial bans on certain behavior of that period did not repress sexuality; instead, he writes that by defining deviance, sexuality was thus "put into discourse" (Foucault, 1990, p. 11), creating a new set of knowledge through which power was expressed. He points to the emergence of "heterosexual" and "homosexual" subjectivities (versus descriptions of desire) as a product of this discourse. Foucault (2003) uses the concept "technologies of power" as an explanation for the techniques or strategies for influencing, shaping, normalizing and determining the conduct of individuals, which ultimately submit subjects to forms of domination. "Truths" about women's ideal body type, for instance, is a technique that invites women to self-surveil their own bodies and diet, or take other drastic measures, to meet a normative standard (Markula, 2003).

Borrowing from the work of Foucault, Cole (1993) suggests taking the technology of sport (such as knowledge, practices, discourses) as the object of study in order to demystify the ways in which bodies are similarly disciplined, reshaped and inscribed. Cooky's (2012) work on girlhood reflects this approach. Following the passage of Title IX, an increasingly amplified type of "girl power" rhetoric has emerged that appears to suggest that the quest for equality is complete. In her analysis of this cultural discourse, Cooky argues that the seemingly empowering rhetoric obscures the emergence of a girlhood subjectivity. Furthermore, this popular expression of girlhood is necessarily limited in its range of representation, thus reflecting the experiences of some girls – but not all. As she writes, "It is here at the intersections of race, class, and gender that the complications and tensions in girls' sport become salient" (Cooky, 2012, p. 224). Thus, her analysis allowed for a discussion of how a seemingly gender-related set of discourses (girl power) function in complex ways to constitute racial and class-based hierarchies among all girls, as well.

Engaging with technologies of power

Foucault suggests that power is not something that can be held by one homogenous group (that is, men in sports) and exercised over others; rather, he saw power as "omnipresent" and continually produced and expressed in everyday practices (Markula and Pringle, 2006, p. 36). He did not deny "global forms of domination" (p. 37), such as sexism or racism, but rather encouraged micro-level analyses in order to understand these social phenomena. Importantly, as noted by Markula and Pringle, Foucault saw power as "productive" (p. 41) in that the expression of power produced subjectivities, policy and social institutions, as well as social transformation. This point of view stands in stark contrast to other forms of power which are conceptualized as repressive and a sort of obstacle to be overcome (Pringle, 2005). Understanding power as omnipresent and productive allows for an optimistic view for change, in that it implies all individuals have the opportunity to engage with technologies of power in small, everyday ways. Foucault called the ability to engage with power relations and problematize one's own ties to identity as "care of the self" and Markula (2003, p. 104) has called for sports scholars to adopt this concept in thinking about how political resistance may occur within sporting spaces.

Thorpe's (2008) study of the discursive constructions of gender in snowboarding culture applies this idea. Through interviews, Thorpe examined how female snowboarders engaged with sexualized discourse, including their process in becoming critically aware of how they are bound to their identity. For instance, in asking one snowboarder about an athlete's decision to pose provocatively in two men's magazines, the woman said, "I have to say 'good on her.' She has a strong, fit and athletic body, so it's probably good for guys and other women to see that she is not a stick figure with balloon boobs" (Thorpe, 2008, p. 213). Thorpe takes these comments in a Foucauldian context in which the woman demonstrates a critical self-awareness about gender and sexuality, and assesses the image in a way that offers an alternative to a normative feminine ideal. The potential counter-discourse on femininity reflects the outcome of caring for the self, in which an individual works to redirect discourses in ways that could prove liberating (McWhorter, 1999).

Conclusion

A post-structural approach diverges from existing research on women in sports media in an important way regarding identity; instead of taking "women" as an essential category, post-structuralists are concerned with thinking about how the category of "woman" is constituted through discursive frameworks. Although institutional critiques have been important in illuminating how biases and taken-for-granted ways of knowing have systematically normalized women's marginalization, it may be useful to adopt a post-structuralist perspective in order to think about how difference is produced through everyday workplace practices and discourse.

Returning to the example from the beginning of this chapter, post-structural theory offers a new way of thinking about the lack of women in sports broadcasting. Assigning female television sports reporters to cover "human interest" stories on the sidelines of football games is one example of a discursive framework that might be addressed by sport communication scholars. Not only is she doing what might be characterized as "woman's work" (for example, reporting on the "softer," off-the-field stories), but she is occupying a space that is less valued in the profession compared with the television booth where the announcers authoritatively inform and explain the game to the viewer. From a post-structural perspective, these types of practices are a technology through which gendered identities are produced; in other words, it is not that female reporters are relegated to working in certain spaces, but that we come to understand the category of a female reporter through seeing her work in those spaces.

A post-structural approach to theorizing diversity would also allow for a more complex discussion of gender. Existing scholarship is nearly silent on issues of sexuality, race, and class, especially in relation to how these identities function as hierarchies among women. In the United States, white and upper-class women most benefit from anti-gender discrimination legislation that is purportedly enacted to help all women (McDonald and Thomas, 2012). Furthermore, discursive frameworks do not affect all women similarly and as Thorpe (2008) argues, women may engage with technologies of power in different ways, depending on their own level of consciousness toward identity. Explanations regarding women's underrepresentation in sports media have largely focused on difference between men and women. Situating women as one group ignores the varying ways in which women engage with bias, a concept often described as intersectionality (McDonald and Thomas). Ultimately, the focus on difference among women may be a powerful direction for future research on sports media workplaces. Questions about who benefits from formal workplace policies regarding gender or cultural shifts in attitudes toward women in sports will be critically important to understanding the state of women in sport as a whole.

Finally, scholars in this area may want to apply the notion of caring for the self to their research; to date, women have been characterized as oppressed, and ideology as something that must be transcended. Foucault's ideas on power offer new ways of understanding the possibilities of resistance, however. It is through discourse, knowledge, and truths that power is expressed, often in ways that are transparent to us. Thus, from a Foucauldian perspective, the "attack point" for creating change is at the level of discourse (McWhorter, 1999, p. 215). Researchers should focus on how sports media professionals engage with discourses of gender, race, class, and sexuality in their everyday experiences and how they redirect that discourse in ways that could be liberating.

References

Acosta, R.V., and Carpenter, L. J. (2012). *Women in intercollegiate sport: A longitudinal national study; thirty three-year update 1977–2012*. New York: Smith College Project on Women and Social Change and Brooklyn College of the City University of New York. Retrieved from http://webpages.charter.net/womeninsport/.

Birrell, S. (2000). Feminist theories for sport. In J. Coakley (Ed.), *Handbook of sports studies* (pp. 61–76). Thousand Oaks, CA: Sage.

Buysse, J. A. M., and Embser-Herbert, M. S. (2004). Constructions of gender in sport: An analysis of intercollegiate media guide cover photographs. *Gender and Society*, 18 (1), 66–81.

Cole, C. L. (1993). Resisting the canon: Feminist cultural studies, sport, and technologies of the body. *Journal of Sport and Social Issues*, 17, 77–97.

Cooky, C. (2012). Do girls rule? Understanding popular culture images of "Girl Power!" and sport. In S. Sprickard Prettyman and B. Lampman (Eds.), *Learning culture through sports: Exploring the role of sports in society* (2nd ed., pp. 210–26). Lanham, MD: Rowman and Littlefield.

Cramer, J. A. (1994). Conversations with women sports journalists. In P. Creedon (Ed.), *Women, media and sport* (pp. 159–180). Thousand Oaks: Sage.

Duncan, M. C. (2006). Gender warriors in sport: Women and the media. In A. A. Raney and J. Bryant (Eds.), *Handbook of sports and media* (pp. 231–52). Mahwah, NJ: Lawrence Erlbaum.

Everbach, T. (2008). Still in the minor leagues: A comparison of women's sports coverage in female- and male-edited newspaper sports sections. *Southwest Mass Communications Journal*, 23 (2), 55–68.

Farhi, P. (2009). For TV's female reporters, it's strictly a sideline job: From NFL to NBA telecasts, the booth still a glass ceiling. *Washington Post*, January 31, p. A1.

Foucault, M. (1990). *The history of sexuality: An introduction* (R. Hurley, trans.). New York: Vintage.

Foucault, M. (1995). *Discipline and punish: The birth of the prison* (A. Sheridan, trans.). New York: Vintage/Random House.

Foucault, M. (2003). *The essential Foucault: Selections from essential works of Foucault, 1954–1984* (revised ed.). P. Rabinow and N. Rose (Eds.). New York: The New Press.

Hall, M. A. (2002). The discourse of gender and sport: From femininity to feminism. In S. Scraton and A. Flintoff (Eds.), *Gender and sport: A reader* (pp. 6–16). London: Routledge.

Hardin, M., and Shain, S. (2006). Feeling much smaller than you know you are: The fragmented professional identity of female sports journalists. *Critical Studies in Media Communication*, 23, 322–38.

Hardin, M., and Whiteside, E. (2006). Fewer women, minorities work in sports departments. *Newspaper Research Journal*, 27 (2), 38–51.

Hardin, M., Simpson, S., Whiteside, E., and Garris, K. (2007). The gender war in US sport: Winners and losers in news coverage of Title IX. *Mass Communication and Society*, 10 (2), 211–33.

Hardin, M. S. Shain, S., and Poniatowski, K. (2008). "There's no sex attached to your occupation": The revolving door for young women in sports journalism. *Women in Sport and Physical Activity Journal*, 17, 68–79.

Heywood, L., and Dworkin, S. L. (2003). *Built to win: The female athlete as cultural icon*. Minneapolis: University of Minnesota Press.

Kian, E., and Hardin, M. (2009). Framing of sport coverage based on the sex of sports writers: Female journalists counter the traditional gendering of media coverage. *International Journal of Sport Communication*, 2, 185–204.

Lapchick, R., Moss II, A., Russell, C., and Scearce, R. (2011). *The 2010–11 Associated Press Sports Editors Racial and Gender Report Card*. Orlando: University of Central Florida College of Business Administration. Retrieved from www.tidesport.org/RGRC/2011/2011_APSE_RGRC_FINAL.pdf.

Markula, P. (2003). The technologies of the self: Sport, feminism, and Foucault. *Sociology of Sport Journal*, 20, 87–107.

Markula, P., and Pringle, R. (2006). *Foucault, sport and exercise: Power, knowledge and transforming the self.* London: Routledge.

McDonald, M. G., and Thomas, C. (2012). The Rutgers women's basketball team talks back: Intersectionality, resistance, and media power. In S. Prettyman and B. Lampman (Eds.), *Learning culture through sports: Perspectives on society and organized sports* (2nd ed., pp. 78–91). Lanham, MD: Rowman and Littlefield.

McWhorter, L. (1999). *Bodies and pleasures: Foucault and the politics of sexual normalization*. Bloomington, IN: Indiana University Press.

Neupauer, N. C. (1998). Women in the male dominated world of sports information directing: Only the strong survive. *Public Relations Quarterly*, 43 (1), 27–30.

Pringle, R. (2005). Masculinities, sport, and power: A critical comparison of Gramscian and Foucauldian inspired theoretical tools. *Journal of Sport and Social Issues*, 29 (3), 256–78.

Ramazanoglu, C., and Holland, J. (2002). *Feminist methodology*. Thousand Oaks, CA: Sage.

Scraton, S., and Flintoff, A. (Eds.). (2002). *Gender and sport: A reader*. London: Routledge.

Smucker, M. K., Whisenant, W. A., and Pedersen, P. M. (2003). An investigation of job satisfaction and female sports journalists. *Sex Roles*, 49 (7–8), 401–7.

Stoldt, G. C., Miller, L. K., and Comfort, P. G. (2001). Through the eyes of athletic directors: Perceptions of sports information directors and other public relations issues. *Sport Marketing Quarterly*, 10 (3), 164–78.

Suggs, W. (2005). *A place on the team: The triumph and tragedy of Title IX*. Princeton, NJ: Princeton University Press.

Thorpe, H. (2008). Foucault, technologies of self, and the media: Discourses of femininity in snowboarding culture. *Journal of Sport and Social Issues*, 32 (2), 199–229.

Tong, R. P. (1998). *Feminist thought* (2nd ed.). Boulder, CO: Westview Press.

Whisenant, W. A., and Mullane, S. P. (2007). Sports information directors and homologous reproduction. *International Journal of Sport Management and Marketing*, 2 (3), 252–63.

Whiteside, E., and Hardin, M. (2010). Public relations and sports: Work force demographics in the intersection of two gendered industries. *Journal of Sports Media*, 5 (1), 21–52.

Whiteside, E., and Hardin, M. (2011). "I don't feel like I'm up against a wall of men!": Negotiating difference, identity and the glass ceiling in sports information. *Journal of Intercollegiate Sport*, 4 (2), 210–26.

Whiteside, E., and Hardin, M. (2012). On being a "good sport" in the workplace: Women, the glass ceiling and negotiated resignation in sports information. *International Journal of Sport Communication*, 5, 51–68.

4

TV BROADCASTING

Toward a pluri- and inter-semiotic approach

Valérie Bonnet and Guy Lochard

Despite clues to a growing interest in this field, there are not many works of research dedicated to the study of TV sportscasting. This lack of production – that we see as patent, considering the importance of sports in contemporary societies, as well as the effects of its broadcasting – can be explained by two factors. The first explanation is that sports lack social as well as scientific legitimacy. In fact, sports could be considered as doubly unworthy of such study, as it is at the crossroad of social and media practices, which are synonymous with alienation and other forms of escapism. The second explanation is the barriers separating fields of study that are specialized in and focused on either the verbal dimension or the visual dimension of this syncretic media discourse. In this chapter, we focus on the latter factor, to take into account what has already been done in these two fields of research and clearly state our own take on this subject.

In terms of the related literature on this subject, we are faced with a two-sided problematic. On the one hand, works on the visual setting of sports scenes are sparse and scattered; a rather astonishing fact when we consider the French movie critic Serge Daney (1998), who was covering tennis for the *Liberation* newspaper in the 1980s. Yet, it is a fact: the shape of semio-aesthetics related to sports gesture and epic drama has yet to be drawn. More systematic analysis has been developed concerning this matter. Some analyses were based on historical, genealogical theories to tackle TV sportscasting as cinema once was. Others formulated theories based on aesthetics and ethics. Lastly, less numerous others tried to put into light differences in TV screenwriting depending on the context, and to explain these through comparative case studies from around the world. Nevertheless, the bibliography related to our subject is less important or cumulative than the one related to the sociology or socio-economics of sportscasting.

There are not many works dedicated to sports announcing either. Despite a few attempts here and there, sports announcing – referring to newspaper articles as well as live play-by-play – has only been dealt with from a general, sociological perspective. Moreover, works in linguistics about the text itself are focusing on that text as an oral genre or as a bearer of

Translated by Yann Descamps, University of Paris 3

recurrent linguistic phenomenon as far as syntax, time and phonology are concerned. In a nutshell, the different aspects of announcing are only tackled as an aside, as examples in some sentence from an article. The dimension of dialogue is most often left aside. Furthermore, analyses of sound material are only made by movie specialists. These mainly aim at the role of sound and, more specifically, the role of voice in the narrative process (for example, Chateauvert, 1996), with debates focusing on the relationship between image and sound in terms of superiority (such as, "which one has the upper ground?").

An alternative model

The methodological, theoretical model that we are introducing here is trying to give answers to these limitations that are based on the fragmented topics and their attendant independence in a variety of disciplines, as different semiotic subjects are too often tackled on their own, with no links with others. This pluri- and intersemiotic model is based on the notion of "apparatus" (*dispositif*) in a semiotic, discursive perspective, in order to embrace the whole complexity of the two-sided relations between filming and announcing, and between verbal and visual setting. This notion of "apparatus" deserves to be explored more deeply, for it is used more and more in scientific and social theories. Its use in our work is a theoretical necessity, and is made explicitly clear in different works that we will only summarize here (for example, Lochard, 2010). Primarily – if not exclusively – used in the context of live shows or series (Bourdon, 1988), this concept leads us to consider that making and directing this type of program is all about taking collective norms of action into account, with these norms having effects on all semiotic levels. Aiming at an intentional meaning, a TV sequence which belongs to the sportscasting genre follows a series of strategies that are dictated by a producing, decision-making group (*instance de production*) comprising people from several groups of professionals (such as journalists, experts, directors, camerapersons).

This work on visual and verbal representation of filmed scenes is not, however, the result of a planned, syncretic enunciation, such as that we can find in classic audiovisual genres on TV or cinema. Because of the cotemporality that exists between the recording and what is recorded, the sportscasting apparatus (*dispositif*) has to deal with a double enunciation, which is spoken by both the announcers and the director. This is also the case for other events that are broadcasted live. Leading to a power struggle which varies depending on the context, this audiovisual scheme of speech can give birth to mutual, regulated forms of links between the verbal and visual enunciations, as well as forms of disruptions between these enunciations (Lochard, 1999). Therefore, to think about what can make these plurisemiotic configurations possible is one of the analyst's main goals. To do so, he has to find specific, productive methodological tools. These tools will not only focus on the program, but will also focus on the entire programming to a larger scale for, as exceptional as it may be, the broadcasting of a sporting event is everything but standing alone. This event is scheduled and broadcasted by a TV institution, which put its brand on the line through the program, and inserted it within a channel schedule, which itself is delivering a macro-discourse illustrating the channel's identity, especially through "inter-programs" (such as trailers) that contribute to station identification.

What is implied in terms of notions and methodology by the examination of the broadcasting is not specific to this kind of program. However, these verbal and visual tools that were created to deal with other types of programs need to be adapted, and a new hierarchy has to be established between parameters of the analysis.

The verbal component

The enunciation allows us to draw links with images as well as to work on several aspects of the material from the text which belongs to the lexicon. For example, *deictic words* (for persons such as *I* or *you*; for places such as *here* or *there*; for time such as *now* or *yesterday*) indicate from where we are talking (that is, how the announcer is handling the live component of broadcasting). *Mode markers* (*modum* vs. *dictum*) indicate where enunciators stand in relation to what is told. In this category, we find adjectives (evaluative or emotional) and substantives (expressing values or revealing the enunciator's place), which indicate where the announcer stands in relation to competitors, the audience or any other actor in the context, and also verbs (expressive ones like *to hope*, or referring to knowledge, like *to consider*). In other words, we have to define where the speaker stands in relation to different elements of the triad: competition/receiver/speaker (that is, with the "apparatus"). The goal is to determine what are the relations between the sport, the media, and the audience, as a result of the audiovisual discourse. Thus, we can question the enunciating efficiency, and – as we cover below – look for the way that meanings are constructed.

This enunciation logically deals with *rhetorical issues* belonging to the art of public speaking. Aristotle's three means of persuasion (ethos, pathos and logos) can be found in sportscasting, with the media sphere replacing the public sphere: thus, the TV announcer's necessary ethos is associated with feelings (through advertisements and their appealing process) and bears elements of rationalization and knowledge (through comments on rules and statistics). These rhetorical issues are less about figures than about *targeted* or *induced effects* created by tools from the art of speech making. Nevertheless, some phenomena need to be underlined in sports announcing, such as psychological essentialism and the use of stereotypes (see Perelman and Olbrechts-Tyteca, 1958). Furthermore, we notice that enunciation is not only about the relationship between a speaker and his speech, it is also between a speaker and others who have an influence on this speech. This relationship with others is particularly important in the context of the media.

This dimension is to be tackled through an "*interactionist*" *angle* taking every aspect of it into account involving the *interplay between agents*, their status and relation to their roles. We can use elements from speech analysis and highlight the dynamic at play in such relations: cooperation (between play-by-play announcer and color commentator) and complementarity (between journalist and expert consultant, interview). In other words, we can notice that agents are looking either to get the advantage or to find a consensus. The interactionist angle also involves notions from different movements in linguistics which enable us to analyze how relations to others are built: coexistence through speech (idiolects, sociolects) that sets the roles for agents (journalist, expert), effects made by quotations and reiterations (rephrasing, specifying, explaining, elaborating), explicit dialogue writing which brings us to the speaker's role in the field (is he a specialist, a greenhorn or a former actor from the field?). It also includes organizational aspects taking into account genres of speech (such as description, narration, argumentation, explanation), how they are linked together (traditionally, the journalist describes, the analyst explains, and both narrate and argue), and speech sequences.

This clearly drawn difference between the two helps the viewer find her or his place, thanks to elements building this relationship of otherness. Using the double-enunciation theory from theatrical studies, we can say that these strategies aim at the interacting agents as much as the audience. They can be about knowledge (of the game's history or its latest evolution, of the sport or the latest news about the athletes) or reading skills (how one feels the moves, the game and, to a larger scale, the evolution of the sport itself). All these contribute to build the agent's credibility, and make her or him more or less relevant.

In essence, they have to identify what is at stake in the situation and story, and take this into account, to make the story livelier and to create a presence effect, without taking the spotlight from the sporting spectacle.

The visual component

If we consider the simultaneous appearances of both modern sports and cinema, and also taking Veray's (2000, p. 75) hypothesis into account (that is, "Our way to film sports on TV finds its origins in early cinema"), we can say that to show moving bodies in sports arenas requires the use of a certain number of processes and techniques also used in cinema.

To define a sport's or competition's mode of representation, we will look at types of shots, points of view, editing patterns, and visual and videogramic capital. For instance, *types of shots* are those that are more likely to be chosen by the director, and thus the *proxemics* regime is applied to the viewer, who is brought closer to, or further from, the sporting scene, depending on shots. Indeed, the director can apply different types of "distances" with the audience, such as a public distance (for example, to be linked with the distance between athletes and the attendance in the stadium through a mid-level shot showing part of the scene, or through a general shot showing the whole scene), a personal or social distance (for example, through waist shots with the feeling to get closer to the athletes' moving bodies), and intimate distance (for example, with now-commonplace close-ups on the face of an athlete in tears after a loss, thanks to technological progresses in optics that bring the audience always closer to the action).

Another aspect involves *points of view* over the scene through directing. First, is the viewer limited to a *uniponctuel* or *biponctuel* regime, as was the case in early TV or in some broadcasting with little technological means (for example, one or two cameras)? In other words, is the audience bound to the single perspective of one of the spectators who is sitting in center court? Or does it enjoy a *pluriponctuel* regime, allowing the spectator to seize the action through multiple angles and to enter sacred places such as locker rooms, thanks to multiple cameras and cameramen? Besides, are these viewpoints anonymous (that is, not sharing the views of an actor from the scene), or are they personalized, with mostly embedded cameras taking the viewer to the athlete's place (for example, racing car driver, parachute, skier) to make him feel what he feels? Or are they surreal shots, offering a towering view over the field, or the entire stadium through suspended or helicopter-carried cameras? There are also *editing patterns* to consider. For instance, how does the shot interact with others following usual syntagmatic patterns? That is another element the analyst needs to look for, trying to identify aesthetic, cognitive effects made by linking shot changes with movements (for example, when a ball disappears off camera and is brought back into view in the next shot), or with moves (for instance, when a referee points at a player who is shown in the next shot) and dramatizing effects made through editing work that shows, alternately, elements of the game and the faces of coaches on the bench.

The last visual component examined when looking at a sporting mode of representation involves *visual capital* and *videogramic capital*. Putting one protagonist or the other in the center of the broadcasting is a decisive element to analyze in the visual staging. How much of the visual capital (amount of time onscreen) does the director dedicate to each protagonist from the filmed scene? Does he only focus on the athletes or does he also show other actors (for example, officials, coaches, relatives)? Are the announcers made invisible and thus becoming *acousmatic* voice-overs? Or, on the other hand, do they often appear onscreen in proportion to their fame, as it is the case mostly with experts who are famous former champions for most of them? This raises another question: is the audience visually out of the screen, or is its relation with athletes in action staged in the broadcast? All this is linked with *social and media identities*, and it highlights the huge differences in how competitions are constructed on TV: the broadcasting is more or less objective, personalized or emphatic, depending on how the director uses visual capital. Furthermore, analyzing visual capital is linked with another operation: analyzing the videogramic capital (that is, the number of appearances onscreen) that is dedicated to each protagonist. It requires counting every single shot and evaluating how many shots are taken of the different agents or types of agents. It is important for visual capital can be distributed in several ways: different rhythms can be produced through editing, with either a few long shots (low videogramic capital) or many quick short shots (high videogramic capital). The former creates a slow pace while the latter creates a staccato pace. TV has moved forward the process of *expertization* of the viewer by using specific techniques (such as slow-motion, replay) more systematically, thus feeding into some scientist type of imagination which is not without consequences, in particular on the way we think of the referee's role. Diana (2000) underlined this consequence while studying the role of slow-motion in soccer, which allows the viewer to have an evaluating power similar to the referee's. It is now part of rugby games, as a video refereeing system using slow-motion and replays to afford questionable is now part of national and international matches.

The sound component

The different characteristics of the announcer's voice (Bourdon, 1988, 1997; Chateauvert, 1996) can be analyzed, as it helps to build effects of ethos and pathos: its volume (for example, tennis announcers tend to whisper), rhythm, sound capital, grain, and tone. The last two elements define the *voice's identity*. In terms of identifying the vocal source, some questions to ponder include: is the voice in (in the shot), synchronous *off* (off the shot but recorded on the spot), or a voice *over* (added from some other place)? All this allows us to define the relation between text and image, and, in particular, the importance of enunciation and relation with the audience (if announcers look at the camera, if there is a double enunciation, and so on). Other elements to be analyzed include contextual sounds, which involve whether the capital source is present, missing, how dense it is, and whether it is to be seen.

Intersemiotic relations

The presence of both text and image in a same message does not translate in a sum (text + image) but in an interrelation (text <=> image), which creates a new added meaning, whose coherence has to be evaluated. The exchange of meanings between both elements (text and image) can either reinforce the filming process or, on the opposite, go against it. This has to be taken into account for the way a game is filmed can change depending on who is filming and who is announcing the game (it can be the case if the director is from another country or is not member of the channel's permanent staff). Thus, we can understand that there is a need to make a list of types of images seen onscreen: elements of context (such as the stadium, city, locker rooms, public, audience), actors from the contest (such as athletes, referees, trainers) and filming elements (such as replays, slow-motion, inserts, split screens).

It is of interest to consider works on advertisement that have explored the *text–image relation*. Even if these works are about still images, they can be adapted to and used in our case. There are three ways of proceeding: starting from the image, starting from the text, and starting from a higher unity built with the text and image (Barthes, 1964). First, let us begin by examining the starting point of the image. The starting point for this analysis would be the anchoring and relaying relations between verbal and visual components that Barthes illuminated. By definition, an image is polysemic and the elements it signifies are changing (connotations). The verbal message allows us to define what is signified and to identify elements from the scene as well as the scene itself. Thus, the verbal component (commentary) helps us to feel the game the right way through descriptions (partial ones) freed from the image (for instance, a tackle can be a great tackle or a violent gesture). The commentary guides the audience through the identifying and interpretation process. Still, we have to be careful, because this guidance works by selecting some elements over others. This selecting process is called "framing" or "focusing". In the relaying relation, the image is completing the text; both elements become part of the same message to a higher level: relaying implies complementarity between the text and image and brings more information (identifying place and actors) that cannot be found in the image (names of players, stats, etc.). These two functions can be found in the same shot, but grasping their own importance is essential to understand and interpret the image.

Next, let us examine the starting point of the text. Leon (1990) chose to do this to see how the image–text relation was organized. He ended by identifying six different functions that the image takes on to complete the text as far as meaning is concerned. The five we found most relevant included approving, implying, invalidating, illustrating, and enunciating. Regarding *approving*, the image is approving what is said while also adding some affect. It produces a sensible representation of what is enunciated by the verbal component (for instance showing crying players singing the national anthem). In terms of *implying*, the image implies what is politically incorrect and cannot be said (for example, when it shows an apology to sports violence). *Invalidating* is when the image contradicts what is said and thus makes it invalid. In terms of *illustrating*, this is when the image illustrates concepts and situations. This function is due to broadcasting's explaining/didactic dimension (through inserts). Lastly, *enunciating* is when the image gives out the identity of the message's sender/receiver.

The third way to proceed involves starting from text–image interrelations as a superior relaying unity. Here, we can borrow from Bardin's (1975) work. Just as they are relevant for advertising, his thoughts can easily be applied to sportscasting, for it is about images that need to be explained, or, on the contrary, images explaining what is announced (through replays). The *informing* message is made of an informing text and a rational image, both completing each other (replays). The *illustrating* message is made of a subjective, connoted text, and a rational text in which we find the meaning of the text, and which sometimes completes it (comments from announcers like "oh, what a beautiful hit!"). The *footnoted* message is made of an informing text and a symbolic, strongly connoted image whose meaning is to be found in or completed by the text (symbolic presence in the stands indicating this person is somebody important). Lastly, the *symbolic* message is made of a subjective, connoted text and a symbolical, strongly connoted image (for example, comments on young ladies in the stands, allusions, private jokes, close-ups on a player's tears).

Five key findings

Being part of a series, like any TV program, a sportscasting program is subject to elements of ritualization, which are different from one sport to another, despite several similarities in sequences (for example, prologue, unfolding of contest, ending, announcing the next episode coming soon). Having to deal with strategies followed through the programming, the produced audiovisual speech is marked by elements of routine, establishing some level of congruence between verbal and visual enunciations. Once made regular, these intersemiotic figures aim at creating several types of effects serving strategies that Charaudeau and Maingueneau (2001) named credibilizing strategy, legitimizing strategy, and priming strategy. The following paragraphs include the five major findings of the current study.

The first major finding involves the concept of *rationalizing*. Implied by the journalist's speech, the principle of seriousness is at the basis of statistics collecting, which is to be found in verbal comments, as well as in visual charts and graphs taking former and current performance indicators into account. These effects of objectification are reinforced by the use of scopic processes such as x-cams or Camcat, offering a synoptic view over the field through towering, high-level shots. Just as it is the case with statistics, these processes are linked with a scientific type of imagination, whose consequence for the way we look at refereeing was remarked earlier. *Creating heroes* is the category for the next result. Some actors become objects of emphasis on the part of announcers; this emphasis being reinforced by a visual focus on them that is noticeable when we consider the *visual capital*. Often part of the journalist's speech, the priming principle is at the basis of this process that turns some of the actors into heroes.

In addition to creating heroes, another key finding involves *making it aesthetic*. Sometimes coupled with rousing music and eloquent praises, slow-motion sequences are the main elements used to build this effect. They can even contribute to the sublimation of some exceptional players, as it is the case in a motion picture dedicated to soccer player, Zinedine Zidane. As an aside, the perfect example to illustrate this is to be found in the 2006 movie *Zidane, Portrait du XXI° Siècle*.

Yet another key finding of the study is categorized as *bringing memories back*. The announcer brings back encyclopedic data (about great players or mythical competitions) with images of the current or former competitions (for example, images from France's victory in the 1998 soccer World Cup during the competition's last edition). In bringing these memories back, he turns them into a legacy or creates positive or negative comparisons between competitors. *Filling the air with suspense* is the last major finding of this study. As noted by Leblanc (1997), this involves hypothetical, fantasy, and futuristic scenarios. Using comments focusing on a possible comeback in the game or the competition in general, and showing statistics validating this possibility, broadcasters insist on the essential uncertainty of sports.

Overall, sportscasting is not only about those regular effects on meaning that are based on the complementarity of verbal and visual components, for it is made of a *two-sided enunciation*. Some unpredicted, unpredictable situations can lead to a split between the verbal enunciation and the visual. Such is the case when the broadcasters face a catastrophe, like the Heysel catastrophe in Belgium or the collapse of Furiani Stadium's stands in France. It is also the case when some less tragic incidents surprise both the announcers and director during the game. In these moments of real live broadcasting, we experience unruled complementary relations, up to dissonance between the visual and verbal components, the latter losing all power over the former because some unbelievable fact just occurred.

One of the main teachings we can draw from the analysis of the apparatus surrounding TV sportscasting (which is generally praised for the uncertainty of its outcome) is to be found in the live component. As organized and planned as it may be, this kind of broadcasting and media construct, just like other live TV programs, cannot be really prepared for take into account another uncertainty: the reality check. However that may be, we can still conclude by saying that broadcasting sports is often more of a pretext to talk about or study something else: holistic thoughts on different things from the media to larger social issues, or more minor thoughts about only one subject, both to be found in the announcing or filming.

References

Bardin, L. (1975). Le texte et l'image. *Communication et Langages*, 26, 98–112.

Barthes, R. (1964). Rhétorique de l'image. *Communication*, 4, 41–2.

Bourdon, J. (1988). Propositions pour une sémiologie des genres audiovisuels. *Quaderni*, 4, 19–36.

Bourdon, J. (1997). Le direct : une politique de la voix ou la télévision comme promesse inaccomplie. *Réseaux*, 81, 61–78.

Charaudeau, P., and Maingueneau, D. (2001). *Dictionnaire de l'analyse du discours*. Paris: Seuil.

Chateauvert, J. (1996). *Des mots à l'image : La voix over au cinéma*. Paris: Méridiens Klincksieck.

Daney, S. (1998). *Le salaire du zappeur*. Paris: Ramsay.

Diana, J.-F. (2000). Les enjeux du ralenti dans la représentation télévisuelle du football: Entre inquisition et requisition. In L. Veray and P. Simonet (Eds.), *Montrer le sport* (pp. 255–69). Paris: INSEP.

Leblanc, G. (1997). *Scénarios du réel* (Tomes 1 et 2). Paris: L'Harmattan.

Leon, P. (1990). Le jeu de la Une et du hasard. Une approche poétique de l'écriture de presse (Unpublished doctoral dissertation). University of Provence, France.

Lochard, G. (1999). Parcours d'un concept dans les études télévisuelles: Trajectoires et logiques d'emploi. *Hermés*, 25, 143–51.

Lochard, G. (2010). Pour une approche sémantique de la notion de dispositif: L'exemple des évènements sportifs. In V. Appel, H. Boulanger, and L. Massou (Eds.), *Les dispositifs d'information et de communication: Concept, usages et objets* (pp. 152–72). Louvain: De Boeck.

Perelman, C., and Olbrechts-Tyteca, L. (1958). *Traité de l'argumentation: La nouvelle rhétorique*. Paris: Presses Universitaires de France.

Veray, L. (2000). Aux origines du spectacle sportif télévisé: Le cas des vues Lumière. In L. Veray and P. Simonet (Eds.), *Montrer le sport* (pp. 75–86). Paris: INSEP.

5

SPORT AS A COMMUNICATION SYSTEM

Ulrik Wagner and Rasmus K. Storm

Can we understand society by claiming that it consists of communication and nothing but communication? According to German sociologist Niklas Luhmann (1927–1998) the answer is: yes! This chapter briefly outlines this grand theory, which puts communication to the fore, and subsequently focuses on sport and mass media and how these two spheres of society are inter-related.

Originally, Luhmann studied law, but a short stay at Harvard University – where he studied under Talcott Parsons – changed his orientation towards sociology. From 1969 until 1993, he held a professorship at the newly established University of Bielefeld in Germany. During the early years, his theory was a kind of elaboration of Parsonian systems theory. But the most interesting turn appeared in the early 1980s, as he started to (re-)introduce new concepts such as autopoiesis, communication, meaning, structural coupling, and world society to his theoretical framework. One of his most important books, *Soziale Systeme*, was published in 1984 (English edition, 1995) giving weight to this endeavor. Over his last ten years, he focused on a theory of distinction and form analysis, which became significant through its incorporation of an inspiration from the *Laws of Form* by George Spencer-Brown (1969). Luhmann's last major contribution to his general social theory about society appeared in *Die Gesellschaft der Gesellschaft* (1997), the year before he died. During his career, he published around 50 books on various topics, such as economics, politics, law, education, love, and mass media, as well as more than 400 articles (Arnoldi, 2001).

Taking Luhmann as our point of departure, the crucial question is: If society consists of nothing but communication, how do we grasp the notion of sport communication? In this chapter – which is an elaboration of Storm and Wagner (2010), with an additional focus on mass media – we will try to answer this question. First we will sketch out the main elements of Luhmann´s grand communication theory, and then move on to focus on how the interrelations between sport and mass media emerge in modern society. While the theory of Luhmann has become an integrated part of the curriculum in some European countries, within disciplines such as management, sociology, and communication studies, it has, however, still not managed to become mainstream within British, North American, and French academic institutions. Therefore, and because of the theoretical complexity, a general introduction is relevant before orientating towards sport and mass media.

Why modern social systems theory?

Why is systems theory relevant in the first place? Why take on a system-theoretical approach to sports studies that are bound up with activities focusing on the subject, when systems theory is often criticized for excluding the subject and the body from its purview? The answer to this question requires some elaboration. Basically, we are presenting a general theory of society that takes a communicative turn in the wake of the general linguistic turn of the social sciences and humanities (Bjerg, 2005), thus intimating that its grandness enables us to provide meaning for various aspects of society, including studies on sport. Communication is put to the fore – it is neither limited to function, when someone is trying to verbalize a message, nor is it a discipline situated at the crossroads between journalism and social science. The society *per se* is communication, but many forms of communication exist.

Functional differentiation, communication, and autopoiesis

One of the central questions of modern systems theory is how modern society is possible? Luhmann's way of answering this question takes the form of a contribution that aims at transcending the level of individual-based agency and to formulating a social systems theory based on communication. His approach is not a theory of social sectors, but rather seeks to develop an ambitious theory of society as such. Luhmann distinguishes between several types of systems: organisms, machines, and social and psychic systems (Luhmann, 2000). We will put aside the first two here and concentrate on psychic and social systems insofar as these are relevant to sport communication studies.

Social communication systems exist on three distinctive levels: interaction systems, organizations, and societies. Simplistic interaction systems require the face-to-face presence of psychic systems; organization systems consist of communication on decision/non-decision and member/non-member, and societies (often named subsystems or functional systems) which are characterized by their abstract level, such as economics, mass media, politics, law, education; and – some would argue – sport. The assumption is that, in a modern era, society is characterized by an increased functional differentiation, owing to the differentiation of symbolic generalized media (Kneer and Nassehi, 1997). Any complex modern society is made possible by functional differentiation. The society is divided into functional subsystems that contribute to the overall system. Money, for example, serves as a symbolic medium for the economic system, while power is the precondition for an autonomous political system. While a functional (societal) system will have a tendency to observe everything through its own lens, so that an economic system will see everything as a matter of payment/non-payment communication, organizational systems organize and demarcate the complexity of the functional systems. For example, sport organizations enact sport communication (to distinguish between winner and losers) by reporting decisions and distinguishing between members and non-members. The latter function aims at limiting the number of persons who are privy to the communication. Thus, while societies are highly inclusive, organizational systems are exclusive. Modern society, through an evolutionary process, has devolved into autonomous areas (spheres of autologics), and modern organizations have the function of organizing these spheres. In this way, modern society does not have to rely on the physical presence of psychic systems, as modern communication media can replace them in some ways (Werron, 2010). Communication about sport is not dependent on the physical presence of all athletes and the audience. Furthermore, none of the functional systems has the ability to determine the communication of other systems. The level of complexity might result from the dominance of one system, but this is not a simple causal relationship (where dominant systems determine the operations in a dominated system). By regarding systems as autonomous, the observer is able to analyze the peculiarities of the system by constantly relating it to, and distinguishing it from, its environment. Thus, a closer look at how social systems produce and reproduce themselves as communication is necessary.

Social systems are more than action as "communication is not a kind of action, because it always contains a far richer meaning than uttering or sending a message alone" (Luhmann, 1990, p. 6). By focusing on communication, this new category tries to grasp the content of a social system. A social system uses communication to produce and reproduce itself and distinguishes itself as a system in relation to its environment. Both social systems and psychic systems operate autonomously. The consciousness (thoughts) of a psychic system is created by itself; nobody else is able to think for you. In a similar way, what belongs to a social system's communication is solely a matter of the system itself. Similarly, social systems operate as closed systems, but, at the same time, they have the ability to observe their environments (openness). The important and controversial distinction between conscious psychic systems and social communication systems implies that social systems are not understood as the sum of psychic systems; psychic systems (often called humans or individuals) appear in the environment of social systems. They behave according to different meaning providing structures that make their respective autonomous operations possible (consciousness versus communication). What "links them together" in a structural coupling is their mutual ability to adapt to each other, such as through language. Psychic systems can irritate (create noise) and penetrate social systems; for example, utterances are not possible without the operations of psychic systems. The disturbing presence of psychic systems in interactional social systems is obvious, but a modern society is characterized by an increased level of organizational differentiation. Establishing organizations therefore creates a society that relies less on all psychic systems and the noise of their presence, but instead is able to produce communication without the physical presence of all involved individuals.

From biology, Luhmann applies the term "autopoiesis" (self-creation) (Maturana and Varela, 1980) to describe how systems not only produce and change their own structures, but also how they produce their own components. In social systems, structures emerge as expectations about communication; for example, sport communication creates expectations that future communication will produce new winners, that football players enter the game dressed in a certain way, swimmers will employ a certain technique. So communication takes place inside social systems, not in their environments, and in a similar way, social systems do not communicate with each other. Social systems might observe how systems in their environments communicate and subsequently use these observations in their own autopoietic communications. This explains a certain feature of social systems. They are operationally closed and yet remain dependent on stimuli from their environments (Luhmann, 2006). This also points to a non-logical communication and the apparent irrationality of some social systems. Doping in competitive sport is not necessarily an irrational interpretation of the quest for victory found in the sport system, but observed by other systems (such as the political) this practice meets scant sympathy once the phenomenon becomes visible and part of their communication (Wagner, 2009). Sport-specific organization creates its own logic, which the outside world occasionally finds very difficult to understand. In a similar way, what a social system (for example, an organization), perceives as its environment is solely a construct of the system itself. What is integrated into the communication from the outside are foreign references elaborated into system-internal information that becomes part of a system's own autopoiesis. Accordingly, a social system selects and transforms unorganized complexity into organized complexity by making it fit into its own communication. Autopoiesis – self-creation – is the concept applied for understanding the process by which systems create and recreate their own elements and what distinguishes them from the environment.

A social system can, therefore, be understood as a complex set of communication enactments that, opposed to its environment, represent a kind of meaning-providing order. This answers the question: "How is society possible?" A system evolves through selection; it has to distinguish itself from its environment in order to be a system. In this sense, it makes sense to see social communication systems as based on meaning: "There is always a core that is taken for granted which is surrounded by references to other possibilities that cannot be pursued at the same time," noted Luhmann (1990). He added that "Meaning, then, is actuality surrounded by possibilities. The structure of meaning is the structure of this difference between actuality and potentiality. Meaning is the link between the actual and the possible; it is not one or the other" (Luhmann, 1990, p. 83). Autopoietic systems constantly rely on the dynamic created by the system-environment distinction in a process where unstable elements of communication are reproduced over and over again. If a living environment disappears, then so does the system. The distinction is constitutive.

What is communication?

Communication, according to Luhmann (1995, 2007), can then be understood as a tripartite selective process. It is a selection of information from a repertory of possibilities, it is a selection of utterances as a form and, lastly, it is understanding (including misunderstanding) defined as the distinction between information and utterance. The definition makes sense when we regard the elements of communication as a distinction between foreign references (information) and self-references (utterance), and communication is only possible when this distinction is understood and creates the condition for future communication (1995). The rejection of former communications indicates understanding and thus successful communication. The tripartite selection is a unit (but analytically decomposable). The autopoiesis of communication is possible because the system, by drawing the distinction between foreign and self-reference, copies itself as a system. One example: Sport is uttered as embodied physical activity that, in the end, results in the information represented by the creation of a winner. The understanding could have been information about anything else (for example, about nursing a patient), but it is in fact a different utterance and this creates a certain unit of information as a basis for subsequent communication. Communication therefore operates recursively by referring to former distinctions that have been drawn. In this process, symbolic generalized media provide the guidelines for a particular communications. Thus, communication is not something that is delimited to one sphere of society, such as the mass media.

The question of agency

Having outlined the concept of communication, it should be clear that this theory does not operate with an agent or agency, even if this agency is more or less hidden. This does not mean, however, that human beings disappear in this theoretical approach: "Of course, one can still say that human beings act. But since that always occurs in situations," noted Luhmann (1995), "the question remains whether and to what extent the action is attributed to the individual human being or to the situation." He added that, "If one wants to bring about a resolution of this question, one must observe, not the human being in the situation, but the process of attribution" (p. xliii). According to Luhmann, action or agency becomes an attribution of communication or a kind of "condensed" communication. This approach means that phenomena that apparently occur as products of rational agents or of individuals in patterns of interdependency suddenly appear in a new context. The theory is somehow an attempt to analyze action without using the category actor; and perhaps – critics will emphasize – this makes the theory too abstract and useless (Hoberman, 2010). In addition to the general introduction to Luhmann's concepts, we have chosen to introduce the ideas of a second-order observation, as this relates to how one can apply the theory as part of an analytical strategy (Andersen, 1999). It can be noted that the application of traditional methods remains a task that far often has been neglected by systems-theoretical contributions, and methodology has been given a lower priority compared with theory development, which is also frequently considered the Achilles' heel of this approach.

The observer as a central figure

As pointed out by Seidl and Becker (2006), every researcher has to choose a way of observing. The researcher has to distinguish his or her observation from other possible observations (Luhmann, 1990, 2000, 2002; see also Arnoldi, 2001). This is a radical but necessary move. Radical because the researcher could have chosen to draw the distinction inherent in his/her observation in a completely different way; necessary because the complexity of the social world demands its own reduction in order to be understood at all. Drawing a distinction is thus an operation that makes the social become visible to the researcher and gives it meaning.

When introducing Luhmann, one must note that modern systems theory does not have a natural point of departure. In other words, the theoretical framework does not provide us with a central aspect that can be judged to be more important than any other (Andersen, 1999). The theory insists that contingency penetrates to the very heart of the social, and every observation made by the systems-theoretical approach is based on this fundamental imperative. It thus seems odd to state that this brief introduction to the ideas of systems theory holds any 'natural' or logical starting point. Nevertheless, the concept of "the observer" seems to be an important concept, which illustrates how a researcher can observe sport and mass media communication. The term "observation" points to the idea of distinction and difference as the fundamental mechanism for reducing complexity. Furthermore, it produces a temporary and contingent picture of the social order – or society, if one prefers that term. Regarding observations as distinctions also implies that one has to imagine distinctions as a unity of a difference between a marked and an unmarked side. Social science thus becomes a second-order observation (Luhmann, 2002). A second-order observation will focus on the distinctions drawn by a first-order observation. But what does this mean? It points to the fact that this distinction could have been drawn otherwise and thereby produced another observation. As Luhmann points out, reality does exist, but no single observation can grasp it in its totality. Therefore, one logical point of departure is to focus on the distinctions that are applied and then ask: *Who is the observer*? (Luhmann, 2002, p. 95).

One "leitmotif" proposed by Luhmann (1995) in *Soziale Systeme* is the distinction between system and environment. Others might distinguish between concept/counterconcept if one planned to conduct a semantic analysis. Modern systems theory encourages the observer to bring various distinctions into play and to use these distinctions. How can we then describe sport? Only by describing what it is not, and only by identifying how it is distinguished from its environment. Soccer can be seen as a game that is based on distinguishing the winner from the loser, using the body as a medium of communication. But the form of the game might be that eleven players are following certain rules of behavior, determining that the ball must not be thrown, and you are not allowed to kick other players. Observing how certain sports are played provides the observer with information on how meaning emerges in sport communication.

The mass media of society

A brief look at modern society reveals that mass media play an important role today. According to Luhmann (2000), mass media are characterized by the use of technology to distribute communication. These technologies have developed and branched off immensely – from printing a book that radically changed European society nearly 600 years ago to the current global use of Facebook, Twitter, and the Internet in general.

In modern society, mass media have differentiated into an autonomous sphere of society. Their communication aims at defining the distinction between information/non-information, which is the binary coding of this societal system. Another significant feature of mass media communication is the impossibility of a direct interaction between sender and receiver. Thus, technology both facilitates mass distribution as well constraining direct linking between message and reception. Thus, ambivalence characterizes the role of mass media. They construct reality and thereby regulate what is considered information in our society. On the other hand, this solely remains autopoietic operations of the system itself. Mass media have no direct access to an audience – the organizational systems producing mass media communication are dependent on expectations and assumptions about the reception of mass media. This cap opens up for a wide range of interpretations, possible rejections and recontextualizations of mass media messages; for instance, when mass media operations are observed by the political system and transformed into political communication. The consequence has been innumerable ramifications within the system of mass media; that is, particular programming of sub-themes that try to direct expectations towards specific areas such as politics, art or sport. Programming becomes a way to orientate the general coding information/non-information.

An additional function of mass media is to serve as the collective memory of society. And again this is highly selective: In order to remember something (information), mass media draw distinctions and leave out certain things (non-information). They construct a social reality, although they cannot decide what reality is. Mass media are constantly on the move. Once something emerges as information, the time factor soon turns it into non-information; so the mass media actually carry within them the seeds of their own obsolescence, which again means that memory is reduced via the evolutionary progress of mass media communication. Retrospective references may awaken the memory of last year's winner of the Wimbledon tennis tournament, but the name of the loser of the semi-finals disappears into oblivion. So, clearly, mass-mediated memory is partial. Oblivion is a precondition for memory – it is one of the forms of mass media communication. Here, we have to focus on connection of the recursiveness and circularity of mass media communication: memory – irritation – arrangement of information – reality construction – memory, and so on. Irritation urges the system to increase its complexity so that it can arrange more information and through this operation provide more information for society. For more than a decade, this ongoing process has led to new sub-areas of mass media. Highly specialized TV channels about pets, sports, news, and pornography are niches that complement traditional mass media broadcasting companies.

Once we have outlined the distinction between information/non-information, construction of reality and collective memory creation as core features of the mass media system, we can claim that the overall function of mass media is to provide society with a sphere that enables and directs the self-observations of society. At one and the same time, this is both accepted and challenged by the systems' environment. Freedom of expression is the concept that most comprehensively encompasses this tension. On the one hand the autopoiesis of mass media is accepted; on the other, its partial construction of a reality is not always unambiguously shared without controversies. The drawing of the prophet Mohammed in a Danish newspaper led to huge conflicts in the Middle East and diplomatic tensions. Reports on Chinese human right violations in Tibet before the 2008 Olympic Games in Beijing were not always a pleasant theme suitable for international politics. Owing to their binary coding, conflicts related to mass media seem unavoidable rather than occasional and temporary. Descriptions of reality are partial and, inevitably, the excluded counterpart will always remain a potential source of irritation.

Sport: A blind spot in systems theory?

Unlike mass media communication, sport has surprisingly not figured in the writings of Luhmann. Sport seems to have been a blind spot in his attempted grand theory. Other scholars have applied Luhmann's ideas to sport, though. Karl-Heinrich Bette (1987), in a volume dedicated to Niklas Luhmann, points to the paradox of a modern society, in which the body is simultaneously and increasingly marginalized and celebrated. The body appears as a minor central theme of political or economic communication. At the same time, the body serves as the indispensable communication medium for sport and for other spheres, such as fashion and health care (which paradoxically is the care of the unhealthy body). In some sectors of modern society, the body is disciplined, whereas in other sectors it emerges as wild and untamed. Bette (1999) points out that, in sport, the body is the cultic object. The interesting aspect is that modern society has produced not one definition of the body, but rather a poly-contextualized one (Bette). This important notion may provide us with a logical understanding of the body and also highlight the tensions that arise because of this relation. Thus, the body only becomes relevant when it fits into the communication of a particular functional system and its binary coding of communication (for example, the body is translated into a market price or a form of political power). In a similar way, competitive sport uses the body as the medium for its communication about winning and losing (Bette). In the German context, Cachay (1988) describes the differentiation of a sport system that initially achieved its functional relevance by providing unique opportunities for education, military service and public health solutions. Following its political role during the era of National Socialism, public health became the primary function of sport. The Norwegian scientist, Jan-Ove Tangen, has approached the question of "how is sport possible?" by stating that the symbolically differentiated medium of sport is the victory and that modern sport is guided by the binary code win/lose, along with the secondary coding improvement/regression (Tangen, 2004).

Drawing on Tangen's idea that the communication of sport mirrors society's lead difference, progress/regress, Storm (2010, 2011) uses the structural coupling between the economic system and the sports system in professional team sports as a frame for answering the question of why European professional sports clubs keep on operating on the brink of insolvency despite the significant increases in revenue enjoyed by the popular sports during the last 30 years. According to Storm, professional team sports clubs can be said to represent one way of operationalizing society's lead difference as the clubs symbolize the constant striving for progress characteristic of modern societies through their use of the double sport codification: win/lose and progress/regress (Storm, 2009; Tangen, 2004, 2010). In the European – as opposed to the American – context, sport codifications rather than the economic code prevail when financial resources are used as a means of achieving the goals of winning and progress, in the majority of professional team sports clubs, instead of the opposite (Storm, 2009, 2010, 2011). Another important aspect that needs further theoretical and empirical elaboration is the function of sport, assuming that sport is a functional communication system of society (Bette, 1999; Cachay, 1988). As mentioned above, Tangen (2004) suggests that sport is a kind of "mirror-function" of society, because modern society needs a system capable of explicitly representing the distinction between progression/regression. Sport serves as a functional system that tests these operations by providing the standardizations, calculations, measurements and quantifications that are common in sport without presenting too much risk to the overall society. One objection might be that similar techniques occur in other functional systems (for example, in economies where stock markets and annual reports serve as measurements and tests that indicate the progression/regression of private corporations). Stichweh (1990) describes the unity of the sport system solely in terms of its ability to provide meaningful communication about embodied performance capabilities. He emphasizes that sport as a differentiated functional system must contribute its own functionality to society and not only be considered as an adjunct of other functional systems. This points to a very interesting question: *Does sport have a unique function?*

Defining sport as a functional system requires theoretical as well as empirical research, because the number of functional systems in a society, according to Luhmann, is an empirical question. Modern systems theory posits an evolutionary process which over time has resulted in the differentiation of autopoietic systems. Therefore, it seems obvious that this development results in more than a few established functional systems which constantly increase in number.

Despite this discussion, it seems beyond any doubt that mass media have integrated sport at a very early stage of modern sports development. Sport has become information – it is a part of modern society's self-description. Werron (2010) outlines how sport historically has been integrated in modern society's self-description as new mass media technologies developed in the 19th century. Another good example of this mutual correlation between sport and mass media is the history of the Tour de France (Wille, 2003). A newspaper company invents this spectacular ride around the country in order to sell papers. This reveals how an organization (here the company running the newspaper) is able to incorporate various communicative forms of logic in its decision making: By integrating road cycling in mass media communication, sport becomes information (the binary code of mass media), the idea of distinguishing the winner from losers is adopted (the binary code of sport), and finally, this enables the company to make a profit from the sale (the binary code of economy). Complex organizations are able to facilitate structural couplings between several functional systems and integrate these in their ongoing communication decisions. Newspapers dedicate sections to sport, TV news often routinely finishes with the sport news, thus allowing institutionalized settings for sport to interpenetrate mass media communication. In that sense, sport stimulates and irritates the mass media – and the mass media accept these stimuli, select useful elements, and leave a lot behind. Sport has become part of the construction of the reality of modern society.

References

Andersen, Å. N. (1999). *Diskursive analysestrategier. Foucault, Koselleck, Laclau, Luhmann*. Copenhagen: Nyt fra Samfundsvidenskaberne.

Arnoldi, J. (2001). Niklas Luhmann: An introduction. *Theory, Culture and Society*, 18, 1–13.

Bette, K.-H. (1987). Wo ist der Körper? In D. Baecker, J. Markowitz, H. Tyrell, and H. Willke (Eds.), *Theorie als Passion – Niklas Luhmann zum 60. Geburtstag* (pp. 600–28). Frankfurt: Suhrkamp.

Bette, K.-H. (1999). *Systemtheorie und sport*. Frankfurt: Suhrkamp.

Bjerg, O. (2005). Die Welt als Wille und System. Oder: Eine Schopenhauerische Kritik der Systemtheorie Luhmanns. *Zeitschrift für Soziologie*, 34, 233–35.

Cachay, K. (1988). *Sport und Gesellschaft. Zur Ausdifferenzierung einer Funktion und ihrer Folgen*. Schorndorf: Hofmann Verlag.

Hoberman, J. (2010). A critical American perspective on sport and the legacy of systems theory. In U. Wagner, R. K. Storm, and J. Hoberman (Eds.), *Observing sport: Modern system theoretical approaches* (pp. 265–74). Schorndorf: Hofmann Verlag.

Kneer, G., and Nasehi, A. (1993). *Niklas Luhmanns Theorie sozialer Systeme. Eine Einführung*. München: Vilhelm Fink Verlag.

Luhmann, N. (1990). *Essays on self-reference*. New York: Columbia University Press.

Luhmann, N. (1995). *Social systems*. Stanford, CA: Stanford University Press.

Luhmann, N. (1997). *Die Gesellschaft der Gesellschaft* (Vols. 1–2). Frankfurt: Suhrkamp.

Luhmann, N. (2000). *The reality of mass media*. Stanford, CA: Stanford University Press.

Luhmann, N. (2002). *Theories of distinction – Redescribing the descriptions of modernity*. Stanford, CA: Stanford University Press.

Luhmann, N. (2006) *Organisation und Entscheidung*. Wiesbaden: VS Verlag für Sozialwissenschaften.

Luhmann, N. (2007). *Indføring i systemteorien*. Copenhagen: Forlaget Unge Pædagoger [Original title: *Einführung in die Systemteorie*].

Maturana, H. R., and Varela, F. J. (1980). *Autopoiesis and cognition: The realization of the living*. Dordrecht: R. Reidel.

Seidl, D., and Becker, K. H. (2006). Organizations as distinction generating and processing systems: Niklas Luhmann's contribution to organization studies. *Organization*, 13 (1), 9–35.

Spencer-Brown, G. (1969): *Laws of form*. London: Allen and Unwin.

Stichweh, R. (1990). Sport – Ausdifferenzierung, Funktion, Code. *Sportswissenschaft*, 20, 373–89.

Storm, R., and Wagner, U. (2010). Observing sport – An introduction. In U. Wagner, R. K. Storm, and J. Hoberman (Eds.), *Observing sport: Modern system theoretical approaches* (pp. 9–31). Schorndorf: Hofmann Verlag.

Storm, R. K. (2009). Samfundets nye kulturpolitik: Sport i oplevelsesøkonomien. *Nordisk Kulturpolitisk Tidsskrift*, 12, 113–39.

Storm, R. K. (2010). Professional team sports clubs and profits: An irreconcilable combination? In U. Wagner, R. K. Storm, and J. Hoberman (Eds.), *Observing sport: Modern system theoretical approaches* (pp. 103–30). Schorndorf: Hofmann Verlag.

Storm, R. K. (2011). Winners and losers in Danish football: Commercialization and developments in European and Danish first-tier clubs. *Soccer and Society*, 12 (6), 737–53.

Tangen, J. O. (2004). *Hvordan er idrett mulig? Skisse til en idrettssociologi.* [*How is sport possible? An outline for a sociology of sport*]. Kristiansand: Høyskole Forlaget.

Tangen, J. O. (2010). Observing sport participation: Some sociological remarks on the inclusion/exclusion mechanism in sport. In U. Wagner, R. K. Storm, and J. Hoberman (Eds.), *Observing sport: Modern system theoretical approaches* (pp. 131–61). Schondorf: Hofmann Verlag.

Wagner, U. (2009). The World Anti-Doping Agency: Constructing a hybrid organisation in permanent stress (dis-) order? *International Journal of Sport Policy and Politics*, 1, 183–200.

Werron, T. (2010). World sport and its public. On historical relations of modern sport and the media. In U. Wagner, R. K. Storm, and J. Hoberman (Eds.), *Observing sport: Modern system theoretical approaches* (pp. 33–59). Schondorf: Hofmann Verlag.

Wille, F. (2003). The Tour de France as an agent of change in media production. In H. Dauncy and G. Hare (Eds.), *The Tour de France 1903–2003: A century of sporting structures, meanings and values* (pp. 128–46). London: Frank Cass.

6

SOCIAL MEDIA AND SPORT COMMUNICATION

Abundant theoretical opportunities

Jimmy Sanderson

A little over a decade ago, communication scholar Robert Craig (1999, p. 119) observed in his award-winning article, "Communication theory is enormously rich in the range of ideas that fall within its nominal scope and new theoretical work on communication has recently been flourishing." In the ensuing time since Craig's declaration, scholars have accomplished much in advancing communication theory, particularly in the emerging field of sport communication (Kassing, 2009; Krizek, 2008; Sanderson, 2011a). Sport communication research is, to use Craig's descriptor, "flourishing." This status has been achieved largely through the willingness of sport communication and sport media researchers to undertake studies that advance communication (including mass communication) theory. Several brief examples include scholars using social identity theory to explain audience perceptions of female sports reporters (Baiocchi-Wagner and Behm-Morawitz, 2011); employing agenda setting theory to analyze Olympic broadcast coverage (Angelini and Billings, 2010); and utilizing dissent to explore Dallas Mavericks' owner Mark Cuban's blogging (Sanderson, 2009). As this volume evidences, sport communication literature is expanding and increasing in prominence. Concurrent with this trek up the mountain of disciplinary acceptance is the necessity for sport communication and sport media researchers to continue integrating and advancing communication theory. The emergence of research investigating social media influences in sport stands as a particularly rich area for this task to be accomplished.

The marriage of social media and sport communication research is in its infancy. Nevertheless, despite its youth, this research track has produced a number of significant studies that have advanced communication theory (Clavio and Kian, 2010; Kassing and Sanderson, 2009a; Hambrick, Simmons, Greenhalgh, and Greenwell, 2010). Valuable work in this research sector is increasing, yet there are a number of theoretical roads that have still to be traversed. The purpose of this chapter is to discuss some of the communication theories that have been utilized in sport and social media research to this point, and then to provide future directions for as of yet, under-utilized or unexplored communication theories. As is explained in Chapter 1 as well, it should be noted that it is impossible to offer every possible theoretical avenue one could travel in this research domain, and scholars interested in this area are encouraged to pioneer their own theoretical pathways.

Current theoretical directions

Researchers investigating social media and sport have employed multiple theoretical frameworks to guide their analyses; however, two theories in particular appear to be prevalent: (a) parasocial interaction, and (b) uses and gratification theory. An overview of how each of these theories has been integrated into social media and sport communication research is now provided.

Parasocial interaction

Parasocial interaction describes how media users relate to and develop relationships with media personae. In their original conceptualization, Horton and Wohl (1956) argued that radio listeners developed bonds of intimacy over time as they persistently consumed media personalities. These bonds prompt audience members to engage media personalities in ways that resemble interpersonal social interaction, but differ as these displays are one-sided and mediated. Since Horton and Wohl's original conception, parasocial interaction has received considerable research attention (Giles, 2002). Early research endeavors focused on traditional mass media channels as scholars explored parasocial interaction with television newscasters (Palmgreen, Wenner, and Rayburn, 1980; Rubin and McHugh, 1987); soap-opera characters (Perse and Rubin, 1989; Rubin and Perse, 1987); and radio and television talk-show hosts (Rubin, 2000; Rubin, Haridakis, and Eyal, 2003). Whereas these efforts were instrumental in advancing parasocial interaction scholarship, sports was curiously overlooked. With the advent of social media, however, sport has become a fertile parasocial interaction research subject (Kassing and Sanderson, 2009a, 2009b, 2010; Sanderson, 2008a, 2008b).

Traditionally, parasocial interaction has been conceptualized as an introspective experience that is usually displayed to those in one's immediate vicinity (for example, communicating to a character while watching television show, talking to others at work). Social media, however, enables sports fans to conveniently and actively communicate parasocial interaction directly to athletes. This capability results in a diverse expression of parasocial interaction behaviors, many of which are quite emphatic (Gleich, 1997). For instance, Kassing and Sanderson (2009a) examined parasocial interaction on cyclist Floyd Landis' blog during three crucial stages of the 2006 Tour de France that ultimately led to Landis winning the Tour (he was later stripped of the title owing to positive tests for performance-enhancing drugs). One of the findings emanating from this study was the significant behavioral effects that parasocial interaction produced, which fans eagerly communicated to Landis. One person noted that after watching Landis, s/he needed to "take the rest of the day off to recover." Others shared how Landis was disrupting their daily lives, characterized by a person who disclosed that s/he was, "reading live updates on my cell phone as I drove 70mph...The whole time I was screaming alone in my car 'Come on Floyd!!!! Just keep going!!!!'"

Sanderson (2008b) noted similar sentiments in parasocial interaction expressions from fans towards Dallas Mavericks' owner, Mark Cuban, while he participated on American Broadcasting Corporation's (ABC) hit television show *Dancing with the Stars*. Sanderson observed that fans: (a) disclosed the emotional intensity they experienced as Cuban performed; (b) conveyed the diligent tasks that they were performing to preserve Cuban's tenure on the show; and (c) advised and counseled Cuban on ways to improve his dancing techniques to make him a stronger competitor. With respect to the second category, examples included, "MC: I sent out an email to EVERYONE, A blast of 14k to vote for you," and

"However after shooting the stills of you and Kym last week working on your routine, I'm telling everyone don't bet against you" (Sanderson, 2008b, p. 161). Others shared their proselytizing efforts:

> My girls are telling everyone at their schools my husband at his work and I am sending out e-mails to all my girlfriends. I know this is a small portion, but sometimes that all adds up!!!...This week I created a bunch of fake email addresses and gave you guys more than 100 votes!!! lol...I will try to think of even more next week.
>
> *(Sanderson, 2008b, p. 161)*

Several important findings stemming from this study, include: (a) that non-playing personnel also are recipients of parasocial interaction from sports fans; and (b) parasocial interaction can induce perception changes, as several people disclosed that in bonding with Cuban, their feelings towards him changed from contempt to adoration.

Parasocial interaction research also has been advanced through findings of parasocial interaction role-reversals, wherein fans give advice to athletes, rather than seek it from them. In their study on Floyd Landis, Kassing and Sanderson (2009a) discovered that fans conveyed diverse counsel related to both cycling and social activities. Examples included, "Get some rest tomorrow and get those legs ready for Saturday!" and "Tell those mechanics to CHECK and DOUBLE CHECK YOUR DAMN BIKE!!!" (Kassing and Sanderson, 2009a, p. 196). Sanderson (2008a) explored parasocial interaction on Boston Red Sox pitcher Curt Schilling's blog and found that fans' advice was stern, bordering on reprimand, such as rebukes for Schilling's perceived incongruence in practicing his Christianity, and in fans' estimation, spending more time blogging than practicing baseball.

As this research depicts, fans are becoming more emboldened in censuring athletes. This behavior has led to the emergence of what has been termed "maladaptive PSI" (Kassing and Sanderson, 2012). Sanderson (2008a), in his study of Curt Schilling, observed this parasocial interaction facet, as fans lambasted Schilling for his overt personality, Republican Party affiliation, and support for United States President George W. Bush, including one person who implied that Schilling's support for Bush made him implicitly accountable for the consequences of the Iraq War.

This summary illustrates several ways that parasocial interaction has been extended through social media and sport research; nonetheless, other fruitful directions await exploration. First, whereas social media have fostered parasocial interaction, they simultaneously create avenues for actual, social interaction. Accordingly, fans navigate between these two spheres in their social media communiqués with athletes and sports figures. Kassing and Sanderson (2012) coined the phrase "circum-social (fan-athlete) interaction" to articulate this revolving interaction pattern facilitated by social media. Future research should investigate how interaction changes as fans rotate between parasocial and social interaction with athletes. Are certain behaviors more prominent in one sphere or another, or do they appear consistently in both contexts? Whereas parasocial interaction is one-sided, it can be argued that athletes experience minimal consequences from maladaptive parasocial interaction, but what happens when the interaction shifts to social?

Second, parasocial interaction encompasses a broad array of behaviors, some of which are still unexplored, and for which sport is well-suited for investigation. For instance, forgiveness is an important relational element, yet this component is missing from the corpus of parasocial interaction research. Athletes and sports figures routinely apologize for both on-the-field and off-the-field miscues, and it would be worthwhile for researchers to explore the extent to which fans extend or withhold forgiveness. Additionally, deception and betrayal also manifest in the sports world and are likely to prompt parasocial interaction. Sports fans often expect loyalty from athletes and sports figures, and when these individuals transgress, strong parasocial interaction is likely to follow. Players voluntarily switching teams and collegiate recruiting are two potentially rich areas where the parasocial interaction repertoire can be expanded, and with fans' propensity to express parasocial interaction via social media, valuable data repositories await.

Uses and gratifications theory

According to uses and gratifications theory (Katz, Blumler, and Gurevitch, 1974), media use emanates from goals, as media consumers select specific, targeted channels to satiate needs and achieve gratification (Clavio and Kian, 2010). Motivations help media users to assess what they stand to gain from consuming a media channel, or what they will lose by avoiding or opting out of that media source. Whereas uses and gratification theory has been extensively applied to traditional media, the emergence of the Internet and social media have created exciting directions for further extension of the theory (Ruggerio, 2000). With respect to social media, researchers have found that social interaction is a primary factor underpinning consumption (Ancu and Cozma, 2009), that communicating with offline friends is a salient motivation for using Facebook (Barker and Ota, 2011), and that the strength of one's habits is a significant predictor of playing social networking games (Wohn, 2012).

Uses and gratifications theory has found a home in social media and sport research. This theory is particularly valuable in understanding why various sports stakeholders use social media (Clavio and Kian, 2010; Frederick, Clavio, Burch, and Zimmerman, 2012), and the content being generated by these individuals (Hambrick, *et al.*, 2010). For instance, Clavio (2008) surveyed college sport message board users and noted four primary areas of uses and gratification for these individuals: (a) interactivity; (b) information gathering; (c) diversion; and (d) argumentation. Clavio and Kian (2010) surveyed Twitter followers of a retired professional golfer and discovered that people followed her because they perceived her to be an expert about her sport, and possessed an affinity for her writing style.

Uses and gratifications theory also has been adopted in social media research in non-mainstream sports such as Mixed Martial Arts (MMA) and the Ultimate Fighting Championship and phenomena such as fantasy sports. Frederick, *et al.* (2012) surveyed consumers of a popular MMA blog and found six primary reasons for accessing the blog: (a) evaluation – criticizing both the blog and the MMA organization; (b) community – sharing interests and experiences; (c) information gathering – obtaining news about MMA; (d) knowledge demonstration – displaying one's intellectual capital about MMA to others; (e) argumentation – debating other fans; and (f) diversion – discussing issues not related to MMA. Ruihley and Hardin (2011) applied uses and gratification to their survey of fantasy sports users to ascertain their reasons for using message boards. They discovered that message boards enhanced the fantasy sport experience through: (a) logistical conversation – discussing transactions, players, or the fantasy league itself with other league members; (b) socializing – trash talking or general conversation with other league members; (c) surveillance – obtaining information beneficial for fantasy sport participation; and (d) advice and opinion – seeking consultation about transactions, players, or other fantasy league matters.

Many of the studies involving uses and gratifications theory are centered on the consumption side of social media, and work is emerging to fill in the other portion. Hambrick, *et al.* (2010), using content analytic methods, discovered that professional athletes used Twitter in the following six ways: (a) interactivity – direct communication with other athletes and fans; (b) diversion – providing non-sports related information; (c) information sharing – offering insights about coaches, teammates or the sport; (d) linking to content – pointing fans to places of interest across the Internet; (e) fanship – sharing their fandom of other sports and athletes; and (f) promotional – endorsing public relations efforts, campaigns, and upcoming games.

This research synopsis illuminates key insights into why sports media consumers use various social media channels, as well as how athletes are using them. However, as with parasocial interaction, there is important work that remains to be done. First, one of the key voices missing in this literature is that of the athlete. This is likely due to the difficulty in obtaining access to athletes, but is imperative that the athlete side of the social media equation be obtained. For instance, what motivations do athletes report for using social media sites? What makes them more apt to use Twitter versus Facebook? How satisfying do athletes find social media? Researchers have outlined several benefits for athletes in using social media (Sanderson, 2011a; Sanderson and Kassing, 2010), but it is crucial to determine whether athletes share these sentiments. Second, most of the social media research invoking uses and gratifications has been centered on Twitter. Whereas Twitter is viewed as the social media channel "of choice" for athletes (Sanderson, 2011a; Sanderson and Kassing, 2011) it would be worthwhile to extend the theory into other social media domains such as Facebook, Tumblr, and Google Plus. What differences and similarities emerge in sports fans who consume one or multiple social media sites to satiate their sports craving?

Suggested theoretical directions

With the above review in place, this section now outlines several theories that are currently under-utilized or untapped and offers ways for them to be woven into the fabric of social media and sport communication research.

Framing

Framing occurs when mass media outlets report news items in ways that guide and shape audience interpretations (Kuypers and Cooper, 2005; Tian and Stewart, 2005). Framing processes are prominent within sports media (Eagleman, 2011; Kian and Hardin, 2009; Sanderson, 2008c) and social media provides athletes with a tool to counteract perceived negative media framing (Sanderson, 2008c). Sanderson (2008c) analyzed how Curt Schilling used his blog to defend himself against allegations that he had faked an injury during the 2004 American League Championship Series. He posited that Schilling's blog served as an outlet to broadly disseminate his defense, and that his efforts were overwhelmingly lauded by fans. Challenging media framing does not, however, lie solely in the purview of the athlete. Indeed, social media allows fans to get involved in this process as well. Sanderson (2010) investigated how fans of professional golfer Tiger Woods used Facebook to counteract media framings related to Woods' marital infidelity. He found that via Facebook, fans perpetuated notions that Woods' unfaithfulness was merely evidence of humanness, a characteristic that had previously been difficult to detect in Woods. Fans also framed Woods' infidelity as a private matter, and together, these framings stood in stark contrast to mainstream media outlets that focused on the sordid details of Woods' extramarital indiscretions.

There are several avenues wherein social media and sport researchers can incorporate framing. First, more work is needed in exploring responses to athletes challenging media framing. Under what circumstances do fans agree or disagree with the athlete? In some cases, introducing alternative frames may elicit bonding between athletes and fans during crisis. For instance, in the spring of 2012, National Football League (NFL) player Jonathan Vilma was suspended for the entire 2012–13 NFL season for allegedly offering financial rewards to his New Orleans Saints teammates to injure other players (Chase, 2012). Vilma has maintained his innocence and has vigorously used Twitter to defend himself, which has resulted in fans rallying to his side and supporting his efforts. A second direction for framing research involves a conceptual corollary – agenda setting (McCombs and Shaw, 1972). Identifying how sport organizations, athletes, and sports reporters use social media to drive their agenda through specific frames, would yield important insights. The sports media landscape has evolved from a narrow ownership to broad playing field (Hutchins and Rowe, 2009). Sports organizations and athletes now compete with sports media organizations to shape and drive messages, and successfully navigating this digital terrain is essential to obtain and sustain public support. How these various sports stakeholders frame their messages will be a valuable contribution to both academics and practitioners.

Predicted outcome value theory

Predicted outcome value (POV) theory deals with initial interaction behaviors and consequences. POV theory suggests that during initial interactions, people make value judgments that are motivated by the desire to reduce relational costs and maximize rewards (Sunnafrank, 1986). POV theory posits that communication behavior in initial interactions is guided by the desire to maximize future outcomes. Accordingly, when one expects positive outcomes, s/he will seek to prolong interaction, promote future contact, and develop the relationship. Conversely, when unfavorable outcomes are expected, individuals will engage in distancing behavior (Ramirez, Sunnafrank, and Goei, 2010). With respect to sport, POV has received scant attention, but in the realm of social media, the theory plays an important role.

One of the trends emanating from social media's societal percolation is employers using social media as resource to investigate prospective employees (Peluchette and Karl, 2010; Roberts and Roach, 2009). This practice is not lost on American collegiate athletic programs, many of which contract with third-parties to monitor student-athletes' social media activity (Sanderson, 2011b). Future research could utilize POV to investigate the role of social media in this realm, particularly as it pertains to athletic recruiting. For instance, is there particular content on a social media site that will prohibit a school from pursuing a potential student-athlete? Or does talent outweigh perceived inappropriate social media use?

This trend also may be occurring in professional sports, and such research has value in this sphere as well. For example, Sanderson (2011b) detailed the case of Zachary Houchins, a college baseball player drafted in 2011 by the Washington Nationals. After the draft, a team fan blog posted tweets from Houchins. The post titled "Nats draft a bigot?" (2011) included sample tweet such as, "My teacher just told me not to worry ab a make up test bc he'll pass me. Whatta boss nigga," and "Time to go and shit on niggas." His last tweet posted on the blog stated, "Gotta watch what I say up here ha," (pp. 505–6). Houchins ultimately returned to college, and his case provides a vivid exemplar of why professional sports teams must be interested in the social media activity of their prospective employees.

Communication privacy management theory

Communication privacy management (CPM) theory was developed by communication scholar Sandra Petronio (1991) to broaden the concept of disclosure. At its core, CPM theory positions communication as a goal-oriented task, and is composed of six propositions. The first proposition contends that private disclosures reveal aspects of the self that are not publicly known, information that people perceive they have the right to control. The second proposition delineates between private, individual, information and public, shared, information. CPM theory posits that individuals choose to share or conceal information based upon criteria that already exists in a particular context, or which emerges through negotiation with others. CPM theory's third proposition contends that people feel vulnerable and violated when they lose control over information release or when privacy is invaded (for example, external monitoring, confidants disclosing information they were instructed to conceal).

CPM's fourth proposition suggests that when people disclose information, others become co-owners of that information, extending privacy boundaries. Disclosers accept responsibility for the information, and receivers have an implied expectation of responsibility. Once information becomes co-owned, the parties must develop privacy rules – CPM theory's fifth proposition. The sixth proposition recognizes that communication and privacy are dialectical tensions (Petronio, 2004). That is, relational partners must balance a need for both expression and concealment, and determine the acceptable balance between public and private. Accordingly, as people distribute information, impose regulations upon that information, and negotiate rules about that information with those to whom they have shared it, one's goals greatly influence their communicative choices (Miller, 2009).

CPM theory was initially applied to interpersonal communication contexts, but scholars are expanding CPM to other contexts, including communication technology (Child, Pearson, and Petronio, 2009; Metzger, 2007). Given CPM theory's underpinnings, it is not difficult to see its value for social media research in sport. Potential topics for investigation include: How do sports teams and athletes negotiate what information is acceptable to broadcast via social media? How do student-athletes feel about their social media activity being monitored by an external third party? What degree of privacy do athletes perceive when using social media? In spite of these promising directions, little work to this point has incorporated CPM. Sanderson (2011b) applied CPM theory to analyze social media policies in Division I collegiate athletics and observed that policies dictated privacy unilaterally. This conclusion stemmed from student-athletes being given numerous content restrictions, with little guidance on how to use social media strategically, and, apparently, little input on these prohibitions. Sanderson argued that shaping privacy rules in this fashion was likely to incite rather than alleviate problematic social media use. As social media is firmly entrenched in sport (Sanderson, 2011a) how sports organizations and athletes negotiate social media use is a vital area where CPM theory can be fruitfully applied.

Conclusion

This chapter illustrates how communication theory has been and can be applied to social media and sport research. Whereas there have been many significant advancements, particularly with parasocial interaction theory and uses and gratifications theory, much remains to be done. This assessment, however, should be met with vigor, not reticence. As sport communication scholars apply and extend communication theory in all areas (not just social media), this burgeoning field will hasten along its liberating trek within the communication discipline. Other scholars will observe how sport communication research extends and advances communication theory, which will further erode barriers to its perceived legitimacy. It is indeed, an exciting time to be conducting sport communication research. Social media stands as an abundant plot eagerly awaiting those willing to cultivate it with their theoretical arsenal.

References

Ancu, M., and Cozma, R. (2009). MySpace politics: Uses and gratifications of befriending candidates. *Journal of Broadcasting and Electronic Media*, 53: 567–83.

Angelini, J. R., and Billings, A. C. (2010). An agenda that sets the frames: Gender, language, and NBC's Americanized Olympic telecast. *Journal of Language and Social Psychology*, 29: 363–85.

Baiocchi-Wagner, E., and Behm-Morawitz, E. (2011). Audience perceptions of female sports reporters: A social-identity approach. *International Journal of Sport Communication*, 3, 261–74.

Barker, V., and Ota, H. (2011). Mixi Diary versus Facebook photos: Social networking site use among Japanese and Caucasian American females. *Journal of Intercultural Communication Research*, 40, 39–63.

Chase, C. (2012). Jonathan Vilma suspended for 2012 season for role in Saints bounty system. Shutdown Corner: A Y! Blog, May 2. Retrieved from http://sports.yahoo.com/blogs/nfl-shutdown-corner/jonathan-vilma-suspended-season-role-saints-bounty-system-155350881.html.

Child, J. T., Pearson, J. C., and Petronio, S. (2009). Blogging, communication and privacy management: Development of the blogging privacy management measure. *Journal of the American Society for Information Science and Technology*, 60, 2079–94.

Clavio, G. (2008). Uses and gratifications of Internet collegiate sport message board users. *Dissertation Abstracts International*, 69(08). ProQuest Digital Dissertations database (Publication No. AAT 3319833). Retrieved from http://gradworks.umi.com/33/19/3319833.html.

Clavio, G. C., and Kian, T. M. (2010). Uses and gratifications of a retired female athlete's Twitter followers. *International Journal of Sport Communication*, 3, 485–500.

Craig, R. T. (1999). Communication theory as a field. *Communication Theory*, 9, 119–61.

Eagleman, A. M. (2011). Stereotypes of race and nationality: A qualitative analysis of sport magazine coverage of MLB players. *Journal of Sport Management*, 25, 156–68.

Frederick, E. L., Clavio, G. E., Burch, L. M., and Zimmerman, M. H. (2012). Characteristics of users of a mixed-martial-arts blog: A case study of demographics and usage trends. *International Journal of Sport Communication*, 5, 109–25.

Giles, D. C. (2002). Parasocial interaction: A review of the literature and a model for future research. *Media Psychology*, 4, 279–305.

Gleich, U. (1997). Parasocial interaction with people on the screen. In P. Winterhoff-Spurk and T. H. A. Van der Voort (Eds.), *New horizons in media psychology: Research co-operation and projects in Europe* (pp. 35–55). Opladen, Germany: Westduetscher Verlag.

Hambrick, M. E., Simmons, J. M., Greenhalgh, G. P., and Greenwell, T. C. (2010). Understanding professional athletes' use of Twitter: A content analysis of athlete tweets. *International Journal of Sport Communication*, 3, 454–71.

Horton, D., and Wohl, R. R. (1956). Mass communication and para-social interaction. *Psychiatry*, 19, 215–29.

Hutchins, B., and Rowe, D. (2009). From broadcast scarcity to digital plentitude. *Television and New Media*, 10: 354–70.

Kassing, J. W. (2009). Editor's introduction. *Electronic Journal of Communication*, 19 (3/4). Retrieved from http://www.cios.org/www/ejc/v19n34tocnew.htm#introduction.

Kassing, J. W., and Sanderson, J. (2009a). "You're the kind of guy that we all want for a drinking buddy": Expressions of parasocial interaction on Floydlandis.com. *Western Journal of Communication*, 73, 182–203.

Kassing, J. W., and Sanderson, J. (2009b). "Is this a church? Such a big bunch of believers around here!": Fan expressions of social support on Floydlandis.com. *Journal of Communication Studies*, 2, 309–30.

Kassing, J. W., and Sanderson, J. (2010). Tweeting through the Giro: A case study of fan–athlete interaction on Twitter. *International Journal of Sport Communication*, 3, 113–28.

Kassing, J. W., and Sanderson, J. (2012). Playing in the new media game or riding the virtual bench: Confirming and disconfirming membership in the community of sport. *Journal of Sport and Social Issues*, September 13, OnlineFirst. DOI: 10.1177/0193723512458931.

Katz, E., Blumler, J. G., and Gurevitch, M. (1974). Utilization of mass communication by the individual. In J. G. Blumler and E. Katz (Eds.), *Uses of mass communications* (Vol. III; pp. 19–32). Beverly Hills, CA: Sage.

Kian, E. M., and Hardin, M. (2009). Framing of sport coverage based on the sex of sports writers: Female journalists counter the traditional gendering of media coverage. *International Journal of Sport Communication*, 2, 185–204.

Krizek, B. (2008). Introduction: Communication and the community of sport. *Western Journal of Communication*, 72, 103–6.

Kuypers, J. A., and Cooper, S. D. (2005). A comparative framing analysis of embedded and behind-the-lines reporting on the 2003 Iraq War. *Qualitative Research Reports in Communication*, 6, 1–10.

McCombs, M., and Shaw, D. (1972). The agenda-setting function of the mass media. *Public Opinion Quarterly*, 36, 176–87.

Metzger, M. (2007). Communication privacy management in electronic commerce. *Journal of Computer-Mediated Communication*, 12, 1–27.

Miller, A. E. (2009). Revealing and concealing postmarital dating information: Divorced coparents' privacy rule development and boundary coordination processes. *Journal of Family Communication*, 9, 135–49.

Palmgreen, P., Wenner, L. A., and Rayburn II, J. D. (1980). Relations between gratifications sought and obtained: A study of television news. *Communication Research*, 7, 161–92.

Peluchette, J., and Karl, K. (2009). Examining students' intended image on Facebook: "What were they thinking?!" *Journal of Education for Business*, 85, 30–7.

Perse, E. M., and Rubin, R. B. (1989). Attribution in social and parasocial relationships. *Communication Research*, 16, 59–77.

Petronio, S. (1991). Communication boundary management: A theoretical model of managing disclosure of private information between martial couples. *Communication Theory*, 1, 311–35.

Petronio, S. (2004). Road to developing communication privacy management theory: Narrative in progress, please stand by. *Journal of Family Communication*, 4, 193–207.

Ramirez, A., Jr., Sunnafrank, M., and Goei, R. (2010). Predicted outcome value theory in ongoing relationships. *Communication Monographs*, 77, 27–50.

Roberts, S. J., and Roach, T. (2009). Social networking web sites and human resource personnel: Suggestions for job searches. *Business Communication Quarterly*, 72, 110–14.

Rubin, A. M. (2000). Impact of motivation, attraction, and parasocial interaction on talk radio listening. *Journal of Broadcasting and Electronic Media*, 44, 635–54.

Rubin, A. M., and Perse, E. M. (1987). Audience activity and soap opera involvement: A uses and effects investigation. *Human Communication Research*, 14, 246–68.

Rubin, A. M., Haridakis, P. M., and Eyal, K. (2003). Viewer aggression and attraction to television talk shows. *Media Psychology*, 5, 331–62.

Rubin, R. B., and McHugh, M. (1987). Development of parasocial interaction relationships. *Journal of Broadcasting and Electronic Media*, 31, 279–92.

Ruggerio, T. E. (2000). Uses and gratifications theory in the 21st century. *Mass Communication and Society*, 3, 3–37.

Ruihley, B. J., and Hardin, R. L. (2011). Message boards and the fantasy sport experience. *International Journal of Sport Communication*, 4, 233-252.

Sanderson, J. (2008a). "You are the type of person that children should look up to as a hero": Parasocial interaction on 38pitches.com. *International Journal of Sport Communication*, 1, 337–60.

Sanderson, J. (2008b). Spreading the word: Emphatic interaction displays on BlogMaverick.com. *Journal of Media Psychology: Theories, Methods, and Applications*, 20, 157–68.

Sanderson, J. (2008c). The blog is serving its purpose: Self-presentation strategies on 38pitches.com. *Journal of Computer-Mediated Communication*, 13, 912–36.

Sanderson, J. (2009). "Thanks for fighting the good fight": Cultivating dissent on Blogmaverick.com. *Southern Communication Journal*, 74, 390–405.

Sanderson, J. (2010). Framing Tiger's troubles: Comparing traditional and social media. *International Journal of Sport Communication*, 3, 438–53.

Sanderson, J. (2011a). *It's a whole new ball game: How social media is changing sports*. New York: Hampton Press.

Sanderson, J. (2011b). To tweet or not to tweet...Exploring Division I athletic departments social media policies. *International Journal of Sport Communication*, 4, 492–513.

Sanderson, J., and Kassing, J. W. (2011). Tweets and blogs: Transformative, adversarial, and integrative developments in sports media. In A. C. Billings (Ed.), *Sports media: Transformation, integration, consumption* (pp. 114–27). New York: Routledge.

Sunnafrank, M. (1986). Predicted outcome value during initial interactions: A reformulation of uncertainty reduction theory. *Human Communication Research*, 13, 3–33.

Tian, Y., and Stewart, C. M. (2005). Framing the SARS crisis: A computer-assisted text analysis of CNN and BBC online news reports of SARS. *Asian Journal of Communication*, 15, 289–301.

Wohn, D. Y. (2012). The role of habit strength in social network game play. *Communication Research Reports*, 29, 74–79.

7

APPLYING PUBLIC RELATIONS THEORY TO INCREASE THE UNDERSTANDING OF SPORT COMMUNICATION

Richard D. Waters

Sports and the communication around informal and formal sporting events play a significant role in the culture of contemporary society. From commercialized professional leagues to pick-up games in neighborhood parks, sports and sport communication have become an integral part of life around the globe by impacting cultural, political, economic, community, and interpersonal relationships. Whether focusing on the business and community negotiations that take place around planning major national and international events, such as the Olympic Games or the Super Bowl, or the relationships between a team, its fans, and their opponents, the underlying communication around these events is critical to shaping our lives whether we are directly or indirectly impacted by the events. As such, academic studies into sports and sport communication need to be pursued using strict social scientific methods and theories that help contextualize the phenomenon to see how they impact society.

Given the impact that sport communication has on many different societal dimensions, it is imperative that the field be examined through the public relations lens. Although frequently stereotyped as publicity and special events by marketing scholars and practitioners based on its early history, contemporary public relations is far more reaching and less one-sided in its practice. In the past 30 years, public relations has shifted from being solely focused on message preparation and delivery to one that is more reflective of long-term relationships and the value that stakeholders bring to an organization (Ledingham, 2006). Cutlip, Center, and Broom (2006, p. 6) define public relations as "the management function that establishes and maintains mutually beneficial relationships between an organization and the publics on whom its success or failure depends". Despite calls for studies into sports management and communication that look into how organizations can improve relationships with their consumers (for example, Mahony and Howard, 2001), little research has been done using public relations framework.

L'Etang (2006) reviewed the state of public relations and sport communication, and found that most of the academic literature that covered sport communication stemmed from the field of marketing. Those that touched on public relations principles took case-study approaches to understand isolated events, such as creating publicity for the National Basketball Association (NBA) (Fortunato, 2000), generating corporate social responsibility opportunities for Super Bowl XL (Babiak and Wolfe, 2006), and examining the effectiveness of crisis communication plans in the aftermath of an athlete's death (Marra, 1998). Though each of these studies used public relations principles and practice as part of their framework, their inclusion of public relations theory was lacking. One study, however, attempted to connect the practice of public relations to the emerging relationship management theory by focusing on how the "Coaches vs. Cancer" campaign used stewardship to foster relationship growth with its supporters (Worley and Little, 2002).

Promising theories for public relations and sport communication studies

Though L'Etang's call for more inquiry into sport communication using public relations theory, little has been done in the past five years. The 2006 plea for more scholarly research outlined several dimensions of sport communication and management practice where public relations could provide knowledge and insights. The dimensions included the management of sporting mega-events, the celebrity of sport, corporate and organizational dimensions of sports and sponsorships, and sports and politics (L'Etang, 2006). While this litany outlined areas of possible, it failed to explicitly connect them to specific public relations theories that would aid in understanding the situation. As such, given the low response from public relations researchers, many of those researching sports and sport communication may be unfamiliar with the nuances of public relations scholarship. This chapter hopes to fill that void by providing an overview of four of the leading public relations theories that may be useful for studying sport communication. In reviewing the four theories, the chapter will use literature from existing sport communication scholarship to demonstrate the connections to public relations, as well as using real-life examples to illustrate how studies may be carried out in the future using public relations theories. The four theories discussed in this chapter include the dimensions of public relations, excellence theory, situational theory of publics, and the principles of dialogic communication.

Dimensions of public relations

The first theory that should be examined centers on the entirety of the practice of public relations. The dimensions of public relations, as proposed by Sha (2007), evolved from Grunig and Hunt's (1984) four models of public relations. Sha revisited the practice of public relations to devise various dimensions that describe what public relations practitioners do on a daily basis in regard to managing relationships with their various stakeholders, ranging from media and government regulators to consumers and activists. The newly proposed dimensions of public relations take the focus off of message creation and dissemination, as was the central point of the four models of public relations, and shift it to the entirety of a practitioner's work.

To better understand this evolution to Sha's (2007) dimensions, it is helpful to briefly review the four models of practice. Press agentry, the first model, came into existence from 1850 to 1900, as historical examples sought publicity using emotion and unfulfilled promises to get the public's attention. Often associated with this model of public relations is Phineas T. ("P. T.") Barnum, ringleader and creator of the Barnum and Bailey Circus, who benefitted from creating and publishing stories "of great interest that were largely fabrications with little news value" (Grunig and Hunt, 1984, p. 28).

In response to the lies and manipulations brought about by press agentry, the second model of public relations – public information – emerged around 1900. This new approach to public relations communication is associated with the name of Ivy Ledbetter Lee, who sought to simply tell the truth and let the public decide if they wanted to be involved with an initiative. In outlining his principles for public relations practice, he stated that his plan was quite simple: "to supply to the press and public of the US prompt and accurate information concerning subjects which it is of value and interest to the public to know about" (Grunig and Hunt, 1984, p. 33).

The two-way asymmetry model reflects the field's understanding of social science concepts of psychology and persuasion as Edward Bernays, Sigmund Freud's nephew, helped to launch the practice of pseudoconversations with stakeholders as a key component of public relations campaigns. Two-way asymmetry is akin to market research, in that practitioners engage with audiences solely to hear their thoughts and opinions so that they can be taken back to the office to design more effective campaigns. A conversation was created, but it was not a genuine one. Legitimate conversation between the organization and stakeholders occurs in the two-way symmetrical model, which began as the field began realigning its focus from message creation and delivery to relationship management.

Scholars have argued that these models are too restrictive and that they should be expanded to describe public relations more accurately (Grunig, Grunig, and Dozier, 2002). Sha (2007) proposed seven dimensions of public relations that reflect its strategic management and tactical communication functions. These four scales that represent the strategy side of public relations include two-way communication, which was conceptualized to focus on an organization's listening and research capabilities; symmetrical communication, which examines how well an organization and stakeholders work with one another to resolve conflict and make decisions; ethical communication, which centers on the underlying intention behind organizational communication and behaviors; and conservation, which determines whether organizations are open to change based on external factors or whether they desire to conserve their own agendas. The three tactical communication scales measure mediated communication, which includes a range of outlets from traditional print and broadcast media to the web and social media; interpersonal conversations held in person, over the phone, and in meetings; and social activities, which included a litany of possibilities, such as dinners, banquets, special events, and lifetime-event gift giving (such as birthdays, anniversaries).

These dimensions have been tested and validated in multiple areas of public relations practice, including cross-cultural communication (Rhee, 2002), consumer affairs (Sha, 2004), and investor relations (Kelly, Laskin, and Rosenstein, 2010). However, these dimensions have not been tested in the sport-communication realm, despite recent published scholarship on several topics that touch on the public relations dimensions. For example, Depken II (2001) examined fan loyalty within the National Football League (NFL) when teams trade star athletes; tapping into Sha's (2007) dimensions, this loyalty is certainly tested when a team may not be as open about its intentions with the trade or ignores public outcry. Additionally, sport organizations are finding that they have to be more focused on two-way and symmetrical communication with fans, as Butler and Sagas (2008) noted a sharp increase in the public's use of Internet fan sites for sport communication rather than the organizations' own websites or sporting news sites.

Sha's (2007) scales present scholars with an opportunity to use valid and reliable scales to measure multiple dimensions of sport communication and management. They could be used to measure both sides' perceptions of key issues within sport management to determine key differences; for example, at the time of writing, the National Hockey League and the National

Hockey League Players Association are currently involved in off-season labor negotiations similar to those that the NFL and NBA have had in the past. They could also be used to measure the overall well-being between fans and sporting teams.

Excellence theory

The excellence theory of public relations resulted from a fifteen-year study of best practices in communication management funded by the International Association of Business Communicators Research Foundation. Using 327 corporate, nonprofit, and government agencies in North America and Europe, the study sought to identify the value that public relations had in organizations based on the role that public relations practitioners had in organization-level decision making and the quality of relationship development with stakeholders (Grunig and Grunig, 1998).

Drawing on quantitative and qualitative measures, the excellence theory derived principles of how public relations should be organized to contribute its potential to organizations. First, public-relations practitioners had to be involved at the management level of an organization to practice excellent public relations. When practitioners were able to play a strategic managerial role, they were used by the organization as much as the legal team to help counsel the organization on important decisions. Involvement in this team did not cause the practitioner to abandon communicating with external audiences, but empowered them to engage in two-way communication with the audiences rather than one-sided messaging to them. Secondly, excellent public relations was only found when the department was not sublimated to marketing or other management functions. When public relations had to report to other organizational departments, the organization was less likely to focus on long-term relationships with stakeholders and more likely to push practitioners to engage in asymmetrical communication (Grunig, Grunig, and Dozier, 2006).

The study found that excellent public relations practice was very strategic in its design and implementation. Whatever communication outlet – special event, newsletter, website, press release – used by an organization was only done so because it met a specific need. Excellent public relations is deliberate in its actions, and it is guided by proactive research based on current conditions. When practitioners fall into a pattern of doing the same activities time and time again, the innovation and excellence have fallen out of reach by the team. A final dimension of the excellence theory found that organizations that were supportive of a participative culture rather than an authoritarian one were more likely to have proactive, excellent public relations (Grunig, *et al.* 2006). When practitioners were not restricted to simply carrying out decisions that were made by management, but allowed to act freely on behalf of the organization, they were more likely to engage in conversations with activists and diverse community groups. The excellence theory found that even though practitioners may be employed by organizations, they ultimately serve as an advocate for both sides' viewpoints. Practitioners that listen and talk with opponents and various community stakeholder groups (for example, LGBT community, Hispanic/Latino community, women) are able to take their concerns back to the decision-making table and help the organization make decisions that best serve everyone involved.

The excellence theory has been used to help understand the success and failures of American owners of soccer teams in the United Kingdom's Barclays Premiere League. American owners who employed public relations strategies as defined by the excellence theory had more hospitable reception by the teams' fans while allowing the team's management to embrace globalization (Coombs and Osborne, 2012). Likewise, conflicts have been examined using practitioner fluidity and ability to converse with activists and community groups in support of a new arena for the Orlando Magic basketball team (Mitrook, Parish, and Seltzer, 2008) and in the placement of Olympic qualifying events in politically charged environments (Yarbrough, Cameron, Sallot, and McWilliams, 1998).

The excellence theory offers several insights for new scholarly studies into sport communication and management. For example, the continuing controversy over the National Collegiate Athletic Administration's ban over sport nicknames or mascots that are deemed hostile or abusive to specific cultures, such as the Florida State Seminoles, the University of North Dakota Fighting Sioux, the San Diego State Aztecs, and the Notre Dame Fighting Irish, could be measured through the excellence theory's approach to handling external groups opposing organizational decisions. The theory could also provide guidance in how to resolve conflict over controversial statements. In May 2012, world boxing champion Manny Pacquiao suggested that gay men must be put to death in a statement opposing gay marriage. His statements generated heated response from the LGBT community and caused his management team a whirlwind of activity as they tried to retain his Nike sponsorship in light of the hostility. The excellence theory of public relations would give guidance on how to handle these situations and provide insights for scholars on how to contextualize them to societal pictures far beyond just the single case study.

Situational theory of publics

Organizations have many different stakeholders, which, when organized into groups around common characteristics, become important publics for public relations practitioners. The situational theory of publics provides a framework for exploring the various factors involved in different publics' attitudes and behaviors toward an organization based on their perceptions of an issue or situation (Grunig, 1997).

According to situational theory of publics, three independent variables – problem recognition, constraint recognition and level of involvement with the issue – predict two dependent variables: information seeking and information processing. Problem recognition is defined as the moment when people recognize that something should be done about an issue or situation, and stop and think about what to do. Constraint recognition happens when people perceive that there may be obstacles in the way of acting related to the problem, and level of involvement is the extent to which people connect with the issue or situation (Grunig, 1997; Hamilton, 1992).

The dependent variables, information seeking and processing, may be passive or active forms of communication. Passive or low levels of information seeking and processing may simply imply that an individual receives or consumes information that is presented to them. Active or higher levels of information seeking and processing, on the other hand, implies that individuals expend effort to locate or consume information about an issue or situation. As Grunig stated, "people communicating actively develop more organized cognitions, are more likely to have attitudes about a situation, and more often engage in a behavior to do something about the situation" (Grunig, 1989, p. 6). Based on these variables, individuals can be considered latent, aware or active publics, a classification system that can help organizations determine information dissemination strategies and create communication campaigns (Aldoory and Sha, 2007). Additionally, those publics who are not impacted by an issue are labeled as nonpublics.

Subsequent studies since Grunig's work have found support for and advanced the situational theory of publics in the sport communication realm. Hopwood (2005) found that leaders of English cricket clubs utilized situational theory unknowingly to decide who to target with their recruitment and marketing efforts, while Ruihley and Hardin (2011) used similar variables to predict who were more likely to participate in fantasy sports leagues. Using sport communication terminology, the active publics may be considered part of the team's fandom. By understanding how the situational theory segments audiences, it is possible for the public relations practitioners to devise strategies to reach these most active fans with key information (Stoldt, Dittmore, and Branvold, 2012).

Using the situational theory of publics to better understand a sport team's fans can help an organization to better prepare to interact with outside sponsors, because they are more likely to know what brands their fans are going to connect with (Hong, 2011), to help understand what marketing strategies to use to draw audiences to games rather than watching them via television (Hall and O'Mahony, 2006), and can be used to decide how to promote consumer purchases of licensed-merchandise (Sierra, Taute, and Heiser, 2012).

Principles of dialogic communication

Kent and Taylor (1998) conceptualized a five-principle framework for maintaining open communications in the virtual age. The principles presented provide detailed guidelines that can be applied to various aspects of public relations, including sport communication. Although they were created originally for an organization's own webpage, scholars have extended the five principles to social media as well. The first principle entails utilization of a dialogic loop to promote exchanges between organizations and their stakeholders. By developing effective dialogic loops, website usage will effectively serve both the organization and its stakeholders. Facilitating conversations can be done through simply providing email addresses of key contacts and offering the ability to either submit a form with questions or concerns or through live two-way interactive communication through a blog, forum, or social media chats.

The second principle centers on the provision of useful information via the website. Website content is at the root of effective virtual relationship building as opposed to generic information that is often masked by flashy graphics and multimedia files. Application of the second principle necessitates that institutions provide useful and detailed information to the public through their websites. The third principle of dialogic communication stresses the importance of updating Internet sites to prompt return visits by viewers. Regularly updating the website gives the public reasons for coming back to learn more about the organization. Regular updates not only promote repeat visitors, but it gives new site viewers fresh information about the institution.

The fourth principle encourages having an intuitive and easily accessible interface through provision of an expressed set of guidelines concerning graphics, typeset, and format. Kent and Taylor (1998) posited that ease of website access assists with the enhancement of the overall web experience for visitors, and is an essential component to building effective online relationships. Ease of navigation and accessibility is integral to an effective website. As such, institutions must maintain a website that utilizes universal formats to reach all potential visitors.

The fifth principle details the area of visitor conservation. The path through a website should be informational, concise, and provides an effortless return to the originating site (Kent and Taylor, 1998). This can be hindered by the existence of dead links and links to other sites that do not offer a return option. Together, the five principles offer an overview for the creation of an effective website use that can enhance dialogic relationships that promote lasting relationships with a sporting team's fan base.

Significant research has been conducted to examine how a variety of sporting entities are using various web-based communication strategies. Clavio (2011) found that American college football programs have been slow to use social media as a communication outlet, and this finding parallels a study of the NFL's web communication approach, which found that the teams' own websites contained more useful information and fostered more dialogue than their Facebook profiles (Waters, Burke, Jackson, and Buning, 2011). However, other research has found that blogs, Twitter, and Facebook have generated favorable responses from Major League Baseball audiences (Dittmore, Stoldt, and Greenwell, 2008) and from Turkish soccer fans (Özsoy, 2011).

As technology and social media become more entrenched in everyday actions, it is going to become more important for sporting organizations to focus on these communication channels. Kent and Taylor's (1998) principles focus on dialogue and interactivity as one key component; however, they do not back away from the importance of having an online presence that is easily understood, navigable, and providing useful information to audiences. The principles force organizations to assess the value of their web presence – whether their own site, their Facebook profile, or any other social media platform that may be used to reach out to audiences. They also give scholars five key variables that can be used to determine whether organizations are succeeding in maintaining a virtual presence that benefits both the sporting team and its fans.

Conclusion

Sport communication and sport management are popular concentrations within many of the leading public relations programs in the USA; however, student interest has not been matched by scholarly interest in the field. After reviewing the current state of the sport communication literature, L'Etang (2006) called for more scholarly endeavors into sport communication using public-relations ideas and approaches, and research began to trickle out in a variety of non-public relations journals and books. Although this chapter has only scratched the surface of the connections between sport communication and public relations theory, it is hoped that linking theoretical constructs to examples of real world examples and to published studies that have already measured similar variables will foster more scholarly research into sport communication using public relations theory.

Ultimately, the four theories discussed in this chapter – the dimensions of public relations, the excellence theory, the situational theory of publics, and the principles of dialogic communication – outline key components of sport management that influence sport communication behaviors. The dimensions of public relations outline the overall strategy and tactical practice of the field, and touch on a variety of dimensions where scholarship could be conducted on sporting teams', athletes', and community sporting groups' management and strategic communicators. The excellence theory of public relations provides additional reference points for sustaining quality, symmetrical public relations programming during times of crises and in conjunction with activist publics. The situational theory of publics allows scholars to segment audiences to better understand who is most likely to become involved with a sporting team based on a variety of constructs, and the dialogic principles of communication outlines five specific criteria that organizations must consider when creating their online presence on websites and social media.

When the management of sporting organizations take time to understand these guiding public relations theories, they are likely to develop and foster mutually beneficial relationship growth with their key audiences. Likewise, sport communication scholars that examine sporting events and communication from these perspectives are likely to see how public relations can bring insights into the management of these endeavors while challenging the boundaries of public relations theory by pushing them into the sport communication context where they have largely been ignored.

References

Aldoory, L., and Sha, B. (2007). The situational theory of publics: Practical applications, methodological challenges, and theoretical horizons. In E. L. Toth (Ed.), *The future of excellence in public relations and communication management* (pp. 339–55). Mahwah, NJ: Lawrence Erlbaum.

Babiak, K., and Wolfe, R. (2006). More than just a game? Corporate social responsibility and Super Bowl XL. *Sport Marketing Quarterly*, 15, 214–22.

Butler, B., and Sagas, M. (2008). Making room in the lineup: Newspaper web sites face growing competition for sports fans' attention. *International Journal of Sport Communication*, 1, 17–25.

Clavio, G. (2011). Social media and the college football audience. *Journal of Issues in Intercollegiate Athletics*, 4, 309–25.

Coombs, D. S., and Osborne, A. (2012). A case study of Aston Villa football club. *Journal of Public Relations Research*, 24 (3), 201–21.

Cutlip, S., Center, A., and Broom, G. M. (2006). *Effective public relations* (9th ed.). Upper Saddle River, NJ: Prentice-Hall.

Depken, II, C. A. (2001). Fan loyalty in professional sports: An extension to the National Football League. *Journal of Sports Economics*, 2, 275–84.

Dittmore, S. W., Stoldt, G. C., and Greenwell, T. C. (2008). Use of an organizational weblog in relationship building: The case of a Major League Baseball team. *International Journal of Sport Communication*, 1, 384–97.

Fortunato, J. A. (2000). Public relations strategies for creating mass media content: A case study of the National Basketball Association. *Public Relations Review*, 26 (4), 481–97.

Grunig, J. E. (1989). Sierra Club study shows who becomes activists. *Public Relations Review*, 15 (3), 3–24.

Grunig, J. E. (1997). A situational theory of publics: Conceptual history, recent challenges and new research. In D. Moss, T. MacManus, and D. Vercic (Eds.), *Public relations research: An international perspective* (pp. 3–38). London: International Thomson Business.

Grunig, J. E, and Grunig, L. A. (1998). The relationship between public relations and marketing in excellent organizations: Evidence from the IABC study. *Journal of Marketing Communications*, 4 (3), 141–62.

Grunig, J. E., and Hunt, T. (1984). *Managing public relations*. New York: Holt, Rinehart and Winston.

Grunig, J. E., Grunig, L. A., and Dozier, D. M. (2006). The excellence theory. In C. H. Botan and V. Hazleton (Eds.), *Public relations theory II* (pp. 21–62). Mahwah, NJ: Lawrence Erlbaum.

Grunig, L. A., Grunig, J. E., and Dozier, D. M. (2002). *Excellent public relations and effective organizations*. Mahwah, NJ: Lawrence Erlbaum.

Hall, J., and O'Mahony, B. (2006). An empirical analysis of gender differences in sports attendance motives. *International Journal of Sports Marketing and Sponsorship*, 7, 334–48.

Hamilton, P. K. (1992). Grunig's situational theory: A replication, application, and extension. *Journal of Public Relations Research*, 4, 123–49.

Hong, J. (2011). Sports fans' sponsorship evaluation based on their perceived relationship value with a sport property. *International Journal of Sport Management and Marketing*, 9 (1/2), 116–31.

Hopwood, M. K. (2005). Public relations practice in English country cricket. *Corporate Communications: An International Journal*, 10 (3), 201–12.

Kelly, K. S., Laskin, A.V., and Rosenstein, G. A. (2010). Investor relations: Two-way symmetrical practice. *Journal of Public Relations Research*, 22 (2), 182–208.
Kent, M. L., and Taylor, M. (1998). Building a dialogic relationship through the World Wide Web. *Public Relations Review*, 24, 321–40.
L'Etang, J. (2006). Public relations and sport in promotional culture. *Public Relations Review*, 32, 386–94.
Ledingham, J. A. (2006). Relationship management: A general theory of public relations. In C. H. Botan, and Hazleton, V. (Eds.), *Public relations theory II* (pp. 412–28). Mahwah, NJ: Lawrence Erlbaum.
Mahony, D. F., and Howard, D. R. (2001). Sport business in the next decade: A general overview of expected trends. *Journal of Sport Management*, 15, 275–96.
Marra, F. J. (1998). Crisis communication plans: Poor predictors of excellent crisis public relations. *Public Relations Review*, 24, 461–74.
Mitrook, M. A., Parish, N. B., and Seltzer, T. (2008). From advocacy to accommodation: A case study of the Orlando Magic's public relations efforts to secure a new arena. *Public Relations Review*, 34, 161–8.
Özsoy, S. (2011). Use of new media by Turkish fans in sport communication: Facebook and Twitter. *Journal of Human Kinetics*, 28, 165–76.
Rhee, Y. (2002). Global public relations: cross-cultural study of the excellence theory in South Korea. *Journal of Public Relations Research*, 14 (3), 159–84.
Ruihley, B. J., and Hardin, R. L. (2011). Beyond touchdowns, homeruns, and three-pointers: An examination of fantasy sports participation motivation. *International Journal of Sports Management and Marketing*, 10 (3/4), 232–56.
Sha, B.-L. (2004). Noether's theorem: the science of symmetry and the law of conservation. *Journal of Public Relations Research*, 16, 391–416.
Sha, B.-L. (2007). Dimensions of public relations: moving beyond traditional public relations models in S. C. Duhe (Ed.), *New media and public relations* (pp. 3–26). New York: Peter Lang.
Sierra, J. J., Taute, H. A., and Heiser, R. S. (2012). Explaining NFL fans' purchase intentions for revered and reviled teams: A dual-process perspective. *Journal of Retailing and Consumer Services*, 19 (3), 332–42.
Stoldt, G. C., Dittmore, S. W., and Branvold, S. E. (2012). *Sport public relations: Managing stakeholder communications* (2nd ed.). Champaign, IL: Human Kinetics.
Waters, R. D., Burke, K. A., Jackson, Z. H., and Buning, J. D. (2011). Using stewardship to cultivate fandom online: comparing how National Football League teams use their websites and Facebook to engage fans. *International Journal of Sport Communication*, 4, 163–77.
Worley, D. A., and Little, J. K. (2002). The critical role of stewardship in fundraising: The Coaches vs. Cancer campaign. *Public Relations Review*, 28, 99–112.
Yarbrough, C. R., Cameron, G. T., Sallot, L. M., and McWilliams, A. (1998). Tough calls to make: Contingency theory and the centennial Olympic Games. *Journal of Communication Management*, 3 (1), 39–56.

8

SPORT, ANALYTICS, AND THE NUMBER AS A COMMUNICATION MEDIUM

Andrew Baerg

WHIP, FIP, BABIP, PECOTA, SCHOENE, PER, DVAR, QBR, GVT, Corsi: Each of these abbreviations and terms represents one component of what has come to be known as advanced metrics or analytics in sport. They all purport to allow sports fans and decision makers new quantitative ways of looking at otherwise familiar sports performances. Sports analytics has been defined as:

> the management of structured historical data, the application of predictive analytic models that utilize that data, and the use of information systems to inform decision makers and enable them to help their organizations in gaining a competitive advantage on the field of play.
>
> *(Alamar and Mehrotra, 2011a, para. 2)*

In some respects, this definition remains somewhat unhelpful, in that this kind of intellectual activity has arguably been occurring in some way since the inception of modern sport (Guttmann, 1978) and, in some instances, in certain pre-modern sports as well (Carter and Kruger, 1990). However, the definition does speak to the more recent purposeful and widespread deployment of quantitative systems as a key cog in individual and organizational decision making in sports.

This chapter explores these developments by concentrating on how numbers function as communication media in sports analytics discourse. The chapter briefly surveys the history of sports analytics before drawing on the work of Bruno Latour and John Durham Peters to address one aspect of the relationship between numbers and communication. It then builds from this theory by turning to sports analytics discourse to argue that their advanced metrics paradoxically reveal that which is hidden and deny what is seen.

Brief history of analytics

Before exploring the number's relationship to analytics, a brief survey of the history of sports analytics is in order. Over the course of the last four decades, a rapidly growing body of work has arisen around new and more elaborate forms of managing, collecting, and analyzing quantitative sports data. One of the first organizations devoting themselves to this task was the Society for American Baseball Research (SABR), founded in 1971 (SABR, 2012). Although not initially exclusively interested in baseball statistics, SABR became attached to the niche field of sabermetrics, a field devoted to the statistical side of baseball. Throughout the 1980s and 90s, sabermetrics devotees like Bill James, Pete Palmer, and John Thorn would publish books on novel ways of looking at the game from a quantitative perspective. Others who saw the virtue of sabermetrics began to apply and extend its methodology to sports like football and basketball near the end of the twentieth century and into the new millennium. Helped along by advances in computing power and new technologies like motion capture that enabled the collection of larger and larger amounts of data, sabermetrics morphed into the broader field of sports analytics (Alamar and Mehrotra, 2011a).

Into the twenty-first century, analytics would become increasingly popular among specialists and non-specialists alike. Among specialists, mathematicians and other scholars began to attend to sports analytics. In 2005, the *Journal of Quantitative Analysis in Sports* published its first issue legitimating scholarly interest in the area. During the first decade of the new millennium, universities like the University of San Francisco and Georgia Institute of Technology began offering courses on sports analytics as well (Alamar and Mehrotra, 2011b).

At a popular level, the release of Michael Lewis' *Moneyball* in 2003 and the book's conversion into the 2011 movie of the same name brought notions attached to sports analytics into the broader culture. Sports analytics has also been given greater attention with mainstream sports media coverage of MIT's annual Sloan Sports Analytics Conference, an event begun in 2007, and the recent development of a similar conference in the United Kingdom at the Manchester Business School first held in 2011. In March 2012, an entire issue of *ESPN The Magazine* was devoted to sports analytics.

A broader history of sports analytics remains yet to be written, yet, if one thing is clear about analytics, it is the field's dependence on numbers as a communication medium. By turning to the work of Latour and Peters, the ensuing section speaks to one aspect of the number's operation as medium, its relation to vision.

The number's mediation of vision

In his work on inscription technologies, Latour (1986) never gets to the point of explicitly discussing numbers as media, yet his work would appear to do everything but. Throughout his journey into and out of visual communication technologies, he consistently refers to the more conventionally media-related categories of time and space and how these technologies shape our experience of time and space. The number becomes an example of one of Latour's visual technologies.

For Latour, numbers render the past visually present and the distant visually proximate. These renderings may operate across several different pasts and distances (see also Porter, 1995). As such, numbers serve as space-binding and time-binding media, with their ability to enable communication across space and time. With their time and space binding capacity, numbers allow for the production of a context of optical consistency. What is seen and recorded in one time and space in a specific way can be subsequently seen and understood upon being transferred to another time and space. Numbers render the witnessing of these individual events comprehensible by making them quiescent, by freezing them, in this optically consistent form. In generating a context of optical consistency, numbers enable two or more vastly different objects to be translated into, barring some unscrupulous act, incorruptible abstract form across space and time. The incorruptibility of the number enables the potential for, in Peters' terms, "systematically undistorted communication" (Peters, 2001, p. 436).

In being optical media technologies, numbers work by allowing for the visualization of that which cannot be seen or cannot yet be seen (Latour, 1986). Numbers enable the aggregation of a series of events and objects that might otherwise be relatively invisible. Not only do they make visible the invisible, numbers also mediate events that one could never experience personally. This property of numbers as a communication medium becomes especially important in a modern society where people are dispersed across great geographical expanses. In being separated across vast spaces, parties who do not and cannot truly know one another will likely experience distrust. As they generate contexts of optical consistency, numbers provide one way to deal with this trust issue (Peters, 2001).

Although McLuhan (1994) speaks of the number's capacity to extend the hand and touch, in working from Latour and Peters, numbers also extend the eye. For numbers to mediate an object or event and position it within a context of optical consistency is to extend the vision of the one deploying the number. This process of translation from event or object into data becomes that much more vital when dealing with multiple events and objects that would be otherwise difficult to explain without numbers. To turn the phenomena under consideration into numbers is to put it in a form that can enable its use in argument.

Sports analytics discourses and vision

To work with this theory and apply it to the discourse of sports analytics is to note a paradox attached to the relation between numbers and vision. On the one hand, as Latour (1986) and Peters (2001) suggest, numbers in sports analytics discourse do indeed enable the sight of what previously could not be seen. In this respect, they extend the eye. Yet, at the same time, numbers are also used to question what is seen, to cast aspersion on what the eye witnesses. As such, within the realm of sports analytics numbers as communication media simultaneously affirm quantitatively mediated vision while rendering a vision divorced from quantification suspicious. The following sections of this chapter address the way sports analytics discourses express this paradoxical relationship to vision and numbers in their communication.

Revealing what can't be seen

First, in discourses of sports analytics, numbers are said to reveal things that cannot be seen. Following Latour (1986) and Peters (2001), they bring objects and events into the sphere of the optical. This notion appears in some of the earliest work in the field, with the word "hidden" appearing in Thorn, Palmer and Reuther's (1984) *The Hidden Game of Baseball: A Revolutionary Approach to Baseball and Its Statistics*, Carroll, Palmer, and Thorn's (1988) *The Hidden Game of Football*, and Bellotti's (1988), *Basketball's Hidden Game: Points Created, Boxscore Defense, and Other Revelations*. However, numbers as this revelatory medium go further back than analytics, even as this discursive theme continues into the present.

Some of sports analytics' forefathers recognized the way that statistical measurement enabled them to possess a vision that they otherwise would not possess. Schwartz (2005a) quotes late-nineteenth-century baseball statistician, Henry Chadwick, and his assessment of how numbers reveal that which is hidden. "Many a dashing general player, who carries a great deal of éclat in prominent matches, has all 'the gilt taken off the gingerbread,' as the saying is, by these matter of fact figures," noted Chadwick. He continued, "And we are frequently surprised to find that modest but efficient worker, who has played earnestly and steadily through the season, apparently unnoticed, has come in, at the close of the race, the real victor" (Schwartz, 2005a, pp. 10–11). Chadwick's numbers enable him to go back in time and to travel to a different place such that the truly best baseball players can be revealed as being productive contributors who would otherwise go unnoticed.

In their 1993 baseball tome, *Total Baseball*, Thorn and Palmer speak of Branch Rickey, former general manager of the Brooklyn Dodgers, as having written a precursor to later sabermetric contributions to baseball knowledge. Rickey's article, in a 1954 issue of *Life*, presented one of the first mainstream contributions to what would become advanced metrics. In a story aimed at debunking some perceived conventional baseball myths, Rickey affirms the way his advanced quantitative formula provides him with new vision. "We can examine with sharper insight the performance of a team or individual over a given period," noted Rickey. He added that "This knowledge can be used to detect flaws that would not otherwise be noted, to give a proper balance to baseball forces, to rearrange batting orders intelligently, to pinpoint problems in pitching" (Rickey, 1954, p. 85). As with Chadwick, Rickey recognizes how numbers provide a revelation that, to the naked eye, would be otherwise inaccessible.

This thread of revelation certainly continues into more recent and advanced forms of analytics found in the annual versions of the *Prospectus* series as well. In Lahman and Greanier's (2002) introduction to the first *Pro Football Prospectus*, they discuss how the performance of various unsung football units has often been lost when compared to the "skill positions" like quarterback, running back, and wide receiver. One of their primary goals in writing the book is to look more closely at groups like offensive and defensive lines and secondaries. Lahman and Greanier (2002, p. 2) maintain that, "Too often, the performance of these groups goes unnoticed, but we put them all under the microscope". The numbers these authors will provide will finally provide a way for fans and decision makers to see an unheralded unit's ability to function. For these authors to deploy the metaphor of the microscope suggests that their calculations will provide sight of what, again, is impossible to see through unmediated observation.

Similarly, in the forward to a recent version of *Hockey Prospectus*, Popilchak and Wilson (2011, p. 389) speak to the virtue of advanced metrics arguing that the Corsi puck possession "metrics give us an idea of the underlying talent that is producing the performance we see as fans". For these writers, hockey fans can only see what players are doing at a surface level and cannot see the subsurface talent behind a given player's production. Hockey analytics holds out the promise that it will reveal this talent and finally put it on display. Again, numbers make visually evident what was once hidden.

In the same publication, Cullen (2011) deploys a visual metaphor as a way to speak to the ways in which advanced hockey metrics enable a clearer vision of player performance. These new hockey statistics represent "an HD picture compared to the black-and-white TV picture presented for so many years" (Cullen, 2011, p. v). With new metrics like goals versus threshold (GVT), ultimate faceoff rating (UFR) and Corsi (a shot attempt, puck possession measure), what is actually occurring in hockey can become apparently crystal clear.

The push for a greater and greater revelation of that which is currently hidden is also heralded by technological advances, present and future. In speaking to the future of baseball's relationship to technology, Fast (2011, p. 89) looks ahead to the day when "detailed and digitized quantification of pitcher mechanics on every pitch thrown in game action" will be available to any who are interested. He goes on to celebrate the possibility that high speed, high definition video and multiple camera angles will enable a totalizing surveillance of pitching biomechanics. These cameras will also be able to reveal "optimal spin-induced movement for various pitch types" (Fast, 2011, p. 92) as a way for pitchers and coaches to maximize the effectiveness of each and every pitch.

As these increasingly complex forms of measurement are deployed, those who mobilize them will continue to see their value in what these measures bring into fans' and sports decision-makers' fields of vision.

Questioning what can be seen

In following Latour and Peters, discourses employed in sports analytics suggest that numbers can reveal what cannot be seen. However, these discourses also frequently place suspicion upon what can be seen away from the mediation of the number. This suspicion is expressed in several different ways.

In one instance, this suspicion is conveyed by a move away from physical comparisons of players. An early version of Jon Hollinger's (2003) *Pro Basketball Prospectus* stresses the importance of a new form of vision he calls the "similarity score." Hollinger justifies his metric of similarity scores by saying that they enable one to differentiate what a player looks like from what that player produces. Similarity scores are employed as a way to compare statistical averages across several categories for the purpose of considering how a player might perform in future seasons. Hollinger creates similarity scores, in part, as a way to dispel myths about how one player physically looks like another claiming that this metric "snaps us out of the habit of comparing players based on visual similarities" (Hollinger, 2003, p. 22). Examining similarity scores subsequently becomes a much more accurate way to see that player and his potential performance than a physical comparison.

Hollinger (2003, p. viii) uses the example of Georgian power forward, Nikoloz Tskitishvili, a player who, at the time of writing, was "incessantly compared to Dirk Nowitzki." Tskitishvili might share some of the same physical characteristics as Nowitzki in having the same skin color, foreign origin, and build, but Hollinger deploys twelve different analytics categories that allow him to question what people are seeing. Based on Tskitishvili's statistical measures and closest similarity score, Hollinger sees the Georgian's career developing much more like that of African-American, journeyman forward, Jonathan Bender, than that of white, German superstar, Nowitzki. Tskitishvili is nowhere near as talented and productive as Nowitzki and, for Hollinger, will not be at any point in the future either. By the time Hollinger speaks of Tskitishvili directly as part of the Denver Nuggets team preview, he goes so far as to say that "Tskitishvili has about as much in common with Dirk Nowitzki as I do with Barbara Walters" (Hollinger, 2003, p. 178). Where others see physical similarities and make comparisons they believe to be viable, Hollinger questions, if not aggressively denies, the conclusions deriving from their vision.

The suspicion of vision is also expressed in explanations for a team's success and failure. In a discussion of the relation between analytics and the measurement of defensive performance, Hollinger (2003) observes how many fans and pundits had made a case for how the Lakers needed an additional shooter around Kobe Bryant and Shaquille O'Neal ahead of the impending season, as a way to rebound from a failed attempt at a fourth consecutive championship. However, Hollinger looks to his metric of defensive efficiency as a way to question what these observers were seeing. Drawing upon the defensive efficiency numbers leads Hollinger to argue that the Los Angeles offense was not the problem during the 2002–03 season. Instead, the team's defense was considerably worse than in previous years and they were abysmal defending the three-point shot. Where many were seeing a Laker deficiency linked to a lack of outside scoring, Hollinger's work denies these observation-based claims.

This suspicion of vision can even be applied to individual game strategies. In the *2011–12 Pro Basketball Prospectus*, Pelton (2011) defends isolation basketball in the face of criticism about how isolation plays often serve as an unsuccessful last ditch effort score. Pelton notes that isolation basketball often comes under fire from those who witness it failing in the playoffs when opponents can scout, and apparently stop, isolation plays more effectively. However, this perceived lack of effectiveness does not hold up under statistical scrutiny. Pelton's quantitative study of play types and their comparative success in producing points reveals how what is seen and the conclusions following from this vision should be denied. His findings demonstrate that isolation plays are only marginally less effective than other types of plays. Pelton argues that isolations get criticized as boring in that, "They don't involve the player and ball movement that make basketball at its highest levels a beautiful game to watch" (Pelton, 2011, p. 340). The boring isolation basketball that is seen should be denied in the face of numbers that speak to its effectiveness relative to other types of plays.

Even as vision is rendered suspicious through advanced statistical comparisons between players, quantitative explanations of team successes and failures and in the debunking of commonly held myths, one of the most prevalent forms of the vision-denying capacity of numbers occurs in discursive clashes arising between experts employing traditional forms of vision and those dependent on analytics as a player assessment tool. Conventional player evaluators have come under fire from analytics-based work and subsequently set out to defend themselves and their commitment to qualitative talent assessment.

In 2005, *Baseball America* (Schwartz, 2005b) set up a discussion between two traditional scouts, Gary Hughes and Eddie Bane, and two baseball analytics writers, Voros McCracken and Gary Huckabay. As the interview unfolded, Hughes and Bain were asked about how they might evaluate a double-A right field prospect. Hughes resorted to conventional baseball wisdom saying that he would "evaluate his [the prospect's] five tools" (para. 54). Hughes went on to add that he wanted to see the player's "swing, the approach at the plate, the show of fear" (para. 57). Bane elaborated on the latter point by saying, "If you show fear, you're gone" (para. 58). Later in the same interview, Bane spoke about evaluating prospects by dogmatically asserting that, "if I see fear in a hitter, I'm not ever coming back. I don't see fear in good big league hitters" (para. 63). Bane later addressed the assessment of pitching talent declaring, "I want [scout] Moose Stubing to find Brendan Donnelly (in the minors) because of how he saw Brendan Donnelly throw, not because of the statistical edge he might have had" (para. 96). With an approach based on traditional forms of scouting vision, Hughes and Bane could come to a quick decision about whether to continue watching the player.

In responding to Hughes and Bane, Huckabay implicitly denied the immediacy of conventional scouting vision for player assessment. "I want to know his age. I want to see his stat lines every year through the minors. I want to know where he's played, what leagues, what parks," asserted Huckabay. "I want to know his defensive numbers, to see what kind of balls he's getting to. If he's making a ton of errors" (Schwartz, 2005b, para. 66). Huckabay makes no reference to the importance of seeing the prospect play in person. He cares little about whether a given batter expresses "fear" or how a player's swing or throw appears. Huckabay is more interested in data that can place the player within the framework of historical analogs (that is, comparable players) and in frameworks that attempt to account for the contexts in which numbers can be produced. To achieve these goals does not require personally witnessing a given player in action. Quantitative data become more trustworthy than the visual signs alerting a scout to a player's potential talent.

In another instance of the conflict between traditional expertise and analytics, former hockey coach and current commentator, Don Cherry, derided the advanced hockey shot attempt metric, Corsi. Cherry's sidekick, Ron MacLean, raised the Corsi statistic during a 2010 broadcast of the popular segment, "Coach's Corner", on the Canadian Broadcasting Corporation's, *Hockey Night in Canada*. MacLean related how a journeyman forward for the Vancouver Canucks, Ryan Johnson, had the worst Corsi rating in the league. Upon hearing that Johnson, one of his typically favored, physically tough, blue collar players, had the worst Corsi rating in the NHL, Cherry demonstrated Johnson's apparent value to his team by showing the audience a series of clips. These clips featured Johnson blocking a series of shots while Cherry passionately argued. "This guy is unbelievable and they call him the worst?" noted Cherry. "I mean, look at the guy! Look at this! And he's the worst player? I'll tell you one thing. Vancouver loves this guy." He added, "I would love to have Ryan Johnson on my team and every coach would have him on [sic] too" (Najak, 2010). With his comments laid over top of a series of clips showing a player doing conventionally intangible and, to his mind, valuable hockey work, Cherry attempted to align his audience's vision with his own expert vision over and against what the Corsi statistics suggested.

This clash can also appear in subtle ways, even when the traditional experts are given some credit for their qualitative knowledge. In the first version of the *Hockey Prospectus* series, Botta (2010) contrasted two types of vision, that of the traditional hockey experts and that of the *Hockey Prospectus* authors. He argued that he would "always stand by what a knowledgeable scout, manager, or coach—in most cases, a lifer in the pro ranks—has to say about players he sees every day on the ice or on video." Botta added, "But on the other hand, the team at *Hockey Prospectus* knows what they're doing. When it comes to evaluating hockey players and teams based on statistics, *based on actual information*, no one in the business does it better" (Botta, 2010, p. v, emphasis added). With this statement, Botta implicitly contrasts the "lifer's" more intuitive, qualitative expertise grounded in that person's vision with the statistical work produced by the *Hockey Prospectus* writers, that which constitutes "actual information." Even though Botta claims to maintain a trust in the traditional expert's vision of what makes a good hockey player, his definition of statistics as "actual information" suggests the opposite. Apparently, the most knowledgeable hockey people do not make decisions grounded in actual information, but only rely on their eyes in what they witness in person or through video. Actual information is implicitly better than the "non-actual" information produced by scouts, managers, and coaches. This line of argument is affirmed later in the same publication when Fryffe (2010) declares that the *Hockey Prospectus* writers aim "to improve our understanding of the game using facts, *not impressions*" (p. 318, emphasis added). With this statement, Fryffe demonstrates a commitment to a more perspicacious vision, one that is oriented around statistical factuality. This form of vision is contrasted to the impression, a vision that is more intuitive and fleeting.

Conclusion

Much more could certainly be said about how numbers operate as communication media. With its focus on how sports analytics discourses deploy numbers as a way to reveal that which is hidden and render suspicious that which can be seen, this chapter has discussed one dimension of how numbers work as communication media in sports analytics discourse.

Sport serves as one of key spaces in culture in which numbers operate as a vital communication medium. Sport also represents something of a unique cultural space, given that considerable amounts of data exist as publically available for aggregation and analysis. The analytics research produced by this aggregation is also comparatively available as well. Certainly, professional sport organizations aim to keep their most advanced statistical measures classified. However, the type of data access that sports fans possess does not occur in other fields like business, education, and medicine, where analytics-oriented approaches have begun to develop momentum. As a consequence, examining how numbers function as a communication medium in sport offers potential insight into how they might operate in other cultural domains, domains that do not allow for the same level of transparency. In this respect, studying this area of sport and communication can serve as a springboard into research in other cultural spaces where these forms of quantification have become increasingly influential.

Further questions can also be asked about additional implications of analytics discourses in sport. What of the place of the typical sports fan in relation to sports analytics? Will this person's vision become marginalized in attempting to participate in conversations about these new forms of measurement in the same way that laypeople become marginalized by scientific rhetoric? Questions could also be asked about the degree to which these metrics shape the rationality of front office personnel and the athletes themselves. Latour suggests that inscription technologies like numbers do not objectify, but they push the object out after extracting data from it such that the extracted data becomes "all that counts" (Latour, 1986, p. 17). Will organization decision makers become devoted to data that selectively reveals and denies and push the object as athlete out? Will athletes understand themselves primarily as data producers rather than as more fully-orbed and complete subjects? As sports analytics gains increasing traction, these kinds of questions will need to be more fully addressed.

Whether numbers are used to reveal that which cannot be seen or render suspicious existing forms of vision, they play a vital role in sport communication. As sports analytics become more and more prominent, the number's mediating capacity should continue to become more prominent as well. These forms of quantitative vision will likely be further extended and usurp forms of vision perceived as obsolete and inadequate. Ultimately, as Fast (2011, p. 94) notes, "There may be little outside of the players' minds that remains out of bounds for [quantitative] analysis, and even there, we will study behavior records to gain a window into players' thinking".

References

Alamar, B., and Mehrotra, V. (2011a). Beyond "Moneyball": The rapidly evolving world of sports analytics, Part I. *Analytics Magazine*, September/October. Retrieved from http://www.analytics-magazine.org/special-articles/391-beyond-moneyball-the-rapidly-evolving-world-of-sports-analytics-part-i.

Alamar, B., and Mehrotra, V. (2011b). Sports analytics, part 2: The role of predictive analytics, organizational structures and information systems in professional sports. *Analytics Magazine*, November/

December. Retrieved from http://www.analytics-magazine.org/november-december-2011/476-sports-analytics-part-2.

Bellotti, R. S. (1988). *Basketball's hidden game: Points created, boxscore defense, and other revelations*. New Brunswick, NJ: Night Work.

Botta, C. (2010). Foreword. In A. Rothstein and T. Seppa (Eds.), *Hockey prospectus 2010–11* (pp. v–vi). Holbrook, NY: Prospectus Entertainment Ventures.

Carroll, B., Palmer, P., and Thorn, J. (1988). *The hidden game of football*. New York: Warner.

Carter, J. M., and Kruger, A. (Eds.). (1990). *Ritual and record: Sports records and quantification in pre-modern societies*. Westport, CT: Greenwood Press.

Cullen, S. (2011). Foreword. In T. Seppa (Ed.), *Hockey prospectus 2011–12* (pp. v–vi). Holbrook, NY: Prospectus Entertainment Ventures.

Fast, M. (2011). Part 2 pitching: Introduction. In B. Lindbergh (Ed.), *Best of baseball prospectus 1996–2011* (Vol. 1; pp. 89–94). Holbrook, NY: Prospectus Entertainment Ventures.

Fryffe, I. (2010). A brief history of statistical analysis in hockey. In A. Rothstein and T. Seppa (Eds.), *Hockey prospectus 2010–11* (pp. 317–20). Holbrook, NY: Prospectus Entertainment Ventures.

Guttmann, A. (1978). *From ritual to record: The nature of modern sports*. New York: Columbia University Press.

Hollinger, J. (2003). *Pro basketball prospectus 2003–2004*. Dulles, VA: Brassey's.

Lahman, S., and Greanier, T. (2002). Introduction. In J. Sheehan (Ed.), *Pro football prospectus 2002*. Washington, DC: Brassey's.

Latour, B. (1986). Visualization and cognition: *Thinking with eyes and hands. Knowledge* and Society: Studies in the Sociology of Culture Past and Present, 6, 1–40.

McLuhan, M. (1994). Number: Profile of the crowd. In W. T. Gordon (Ed.), *Understanding media: The extensions of man* (pp. 145–59). Corte Madera, CA: Gingko.

Najak, S. (2010) (Producer). *Hockey Night in Canada* [television broadcast]. Toronto, ON: Canadian Broadcasting Corporation, March 27.

Pelton, K. (2011). In defense of the isolation. In B. Doolittle and K. Pelton (Eds.), *Pro basketball prospectus 2011–12* (pp. 339–40). Holbrook, NY: Prospectus Entertainment Ventures.

Peters, J. D. (2001). "The only proper scale of representation": The politics of statistics and stories. *Political Communication*, 18, 433–49.

Popilchak, R., and Wilson, K. (2011). Possession is nine-tenths of the law: Corsi revisited. In T. Seppa (Ed.), *Hockey prospectus 2011–12* (pp. 385–89). Holbrook, NY: Prospectus Entertainment Ventures.

Porter, T. M. (1995). *Trust in numbers: The pursuit of objectivity in science and public life*. Princeton, NJ: Princeton University Press.

Rickey, B. (1954). Goodbye to some old baseball ideas: "The Brain" of the game unveils formula that statistically disproves cherished myths and demonstrates what really wins. *Life*, August 2, 78–89.

SABR (2012). Society for American Baseball Research. The SABR Story. Retrieved from http://sabr.org/about.

Schwarz, A. (2005a). *The numbers game: Baseball's lifelong fascination with statistics*. New York: St. Martin's.

Schwarz, A. (2005b). The great debate. Durham, NC: Baseball America. Retrieved from http://www.baseballamerica.com/today/features/050107debate.html.

Thorn, J., Palmer, P., and Reuther, D. (1984). *The hidden game of baseball: A revolutionary approach to baseball and its statistics*. New York: Doubleday.

Thorn, J., and Palmer, P. (1993). Part II: Introduction. In J. Thorn and P. Palmer (Eds.), *Total baseball* (3rd ed., pp. 602–18). New York: Harper Collins.

9

RESEARCH METHODOLOGIES IN SPORT COMMUNICATION

Merryn Sherwood and Matthew Nicholson

This chapter explores the methodologies that are most commonly employed in the field of sport communication research, primarily via a meta-analysis of prominent research published in peer-review journals and reputable edited book collections. Every attempt has been made to be as comprehensive as possible within the context of a burgeoning field of literature associated with sport communication and the limitations of a solitary chapter. On the basis of the meta-analysis conducted, the chapter also compares the field of sport communication to the field of communication more generally, and in doing so, enables some implications for the future of sport communication research to be explored.

When Wenner (1989) first proposed a research agenda for the field of sport communication, or 'MediaSport,' it was driven by the increasing commercialization of both sport and media. Sport was no longer a peripheral player, with multi-million dollar broadcast rights deals tipping it into the territory of big business. Not only that, sport had an important role to play in society, as a vehicle for social and cultural development. Over the past 20 years, with the internet age fuelling hyper-globalization, it is not surprising that Gantz (2011) has stated that the field of media and sport research is now "enormous." The amount of research that concerns MediaSport, and the four areas that Wenner proposed in his transactional model of media – institutions, media texts, audiences, and the places where they intersect – now "reflects the work of psychologists, sociologists, anthropologists, economists, physiologists, historians, communication scientists, rhetorical and cultural/critical scholars" (Gantz, 2011, p. 1). In a recent edited academic book focusing on sport media, Billings compiled a list of significant contributions to sport media scholarship; the list contains over 400 entries, including articles in more than 70 different journals. As the author stated in his conclusion, "the amount of seminal sport communication scholarship produced over the past three decades is astounding and, moreover, exceeds the overarching systemic structures that should support it" (Billings, 2011, p. 181).

This presents challenges for a comprehensive analysis of research methods used in the study of sport media or communication, given that both the focus of this research and where it is published has increased exponentially in the past 20 years. Not only has sport communication been a focus of new journalism journals, such as *Journalism*, *Journalism Practice*, and *Journalism*

Studies, there are now two peer-reviewed sport communication journals, with more in development. The *International Journal of Sport Communication* has been published since 2008, and the *Journal of Sports Media* since 2006. Other journals have also commissioned special issues focused on sport media, such as *Media International Australia* (1995 and 2011) and *Public Relations Review* (2008). While there are established meta-analyses of communication research methods (Cooper, Potter, and Dupagne, 1994; Kamhawi and Weaver, 2003; Riffe and Freitag, 1997; Trumbo, 2004), the breadth of sport media research means that simply replicating these studies would not have accurately covered the field. Therefore, guidelines were established to provide some useful and necessary limitations for this chapter. Firstly, sport communication was defined as any research that concerned the four different areas of research Wenner (1989) proposed in *Media, sport and society*: institutions, texts, the audience, and where these interact. We also acknowledged the definition provided by Pedersen, Laucella, Miloch, and Fielding (2007), that "sport communication is a process by which people in sport, in a sport setting, or through a sport endeavour, share symbols as they create meaning through interaction" (p. 196). The sample of research was then compiled by searching peer-reviewed journals in the field of sport management, sport sociology, journalism, and mass communication, as well as specific sport media journals. Search terms used were sport, sports, sports journalism, sports media, and sports communication. Journal articles were chosen as the main focus for this examination of research methods, as Weaver and Wilhoit (1988) stated, they are viewed as the "the nerves of a discipline," while edited academic books that explicitly concerned sport communication were also included.

The journals reviewed for this chapter included the *International Review for the Sociology of Sport*, *Journal of Sport Management*, *Journal of Sport and Social Issues*, *Sport Management Review*, *International Journal of Sport Communication*, *Journalism*, *Journalism Studies*, *Journalism Practice*, *Journalism and Mass Communication Quarterly*, *Media, Culture and Society*, *New Media and Society*, *Howard Journal of Communications*, *Mass Communication and Society*, *Journal of Broadcasting and Electronic Media*, and *Media International Australia*. Given that some of the most important work in this field has also been published in edited academic books, these were also included in this sample. First, each article or book chapter was scanned, to determine whether the article or chapter was the result of original and empirical research. Meta-analyses, commentaries, conceptual work, and other articles and chapters that did not contain an original research study were excluded. Second, each article and book chapter from the smaller sample was then analyzed for the method employed by the researcher or research team.

Overall, the analysis of research methods conducted reveals that most of the sport communication research has occurred in one section of the transactional model that Wenner originally proposed over 20 years ago. Wenner's model of analysis within *Media, sport and society* included four primary elements: the media sports production complex, the content of media sports, the audience, and the social system in which these elements relate to each other. In the updated *MediaSport*, published nine years later, Kinkema and Harris (1998) stated, in their review of sport media scholarship, that the majority of research had occurred in three of those areas – with the major focus on one, the messages or content of mediated sport texts. An analysis of research conducted and published since 1998 confirms Kinkema and Harris' previous findings, and it is therefore not surprising that the research method that matches this form of inquiry – content analysis – is still the most widely used method within the sport communication field. While survey research, qualitative interviews, case studies, and the experimental method have also been used in sport media research, and the focus of these studies has widened, this chapter illustrates the diversity in research methods is yet to reflect the broader agenda of sport communication studies. Each of the most common methods in sport communication research will now be discussed in turn.

Content analysis

A widely recognized definition for content analysis is a research technique "for making replicable and valid inferences from texts (or other meaningful matter) to the contexts of their use" (Krippendorff, 2004, p. 18). As Krippendorf detailed in his extensive exploration of the history and use of this method, content analysis has a long history, from its first use to analyze newspaper content in 1893, to unraveling propaganda during World War II and, since the early 1950s, as a widely used research technique by all academic disciplines. Content analysis can be quantitative or qualitative, as researchers can either use it to analyze texts for the amount of words used or the number of descriptors mentioned, for example, or use it to thematically decode media texts. Given that media texts are the largest area of sport communication studied, this has become the method most often employed in sport communication research. It is clear from analysis conducted as part of this chapter that content analysis is being consistently used to predominantly analyze media texts on two different platforms – newspapers and television commentary – to investigate three major areas of representation: gender, race, and nationality.

The use of content analysis to determine how gender is represented in mediated texts is one of the largest areas of research. The two largest sub-sets of this research are the examination of gender within printed content, such as newspapers or magazines (Crossman, Hyslop, and Gutrie, 1994; Cuneen and Sidwell, 1998; Denham and Cook, 2006; Eastman and Billings, 1999; Hardin, Dodd, and Lauffer, 2006; Harris and Clayton, 2002; Higgs and Weiller, 1994; Higgs, Weiller, and Martin, 2003; Jones, Murrell, and Jackson, 1999; Kinnick, 1998; Lumpkin and Williams, 1991; McCree, 2011; Messner, Duncan, and Cooky, 2003; Pedersen, 2002; Shifflett and Revelle, 1994; Stone and Horne, 2008; Travers, 2011; Vincent, 2004; Vincent, Pedersen, Whisenant, and Massey, 2007; Wann, Schrader, Allison, and McGeorge, 1998; Whiteside, Simpson, and Hardin, 2007), and gender in television commentary or television coverage (Angelini, Macarthur, and Billings, 2012; Billings, Angelini, and Eastman, 2008; Billings, Angelini, and Eastman, 2005; Billings, *et al.*, 2006; Billings, Halone, and Denham, 2002; Blinde, Greendorfer, and Shanker, 1991; Caple, Greenwood, and Lumby, 2011; Capranica and Aversa, 2002; Coventry, 2004; Eastman and Billings, 1999; Eastman and Billings, 2000; Greer, Hardin, and Homan, 2009; Halbert and Latimer, 1994; Hallmark and Armstrong, 1999; Higgs and Weiller, 1994; Higgs, Weiller and Martin, 2003; Messner, Duncan, and Wachs, 1996).

In terms of ethic representations, one of the first content analyses was conducted by Rainville and McCormick (1977), who compared the description of black and white players in professional football. The representation of African American athletes has since been a large area of focus (Byrd and Utsler, 2007; Cunningham and Bopp, 2010; Mastro, Blecha, and Atwell Seate, 2011; Rada, 1996; Rada and Wulfemeyer, 2005; Ronald, 2009; Smith and Berry, 2000), while new studies have focused on different ethnicities (Malcolm, Bairner, and Curry, 2010), or representations of nationality (Billings, Angelini, and Wu, 2011; Billings, MaCarthur, Licen, and Wu, 2009; Billings and Tambosi, 2004; Buffington, 2012; Garland and Rowe, 1999; Lee and Maguire, 2009; Scott, Hill, and Zakus, 2012; Cho, 2009). There is also an increasing area of literature that addresses two or more of these frameworks at once, such as gender and race (Coventry, 2004; Daddario and Wigley, 2007; Eastman and Billings, 2001), gender and nationality (Borcila, 2000), race and nationality (Jackson, 1998) and gender, ethnicity and nationality (Billings and Angelini, 2007; Billings, *et al.*, 2008; Billings and Eastman, 2002; Van Sterkenburg and Knoppers, 2004). There have been other content analyses that explore the focus of sports articles in print media, and whether they hold true to the statement that sports section is the "toy department" of the newsroom (Rowe, 2007) and to compare web-first sports coverage in the UK and Australia (English, 2011).

It is evident from the analysis conducted for this chapter that the size and scope of content analysis research differs greatly. Although the stated rationales and methodology sections of the various articles and chapters reveal very little on this issue, it may be surmised that the size and scope of much content analysis research is dependent on access to human resources and budget constraints. Content analysis of mediated sport texts has been the most popular form of sport communication research because of the accessibility of the texts, which are either freely available or can be accessed/recorded at minimal cost. By contrast, the analysis of televised texts is typically very expensive because it is often laborious and repetitive.

Surveys

Surveys, in all their forms, have become a mainstay of much academic research, particularly in the social sciences. Depending on design, surveys or questionnaires can be used to obtain quantitative, qualitative, or a mixture of quantitative and qualitative data, however the primary aim in conducting a survey is to derive statistics from a certain area of the population, or sample. Surveys, including self-completed questionnaires, postal questionnaires, or online questionnaires, have been used to establish some important research in the sport communication field, such as the background, values, and profile of sport journalists.

Some landmark studies in this field include Garrison and Salwen (1989; 1994), who posted a survey to members of the American Associated Sports Press, using a five-point Likert-type scale to judge responses to statements concerning ethics, education, and professionalism. Nicholson, Zion, and Lowden (2011) replicated and added to Henningham's (1995) paper-based study by emailing a link to an online survey to the entire cohort of Australian sport journalists. All four of these studies offer important insights regarding sport journalists' demographics and attitudes towards ethics and professionalism. Other surveys that have investigated sport journalists include whether blogging has had an impact on sport journalists traditional journalistic paradigms (Schultz and Sheffer, 2007), and whether ethics is still an issue in newspaper sport departments (Hardin, 2005a). Surveys have also been used to examine audiences: Wann and Branscombe (1990) used a survey to measure strategic self-presentation within a group of sport fans, while both Clavio and Kian (2010) and Cheever (2009) used an online survey to determine uses and gratifications of different sport fans. There have also been a number of studies that explore how audiences view and react to televised sports in different contexts (Gantz, Wang, Paul, and Potter, 2006; Johnson and Schiappa, 2010; Schweitzer, 1992). A number of studies have surveyed either female sport journalists (Hardin and Shain, 2005), or the wider sport communication workforce (Hardin, 2005b; Sheffer and Schultz, 2007; Whiteside and Hardin, 2010), in order to examine the issue of gender in the sport communication workforce.

Like content analysis research, survey research differs in size and scope. Because most surveys deployed in sport communication research are designed to answer research questions quantitatively, the data collected can be analyzed relatively quickly, cheaply, and effectively. The transition from paper-based surveys to modern online equivalents has made the survey a relatively cheap option for the vast majority of social science research; however, the ability to capture a random sample has declined somewhat. For much of the research examined for the purpose of this chapter, the issue of randomness was of little importance.

Case studies and ethnographies

Two different qualitative research methods – case study and ethnography – have been included together here, as they have been used as overlapping methods in sport communication research. As Creswell (2007) noted, the major difference between them is participant observation; in ethnography the researcher also takes part in the creation of culture, while in a case study there is typically only non-participant observation. Creswell defined a case study as a qualitative approach in which the investigator explores a bounded system (case), or multiple bounded systems (cases) over time, through detailed in-depth data collection involving multiple sources of information, and reports a case description and case-based themes. Ethnography is a qualitative design in which the researcher describes and interprets the shared and learned patterns of values, behaviors, beliefs and language of a culture sharing group (Harris, 2001).

There have been some landmark case studies or ethnographies in sport communication, all centered on the production of sport for television (Gruneau, 1989; MacNeill, 1996; Stoddart, 1994). Gruneau conducted observations of the production of a Canadian Broadcasting Corporation (CBC) broadcast of a World Cup downhill ski race held in Whistler, British Colombia, while Stoddart's study encompassed two summers of three Australian broadcasters' production of golf. Both uncovered important information about the factors that influence the production of sport for a televised audience. MacNeill's study went even further, recording minute detail on the production of Olympic ice hockey, including camera positions and types of shots to detail the factors that impact on sports production. Another significant case study is the work of Lowes (1999), in which the researcher spent four months conducting non-participant observation in a Canadian newspaper office, and also interviewed sports teams' media managers, in order to establish how work routines employed by news workers led to the manufacture of sports news. Similarly, Mitrook, Parish, and Selzter (2008) examined the Orlando Magic's public relations strategy by conducting interviews with staff and analyzing media texts. There is also an area of research that self-identifies as "case studies," but does not align with the traditional qualitative method defined as by Creswell (2007), as its studies involve the examination of media texts as they relate to a particular incident or time (Banagan, 2011; Batchelor and Formentin, 2008; Boyle, Dinan, and Morrow, 2002; Collins, 1998; Coulter, 1986; Fortunato, 2000; Sanderson, 2008; Serazio, 2010; Tamir and Galily, 2011).

Of all the research methods featured in this chapter, true case study and ethnographic research is perhaps the most time consuming for the researcher. Content analysis and survey research can both be time compressed if need be. By contrast, case study and ethnographic research requires the researcher to devote a large amount of time, as well as to follow the schedule and habits of the organization(s) and people who are being investigated. Relative to studies examined throughout the analysis of this chapter, intensive case study and ethnographic research is often successfully employed by graduate students or researchers on sabbatical, for example.

Mixed methods

For the purposes of this chapter, mixed methods research was defined as any combination of qualitative and quantitative research used in one study, which is not otherwise categorized as a research method on its own right. There are a number of studies in the sport communication field that have utilized this approach, perhaps illustrating that mixed methods is a growing research methodology.

The majority of studies identified as mixed methods combine interviews with a form of quantitative analysis. Bruce (2004) explored race in televised sport by combining a content analysis of basketball commentary from the USA (NBA and NCAA Division I) and qualitative interviews with eleven male basketball commentators. Other studies to employ this method include Bernstein (2000), who examined globalization with content analysis of Olympic newspaper coverage in Britain and Israel and interviews with journalists and Eastman, Brown, and Kovatch (1996), who conducted a qualitative content analysis of mediated texts and interviews with five CBS production executives, to explore political messages surrounding the Barcelona Olympics. Another common mixed method approach has been the use of surveys and follow-up in-depth qualitative interviews, which have been used by Salwen and Garrison (1998) and Reinardy (2007) to examine sports journalists. Mixed methods has also been used in historical sports communication research, with Cressman and Swenson's (2007) analysis of documents and interviews exploring why CBS broadcast the first season of the NFL in the USA.

Experimental research

While experimental research is a very small component of the sport communication field, there are some significant examples of this method being employed in order to examine audience reactions to televised sport. Bryant, Comisky, and Zillmann (1981) showed clips of sports with varying level of violence to 38 male and 38 female participants and found that "at least for male viewers, a high degree of aggressiveness is a critical ingredient of the enjoyment of watching sports contests" (Bryant, *et al.*, 1981, p. 256). Angelini (2008) also examined gender using an experimental design, using video clips to explore the difference in watching male and female athletes. The other issue that has been explored in experimental design is the sport and violence nexus. Raney and Depalma (2006) explored the relationship between the levels and contexts of sport violence and viewer enjoyment, mood, and perceptions of violence, while Raney and Kinnally (2009) investigated perceived violence and enjoyment across different intercollegiate (American) football contests between two heated rivals.

Other common methods

Qualitative interviews are becoming more prominent with the sport communication research field, although not to the point that they can be considered one of the major methodologies. Gantz and Wenner were early adopters of the interview, using large-scale telephone interviews to explore televised sport viewing patterns (Gantz, Wenner, Carrico, and Knorr, 1995; Gantz and Wenner, 1991). A large focus of studies employing qualitative interviews involves sport communication industry work practices, such as female sport journalists (Hardin and Shain, 2006; Hardin and Whiteside, 2009), television broadcasters (Billings, 2009), the new breed of Australian internet sports journalists (Lange, Nicholson, and Hess, 2007), Israeli sport journalists (Tamir and Galily, 2011), and public relations and marketing staff in New Zealand rugby (Scherer, 2007). Bruce (1998) also used interviews to explore the reactions of female basketball fans to televised coverage.

Comparison to non-sport communication literature

While sport journalism has been labeled the "toy department" compared with its news journalism counterparts, Boyle (2006) noted that perhaps sport journalism has more in common with its news counterparts than first thought. This is also evident in terms of the overall mass communication and journalism fields of research, as similar methods have been used to investigate similar themes in both the sport communication and mass communication fields.

Overall, analysis of the sport communication literature has revealed that content analysis and surveys have been the most commonly employed research methods – and quantitative versions of each have dominated. Cooper, Potter, and Dupagne (1994) conducted the first major meta-analysis of methods in communication research and found, in a review of ten leading communication journals from 1965 to 1989, that the majority (57.8 percent) of published mass media research articles used quantitative methods. In a direct replica of this research, Trumbo (2004) found that almost the exact quantitative percentage (57 percent) for the years from 1990 to 2000. In a meta-analysis of research in journalism journals from 1984 to 1999, Kamhari and Weaver (2003, p. 13) found that over 60 percent of research was quantitative; surveys and content analysis "far exceeded any other method of data gathering in the 1980s and 1990s". That content analysis is the major form of enquiry is not surprising, as Kolmer (2008, p. 117) noted it has become "an important method of journalism research as a principal tool for analysing the products of journalistic activity".

In terms of the amount of qualitative research found in the mass communication field, Kamhami and Weaver (2003) found there was only a four percent increase in the number of qualitative studies from the early 1980s to late 1990s, emphasizing the idea that qualitative research has become more common is false. The small amount of mixed methods research, or combination of qualitative and quantitative studies, also aligns with the trend in sport communication research. The frequency of research that does not have a clearly defined methodology is also prevalent in journalism and communication journals, however this may also be a representation of the wider academic focus on importance of method over time.

Future implications

As is evident from this review of sport communication research methodologies, sport communication scholars have made inroads since Wenner's original call for a research agenda in media and sport. While the majority of research has been undertaken through quantitative content analysis and surveys, these methods have allowed sport scholars to contribute a great deal in understanding sport's roles in the construction of race, nationality, and gender (Billings, 2011). There has also been a wide sampling of other research methods, including case studies, ethnography, qualitative interviews, and experimental research, which have helped to contribute to our understanding about the ways in which sport is produced and consumed.

However, a re-examination of Wenner's original research agenda from 1989 sheds light on gaps that still exist. He proposed that "getting an accurate view of the media and sports relationship in society will require understanding from a variety of perspectives" (Wenner,

1989, p. 25). His transactional model allowed for this. Its four different areas – institutions, texts, audiences, and where they meet – showed not only that the MediaSport world is multifaceted, but also that all the players in it are inextricably entwined. It is clear that the research gap exists in the areas of interactions and connections. As this chapter's examination of sport communication literature demonstrates, there is a plethora of research that examines different elements of sport media, yet, as Shoemaker and Reese (1990, p. 649) pleaded of communication researchers, the discipline is in danger of being "stuck on a plateau" because "most content analyses are not linked in any systematic way to either the forces that created its content or to its effects". Given that sport communication already encompasses so many different disciplines and approaches, research that addresses the production and consumption of sport communication from the point of view of many stakeholders is integral to the future of the discipline.

The method that clearly stands out is a mixed methods approach. While content analysis of mediated texts could still be conducted, these studies would be strengthened by the addition of qualitative interviews from different stakeholders, to illustrate underlying meaning, as Bruce (2004) and others have found using a mixed methods approach. More ethnography and case studies would also be valuable additions to the field, particularly given sport communication now exists in a rapidly changing environment. The past ten years have revealed a dramatic change in the ways that we produce and consume media, with the advent of social media platforms like Facebook and Twitter, video sharing networks like YouTube, and photo sharing sites like Instagram; these can all be consumed anytime, anywhere on internet-enabled mobile devices. While there is evidence to suggest that sport journalists and fans are using this technology to interact, report, and consume sports media, there is little research that has examined how this new technology is being utilized in the field of sport communication. A case study of sport bloggers, an ethnography of digital news production, or a mixed methods approach of surveys and interviews with the audience that consumes the sport product to explore whether it is meeting their needs are just some of the research projects and methodologies that could offer important insights to both academia and industry.

References

Angelini, J. R. (2008). Television sports and athlete sex: Looking at the differences in watching male and female athletes. *Journal of Broadcasting and Electronic Media*, 52 (1), 16–32.

Angelini, J. R., Macarthur, P. J., and Billings, A. C. (2012). What's the gendered story? Vancouver's prime time Olympic glory on NBC. *Journal of Broadcasting and Electronic Media*, 56 (2), 261–79.

Banagan, R. (2011). "The Decision", a case study: LeBron James, ESPN and questions about US sports journalism losing its way [online]. *Media International Australia, Incorporating Culture and Policy*, 140 (Aug), 157–67.

Batchelor, B., and Formentin, M. (2008). Re-branding the NHL: Building the league through the "My NHL" integrated marketing campaign. *Public Relations Review*, 34 (2), 156–60.

Bernstein, A. (2000). "Things you can see from there you can't see from here." *Journal of Sport and Social Issues*, 24 (4), 351–69.

Billings, A. C. (2009). Conveying the Olympic message: NBC producer and sportscaster interviews regarding the role of identity. *Journal of Sports Media*, 4 (1), 1–23.

Billings, A. C. (2011). Reaction time: Assessing the record and advancing a future of sports media scholarship. In A. C. Billings (Ed.), *Sports media: Transformation, integration, consumption* (pp. 181–90). New York: Routledge.

Billings, A. C., and Angelini, J. R. (2007). Packaging the Games for viewer consumption: Gender, ethnicity, and nationality in NBC's Coverage of the 2004 Summer Olympics. *Communication Quarterly*, 55 (1), 95–111.
Billings, A. C., and Eastman, S. T. (2002). Selective representation of gender, ethnicity, and nationality in American television coverage of the 2000 Summer Olympics. *International Review for the Sociology of Sport*, 37 (3–4), 351–70.
Billings, A. C., and Tambosi, F. (2004). Portraying the United States vs. portraying a champion: US network bias in the 2002 World Cup. *International Review for the Sociology of Sport*, 39 (2), 157–65.
Billings, A. C., Halone, K. K., and Denham, B. E. (2002). "Man, that was a pretty shot": An analysis of gendered broadcast commentary surrounding the 2000 Men's and Women's NCAA Final Four basketball championships. *Mass Communication and Society*, 5 (3), 295–315.
Billings, A. C., Angelini, J., and Eastman, S. (2008). Wie Shock: Television commentary about playing on the PGA and LPGA Tours. *Howard Journal of Communications*, 19 (1), 64–84.
Billings, A. C., Angelini, J. R., and Eastman, S. T. (2005). Diverging discourses: Gender differences in televised golf announcing. *Mass Communication and Society*, 8 (2), 155–71.
Billings, A. C., Angelini, J. R., and Wu, D. (2011). Nationalistic notions of the superpowers: Comparative analyses of the American and Chinese telecasts in the 2008 Beijing Olympiad. *Journal of Broadcasting and Electronic Media*, 55 (2), 251–66.
Billings, A. C., Brown, C. L., Crout, J. H., Mckenna, K. E., Rice, B. A., and Timanus, M. E. (2008). The Games through the NBC lens: Gender, ethnic, and national equity in the 2006 Torino Winter Olympics. *Journal of Broadcasting and Electronic Media*, 52 (2), 215–30.
Billings, A. C., Craig, C. C., Croce, R., Cross, K. M., Moore, K. M., Vigodsky, W., and Watson, V. G. (2006). "Just one of the guys?" Network depictions of Annika Sorenstam in the 2003 PGA Colonial Tournament. *Journal of Sport and Social Issues*, 30 (1), 107–14.
Billings, A. C., Macarthur, P. J., Licen, S., and Wu, D. (2009). Superpowers on the Olympic basketball court: The United States versus China through four nationalistic lenses. *International Journal of Sport Communication*, 2, 380–97.
Blinde, E. M., Greendorfer, S. L., and Shanker, R. J. (1991). Differential media coverage of men's and women's intercollegiate basketball: Reflection of gender ideology. *Journal of Sport and Social Issues*, 15 (2), 98–14.
Borcila, A. (2000). Nationalizing the Olympics around and away from "vulnerable" bodies of women. *Journal of Sport and Social Issues*, 24 (2), 118–47.
Boyle, R. (2006). *Sports journalism: Context and issues*. Thousand Oaks, CA: Sage.
Boyle, R., Dinan, W., and Morrow, S. (2002). Doing the business? *Journalism*, 3 (2), 161–81.
Bruce, T. (1998). Audience frustration and pleasure. *Journal of Sport and Social Issues*, 22 (4), 373–97.
Bruce, T. (2004). Marking the boundaries of the "normal" in televised sports: The play-by-play of race. *Media, Culture and Society*, 26 (6), 861–79.
Bryant, J., Comisky, P., and Zillmann, D. (1981). The appeal of rough and tumble play in televised professional football. *Communication Quarterly*, 29 (4), 256–62.
Buffington, D. T. (2012). Us and them: US ambivalence toward the World Cup and American nationalism. *Journal of Sport and Social Issues*, 36 (2), 135–54.
Byrd, J., and Utsler, M. (2007). Is stereotypical coverage of African–American athletes as "Dead as Disco"? An analysis of NFL quarterbacks in the pages of *Sports Illustrated*. *Journal of Sports Media*, 2 (1), 1–28.
Caple, H., Greenwood, K., and Lumby, C. (2011). What league? The representation of female athletes in Australian television sports coverage. *Media International Australia, Incorporating Culture and Policy*, 140 (Aug), 137–46.
Capranica, L., and Aversa, F. (2002). Italian television sport coverage during the 2000 Sydney Olympic Games. *International Review for the Sociology of Sport*, 37 (3–4), 337–49.
Cheever, N. (2009). The uses and gratifications of viewing mixed martial arts. *Journal of Sports Media*, 4 (1), 25–53.
Cho, Y. (2009). Unfolding sporting nationalism in South Korean media representations of the 1968, 1984 and 2000 Olympics. *Media, Culture and Society*, 31 (3), 347–64.

Clavio, G., and Kian, T. M. (2010). Uses and gratifications of a retired female athlete's Twitter followers. *International Journal of Sport Communication*, 3, 485–500.

Collins, R. (1998). Supper with the devil – a case study in private/public collaboration in broadcasting: The genesis of Eurosport. *Media, Culture and Society*, 20 (4), 653–63.

Cooper, R., Potter, J., and Dupagne, M. (1994). A status report on methods used in mass communication research. *Journalism Educator*, 48 (4), 54–61.

Coulter, B. J. (1986). The Canadian press and the problem of responsible journalism: An Olympic case study. *Journal of Sport and Social Issues*, 10 (2), 27–48.

Coventry, B. (2004). On the sidelines: Sex and racial segregation in televised sports broadcasting. *Sociology of Sport Journal*, 21 (3), 322–41.

Cressman, D. L., and Swenson, L. (2007). The pigskin and the picture tube: The National Football League's first full season on the CBS Television Network. *Journal of Broadcasting and Electronic Media*, 51 (3), 479–97.

Creswell, J. W. (2007). *Qualitative inquiry and research design: Choosing among five approaches*. Thousand Oaks, CA: Sage.

Crossman, J., Hyslop, P., and Gutrie, B. (1994). A content analysis of the sports section of Canada's national newspaper with respect to gender and professional/amateur status. *International Review for the Sociology of Sport*, 29 (2), 123–31.

Cuneen, J., and Sidwell, M. J. (1998). Gender portrayals in *Sports Illustrated for Kids* advertisements: A content analysis of prominent and supporting models. *Journal of Sport Management*, 12 (1), 39–50.

Cunningham, G. B., and Bopp, T. (2010). Race ideology perpetuated: Media representations of newly hired football coaches. *Journal of Sports Media*, 5 (1), 1–19.

Daddario, G., and Wigley, B. J. (2007). Gender marking and racial stereotyping at the 2004 Athens Games. *Journal of Sports Media*, 2 (1), 29–51.

Denham, B. E., and Cook, A. L. (2006). Byline gender and news source selection: Coverage of the 2004 Summer Olympics. *Journal of Sports Media*, 1 (1), 1–17.

Eastman, S. T., and Billings, A. C. (1999). Gender parity in the Olympics. *Journal of Sport and Social Issues*, 23 (2), 140–70.

Eastman, S. T., and Billings, A. C. (2000). Sportscasting and sports reporting. *Journal of Sport and Social Issues*, 24 (2), 192–213.

Eastman, S. T., and Billings, A. C. (2001). Biased voices of sports: Racial and gender stereotyping in college basketball announcing. *Howard Journal of Communications*, 12 (4), 183–201.

Eastman, S. T., Brown, R. S., and Kovatch, K. J. (1996). The Olympics that got real? Television's story of Sarajevo. *Journal of Sport and Social Issues*, 20 (4), 366–91.

English, P. (2011). Online versus print: A comparative analysis of web-first sports coverage in Australia and the United Kingdom [online]. *Media International Australia, Incorporating Culture and Policy*, 140 (Aug), 147–56.

Fortunato, J. A. (2000). Public relations strategies for creating mass media content: A case study of the National Basketball Association. *Public Relations Review*, 26 (4), 481–97.

Gantz, W. (2011). Reflections and suggestions for scholarship in sports and media. In A. C. Billings (Ed.), *Sports media: Transformation, integration, consumption*. New York: Routledge.

Gantz, W., and Wenner, L. A. (1991). Men, women, and sports: Audience experiences and effects. *Journal of Broadcasting and Electronic Media*, 35 (2), 233–43.

Gantz, W., Wang, Z., Paul, B., and Potter, R. F. (2006). Sports versus all comers: Comparing TV sports fans with fans of other programming genres. *Journal of Broadcasting and Electronic Media*, 50 (1), 95–118.

Gantz, W., Wenner, L., Carrico, C., and Knorr, M. (1995). Televised sports and marital relationships. *Sociology of Sport Journal*, 12 (3), 306–23.

Garland, J., and Rowe, M. (1999). War minus the shooting? *Journal of Sport and Social Issues*, 23 (1), 80–95.

Garrison, B., and Salwen, M. (1989). Newspaper sports journalists: A profile of the "profession". *Journal of Sport and Social Issues*, 13 (2), 57–68.

Garrison, B., and Salwen, M. B. (1994). Sports journalists assess their place in the profession. *Newspaper Research Journal*, 15 (2), 37–49.

Greer, J. D., Hardin, M., and Homan, C. (2009). "Naturally" less exciting? Visual production of men's and women's track and field coverage during the 2004 Olympics. *Journal of Broadcasting and Electronic Media*, 53 (2), 173–89.

Gruneau, R. (1989). Making spectacle: A case study in television sports production. In L. A. Wenner (Ed.), *Media, sports and society* (pp. 134–54). Newbury Park, CA: Sage.

Halbert, C., and Latimer, M. (1994). "Battling" gendered language: An analysis of the language used by sports commentators in a televised coed tennis competition. *Sociology of Sport Journal*, 11 (3), 298–303.

Hallmark, J. R., and Armstrong, R. N. (1999). Gender equity in televised sports: A comparative analysis of men's and women's NCAA division I basketball championship broadcasts, 1991–1995. *Journal of Broadcasting and Electronic Media*, 43 (2), 222–35.

Hardin, M. (2005a). Survey finds boosterism, freebies remain problem for newspaper sports departments. *Newspaper Research Journal*, 26 (1), 66.

Hardin, M. (2005b). Stopped at the gate: Women's sports, "reader interest" and decision making by editors. *Journalism and Mass Communication Quarterly*, 82 (1), 62–77.

Hardin, M., and Shain, S. (2005). Strength in numbers: The experiences and attitudes of women in sports media careers. *Journalism and Mass Communication Quarterly*, 82 (4), 804.

Hardin, M., and Shain, S. (2006). "Feeling much smaller than you know you are": The fragmented professional identity of female sports journalists. *Critical Studies in Media Communication*, 23 (4), 322–38.

Hardin, M., and Whiteside, E. (2009). Token responses to gendered newsrooms. *Journalism*, 10 (5), 627–46.

Hardin, M., Dodd, J. E., and Lauffer, K. (2006). Passing it on: The reinforcement of male hegemony in sports journalism textbooks. *Mass Communication and Society*, 9 (4), 429–46.

Harris, J., and Clayton, B. (2002). Femininity, masculinity, physicality and the English tabloid press. *International Review for the Sociology of Sport*, 37 (3–4), 397–413.

Harris, M. (2001). *The rise of anthropological theory: A history of theories of culture*. Walnut Creek, CA: AltaMira.

Henningham, J. (1995). A profile of Australian sports journalists. *ACHPER Healthy Lifestyles Journal*, Spring, 13–17.

Higgs, C. T., and Weiller, K. H. (1994). Gender bias and the 1992 Summer Olympic Games: An analysis of television coverage. *Journal of Sport and Social Issues*, 18 (3), 234–46.

Higgs, C. T., Weiller, K. H., and Martin, S. B. (2003). Gender bias in the 1996 Olympic Games. *Journal of Sport and Social Issues*, 27 (1), 52–64.

Jackson, S. J. (1998). A twist of race: Ben Johnson and the Canadian crisis of racial and national identity. *Sociology of Sport Journal*, 15, 21–40.

Johnson, T. C., and Schiappa, E. (2010). An exploratory study of the relationships between televised sports viewing habits and conformity to masculine norms. *Journal of Sports Media*, 5 (1), 53–78.

Jones, R., Murrell, A. J., and Jackson, J. (1999). Pretty versus powerful in the sports pages. *Journal of Sport and Social Issues*, 23 (2), 183–92.

Kamhawi, R., and Weaver, D. (2003). Mass communication research trends from 1980 to 1999. *Journalism and Mass Communication Quarterly*, 80 (1), 7–27.

Kinkema, K. M., and Harris, J. C. (1998). MediaSport: Key research and emerging issues. In L. A. Wenner (Ed.), *MediaSport* (pp. 27–54). London: Routledge.

Kinnick, K. N. (1998). Gender bias in newspaper profiles of 1996 Olympic athletes: A content analysis of five major dailies. *Women's Studies in Communication*, 21 (2), 212–37.

Kolmer, C. (2008). Methods of journalism research – Content analysis. In M. Loffelholz and D. Weaver (Eds.), *Global journalism research: Theories, methods, findings, future* (pp. 117–30). Malden, MA: Blackwell.

Krippendorff, K. (2004). *Content analysis: An introduction to its methodology*. Thousand Oaks, CA: Sage.

Lange, K., Nicholson, M., and Hess, R. (2007). A new breed apart? Work practices of Australian internet sport journalists. *Sport in Society: Cultures, Commerce, Media, Politics*, 10 (4), 662–79.

Lee, J. W., and Maguire, J. (2009). Global festivals through a national prism. *International Review for the Sociology of Sport*, 44 (1), 5–24.

Lowes, M. D (1997). Sport page: A case study in the manufacture of sports news for the daily press. *Sociology of Sport Journal*, 14, 143–59.
Lowes, M. D. (1999). *Inside the sport pages: Work routines, professional ideologies and the manufacture of sports news*. Toronto: University of Toronto Press.
Lumpkin, A., and Williams, L. D. (1991). An analysis of *Sports Illustrated* feature articles, 1954–1987. *Sociology of Sport Journal*, 8 (1), 16–32.
MacNeill, M. (1996). Networks: An ethnography of CTV's production of 1988 Winter Olympic ice hockey tournament. *Sociology of Sport Journal*, 13, 103–24.
Malcolm, D., Bairner, A., and Curry, G. (2010). "Woolmergate": Cricket and the representation of Islam and Muslims in the British press. *Journal of Sport and Social Issues*, 34 (2), 215–35.
Mastro, D. E., Blecha, E., and Atwell Seate, A. (2011). Characterizations of criminal athletes: A systematic examination of sports news depictions of race and crime. *Journal of Broadcasting and Electronic Media*, 55 (4), 526–42.
McCree, R. D. (2011). The death of a female boxer. *Journal of Sport and Social Issues*, 35 (4), 327–49.
Messner, M. A., Duncan, M. C., and Wachs, F. L. (1996). The gender of audience building: Televised coverage of women's and men's NCAA Basketball. *Sociological Inquiry*, 66 (4), 422–39.
Messner, M. A., Duncan, M. C., and Cooky, C. (2003). Silence, sports bras, and wrestling porn. *Journal of Sport and Social Issues*, 27 (1), 38–51.
Mitrook, M. A., Parish, N. B., and Seltzer, T. (2008). From advocacy to accommodation: A case study of the Orlando Magic's public relations efforts to secure a new arena. *Public Relations Review*, 34 (2), 161–8.
Nicholson, M., Zion, L., and Lowden, D. (2011). A profile of Australian sport journalists (revisited). *Media International Australia, Incorporating Culture and Policy*, 140 (Aug), 84–96.
Pedersen, P. M. (2002). Examining equity in newspaper photographs. A content analysis of the print media photographic coverage of interscholastic athletes. *International Review for the Sociology of Sport*, 37 (3–4), 303–18.
Pedersen, P. M., Laucella, P. C., Miloch, K. S., and Fielding, L. W. (2007). The juxtaposition of sport and communication: Defining the field of sport communication. *International Journal of Sport Management and Marketing*, 2 (3), 191–207.
Rada, J. A. (1996). Color blind-sided: Racial bias in network television's coverage of professional football games. *Howard Journal of Communications*, 7 (3), 231–9.
Rada, J. A., and Wulfemeyer, K. T. (2005). Color coded: Racial descriptors in television coverage of intercollegiate sports. *Journal of Broadcasting and Electronic Media*, 49 (1), 65–85.
Rainville, R. E., and McCormick, E. (1977). Extent of covert racial prejudice in pro footballers announcers' speech. *Journalism Quarterly*, 54, 20–6.
Raney, A. A., and Depalma, A. J. (2006). The effect of viewing varying levels and contexts of violent sports programming on enjoyment, mood, and perceived violence. *Mass Communication and Society*, 9 (3), 321–38.
Raney, A. A., and Kinnally, W. (2009). Examining perceived violence in and enjoyment of televised rivalry sports contests. *Mass Communication and Society*, 12 (3), 311–31.
Reinardy, S. (2007). Satisfaction vs. Sacrifice: Sports editors assess the influences of life issues on job satisfaction. *Journalism and Mass Communication Quarterly*, 84, 105–21.
Riffe, D., and Freitag, A. (1997). A content analysis of content analyses: Twenty-five years of Journalism Quarterly. *Journalism and Mass Communication Quarterly*, 74 (3), 515–24.
Ronald, B. (2009). It hurts the team even more: Differences in coverage by sports journalists of White and African-American athletes who engage in contract holdouts. *Journal of Sports Media*, 4 (1), 55–84.
Rowe, D. (2007). Sports journalism: Still the "toy department" of the news media? *Journalism*, 8 (4), 385–405.
Salwen, M. B., and Garrison, B. (1998). Finding their place in journalism: Newspaper sports journalists' professional "problems." *Journal of Sport and Social Issues*, 22 (1), 88–102.
Sanderson, J. (2008). "How do you prove a negative?" Roger Clemens's image-repair strategies in response to the Mitchell report. *International Journal of Sport Communication*, 1 (2), 246–62.

Scherer, J. (2007). Globalization, promotional culture and the production/consumption of online games: Engaging Adidas's "Beat Rugby" campaign. *New Media and Society*, 9 (3), 475–96.

Schultz, B., and Sheffer, M. L. (2007). Sports journalists who blog cling to traditional values. *Newspaper Research Journal*, 28 (4), 62–76.

Schweitzer, K. (1992). Perception of threatening events in the emotional aftermath of a televised college football game. *Journal of Broadcasting and Electronic Media*, 36 (1), 75–82.

Scott, O. K. M., Hill, B., and Zakus, D. H. (2012). When the home team is not featured: Comparison of two television network commentaries during broadcasts of the 2006 FIFA World Football Cup. *Sport Management Review*, 15 (1), 23–32.

Serazio, M. (2010). When the sportswriters go marching in: Sports journalism, collective trauma, and memory metaphors. *Critical Studies in Media Communication*, 27 (2), 155–73.

Sheffer, M. L., and Schultz, B. (2007). Double standard: Why women have trouble getting jobs in local television sports. *Journal of Sports Media*, 2 (1), 77–101.

Shifflett, B., and Revelle, R. (1994). Gender equity in sports media coverage: A review of the NCAA News. *Journal of Sport and Social Issues*, 18 (2), 144–50.

Shoemaker, P. J., and Reese, S. D. (1990). Exposure to what? Integrating media content and effects studies. *Journalism and Mass Communication Quarterly*, 67 (4), 649–52.

Smith, E., and Berry, B. (2000). Race, sport and crime: The misrepresentation of African Americans in team sports and crime. *Sociology of Sport Journal*, 17 (2), 171–97.

Stoddart, B. (1994). Sport, television, interpretation and practice reconsidered: Televised golf and analytical orthodoxies. *Journal of Sport and Social Issues*, 18 (1), 76–88.

Stone, J., and Horne, J. (2008). The print media coverage of skiing and snowboarding in Britain. *Journal of Sport and Social Issues*, 32 (1), 94–112.

Tamir, I., and Galily, Y. (2011). The human factor in the historical development of the media: Israeli sports pages as a case study. *International Journal of the History of Sport*, 28 (18), 2688–706.

Travers, A. (2011). Women's ski jumping, the 2010 Olympic Games, and the deafening silence of sex segregation, whiteness, and wealth. *Journal of Sport and Social Issues*, 35 (2), 126–45.

Trumbo, C. W. (2004). Research methods in mass communication research: A census of eight journals 1990–2000. *Journalism and Mass Communication Quarterly*, 81 (2), 417–36.

Van Sterkenburg, J., and Knoppers, A. (2004). Dominant discourses about race/ethnicity and gender in sport practice and performance. *International Review for the Sociology of Sport*, 39 (3), 301–21.

Vincent, J. (2004). Game, sex, match: The construction of gender in British newspaper coverage of the 2000 Wimbledon Championships. *Sociology of Sport Journal*, 21, 435–56.

Vincent, J., Pedersen, P. M., Whisenant, A., and Massey, D. (2007). Analysing the print media coverage of professional tennis players: British newspaper narratives about female competitors in the Wimbledon Championships. *International Journal of Sport Management and Marketing*, 2 (3), 281–300.

Wann, D. L., and Branscombe, N. R. (1990). Die-hard and fair-weather fans: Effects of identification on BIRGing and CORFing tendencies. *Journal of Sport and Social Issues*, 14 (2), 103–17.

Wann, D. L., Schrader, M. P., Allison, J. A., and McGeorge, K. K. (1998). The inequitable newspaper coverage of men's and women's athletics at small, medium and large universities. *Journal of Sport and Social Issues*, 22 (1): 79–87.

Weaver, D., and Wilhoit, G. C. (1988). A profile of JMC educators: Traits, attitudes and values. *Journalism Educator*, 43 (2), 4–41.

Wenner, L. A. (1989). *Media, sports and society*. Newbury Park, CA: Sage.

Whiteside, E., and Hardin, M. (2010). Public relations and sports: Work force demographics in the intersection of two gendered industries. *Journal of Sports Media*, 5 (1), 21–52.

Whiteside, E., Simpson, S., and Hardin, M. (2007). The gender war in US sport: Winners and losers in news coverage of Title IX. *Mass Communication and Society*, 10 (2), 211–33.

10

ATHLETE–MEDIA COMMUNICATION

A theoretical perspective on how athletes use and understand gendered sport communication

Elsa Kristiansen and Trygve B. Broch

Since the 1990s, the volume of journalistic sport reports has rapidly increased. According to Sage (2010), the media's presence in contemporary society now involves two social roles: to *communicate* information about (sports) people and (sports) events, and to provide entertainment. Maguire and colleagues argue that *mediated sport* as entertainment even plays an important part in our social existence and shapes our understandings of social life (Maguire, Jarvie, Mansfield, and Bradley, 2002). Consequently, the media are not neutral communicators. Rather, sport as a cultural and mediated phenomenon avails the inscription of national, local, and global meanings that should be critically examined. Furthermore, sport through the journalistic lens has become a means to portray ideal images of selves, others, and organizations to large audiences. The cultural *omnipresence* of sport communication *through mass media* has developed into an institutional complex of enormous social, cultural, political, and economic importance (Sage, 2010).

Clearly, this development has an impact on both aspiring youths and elite athletes exposed to the media. First, young athletes may look to elite athletes for inspiration. However, elite athletes are not only role models for their sport skills and talents, they also comprise a set of idolized personal characteristics such as morality, citizenship, and wisdom (Addis, 1996). Second, the intense media focus also influences elite athletes who may conceive positive media attention as additional motivation. Conversely, negative or critical journalistic reports may affect the athletes' preparation and self-confidence in a negative manner (Gauntlett, 2008). Elite athletes are not only confronted by success and failure, they also have to cope with the media's cultural ideals. Mediated sport communication for example form elite athletes through nationalistic (Billings, MacArthur, Licen, and Wu Dan, 2009) and gendered (Broch, 2011; Sisjord and Kristiansen, 2008) lenses. Consequently, when elite athletes communicate who they are (or whom they are expected to be) to the media, the media do not necessarily return the favor in a neutral manner.

In this chapter, Connellist perspectives are applied to explore how gendered sport communication is used and understood by Norwegian teenage athletes and elite athletes. After presenting the theoretical framework, the chapter is divided into two discussion sections: teenagers and elite athletes. The first section illustrates how media images are used in specific Norwegian sport cultures and what gendered meanings are derived from sport communication to inform the young athletes' sport practice. The second section discusses how elite athletes use and negotiate gendered media imagery during their athletic careers. The two sections also illustrate how inspiration drawn from Connell's theories can be applied in two different methodological settings; namely, to analyze empirical data collected though participant field observations among Norwegian teenage athletes and then interviews of elite athletes.

Gendered sport communication

To understand how athletes use and understand sport communication, theoretical inspiration is drawn from Connell's perspectives regarding gender. Fundamental to our analysis is Connell's conception of gender as a social structure involving a specific relationship with bodies:

> Gender is the structure of social relations that centers on the reproductive arena, and the set of practices (governed by this structure) that bring reproductive distinctions between bodies into social processes.
>
> *(Connell, 2002, p. 10)*

With regard to male and female bodies, sport at times exaggerates gendered stereotypes (such as men building muscle mass), at times mythologizes (for example, glorifying muscular male athletes' achievements), and at times complicates (for example, strong and powerful female athletes glorified) structured gender binaries and cultural stereotypes centered on the reproductive arena. Furthermore, there are usually significant differences of bodily appearance between a long-distance runner and an American football player, even big differences between a linesman and a wide receiver. Implicitly, there are many ways of being a man or a woman. In Connell's (1995) wording, there are many masculinities and femininities. Nevertheless, all men and women in some manner relate to gendered expectations regarding what is gender appropriate behavior and appearance in any given culture and historical period.

When athletes, coaches, and media exaggerate, mythologize, and complicate gender binaries and norms, they are sometimes induced by the structure of gender. Connell (1987) argues that gender relations are always power relations that can induce persons to challenge or reinstate hegemonic conceptions of appropriate gender relations. Accordingly, hegemonic masculinity (Connell, 1987, 1995, 2000) constitutes the ideal definition of masculinity that occupies the dominant position in any given pattern of gender relations; superior to other subordinated masculinities and all femininities. Hegemonic masculinity represents a symbolic practice and an ideal often associated with heterosexuality, authority, strength, and physical toughness. On the other hand, emphasized femininity – which is hegemonic masculinity's complementary and dichotomous opposite – is oriented to accommodate the interests and desires of men, and often characterized by a display of sociability, receptiveness, and passivity, rather than technical competence. Though emphasized femininity, as hegemonic masculinity, is conceived as a cultural ideal, it can never obtain a hegemonic position at the top of the gender hierarchy theorized by Connell. It is also significant to note that few men perform and/or embody prototypical hegemonic masculinity (Connell, 2000), and very few women embody emphasized femininity in most of their everyday encounters. However, through fictional male and female characters (for example, Hollywood movie heroes and heroines) and exceptional men and women, who succeed and display contextually ideal (almost fictional) forms of masculinity and femininity (like some sport heroes), some men and women come to symbolically represent a hegemonic masculinity and the emphasized femininity ideal.

Connell (1995, 2000) gives an account of gender relations in a variety of social institutions, including organized sports. Behavior characterized by muscular strength, authority, courage, heterosexuality, and the ability to endure pain and to use violence in combination with physical skills has been analyzed to represent the hegemonic form of masculinity, both within the performance (Messner and Sabo, 1994) and the mediation (Broch, 2011; Messner, 2002; Pedersen, Whisenant, and Schneider, 2003) of many male sports. This ideal of hegemonic masculinity has also been analyzed as a structural barrier women and girls have to negotiate to be accepted as gender appropriate female athletes (Coakley, 2007; Sisjord and Kristiansen, 2008). This chapter is inspired by Connell's theory and explores how both teenage and adult elite athletes use and understand gendered sport communication.

Teenage athletes

To investigate how young Norwegian handballers use and understand gendered sport communication, participant field observations in Norwegian team handball culture were carried out. During the 2011–2012 handball season, one of the chapter authors (Broch) followed a team for fifteen-year-old boys and a team for thirteen-year-old girls. The boys' team consisted of about 25 athletes, with a man in his early 20s as their coach. The girls' team also numbered approximately 25 players, and were coached by one man and one woman, who were both in their late forties. They were also both former elite handballers. Participant field observations took place on the ground and in the midst of the handball action. This is an ideal situation to explore how media images are used and understood in everyday practice. Notes on verbal, nonverbal, textual, and symbolic practices with a focus on detailed descriptions, what Geertz (1973) defines as "thick descriptions", were written down. This method focuses cultural nuances, behavioral variations, and facets more than the socially generalizable. The researcher's role included participation in the coaching staff, managing and assisting the head coach during practices and games, and partaking in the practice of handball play among the athletes (play specific activities and drills when the group was shorthanded).

Shortly after arriving on site and spending time with the informants, their use of media messages to construct and induce meaning was manifest. Both the girls and boys watched elite televised representations of Norwegian elite handball. All three coaches made instructional references to televised performances of handball:

> Peter stops the girl's play sequence by shouting "What's most important ALWAYS keep your eyes on the goal! Look here" Peter picks up the ball and with his 220 lbs heavy, 6 foot 8 inches tall body, thunders toward 13 years old Lisa on defense. Lisa covers her eyes and bends her neck and shoulders in fear "If the defender does not engage, it will bang! Trine Haltvik probably scored 10.000 goals by banging the ball passed defenders" Peter illustrates by throwing his arm at Lisa's neck and shoulders. "If the defender does tackle, it will be room for the winger, and you can go all Håvard Tvedten on them" Peter laughs and smiles to Emily positioned on the wing.
>
> *(Field notes)*

Trine Haltvik and Håvard Tvedten are two of Norway's most renowned handballers, respectively from the women's and men's national teams. Haltvik is well known for her hard-nose no-fear attitude and Tvedten for his elegant technique and artistic handball skills. Within Connell's (1995) framework, these two athletes represent particular ways of being a woman and a man, both found appropriate by the coach to inform the girls' handball practice. Connell's (1987, 1995) gender hierarchy, however, meets a difficult explanatory task when applied in the Norwegian handball practice observed. In Norway, the contact sport of handball is dominated, actually defined as a sport for women (Goksøyr, 2008; von der Lippe, 2010). Through international achievements, media exposure and an approximate of 70 percent female participants it has been the women who have resided the hegemonic position within Norwegian handball. Norwegian elite female handballers have for quite some time now served as exemplary models for both girls and boys (Broch, 1995). Similar remarks and use of elite role models, as empirically manifested above, to guide, color, and inform the teenagers' handball skills where observed repeatedly throughout the period of observations. When the boys' team performance had gone astray, the team's coach presented the Norwegian elite female team named Larvik as an exemplary model to the boys:

> Larvik is a good example. They [the women] are regarded as the *best team* in all the matches they play in the Norwegian elite league. Always being a favorite, that's a lot of pressure; it makes it hard to succeed. But they [Larvik] *always* sweep the floor clean, they *crush all adversaries*; that's how we must play, that's the attitude and mindset we need. Larvik is a great example.
>
> *(Field notes)*

The boys' coach never mentions that Larvik is an elite *women's team*; it is tacit knowledge that it is the most successful Norwegian women's club, both domestically and internationally. In the Norwegian handball culture observed, both mediated female and male role models were used to induce young masculinities and femininities. In the case of successful styles of play, the sex of the role models seemed less important to the coaches than the handball specific achievement of the idol. The emphasized style of play presented by the girls' coach was very similar to the hegemonic style of play proposed in the boys' team; as shown in the above note, women's handball even explicitly informed the boys' practice.

Female handball was, however, not the only inspirational media asset understood as informative for the boys' handball practice. The boys' team adopted a Hollywood narrative to inform and enhance the players' pre-game routine. The narrative is an audio excerpt that the coach and team had downloaded to an iPhone and connected to a boom box. An auditory excerpt from the movie *Any Given Sunday*, the speech sequence performed by actor Al Pacino, was played in the locker-room just before game-time:

> You find out life's this game of inches, so is football...On this team we fight for that inch. On this team we tear ourselves and everyone else around us to pieces for that inch. We claw with our fingernails for that inch. Because we know when we add up all those inches, that's gonna make the fucking difference between winning and losing! Between living and dying!... I'll tell you this, in any fight it's the guy who is willing to die who is gonna win that inch....Now, what are you gonna do?
>
> *(Donner, Halsted, Townsend, and Stone, 1999)*

It the context of the pregame routine, Pacino's speech attained a dynamic gendered potential in the specific boys' team. As soon as the handball coach presses the play button, the end – and supposed to be climax – of the handball team's pregame routine commenced:

> After the warm-ups, the boys gather in the narrow locker-room. There is not much time left; some last words from the coach, put on jerseys, pack the bags, and the game can start. The boys are spread out on the benches and the coach has prepared the boom box: 'Ok guys!'. During the next 3 minutes the boys are quiet, but the locker-room is loud. From the boom box streams a Hollywood-ambiance, bass, treble, and a musk male voice thunders between the naked walls. Accompanied by a symphonic orchestra the message urges us all: 'Now, what are you gonna do?'. The boys clap their hands, holler and get on their feet – we take the field invigorated.
>
> *(Field notes)*

As in the movie, the handball players respond to the coach's request and get on their feet, ready and supposedly pumped for the game. This pre-game routine was repeated on several occasions and with varying intensity, but always ended by mimicking the movie. The speech's moral value and meaning was also presented by the coach as a team motto, a standard signifying an appropriate reputation of the team, and as an inspirational resource for practice and game exertion.

In a Connellist framework, the active use of the Hollywood narrative can be analyzed as a means to inscribe the boys' handball practice with additional masculine meaning. It becomes a metaphoric tool to connect their handball activity to a hegemonic masculine ideal presented by Hollywood producer, Oliver Stone. In relation to the season observed, the use of the Pacino speech can hardly be analyzed as reinstating a global hegemonic gender hierarchy within the Norwegian handball context. After all, handball is in Norway a women's sport where specific women are role models for both girls and boys. Applying cultural thick description suggests that the structural gender hierarchy does not always manifest itself empirically. Explicitly, in particular contexts women are not always subordinate to men. However, in line with Connell's (1995) argument, the speech offers the Norwegian boys' team an ideal masculinity that avails proud boys practicing a culturally defined women's sport. It offers a hegemonic masculine ideal to aspire in play, an ideal that stratifies the team in regards to a masculine hierarchy where particular styles of play are valued more than others.

Elite athletes

Athlete–media communication became a hot topic when one of the chapter authors (Kristiansen) interviewed female (United States in 2010) and male elite (Europe in 2008) soccer players. To highlight the athletes' perceptions on how they and the media communicate gender, the narratives of four athletes are presented. The two merited female athletes with an Olympic gold medal as the peak of their career, also represent different continents. The two male athletes, on the other hand, had long careers on their respective national teams, and experience from several European leagues.

The athlete–media relationship is potentially a stressful relation. Usually, elite athletes have an ambivalent relationship with journalists and their coverage (Kristiansen and Hanstad,

2012); the journalists chase the athletes for a story, and the athletes need the journalist to be visible in the media. As one emphasized:

> You must make your own rules on how you will behave, and always question their [the journalists] motives so they don't catch you off guard. During these past few years the journalists have never asked me questions about team conflicts, conflicts with the coach and other types of "scandals". I did not give journalists the answers they wanted. Team conflicts must be, after coverage of superb victories, the media's favorite theme.
>
> *(Male soccer player)*

Apparently, it is not easy communicating athletic skills when the journalists rather prefer success, scandals (Kristiansen and Hanstad, 2012), and entertainment (Sage, 2010). To address the increasing journalistic attention and tabloidization, elite athletes now learn and practice a range of different types of coping strategies (Kristiansen and Roberts, 2011). Furthermore, the athletes also learn the gendered codes that possibly enhance their sport-media value. When becoming professional sport communicators, some athletes come to earn a lot of money, while others realize that they do not communicate masculinities and femininities that live up to the gendered expectations of the media:

> In order to get some media attention you have to be this bombshell, this beautiful bombshell like Brandi Chastain that everyone wants to have sex with. You must be kind of good on the playing field, for sure, but even sometimes that doesn't matter like Anna Kournikova. I think it is really tricky where, again, people can disguise attention or media can say that they are given attention, but sometimes it is quite ambiguous as so why is that person or that particular somebody get that particular attention. Whoever it is…it is never about performance first in female sport. It is always about the hot-factor.
>
> *(Female soccer player)*

In line with previous Connellist research (Sisjord and Kristiansen, 2008), elite athletes' comprehensions of selves do not always correspond with the media's market strategies. The soccer player above argued that athletes are valued more within the sport-media complex if they are conventionally and heterosexually attractive. In Connell's (1995) terminology, the symbolic and bodily display of emphasized femininity and traditional heterosexual attractiveness is valued more than the technical competence of female athletes. Brandi Chastain, who is mentioned in the quote, is an excellent example. She rose to prominence after the 1999 FIFA World Cup. The dominant theme in the media, however, did not concern Chastain's accomplishments on the field. Instead, coverage focused on Chastain stripping, pulling off her jersey, and revealing her sports bra after converting the winning penalty in the final. Messner (2002, p. 98) later argued that this media focus was "humorous sexualisation" of women athletes.

Chastain got the headlines when undressing, and many female athletes have strategically "come to terms" with this particular media focus. Swimmer Amanda Beard and figure skater Katarina Witt are two on a long list of athletes stripping for *Playboy*. *Playboy* and other media become outlets for female athletes to display and reinstate emphasized feminine selves in economically and symbolically viable terms. The naked body is, however, not the only bodily way of displaying emphasized femininity. The female athletes interviewed argued that the display of and focus on selves as heterosexual wives and mothers are also appropriate athlete–media communication:

> I feel that the media focused a lot on the fact that I am a mother. I guess that is one way of saying that I am not lesbian, but I would have preferred a more thorough focus on my athletic achievements instead. I guess soccer is still a sport for men, and female players often get labeled butch lesbians.
>
> *(Female soccer player)*

The interviewee felt that the media preferred a heterosexually "straight" focus. This media focus created a gendered tension, here resolved by the strategic display of emphasized femininity through a practiced nuclear family. She partly explained this need for symbolic displays of femininity as a result of the masculine context of her soccer practice. Emphasized femininity becomes a means to reinstate a specific gendered identity that is symbolically contested by her contextual practice. When the gender hierarchy is disturbed in this manner emotional responses like distrust and disgust may be provoked (Connell, 2002). Seemingly, it may produce invisibility in the media as well. The more female athletes blur the gender binaries, the more their sexual orientations tend to be discussed or hinted at in the media. This was particularly explicit during the peak of female soccer during the 1999 World Cup, as one of the female players interviewed recalled:

> So many questions were about sexuality, but in fact, the substance of what they were asking had nothing to do with how talented, how great we were, and yeah, maybe every now and then the history that we were making, but, they had all these other questions that seemed to sabotage the greatness of who we were and what our team was accomplishing.
>
> *(Female soccer player)*

The media's focus on sexual orientation sabotaged, or policed, the transformative power and possible impact of the female sport achievements (Messner, 2002; Sisjord and Kristiansen, 2008). In light of Connell's (2002) theory, the frustration expressed is a result of an overall structure of gender relations. When female athletes invade not only the traditionally male sport field but also the heavily masculine media sport field, these female athletes are portrayed through the hegemonic masculine gaze; foremost receiving media attention when heterosexually appealing and sexually available. Otherwise, the female athletes articulated that they often felt "invisible" in the media and that their omitted accomplishments did anger them, like "wait a minute, I just scored?"– as one interviewee expressed. Coverage of women's sports is not concomitant with the coverage of men's sport (Coakley, 2007), and not all men's sports share prime time equally. Hence, the sports media can be analyzed as reinforcing hegemonic masculinity and stratifying other masculinities and femininities in sport. Research indicates that both male and female journalists are equally responsible for the under-represented coverage of female athletes (Pedersen, *et al.*, 2003). Boyle and Haynes (2000) noted that media visibility creates corporate interest, which in turn creates economic sponsor profits for sports and athletes. Consequently, female athletes are forced to negotiate their sport accomplishments, lack of income, earning power, and media visibility in a culture that celebrates specific gender norms. Analytically, Connell's theoretical framework manifests that these negotiations relate to the structure of gender, a structural media-sport dynamic previously analyzed by Messner as "a powerful reaffirmation of masculine (male) privilege" (Messner, 2002, p. 76).

Until now, female athletes' negotiation of sport communication has been discussed. How do gender norms shape the male athlete–media relation? Is it an advantage for men to display the binary and stereotypic opposition to emphasized femininity when within the sport-media complex? One of the female athletes pointed out that being fortunate with looks is also profitable for men:

> In many ways I think sex sells for both genders. I am not an idiot. Wayne Rooney doesn't get probably some of the sponsorships that Christian Ronaldo does...because of how, you know...gorgeous Ronaldo is, but Wayne Rooney definitely does not miss out of any attention because of his performance.
>
> *(Female soccer player)*

Is hegemonic masculinity in contemporary capitalist societies reshaped by consumerism into an objectified ideal-to-be-bought often analytically linked to notions of femininity? To fluctuate in the spotlight may also have an impact on male athletes' perceptions of beautiful selves, as one of the male interviewees expressed:

> One of my friends who won Champions League at a very young age and is considered very successful, have changed so much the last couple of years because of his fame and popularity as a footballer. He became one of many I have seen change because he received media attention; suddenly he got headlines because of *hairstyle, girlfriend, fashion and lifestyle.* I have seen guys using an hour in front of the mirror before press conferences in order to take care of their "image" and "look". I don't know...Media can be very straining if you act out as they want.
>
> *(Male soccer player)*

Obviously, in soccer, appearance and look matter for both women and men. David Beckham is often used as an exemplary illustration. With firm footing in his masculine athleticism, he has had the possibility to maneuver an androgynous blend of emphasized and hegemonic opposites. As Cashmore (2006) sums up, he is "straight, but adored by gay men; male, but with a penchant for nail varnish, body-waxing, and androgynous attire (Cashmore, 2006, p. 233). Equally, the quote above reveals, some players disregard this development in soccer, while others are almost ridiculed when trying to stage a commodified image. The finding of men communicating specific notions of beauty for the same reasons as women – to increase economic sponsor profits – was further nuanced by one of the male athlete interviewee's negotiation of his display of profitable masculinity in contrast to athletic focus:

> I have often been asked about the way I celebrate penalty shots – I look "weird". Sometimes I even drop the goal celebration, but the thing is; I have never considered or planned how to celebrate the goals. Some like running away from team mates, while others take off their shirt. If I did something like that I would lose my focus and not score.
>
> *(Male soccer player)*

How female and male players celebrate goals is often debated both in the media and in the locker-room. The interviewee above reflects on his position in the media spotlight, but concludes he needed all his energy to focus on the game. Other players act in accordance with believed media expectations. Comparative perspectives on male and female athletes explicitly manifest that differences among men and women are as binary as the gender binary itself.

Conclusion

How mediated sport is used and understood by young and elite athletes is an understudied topic (Kristiansen and Lines, 2013). In particular, and as indicated above, the study of the athlete–media relation can also become a tool to explore how gendered structures are contested, transformed, and reinstated through athlete–media communication. The role models presented for young athletes, may have a resilient impact on how they in later adult life will comprehend gendered selves and others. As shown above, gendered comprehensions also shape elite athletes' communication with the media.

Participant field observations over an extended period of time complicate the Connellist framework introduced in this chapter. A Geertzian perspective manifests social life as more complex and nuanced than reflected by Connell's gender hierarchy model. The empiric materials indicate that ideal constructions of emphasized femininity and hegemonic masculinity should hardly always be analyzed as binary and stereotypical oppositions. However, significant metaphoric elements, like the Hollywood narrative applied by the handball coach, can also link a specific handball culture to global symbolic and structured gendered meanings.

Interviews of both male and female athletes additionally avail a similar analytic potential to reflect gender as multifaceted, but still induced by what Connell defines as the structured relation of gender. Significant cultural definitions of emphasized femininity and hegemonic masculinity shape opportunities of media visibility for both male and female elite athletes. The interviewees communicate a desired focus on athletic skills, while at the same time they negotiate norms of gender-appropriate appearance. Sport communication for men and women is still induced by normative displays of the male and female binary. This structural negotiation and active use of gendered meaning to inform, understand, and portray selves and others is accordingly manifested in aspiring and elite athletes' practice, as well as in the sport media's strategies. In a time when many gender binaries are transgressed, perspectives on the athlete–media relationship can illuminate how sport communication is understood and used to negotiate and enhance specific images of gendered selves and others.

References

Addis, A. (1996). Role models and the politics of recognition. *University of Pennsylvania Law Review*, 144, 1377–468.

Billings, A. C., MacArthur, P. J., Licen, S., and Wu D. (2009). Superpowers on the Olympic basketball court: the United States versus China through four nationalistic lenses. *International Journal of Sport Communication*, 2, 380–97.

Boyle, R., and Haynes, R. (2000). *Power play. Sport, the media and popular culture*. Essex: Pearson Education.

Broch, H. B. (1995). Håndball er ingen frøkensport: antropologiske perspektiver på aldersbestemt håndball for gutter og jenter [Handball is no ladies game]. *Barn*, 2, 21–38.

Broch, T. B. (2011). Norwegian Big Bang Theory: Production of gendered sound during team handball broadcasts. *International Journal of Sport Communication*, 4, 344–58.

Cashmore, E. (2006). *Celebrity/Culture*. New York: Routledge.
Coakley, J. (2007). *Sports in society: Issues and controversies* (9th ed.). Boston: McGraw-Hill Higher Education.
Connell, R. (1987). *Gender and power: Society, the person, and sexual politics*. Stanford, CA: Stanford University Press.
Connell, R. (1995). *Masculinities*. Cambridge, UK: Polity Press.
Connell, R. (2000). *The men and the boys*. Berkeley, CA: University of California Press.
Connell, R. (2002). *Gender*. Cambridge, UK: Polity Press.
Donner, L. S. D., Halsted, D., Townsend, C. (Producers), and Stone, O. (Director). (1999). *Any Given Sunday*. United States: Warner Bros.
Gauntlett, D. (2008). *Media, gender and identity. An introduction* (2nd ed.). London: Routledge.
Geertz, C. (1973). *Thick description: Toward an interpretive theory of Culture. The interpretation of cultures: Selected essays by Clifford Geertz*. New York: Basic.
Goksøyr, M. (2008). *Historien om norsk idrett*. Oslo, Norway: Abstrakt Forlag.
Kristiansen, E., and Hanstad, D.V. (2012). Journalists and Olympic athletes: A Norwegian case study of an ambivalent relationship. *International Journal of Sport Communication*, 5, 231–45.
Kristiansen, E., and Lines, G. A. (2013). Media. In A. Papaioannou, and D. Hackfort (Eds.), *Concepts in sport and exercise psychology*. London: Taylor and Francis.
Kristiansen, E., and Roberts, G. C. (2011). Media exposure and adaptive coping in elite football. *International Journal of Psychology*, 42, 339–67.
Maguire, J., Jarvie, G., Mansfield, L., and Bradley, J. (2002). *Sports worlds: A sociological perspective*. Champaign, IL: Human Kinetics.
Messner, M. A. (2002). *Taking the field: Women, men and sports*. Minneapolis, MN: University of Minnesota Press.
Messner, M. A., and Sabo, D. F. (1994). *Sex, violence and power in sports: Rethinking masculinity*. Freedom, CA: Crossing Press.
Pedersen, P. M., Whisenant, W. A., and Schneider, R. G. (2003). Using a content analysis to examine the gendering of sports newspaper personnel and their coverage. *Journal of Sport Management*, 17, 376–93.
Sage, G. H. (2010). *Globalizing sport: How organizations, corporations, media, and politics are changing sports*. London: Paradigm.
Sisjord, M. K., and Kristiansen, E. (2008). Serious athletes or media clowns? Female and male wrestlers' perceptions of media constructions. *Sociology of Sport Journal*, 25, 350–68.
von der Lippe, G. (2010). *Et kritisk blikk på sportsjournalistikk*. Kristiansand, Norway: IJ-forlaget.

SECTION II

Traditional media associated with sport communication

11

A GLOBAL CRISIS?

International perspectives on the state of print sport media

Matthew H. Zimmerman, Ilan Tamir, Holger Ihle, Jörg-Uwe Nieland, and Jianjun Tang

With losses in advertising, readership, and prestige, the decaying state of news media in the US has become such a well-known fact that even works of drama feature it as a plot point (Sepinwall, 2012). After enjoying a prominent place in the societal firmament for decades, print sports media in the US experienced a precipitous decline in recent years. With the demise in the early 1990s of the short-lived *National Sports Daily*, there have been no print US sports dailies distributed nationally. The country's two main print sports magazines, *Sports Illustrated* and *ESPN The Magazine*, each regularly report circulations of approximately two million (Friedman, 2010), but this figure is possibly aided by various subscription discounts available to consumers.

There is not a complete consensus regarding the reasons for print media's ongoing demise. In an examination of Canadian media conglomerates, Winseck (2010) noted the rise of new online communication technologies and their respective ownership, including the Google and YouTube partnership, Facebook, and Wikipedia. These newer, well-funded online outlets cut into traditional media's role as gatekeepers of information and ideal places to advertise (Edmonds, 2012). However, Winseck also argued that the decline in print media was not necessarily due to the Internet and these technologies, but rather were a result of circumstances, including the global economic crisis and media consolidation.

While the current state of print media in the US is accepted to be troubled, it is worth discussing how various factors – both global and local – have affected print sports media in other nations. In this chapter, researchers present a comparative set of examples that display the current state of print media in different parts of the globe. Authors from Israel, Germany, China, and the US present their research in the following sections.

Print sport journalism in Israel

Despite Israel's young age (the state was only established in 1948), Israeli sports media have managed to undergo fascinating processes that reflect, to a great extent, many of the challenges that face media in general and sports media in particular in recent years. The development of media, posited Caspi, constitutes a "historical wheel" comprising four stages, which explains the presence of various media side by side (Caspi, 1993, p. 115). The first stage is the breakthrough, in which attention focuses on the very emergence of the medium, while temporarily abandoning the old media forms. The second stage gives rise to the establishment of the new medium. The next stage, defensiveness, occurs when a newer medium threatens to a certain extent the current media equilibrium. The defensiveness regarding the old media forms stems from the fear of significant regression in cuts from their consumers. The adaptation of the fourth stage delineates the new media reality, which is a result of coping with the media forms in the previous stages. Adjustment to the existence of the new medium can also express itself as surrender, meaning the fading away or disappearance altogether of the older media forms, or in changes and adjustments of the functions served by these older media. The Israeli sports media has passed three waves, or wheels, in Capsi's (1993) terms.

The breakthrough stage of Israeli sports journalism began shortly before the establishment of the state with the emergence of private sports journals, whose distribution was irregular and whose reviews were characterized by blatant political biases and preferences. The introduction of the sports sections in the daily evening newspapers did not significantly change this reality. The establishment of sports media was tied to the sports editors' attempts to professionalize the sports journalism occupation and raise it above the narrow political considerations. This media situation, which many of the sports journalists tried to change, was a course that helped lead toward the establishment of *Sports News* (*Hadashot Hasport*), which, at the time, was defined as the most important sports-related publication in Israel. The economic reality – that is, sports journalism's struggles to survive – was the second course. A handful of individuals tried to establish quality sports journalism, practically out of thin air. They were nicknamed the 'founding generation' or the 'national team' of sports journalists in Israel (Porat, 1987). The emergence of *Sports News* in 1954 was an innovation in the landscape of Israeli journalism. The paper, which circulated for about three years, set new standards of work which influenced the norms of subsequent generations, affecting the entire scope of journalism.

In the public domain, the paper enjoyed tremendous success, and became a central factor in determining the sports agenda in Israel. The paper established the accepted standard in sports review. For example, *Sports News* insisted on writing its stories in Hebrew. To achieve this, the staff needed to generate new words to illustrate different functions and situations that arose in the world of sports (such as goal, offside, defender, or tackle). The paper broadened the scope of the coverage, although football was always in the center of attention. Even international sporting events earned a place in the paper. For the first time, *Sports News* decided to score athletes following a game, and offered training courses for sports journalists and broadcasters. In the years that followed, many sports journalists were graduates of these classes. In *Sports News*' footsteps came the predecessors of televised sports broadcasts (1968: "A Look at Sports" weekly roundup of sports events) and radio-broadcast sports (1970: "Songs and Goalposts" live weekly broadcast of football games in Israel).

The 1980s had already heralded the breakthrough of an additional wave of media development in Israel. The focus was centered on the expansion of the sports sections of the daily newspapers, especially the emergence of the newspaper *News* (*Hadashot*) in 1984, which was considered to be a sometimes anti-establishment publication. *News*, as part of its younger persona, dedicated a considerable portion of its space to sports review. In its wake, the larger daily papers were forced to expand their sports coverage. Thus, the two main newspapers, Yedioth Aharonoth and Maariv, doubled and sometimes tripled the volume of their sports sections, with an average of six pages daily at the time. In light of the recruitment processes of the new and renewed sports sections, and their general management, the older generation of journalists expressed aggressive opposition to the appearance of *News* and the ever-growing circulation of local journals, which dedicated a significant amount of coverage to sports. The defensive phase took on a hostile quality as the veteran journalists lashed out (Rosenblatt, 1987). The criticisms addressed the new journalists' abilities and understanding of their field. Also assailed were the new journalists' training and management, which, in the older generation's opinion, bordered on crossing ethical lines. Among other criticisms were the supposed importance placed on the visibility of their names in the newspapers, their writing or the perceived professional shallowness that typified their work. There was a consensus among the veteran sports journalists that their young heirs were forging sensitive and unhealthy ties with associations, politicians, coaches, and athletes. Yet the senior journalists, who had expressed sharp disappointment at the new generation, actually found their place in the new media environment. The people from *Sports News* were absorbed into the larger dailies, often in editorial positions.

One significant indicator of the professional establishment of the journalist in this generation was the shift of the sports journalist into parallel journalistic spheres that were considered serious and established. Journalists who were identified with the advent of the second wave moved into areas of political and military review. Sports journalism thus earned recognition for its professionalism, despite the criticism it drew a few years earlier.

At the turn of the century, during an era that gave rise to local sports media, the intermediate generation of sports journalists was also forced to defend itself. This time, the emergence of the third wave came from outside the traditional printed journalism. In large part, it reflected the significant challenges facing print media worldwide. The 1990s introduced three new players that transformed sports media. The multiple-channel television that had begun to gain popularity in Israel was a fertile breeding ground for two televised entities: The Sports Channel and Charleton, which had begun to broadcast sports in 1990. By 2012, these two bodies held nine broadcasting channels on cable and satellite television. In 1999, another sports channel, One, was established to compete against the sports channel, Sport5. These new bodies introduced a new and even younger generation of journalists that again changed the rules of the game.

The new organizations opened the opportunity for women to cross into the previously closed world of sports media. Similar to the first wave, the new criticism attacked the supposed unreliability of female journalists and their problematic management, especially regarding any issue pertaining to the mixing of professional and personal life. The verbal assaults on this new generation of female journalists reflect the generational turnover that represents the loss of hegemony in printed sports media. There was also a distinct defensiveness against the feminization of sports media, which expresses the loss of the masculine hegemony in sports review (Tamir and Galily, 2011).

A critical analysis of repetitive journalistic defensiveness, in a framework of conflicting approaches, can lend an additional viewpoint. One of the claims associated with the critical approach in regard to the journalistic profession posits that the certain professions forged a status of professionalism and then earned social recognition for the end goal of retaining their own professional monopoly. Accordingly, members of the first incarnation of sports journalism saw themselves as an exclusive professional body by virtue of belonging to the founding generation of journalists. They had difficulty accepting new members as well as with the diminishing boundaries that separate distinct professionals. The second wave of journalistic defensiveness revealed a double challenge: the loss of professional distinction, as occurs in any turnover of personnel, and the collapse of the gender hegemony. Sports media, which represents the body of sports knowledge, was a clear bastion of masculinity as an expression of the connection that binds sports and men. The profession struggled to accept the increasing feminine presence as a significant group rather than individuals, since it viewed this femininity as a collapse of the strength of that bond. Thus, it can be seen that the criticism toward women in sports media, while reminiscent of the criticism hurled at the intermediate generation, is more aggressive in its content. It is a defensive battle waged against a foreign body that is trying to usurp the existing power.

The sport press in Germany

The German print media considers March 23, 1886 as the birthday of the sports section. Among other events, the *Münchener Neueste Nachrichten* reported on a bet between a horse car and a runner, as well as results of horse races (Eggers, 2009). Until the First World War, the majority of the prestigious papers followed, with small columns about sport. The local sporting events were emphasized within the coverage. During this period, only a few reports were written by (professional) sport journalists, with the newspapers and magazines relying on the reports of athletes as correspondents.

Sports journalism in Germany had its first heyday during the Weimar Republic (1918–1933). At that time, all major papers had a sports desk with a major emphasis on football. *The Kicker* was founded in 1920 and magazines such as the *Fußball* and the *Fußballwoche* emerged quickly as rivals in the 1920s. The magazines were used as official partners by the German Football Association (DFB). With the beginning of the Third Reich, sports journalism went through a major caesura. The market for sport magazines slowed, and Jewish sport journalists were not allowed to work anymore (Eggers, 2009).

After the Second World War, sport was treated as an orphan by the transregional daily newspapers (such as the *Frankfurter Rundschau, Süddeutsche Zeitung*). Sports journalists were considered outsiders. However, the tabloid press including flagship, the *Bild*, founded in 1952, put a lot of emphasis on sports coverage. It was no coincidence that the *Kölner Express* hit the market in conjunction with the introduction of the *Bundesliga* in 1963 (Eggers, 2009). Also, the sports newspaper *Deutsches Sport-Echo* was published daily in East Germany. It reported on all Olympic sports and enjoyed great demand, but ceased publication after the 1990 German Reunification. As noted by Eggers, other journals such as the *Fußballwoche, Leichtathletik* or *Handball* were read frequently in the GDR.

At the time of the last press statistical survey (2011), researchers counted 1,509 daily newspapers (Reitze, 2011). Reitze also noted that the number of copies sold was reported to be 19.1 million. This number also contained the various local editions of single newspapers. These mainly differed regarding regional, local and subregional information. In 2011, as detailed by Reitze, there were a total of 369 newspaper titles. However, this lower number of titles can be explained when considering the so called Publizistische Einheiten. A Publizistische Einheit includes all titles (including editions) for which a complete editorial team is responsible. A complete editorial team creates the basic parts of the newspapers, mainly the (transregional) political, economic and sport sections. There were, according to Reitze, 133 Publizistische Einheite in Germany in 2011. Therefore, what on first view looks like a lot of variety with more than 1,500 newspaper editions, is attributable to a much smaller number of editorial teams. Thus, the proportion of editions, titles, and Publizistischen Einheiten is an indication for the concentration on the German print media market, which has been decreasing for considerable time as of this writing. The number of newspaper editions declined by ten percent from 1990 to 2011. However, there was a 16 percent decline in Publizistischen Einheiten during the same time period (Reitze, 2011). Not only has the number of local editions gone down, but more editions are compiled by fewer complete editorial teams. As a result, the variety of coverage within the German newspaper market diminished. A much more sweeping decrease can be detected in the total editions of the daily press, which declined by 30 percent since 1990.

In fact, 2012 saw the highest concentration in the German newspaper market, measured against the shares of publishers on the total number of editions sold (Röper, 2012). Röper noted that 58 percent "of all newspaper copies – came from the ten leading publisher groups. This is the highest number since this row of analysis started in the 1970s." Röper added that over 44 percent of all of Germany's daily newspaper circulations were printed by the "five companies with the widest circulation" (Röper, 2012, p. 272). The decline in circulations and the drop in the advertising market in 2000 led to the breakaway of the main financial framework for the funding of newspaper journalism (Röper, 2012), followed by a reduction in staff. In 2011, as noted by Röper, 12,966 journalists worked in the editorial teams of German weekly and daily newspapers – a decline of 20 percent since 2000. In addition, the situation brought losses in quality, mainly in the local coverage. "Some local sections are similar to a patchwork these days," stated Röper. "Sometimes only the smaller part of an edition is produced autonomously. The bigger part consists of copies of other material" (Röper, 2012, p. 270). In contrast is the pattern within the consumer publications sector. Since 1990, there has been an increase in the number of titles as well as the number of sold editions. In 1990, 565 different titles were on the market, while in 2011, 897 titles were published, an increase of 59 percent. However, the sold editions only increased by 3.1 percent. While there were more magazine consumers, there were fewer readers per title. The most title variety can be found within the journal sector. There were 1,154 journal titles, which are bought by 12 million readers. In this sector, the number of titles rose by 28 percent since 1990, but the number of readers went down by a quarter (Röper, 2012).

It is noteworthy that the German print media market lacks a purely sport-related newspaper, despite the fact that in France, Spain, and Italy, *L'Equipe*, *Marca*, and *La Gazzetta dello Sport*, respectively, are often the most-read publications (Zubayr and Gerhard, 2004). Germany-based individuals aged fourteen and older were asked what topics they most preferred, and more than a quarter of the respondents replied they were "very interested" in sport while over 21 percent expressed "some interest" (Mende, Oehmichen, and Schröter, 2012, p. 10). Thus, a combined 47.1 percent have at least "some interest" and is a potential audience for sports content in the media. Sport occupied the sixth position in the ranking of topics of interest. Asked which topics they sought information on through the media, 66.8 percent of the people who had at least "some interest" in sport reported they had gained information on sport (Mende, *et al.*, 2012, p. 11). Two-thirds of the sample received information through television. One-third caught up on sport in the daily press, and 25.6 percent listened to radio broadcasts. Online media were used by 17.6 percent of respondents. These findings seem to align with the specific features of sport coverage in the daily press. While, in particular, the transregional sections of the newspapers are dominated by national and international mega events, most local daily newspapers also inform about local sport happenings, in which readers take a great interest. As noted by Schwier and

Schauerte (2007, p. 204), nearly 40 percent of respondents "stated that they preferably read reports about local and regional performance tiers in the daily newspaper". The sports desks of the daily newspapers are faced with a twofold challenge: they must gain young readers, and become more attractive for advertisers (Kamp, 2012). The daily newspaper meets this challenge by providing an additional option to television.

With the decline in circulations and advertising revenues, working conditions on the sports desk have changed. Permanent positions became very rare (Kamp, 2009). As the demands on sport journalists increased, the working conditions became worse, and the environment more difficult. In addition, there is an orientation toward entertainment in the transitional newspapers. Many publishing companies act according to the principle of online first.

The sport magazines establish the basis of sport coverage. A look at the titles within the consumer publications and also the professional journal sections revealed that there is a difficult-to-assess variety of titles within the sport area (Schwier and Schauerte, 2007). A ten-year analysis of the sport magazine market showed that this type of magazine lost circulation in Germany, declining by six percent between 1998 and 2008. At the same time, the total number of titles registered with the Informationsgemeinschaft zur Feststellung der Verbreitung von Werbeträgern (IVW) increased by 17 percent (Kleinjohann 2009). In early 2012, 70 sport magazines, devoted to 21 different sports, were listed by the Audit Bureau of Circulations (IVW, 2012). The variety of titles spread among 56 publishing companies. For 15 of the 21 sports, there were at least two publishing companies which published the two relevant titles (with the exception of triathlon and shooting sports). Over the years, the *Kicker* and the *Sport Bild* have established themselves as the two leading sport magazines, both dedicating coverage to sport in general although their main emphasis is on football. According to Reitze (2011), ten percent of all print media readers also read sport magazines and sport publications were mostly read by men (6.71 million readers, compared with 0.44 million women).

Print sport media in China

Print sport media have seen a long history since the People's Republic of China was founded in 1949. Their development and evolution, affected by various factors, can be divided into four phases of modern Chinese history. For each period of time, print sports media have played a different role in sport communication in China.

The first phase, which lasted from 1949 to 1978, marked the emergence of sport media with the founding of new China. The mainstream print sport media at the time were characterized by one sports newspaper and one sports magazine. In 1950, *New Sports*, the earliest nationwide sports magazine in China, was founded. Eight years later, the first sports newspaper in China, *Sports Daily*, published its inaugural issue. Both belonged to the State General Administration of Sports. During this period, print sport media in China were a part of government media rather than independent business entities. Almost all of the sports coverage was expected to stay aligned with the work and policies of the new government and Communist Party of China. In effect, they acted as spokespersons or mouthpieces, helping create a favorable image of the nation, the Party and government. When Rong Guotuan won China's first world table tennis championship in August 1959, *New Sports* featured his success in a lead article. The article stated, "Rong Guotuan achieved success not by accident, but because of the education and cultivation of the party by which his political consciousness was enhanced so that he had enough confidence to bring his skills into full play" (Hua, 1959, p. 4).

Shortly after Wu Chuanyu won China's first 100-meter swimming championship, Huang (1953) stated that "Chuanyu's terrific skills and remarkable achievements prove to the world that Chinese people have said farewell to what used to be described by the Western world as the sick man of East Asia." Huang added that "the wisdom, talent, and healthy bodies of Chinese people are not inferior to any other nation" (Huang, 1953, pp. 24–5).

The second phase occurred from 1978 to 1994, when print sport media featured an increasing number of sports newspapers and magazines. *Soccer* and *Titan Weekly*, the two most influential and authoritative sports newspapers as of 2012, began publication in 1980 and 1988, respectively. Another very important sports newspaper was *Ball News*, established in 1988 by Liaoning Daily Group, a newspaper group in the northeast region of China. Based on China's first sports newspaper, *China Sports Daily* was formally launched in 1988. In addition, such sports magazines as *Soccer World*, *China Volleyball*, *Track and Field*, *Table Tennis World*, and *China Martial Arts* also came into being in the early 1980s. By the end of the decade, there were approximately 80 print sports publications in China.

The rapid expansion of print sport media was largely due to the economic development in China as well as the outstanding performance of Chinese athletes in the world sporting arena. Thanks to the economic reform that began in 1978, the economy in China developed rapidly and sparked the tremendous growth of sports nationwide. When the Chinese national women's volleyball team won five consecutive world championships in the 1980s, that success ignited a surge in the popularity of women's volleyball throughout China, and the victorious women became a source of great pride and honor for Chinese people. In addition, at the Summer Olympic Games in 1984, Chinese athletes made an historic breakthrough with 15 gold medals, which stimulated China's enthusiasm for sports.

The third phase is from 1994 to 2000, the golden age of print sport media in China. In 1994, a commercialized professional soccer league, the Chinese National Football Jia A League, made its debut. Sports in China developed rapidly following the inception of professional soccer. Soccer became the most popular game in China and more and more individuals, especially young people, showed great interest in consuming soccer news. Accordingly, almost all of the sport newspapers highlighted soccer games both at home and abroad, reporting results from the main professional leagues in England, Italy, and Spain. To respond to the popularity of professional soccer, two other noteworthy sports newspapers were established: *China Soccer Post* in 1994 and *Southern Sports* in 2000. During this period, the circulation of most sport newspapers hit a record high, with *Soccer* and *Titan Weekly* reaching a circulation of two million per issue.

The fourth or the last phase of print sport media in China began in 2001. It is a stage of reshuffling for print sport media in China, marked by the cease in publication of several renowned sport newspapers. In September 2002, *21 Century Sport Weekly* closed after only six months. In 2005, *Ball News* and *Southern Sports* each published their last issue. *China Soccer Post*, which had chronicled the Chinese soccer league for 15 years, closed its doors in 2009.

Two factors led to the collapse of print sport media in China. First, the rise of new media, especially the Internet, was attracting more and more young people away from the traditional mass media. It sounds reasonable when some experts say that new media helped bring down print sport media, since they have the advantages in timeliness, distribution, and availability which traditional media lack. Second, the fall in soccer's competitive level and the deterioration of the market for the soccer league, now called the Chinese Super League, are also contributing factors. Soccer corruption became a very serious problem, and many soccer officials and players have been prosecuted for match fixing, gambling, and bribery. The former glamour and prosperity of soccer has vanished, and Chinese sports fans have become less interested in the games. As a result, with the exception of a few large sport media outlets such as *Soccer* and *Titan Weekly*, most print sport media revolving around soccer coverage are doomed to fail. To survive the media market, many print sport media outlets, including *Titan Weekly*, are making some reforms and trying to balance different sports topics, with the National Basketball Association taking a prominent position in many print sport media outlets.

As for the future of print sport media in China, the founding of sport media groups is becoming a trend. *Titan Weekly* has already developed into a large sport media group consisting of sports newspapers, sports magazines, sports websites, and even sport radio and TV programs, with *China Sport Daily* following a similar model. For the time being, and even in the future, the print sport media market will be under the control of the two media groups, as well as *Soccer*. Local print sport media, such as *Oriental Sports Daily* in Shanghai and *Yangtze Sports Daily* in Jiangsu, must fight for survival.

Print sport media in the US

A recent report by the Organization for Economic Cooperation and Development indicated that stateside newspaper circulation numbers had fallen by 30 percent between 2007 and 2009. This represented the largest such drop in the world, ahead of the United Kingdom (25 percent), Greece (20 percent), Italy (18 percent), and Canada (17 percent) (Robinson, 2009). The concurrent decline in print advertising, combined with the ability for consumers to gain access to news on portable devices (such as SmartPhones, iPads, Kindles), led to speculation that US-based newspapers may potentially consider a move to an online-only model (Palser, 2009). While that has not occurred as of yet, placing content online did not lose print media its overall audience. A 2011 study indicated that two-thirds of US Internet users over the age of 18 were visiting newspaper websites. In addition, more people sought news through their mobile devices (Sadowski, 2011). However, despite the retention of much of its audience online, US print media revenues suffered. The *State of the News Media Report 2012* noted that, for most of 2011, US print advertising losses outpaced online advertising increases by an eight-to-one margin (Pew Research Center 2012). Newspapers attempted to reclaim lost revenues through measures such as online pay walls and the Associated Press' agreements with news companies to collect royalties from news aggregators (Mitchell and Rosenstiel, 2012). As US newspapers lost advertising, online companies gained revenue. In 2011, Internet juggernaut Google brought in US$37.9 billion in revenue, US$4 billion more than the entire newspaper industry combined (Edmonds, 2012).

In an effort to maintain profits as advertising declined, US newspapers cut staff at high rates. For example, in June of 2012, announcements of a total of 600 layoffs at newspapers including the *New Orleans Times-Picayune* and the *Birmingham (Alabama) News* prompted a writer at the Poynter Institute for Media Studies to note that the high number of job losses was not a record mark. In February of that year, media ownership giant Gannett offered buyouts for 665 employees, less than a year after it had laid off more than 700 newspaper employees and four years after more than 2,100 Gannett employees lost their jobs. Newspaper publisher McClatchy laid off 1,600 employees in 2009, while Time Inc. cut more than 1,000 workers in a recent two-year span (Sonderman, 2012). In 2012, the *Times-Picayune* lost nearly half of its newsroom staff, and the *Birmingham News* went from 102 newsroom employees to 41. In addition to the *Times-Picayune's* layoffs, the newspaper also sought to cut costs by cutting publication to only three days a week (Robertson, 2012). The image of the print newspaper as a dying medium in the US begat the site *NewspaperDeathWatch.com*, which compiles news regarding print media (for example, ownership, layoffs, financial solvency). The front page of the site also features a list of shuttered newspapers under the heading "R.I.P. US metropolitan dailies that have closed since this site was created in March, 2007" (Gillin, 2012). As noted on the website, these include defunct print outlets in major cities such as Denver's *Rocky Mountain News*, the *Honolulu Advertiser*, and the *Cincinnati Post*.

The drop in revenue for print properties stateside has been described as "precipitous and permanent" (Palser, 2009, p. 44). Yet, rather than noting a lack of adjustment to a changing media world by either themselves or the outlets they worked for, some journalists place the responsibility for print media's ongoing demise on the financial world (for example, "Wall Street") (Usher, 2010). Few definitive answers exist regarding the future of print sports media in the US. Continued declines in staffing levels and the resulting increased workload on the remaining staffers, technology, declines in revenue, and possible changes in news focus are all factors that contribute to the continued shifts in print sports media (Reinardy, 2010). Further, the Internet's ongoing effect on newspaper journalism cannot be predicted (Benson, Blach-Orsten, Powers, Willig, and Zambrano, 2012).

Conclusion

Four separate perspectives from four very different regions have provided an idea of the state of print sport media. While factors including the rise of new media and losses in advertising have had an effect on the state of sports media in the US, China has seen the decline of its most popular sport – soccer – help to lead to a decline in sport media. In Israel, previous generations' need to protect their position has been challenged, while Germany's losses in revenue and circulations mirror the struggles of print media outlets in the US. As scholars and educators attempt to determine the best course (or courses) of action regarding the preservation and survival of print sports media, it is clear that no universal solution exists, as the challenges and obstacles differ from region to region.

References

Benson, R., Blach-Orsten, M., Powers, M., Willig, I., and Zambrano, S. (2012). Media systems online and off: Comparing the form of news in the United States, Denmark, and France. *Journal of Communication*, 62 (1), 21–38.

Caspi, D. (1993). *Mass media* (Vol. A: Sections 1–4). Tel Aviv: The Open University.

Edmonds, R. (2012). 6 trends for newspapers in 2012, from Sunday boom to an executive bust. *Poynter*. St Petersburg, FL: Poynter Institute, March 19. Retrieved from http://www.poynter.org/latest-news/business-news/the-biz-blog/166575/6-trends-for-newspapers-in-2012/.

Eggers, E. (2009). Geschichte des Sportjournalismus. In T. Horky, T. Schauerte, J. Schwier, and DFJV (Hrsg.) (Eds.), *Sportjournalismus* (pp. 15–26). Konstanz: UVK.

Friedman, J. (2010). ESPN-SI: National magazine showdown. *Market Watch*, March 17. Retrieved from http://articles.marketwatch.com/2010-03-17/commentary/30760981_1_si-sports-illustrated-national-magazine.

Gillin, P. (2012). R.I.P. US metropolitan dailies that have closed since this site was created in March, 2007. *Newspaper Death Watch*, col. 1. Retrieved from http://newspaperdeathwatch.com/.

Hua, X.W. (1959). World champion Rong Guotuan. *New Sports*, 149 (8), 4–6.

Huang, Z. (1953). Chinese athletes in Bucharest. *New Sports*, 35 (10), 24–5.
IVW. (2012). *Publikumszeitschriften mit nationaler Verbreitung: Sportzeitschriften*. Informationsgemeinschaft zur Feststellung der Verbreitung von Werbeträgern. Retrieved from http://daten.ivw.eu/index.php?menuid=1141andu=andp=andb=alleandsv=214andsb=214andt=Publikumszeitschriften+mit+nationaler+Verbreitungandtsub=SPORTZEITSCHRIFTEN.
Kamp, H.-C. (2009). Sport in Tageszeitungen. In T. Horky, T. Schauerte, J. Schwier, and DFJV (Hrsg.) (Eds.), *Sportjournalismus* (pp. 125–54). Konstanz: UVK.
Kleinjohann, M. (2009). Sportzeitschriften. In T. Horky, T. Schauerte, J. Schwier, and DFJV (Hrsg.) (Eds.), *Sportjournalismus* (pp. 155–70). Konstanz: UVK.
Mende, A., Oehmichen, E., and Schröter, C. (2012). Medienübergreifende Informationsnutzung und Informationsrepertoires: Fernsehen, Radio, Zeitung und Internet im Vergleich. Media Perspektiven, 1, 2–17.
Mitchell, A., and Rosenstiel, T. (2012). Overview. In Pew Research Center. *The state of the news media 2012: An annual report on American journalism*. Project for Excellence in Journalism. Retrieved from http://stateofthemedia.org/2012/overview–4/.
Palser, B. (2009, June/July). Stopping the press. *American Journalism Review*. Retrieved from http://www.ajr.org/article.asp?id=4766.
Pew Research Center (2012) *The state of the news media 2012: An annual report on American journalism*. Project for Excellence in Journalism. Washington DC: Pew Research Center. Retrieved from http://stateofthemedia.org/2012/overview-4/.
Porat, Y. (1987). Forty years later. *The Journalism Yearbook*, 115.
Reinardy, S. (2010). Need for speed onto Internet clashes with journalistic values. *Newspaper Research Journal*, 31 (1), 69–83.
Reitze, H. (Ed.). (2011). *Media Perspektiven Basisdaten 2011: Daten zur Mediensituation in Deutschland*. Frankfurt: Media Perspektiven.
Robertson, C. (2012, June 12). New Orleans struggles with latest storm, newspaper layoffs. *New York Times*. Retrieved from http://www.nytimes.com/2012/06/13/us/new-orleans-struggles-with-latest-storm-newspaper-layoffs.html?_r=1andpagewanted=all.
Robinson, J. (2009). UK and US see heaviest newspaper circulation declines. *The Guardian*, June 17. Retrieved from http://www.guardian.co.uk/media/2010/jun/17/newspaper-circulation-oecd-report.
Röper, H. (2012). Zeitungsmarkt 2012. In *Media Perspektiven*, 5, 268–85.
Rosenblatt, Y. (1987). The barks are not serious. *The Journalism Yearbook*, 116–19.
Sadowski, C. (2011). Newspaper websites post consecutive quarterly traffic increase. Newspaper Association of America, July 12. Retrieved from http://www.naa.org/News-and-Media/Press-Center/Archives/2011/Newspaper-Websites-Post-Consecutive-Quarterly-Traffic-Increase.aspx#.UG1c4I5XvGs.
Schwier, J., and Schauerte, T. (2007). Nutzung von Sportangeboten in den Medien. In T. Schierl (Ed.), *Handbuch Medien, Kommunikation und Sport* (pp. 200–11). Schorndorf: Hofmann.
Sepinwall, A. (2012). Review: USA's 'Political Animals' takes compelling look at an alternate Clinton family. HitFix, July 11. Retrieved from http://www.hitfix.com/whats-alan-watching/review-usas-political-animals-takes-compelling-look-at-an-alternate-clinton-family.
Sonderman, J. (2012). 600 newspaper layoffs in one day is, unfortunately, not a record. *Poynter*, June 13, updated June 14. Retrieved from http://www.poynter.org/latest-news/mediawire/177145/600-newspaper-layoffs-in-one-day-is-unfortunately-not-a-record/.
Tamir, I., and Galily, Y. (2011). The human factor in the historic development of means of communication. *International Journal of the History of Sport*, 28 (18), 2688–706.
Usher, N. (2010). Goodbye to the news: how out-of-work journalists assess enduring news values and the new media landscape. *New Media and Society*, 12 (6), 911–28.
Winseck, D. (2010). Financialization and the "Crisis of the media": The rise and fall of (some) media conglomerates in Canada. *Canadian Journal of Communication*, 35 (3), 365–93.
Zubayr, C., and Gerhard, H. (2004). Zur Nachfrage nach Sportangeboten in den Medien. In H. Schramm (Ed.), *Die Rezeption des Sports in den Medien* (pp. 28–48). Köln: Halem.

12

SPORTS REPORTING AND JOURNALISTIC PRINCIPLES

Thomas Horky and Barbara Stelzner

Journalists are modern story-tellers. They convey true stories in an engaging and relevant manner. Journalism differs from fiction because not only does it deal with real events that are being (meant to be) reported in an accurate manner, but also because it is expected to follow binding rules and guidelines. However, topics covered by sports journalism have distinct characteristics that often differ from the topics covered by other journalistic beats. This chapter considers how the often emotional and affective themes covered in sports journalism have led to a problematic relationship with journalistic norms and principles. The analysis builds on a previous article published by Hans-Jörg Stiehler and one of the authors (Stiehler and Horky, 2009).

Norms and principles of journalism

Journalism as practiced in modern Western societies fulfills dual roles. Print and broadcast media are seen as social institutions, which are expected to serve the common good and are bound by the principles of educating the public, and moral values such as truthfulness, lawfulness, and freedom of speech. However, media are also businesses which are driven by economic interests, such as reach, competition, deadlines and revenues. This "inherent schizophrenia" (Weischenberg, 1998, p. 171) leads to contradictions between what the media are supposed to deliver from a commercial point of view and what is expected of them in terms of their role as the "Fourth Estate". In order to protect the latter, many countries have introduced guidelines for journalists. In Germany, the Press Council has established a press codex (Deutscher Presserat, 2006) which safeguards the key principle of press freedom and reminds journalists of their basic duties to society.

These principles are, in many cases, based on self-regulation and have set the norms for journalistic work. In Germany, they are being monitored by the Press Council. Any infringements can lead to an official warning. Other countries operate in a similar fashion (for example, in the US, one could refer to the *Principles of Journalism* (Project for Excellence in Journalism, 2012). These norms are based on four key recommendations (Weischenberg, 1998, p. 196). First, reporting has to be truthful and independent from commercial or other interests. Second, information gathering has to be based on fairness and honesty. Third, journalists have to protect the rights of any individuals about whom they are reporting. Fourth, special caution should be exercised in the case of serious crimes. Guidelines for specialist journalistic beats are the exception rather than the rule (for example, in Germany, reporting on medical issues is being covered by a number of policies). The above mentioned characteristics of sports journalism suggest that norms are handled differently in this area. This assumption will be stress-tested in due course with the help of an evaluation of the particularities of sports as well as sports reporting.

Storytelling in sports journalism

Sport, as portrayed and stage-managed by the media, is not about physical exercise. We might as well call this phenomenon "media sports". This stands for the correlation between sports and media which has developed over the past few decades. It is the result of global practices which can be summarized with the term mediatization that is, the penetration of social structures by the technological, economic, and institutional aspects in which media are engaged. They are not limited to sports reporting but manifest themselves more distinctly in this area. The media exercise a type of selective adaptation. They focus in particular on high-performance and the most popular sports (that is, the media reality of sports). On the other side of the equation, sports adapt to what media can exploit most effectively and engagingly to serve consumers' wants and needs.

The phenomenon of media sports goes back to developments such as the establishment of professional baseball leagues in the US (1876), soccer leagues in England (1888), the revival of the Olympic Games in 1896, and the launch of the Tour de France by the French sports magazine *L'AUTO* in 1903. Even earlier examples include boxing and horse racing: the rulebook for boxing was first published in 1743 (London Prize Rules) and adapted in 1876 (Queensberry Rules). Professional horse racing saw the inception of the Jockey Club in 1750 and the inaugural Epsom Derby in 1780. These dates coincided with the growing popularity of sports betting and an increased focus on audiences. Over the course of time, the media caught up with developments: initially in print, later on radio, newsreels in cinema, television, the Internet and other communication channels.

Sport events are not only reported or commented on, but have their own narrative, with its own language, syntax and semantics. This narrative and theatrical gestus is key to the public's and the media's fascination with sport. Sport offers all the ingredients of an Aristotelian drama: protagonists with defined roles, unity of place, time and action, concepts like winning and losing, fortune and misfortune, breaking the rules vs. fair play, friendship and animosity, and certainty and uncertainty. Sport portrays modern myths that have been updated from the past. They manifest themselves in intrinsic sporting myths such as the "friendly meeting" or "sportsmanship" of the British tradition (Eisenberg, 1995, p. 89), or the ideal of peaceful rivalry during the Olympic Games. They also manifest themselves in, originally non-sports related, motives such as David and Goliath and Cain and Abel. Sports events are modeled on stories about individuals' fates. They resemble the typical plots of soap operas and offer a projection screen for any type of emotion. They satisfy the need to belong to one place in the era of globalization, or the craving for comfort in a world of soulless bureaucracy and technology. Thus, sport is an easy conversation topic, whether in sport clubs, at the water cooler or in the pub. This, in turn, is reflected in today's sports coverage, with its huge number of experts commenting before, during and after an event. Last but not least, the media love sport because it offers an intriguing opportunity to exploit different types of revenue streams: Advertising and sponsoring around an event, advertising channels inside arenas and stadiums, and competitors who often resemble walking, running, or cycling billboards.

The basic structures of today's mediatized sports environment has developed over the past 50 years and gathered pace since the 1980s. Media and sports have adapted to each other in order to maximize their entertainment potential. They zoom in on conflict, suspense, charisma, strategy, rules, measurable results (such as victory, draw, loss, record), and the increasingly complex nature of (serial) competitions (for example, tournament, leagues). In terms of the tools used, media sports are a type of informative journalism. However, as is noted in the chapter below, media sports occasionally follow their own rules which differ from those of traditional informative journalism.

The growing relationship between sport and media over the past few decades can be summarized as a movement from when sports were covered by the media to today where the two are inextricably linked as *media sport* (Foltin and Hallenberger, 1994). This phrase describes two trends. First, it describes changes in the structure of competitions in terms of rules, sport types, locations, and the like. They now adapt to the requirements of media, especially TV. For example, there are more and more sports added to key events (such as the Olympic Games) and competitions have been expanded (for example, the Football World Cup) in order to produce a constant stream of coverage at the highest level (which has led to the virtual downgrading of national championships to qualification rounds for international events). The second trend is the medial presentation of sports, which has contributed to the development of television entertainment. Both of the above trends are mutually dependent and should, arguably, be analyzed in the context of infotainment. This has been proven empirically (Früh and Wirth, 1997). From the sender's point of view, "infotainment" is an amalgamation of informative and entertaining content and styles. It can be seen as a strategy to increase awareness and make reception more palatable, a strategy that can also be applied to sports coverage (Horky, 2001; Kinkema and Harris, 1998; Stiehler, 1997).

Infotainment follows basic principles, such as dynamization, emotionalization, narrativization, and the allocation of relevance. It goes without saying that a number of developments in sport (for example, moving them into city centers, making competitions more transparent) help to increase their attractiveness but are not necessarily part of the infotainment concept. In the following infotainment categorization, changes in sports competitions are separated from changes in TV sports coverage even though there are obvious connections between the two.

As noted above, one of the primary principles of infotainment is dynamization. This involves speed, the unexpected, and the unusual (seen from a content and format point of view). Examples of changes in sports competitions based on dynamization include short or mini competitions (for example, skiing, biathlon, skating), animations in stadiums, and musical and show displays before and during a competition. Examples of changes in TV sports coverage as a result of dynamization include sequence of pictures, camera angles, running cameras, flying eyes, and the like. Also included in this are displays of graphics with additional information (such as time, speed, distance, virtual yellow jersey).

Another infotainment principle is emotionalization, which involves stimulus, verbalization, and visualization of emotions. Examples of changes in sports competitions based on this principle includes framing with rituals (for example, during the opening, closing, and medal ceremonies), building suspense at the end of the competition (such as golden goal, sudden death, tiebreak) or with the structure of contests (for example, increasing number of final stages), systematizing the organization of records (for example, pacemakers in long-distance running), animating the audience (for example, "applaud now"), using functional but body-enhancing (that is, sexy) outfits, and choreographing celebrations. Examples of changes in TV sports coverage as a result of emotionalization include such activities as using emotional language, engaging in hero worship and demolition, and providing close-ups (that is, faces as mirrors of emotions).

Narrativization is yet another aspect of infotainment. This involves the embedding of sports reporting into storytelling. Examples of this in relation to changes in sports competition are providing narrative logic of individual sports (for example, who wins and how), labeling of contents based on the modus of movie titles (for example, "The Rumble in the Jungle"), and engaging in commentary on location. There are also changes in TV sports coverage-related narrativization. For instance, this involves the daily follow-ups about international, national, and regional heroes on sport channels or news programs with fixed sports slots (such as German Bundesliga, Formula 1). It also includes all-sports talk shows, a focus on stars and celebrities, extensive pre-and post-match reports, and dedicated cameras which zoom in on individual competitors, managers, and other important people.

The fourth involves the allocation of relevance. This is concerned with upsizing (hyping) the importance of competition. Examples of changes in sports competitions based on this infotainment principle are the introduction of rival contests and the classification of competitions into hierarchies (for example, the World Cup, Champions League). There are also numerous examples of this principle involved with changes in TV sports coverage. One example of this would be how, on the international level, there is a focus on high-performance sports, and on the national level, sports are covered according to their popularity in individual countries (for example, rugby and horseracing in England; Gaelic sports in Ireland; football, basketball, golf, and ice hockey in the US; cricket and hockey in India). Other examples include the transformation of competitions into events with show character and the turning of title bouts/races into duels.

These developments have gone hand in hand with the introduction of video screens at sports events which add to the unique live atmosphere by providing extra layers of information which the audience can otherwise only get on television. This applies in particular to sports which cannot be followed in their entirety on location (for example, cycling, marathons, golf, sailing, car rallies). It also applies to key decisions during a competition (for example, did the ball cross the line?) which can only be judged properly with the help of technology such as replays or slow motion images.

Specific characteristics of sports journalism

Key principles and guidelines of journalism in general have been mentioned above. Sports journalism follows similar rules. However, it also differs from other journalistic beats. Sport is a subsystem of society which can be described as a combination of play and culture in the context of their original roles as entertainment and recreation. One has to bear in mind that sports (as portrayed by the media) is play that is staged – professionally, scientifically and commercially – for and in front of the public. The correlation between sports and economic, political, technological, and social processes can transform play into a very serious business for audiences and media alike. Sports journalism takes place in a world it has created itself through staging drama, highlights, crises, successes, and failures. The self-dramatization of sports and its dramatization through media go hand in hand with each other and form an inseparable unit. Modern sports journalism should reflect on that and, where necessary, include it in its coverage.

Based on those special circumstances, we can use three ways to describe characteristics and trends in modern sports journalism. The first way is from the "greatest pastime in the world" into the heart of society. Because of its entwinement with other parts of society and the public's interest, sport is not only play. It is an economic factor – a stage for local, regional, and national grandstanding and a platform for political influence. As a consequence, sport moves into the limelight of the public's and media's attention, particularly in the case of large tournaments. Olympic Games, World and European Championships in popular sports have the power to change the news agenda, dominate program schedules and justify the production of special supplements in magazines and newspapers. This illustrates the role that large sports events play not only in the public discourse but on all levels of society. The result is curiously ambivalent, because there is not only a growing danger of the political and commercial instrumentalization of sports, but also of a growing awareness for this phenomenon. Both lead to more coverage in terms of volume and the range of topics chosen.

The second way is from reporting to other narrative formats. The beginning of sports journalism was dominated by news and straight-forward news reports. Since then, the variety of different narrative formats has grown. In television, this can be explained with simple economics: TV rights for soccer, the Olympic Games, and large tournaments plus huge production costs are more easily digested when video material is spread over larger parts of the schedule and recycled. Ironically, fringe programming, which can take up more than twice the time of an actual competition, is often forced upon broadcasters because of a lack of picture rights. Print and rightless broadcasters can only compete with the Internet and rights holders if they offer additional analysis, valuable background information and rich context.

The third way is from sports events to thematic variety. Sports journalism focuses on sports events. But what is an event? It is definitely more than the contest itself. It is worth mentioning three aspects that do not only enable but also force medial thematization. The first aspect is that there is a clear correlation between sport and other parts of society. Some economic and political aspects of sports might stay in the background; others such as political intervention (see the Olympic Summer Games in 1980 and 1984; the European Football Championships 2012), or doping can become relevant. The second aspect is that many sporting achievements are the result of professional teamwork. This increases the number of people media can choose as interview partners, commentators, or sources for backgrounders. The third aspect is that many sports protagonists have personality traits and whims which are often the basis for turning them into high achievers (or failures). Sport gives birth to stars that fit into the glamorous media system of producing celebrities. Hero worship, soft news about stars' private lives, and gossip are part and parcel of contributing to the public's trust (or mistrust) in public figures. Tabloid journalism is a prerequisite for the successful reception of sports which is driven by edge of the seat rooting for one's heroes and built on a quasi parasocial connection.

Problems between sports and sports journalism

As mentioned at the beginning of this chapter, journalism is based on norms that are enshrined in guidelines on journalistic quality. However, sports reporters are coming more and more under scrutiny: sport as portrayed by the media is turning increasingly into a circus, some sports journalists have turned from critical eyewitnesses into entertainment vendors, often lack distance and behave more like fans than neutral observers. Sports journalism, like any other journalism, bears specific risks which lead to questions about quality (Bucher and Altmeppen, 2003). The discrepancy between journalistic norms and their being observed by sports journalists can be illustrated by the examples of doping, involvement, and constraints.

Regarding doping, the death of the German heptathlete, Birgit Dressel, in 1987 made the front page of Germany's largest news magazine, *Der Spiegel* (Horky, 2012). It was the first large-scale lead story on doping. In due course, other athletes (such as Ben Johnson, Marion Jones, Jan Ullrich, Claudia Pechstein) were also exposed and became subject of a plethora of suspicions that sports journalists have never managed to catch up with. The use of performance-enhancing drugs was nothing new in 1987. It has long been one of the core challenges of modern sports. Why do so few sports journalists cover this issue? Why do newsrooms shy away from in-depth research on the topic? Sure: almost all media pay attention when a well-known athlete is found guilty of doping. As a matter of fact, media coverage is one of the reasons why sport faces up to drug use. But the context is often only scrutinized from the perspective of the athlete in question or the duped audience. A structural analysis of the problem is missing. In fact, doping is one of the biggest challenges of sports journalism because it throws up uncomfortable questions. Do journalists (or their employers) want to report on a topic that turns off viewers, listeners and readers? It is proven that doping impacts on ratings and circulation. Yes, bad news can attract interest; unless, it seems, when it has to do with doping. The only solution to this conundrum is a new way of thinking and a turning away from the relentless prioritization of speed, exclusivity and emotions.

In terms of involvement, there are aspects related to closeness and distance. For example, the motto of a German sports niche channel is "We are not just bystanders...we are in the thick of it." This motto is often interpreted as a criticism of sports journalism. This is not fair as sports journalists are actually directly affected by what happens on their beat. Journalists from other walks of life know this phenomenon equally well; Leyendecker (2006, p. 228) has described it as a "sticky affinity". Sporting defeat can lead to financial consequences: sports that do not perform get neglected, teams which get relegated receive less attention, advertising revenues shrink, travel budgets get cut, and it is not only the sport or the team whose importance diminishes but also the reporter who covers the beat. For example, the failure of a (German) team to qualify for a World or European Championship can lead to fewer journalists receiving accreditation. Failure also leads to less audience interest, which results in financial losses for media outlets. Thus, qualification is not only an exciting and occasionally dramatic topic for story-telling but also a competition for leads, column inches and future work assignments.

Another example of the discrepancy between journalistic norms and their being observed by sports journalists relates to economic and emotional constraints. Other economic circumstances that influence aspects of sports reporting include a channel losing TV rights to an event, as commentators often end up being surplus to requirements. In Germany, there has been a medial migration of sports journalists that follow TV rights from one channel to the next. The more popular ones easily find lucrative alternatives, the less well-known commentators often end up on obscure niche channels or on the dole. It is true that emotional and economic involvement also exists in other journalistic branches (such as politics, business). However, these examples of private and professional entanglement seem to be much less emotional and problematic than sports journalists who act like fans. When a party a journalist is a member of loses an election, he/she can still report on the party in opposition or the new party in power. This cannot be compared with a journalist's core team being relegated and generating much less interest. It often leads to the journalist being forced to find a different specialist topic. Also, being a fan becomes even more complex when dealing with national events. Which journalists dare to argue against their own national team or condemn the tactical foul (fair foul) which will secure victory for the home side? Big events are followed by millions who root for their team. This hampers journalists' ability to take a critical position. Sports reporting has been struggling with this for some time without coming up with a convincing solution.

Journalistic norms undermined in sports reporting

The cited examples show the areas which can threaten journalistic norms and principles in sports journalism. These specific dangers lead to the question of quality and honest attitude of sports journalists. As noted by Horky, Schauerte, and Schwier (2009), in terms of the journalistic norm involving variety of sources and different points of view, the dangers in sports journalism relate to monopoly rights (such as TV, radio) which undermine variety. Regarding the journalistic norm of relevance, Horky and colleagues point out that the dangers in sports journalism consist of limited focus on national heroes, top sports, and media sports (for example, excess, stylization, staging). They point out that the journalistic norm of professionalism (for example, fairness, neutrality, correctness, analysis) is being undermined in sports reporting through biases, nationalism, beautifying short reports, clichés, and stereotypes. The norm of rightfulness is being undermined by discrimination in sports reporting. Independence of the business and independence of the individual are being undermined by the influence of commercial partners with the former and embedded journalists with the latter. Horky and colleagues add that the journalistic norm of separation between commercial and editorial content is being threatened by sponsoring, product placement, and permanent advertising. Lastly, they note that the journalistic norm of separation between facts and opinions is being undermined in sports journalism through the blurring of the lines between facts and excessive commentary, emotion, and opinion.

The journalistic norms and related dangers in sports journalism detailed above serve to illustrate the particularities of and dependencies in sports journalism that require a discussion about ethics. The rest of this section covers seven (ethical) threats in sports journalism which will be characterized as "traps" in due course. The first threat involves the patriotism trap. Sports reception is likely to be less interesting and entertaining if it does not contain a minimum amount of playful bias. Neutral observers in the audience are an exception. Recipients therefore tolerate to a certain extent that sports journalists represent the perspective of their own side. That is because sports journalists are also sports recipients and have natural preferences for local, regional and national athletes. This type of bias contradicts neutral and balanced reporting as it interprets the reality from a distinctively subjective point of view. The second threat is the monopoly trap. Top-quality journalism relies on diversity of sources and points of view. However, in media sports, broadcast rights are being sold for enormous sums leading to monopolies in reporting and thematic constraints with regards to the use of the material. The result is media companies co-owning sports events. This does not have to but can be problematic.

The third threat is the thematization trap. High-quality journalism selects, judges, and publishes material according to relevance. The journalistic system filters out what is pertinent and what is not. However, this leads to media outlets adopting identical news agendas and is particularly prevalent in sports journalism: the importance of tangible results lifts the need for information above that for background analysis and journalistic evaluation. The emphasis on ratings encourages "more of the same" (that is, a select view of top or media sports – in Germany, for example, football and national celebrities). The result is a lack of varied (and relevant) reporting on other aspects of sporting life. In addition to this thematization trap, there is the emotional trap. Sport – with its highly affective content and its large degree of personal involvement – provokes an emphasis on emotions. Instead of educating the viewer with neutral analysis, results and events are being presented with a magnifying glass on sentiment (such as in flash interviews) or with a lack of distance. These stereotypes lead to gray areas with regards to the journalistic norm of separating facts from opinion. The result is sports journalism that is full of clichés and manipulated by 'meaningful' images.

The fifth threat is the dependency trap. Quality journalism is based on the principle of impartiality. However, dependencies on publishers, shareholders, or advertisers, as well as government influence can undermine the control function of the Fourth Estate. TV channels and other media outlets are often not only a direct sponsor or license holder and thus co-manager of the events they report on; in some cases they conceive events in order to initiate reporting on them (for example, Tour de France). This can, on the one hand, lead to distinct dependencies on the corporate level (that is, the financing of sports events, teams, or individual broadcast programs). Individual actors, whether reporters or sports personalities, can, on the other hand, become equally dependent through close relationships (Leyendecker, 2006). A lack of distance between the subject and object of reporting can produce an inappropriate glorification of individuals.

The last two threats involve staging and advertising. Thus, the sixth threat is labeled the staging trap. The distinction between self- and third-party dramatization is a core challenge that high-quality journalism has to address. Problems occur when sports journalists become slaves to the requirements of medial staging. Loss of authenticity does not only kick in when the analysis of a sports event fails to adhere to normative journalistic rules (for example, wrestling). Staging that focuses primarily on the media-adequate presentation of sports events is equally dangerous. The seventh threat is titled the advertising trap. Sports journalism is perforated by sponsorship and advertising because commercial partners jump on emotional appeal and media interest. The media's economic need to recoup costs does the rest. This leads to an increasingly complex entanglement of commercial and editorial content. This could result in future sports reporting not being perceived as journalism but being replaced by (biased) public relations or other types of communication.

Guidelines for sports journalism

The above mentioned threats to key journalistic principles and traps that have been identified support the call for ethical guidelines in sports journalism. Recently, the Association of German Sports Journalists took this on board and issued its own guidelines. While the document the association produced is 51 pages overall, the first page provides eight key guidelines. The first ethical requirement that the Verband Deutscher Sportjournalisten [VDS] declared that sports journalists should agree to observing detailed that:

> The professional privilege that is enshrined in Article 5 of the German Constitution, the Declaration of Human Rights, the Council of Europe Convention and in national laws

> governing the press, in broadcasting legislation and national treaties has to be applied by sports journalists in a responsible and morally unimpeachable manner.
>
> *(Verband Deutscher Sportjournalisten, 2010, p. 1)*

The second ethical objective promoted by the organization is that sports reporters "resist any nationalistic, chauvinistic, racial, religious or political defamation or discrimination." The third guideline noted that, "Sports journalists perform a public control function. They cover and evaluate all aspects of their field. They champion a humane, doping- and corruption-free sporting environment." The next ethical requirement put forth by VDS was that "Sports journalists will not allow themselves to be monopolized or exploited. They protect their journalistic impartiality and turn down invitations or gifts that could undermine their independent status." The fifth noted that, "Sports journalists protect the dignity of man and observe principles of safeguarding personality and privacy. They have to consider all consequences of their reporting on individuals' lives." The next ethical requirement proposed by the organization explained that, "Basic journalistic principles include thorough research, accurate citation and the use of unambiguous language. Sports journalists are committed to reporting truthfully and objectively." The seventh ethical objective involved noting that professional sport industry journalists are, "faithful to journalistic quality. They aspire to a high level of education and training in their profession." The last ethical guideline suggested by the association noted that sports reporters should "behave in a fair manner, are transparent in criticism of others and pledge mutual esteem" (Verband Deutscher Sportjournalisten, 2010, p. 1). It is our suggestion that the above eight guidelines put forth by VDS could form the basis for future proposals on ethics in sports journalism.

References

Bucher, H.-J., and Altmeppen, K.-D. (2003). *Qualität im Journalismus. Grundlagen – Dimensionen – Praxismodelle*. Wiesbaden: VS.

Deutscher Presserat. (2006). *Publizistische Grundsätze (Pressekodex)*. Bonn: Richtlinien für die publizistische Arbeit nach den Empfehlungen des Deutschen Presserats.

Eisenberg, C. (1995). *Gesellschaftsgeschichte des bürgerlichen Sports. England und Deutschland vom 18. bis zum frühen 20. Jahrhundert*. Hamburg: Habilitationsschrift am Fachbereich Geschichtswissenschaft der Universität.

Foltin, H. F., and Hallenberger, G. (1994). Vom Sport im Fernsehen zum Fernsehsport. Zur Geschichte und aktuellen Situation der Sportsendungen. In H.-D. Erlinger and H. F. Foltin (Eds.), *Unterhaltung, Werbung und Zielgruppenprogramme* (pp. 113–41). München: Fink.

Früh, W., and Wirth, W. (1997). Positives und negatives Infotainment. Zur Rezeption unterhaltsam aufbereiteter TV-Information. In M. Haller and G. Bentele (Eds.), *Aktuelle Entstehung von Öffentlichkeit. Akteure – Strukturen – Veränderungen* (pp. 367–82). München: UVK Medien.

Horky, T. (2001). *Die Inszenierung des Sports in der Massenkommunikation. Theoretische Grundlagen und Analyse von Medienberichterstattung*. Jesteburg: Xox.

Horky, T. (2012). Den Sportjournalismus an seiner Ehre packen. *Vocer*, May 22. Retrieved from http://www.vocer.org/de/artikel/do/detail/id/192/den-sportjournalismus-an-seiner-ehre-packen.html,%20aufgerufen%20am%2011.06.2012.

Horky, T., Schauerte, T., and Schwier, J. (Eds.). (2009). *Sportjournalismus*. Konstanz: UVK.

Kinkema, K. M., and Harris, J. C. (1998). MediaSport studies: Key research and emerging issues. In L. A. Wenner (Ed.), *MediaSport* (pp. 27–54). London/New York: Routledge.

Leyendecker, H. (2006). Klebrige Nähe. Anmerkungen zur Korruption im modernen Sportjournalismus. In J. Weinreich (Ed.), *Korruption im Sport* (pp. 228–40). Leipzig: Forum.

Project for Excellence in Journalism. (2012). *Principles of Journalism*. Journalism.org. Pew Research Center's Project for Excellence in Journalism. Retrieved from http://www.journalism.org/resources/principles.

Stiehler, H.-J. (1997). Mediensport als Unterhaltung. Allgemeinplätze zu medialen Inszenierungen. *Soziale Wirklichkeit. Jenaer Blätter für Sozialpsychologie und angrenzende Wissenschaften*, 1 (3/4), 279–89.

Stiehler, H.-J., and Horky, T. (2009). Themen für Sportjournalisten. In T. Horky, T. Schauerte, and J. Schwier (Eds.), *Sportjournalismus* (pp. 63–78). Konstanz: UVK.

Verband Deutscher Sportjournalisten. (2010). *Satzung des Verbandes Deutscher Sportjournalisten e.V.* Mannheim: Verband Deutscher Sportjournalisten. Retrieved from http://www.sportjournalist.de/de/Service/.

Weischenberg, S. (1998). *Journalistik-Medienkommunikation: Theorie und Praxis. Band 1: Mediensysteme, Medienethik, Medieninstitutionen* (2nd ed.). Wiesbaden: Westdeutscher Verlag.

13

CHRONICLING SPORT, BRANDING INSTITUTIONS

The television sports documentary from broadcast to cable

Travis Vogan

Many of documentary film's most renowned works take sport as their topic. These productions celebrate sport's beauty, explore its history, and probe its complex and intimate relationship to society. Leni Riefenstahl's *Olympia* (1938) – perhaps the most infamous sports documentary ever made – is a Nazi-funded celebration of the 1936 Berlin summer Olympic Games. Steve James' *Hoop Dreams* (1994) interrogates the common myth that basketball provides a realistic means through which young inner-city African American men can improve their economic circumstances. Leon Gast's Academy Award-winning *When We Were Kings* (1996) uses the 1974 "Rumble in the Jungle" (wherein Muhammad Ali beat the younger and heavily favored George Foreman to regain the heavyweight boxing title) to consider the intersections among sport, race, and politics. Though distinct in form and purpose, each of these now canonical documentaries suggests that sport provides a lens through which to illuminate and comment on society's values, beliefs, and attitudes.

Television sports documentaries explore the same aesthetic, historical, and sociopolitical concerns. However, they are also shaped by institutional, industrial, and economic factors specific to the medium. For instance, documentary is traditionally connoted as more contemplative and sophisticated than other television genres (Curtin, 1995; Watson, 1994). In fact, Federal Communication Commission Chair Newton Minow cited documentary as one of the few genres within the "vast wasteland" (Minow, 1964, p. 65) of TV that realizes the medium's potential to enrich, inspire, and educate. Building upon these attitudes, sport media institutions have consistently used television documentaries to build distinct, respectable, and profitable identities.

ABC Sports, NFL Films, HBO Sports, and ESPN illustrate how sport media outlets use television documentaries to construct, promote, and maintain their brands. While these are far from the only organizations that produce sports documentaries for television, they usefully explain the role documentary has served in establishing powerful images for sport media outlets over time and in the contexts of broadcast and cable TV. Furthermore, these outlets often use each other to create and strengthen their brands, whether by co-producing documentaries, using other companies' works to fill programming schedules, or simply defining themselves in opposition to one another. These organizations' varied practices and the intersections among them suggest that television sports documentaries are as invested in building institutional identities as they are in exploring sport's meaning and history.

During the late 1950s, ABC was America's least popular major television network. Industry insiders mockingly called it the "almost broadcasting company." Sports coverage provided a key instrument through which the network established respectability and increased its number of affiliates. In 1959, ABC competitor NBC discontinued *Gillette Cavalcade of Sports* – a collection of Gillette-sponsored sports programming that included a popular Friday evening boxing program – to make room for content it believed would have broader appeal (Rader, 1984; Sugar, 1978). Gillette brought its sizable sports advertising budget to ABC on the condition that the network attach the razor manufacturer to its Wednesday night boxing package. The eight million dollars that Gillette gave ABC was more than the network had spent on sports programming over the course of its entire history. ABC used Gillette's investment to create ABC Sports, America's first network sports division. Shortly after its development, ABC Sports purchased the rights to telecast NCAA football (1960) and created *Wide World of Sports* (1961).

ABC Sports paired its increased sports programming with a more dramatic aesthetic approach established by producer, Roone Arledge. Arledge believed typical sports telecasts did little to reproduce the thrills of attending a game. He thus innovated an "up close and personal" method that both brought viewers closer to sporting events and emphasized their drama. Arledge postulated that this style would broaden telecasts' appeal beyond the typical sports fan. In a memo he penned to explain this new approach to his network colleagues, Arledge (2003) claimed that ABC Sports would increase the number of cameras it used and would borrow from a variety of nonfiction television genres in order to "heighten the viewer's feeling of actually sitting in the stands" and "add show business to sports" (Arledge, 2003, p. 30–1). Taking Arledge's manifesto as their guide, ABC Sports' college football broadcasts would include pre-game documentary segments that framed contests with dramatic storylines, incorporate shots of fans and coaches' reactions to important plays, and highlight the pageantry surrounding featured contests.

Beyond its college football telecasts, ABC Sports showcased its "up close and personal" approach with *Wide World of Sports*, a non-live program that covered an eclectic mixture of popular, international, and obscure sporting events, from sumo wrestling in Japan to log rolling in Wisconsin. From a practical standpoint, *Wide World*, which debuted in April 1961, capitalized on the gap between the football and baseball seasons and the relative scarcity of sports television during the summer months. Moreover, ABC could acquire broadcasting rights to many of the little known sporting events that *Wide World* covered for a fraction of the price that more popular sports demanded. But securing popular sporting events was not necessary for *Wide World* to achieve its goal of emphasizing athletic competition's excitement. The program's documentary segments used athletic events as starting points from which to create gripping and inspiring stories. As the voice-over portion of *Wide World*'s introduction declares, the program "span[s] the globe to bring you the constant variety of sport: the thrill of victory, the agony of defeat, the human drama of athletic competition."

Though not explicitly polemical, *Wide World*'s short documentary pieces also often probed sport's sociopolitical dimensions. For instance, the program sympathetically covered Muhammad Ali's controversial refusal to serve in Vietnam, and it provided celebratory coverage of women's athletics well before Title IX's 1972 passage. In 1976, *Wide World* even documented a Harlem Globetrotters exhibition at Attica Correctional Facility, the site of a deadly riot six years earlier. *Wide World*'s segment on the Globetrotters' visit to Attica, which sport historian Bert Sugar describes as a "sociological documentary on penology" (Sugar, 1978, p. 125), used the game to provide a glimpse of post-riot life in the prison.

Wide World helped to mythologize sports figures like Ali and daredevil motorcyclist Evel Kneivel, and it transformed host Jim McKay and commentator Howard Cosell into national celebrities. Along with ABC Sports' innovative live broadcasts, *Wide World* established the network division as the leader in American sports television and set the foundation for its groundbreaking coverage of the 1968 Olympic Games and its 1970 development of *Monday Night Football.* Furthermore, ABC Sports' documentary-driven production practices brought the entire network greater renown. By the middle 1970s, ABC was America's most popular television network, a stark contrast to its days as the "almost broadcasting network."

Like ABC, the National Football League (NFL) struggled to build its reputation during the late 1950s and early 1960s. At the beginning of the 1960s, professional football was America's third most popular sport, behind both professional baseball and college football. By the end of the decade, the NFL would be the nation's most prominent and profitable sports spectacle. It partly owed this dramatic shift in status to its development of NFL Films, the league's subsidiary documentary film production company.

NFL Films began as Blair Motion Pictures, an independent production company owned and operated by retired Philadelphia overcoat salesman, Ed Sabol. Building upon Arledge's aesthetic method, Sabol strove to produce films that both emphasized games' dramatic qualities and displayed details not typically seen on television broadcasts. In 1962, Sabol purchased the rights to film the NFL Championship and created *Pro Football's Longest Day*, a 28-minute documentary that depicted the contest as a geopolitically inflected battle of wills between the Green Bay Packers and New York Giants. Upon viewing Blair Motion Pictures' production, NFL commissioner Pete Rozelle named it the finest football film he had ever seen (MacCambridge, 2005).

After producing similarly successful films for the NFL's two subsequent championship games, Sabol proposed that the league incorporate Blair Motion Pictures as a permanent in-house production company. Sabol's proposal tapped into Rozelle's established preoccupation with creating and publicizing a positive image for the league. Upon Rozelle's urging, the NFL purchased Blair Motion Pictures in 1964 for US$280,000 – a US$20,000 investment from each of the league's then fourteen teams. Ed Sabol served as president while his son Steve – who took over as president in 1987 – developed the company's aesthetic approach. Since its incorporation, NFL Films has documented every NFL game and produced thousands of celebratory made-for-television documentaries.

Although sports television was increasing in popularity during the 1960s, the NFL was only present on the medium during live broadcasts of its games, short recaps of those games on the evening news, and a few scattered highlight programs. Aside from sporadic national broadcasts, most of these representations had a regional focus and were available only to those who lived near an NFL franchise. NFL Films started to provide halftime highlights for network football broadcasts and produced several nationally syndicated programs, such as *NFL Game of the Week*, *This is the NFL*, and *NFL Action*. The programs educated viewers about the league and its players, contextualized the past week's games, and created anticipation for upcoming contests. More importantly, they gave the NFL a national presence on television throughout the entire week and year.

Just as significant as its enhancement of the league's visibility, NFL Films' productions give the league meaning. However, unlike newspaper reports or live telecasts, the company's films are designed to create a positive mythology for the NFL that distinguishes it from other sport organizations. NFL Films both documents the league's history and positions it as a heroic institution characterized by awe-inspiring moments and epic battles. The company typically uses a combination of ground level slow motion, baritone voiceover narration, symphonic scores, on-field sound, montage editing, and 16-mm color film to transform the organization's players and coaches into "legends of autumn" who partake in "cruel rites of manhood" on the "100-yard universe" of professional football.

Moreover, NFL Films is organized around an effort to create moving experiences. Steve Sabol (as cited in Block, 1972) claims that the main objective of the company's documentaries is "to give the viewer goose pimples" (Block, 1972, p. 17). These visceral spectacles reinforce the romantic mythology the company fashions and further set the NFL apart from its competition. NFL Films represents powerful hits as cringe-inducing moments of violence and winning touchdowns as uplifting feats of triumph. In doing so, it presents the NFL as an organization that furnishes these unique thrills. NFL Director of Broadcasting, Val Pinchbeck (as cited in Macnow, 1988), maintained that NFL Films documentaries "may have done more to promote professional football than anything other than the games themselves" (Macnow, 1988, p. 44). Along similar lines, *Sports Illustrated*'s Austin Murphy (1999) called the company "perhaps the most effective propaganda organ in the history of corporate America" (Macnow, 1988, p. 82).

One of the most successful ways in which NFL Films publicized the league during its first decades of operation was through a weekly halftime highlight package it produced for ABC's *Monday Night Football*. In addition to *Monday Night Football*'s "up close and personal" representation of the games, Arledge sought to devise a way for the prime time program to retain viewers throughout the featured contests' halftime periods. Traditionally, television broadcasts used halftime periods to recap the first half's action, speculate on the upcoming half, and perhaps comment on the league's other games. While halftime programming was decidedly less exciting than the game action, daytime Sunday telecasts did not typically have to contend with significant competition. *Monday Night Football*, however, aired in simultaneity with established prime time programs. The NFL Films-produced and Howard Cosell-narrated highlight package of the previous day's league games helped ABC to keep viewers tuned in through halftime.

Each Sunday, ABC would select a number of games it wanted NFL Films to feature in the halftime highlight package. Immediately after those games, the film NFL Films shot was rushed back to the company's headquarters to be developed and edited. NFL Films producers would work through the night to finish the highlight package by Monday morning, when it would be flown to the site of that evening's game. Cosell would record his narration, often extemporaneously, just hours before kickoff. In addition to Cosell's narration, the highlights featured NFL Films' signature ground-level slow motion and montage editing. The highlight package quickly became a distinguishing feature of *Monday Night Football*. The Washington Post's Leonard Shapiro claimed that the highlights were "as much of an institution as *Monday Night Football* itself" (Shapiro, 1981, p. TV5). "Even in blowouts," football historian Michael MacCambridge writes, "the audience numbers stayed strong through the halftime package" (MacCambridge, 2004, p. 279). NFL Films' *Monday Night Football* highlights used the prime time program's visibility to popularize further the mythology the company constructs for the NFL. Simultaneously, the highlight package, which was discontinued after Cosell's 1983 departure from *Monday Night Football*, solidified ABC Sports' position as America's most innovative and renowned sports television outlet.

Sports documentaries serve similar purposes in cable television. HBO Sports, the premium cable channel HBO's sports programming division, has consistently used documentaries to build the organization's prestigious brand, which it famously advertises with the tagline "It's Not TV, It's HBO." In 1999, HBO Sports received a Peabody Award for its "consistently superb series of documentaries" and its productions have won multiple Emmy Awards in both the "Outstanding Sports Documentary" and "Outstanding Sports Journalism" categories.

HBO Sports primarily creates journalistic and historical documentaries. For instance, *Real Sports with Bryant Gumbel* (1995–present) features investigate reportage, biographical profiles, and human-interest pieces. In 2004, *Real Sports* produced an Emmy Award and Alfred L. DuPont-Columbia University Award-winning story that used hidden cameras to expose the enslavement and trafficking of young Bangladeshi and Pakistani boys into the United Arab Emirates to serve as jockeys in the country's popular camel races. The segment led to a ban in the UAE against using children under fifteen years old as jockeys. In 2008 and 2010, *Real Sports* produced Emmy-winning investigative pieces that examined the link between sport-induced head trauma and brain damage. Similar to the program's examination of enslaved camel jockeys, these segments precipitated greater awareness of concussions' potential long-term effects that has motivated the NFL and other sport organizations to treat these injuries with greater care.

HBO Sports' *Sports in the 20th Century* documentary series recounts a combination of canonical, inspirational, and controversial stories from sport's past. The productions typically adopt a consistent, and even somewhat formulaic, set of aesthetic conventions that include voiceover narration, interviews with witnesses and experts, and archive footage to shed new light on familiar topics and to revisit significant but largely forgotten sports stories. For instance, *Do You Believe in Miracles? The Story of the 1980 US Hockey Team* (2001) reflects on the "miracle on ice" wherein the US Olympic hockey team surprisingly beat the heavily favored Soviet Union. The film nostalgically outlines how the team's unlikely triumph composed a point of national pride during a turbulent moment in American history. Similarly, *Dare to Dream: The Story of the US Women's Soccer Team* (2005) traces this team's history from its humble beginnings as an obscure curiosity in 1985; outlines its ascent into the national and global spotlight; and praises its positive impact on popular attitudes toward women's sport. In contrast to *Do You Believe in Miracles* and *Dare to Dream*'s celebratory focus, *Assault in the Ring* (2009) reflects upon a scandalous 1983 welterweight boxing match between rising star Billy Collins Jr. and journeyman Luis Resto. Resto unexpectedly beat Collins. However, it was later discovered that Resto's trainer had illegally removed padding from the boxer's gloves to increase the force of his punches. The film examines how the infamous and tragic bout impacted Collins, who was subsequently forced to retire because of damages sustained to his eye, sank into depression, and was killed the following year in a drunk driving accident; and Resto, who was sentenced to two and a half years in prison for his involvement in the incident and has since struggled to gain redemption.

Throughout HBO Sports' history, NFL Films has helped the division to develop and strengthen its association with the documentary genre. For example, NFL Films provided most of the footage used in *Inside the NFL*, a weekly seasonal program that features a combination of highlights, interviews, and studio analysis. *Inside the NFL*, which began in 1977, was HBO's longest-running program until its 2008 cancellation (it was immediately picked up by HBO competitor Showtime). Similar to the purpose NFL Films' halftime highlights served for *Monday Night Football*, the company's recognizable conventions distinguished *Inside the NFL* from the majority of football programs, and, by extension, set HBO Sports apart from the other sport media outlets that cover the NFL. Beyond Inside the NFL, NFL Films co-produced several of HBO Sports' *Sports in the 20th Century* documentaries, such as *Unitas* (1999); *Lombardi* (2010), which won the 2011 Emmy for Outstanding Sports Documentary; and *Namath* (2012). HBO Sports used NFL Films' enormous archive of game footage and interviews to enhance these documentaries' authenticity and drama. Moreover, as NFL Films' documentary practices have helped HBO Sports to build prestige, NFL Films – as well as the league it represents – benefits from its alliances with HBO Sports' powerful brand.

NFL Films has recently helped HBO Sports to forge a niche within the increasingly popular genre of reality television with *Hard Knocks*, a co-production that provides a behind-the-scenes glimpse into a particular NFL team's preseason training camp and chronicles the obstacles its players and management endure while preparing for the season. The Emmy-winning program builds drama through focusing on a combination of coaches struggling to meet owners and fans' expectations, rookies adjusting to the rigors of professional football, and veterans striving to make the team. *Hard Knocks*' success prompted HBO Sports to develop *24/7*, a more frequently produced reality series that covers the lead-up to significant sporting events. For instance, 2010 and 2011 installments of *24/7* documented the weeks prior to the National Hockey League's annual Winter Classic. HBO Sports also often uses *24/7* to publicize and dramatize the boxing matches HBO offers through its pay-per-view service, HBO PPV.

HBO Sports' wide-ranging and celebrated productions have established the outlet as contemporary television's most recognized and celebrated producer of sports documentaries. While HBO Sports stood unrivaled as the leader of the television sports documentary genre throughout much of the 1990s and 2000s, in 2008 the cable outlet ESPN's subsidiary production company ESPN Films began to compete aggressively for market share.

ESPN was not always the "worldwide leader in sports." In fact, during the organization's early years its relatively meager programming budget only allowed it to purchase rights to unpopular and obscure sporting events. Tape-delayed telecasts of Australian rules football and drag racing were commonplace. The only connections ESPN had to the most popular US sport organizations were the highlights and commentary it provided on its flagship studio program *SportsCenter*.

NFL Films' documentary programs, which were well within ESPN's limited economic reach, allowed the fledging cable channel to establish a valuable association with the NFL – which had firmly established itself as America's most popular sport organization by ESPN's 1979 birth. ESPN quickly became the principal outlet for NFL Films' syndicated programs. In 1987 the Washington *Post*'s Norman Chad sarcastically observed that NFL Films provided so much of ESPN's programming that if the film production company ever folded, "ESPN might have to change its name to EPN," (Chad, 1987, p. B2) taking the word "sports" out of its moniker.

Building in part upon the relationship it established with NFL Films, ESPN steadily gained respectability and greater carriage from cable providers throughout the 1980s. Rather than compete with the increasingly powerful 24-hour cable channel, in 1984 ABC purchased a majority stake in it. The network supplied ESPN with ABC Sports programming – including re-runs of *Wide World of Sports* – and allowed the channel to benefit from its established brand. However, as ESPN continued to grow and expand, it eventually became even more firmly identified with sports television than ABC Sports. In fact, when the Walt Disney Company acquired ABC in 1996, CEO Michael Eisner (as cited in Smith, 2009) called ESPN the "crown jewel" (Smith, 2009, p. 17) of the acquisition. In 2006, ABC rebranded its sports programming from ABC Sports to "ESPN on ABC" to take advantage of the cable outlet's renown.

While ESPN now has the most valuable brand in American and global sport media, it is not traditionally known for its documentaries. In 2008, ESPN rebranded its subsidiary production company ESPN Original Entertainment as ESPN Films and shifted its focus to documentary in order to capitalize on the genre's increasing popularity. Dan Klores' *Black Magic* (2008) was the first documentary produced under the ESPN Films banner. The film, which received a Peabody Award, examined basketball at historically Black colleges and universities during the civil rights movement. The subsidiary's second production, Spike Lee's Kobe *Doin' Work* (2009), focused thirty cameras on Los Angeles Lakers star, Kobe Bryant, during a single game, to provide an intimate glimpse into his prodigious play.

30 for 30 (2009–2010), a series of 30 documentaries made by 30 commissioned filmmakers to celebrate ESPN's 30th anniversary, more emphatically announced ESPN's enhanced investment in the documentary genre. The series covered a range of topics related to sport's history since 1979 and featured a diverse roster of high-profile directors, such as Peter Berg, Barbara Kopple, Barry Levinson, Albert Maysles, and John Singleton. ESPN Films launched *30 for 30* in October 2009 with Berg's King's *Ransom*, which explores Wayne Gretzky's 1988 trade from the Edmonton Oilers to the Los Angeles Kings and the profound effects it had on the National Hockey League. The series' remaining films premiered intermittently over the course of the following year. *30 for 30*'s mission statement (ESPN Films, 2009) describes the project as "[a]n unprecedented documentary series featuring thirty films from some of today's finest storytellers." Building upon this statement, ESPN Films' various marketing and promotional materials frame the series as a uniquely artful and ambitious undertaking in the history of sports television.

Bill Simmons (ESPN.com columnist, Editor-in-Chief of ESPN's Grantland.com, and host of the popular B.S. Report podcast) conceived of and developed *30 for 30*. Simmons wondered how ESPN, with its mammoth archive of sports footage, could justifiably claim to be the "worldwide leader in sports" without consistently producing documentaries. "It seemed like every time HBO released a sports documentary that it was a big deal," Simmons (2010) writes, "and meanwhile ESPN has all this material and expertise and is not engaging this area." Simmons believed a documentary series would both make use of ESPN's then dormant archive and help the outlet forge a niche within a sports television genre typically recognized as the domain of HBO Sports. In an interview with the *New York Times*, he even jokingly claims (as cited in Sandomir, 2009, p. B17) to "want nothing more than to destroy them [HBO Sports]". Along more diplomatic lines, ESPN Executive Vice President for Content, John Skipper (as cited in Sandomir, 2009, p. B17), asserts that "we [ESPN Films] want to be the first stop for documentary makers to tell great stories" and suggests that *30 for 30* is designed to establish this new role for ESPN Films.

In a segment of a *30 for 30* podcast that Simmons hosted during the series' initial run, he and fellow Executive Producer, Connor Schell, complained that HBO Sports documentaries are designed for older viewers and that their repetitive formal conventions have made the genre stale. In contrast, they claim that ESPN Films encourages artfulness and innovation (Simmons, 2010). After HBO Sports received the 2010 Emmy Award for Outstanding Sports Documentary, an honor it was receiving for the third year in a row, the subsidiary's President, Ross Greenburg, was asked his opinion about the competition that ESPN Films' documentaries posed. He dismissed ESPN Films' work as shoddy. To illustrate his point, Greenburg (as cited in Hiestand, 2010, p. 3C) likened the experience of watching HBO Sports' documentaries to "walking into a gallery and seeing [Michelangelo's] David" and compared ESPN Films' productions to "something I chipped out when I was 10". Moreover, he asserted (as cited in Hiestand, 2010, p. 3C) that HBO Sports "will always feel" that it "owns" the Outstanding Sports Documentary category.

To distinguish itself from its traditionally more prestigious competitor, ESPN Films advertised *30 for 30* productions' formal diversity and suggested the series' aesthetic variety is a consequence of its films' derivation from their commissioned directors' unique and celebrated creative approaches. As contributing director, Alex Gibney (as cited in Sandomir, 2009), notes, "HBO has their format, but [its documentaries] are rigorously produced with exactly the same style... *30 for 30* is doing just the opposite. They're saying, 'each one of these is going to be wildly different'" (Sandomir, 2009, p. B17). Expanding upon Gibney's statement, Simmons (as quoted in Coyle, 2010, para. 5) argues that ESPN's willingness to let filmmakers "explore their vision" made *30 for 30* "more creative" than the "producer-controlled" content that its competition constructs. Whereas HBO Sports does not generally call attention to the individuals hired to construct its documentaries, ESPN Films emphasizes *30 for 30*'s renowned filmmakers to increase the series' value and distinguish it from its competitor's productions.

In 2010, *30 for 30* won a Peabody Award as well as the International Documentary Association's "Distinguished Continuing Series" prize. Furthermore, ESPN Films has continued to produce a steady stream of documentaries after *30 for 30* ended, establishing ESPN as a fixture in the genre. Beyond competing with HBO Sports, and adding a new element to its increasingly powerful and diversified brand, ESPN's amplified commitment to producing documentaries augments the organization's broader institutional ambition to build and assert its image as the "worldwide leader in sports."

Partly in response to ESPN Films' success, HBO Sports has developed a new documentary series in cooperation with the weekly magazine, *Sports Illustrated*, which, like HBO, is owned by Time Warner. *Sport in America: Our Defining Stories*, which premieres in 2013, sets out to examine America's "national character" through sport's greatest and most inspirational moments. While developing the project, HBO Sports and *Sports Illustrated* encouraged fans to upload videos to the *Sport in America* website wherein they recount sports moments that significantly impacted their lives. The producers plan to use some of the participating fans in the documentary series. Similar to its collaborations with NFL Films, then, HBO Sports employs *Sports Illustrated*'s powerful brand to amplify *Sport in America*'s value and to protect its fragmenting market share of the television sports documentary.

While the sports documentary spans the history of television, the genre has recently amplified in popularity. An increasing number of sport media outlets produce television documentaries that claim to examine sport's meaning and history. For instance, the NFL Network's NFL Films-produced *America's Game* series celebrates each Super Bowl-winning team's championship season. Similarly, Showtime's *The Franchise* seeks to capitalize on the renown of HBO Sports' *Hard Knocks* and *24/7* by following a Major League Baseball team prior to and during its season. As with ABC Sports, NFL Films, HBO Sports, and ESPN's documentary films and programs, these productions do not merely investigate sport's significance. They also work to construct distinct identities for the outlets that create them within the increasingly crowded contemporary sport media landscape. With *America's Game*, the still nascent NFL Network uses NFL Films to help establish a valuable niche in cable sports television. *The Franchise* aids Showtime's efforts to compete with rival premium cable channel

HBO. The history of the television sports documentary is therefore marked both by these productions' examinations of sport and the institutional, economic, and industrial factors that inform their construction. It is necessary to consider these medium-specific factors to understand this sports television genre's history, development, and uses. Moreover, and more broadly, the genre explains how some of sport media's most influential institutions have worked – sometimes in collaboration, sometimes in opposition – to build, expand, and strengthen their brands.

References

Arledge, R. (2003). *Roone: A memoir.* New York: HarperCollins.

Block, A. (1972). The 27th team. *Philadelphia Inquirer*, December 10, 17–22.

Chad, N. (1987). With ESPN, stay alert to the web it weaves. *Washington Post*, December 19, B2.

Coyle, J. (2010). ESPN hands off to filmmakers, and they run with it in '30 for 30'. *PressofAtlanticCity*, May 4. Retrieved from http://www.pressofatlanticcity.com/life/article_586672af-14dd-5771-8319-4a62d6031bcc.html.

Curtin, M. (1995). *Redeeming the wasteland: Television documentary and cold war politics.* New Brunswick, NJ: Rutgers University Press.

ESPN Films. What is *30 for 30.* (2009). Retrieved from http://30for30.espn.com/.

Hiestand, M. (2010). HBO Sports stakes out sports documentary turf. *USA Today*, April 27, 3C.

MacCambridge, M. (2004). *America's game: The epic story of how pro football captured a nation.* New York: Random House.

Macnow, G. (1988, September). NFL Films is scoring high. *Nation's Business* 76 (9), 44–7.

Minow, N. (1964). Television and the public interest. In N. Minow (Ed.), *Equal time: The private broadcaster and the public interest* (pp. 45–69). New York: Atheneum.

Murphy, A. (1999). The path to power. *Sports Illustrated*, 91 (8), 82.

Rader, B. (1984). *In its own image: How television has transformed sport.* New York: The Free Press.

Sandomir, R. (2009). For 30th anniversary, ESPN hands camera to someone else. *New York Times*, September 29, B17.

Shapiro, L. (1981). Halftime highlights got you down? Don't blame Howard. *Washington Post,* November 29, TV5.

Simmons, B. (2010). 30 for 30: Schell and Dahl. Interview with Connor Schell and John Dahl. 30 for 30 podcast with Bill Simmons. *ESPN Audio*, December 10, 55 min. Retrieved from http://espn.go.com/espnradio/play?id=5900091.

Smith, A. (2009). *ESPN the company: The story and lessons behind the most fanatical brand in sports.* Hoboken, NJ: Wiley.

Sugar, B. (1978). *"The thrill of victory": The inside story of ABC Sports.* New York: Hawthorn.

Watson, M. (1994). *The expanding vista: American television in the Kennedy years.* Durham, NC: Duke University Press.

14

SPORTS BROADCASTING

History, technology, and implications

Brad Schultz and Wei Wei

In 1920, the National Football League (NFL) was still a shaky proposition, with teams forming and failing on almost a weekly basis. When twelve of the league's founders met to discuss a formal organization, the team entrance fee was a mere US$100. "There wasn't one hundred dollars in the room," said George Halas, who founded the Chicago Bears franchise, "but still each of us put up one hundred dollars for the privilege of losing money" (McDonough, 1994, p. 25). Today, the NFL is a multi-billion dollar conglomerate, with offices in five countries on three continents. In its valuations of NFL teams, *Forbes* estimates that the 32 teams in the league annually bring in a combined US$8.3 billion in revenues. The Dallas Cowboys are currently ranked as the NFL's most valuable franchise at US$1.85 billion, but even the "poorest" team, the Jacksonville Jaguars, is worth US$725 million (Badenhauser, 2011).

There are myriad reasons for the growth of the NFL, but certainly the broadcast media have played a pivotal role. In 1962, the league sold the rights to televise its games to CBS for US$4.65 million. The league's 2012 contract is worth US$17.6 billion, paid over eight years by CBS, FOX, NBC, and ESPN, and that does not include additional millions the league earns from its "Sunday Ticket" subscription package. Television rights fees for the NFL have increased 10,000 percent since 1970, and eleven of the twenty highest-rated television shows of all time are Super Bowl games. Television revenue has also generated huge profits for other leagues and organizations. FOX is in the middle of a six-year, US$2.5 billion deal to televise Major League Baseball (MLB), while ESPN is paying US$851 million. In addition, major professional teams gain money by selling broadcast rights to local stations. The National Basketball Association (NBA) has more than doubled its television rights revenue since 1994, and now earns US$2.4 billion over six years from ABC, ESPN, and Turner Sports.

Historical development

The modern sports landscape is dominated by the role of broadcasting and the growth of media technologies, and the seeds for such growth were planted more than a century ago. Sowell (2008) argues that the development of the telegraph in the 1840s led to national sports coverage in the US, creating an interest in sports through its ability to connect large audiences.

In the late 1800s, the emerging film industry was often used to record and distribute athletic events. In 1894, Thomas Edison staged, filmed and distributed a boxing match between Michael Leonard and Jack Cushing. For 60 cents audiences could watch the six-round bout in a peep show kinetoscope and it "created a sensation" (Gamache, 2010, p. 86). Just in St. Louis, films of the 1908 World Series packed two movie houses twice a day for a week (Seymour, 1989). In 1913, Western Union paid each MLB team US$17,000 per year over five years for the telegraph rights to the games. The movie industry purchased the rights to film and show the highlights of the 1910 World Series for US$500, a figure that team owners managed to increase to US$3,500 for the following season (Haupert, 2007).

The next broadcast breakthrough was radio. As early as 1912, F. W. Springer and H. M. Turner began to broadcast accounts of University of Minnesota's home football games to a sparse audience (Smith, 2001). In 1920, Japanese domestic middle school's baseball matches were often broadcast to local listeners (Hashimoto, 1992). In April 11, 1921, sportswriter Florent Gibson of the *Pittsburgh Post* was asked to give a blow-by-blow description of a prizefight, and he may have been one of the first play-by-play commentators in the world (Catsis, 1995). Later that year, a former Australian cricket player, Len Watt was handed a microphone to describe a cricket match in Sydney (Steen, 2008).

By the 1920s, radio used sports programming to become a powerful mass medium. In 1922, radio helped the World Series to reach an estimated audience of one million listeners, which did not include crowds of fans who gathered around loudspeakers in New York and New Jersey (Halberstam, 1999). The 1923 boxing match between Jess Willard and Luis Firpo attracted a broadcast audience of two million (Owens, 2006), while another heavyweight title fight between Jack Dempsey and Gene Tunney in 1927 generated thousands of dollars worth of sales for radio receivers (Betts, 1974). The 1923 fight in New York between Firpo and Dempsey for the world heavyweight title in New York marked the first broadcast in South America. The following year, Africa's first broadcast was a rugby match from Cape Town (Booth, 2008). By 1927, NBC had sufficiently developed a US network to the point that it could broadcast the Rose Bowl between Stanford and Alabama, a game that marked the first live, coast-to-coast broadcast of a sporting event on radio.

Europe was at the forefront of television sports broadcasting, which made its debut in 1936 when the Germans covered the Garmisch-Partenkirchen Winter Olympics on a delayed basis (Wei, 2012). The Summer Olympics from Berlin later that year are largely regarded as the first live television sports transmission, as two German networks provided a total of 138 viewing hours to those watching in special viewing booths in Berlin and Potsdam (OBSV, 2012). The following year, BBC Television hired Harry Mallin to commentate on an England versus Ireland amateur boxing contest from the Alexander Palace on February 4, 1937 (Owens, 2007), followed by the Wimbledon tennis tournament in June.

The first television broadcast of a baseball game in the US occurred on August 26, 1939, but featured only two cameras. Reception was fairly poor, but hardly anyone seemed to notice as only about 400 sets existed in New York to pick up the signal. The *New York Times* noted, "Television set owners as far away as 50 miles viewed the action" between the Reds and Dodgers from Brooklyn (Baseball-statistics.com, 2001, para. 12). Pro football also televised its first game in 1939, which consisted mostly of fuzzy camera shots of the player with the ball. Cameramen were frequently faked out, and, on several occasions, announcers had to invent intricate lateral passes to explain why the home viewer could not see the ball. Coverage slowly improved, but even by 1948 in a broadcast of the college football game between Oklahoma and Texas on WBAP-TV, the bands that performed at halftime had to stay in between the 35-yard lines so as to remain in range of primitive cameras (Heard, 1980).

Despite those rocky beginnings, television soon became an even more dominant force than radio. Television sports exploded throughout the 1950s and 60s, as the networks dramatically increased their production and distribution of live sports content. The networks jockeyed with each other for exclusive broadcast rights for popular events such as the Olympics, NFL, MLB, and the NBA. CBS was the first network to broadcast the Olympics in the US, but the rights eventually passed to ABC and now NBC. In 1960, CBS spent only US$50,000 to televise the Winter Games from Squaw Valley, California. In 2011, NBC paid US$4.38 billion for the rights to four Olympic Games starting in 2014 (SB Nation, 2011).

Network competition helped increase the value of television rights fees, but the Sports Broadcasting Act of 1961 also played a vital role. Up until that time NFL teams were required by anti-trust law to individually negotiate their own television rights deals. "It was a growth that was kind of segmented," said long-time Cowboys' general manager Tex Schramm. "The Chicago Bears and Chicago Cardinals had their own networks. George Preston Marshall and the Washington Redskins had their southern network. And (the Rams) tried to have the west coast network" (Sabol, 1998). NFL Commissioner Pete Rozelle stepped in and convinced owners that they needed to share television revenues equally. Congress approved, and in 1962, the first league-wide television contract began.

Televised sports content was controlled by ABC, CBS, and NBC until more competition came along in the 1970s. Ted Turner's WTBS began distributing Atlanta Braves games through national cable and suddenly the networks began to lose their power. This was accelerated through the development of the Internet, digital delivery systems and interactive communication. Today, there are more content providers than ever before and more people watching. The worldwide viewership for the Summer Olympics continues to grow – 3.6 billion for Sydney in 2000, 3.9 billion for Athens in 2004, 4.7 billion for Beijing in 2008 in 2008, and 4.8 billion for London in 2012 ("Cumulative," 2012).

Changes and implications

The broadcast media played a central role in what McChesney (1989, p. 54) called the "nationalization" of sports, which is one sense is the transition from pastime to commercial enterprise. Frey and Eitzen (1991) called this the commoditization of sport, or "the evolution of sport from a playful, participation-oriented activity to one that resembles a corporate form guided by the principles of commercialism and entertainment" (Frey and Eitzen, 1991, p. 503). Historically, professional sports have relied on ticket sales, which is why baseball owners in New York were reluctant to broadcast their games on the radio. Fearing that giving away the product for free would hurt game attendance, all three New York baseball teams had a ban on live radio broadcasts as late as the 1930s. The ban was broken in 1938 when Larry MacPhail took over the Brooklyn Dodgers and immediately signed a deal with 50,000-watt station WOR. In one year sponsors paid more than US$100,000 in advertising, and while the Dodgers struggled on the field their attendance actually increased (Golenbock, 1984). By 1935, CBS, NBC, and Mutual were all broadcasting baseball on a national basis. In 1937, rights to broadcast the World Series on radio were worth US$100,000; in 1949, Gillette signed a seven-year, US$1 million deal to become the exclusive radio sponsor of the World Series and All-Star games (Broadcasting, 1970).

Thus, in modern sport, "Attracting spectators and media sponsorships becomes more important than the playing process because sport is now driven by profit and the market" (Frey and Eitzen, 1991, p. 508). A typical example is the Green Bay Packers, a team ranked by Forbes as the tenth most valuable of the NFL's 32 teams. In 2012, the Packers earned US$276 million in operating revenues, of which US$52 million came from ticket sales, while broadcasting and media fees accounted for US$109 million (Forbes, 2012). NFL revenue as a whole "rose 5.8 percent to US$8 billion on higher television income" (McLuskey, 2010, para. 4).

It could be argued that the economic impact of broadcasting has fundamentally altered how US sports are organized, contested and consumed. Broadcast fees have made sports so profitable that players have challenged team owners for larger shares of media riches. Player salaries have increased dramatically since the 1970s, in part because of the increase in broadcast rights fees. Such fees have also led to player empowerment in a collective sense. It was the unequal distribution of local broadcast fees, and a corresponding desire by owners to impose a salary cap, that led MLB players to go on strike in 1994. Owners argued that unless teams shared local broadcasting revenue, small market teams would unduly suffer (Staudohar, 1997). The NFL lockout of 2011 was largely due to team owners renegotiating network television contracts to secure US$4 billion that would be paid even if no games were played (Jensen, 2011).

New broadcast technologies such as the Internet, Twitter, and social media such as Facebook have changed the nature of athlete-media interaction, allowing athletes to bypass the traditional media such as newspapers and television and take their message directly to fans. Such technology is now interactive and allows athletes to communicate directly with fans. "We're hitting (Twitter) hard," said NBA player Chris Bosh. "You can put up what you're doing. Or if you have a question, you'd be surprised how much people know. You can be, like, 'I need directions to this spot. People will tell you'" (Feschuk, 2009, para. 5). Gregory (2009, para. 6) notes that Twitter and other new media technologies have the potential to "change the athlete/fan interaction forever". In 2012, the website tweeting-athletes.com reported that soccer stars Cristano Ronaldo (14.2 million) and Kaka (13.5 million) had the most Twitter followers of any athletes in the world.

These same broadcast technologies have opened up several areas for sports consumers, who have many more choices and options in terms of channels, content and opportunities for feedback. Providers found that customers would pay extra fees, usually between US$30 and US$50, for special events such as championship boxing fights. The boxing match between Oscar de la Hoya and Floyd Mayweather in 2007 set a record with 2.15 million pay-per-view purchases and earned US$120 million, making it the richest bout in history (New York Times, 2007). Pay-per-view has also become popular with consumers who cannot see certain games or teams in their local area. Most major sports leagues, including the NFL, NBA, MLB, and NHL, offer out-of-market programming for an additional fee. The NFL has more than 18 million subscribers to its Sunday Ticket programming, which allows consumers to watch up to 14 games per weekend on satellite television (Lieberman, 2009). In a similar way, sports leagues are using satellite radio to reach consumers. In addition to dozens of specialized sports channels, Sirius XM satellite radio currently has an eleven-year deal worth US$650 million to carry MLB games (Walker, 2009).

In addition to increasing consumption options, sports broadcasting has shifted communication from a one-way, static model to a two-way, interactive process in which audiences play a much more participatory role. The sports fans of 2012 not only have seemingly unlimited, instant access to content through message boards, fan forums, and blogs, they can also create, distribute and share their own information. Hundreds of fans have created dedicated websites to coverage of their favorite teams, and in some cases these sites rival traditional coverage offered by newspapers and magazines (Lemann, 2006). Sports broadcasting technologies have also had a strong practical impact on athletic events. The growing importance of television rights fees often dictates when and where games take place, and many events begin at odd hours to accommodate broadcast schedules. College basketball's Midnight Madness, in which teams begin practice at the first possible moment after 12 a.m. on the first practice day allowed by the NCAA, is a recent development for the benefit of television cameras. "You folks (the networks) are paying us a lot of money to put this game on television," former Alabama football coach Bear Bryant once commented. "If you want us to tee it up at two in the morning, then that's when we'll tee it up" (as cited in Schultz, 2001, p. 18).

One of the most visible manifestations of broadcast technology is the use of instant replay. It began during the telecast of a college football game in 1963 as an added feature for television audiences, but it has since become an important element of how games are played. Almost every professional and college sports league in the US now uses replay in some form to review action on the field, and in some cases replay has directly determined the outcome of games. According to Brennan, "Over the years, the NFL, NBA, NHL, some NCAA sports and major tennis tournaments have realized (reluctantly, in some cases) that there was no avoiding the use of instant replay to help govern their games" (Brennan, 2008, para. 5). The NFL has the longest, most extensive, and in some cases most controversial, replay system among professional leagues. "If people sitting in their living rooms can see a play is called incorrectly," said former NFL coach Don Shula, "then we should be able to see it, too" (Brennan, 2008, para. 3).

Broadcast globalization

In part because of broadcasting technologies, sport is now an interconnected global enterprise that thrives far beyond the US. Americans tend to think of the Super Bowl as a worldwide sporting phenomenon, and indeed, the 2011 Super Bowl between Pittsburgh and Green Bay had 111 million viewers, the largest audience for any single television show in US history (Sweeney, 2011). But that figure is dwarfed by the 2010 World Cup, which was broadcast to 214 countries and reached a cumulative audience of more than 26 billion, including 715 million for the championship match (Michaels, 2010).

Gratton and Solberg (2007) argue that European sports broadcasting lagged behind the US model because it began primarily on public channels and was heavily regulated. Not until the late 1980s did deregulation and competition emerge to drive up rights fees, and today much European sports content, particularly soccer, has transitioned exclusively to pay channels. The effect of competition combined with new media technologies have opened up sports broadcasting in Europe, Asia and South America, and have allowed those areas not only to broadcast to their own people, but also to export sports content to other countries, including the US.

Today, television coverage of global mega-events is usually produced by international co-operations. The Olympic Broadcasting Service began in 2001 and it now selects and oversees the companies that provide coverage of the Olympic Games. In recent Olympics, track and field events were produced by NRK (Norway) and SVT (Sweden), badminton, table tennis and modern pentathlon were produced by CCTV (China), and broadcasters from the host country were responsible for parts of soccer and basketball matches (Wei, 2012). The World Cup matches have been produced by HBS (Switzerland) since 1998 (Wei, 2011a). This international cooperation is essential for nations that cannot broadcast on their own. For the 2011 Astana-Almaty Asian Winter Games, HBS was appointed by the host nation Kazakhstan to broadcast the event. With the technological help of HBS, Qatar-based Al Dawri and Al Kass produced the 2011 AFC Asian Cup, establishing a world record with 51 different cameras broadcasting a single soccer game (Wei, 2011b).

Thus, in some ways international cooperation has made the larger broadcast organizations even more dominant. Eurosport, a leading television sports company across Europe, broadcasts in 20 languages and covers the whole of the continent (except for France and the UK) with the same video feed. Ireland-based Setanta Sports provides sports programs to Europe, North America, the Far East, Australia and dozens of African countries (Wei, 2012). Eurosport currently has multiple channels, including Eurosport 2 and Eurosportnews channels, to cover the Asian-Pacific area (Chalaby, 2009).

The 2008 Beijing Olympics demonstrated the popularity of sport in China, and international broadcasters are making a strong effort to reach growing Chinese audiences. US broadcasters and sports organizations are particularly involved in exporting content to China and around the world. When Yao's Ming's Houston Rockets played Yi Jianlian's Milwaukee Bucks on November 9, 2007, more than 200 million people in China watched the game on 19 different networks, making it the most viewed NBA game in history (Associated Press, 2007). The NBA distributes its games in more than 40 different languages to 215 different countries, and in 2011 the league showed its annual All-Star game live and in 3-D to more than 100 cinemas in Belgium, Italy, Germany, and Mexico. "For the first time, international basketball fans are going to have the opportunity to see NBA All-Star like never before," said Matt Brabants of the NBA's International Division, "on the big screen in cinemas with a special courtside seat to all the action—in 3D" (TVTechnology, 2011, para. 2).

The NFL is also using the media to expand its product overseas. The league began playing exhibition games in Europe in 1986 and created a developmental league based in Europe called the World League of American Football. The league went through several incarnations before the NFL pulled the plug in 2007, and while the NFL has hopes of a permanent presence overseas it is still reaching out to foreign audiences through high definition television, the Internet, and other media technologies. "We will continue to build our international fan base by taking advantage of technology and customized digital media that make the NFL more accessible on a global scale than ever before and through the regular-season game experience" (para. 3), said Mark Waller, senior vice president of NFL International. "The time is right to re-focus the NFL's strategy on initiatives with global impact, including worldwide media coverage of our sport and the staging of live regular-season NFL games" (National Football League, 2007, para. 2).

Future challenges

The essence of sport has always been the personal experience: the pageantry, color, and excitement of live athletic competition. But broadcasting has fundamentally altered this experience and made it much easier, and in some cases more satisfying, to watch at home. Not long after MLB began televising games on a regular basis, then-MLB Commissioner Ford Frick observed, "One of the jobs that baseball has to do is keep television from making the show too good. The trouble is that television wants the viewer to see the game better than the fan in the ballpark" (Arledge and Rogin, 1966, p. 100).

Today, the viewer often does see the game better, thanks to high definition, multiple camera angles, and large screen resolution. While live attendance at sporting events has not yet unduly suffered, especially for professional football, even the popular NFL has recently witnessed drops in overall attendance and average attendance (McCarthy, 2010). Thus, one of the challenges in the 21st century is to use broadcasting technology as a means of improving the live experience. In 2009, the Cowboys opened a US$1.2 billion, 100,000-seat stadium equipped with a 60-yard-long high-definition (HD) videoboard suspended 90 feet above the field. The following season, both NFL teams in New York began play in a similar US$1.6 billion facility, and almost all NFL stadiums in 2011 have HD screens and wireless Internet access. "We aren't just going to invest on new technologies that serve people at home," says Brian Rolapp, the NFL's vice president for digital media. "We will continue to invest to make the stadium experience better" (Leahy, 2010, para. 43).

While programming on a 60-yard screen may seem interesting, the key to sports content may lie on a screen no bigger than six inches. Mobile television – making programming available on cell phones and hand-held computers – is the next frontier for sports content providers. According to Jessell (2011, para. 6), "broadcasting's real future is mobile. Smart phones will gradually replace all the dumb phones and everybody with have a TV receiver in their pocket or purse". While the concept of "TV Everywhere" continues to evolve, "All mobile TV trials to date have shown that sport on mobile TV will be a success story," says Kieran Mahon, media development manager at Vodafone. "Sport on mobile TV has the capacity to generate billions of dollars every year" (Wilson, 2006, paras. 9–10).

Mobile television is an area where sports broadcasters can maintain profitability in an uncertain media environment. Costs and rights fees have risen dramatically in recent years, owing mainly to increased competition among various network, cable and satellite programmers. Such costs will ultimately be pushed on to consumers through increased subscription and access fees. More events will continue to transition from free, over-the-air broadcast channels to cable and pay outlets, such as the college football Bowl Championship Series, which, in 2011, moved from Fox to ESPN. "I think that there's cord cutting because of the economic factor, where rates continue to rise for people and they can't stomach the whole cost," said Derek Chang, executive vice president of content strategy and development for DirecTV. "Going back to whether or not customers will ultimately bear the freight is something that everyone is cognizant of and trying to assess what the tolerance level there is" (Ourand, 2011, para. 36).

But even in an environment in which many media outlets are folding, streamlining or reducing workforce (Hirschorn, 2009), sports broadcasting is strong and should remain robust well into the future. Economically, culturally and technologically, it is the golden goose of 21st century media; seemingly impervious to downturns, contractions and fragmentation. "The value of the sports content is increasing as it becomes more and more difficult to get people in front of a set — and a specific demographic in front of a set," said Sean McManus of CBS Sports. "Sports is still able to attract that demographic, and it's pretty consistent in terms of the people it brings to the set. That isn't true of a lot of other programming on television" (Ourand, 2011, para. 48).

References

Arledge, R., and Rogin, G. (1966). It's sports...it's money...it's TV. *Sports Illustrated*, April 25, 92–106.

Associated Press. (2007). Yao Ming's Rockets beat Yi Jianlian's Bucks, 104–88. *ESPN NBA*, November 7. Retrieved from http://sports.espn.go.com/espn/wire?section=nbaandid=3103080.

Badenhausen, K. (2011). The NFL's most valuable teams. *Forbes*, September 7. Retrieved from http://www.forbes.com/sites/kurtbadenhausen/2011/09/07/the-nfls-most-valuable-teams/.

Baseball-statistics.com (2001). Ebbetts Field. *Baseball-statistics*. Retrieved from http://www.baseball-statistics.com/Ballparks/LA/Ebbetts.htm.

Betts, J. R. (1974). *America's sporting heritage: 1850–1950*. Reading, MA: Addison-Wesley.

Booth, D. (2008). *Talking of sport: The story of radio commentary*. Cheltenham, UK: Sports Books.

Brennan, C. (2008). Baseball still missing the call on instant replay. *USA Today*, May 29. Retrieved from http://www.usatoday.com/sports/columnist/brennan/2008-05-28-Replay_N.htm.

Catsis, J. (1995). *Sports broadcasting*. Chicago: Nelson-Hall.

Chalaby, J. (2009). *Transnational television in Europe: Reconfiguring global communications networks*. London: I. B. Tauris.

Cumulative TV-viewership of the Olympic Summer Games worldwide from 1996 to 2012. (2012). Statista. Retrieved from http://www.statista.com/statistics/236692/total-number-of-tv-viewers-of-olympic-summer-games-worldwide/

Feschuk, D. (2009). Bosh, NBA all a-Twitter over latest blogging fad. *Toronto Star*, February 17. Retrieved from http://www.thestar.com/Sports/NBA/article/588483.

Forbes. (2012). Green Bay Packers. *Forbes*, August. Retrieved from http://www.forbes.com/teams/green-bay-packers/.

Frey, J. H., and Eitzen, D. S. (1991). Sport and society. *Annual Review of Sociology* 17, 503–22.

Gamache, R. (2010). Genealogy of the sportscast highlight form: From peep show to projection to hot processor. *Journal of Sports Media,* 5 (2), 77–106.

Golenbock, P. (1984). *Bums*. New York: Pocket Books.

Gratton, C., and Solberg, H.A. (2007). *The economics of sports broadcasting*. New York: Routledge.

Gregory, S. (2009). Twitter craze is rapidly changing the face of sports. *Sports Illustrated*, June 5. Retrieved from http://sportsillustrated.cnn.com/2009/writers/the_bonus/06/05/twitter.sports/2.html.

Halberstam, D. (1999). *Sports on New York radio: A play-by-play history*. Lincolnwood, IL: Masters.

Hashimoto, K. (1992). *History for Japanese broadcasting*. Tokyo: Osamu Press.

Haupert, M. J. (2007). The economic history of major league baseball. *EH.net Encyclopedia*, December 3. Retrieved from http://eh.net/encyclopedia/article/haupert.mlb.

Heard, R. (1980). *Texas vs. Oklahoma: When football becomes war*. Austin, TX: Honey Hill.

Hirschorn, M. (2009). End times. Can America's paper of record survive the death of newsprint? Can journalism? *Atlantic Magazine*, January–February. Retrieved from http://www.theatlantic.com/magazine/archive/2009/01/end-times/307220/.

Jensen, S. (2011). NFL lockout upheld by appellate court. *Chicago Sun-Times*, May 16. Retrieved from http://www.suntimes.com/sports/5420096-417/nfl-lockout-upheld-by-appellate-court.html.

Jessell, H. A. (2011). Broadcasting's future is all about mobile. *TVNewsCheck*, May 20. Retrieved from http://www.mobile500alliance.com/press/Jessell_060211.html.

Leahy, S. (2010). HDTV and technology pit NFL stadiums vs. fans living rooms. *USA Today*, September 1. Retrieved from http://www.usatoday.com/sports/football/nfl/2010-08-31-nfl-hd-v-stadium-or-living-room_N.htm.

Lemann, N. (2006). Amateur hour. *New Yorker*, August 7. Retrieved from http://www.newyorker.com/archive/2006/08/07/060807fa_fact1.

Lieberman, D. (2009). DirecTV offers NFL Sunday Ticket via Internet in NY trial. *USA Today*, August 17. Retrieved from http://www.usatoday.com/tech/news/2009-08-16-broadband-directv-football_N.htm.

McCarthy, M. (2010). NFL: attendance likely to fall for third straight season in 2010, to lowest level since 1998. *USA Today*, September 1. Retrieved from http://content.usatoday.com/communities/thehuddle/post/2010/09/nfl-attendance-likely-to-fall-for-third-straight-season-in-2010-to-lowest-level-since-1998/1.

McChesney, R. (1989). Media made sport: A history of sports coverage in the United States. In L. Wenner (Ed.), *Media, sports and society* (pp. 49–69). Newbury Park, CA: Sage.

McDonough, W. (Ed.). (1994). *75 seasons: The complete story of the National Football League, 1920–1995*. Atlanta: Turner.

McLuskey, D. (2010). Dallas Cowboys top Forbes magazine list as NFL team values have first drop. Bloomberg, August 25. Retrieved from http://www.bloomberg.com/news/2010-08-26/dallas-cowboys-top-forbes-list-as-nfl-team-values-have-first-decline.html.

Michaels, S. (2010). World Cup viewing figures prove that this really is the world's game. *Goal.com*, May 29. Retrieved from http://www.goal.com/en/news/1863/world-cup-2010/2010/05/29/1947801/world-cup-viewing-figures-prove-that-this-really-is-the-.

National Football League. (2007). NFL Europa closes. *NFL.com*, August 3. Retrieved from http://www.nfl.com/nfl-europa-closes.

New York Times (2007). Mayweather victory sets pay-per-view mark. *New York Times*. May 10. Retrieved from http://query.nytimes.com/gst/fullpage.html?res=9C03E4D61731F933A25756C0A9619C8B63andref=oscardelahoya

OBSV. (2012). *Olympic Broadcasting Service*, February 11. Retrieved from http://obsv.ca/.

Ourand, J. (2011). How high can rights fees go? *SportsBusiness Journal*, June 6. Retrieved from http://www.sportsbusinessdaily.com/Journal/Issues/2011/06/06/In-Depth/Rights-Fees.aspx.

Owens, J. (2006). Sports coverage on radio. In A. Raney and J. Bryant (Eds.), *Handbook of sports media* (pp. 117–29). Mahwah, NJ: Lawrence Erlbaum.

Owens, J. (2007). *Television sports producing*. Amsterdam: Focal Press.

Broadcasting. (1970). Radio's Version of "Who's on First?": Many claims have been made, but radio's paternity is still a question. In J. Miller (Ed.), *History of American Broadcasting*, November 2. Retrieved from http://jeff560.tripod.com/70.html.

Sabol, S. (Producer). (1998). *Replay! The history of the NFL on television* [Television show]. United States: NFL Films.

SB Nation (2011). TVBizwire: Sports Flashes: NBC Wins Olympics With Bid Topping US$4 Billion; Tiger Withdraws From Upcoming US Open. *TV Week*, June 7. Retrieved from http://www.tvweek.com/blogs/tvbizwire/2011/06/nbc-awarded-rights-to-olympics.php.

Schultz, B. (2001). *Sports broadcasting*. Woburn, MA: Focal.

Seymour, H. (1989). *Baseball: The golden age*. New York: Oxford University Press.

Smith, R. (2001). *Play-by-play: Radio, television, and big-time college sport*. Baltimore: Johns Hopkins University Press.

Sowell, M. (2008). The birth of national sports coverage: An examination of the New York Herald's use of the telegraph to report America's first 'championship' boxing match in 1849. *Journal of Sports Media*, 3 (1), 47–69.

Staudohar, P. (1997). The baseball strike of 1994–95. *Monthly Labor Review*, March: 21–7.

Steen, R. (2008). *Sports journalism: A multimedia primer*. London: Routledge.

Sweney, M. (2011). Super Bowl 2011 draws highest ever audience for US TV show. *The Guardian*, February 8. Retrieved from http://www.guardian.co.uk/media/2011/feb/08/super-bowl-highest-ever-audience.

TVTechnology. (2011). NBA to show 3D all-Star game in overseas cinemas. *TVTechnology*, February 15. Retrieved from http://www.tvtechnology.com/article/113800.

Walker, D. (2009). Sirius XM deal good for baseball, too. *Milwaukee Journal Sentinel*, February 17. Retrieved from http://www.jsonline.com/blogs/sports/39732137.html.

Wei, W. (2011a). Reading the myth: Semiotic research on 2010 World Cup South Africa's television broadcasting. *China Sport Science and Technology*, 47 (2), 47–51.

Wei, W. (2011b). Research on image narratives of AFC 2011 Asian Cup's television broadcasting. *TV Research*, 18 (4), 62–4.

Wei, W. (2012). *History of international sports broadcasting*. Beijing: China Radio and Television Publishing House.

Wilson, B. (2006). Mobile TV sports viewing is on the move. *BBC News*, November 19. Retrieved from http://news.bbc.co.uk/2/hi/business/6153536.stm.

15

THE GLASS CEILING AND BEYOND

Tracing the explanations for women's lack of power in sports journalism

Erin Whiteside and Marie Hardin

The Association for Women in Sports Media (AWSM), a networking organization for women in sports-media careers in the US, commemorated its 25th anniversary in 2013. For AWSM, certainly, there was reason to celebrate, as it reviewed changes in the mediated sports landscape over the past three decades. Women are now more visible on sports cable television and as columnists or writers for major sports publications than ever. It is impossible, for instance, to watch ESPN's signature show, *SportsCenter*, without seeing women reporting stories and perhaps anchoring the desk. Women dominate the "sideline reporter" position in game broadcasts of college and professional sports.

The increased visibility and opportunity did not come easily. The history of women covering sports in the US is one of struggle. The right of female sports reporters to have the same access as their male counterparts, for instance, was decided in a 1978 decision by a federal judge after *Sports Illustrated* writer, Melissa Ludtke, was barred from Major League Baseball (MLB) locker rooms (Ricchiardi, 2005). Still, well beyond that legal victory, female sports-writers faced "a gauntlet of intimidation" on the job (Ricchiardi, 2005, p. 59). Perhaps the most famous – and ugly – example of the struggle for women to have the opportunity to cover sports, without harassment, was that of sportswriter Lisa Olson, who was harassed in a National Football League (NFL) locker room in 1990 and subsequently filed a lawsuit.

Although incidents of blatant harassment have subsided (but not disappeared – the harassment of Mexican sports reporter Ines Sainz at an NFL training facility in 2010 received a great deal of media attention), women in the field face other roadblocks to thriving in a staunchly male-dominated profession (Ricchiardi, 2005). The percentage of women covering sports has not climbed substantially in the past decade, and top-level positions in most sports departments continue to be dominated by men. Long-time sports reporter Joanne Gerstner (2005) wrote in a column for the trade publication *Editor and Publisher*, women might secure entry-level jobs but are discouraged from moving up. "I've had [AWSM] members tell me stories of applying for jobs as editors or columnists, only to be told that the paper wasn't 'ready' to have a woman in that position," noted Gerstner. "Others have had editors openly question them at job interviews about their family plans or how they would juggle children and being an editor. Would a man receive these same illegal questions?" (Gerstner, 2005, p. 5).

Scholarly research into the status of women in sports journalism has documented the progress – and lack thereof – that women have made in the field, and the reasons sports departments remain generally unwelcoming places for women to build careers. Scholars have argued that the role of women in the production of mediated sports has implications for the ways sports are culturally understood and covered; the role of women in mediated sports is also one important indicator for fulfillment of the promise of Title IX, the US law protection equality of opportunity in sport for girls and women. This chapter reviews research focusing on the roles, opportunities and representation of women in US sports journalism.

Women in sports departments: The research

Research tracking the demographics of sports departments and the experiences of female sports journalists began in earnest during the mid-1990s. Little was published before that outside the anecdotal, first-person accounts of reporters such as Susan Fornoff (*Lady in the locker room*, 1993) and Alison Gordon (*Foul balls: Five years in the American League*, 1984), and coverage of court challenges waged on behalf of female reporters who had been harassed or barred from locker rooms, such as Ludtke and Olson.

Cramer (1994) and Miller and Miller (1995) were among the first to publish scholarly accounts examining the environment for women covering sports. Cramer interviewed 19 female sports journalists, each with an average of 11 years' experience, about their jobs and about women's sports coverage. The women who were interviewed expressed ambivalence about their careers, citing excitement of the beat and travel as reasons for staying with their jobs but the demands on their time as a drawback. Most said their supervisors supported them but also that they had been sexually harassed or assaulted on the job. Others described difficulties in gaining interviews with athletes who refused to talk to female reporters. The women also saw covering women's sports as a way to stall their careers because of the low status of women's sports in their newsrooms. They believed that, as more women entered sports departments, the stature of women's sports would inevitably increase.

Survey research of women in the industry

Miller and Miller were among the first to publish the first of a handful of studies surveying members of the AWSM about their experiences covering sports. The scholars asked the members about their experiences in newsrooms, interacting with reporters, editors, and managers. Generally, respondents characterized sexual discrimination and even harassment as routine. When women are hired, "[T]hey are expected to know less and adhere to higher standards of performance while tolerating lower salaries, less desirable assignments, and sexist comments in the workplace" (Miller and Miller, 1995, p. 888). In a survey of 89 AWSM members several years later for a master's thesis (Hoshino, 1998), respondents expressed frustration at being passed over for promotions and at salary inequities. Almost half (48 percent) of respondents also reported being sexually harassed, oftentimes by sources and in locker rooms.

Studies since 2000 generally echoed the findings of earlier research. Smucker, *et al.*'s (2003) survey of AWSM members who work at daily newspapers found that, although they expressed general satisfaction with their careers, they were not satisfied with the opportunities for advancement. A survey of 144 AWSM members by Hardin and Shain, (2006a), found similar results. Most said they were satisfied with their jobs, but more than half reported having experienced sexual discrimination in the newsroom and in the field when reporting stories. A strong majority (85 percent) said they believed that discrimination was a barrier for women in the field. Respondents also noted long hours, relatively low pay, and a lack of opportunities for advancement as reasons they considered leaving the profession (Hardin and Shain, 2005). Hardin and Shain, who also assessed the career spans of the participants, observed that the average career span for women in the field was short; only a few persisted for more than ten years.

Hardin and Shain also conducted focus groups with women who worked in sports journalism at varying levels. Participants, who ranged in age from 25 to 60, described the work they did in positive terms: "It's an unbelievably rewarding and exciting profession" (Hardin and Shain, 2005, p. 28) one participant said, which was typical of responses about the nature of work covering sports. They saw gender-related discrimination as a routine part of the job, however. They also believed that efforts by sports departments to hire a woman in order to diversify worked to help them secure entry-level jobs; however, they felt that once hired, they were under constant pressure to "prove themselves" (Hardin and Shain, 2005, p. 29) and were unlikely to be promoted.

Studies on demographics and hiring

The first scholarly studies aimed at providing a baseline understanding of the demographics in newspaper sports departments and whether women were not, indeed, likely to be promoted, was not published until 2006. Until that point, the ratio of women to men covering sports had not been systematically tracked. An informal survey by Associated Press Sports Editors (APSE) in 1999 found that only ten percent of sports reporters were women (Skwar, 1999). Another informal survey of 50 newspaper sports departments in 2001 showed that women constituted about 13 percent of employees, and just two of the 50 sports departments had a female sports editor (Etling, 2002). Research indicates that many sports editors (41 percent, according to a 2005 survey) believe they do not have an ethical obligation to increase the number of women working in sports departments (Hardin, 2005).

Two empirical studies looking at sports department demographics were published in 2006. Hardin and Whiteside (2006) surveyed sports departments at the top 200 circulation US newspapers and found that just 11 percent of all sports-department personnel were women. Newspapers with the highest circulations (more than 250,000) employed a slightly higher percentage of women: 13 percent. Overall, one in ten women was in a supervisory role; most were reporters. Another study published the same year, but surveying members of the APSE, an industry group of 300 newspapers, found that women were almost 13 percent of total staffs for those publications that participated (Lapchick, Brenden, and Wright, 2006). Lapchick and colleagues' most recent study of participating APSE-member sports departments, published in 2010, found that women were about 11 percent of all sports staffers (Lapchick, Moss II, Russell, and Scearce, 2010). Far less research has been conducted on the ratio of women to men in television sports production; one study, in 2006, put the percentage of women working in sports in the top-50 US television markets at 11 percent (Hardin, Genovese, and Yu, 2009).

Sports departments are far less diverse, in terms of their ratio of women, than other areas of the newsroom. Demographic data for US newsrooms shows large differences in the representation of women in various roles. In 2006, for example, women constituted 40 percent of reporters across all areas of the newsroom, compared with just ten percent in sports. The biggest disparity is in supervisory roles, where, in 2006, women comprised more than one-third of editors in other parts of the newsroom (compared with seven percent in sports; Hardin and Whiteside, 2006).

Theorizing women's subordinate status

Scholars who have studied the working conditions for female journalists suggest that sports departments are a space within newsrooms where a number of complex dynamics intersect – including those involving the norms of news production and cultural understandings of sport – to create unique challenges for women (Hall, 1996; Miloch, Pedersen, Smucker, and Whisenant, 2005; Staurowsky and DiManno, 2002). For instance, a survey of sports editors found that about a quarter of participants believed that women are naturally less athletic than men and half of those surveyed saw Title IX as "unjust to men's sports" (Hardin, 2005, p. 73). These attitudes reflect the process of hegemonic masculinity, or the "pattern of practice" that upholds male privilege and contributes to the maintenance of patriarchy (Connell and Messerschmidt, 2005, p. 832). Hegemonic masculinity stems from the more general notion of hegemony, a theory first conceptualized by the Italian theorist Antonio Gramsci that refers to the process by which individuals consent to their own domination and internalize certain ideology as commonsense and natural. Importantly, hegemony does not mean control via force, and indeed, Gramsci was most interested in the process by which working-class individuals during the industrial period appeared to willingly subscribe to prevailing norms about their class status and, despite their overwhelming numbers, accept their role as subordinates to an elite few.

Hegemonic masculinity

Sports are often described as a hegemonic institution because its organizational practices and discursive frameworks function to normalize women's inferiority and continually provide the justification for their (accepted) marginalization. Going further, sports are a space in which an ideal type of masculinity is celebrated; examples include the visibility and cultural primacy bestowed on men's sports in which strength and power are fully on display, the glorification of athletes who play through pain, as well as the militaristic narratives that often encompass major sporting events. Over time this pageantry transforms sporting spaces into essentially male spaces, making women's inclusion seem illogical and unwarranted (Messner, 2002). Further, because gender is conceptualized as two concepts on opposite ends of a binary pole, women face cultural sanctions for embodying masculine traits. Ultimately, the celebration of all things masculine is protected as a benefit that only men earn the privilege of enjoying. Stereotypes about the "butch" female athlete are one reflection of how such ideology functions as a lens through which meaning is constructed (Griffin, 1998). Such commonsense logic about women's lack of fit in sports explains the challenges that women face in sports media careers, and it is this deployment of such ideology over time that undergirds the maintenance of hegemonic masculinity.

Regarding hegemonic masculinity in sports journalism, overtly sexist discourse still occurs (for example, MLB, 2012); such discourse invites viewers to consider women not as capable and professional figures in sports but as sexual objects, and, more generally, reasserts men as the rightful embodiment of athleticism. However, overtly sexist discourse is generally frowned upon in a day and age where girls are routinely educated about their limitless potential in all fields, including those traditionally dominated by men. Thus, the expression of hegemonic masculinity is often more subtle. One oft-cited example is the relative paucity of women's sports content published or aired by sports media outlets. The lack of visibility given to women's sports conveys a lack of legitimacy, and is a practice that renders men's sports as "authentic sports, and women's a pale comparison" (Duncan, 2006, p. 236). Sports journalism practices and value systems function in a similar way. In long interviews, Hardin and Shain (2006b) noted how women in the industry recognized their lack of power and inability to gain respect on men's terms. At the same time, however, the women in their study used gendered labels to criticize women who did succeed – describing those women as "too bossy" or as using their sexuality in unethical ways (Hardin and Shain, 2006b, p. 335). Because the pursuit of power was seen as violating gender norms, it was ultimately rendered as a negative ambition for women. When dominant ideology functions as a lens for meaning-making in a way that privileges men as it did in this case, the hegemony in the sports department "retains its power" (Hardin and Shain, 2006b, p. 335). Dominant ideology also provides justification for a division of labor that favors men. Women are often denied opportunities for covering high profile assignments, like the World Series (Ricchiardi, 2005). Further, survey data has shown that women feel pigeonholed into covering women's sports; in the male-defined culture of sports journalism, such sports are considered lower value, and thus low-status beats (Cramer, 1994; Miloch, *et al.*, 2005). Access to highly valued assignments (men's sports) is critical to the promotion process, making a gendered division of labor especially problematic for women.

The process by which women's marginalization is normalized, also happens through the deployment of ideology related to workplace routines considered commonsense. Women may be viewed as ill-fitted for leadership positions because of prevailing norms related to the news production process in which reporters are expected to be available at all times (Robinson, 2005). When hours at work are privileged over quality work output, total availability is then transformed into competence; doing so puts individuals with families and other non-work priorities at a decided disadvantage. Furthermore, in sports, most events happen at nights and weekends, a time when the primary caretaker is usually required to be home with children. Despite cultural shifts in attitudes toward childrearing, women still report a pessimistic outlook about the prospect of raising a family and building a successful career in sports journalism (Hardin and Whiteside, 2009; Hardin, Shain, and Poniatowski, 2008). The lack of institutional childcare support, combined with ideology that dictates women as naturally better suited as the primary caretaker function simultaneously to create unique challenges for women in an environment where total allegiance to the profession is considered a hallmark of the ideal worker.

Tokenism

Research has demonstrated that few women stay in sports journalism over the entirety of their professional careers; these high turnover rates are consistent with scholarship on tokenism, which examines the experiences of minorities in group settings. Tokens are often viewed as representatives of a category and are evaluated based on stereotypes of the category they represent (Kanter, 2003). This process explains why so many women in sports journalism report feeling pressure to prove their worth. Lingering stereotypes about women's lack of athletic aptitude and knowledge related to sports in general create a set of expectations that women must overcome as long as they occupy a token status. As one woman explained to researchers about her early days on the job, "I felt right away that I needed to prove myself because I wanted them to respect me as their equal and as someone who had equal sports knowledge as them" (Hardin and Whiteside, 2009, p. 637). In an open-ended question on a survey by Miloch, *et al.* (2005), female sports reporters were asked about advice they would give young women; the top answer was "know your stuff," a comment that hearkens to questions about women's competence in sports (Miloch, *et al.*, 2005, p. 227). Men are not subject to such evaluations, as their sports knowledge is considered a given by way of their gender, an example of a type of invisible privilege enjoyed by men.

As a symbol of difference, tokens are highly visible; Kanter (2003) suggests that tokens respond to that visibility in three ways, including: 1) over-achieving in order to assuage concerns about their competence; 2) seeking ways to turn their visibility into an advantage; and 3) working to blend in and thereby minimize their difference. Because of their minority status, it is a risk to challenge dominant workplace value systems and indeed, much research on women in sports journalism has noted the ways in which women appear to subscribe to cultural norms that otherwise cement their outsider status. In interviews, female sports journalists resist indicting problematic workplace cultures and instead focus on adapting to issues like perceived gender discrimination. Doing so allows women to assimilate and – as much as possible – essentially minimize their difference. Hardin and Shain (2006b, p. 331) also noted how women in their study used the idea of developing a "thick skin" as a coping mechanism when facing questions about their competence.

Others may actively work to position their gender as an advantage. For example, women have described seeing their gender as a useful tool in garnering interviews their many male colleagues may be otherwise unable to secure; although such strategies may provide a short-term benefit, they also ultimately limit the possibilities of increased gender diversity. After all, if being a "scarce commodity" as a female sports journalist is an advantage, there is no motivation among women to relinquish that advantage. Furthermore, allowing sexist jokes to continue unabated, or coping with unwarranted criticism of one's aptitude by ignoring it, may create a sense of acceptance, but also facilitates the maintenance of a system that delegitimizes women's status (Claringbould, Knoppers, and Elling, 2004).

Hegemony is at its most powerful when individuals see the opportunity for resistance as futile and accept the given power structure as natural. The resistance among women to challenging sexual harassment and discrimination noted by Hardin (2005), Miller and Miller (1995), and others is evidence of how hegemony works. Women should not be blamed for failing to take a more activist role, however; as tokens they have little power to challenge a system that in many ways is organized to normalize their outsider status.

In working to relieve women from the pressures of token status, scholars have advocated increased attention to diverse hiring practices. The industry has followed suit and the lack of diversity is an issue that is routinely discussed in industry publications. Yet, improvements in gender diversity have not materialized. One reason may be the practice of homologous reproduction, or the process of hiring individuals that match the characteristics of those making such employment decisions (Whisenant and Mullane, 2007). Given that (white) men occupy the vast majority of leadership and authority positions in sports journalism, attention should be given to how this process may be manifest in sports. Related, women have reported feeling on the outside of informal networks; these types of (male-dominated) groups are essential to gaining access to opportunities that may lead to promotions (Kanter, 2003).

Conclusions: Remedies for change

Scholars have suggested several remedies for addressing the ongoing problems facing women in the industry. As tokens, women hold little power and face great risks in challenging workplace value systems that privilege men. It is no wonder that few women cite sexual harassment or gender discrimination as reasons for leaving the industry. The recognition about their lack of power may also explain why aspiring sports journalists resist labeling themselves as feminists (Staurowsky and DiManno, 2002).

However, research has noted that once tokens reach a critical mass of 15 percent of any given group, change becomes more realistic (Grey, 2002). Thus, the tandem goals of hiring, coupled with a focus on retention, may aid women in reaching a critical mass in sports journalism. Once they do so, women may feel safer in challenging comments or practices that question their legitimacy. A critical mass may also help raise awareness of issues uniquely facing women. A longitudinal study has shown that female sports journalists routinely report feeling pessimistic about the prospect of balancing work and family (Hardin, Shain and Poniatowski, 2008; Hardin and Whiteside, 2009). Women have suggested that flex-time or on-site childcare would help in that regard (although such programs would have to be used by everyone – men in included – or as Hardin, *et al.* (2008) point out, they would simply function to further mark women's difference).

Perhaps a less obvious challenge facing women is gaining access to informal networks. Kanter (1977, p. 181) notes that, often in organizations, lower-level workers are aided through what she calls "sponsorship" from someone in a leadership position. The sponsor aids in everything from mentorship to more informal assistance, including creating opportunities for networking, social invitations, and so on. Sponsorship is extraordinarily valuable in that it is an outward indicator of an association with power; although such a relationship is important for all workers, it may be especially so for women, who "need even more the signs of such influence and the access to real power provided by sponsors" (Kanter, 1977, p. 183). Because, as Claringbould, *et al.* (2004, p. 710) note, sports journalism is so "skewed" in favor of (white) men, it is critical that advocacy groups work to create sponsorship opportunities for women. One such group is AWSM, and scholars such as Hardin and Shain (2006a) and others have encouraged the organization to continue its efforts to fill this void. Staurowsky and DiManno also urge faculty members to consider the issues presented in this chapter when advising female students. They suggest faculty work toward uncovering internships that may be especially hospitable to women, and address these issues with potential employers. Most importantly, they urge faculty to avoid leaving young female sports journalists "to take on the system in isolation" (Staurowsky and DiManno, 2002, p. 154).

Although these ideas may provide a short-term benefit, improving opportunities for women in sports journalism may only happen once commonsense understandings about gender and sports change (Hardin, *et al.*, 2008; Hardin and Shain, 2006b). Advocating for increased and better women's sports coverage may be one way such a shift could occur; seeing more women engaged in athletic pursuits – especially strength sports in which women use their bodies in powerful ways – disrupts cultural norms about sports and gender that may prove liberating for women. However, when women are covered, too often their athleticism is downplayed in favor of narratives that showcase normative femininity. The *Sports Illustrated* 2010 Olympics preview issue is one example (Russo, 2010). In putting Lindsay Vonn on its cover, the magazine made a pointed shift in its practice of featuring male athletes nearly exclusively (Bishop, 2003). Yet Vonn's athleticism was not on display; rather, the image hinted at her sexuality and invited the viewer to consume Vonn as an object, rather than an active, athletic subject. Discourse that consistently downplays women's athleticism guards against challenges to male superiority in sports and normalizes women's outsider status. Interestingly, more women in the industry may provide an antidote to problematic depictions of female athletes (for example, in a content analysis, Kian and Hardin (2009) found that women used less stereotypical frames when covering female athletes compared with men). Changing the way women's sports are covered is critical to addressing the persistent lack of diversity in sports journalism. Ultimately, as Hardin and Shain (2006b) note, women are unlikely to earn acceptance in sports journalism until they earn acceptance in sports.

References

Bishop, R. (2003). Missing in action: Feature coverage of women's sports in *Sports Illustrated*. *Journal of Sport and Social Issues*, 27 (2), 184–94.

Claringbould, I., Knoppers, A., and Elling, A. (2004). Exclusionary practices in sport journalism. *Sex Roles*, 51 (11/12), 709–18.

Connell, R. W., and Messerschmidt, J. W. (2005). Hegemonic masculinity: Rethinking the concept. *Gender and Society*, 19 (6), 829–59.

Cramer, J. (1994). Conversations with women sports journalists. In P. Creedon (Ed.), *Women, media and sport: Challenging gender values* (pp. 159–80). Thousand Oaks, CA: Sage.

Duncan, M. C. (2006). Gender warriors in sport: Women and the media. In R. Raney and J. Bryant (Eds.), *Handbook of sports and media* (pp. 231–52). Mahwah, NJ: Lawrence Erlbaum.

Etling, L. (2002). An uphill climb. APSE Special Report. *Dallas Morning News*, June. Retrieved from http://archive.apsportseditors.org/jun2002/5-7etling.html.

Fornoff, S. (1993). *Lady in the locker room: Uncovering the Oakland Athletics*. Urbana, IL: Sagamore.

Gerstner, J. (2005, April). Women aren't getting a fair shake in sports, either. *Editor and Publisher* 138 (4), 5.

Gordon, A. (1984). *Foul balls: Five years in the American League*. Toronto: McClelland and Stewart.

Grey, S. (2002). Does size matter? Critical mass and New Zealand's women MPs. *Parliamentary Affairs*, 55, 19–29.

Griffin, P. (1998). *Strong women, deep closets: Lesbians and homophobia in sport*. Champaign, IL: Human Kinetics.

Hall, A. (1996) *Feminism and sporting bodies: Essays on theory and practice*. Champaign, IL: Human Kinetics.

Hardin, M. (2005). Stopped at the gate: Women's sports, "reader interest," and decision making by editors. *Journalism and Mass Communication Quarterly*, 82 (1), 62–77.

Hardin, M., and Shain, S. (2005). Female sports journalists: Are we there yet? 'No.' *Newspaper Research Journal*, 26 (4), 22–35.

Hardin, M., and Shain, S. (2006a). Strength in numbers? The experiences and attitudes of women in sports media careers. *Journalism and Mass Communication Quarterly*, 82 (4), 804–19.

Hardin, M., and Shain, S. (2006b). "Feeling much smaller than you know you are": The fragmented professional identity of female sports journalists. *Critical Studies in Media Communication*, 23 (4), 322–38.

Hardin, M., and Whiteside, E. (2006). Fewer women, minorities work in sports departments. *Newspaper Research Journal*, 27 (2), 38–51.

Hardin, M., and Whiteside, E. (2009). Token responses to gendered newsrooms: Factors in the career-related decisions of female newspaper sports journalists. *Journalism*, 10, 627–46.

Hardin, M., Genovese, J., and Yu, N. (2009). Privileged to be on camera: Sports broadcasters assess the role of social identity in the profession. *Electronic News*, 3 (2), 80–93.

Hardin, M., Shain, S., and Poniatowski, K. (2008). There's no sex attached to your occupation: The revolving door for young women in sports journalism. *Women in Sport and Physical Activity Journal*, 17, 68–79.

Hoshino, K. (1998). *Job satisfaction and status of women sports journalists.* Master's thesis, California State University, Fresno.

Kanter, R. (1977). *Men and women of the organization.* New York: Basic Books.

Kanter, R. (2003). Men and women of the corporation. In R. J. Ely, E. G. Foldy, and M. A. Scully (Eds.), *Reader in gender, work, and organization* (pp. 34–48). Malden, MA: Blackwell.

Kian, E. M., and Hardin, M. (2009). Framing of sport coverage based on the sex of sports writers: Female journalists counter the traditional gendering of media coverage. *International Journal of Sport Communication*, 2, 185–204.

Lapchick, R., Brenden, J., and Wright, B. (2006). *The 2006 racial and gender report card of the Associated Press Sports Editors.* College of Business Administration, University of Central Florida. Retrieved from http://web.bus.ucf.edu/sportbusiness/?page=1445.

Lapchick, R., Moss II, A., Russell, C., and Scearce, R. (2010). *The 2010–11 Associated Press Sports Editors racial and gender report card.* College of Business Administration, University of Central Florida. [www.tidesport.org/RGRC/2011/2011_APSE_RGRC_FINAL.pdf.

Messner, M. A. (2002). *Taking the field: Women, men, and sports.* Minneapolis: University of Minnesota Press.

Miller, P., and Miller, R. (1995). The invisible woman: Female sports journalists in the workplace. *Journalism and Mass Communication Quarterly*, 72, 883–9.

Miloch, K., Pedersen, P. M., Smucker , M. K., and Whisenant, W. A. (2005). The current state of women print journalists: An analysis of the status and careers of females in newspaper sports departments. *Public Organization Review: A Global Journal*, 5 (3), 219–31.

MLB. (2012). Ball girl makes nice grab. *MLB.com*, June 20. Retrieved from http://mlb.mlb.com/video/play.jsp?content_id=22457337.

Ricchiardi, S. (2005). Offensive interference. American Journalism Review, January, 58–62.

Robinson, G. J. (2005). *Gender, journalism and equity: Canadian, US, and European perspectives.* Cresskill, NJ: Hampton.

Russo, M. (2010). It's all about Vonn anatomy. *Minneapolis Star-Tribune*, February 11. Retrieved from http://www.startribune.com/sports/olympics/84073732.html?elr=KArksi8cyaiUg7Kk8P3iUiD3aPc:_Yyc:aUU.

Skwar, D. (1999). Women's sports gain the spotlight. *APSE Newsletter*, August: 14.

Smucker, M. K., Whisenant, W. A., and Pedersen, P. M. (2003). An investigation of job satisfaction and female sports journalists. *Sex Roles*, 49, 401–7.

Staurowsky, E. J., and DiManno, J. (2002). Young women talking sports and careers: A glimpse at the next generation of women in sport media. *Women in Sport and Physical Activity Journal*, 11, 127–41.

Whisenant, W. A., and Mullane, S. P. (2007). Sports information directors and homologous reproduction. *International Journal of Sport Management and Marketing*, 2 (3), 252–63.

16

UNDERSTANDING THE BIGGEST SHOW IN MEDIA

What the Olympic Games communicates to the world

Andrew C. Billings and Natalie Brown

In an age of fragmented media consumption, the anomalies are the media offerings that still offer tremendous demographic reach. Programs such as *American Idol* and *Dancing with the Stars* draw a multitude of ages and backgrounds within a weekly viewership of 20–25 million Americans (Seidman, 2011). The Super Bowl offers a singular yearly rating that is the envy of all US media content, drawing over 100 million viewers, regardless of the teams that are playing or the media markets in which they reside. The men's FIFA World Cup soccer tournament offers reach beyond a single nation, with billions of people watching at least part of a game (FIFA Online, 2011). However, one consistent major player within all megasports (and mega-media) offerings has been the Olympic telecast. In a variety of ways, the Olympics represents the most epic scope of all: billions of people watching among virtually every nation, over 200 different nations competing, and 17 consecutive days in which the Olympic telecast dominates all media coverage: often morning, afternoon, evening, and late-night (Billings, 2008).

Because of the tremendous size and diversity of the audience within a plethora of media formats (television, newspaper, Internet, magazines, radio, and more), a great deal of scholarly examination has been devoted to the manner in which the Olympics are conveyed worldwide as well as the lessons we can learn from these depictions (see Real, 1989; Puijk, 1997). These discussions have involved issues such as politics (Espy, 1979; Larson and Park, 1993), power (Larson and Park, 1993; Schaffer and Smith, 2000), gender (Toohey, 1997; Billings, 2008), nationalism (Bairner, 2001; Billings and Angelini, 2007), ethnic representation (Hartmann, 1996; Sabo, Jansen, Tate, Duncan, and Leggett, 1996), (dis)ability (Brittain, 2009), and many, many more. In essence, these scholars collectively argue that sport is not just a microcosm of society, but that society is a microcosm of sport; to learn about the Olympics is to learn about the state of the world today (see Dayan and Katz, 1992) – the issues that matter to us and the manner in which we discuss them.

In many ways, the "Olympic ideal" runs counter to these discussions as academicians have analyzed them. This "ideal" argues that individuals, rather than nations, can compete every four years without restriction based on their politics, identity, or economic status. However, when the competition is actually held, media gatekeepers (and, increasing, at-home enthusiasts turned social media producers) describe the competitions within troubling terms of "us" vs. "them" and "hero" vs. "villain". This chapter will provide the broad strokes of Olympic media coverage by outlining (a) Olympic production tendencies, (b) Olympic media content trends, (c) Olympic effects research findings, and (d) paths for better understanding of what the Olympics communicates to the world.

Production messages

Viewers/consumers comprehend Olympic events by incorporating established media frames (Goffman, 1974) during the telecast of the Olympic Games. These media frames jointly work to showcase the unique blend of culture, politics, national pride, and sporting spectacle that defines the Olympics. Sportscasters and producers use these frames to package the rhetorical narratives of the Olympic Games, helping viewers to interpret and evaluate the information they are receiving (Neuman, Just, and Crigler, 1992). Consistent with foundational tenets of agenda setting theory (McCombs and Shaw, 1972), viewers are subconsciously triggered to conclude which competitions and athletes are "newsworthy" according to their relayed prominence in the media (for example, the hour in which they are shown on television, the prominence/salience of a headline or webpage; Eastman and Billings, 2000) as well as the extent of coverage devoted to them (such as the article or airtime length; Adams and Tuggle, 2004).

Compared with content and effects research, relatively little has been ascertained to understand how production choices are made and whether macro-level impacts on societal attitudes are as much a part of the equation as ratings, timing, and economic realities. Still, two major messages can be articulated about Olympic media production.

Production message #1

The first production message is that advanced preparation allows for the funneling from virtually infinite (number of Olympic stories) to finite (number of programming hours). Television producers make overt decisions regarding which competitions to highlight and which to exclude based on ratings and demographic breakdowns internal to those ratings. NBC, the US network that has possessed exclusive broadcast rights to the Games since 2000, has dispersed Olympic content across multiple channels, developing another way to signal importance of certain sports. The option of showing events on either network or ancillary cable channels (such as MSNBC, USA, Bravo) allows producers to focus their base/home network (NBC) coverage on events that maintain the largest demographic desires (such as swimming, gymnastics, figure skating), while not eliminating sports that might be geared for a more targeted/niche audience (like boxing, curling, bobsledding).

These production decisions of what to show (selection), what to show a lot of (emphasis), and what to leave out (exclusion), shape the Olympic experience of viewers/consumers (Gitlin, 1980). The Olympics provides millions of viewers with a dynamic spectacle filled with dramatic events of humans achieving impossible feats in the unpredictable environment of sport (Morris and Nydahl, 1985). Yet, Olympic producers and broadcasters believe they never prioritize drama and spectacle at the expense of an unbalanced broadcast.

Little research has truly been able to tap into the mediated Olympic production mechanism, but we do have some basic parameters uncovered in the previous scholarly work that does exist. The planning for each Olympic broadcast begins seven years prior to the start of the Games when the host nation is selected. Olympic producers must identify "big ticket" events at each Olympic venue and program them in a way to acquire the largest possible audience for the greatest possible duration, even if the result is a significantly tape-delayed version of the Games that NBC refers to as "plausibly live" (Billings, 2008, p. 50). This massive "jigsaw puzzle" (p. 85) will, hopefully, render main storylines that will help attract and maintain large audiences.

With well over 10,000 athletes from over 200 countries competing on the world's grandest stage during the Summer Games and over 2,600 athletes from over 80 nations competing in the Winter Games (International Olympic Committee, 2011), the Olympics has a virtually limitless number of potential storylines that must be addressed by producers. The editorial staff consists of writers and producers who select stories that they believe should be conveyed to the audience through profiling or promoting certain athletes leading up to their competition date. The editorial staff identifies the stories that *must* be told, the stories that *should* be told, and the stories that *could* be told if time permits (Billings, 2008, p. 38). In 2008, Michael Phelps' pursuit of a record eight gold medals in swimming was obviously promoted as one of the main storylines of the Beijing Olympics. Advanced promotion of this storyline paid big dividends for NBC producers (in the form of ratings and perceived prescience), while many others have not (such as hyping Michelle Kwan in the 2006 Games only to have her withdraw with an injury before the Opening Ceremonies.)

Production Message #2

The second production message is that "Heroes vs. villains" is an acceptable construct; "us vs. them" is not. As George Orwell famously summarized, international sport represents "war without shooting" (cited in Billings, 2008, p. 11). This remains a chief concern among Olympic producers: producing a broadcast free of biased reports and commentary. In fact, NBC Coordinating Producer Molly Solomon identified that NBC's "cardinal rule" prohibits the use of personal pronouns (like "we," "us," and so on) to refer to American teams or athletes (Billings, 2008, p. 44), a tendency that many other countries readily employ (Billings, Angelini, and Wu, 2011). Producers believe this "us vs. them" prohibition relates NBC's production goals of chronicling history rather than relaying an Americentric rendering.

However, Langer (1981) wrote that sports media often places athletes in traditional storytelling roles of protagonist and antagonist constructions that form interesting narratives used to captivate audiences. In the 2008 Olympics, China expressed their intention to beat the United States in the medal count, thereby showcasing their status as a major world power (Billings, *et al.*, 2011). Producers complied with this story by displaying on-screen medal counts for the first time in recent history, presumably justified as *reporting* a story that created protagonists and antagonists rather than *creating* this dichotomy.

Often, the creation of heroes and villains presents ties to gender and ethnic impacts as well. For instance, the need to promote interesting, new, compelling stories inevitably includes women athletes in a fair greater share than other forms of sports media, even if there is still a historical gender gap that exists in coverage (Duncan, 2006). The story-hero dynamic creates interesting stories from racialized points of view as well. Producers claim that the richness of a story drives coverage more so than an athlete's ethnicity, yet sometimes ethnicity provides part of the richness to the story itself. In the cases of Vonetta Flowers (bobsledding) and Shani Davis (speed skating), being the first black Americans to win gold medals in their respective sports created winning storylines for the broadcast. Through it all, NBC producers maintain a belief that their telecast is the "least jingoistic of all modern Olympic coverage" through its commentary (Billings, *et al.*, 2011, p. 255). Yet, the realities of whether this is true is played out in the larger amount of literature related to Olympic content.

Content messages

By far the largest area of Olympic media research involves analysis of on-air content, at least partly because mass events such as the Olympics are "easily related to myriad issues concerning socialization, interpersonal communication, value formation, racial and gender assessments, and the balance of political power" (Wenner, 1989, p. 16). Thus, decades of research have been focused on how these types of issues manifest within the overarching dialogue surrounding the Olympics, particularly within the 23 percent of coverage that is not deemed "play-by-play" but rather "color" commentary (Bryant, Comisky, and Zillmann., 1977). Repeatedly, issues of representation and cultural transformation (see Whannel, 1992) become problematic within Olympic media when analyzed through an identity-oriented lens. In contrast with the previous section on Olympic media production – where conclusions are meager when determining the messages explicitly or implicitly sent to the masses, there are three macro-level messages often relayed in Olympic media content.

Content message #1

The first content message is that it is okay to promote your home country, as long as you are not xenophobic about it. The most consistent and perhaps problematic finding within these content analyses involves the degree in which Olympic media offerings are altered to promote national identities over larger, Olympic ideals (see Min and Zhen, 2010). Real (1989) studied the extent of nationalism within a variety of Olympic media forms and throughout a multitude of nations, concluding that the question was not *whether* home nations would be made more salient through greater promotion, hype, and perceived drama but rather the *extent* to which a home nation is promoted. He found that all nations promoted their athletes at rates substantially higher than their achievements would warrant, but that some nations did so at rates five times higher than others. In more recent analyses, Billings (2008) reported that the United States coverage on NBC always hyped American athletes at a higher rate than medals would warrant, but American athletes were highlighted triple that expected rate in the Winter Games and more than quadruple that rate in the Summer Games.

Thus, nationalism becomes the proverbial "fly in the ointment" of internationalized sports such as the Olympics (Sabo, *et al.*, 1996, p. 19), and that promotion happens regardless of nation (see Allison, 2000). The question becomes whether the coverage becomes egregiously nationalistic using personal pronoun and "us vs. them" dichotomies or whether the biases are not necessarily promoting the nation as much as shifting the amount of media exposure to gain higher ratings and advertiser rates.

Content message #2

The second content message is that women will not be described as equals to men, but they will be highlighted far more favorably than in any other sport. Whether one is examining the Winter Olympic telecast (in which women are shown approximately 40 percent of the time in the US; Billings and Angelini, 2007) or the Summer Olympic telecast (in which women are shown 48 percent of the time in the US; Billings and Angelini, 2007) one can conclude two things: (a) women are not shown as much as men and (b) this is still far better than any other form of sports media representation. Previous studies have found that women receive proportional coverage in the single digits in sports news programs (Adams and Tuggle, 2004), newspapers (Eastman and Billings, 2000), and overall media exposure (Messner and Cooky, 2010). The 1996 Olympics was promoted in the United States as the "Games of the Women," largely because it occurred 24 years after Title IX legislation produced a new generation of women who matured as athletes in a more robust environment for women's sports. Yet, proportions remain remarkably steady, showing that women receive a solid share of coverage, and yet not an equal amount when compared with men.

Olympic coverage has also not been revealed as overtly sexist the way other forms of sports media have been known to be (Davis, 1997; Messner, 1993). However, Olympic coverage has been frequently offered in ways that nonetheless covertly undermine the efforts of women athletes. What was previously dubbed a dichotomy of the "pretty vs. the powerful" (Jones, Murrell, and Jackson, 1999) is now far more nuanced, with different forms of divergent dialogue being revealed in each Olympics. The most common of these themes has involved the hyping of men's successes because of perceived strength and experience advantages while promoting the notion that females fail because of their lack of composure (see Billings, Angelini, and Duke, 2010; Tuggle, Huffman, and Rosengard, 2007). Such linguistic differences can undermine the achievements of women athletes, even at this pinnacle of athletic achievement, simply by employing different types of words in a sports media telecast (see Halbert and Latimer, 1994).

Content message #3

The third content message is that race will be something seen but not spoken about in an Olympic Games. Given the sensitive nature of discussing race and ethnicity within any form of societal interaction, one can understand why sports producers and announcers are reluctant to share insight about the subject to the masses. Nonetheless, the avoidance of this topic is quite troubling, particularly when noting how scholars have found that athletes of different ethnicities are described in "color-coded" (Rada and Wulfemeyer, 2005, p. 65) manners (see also Hoberman, 2007; Wonsek, 1992).

When asked about race, even NBC President of Sports and Olympics, Dick Ebersol, treated the issue as important, but not something to dwell on, noting that: "Whatever's about to come out of my mouth will be the first time that I've ever even thought about this" (Billings, 2008, p. 49). Content analyses have nonetheless shown ethnic differences, but such studies (see Billings and Eastman, 2003; Billings and Angelini, 2007) noted limitations in (a) the lack of relative ethnic diversity in the Winter Games (with over 85 percent of athletes identifying as "white" and making cross-race comparisons difficult to statistically determine) and (b) linguistic differences in the Summer Games could just as easily be the result of event stacking (given that the ethnic composition of athletes competing in the 100m swimming final is nearly a polar opposite of the 100m track final). In sum, virtually all parties involved in Olympic media ranging from producers and announcers to at-home viewers agree that race and ethnicity are important issues, yet these topics receive little focus within the Olympic telecast.

Effects messages

While content analyses reveal systematic differences within Olympic telecasts, it is imperative to understand the effects these skewed renderings have on an audience. Gerbner, Gross, Morgan, and Signorelli (1986) detailed how biased messages that are present in media affect both light and heavy viewers of the Games. When applied to Olympic research, heavier viewers of the Olympics are more likely than light viewers to align their views more closely with the messages being presented during the telecast (Billings, 2008). While studies have shown that viewer behaviors can be affected by televised sports programming (Gantz and Wenner, 1991), there is also evidence that these biased mediated messages do not always cause the audience to accept that specific version of Olympic "reality" (Billings and Angelini, 2007; Tuggle and Owen, 1999).

The Olympic telecast exposes millions of Americans to multiple hours of programming per day; thus, affording an unparalleled opportunity for prolonged exposure to mediated messages. Audiences can also regard NBC's telecast of the Olympic Games as chronicling history. Viewers are drawn to the unpredictable nature of the Games that present the inherent drama of watching athletes attempt great physical achievements. This combination of prolonged exposure and realism of content has the potential power to cause dramatic attitudinal shifts within the audience (Bandura, 1986; Potter, 1986), leading to our three messages that Olympic media conveys to the word regarding effects.

Effects message #1

The first effects message is that the Olympic telecast facilitates nationalistic pride that can cause an audience to overestimate its nation's success. As previously mentioned, content analyses have revealed that American men receive more coverage during the Olympic Games than American women, and white athletes are shown much more frequently than athletes of other races. While NBC works to include compelling stories from other nation's athletes, it cannot be ignored that the primary focus of the telecast and the audience lies in how American athletes fare in each competition. Therefore, it should come as no surprise that when asked to recall the number of medals won during the 2006 Torino Winter Olympics, respondents believed that 30 percent of medals were won by the United States, almost three times the 11 percent of the awarded medals the US actually won (Billings, 2008). This result added to the belief that the Olympic telecast can foster a sense of self-importance stemming from a false belief that a home nation is performing dramatically better than it actually is.

However, distance from the Games only resulted in an escalated form of this effect; respondents who were questioned four weeks after the Closing Ceremonies guessed that the US won the 33.9 percent of medals. Over time, the actual results viewers witnessed during the Olympic Games diminished from memory. The results faded; the nationalistic feelings amplified.

Effects message #2

The second effects message is that audiences believe Olympic content is skewed toward US men athletes because they are more successful than US women athletes. Olympic viewers have also been asked to evaluate the perceived gender gap in Olympic coverage (Billings, 2008). When asked what the gender gap was within the 2006 Torino coverage, both light and heavy viewers gave approximations that were within one percentage point of the actual gender gap in coverage. Men athletes received 60 percent of the coverage and audiences roughly knew this. Yet, the interesting component regarding gender in the telecast is found when viewers were asked to approximate the number of medals won by both US men and US women. Respondents approximated that male athletes won 54.5 percent of the awarded Olympic medals. However, in reality, male athletes accounted for 44 percent of awarded medals in Torino. Thus, there is another gap between the audience's perception and reality. Clearly, Olympic viewers understand that they are watching coverage that features more male athletes than female athletes. Yet, they assume the gender gap is directly attributed to the performances of male and female athletes. Audiences have formed an inaccurate causal relationship between clock-time and medal counts.

Effects message #3

The third effects message is that audiences perceive the Winter Olympic Games to be much more ethnically diverse than they are in reality. The largest difference between audience perception and Olympic reality occurred in the estimated amount of ethnic diversity among Olympic medalists (Billings, 2008). In the 2006 Winter Games in Torino, over 85 percent of medalists self-identified as white/Caucasian. Yet, viewers dramatically underestimated this number by assuming that white athletes accounted for only 50 percent of awarded medals. While respondents estimated that black athletes won one-sixth of all awarded medals, Shani Davis was the only black athlete to win a medal for any country in Torino, with his two medals accounting for less than one percent of all awarded medals.

These results support Ebersol's claim that NBC does not give much consideration to discussing racial implications during the telecast. This lack of discussion seems to have affected the audience's perception of the ethnic makeup of the Winter Games. Clearly, the audience does not grasp the fact that the Winter Games lack the same levels of diversity observed during the Summer Games. This was especially seen in the fact that respondents estimated that 6.8 percent of medalists were Middle-Eastern, despite the fact that virtually all Middle-Eastern countries chose not to compete in the Winter Games. By NBC choosing not to discuss the ethnic makeup of the Games during the telecast, audiences are left with a great misunderstanding of the participants within this global spectacle.

Future media formats and trends

The future of Olympic media will likely be impacted from the mediums used to render the Games more than changes within the format of the competition itself. While the competition will remain similar in length and format for the immediate future, the manner in which people consume the Olympics continues to change dramatically (Marshall, Walker, and Russo, 2010). Given athletes' propensity to interact with their fans via Facebook status updates and Twitter feeds (Sanderson, 2011), both the perceived "liveness" and the interactivity between athlete and fan will continue to change immeasurably. In the face of a strong headwind against the "plausibly live" format, networks like NBC will be challenged to offer a duality of Olympic programming: one that is to be consumed immediately via an Internet offering based on expansive coverage (that is, every sport and event being found on a website, providing certain promotional and commercial caveats) and another offered on television based on specialized, snack-sized coverage (that is, primetime telecasts featuring a small number of events and stars, packaged in media "chunks" to be programmed like the aforementioned jigsaw puzzle over the course of a night).

Nonetheless, the future of Olympic media still appears to primarily reside in the "old" media formats of television and newspapers more than the multitude of new media offerings. Given the extremely high ratings the Olympic telecast continues to garner regardless of tape-delay and other more immediate sources (see Hiestand, 2008) that clutter the producer–viewer relationship, it is fair to conclude that new media will exert a greater impact on Olympic media (see Hutchins and Mikosza, 2010) without, at least in the immediate future, offering a direct replacement threat to the televised Games. As much as many may assume the Internet chimes a death knell for traditional media, television viewing continues to increase and still is at peak levels (Keller, 2010). Thus, Olympic media of the future promises to marry traditional and new media formats more than compete within them.

This chapter has predominantly focused on the role Olympic media has in shaping the way American society views the Games – often subsequently connecting them to their worldviews and attitudes about other nation states. However, an increasing amount of scholarship has delved into the content and impact of how the Olympics is conveyed to a wide variety of nations and audiences (see Ning, Zhongshi, and Fei, 2011; Zhang, 2011), finding that opinions are, indeed shaped by this biggest show of all media offerings.

References

Adams, T., and Tuggle, C. A. (2004). ESPN's SportsCenter and coverage of women's athletics: It's a boy's club. *Mass Communication and Society*, 7, 237–48.

Allison, L. (2000). Sport and nationalism. In J. Coakley and E. Dunning (Eds.), *Handbook of sports studies* (pp. 344–55). London: Sage.

Bairner, A. (2001). *Sport, nationalization, and globalization: European and North American perspectives*. Albany, NY: SUNY.

Bandura, A. (1986). *Social foundations of thought and action: A social cognitive theory*. Upper Saddle River, NJ: Prentice Hall.

Billings, A. C. (2008). *Olympic media: Inside the biggest show on television*. London: Routledge.

Billings, A. C., and Angelini, J.R. (2007). Packaging the games for viewer consumption: Nationality, gender, and ethnicity in NBC's coverage of the 2004 Summer Olympics. *Communication Quarterly*, 55 (1), 95–111.

Billings, A. C. and Eastman, S. T. (2003). Framing identities: Gender, ethnic, and national parity in network announcing of the 2002 Winter Olympics. *Journal of Communication*, 53 (4), 369–86.

Billings, A. C., Angelini, J. R., and Duke, A. H. (2010). Gendered profiles of Olympic history: Sportscaster dialogue in the 2008 Beijing Olympics. *Journal of Broadcasting and Electronic Media*, 54 (1), 9–23.

Billings A. C., Angelini, J. R., and Wu, D. (2011). Nationalistic Notions of the Superpowers: Comparative Analyses of the American and Chinese Telecasts in the 2008 Beijing Olympiad. *Journal of Broadcasting and Electronic Media*, 55 (2), 251–66.

Brittain, I. (2009). *The Paralympic Games explained*. New York: Routledge.

Bryant, J., Comisky, P., and Zillmann, D. (1977). Drama in sports commentary. *Journal of Communication*, 27, 140–9.

Davis, L. R. (1997). *The swimsuit issue and sport: Hegemonic masculinity and Sports Illustrated*. Albany, NY: SUNY.

Dayan, D., and Katz, E. (1992). *Media events: The live broadcasting of history*. Cambridge, MA: Harvard.

Duncan, M. C. (2006). Gender warriors in sport: Women and the media. In A. Raney and J. Bryant (Eds.). *Handbook of sports and media* (pp. 231–52). Mahwah, NJ: LEA.

Eastman, S. T., and Billings, A.C. (2000). Sportscasting and sports reporting: The power of gender bias. *Journal of Sport and Social Issues*, 24 (1), 192–12.

Espy, R. (1979). *The politics of the Olympic Games*. Berkeley, CA: University of California Press.
FIFA Online. (2011). Almost half the world tuned in at home to watch 2010 FIFA World Cup South Africa. *FIFA.com*, July 11. Retrieved from http://www.fifa.com/worldcup/archive/southafrica2010/organisation/media/newsid=1473143/index.html
Gantz, W., and Wenner, L. (1991). Men, women, and sports: Audience experiences and effects. *Journal of Broadcasting and Electronic Media*, 35, 233–43.
Gerbner, G., Gross, L., Morgan, M., and Signorelli, N. (1986). Living with television: The dynamics of the cultivation process. In J. Bryant and D. Zillmann (Eds.), *Perspectives on media effects* (pp. 17–40). Hillsdale, NJ: Erlbaum.
Gitlin, T. (1980). *The whole world is watching: Mass media in the making and unmaking of the New Left*. Berkeley, CA: University of California.
Goffman, E. (1974). *Frame analysis: An essay on the organization of experience*. New York: Harper and Row.
Halbert, C., and Latimer, M. (1994). "Battling" gendered language: An analysis of the language used by sports commentators in a televised coed tennis competition. *Sociology of Sport Journal*, 11, 298–308.
Hartmann, D. (1996). The politics of race and sport: Resistance and domination in the 1968 African American Olympic protest movement. *Ethnic and Racial Studies*, 19 (3), 548–66.
Hiestand, M. (2008). NBC scores mixed bag of pros, cons. *USA Today*, August 25, p. 3C.
Hoberman, J. (2007). Race and athletics in the twenty-first century. In J. A. Hargreaves and P. Vertinsky (Eds.), *Physical culture, power, and the body* (pp. 208–31). London: Routledge.
Hutchins, B., and Mikosza, J. (2010). The web 2.0 Olympics. Convergence: *Journal of Research into New Media Technologies*, 16 (3), 279–97.
International Olympic Committee (2011). Olympic Games. *Olympic.org*. Retrieved from http://www.olympic.org/olympic-games.
Jones, R., Murrell, A. J., and Jackson, J. (1999). Pretty versus powerful in the sports pages: Print media coverage of US Women's Olympic gold medal winning teams. *Journal of Sport and Social Issues*, 23 (2), 183–92.
Keller, R. (2010). Home television viewing at an all-time high. *Hufflepost TV*, March 10. Retrieved from http://www.aoltv.com/2010/05/03/home-television-viewing-at-an-all-time-high/.
Langer, J. (1981). Television's personality system. *Media, Culture, and Society*, 3 (4), 351–65.
Larson, J. F., and Park, H. S. (1993). *Global television and the politics of the Seoul Olympics*. Boulder, CO: Westview.
Marshall, P., Walker, B., and Russo, N. (2010). Mediating the Olympics. *Convergence: The Journal of Research into New Media Technologies*, 16 (3), 263–78.
McCombs, M. E., and Shaw, D. L. (1972). The agenda-setting function of mass media. *Public Opinion Quarterly*, 36, 176–87.
Messner, M. (1993). *Power at play*. Boston: Beacon.
Messner, M. A., and Cooky, C. (2010) *Gender in televised sports: News and highlights shows, 1989–2009*. Los Angeles: USC Center for Feminist Research. Retrieved from https://dornsifecms.usc.edu/assets/sites/80/docs/tvsports.pdf.
Min, W., and Zhen, X. (2010). Mirroring the Olympic Games – The Beijing 2008 Olympic Games in the American media. *International Journal of the History of Sport*, 29 (9–10), 1794–808.
Morris, B., and Nydahl, J. (1985). Sports spectacle as drama: Image, language, and technology. *Journal of Popular Culture*, 18 (4), 101–10.
Neuman, W. R., Just, M. R., and Crigler, A. N. (1992). *Communication knowledge: News and the construction of political meaning*. Chicago: University of Chicago Press.
Ning, W., Zhongshi, G., and Fei, S. (2011). Message, perception, and the Beijing Olympics: Impact of differential media exposure on perceived opinion diversity. *Communication Research*, 38 (3), 422–45.
Potter, W. (1986). Perceived reality and the cultivation hypothesis. *Journal of Broadcasting and Electronic Media*, 30, 159–74.
Puijk, R. (1997). *Global spotlights on Lillehammer: How the world viewed Norway during the 1994 Winter Olympics*. Luton: University of Luton Press.

Rada, J., and Wulfemeyer, K.T. (2005). Color coded: Racial descriptors in television coverage of intercollegiate sports. *Journal of Broadcasting and Electronic Media*, 49, 65–85.

Real, M. R. (1989). *Super media: A cultural studies approach*. Newbury Park, CA: Sage.

Sabo, D., Jansen, S. C., Tate, D., Duncan, M. C., and Leggett, S. (1996). Televising international sport: Race, ethnicity, and nationalistic bias. *Journal of Sport and Social Issues*, 20, 7–21.

Sanderson, J. (2011). *How social media is changing sports: It's a whole new ballgame*. New York: Hampton.

Schaffer, K., and Smith, S. (Eds.). (2000). *The Olympics at the millennium: Power politics and the Games*. Piscataway, NJ: Rutgers University Press.

Seidman, R. (2011). TV ratings broadcast top 25: 'American Idol,' 'The Voice,' 'Modern Family,' 'Dancing with the Stars,' 'NCIS' top week 34 viewing. *TV By the Numbers*, May 17. Retrieved from http://tvbythenumbers.zap2it.com/2011/05/17/tv-ratings-broadcast-top-25-american-idol-the-voice-modern-family-dancing-with-the-stars-ncis-top-week-34-viewing/92944/.

Toohey, K. (1997). Australian television, gender and the Olympic Games. *International Review for the Sociology of Sport*, 31 (1), 19–29.

Tuggle, C. A., and Owen, A. (1999). A descriptive analysis of NBC's coverage of the centennial Olympics. *Journal of Sport and Social Issues*, 23 (2), 171–83.

Tuggle, C. A., Huffman, S., and Rosengard, D. S. (2007). A descriptive analysis of NBC's coverage of the 2004 Summer Olympics. *Journal of Sports Media*, 2 (1), 53–76.

Wenner, L. A. (1989). Media, sports, and society: The research agenda. In L. A. Wenner (Ed.), *Media, sports and society* (pp. 13–48). Newbury Park, CA: Sage.

Whannel, G. (1992). *Fields in vision: Television sport and cultural transformation*. London: Routledge.

Wonsek, P. L. (1992). College basketball on television: A study of racism in the media. *Media, Culture and Society*, 14, 449–61.

Zhang, L. (2011). Stereotypes of Chinese: Media use and Olympic Games. *China Media Research*, 7 (3), 64–71.

17

THE STATE OF THE SPORTS PRESS

Reflections on an international study

David Rowe

Introduction: The place of print in sport and sport in print

Organized media reporting and commentary on sport began in the eighteenth century in the medium of print, and was supplemented in the twentieth century by radio. For the last half-century, broadcast television has been the dominant sport medium, although it can be claimed plausibly that the Internet and mobile technologies are beginning to challenge, if not supplant it (Hutchins and Rowe, 2012). As successive waves of new media technology have emerged and developed, it is conventional to pronounce the "end" of its predecessors. At present, for example, "old" or "legacy" media such as newspapers and television are consistently discussed in the context of crisis, decline or demise, but on closer inspection provide instances of resilience, adaptation, and multi-media user practices (see, for example, various contributions to Franklin, 2009; Katz and Scannell, 2009; Turner and Tay, 2009). Print-based sports journalism, then, remains an important component of the "media sports cultural complex" (Rowe, 2004), albeit one that, like the newspaper itself, is clearly under pressure, especially in mature digital media environments.

Newspapers with substantial sport content[1] continue to be popular and influential for several reasons. They conventionally employ more journalists than other media such as television and radio, and so produce a greater range of content that is necessarily less tied to direct sport event commentary. Thus, newspapers retain significant elements of their agenda setting leadership in sports discourse that, in the twenty-first century, is now easily disseminated via online media. For this reason, although the circulation and sales of the paper versions of the news may be falling, their readerships are often actually increasing via, in particular, the global availability of news websites that carry the sport texts written in the first instance by sport journalists trained in print and still writing under old, established mastheads. At the same time, the decline of newsprint titles is highly variable across the world – it is more marked in some Western markets (notably the United States) than in others (such as those in northern Europe, including Iceland, Norway and Sweden, and Japan, where over 80 percent of the population still reads a daily newspaper), while in parts of Asia and South America newspapers are actually booming according to the newspaper industry's most recent annual research report:

> Globally, daily newspaper distribution reached 540 million copies in 2008, but has declined by 3.9% since. But within this, sales in Asia have risen by 15% between 2006 and 2010, and 5% in the most recent year. Latin America has also seen newspaper growth. In Europe and North America, the picture has been less encouraging, with circulations falling 20% in North America since 2006 and by 10% across Western and Eastern Europe.
>
> The marked differences between the mature and developing markets are instructive… Such patterns are also reflected in the variance in the number of titles. Overall since 2006, the number of paid-daily newspapers published across the world has risen by 12.3% to 14,853.
>
> *(World Association of Newspapers and News Publishers, 2012, para. 7–10)*

Sports journalism originating in newspapers may be increasingly globally available online, but it is still largely produced out of individual countries and usually tailored towards nationally constituted and regional/local readerships (see discussion below). Thus, while it is probably premature to propose a phenomenon that can be called *global* sports journalism, there are features of different national sports journalism environments that, when examined alongside others, may indicate established patterns and new trends that can be regarded as at least *international* in nature. This chapter, then, reflects on the findings of the International Sports Press Survey 2011,[2] a content analysis that was conducted under the auspices of the Denmark-based non-government organization *Play the Game.*[3] The 2011 survey, involving newspapers from 22 countries (Table 17.1) in the data reported here,[4] sought to replicate and extend a 2005 Survey that involved ten countries, at that time the largest ever conducted on the international sports press. The latest survey, although limited both by continental/regional/national over-representation and under-representation, constitutes an even larger data set that is so far unmatched in its scale and ambition. Some changes to the international sports press in the crucial early years of the 21st century are addressed, considering national variations and trends that may point, with appropriate analytical caution, towards the international and, ultimately, the global. The chapter also takes advantage of the enhancement of the 2011 survey – measuring coverage of sport across the whole newspaper rather than confining it to the sports pages – to consider (briefly) the wider presence of sport, while also raising issues of purpose and quality in print sport journalism.

Before addressing the survey it is important to contextualize it with regard to the standing of sports journalism within journalism and societal culture. It is fair to observe that sports journalism and, indeed, sports journalists themselves have something of a "down market" reputation (Boyle, 2006; Boyle, Rowe, and Whannel, 2010) except among leading columnists, especially in the USA, where those who are established and well-regarded tend to be called sports *writers*. This image problem is, in part, derived from the relatively low level of educational attainment of sports journalists in countries such as Britain and Australia (again, less applicable to the USA context; see Rowe, 2004) and, correspondingly, to comparatively limited possession of "cultural capital" (Bourdieu, 1984), which can be defined here as the symbolic authority and power that can be derived from the command of elite, specialized knowledge. Reporting on popular contact sports performed and consumed frequently by working-class men does not tend to confer on the sports journalist the sociocultural prestige that is asserted by (though not necessarily ascribed to) peers in journalistic rounds with greater *gravitas*, such as institutional politics, international affairs, and economics. Indeed, unlike some of the spheres of journalism where knowledge is more hierarchically ordered and

TABLE 17.1 Surveyed newspapers

	Countries	*Newspapers*
1	Australia	*The Australian, Herald Sun, West Australian , Sydney Morning Herald*
2	Brazil	*O Globo, Meia Hora, Tribuna de Minas*
3	Canada	*The Globe and Mail, The Toronto Sun, The Toronto Star*
4	Denmark	*Politiken, Ekstra Bladet, Fyens Stiftstidende, Morgenavisen Jyllands-Posten, Berlingske, B.T.*
5	England	*The Telegraph, The Guardian, Daily Mirror, The Independent, Brighton Argus, The Telegraph* (Regional)*, The Times* (England)
6	France	*Le Figaro, Aujourd'hui en France, La Voix du Nord, Le Monde*
7	Germany	*Frankfurter Allgemeine Zeitung, BILD, Hamburger Abendblatt, Sueddeutsche Zeitung, Express, Westdeutsche Allgemeine Zeitung, Koelner Stadtanzeiger, die tageszeitung, Berliner Zeitung*
8	Greece	*Kathimerini, Ta Nea, Aggelioforros or Makedonia*
9	India	*The Hindu, The Times of India, Dinamani*
10	Malaysia	*The New Straits Times, The Star (Malaysia), Berita Harian*
11	Nepal	*Kantipur, Nagarik, Adarsha Samaj*
12	New Zealand	*The New Zealand Herald, The Waikato Times*
13	Poland	*Gazeta Wyborcza, Fakt, Polska Glos Wielkopolski*
14	Portugal	*Jornal de Noticias, Correio da Manha, Diario de Coimbra*
15	Romania	*Jurnalul National, Click, Adevarul*
16	Scotland	*The Herald, Daily Record, The Scotsman*
17	Singapore	*The Straits Times*
18	Slovakia	*SME, Novy Cas*
19	Slovenia	*Delo, Slovenske Novice, Primorske Novice*
20	South Africa	*The Times (South Africa), Daily Sun, The Argus*
21	Switzerland	*Neue Zuercher Zeitung, Blick, Tages-Anzeiger, Le Matin, Le Temps, 24 heures*
22	USA	*Washington Post, USA Today, New York Post, The Tennessean*

commanded, it is the very popularity of sports culture that lends itself to a wider distribution of competence. That is, the claim that everyone who has played a little sport and, ironically, read many sport reports while also watching a lot of it on television, knows as much about it as any sports journalist who is fortunate enough to be paid to cover it, undermines the sports journalist's standing. Negative reputations of sports journalism and journalists are, as noted, variable across national contexts, and also no doubt connected to the often low position of journalists in general on scales of occupational prestige and trust in countries with major media sectors (such as the UK and USA). Thus, for example, a British study found that, between 2003 and 2010, trust in broadsheet journalists declined by 24 percent to 41 percent, and for tabloid journalists (who are most closely associated with high levels of sports coverage in comparison to "hard" news) it fell by four percent to only ten percent (Kellner, 2010).[5] These broader societal considerations of media and journalism form an important backdrop to any analysis of survey findings of the products of sports journalists and the power of sports news.

The 2011 International Sports Press Survey: Visuality, presentational form, and sources

It should be emphasized that the discussion here is concerned with the "broad brush" aspects of the international survey (as summarized in Table 17.2). It does not, for example, break down findings within individual countries or weight them according to the proportion of articles. Nor is the survey globally representative – as is readily apparent, Europe (especially northern) is over-represented in accounting for 63 percent of the total article count, and Asia, Africa (both bolstered in the later iteration of the survey not addressed here), and South America under-represented (see Table 17.3), while the temporal sampling compression into four months (April to July) does not take into account the seasonality of sport within and between hemispheres. Nonetheless, the survey provides, as the largest such exercise ever undertaken, a very useful "snapshot" of the state of the sport press in several countries that can be isolated and combined for a range of analytical purposes.

TABLE 17.2 Number and percentage of articles from participating countries

Countries	*Articles*	
	(*n*)	(%)
Australia	1,671	9.1
Brazil	559	3.0
Canada	837	4.6
Denmark	1,522	8.3
England	2,554	13.9
France	475	2.6
Germany	1,899	10.4
Greece	669	3.6
India	544	3.0
Malaysia	1,159	6.3
Nepal	186	1.0
New Zealand	382	2.1
Poland	815	4.4
Portugal	391	2.1
Romania	283	1.5
Scotland	962	5.2
Singapore	251	1.4
Slovak Republic	256	1.4
Slovenia	502	2.7
South Africa	522	2.8
Switzerland[a]	1,223	6.7
USA	676	3.7
Total	18,338	100.0[b]

[a] (French and German languages combined)
[b] Rounded total

TABLE 17.3 Percentages of surveyed articles by continent

Continents	*Article contribution*	
	(*n*)	(%)
Africa	522	2.8
Asia	2,140	11.7
Australasia	2,053	11.2
Europe	11,551	63.0
North America	1,513	8.3
South America	559	3.0
Total	18,338	100.0

Among the notable findings of the survey is the affirmation – or, perhaps, reaffirmation – of the *visuality* of print sport journalism. While still photography has long been an important feature of sport in newspapers and magazines (Rowe, 2004), the visual power of television and the internet is such that written text must now be even more substantially "spiced" with photographs. Figure 17.1 reveals that almost two-thirds of surveyed newspaper articles on sport contained at least one photograph, with over 16 percent containing two or more. Indeed, the total number of photographs (over 17,000) almost matched the total for articles (18,338). The combination of text and still photograph is, then, still potent alongside the appeal of voice and the moving image. This more "contemplative" mode of mediated sport contrasts notably with the emphasis in live broadcast sport on observing real-time movement with often-excited commentary. Deprived of "liveness" in this way, the print sport text is either prospective (anticipating a coming sport event) or retrospective (describing and

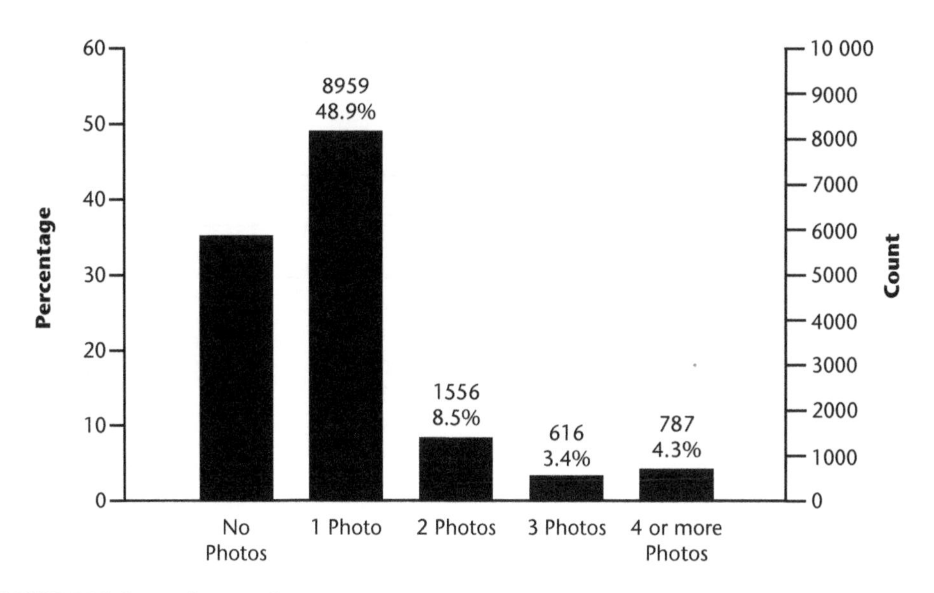

FIGURE 17.1 Sport photographs

analyzing a sport event that has occurred). The primary function of the photograph in this case is identification (necessary because words are arbitrary signifiers of their referents) and illustration (a striking "frozen" image that frequently captures key characteristics of movement) of its subject. This text/image combination has enduring appeal to audiences, and is replicated on sport news websites, which can provide not only substantial galleries of sport images but may also be supplemented by moving/action images in the context of convergent media. Illustrative sports photography close to the expository text cannot match the immediacy and dynamism of video, but its capacity to contextualize and "anchor" information persists and develops within the structured print sport news story.

The survey also demonstrates that the visuality of the sports press is accompanied by a resilient news orientation: as Table 17.4 indicates, "News" was a strong article form (40.4 percent) coming second only to the "Report, Story, Feature" category (44.4 percent), which also contains a substantial news component and is difficult to differentiate from news. These findings suggest that the sports press retains a traditional agenda-setting fourth-estate role of revealing new information, as well as reporting and elaborating on what has already occurred (especially during competitive sport encounters). Yet, despite any intuitive impression that sport news and coverage is everywhere in the newspaper, 90.7 percent of sport stories in the survey came from the sports sections of the newspapers (excluding "tear outs" and other specialist supplements, which were not counted). In other words, despite sport's enormous media visibility, most articles about it remain confined to a dedicated sport section within the newspaper. These have, indeed, grown in size and density in many newspaper markets (Rowe, 2007), meaning that the sports desk clearly retains its prime position within many newspapers around the world.

The broad presentational types of article, though, do not give an indication of textual quality. One characteristic that is often used as a proxy for news quality is the selection, number, and range of sources (Coleman and Ross, 2010), according to the general assumption that quantity and diversity of sources used in an article provide an indication of comprehensiveness, perspectival variety and the requisite "labor" devoted to article preparation. Table 17.5 reveals that 26.5 percent of surveyed articles had no sources and 40.5 percent had only one, while only

TABLE 17.4 Presentational form in sport journalism

Form of presentation	*Articles*	
	(*n*)	(%)
News	7,402	40.4
Report, story, feature	8,139	44.4
Interview	680	3.7
Specific commentary story, column	1,366	7.4
Portrait	475	2.6
Gloss, satire	123	0.7
Other	102	0.6
Unclear	51	0.3
Total	18,338	100.0[a]

[a] Rounded total

TABLE 17.5 Sources

Number of sources	*Number of articles*	*Percentage*
No (0) sources	4856	26.5
One (1) source	7436	40.5
Two (2) sources	3498	19.1
Three (3) or more sources	2218	12.1
Unable to measure	308	1.7
Missing case	22	0.1
Total	18,338	100.0

12.1 percent had three or more. Furthermore, almost six of every ten (58.8 percent) of the sources used were from the sport world itself (especially athletes, coaches, managers, and sport organizational spokespeople), with little use of sources beyond this sphere.

These findings give some weight to the criticism of sport as the "toy department" of the news media in the sense that it appears relatively self-enclosed, focusing on a small number of subjects and "protagonists" (over half of whom were athletes, most of whom were male). This apparent insularity could be challenged or reinforced according to the sex/gender composition of the sport journalism workforce, which was surveyed via author bylines. If newspaper sports journalism principally involves men writing about men for the benefit of other men, it is open to the charge that the sports media are complicit in the reproduction of male hegemony in a pivotal domain of popular culture.

Sex/gender, "the world game", and dominant sports

The autonomous sports desk may continue to replicate itself in the newspaper, but is that desk still male dominated? The survey set out to determine the gender composition of newspaper-based sports journalism in exploring not just the product of sport journalism, but also who produces it. A total of 61.7 percent (11,311) of articles about sport had a journalist's byline (itself an indication that sports journalists are by no means anonymous "content providers") and, of these, 91 percent were males (see Table 17.6), with less than eight percent being women (and less than one percent "mixed").

It is readily apparent, then, that sports journalism according to the findings of this survey mirrors the male domination of the sports that it covers. Although, in measuring coverage of individual sports, the survey did not expressly separate male and female sports, it is evident that press coverage concentrated on a restricted range of professional sports, and that these involved mostly male sport competitions. Thus, Figure 17.2 shows an intensive focus on a single sport – association football (soccer) – which received more article coverage than the combined top eight other sports and a composite category of nominated other sports.[6] This survey result was to some degree produced by an over-representation of "soccer nations" among the participating countries, but it is remarkable that several weeks of the survey period were outside the soccer season in most of them. While individual "mixed" sports like tennis and golf are represented in the top ten, the majority are male-dominant team sports that can be said to monopolize much of the sports press in many countries. Thus, it can be concluded,

TABLE 17.6 Sex/gender of named journalists

Sex/gender of journalists	*Articles*	
	(*n*)	(%)
Male	10,324	91.3
Female	848	7.5
Both	46	0.4
Not specified	73	0.6
Missing cases	20	0.2
Total	11,311	100.0

as others have argued for many years (see, for example, Creedon, 1994), that sports journalism does little to challenge male sport hegemony – and, indeed, can be seen to contribute powerfully to its reinforcement.

These survey findings, apart from suggesting that soccer's claim to be the "world game" is compelling, also reveal that newspaper coverage is heavily concentrated on a relatively small number of (mainly male) sports. This is not a peculiar characteristic of newspapers, though, as it is also demonstrably the case regarding international sports television (see Rowe, 2011), with the commercial logic of the media sports cultural complex tending, paradoxically, to narrow rather than broaden the horizons of the world of sport in terms of the distribution of sports coverage. Given that the survey measured sports coverage in regional, metropolitan and national broadsheet and tabloid newspapers from several countries, it is instructive also to address their spatial as well as sport-specific coverage.

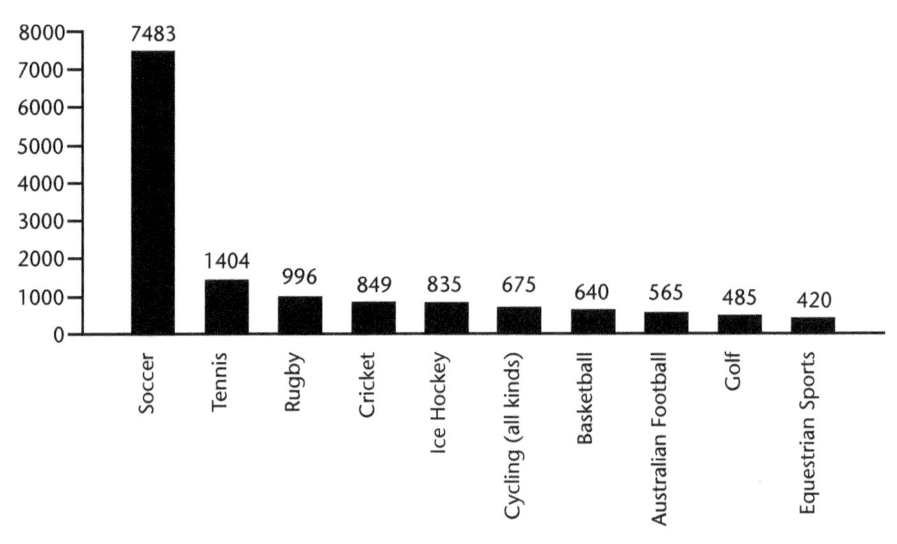

FIGURE 17.2 Top ten sports (only the primary sport in each article)

Spaces of sports journalism

Sport takes place at different levels (from contests focused on cities/regions to global tournaments) and in a range of contexts (from the municipal sports field to the "cathedral" stadium of world sport). Table 17.7 is broadly consistent with developments in professional sport in modernity, with nationally and internationally focused sport dominating the local/regional level. Just as sport developed from highly localized environments to embrace national and then international competition (Guttmann, 1978), media coverage followed and, indeed, induced this spatial and organizational expansion. The similar weighting of national (45.5 percent) and international (43.1 percent) levels of sport found in the survey indicates the prominence of the nation as a key organizing context in contemporary sport – newspapers here are covering sporting contests both within (that is, nationwide) and between nations.

While it can be expected that international coverage will be more intense if a national representative (as team or individual) is engaged in competition, there is also a considerable degree of "disinterested" coverage. Thus, as Table 17.8 reveals, while over one-third (35.5 percent) of articles dealing with international events focused on a country's participating nationals, approaching half (46.3 percent) did not. The most plausible explanation for this pattern is that many major international events do not include a large number of countries but are of interest to a wide international sports spectatorship. Thus, events covered during the survey like the UEFA Champions League and the Tour de France attract viewers irrespective of participation by their national compatriots, with the increased global circulation of professional athletic labor, diasporic spectatorship, and major sports brand promotion and broadcast rights stretching media and audiences in various directions (Rowe, 2011).

Despite the global mobility of sports, athletes, television images, and newspaper texts, as Figure 17.3 indicates, Europe and North America continue to dominate sport and its newspaper coverage. While, as previously noted more than once, these continents (especially the former) dominated the iteration of the survey reported here (and so, perhaps, it can also be observed that they dominate media sport research and scholarship), the survey findings are not inconsistent with the main directions of the global flow of media sport from West to East. Although these flows are not entirely unidirectional and do not represent absolute media sports imperial domination, they do register the power of Western sports brands, such as the English Premier League and the National Basketball Association, to be both the source of media coverage in their own countries and regions, and to be promoted and "sold" successfully to developing markets, especially in the Asia-Pacific region (Rowe 2011).

TABLE 17.7 Spatial focus of newspaper sport articles

Level	*Articles*	
	(*n*)	(%)
Local/regional	2,038	11.1
National	8,351	45.5
International	7,905	43.1
Missing cases	44	0.2
Total	18,338	100.0[a]

[a] Rounded

TABLE 17.8 Focus on national sport participants abroad

Focus on nationals abroad	*Articles*	
	(*n*)	(%)
Yes	2,807	35.5
No	3,657	46.3
Not able to specify	100	1.3
Missing cases	1,341	17.0
Total	7,905	100.0[a]

[a] Rounded

It was noted above that newspapers, which are experiencing a decline in many Western countries, are booming in parts of Asia (and also South America). Commensurately, the rise of sport in Asia (as signified by, for example, China's hosting of the 2008 Olympic Games and India's Premier League initiative in cricket) might be expected to lead to the development of sports journalism in that continent. But this is not only a question of importation and replication of established models of sports journalism. Of particular interest to scholars of sport communication is the extent to which, as it develops in new contexts, sports journalism may diverge from the patterns of mediation established in other places in earlier epochs.

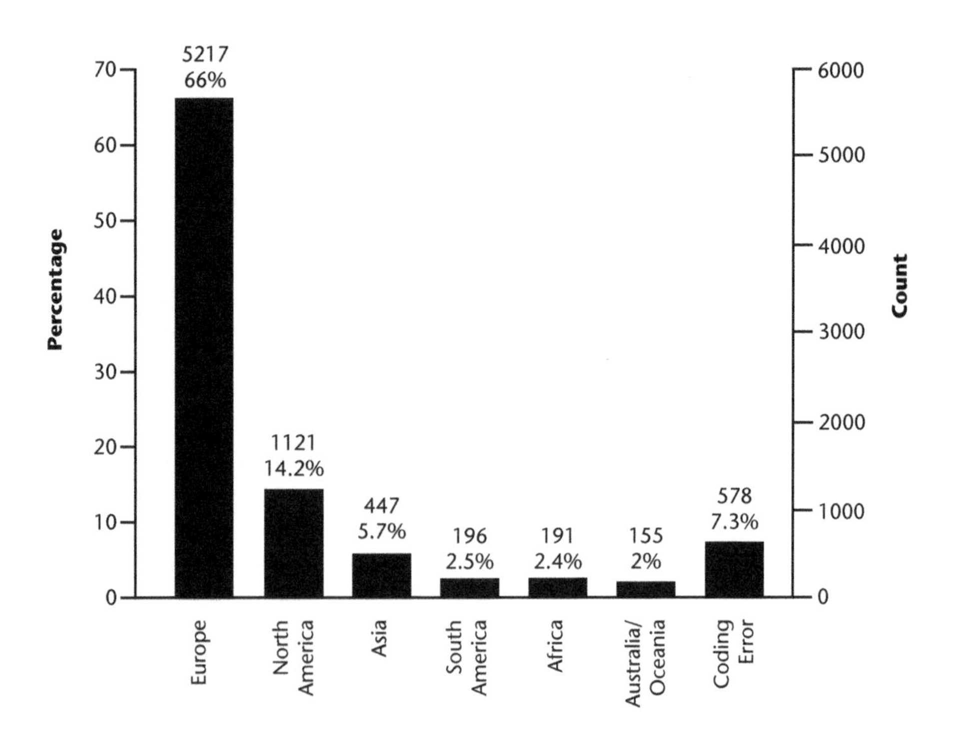

FIGURE 17.3 Continental distribution of reported sports events

Conclusion: Sport communication and the newspaper: Time and tide

Newspaper sports journalism is a very substantial global enterprise with many national variations, and it would be unwise to seek to advance over-extended conclusions based on a 22-country survey and the sample of composite findings addressed here. However, the International Sports Press Survey 2011 provides some valuable pointers towards the state of the press and, by extension, reader habits and expectations (though these latter could not be addressed within a content analysis and, therefore, must be imputed here). Broadcast sport, not all of which involves "live" sport performance, requires a more concentrated, directed kind of audience attention that involves watching and listening to a presented media text. The flexibility of the printed form (even at a time of its progressive transfer to online and mobile platforms) creates more opportunities for audiences to select and "pace" their engagement with the "non-live" text. Thus, for example, newspapers (especially tabloid) retain some advantage in the context of sports audiences engaged in commuting via public transport who are freed from the technological constraints of reception and of contextual factors such as insulation from "noise". When combined with the "news-breaking" capability of newspapers with substantial, specialist sport "beat" reporter cohorts, it is not surprising that the print form retains a substantial presence in the face of rapid change in media communication technologies, practices and uses (Hutchins and Rowe, 2012). However these changes transpire – and the predictive success of "media futurists" has been signally limited – there is no certainty that changes in media technology will correspond to substantive changes in sports journalism itself.

Thus, the snapshot of international sports journalism discussed here can helpfully reflect on the direction of sports journalism irrespective of its specific medium – routines of sports journalism can be established and reproduced across media and time periods. As mentioned, the 2011 survey sought to replicate, as far as possible, an earlier one conducted in 2005 (Schultz-Jorgensen, 2005). However, there were substantial differences between the surveys, not least the much smaller scope of the earlier survey (which sampled, at a time of year close to the 2011 study, ten countries, 37 newspapers, and 10,007 articles).[7] Despite these variations, it is possible to compare their findings in some respects. For example, the comparative Table 17.9 reveals that, while there was a decline in the proportion of named male journalists (63.2–

TABLE 17.9 Sex/gender of named journalists, 2005 and 2011 International Sports Press Surveys

Sex/gender of journalists	*2011 articles*		*2005 articles*	
	(*n*)	(%)	(*n*)	(%)
Male	10,324	56.3	6,326	63.2
Female	848	4.6	465	4.6
Both	46	0.3	77	0.8
Not specified	7,100	38.7	3,139	31.4
Missing cases	20	0.1	–	0.0
Total	18,338	100.0	10,007	100.0

Note. Unlike the 2011 survey, the 2005 survey had no categories to identify sources such as agencies or pseudonyms, so for the 2005 survey these sources have all been coded as "Not specified". Hence, for the purpose of comparison, the categories, "Agency", "Two or more agencies", "Pseudonym", "No source" and "Coding error" in the 2011 survey have all been categorized as "Not specified" in this table.

56.3 percent), the proportion of female journalists named as providing newspaper sports stories remained static at 4.6 percent, with most of the change accounted for by a reduction in bylines produced, in part, by greater news agency syndication. The larger country spread and sample in 2011, therefore, did not offer any indication of an improved gender balance in sport-related journalism, despite encompassing almost ten percent of stories that were not confined to the sports pages.

Empirical research is always subject to methodological limitations and interpretive variations, which are evident in the case of an international content analysis that took in many thousands of newspaper sport stories in a range of newspapers in several countries. However, these findings provoke some telling, though not conclusive reflections on the state of the contemporary sports press, including that: while newspapers tend to be thought of as primarily about written text, the text-image-sport relation is crucial; and that the newspaper sports world tends to be enclosed and auto-referential, and hierarchical in terms of sports, sex/gender, nation, and global position. Analytical observations of this kind are by no means final, but operate as invitations to sport communication scholars to explore and test them through specific and comparative research. On the evidence presented here, the sports press remains a powerful force in shaping both the ways of seeing sport and the sports that can be seen.

Notes

1 This chapter is concerned with the sport pages within general newspapers, rather than specialist sport newspapers. These remain important in some national markets (such as in southern European countries like Greece and Spain, where association football in particular is highly popular) but in decline in others (such as the United Kingdom and Australia).

2 The survey covered fourteen days of publication between April 15, 2011 and July 2, 2011 on a rolling basis (excluding Sunday newspapers if not comparable to weekday editions), with a total of 18,338 articles from 81 newspapers in 22 countries incorporated in the data reported here. Each nationally based team selected the biggest broadsheet and tabloid newspaper, a regional title and additional newspapers as desired. Switzerland was divided into German and French language newspapers in the survey, but is regarded here as one country within the Swiss Confederation. Newspapers for Scotland and England were separated as two countries within the United Kingdom.

3 The survey was led by Thomas Horky (Macromedia University of Applied Sciences, Hamburg) and Jörg-Uwe Nieland (German Sport University, Cologne), who coordinated the researchers in participating countries. I would like to thank, apart from the aforementioned coordinators, the other members of the Australian research team, Rachel Payne (Play the Game) and Peter Lorentzen (Deakin University), and Vibha Bhattarai Upadhyay at the University of Western Sydney for her research assistance on this chapter.

4 Five countries – Kenya, Trinidad and Tobago, Uganda, Zambia, and Saudi Arabia – were subsequently included, but their data were not available to the author at time of writing.

5 The Leveson Inquiry (2012) into the "culture, practices and ethics of the press" and the "extent of unlawful or improper conduct" within News International and other media organizations is likely further to reduce journalistic prestige and trust in future surveys.

6 A series of other sports and missing cases made up the rest, but the domination of soccer is striking. Coverage of tennis in the articles was boosted seasonally by international events like French Open (May 22 to 5 June 2011) and Wimbledon (20 June to 3 July 2011), as was cycling via events like Giro d'Italia (7–29 May 2011) and the pre-tournament coverage of the Tour de France (2–24 July 2011). Cricket had recently had its World Cup (19 February to 2 April 2011) and, in the 2011 Survey, was more prominent than in its smaller 2005 predecessor with the inclusion of India, New Zealand and South Africa, where cricket is popular, in addition to Australia. Of particular note here

is the establishment of the Indian Premier League in 2008 – one of the world's richest sports tournaments – which has raised the international profile of cricket. The single category "rugby" is inflated in this instance by combining two codes – rugby union and rugby league.

7 The countries in common were Australia, Denmark, England, Germany, Romania, Scotland, Switzerland, and USA, with Austria and Norway not participating in 2011.

References

Bourdieu, P. (1984). *Distinction: A social critique of the judgement of taste.* London: Routledge and Kegan Paul.

Boyle, R. (2006). *Sports journalism: Context and issues.* London: Sage.

Boyle, R., Rowe, D., and Whannel, G. (2010). "Delight in trivial controversy?" Questions for sports journalism. In S. Allan (Ed.), *Routledge companion to news and journalism studies* (pp. 245–55). London: Routledge.

Coleman, S., and Ross, K. (2010). *The media and the public: 'Them' and 'us' in media discourse.* Oxford: Wiley-Blackwell.

Creedon, P. J. (Ed.). (1994). *Women, media and sport: Challenging gender values.* Thousand Oaks, CA: Sage.

Franklin, B. (Ed.). (2009). *The future of newspapers.* London: Routledge.

Guttmann, A. (1978). *From ritual to record: The nature of modern sports.* New York: Columbia University Press.

Hutchins, B., and Rowe, D. (2012). *Sport beyond television: The internet, digital media and the rise of networked media sport.* New York: Routledge.

Katz, E., and Scannell, P. (Eds.). (2009). The end of television? Its impact on the world (so far). *Annals of the American Academy of Political and Social Science*, 625 (1). Special issue.

Kellner, P. (2010). Number cruncher: A matter of trust. *Prospect*, September 22. Retrieved from http://www.prospectmagazine.co.uk/magazine/peter-kellner-yougov-trust-journalists/.

Rowe, D. (2004). *Sport, culture and the media: The unruly trinity* (2nd ed.). Maidenhead: Open University Press.

Rowe, D. (2007). Sports journalism: Still the 'toy department' of the news media? *Journalism: Theory, Practice and Criticism*, 8 (4), 385–405.

Rowe, D. (2011). *Global media sport: Flows, forms and futures.* London and New York: Bloomsbury Academic.

Schultz-Jorgensen, S. (2005). The world's best advertising agency: The sports press. *International sports press survey 2005.* Copenhagen: House of Monday Morning: Play the Game. Retrieved from http://www.playthegame.org/upload/sport_press_survey_english.pdf.

The Leveson Inquiry. (2012). Leveson Inquiry: Culture, practice and ethics of the press. *The Leveson Inquiry.* Retrieved from http://www.levesoninquiry.org.uk/.

Turner, G., and Tay, J. (Eds.). (2009). *Television studies after TV: Understanding television in the post broadcast era.* London and New York: Routledge.

World Association of Newspapers and News Publishers. (2012). *World press trends 2011.* Retrieved from http://www.wan-ifra.org/articles/2012/04/17/world-press-trends-2011.

18

THE IMPACT OF SPORT PUBLICITY ON FANS' EMOTION, FUTURE PREDICTION, AND BEHAVIORAL RESPONSE

Dae Hee Kwak and Yu Kyoum Kim

Sport is a part of everyday life in contemporary society. Sport can shape relationships at every level, including diplomatic, cultural, economic, organizational, community, and interpersonal (L'Etang, 2006). Consumer demand for watching mediated sporting events and related content continues to soar. Research has shown that sports fans are unique and different from consumers of other media entertainment genres in terms of their media use. Sports fans seem generally motivated to search for information about their favorite teams, players, and coaches. They are not only emotionally involved in a game's outcome, but also are motivated to search for additional content before and after an event (Gantz, Wang, Paul, and Potter, 2006). Because of the rapid growth of digital media technology, fans can read articles, view highlights, or even tweet about a play that just happened through their personal devices (such as mobile phones, tablet PCs), while watching a game on television.

Of all of these various forms of communication, the focus of the current chapter is publicity. From a communication standpoint, publicity is considered a more credible source of information and is more persuasive than other marketer-driven messages such as advertising (see, for example, Bond and Kirshenbaum, 1998; Ries and Ries, 2002). However, the impact of publicity on sports fans is poorly understood. To date, limited research has explored how sports consumers process positive and negative publicity about a professional team (see Funk and Pritchard, 2006). Although sports fans are willing to pay for exclusive content to gain access to richer information (Hammervold and Solberg, 2006), little is known about what sport publicity does to sports consumers' thoughts and behaviors.

This chapter explores the impact of sport publicity on fans' emotions, future predictions, and behavior from a consumer behavioral perspective. In discussing the impact of positive and negative publicity on sports fans, several communication theories (balance theory, cognitive dissonance theory, and mood management theory) are briefly reviewed to explain why fans seek out information and how they cope with it. A comprehensive model of sport publicity processing that integrates internal factors, processing mechanisms, and various fan reactions is presented herein.

Motivation for seeking sport information

In the mid-1950s, media researchers began to realize that audiences are more active and heterogeneous than were previously believed. Work in balance theory (Heider, 1958) and cognitive dissonance (Festinger, 1957) can help us understand why people seek out information that is consistent with their attitudes and beliefs and avoid information that they know will conflict with their existing attitudes and beliefs: this is because individuals are motivated to achieve balance and avoid cognitive dissonance. Festinger's cognitive dissonance theory further suggests that when people encounter counter-attitudinal information, they search for means to alleviate the dissonance such information produces.

Given that winning is only available to one competitor in the competitive sport setting, sporting events represent a type of action that will consistently promote fans' need for information. According to Zillmann (1996, p. 202), "hopes and fears are inseparably intertwined in the apprehensions that produce suspense". Therefore, before a sporting event or a season, highly identified fans will experience mixed feelings of hope and fear coupled with the cognitive state of uncertainty. These heightened feeling states create greater suspense among fans when consuming sporting events (Zillmann, 1996). Therefore, prior to a game, it is likely that fans are motivated to choose information that will reinforce their existing belief system ("my team will be successful this season") and avoid negative information about the team. The underlying premise of this selective exposure is that people are motivated to reduce cognitive dissonance and distress and pursue balance within their psychological system. So, individuals will choose information that will make them feel comfortable and safe. Being a fan of a team means that one has to cope with continuous distress caused by outcome uncertainty. Before a game, for instance, individuals who care for the outcome (highly identified fans) will experience strong anticipated emotion (hope and fear) which will increase levels of arousal and distress. Subsequently, fans will tune into information that is congruent with their attitudes and beliefs to alleviate that distress.

When a game is over, information seeking will be dependent upon the game outcome – win or loss. If the team wins, fans will "bask in reflected glory" (BIRG; Cialdini, *et al.*, 1976) by visiting the team's website (Boen, Vanbeselaere, and Feys, 2002). Boen and colleagues empirically demonstrated that the number of team website visitors were significantly higher after the team's victory than after a loss or a draw against an opponent. They found the online BIRG phenomenon by examining the number of unique website visitors after each match. This finding further illuminates that fans are motivated to search for attitude-congruent information after their team's win.

The findings by Boen and colleagues indicate that fans will be motivated to seek more (attitude-congruent) information that further extends or maintains their excitement and feelings of vicarious achievement from the win. On the other hand, when the team fails, fans will "cut off reflected failure" (CORF) by temporarily distancing themselves from the team (Snyder, Lassegard, and Ford, 1986). Fans of a losing team will refer to the team as "they" instead of "we" and will avoid public association with a losing team. Research has shown that fans reading negative publicity about the team are less likely to accept team-related promotions than fans reading positive publicity about the team (Kwak, Kim, and Hirt, 2011).

The notion of BIRG/CORF is grounded in social identity theory (Tajfel and Turner, 1979), which offers an interesting framework to understand these identity management tactics. According to social identity theory, people strive for a positive social identity. "Social identity" refers to the cognitive, emotional, and evaluative connotations of belonging to groups. Therefore, strong identification with a team makes almost no distinction between the fan and the team. While BIRG behavior has been well documented in the literature, fans' CORF behavior is relatively little understood. This might be because coping with counter-attitudinal events is far more complex than attitude congruent situations (Tormala and Petty, 2004).

Depending on the strength of team identification, various forms of resistance take place to cope with attitude incongruent messages. While some might repair their moods by bolstering their initial attitude toward the failing team ("I love this team no matter what"), some may temporarily disconnect the association with the team, while some may derogate the source by discounting the credibility of the writer. Some empirical findings suggest that resisting counter-attitudinal attack can even help strengthen the initial positive attitude (Tormala and Petty, 2004), supporting the adage that "what doesn't kill us makes us stronger." This is based on the assumption that fans will not easily change their favorite teams merely based on the teams' performance. For instance, a Boston Red Sox fan would not (perhaps never) switch to support the New York Yankees simply because of the team's performance level. Therefore, when one's favorite team losses, it is expected that fans will experience greater cognitive dissonance, which will stimulate them to actively seek out alternatives (for example, positive publicity, blasting opponent, accusing referees) to reduce their negative feelings. The notion of resistance to counter-attitudinal message will be discussed in more detail later in this chapter.

Another theoretical perspective that can help explain the fan motivation for information seeking is mood-management theory. Studies have consistently shown that media content has a mood-eliciting property that can alter a viewer's mood state. Mood-management theory posits that viewers utilize specific media content to alleviate negative feelings and to maximize the intensity of positive feelings (see, for example, Knobloch and Zillmann, 2002). Mood-management theory can complement the social identity theory by clarifying why fans may still BIRG or CORF even in the absence of the eyes of others (compare Boen, *et al.*, 2002). For instance, promoting mood-congruent behavior (such as visiting the team's website following a win) does not necessarily have to involve the identity management process. Fans might visit the team's website or read articles about the team to simply extend their positive feelings after a win. Likewise, fans may select articles that support their existing attitudes and help repair negative feelings triggered by a team's failure. Although further empirical evidence should be gathered to advance this line of inquiry, mood-management theory posits that individuals' psychological and sociological needs can be addressed by media content (Chang, 2006). Therefore, mood-management principles can also explain selective media exposure among sport fans.

To summarize the motivation of team-related publicity processing, processing mechanisms, and its consequences, the sport publicity processing model is presented in Figure 18.1. The figure illustrates that individual difference factors (for example, commitment, identification, mood state) motivate exposure to team-related publicity. As briefly discussed earlier, viewing and processing publicity can be explained by various theoretical perspectives such as balance theory, cognitive dissonance, BIRG/CORF, and selective exposure. These theories help explain the underlying motivation for seeking sport-related information. Processing either positive or negative publicity leads to various emotional, cognitive, and behavioral responses. The model also shows that when an individual is exposed to a counter-attitudinal (negative) message, the individual then will seek out various strategies to resist that information (Jacks and Cameron, 2003).

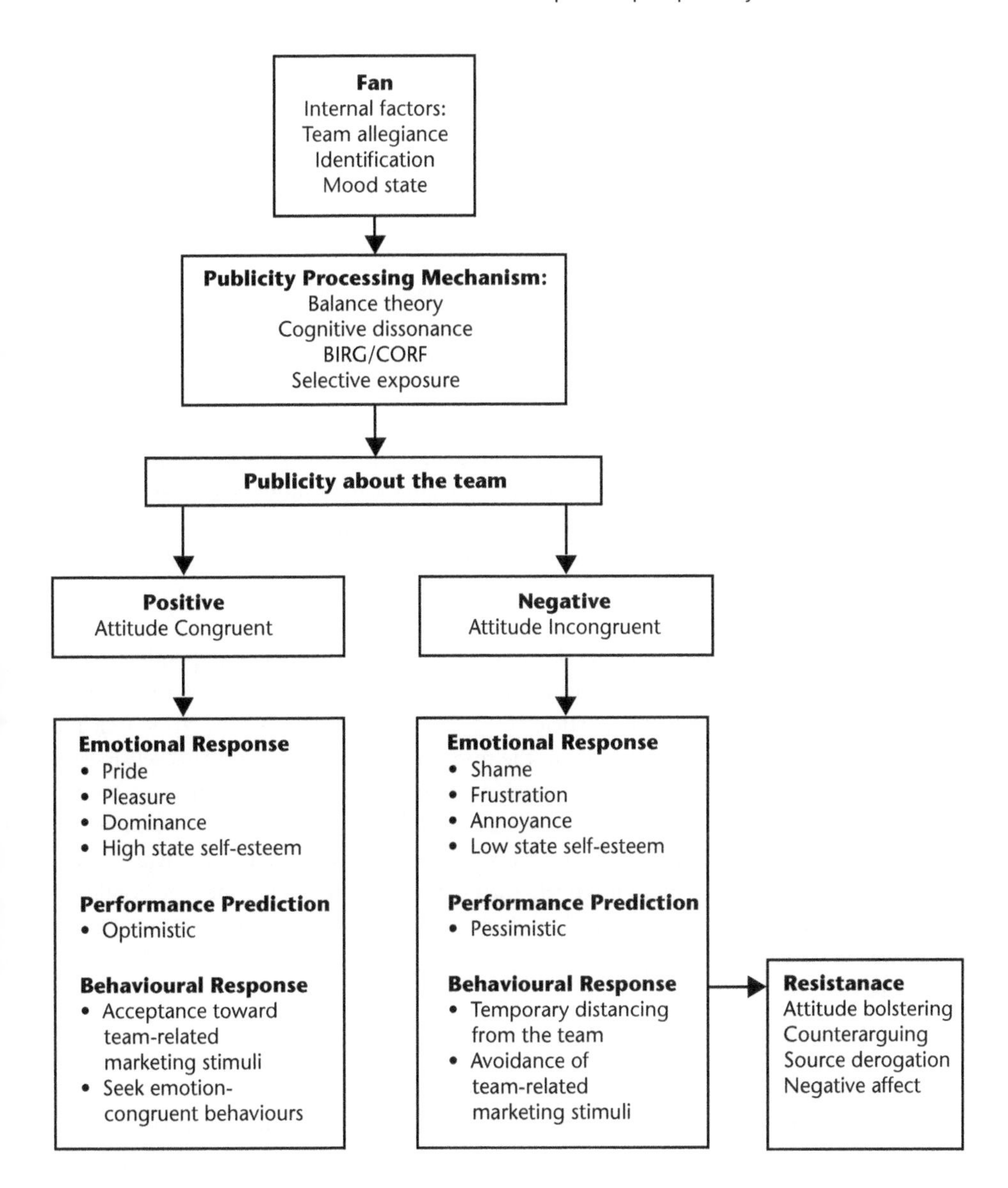

FIGURE 18.1 A model of sport publicity processing

Publicity impact on emotion and state self-esteem

Undoubtedly, sport provides a unique opportunity to understand how emotions operate in people's minds. The vicarious consumption of competitive sporting events is like an emotional rollercoaster (Madrigal and Dalakas, 2008). The intensity of the experience cannot be overstated since for those diehard fans, they perceive the team's success (or failure) as personal success (or failure) (Hirt, Zillmann, Erickson, and Kennedy, 1992). Research has shown that even reading a sports page can elicit strong emotional feelings in fans (Kwak, *et al.*, 2011; Wann and Branscombe,

1992). For instance, Kwak and colleagues found that fictitious articles about a university's men's basketball team induced different emotional responses among the university's students. Message valence was manipulated (positive, negative, and neutral) in the study and the valence had significant effects on eliciting different emotional feelings. A positive piece of publicity evoked more positive emotions, while a negative piece elicited more negative emotions. The study measured both basic-level emotions (pleasure, arousal, and dominance) and self-conscious emotions (pride and shame) and demonstrated that publicity affected all these emotional feelings. Findings suggest that reading a short written message about the team was sufficient to change respondents' emotional states. In line with Hirt, *et al.*'s (1992) findings, fans attributed the stimuli (publicity about their team) as personal experience and felt pride and shame, depending on the valence. Therefore, findings suggest that a single exposure to either positively or negatively framed publicity can easily stir up emotions in sport fans.

Additionally, a team's performance can also influence one's state of self-esteem. Hirt and colleagues (1992) found that the team's success or failure significantly affected state of self-esteem. Fans viewed themselves more positively after a win and more negatively after a loss. We also found that reading a positive article about the team can enhance a fan's state of self-esteem. Undergraduate students were asked to respond to the state of self-esteem scale immediately after reading either positive, negative, or neutral publicity about the team. There was a significant mean difference between positive publicity and neutral publicity, respondents in the positive condition reporting higher levels of state self-esteem ($M_{self\text{-}esteem} = 33.47$; $SD = 5.26$) than respondents who read a neutral article ($M_{self\text{-}esteem} = 29.95$; $SD = 5.04$) ($p < .05$). This finding suggests that positive publicity about the team can temporarily boost fans' self-regard.

To summarize, sport publicity has emotion-eliciting properties that can trigger different emotional feelings in fans' mind. Simply reading an article about one's favorite team evoked strong emotional responses among respondents. Additionally, fans in the positive message condition viewed themselves more positively than the fans in the neutral message condition. Therefore, empirical evidence suggests that sport publicity can shift one's transitory feeling states as well as state self-esteem.

Publicity impact on future performance prediction

After a team's win, fans become more optimistic about the team's future performance. Hirt, *et al.* (1992) found that fans were more optimistic about the team's future performance after a win than a loss. Enhanced self-esteem and positive emotions triggered from winning may have increased their confidence in the team's future performance. On the other hand, negative affect elicited from a loss may have reduced available resources to believe that the team will succeed in the future. However, the effect of publicity on fans' performance prediction remains unknown. Thus, Kwak, *et al.* (2011) further replicated this phenomenon by using sport publicity as research stimuli. Using an online experiment, the scholars developed three fictitious sport articles (positive, negative, and neutral) about the university's men's basketball team, and undergraduate students ($N = 157$) were recruited to participate in this study. Respondents were randomly assigned to read one of three articles and then respond to three questions asking about the team's future performance:

- How many total games do you think the team will win this season? (0–33 regular season games);

- How many conference games do you think the team will win this season? (0–18 regular conference games);
- What is the probability (percentage) that the team would play in the NCAA Tournament this season? (0–100 percent).

As expected, in a study not yet published, the chapter authors found that publicity valence had a significant effect on performance prediction. For instance, respondents in the positive publicity condition expected the team to win more regular season games and conference games than respondents in the negative publicity condition. Additionally, respondents in the positive publicity condition were more optimistic than respondents in the negative publicity condition about the team's probability of playing in the NCAA tournament ("March Madness"). Taken together, preliminary findings suggest that publicity valence can also influence fans' projection of their team's future performance (compare Hirt, *et al.*, 1992).

Publicity impact on behavior

While the influence of publicity on emotional response and future performance prediction has been discussed, one would wonder if written communication can change behavioral response. Although this question begs more empirical research, some evidence exists that positive and negative publicity may influence behavioral change (Kwak, *et al.*, 2011). In order to explain how publicity affects behaviors, two motivational systems which underlie behavior – the behavioral activation system (BAS) and the behavioral inhibitory (or avoidance) system (BIS) are discussed herein (Gray, 1990).

The BAS is believed to regulate approach motives, in which the goal is to move toward signals of reward (Gray, 1990). According to Gray, this system is responsible for the experience of positive emotions such as hope, elation, and happiness. Therefore, positive publicity about one's favorite team will motivate goal-directed behaviors to maintain positive feelings triggered by an article. In an experimental study, Kwak, *et al.* (2011) found that fans who read a positive article about a team were more likely to accept a team-related promotional item (schedule card) than fans who read a negative article. A positive message influenced participants to approach toward desired goals.

On the other hand, the BIS is considered to regulate aversive motives, in which the goal is to move away from something unpleasant (Gray, 1990). When reading a negative article about a team, a fan may experience unpleasant feelings and such unpleasant feelings may activate the BIS, motivating the fan to temporarily stay away from the source of negative stimuli – the article or the team. It inhibits behavior that may lead to negative or painful outcomes. Fans will try to avoid a situation which exacerbates negative feelings. For instance, some fans may leave the stadium or arena even before the final whistle if their team has no chance to come back. These fans may not want to see their team suffer until the end of the game and thus may want to avoid that situation to alleviate negative feelings.

Kwak, *et al.* (2011) found that respondents in the negative article condition were significantly less likely to accept a team-related promotional item than respondents in the positive and neutral conditions. They wanted to avoid a situation that would aggravate their negative feelings (such as shame). Recently, research has shown that when publicity is coupled with advertising, positive publicity will further boost consumer attitudes regarding purchase intentions while negative publicity will cause even more negative evaluation of an advertised product (Kim, Yoon, and Lee, 2010; Kwak, Lim, and Kwon, 2012). In Kwak, *et al.*'s (2012) study, the scholars found that positive publicity enhanced the licensed product's perceived value and purchase intentions regardless of its product category (utilitarian vs. symbolic). These findings suggest that publicity can further embed symbolic meanings of a product associated with that publicity.

Practitioners may find publicity a useful marketing strategy to increase team-related purchase behaviors (such as licensed products, tickets). Before the start of a new season, when hopes are high, communicating a positive projection of the team's performance may add greater product value than neutral or negative information. Because it may be difficult for teams to control messages from mainstream media outlets (for example, ESPN, *Sports Illustrated*), social media could serve as an effective outlet for targeted communication. For instance, the University of Michigan has its own football team Facebook page (www.facebook.com/michiganfball) and uses it as a viable platform to communicate with over 890,000 enthusiastic supporters. In 2012, the Facebook page posted front and back images of a new licensed t-shirt with the message "Now, you're ready for kickoff." The T-shirt has "2012 Michigan Football Team 133" in large print on the front, and "11 national titles, 42 conference championships, 3 Heisman Trophy winners, 41 bowl game appearances, most wins in college football, largest stadium in America" printed on the back. The link to the online store to purchase the product was provided with the images. Two days after it was first posted, 4,174 fans "liked" it and 347 fans "shared" the information, while more than 170 fans left a comment on the product. Fans were highly engaged with the product, and their comments were mostly favorable toward it (for example, "Where can I get one?", "Go Blue! Love it!", "I need one of those", "I am ready for some football"). This is an interesting example, because the product itself articulates the team's quality (tradition) above and beyond the mere exposure of the brand (UM logo). Thus, teams may find this form of communication and product development strategy useful for engaging with their fans and increasing licensed merchandise sales.

Overall, findings from an experimental study suggest that publicity has a significant impact on respondents' behavioral responses to team-related marketing stimuli. In line with the BAS/BIS framework, a positive article seems to trigger an approach tendency while a negative article seems to activate the inhibitory system. Obviously, more systematic research is needed in this area to further examine the impact of publicity on emotional, cognitive and behavioral responses in sport fans.

Negative publicity and resistance

While it is presumable that positive messages will always boost fan confidence and make fans feel good about themselves, processing negative messages seems far more complicated than processing attitude-congruent messages. A strong emotional attachment established with the team would make it difficult to accept counter-attitudinal messages. Personally important attitudes are difficult to change (Eagly and Chaiken, 1993; Petty and Krosnick, 1995). As briefly noted previously, an increasing body of communication research has been devoted to understanding how people resist attitude-incongruent messages (see Knowles and Linn, 2004 for a detailed review of resistance).

Communication research has identified several strategies people use to resist persuasion. Among them are counter-arguing, attitude bolstering, source derogation, negative affect, and selective exposure (Jacks and Cameron, 2003). Counter-arguing involves direct rebuttal of arguments ("I don't believe it") (see, for example, Cameron and Jacks, 1999; Zuwerink and Devine, 1996). In contrast, attitude bolstering involves generating thoughts that are consistent with one's original attitudes and beliefs without directly refuting arguments ("I like my team no matter what") (for example, Jacks and Cameron, 2003). Source derogation involves insulting the source, criticizing his or her expertise or trustworthiness ("He does not know anything about my team") (see, for example, Festinger, 1957; Kwak, Kim, and Zimmerman, 2010). Negative affect involves responding to an attitude-incongruent message by getting angry, irritated, or upset ("This makes me frustrated") (for example, Jacks and Devine, 2000). Lastly, selective exposure involves resisting a counter-attitudinal message by leaving the situation or actively avoiding the message (see, for example, Frey, 1986). Although each of these resistance strategies appears in the communication literature, they have never been examined in the sport publicity context.

In an unpublished study conducted by the chapter authors, Kwak and Kim examined this resistance phenomenon within the sport publicity setting by exposing college students ($N = 93$) to a negative article about their university's basketball team. Using a free-thought listing technique, respondents were asked to write down anything that was going through their minds when reading the article. Responses then were coded based on Jacks and Cameron's (2003) typology of resistance. Similar to Jacks and Cameron, four resisting strategies were identified: about 31 percent of the responses were related to counter-arguing, about 38 percent of the responses were related to negative affect, about 16 percent of the responses were related to source derogation, and about 11 percent of the responses were related to attitude bolstering. Some specific comments were: "It was just an article so the person writing the article probably wasn't anyone important," "This writer doesn't understand XXX basketball" (source derogation); "This is embarrassing. Feel bad for the players" (negative affect); "He is just writing an article to state the obvious that we are re-building" (counter-arguing). The preliminary findings of this study hint that negative publicity about the team will evoke a fair amount of counter-arguing and negative affect. However, more systematic research is needed to examine the conditions under which other strategies might be effective in resisting negative information about the team.

Conclusion

Compared with other forms of marketing communication, the impact of publicity has been neglected in the sport communication and sport management literature. Although sport-related information is pervasive in our everyday life, little attention has been paid to the impact of publicity on emotional, cognitive, and behavioral responses among sport consumers. Based on the communication literature and empirical research in this area, a sport publicity processing model has been presented here to explain fan motivations, processing mechanisms, and various outcomes (emotional, cognitive, and behavioral) associated with processing publicity. Further, the notion of resistance in processing counter-attitudinal messages is also included in the model.

Several communication theories help understand why fans crave team-related information. Balance theory and cognitive dissonance theory focus on the valence of messages (attitude congruent vs. attitude incongruent) and how they motivate information processing. In contrast, mood management theory and BIRG/CORF theory explain how approach/avoidance tendencies triggered by message valence affect fans' feelings, decisions, and behaviors. Research on resisting persuasive messages provides additional insights into how fans process attitude-incongruent messages. Empirical findings suggest that sport publicity can significantly affect how fans feel, think and make decisions. When dealing with negative publicity, fans use various strategies (for example, counter-arguing, negative affect, source derogation, attitude bolstering) to counter attitude-incongruent messages.

Obviously, more systematic research is needed in this area. In particular, one area that needs further examination is the influence of user-generated content. With the explosive growth of social network sites, examining the relative persuasive strengths of different source characteristics (team-generated vs. mainstream media-generated vs. fan-generated) may be an interesting avenue for future research. Another underdeveloped line of research is the role of resistance in team–fan relationship constructs. Findings from communication research have been inconsistent with respect to whether resistance augments or diminishes initial attitudes (compare Tormala and Petty, 2004). Future research along these lines will further extend our understanding of sport publicity and its impact on sport fans.

References

Boen, F., Vanbeselaere, N., and Feys, J. (2002). Behavioral consequences of fluctuating group success: An internet study of soccer-team fans. *Journal of Social Psychology*, 142, 769–81.

Bond, J., and Kirshenbaum, R. (1998). *Under the radar: Talking to today's cynical consumer*. New York: John Wiley and Sons.

Cameron, K. A., and Jacks, J. R. (1999). *Modes of resisting attitude change: An experimental approach*. Poster presented at the meeting of the Midwestern Psychological Association, Chicago, IL.

Chang, C. (2006). Beating the news blues: Mood repair through exposure to advertising. *Journal of Communication*, 56: 198–217.

Cialdini, R. B., Bordon, R. J., Thorne, A., Walker, M. R., Freeman, S., and Sloan, L. R. (1976). Basking in reflected glory: Three field studies. *Journal of Personality and Social Psychology*, 34, 366–75.

Eagly, A. H., and Chaiken, S. (1993). *The psychology of attitudes*. New York: Harcourt Brace.

Festinger, L. (1957). *A theory of cognitive dissonance*. Evanston, IL: Row, Peterson.

Frey, D. (1986). Recent research on selective exposure to information. *Advances in Experimental Social Psychology*, 19, 41–80.

Funk, D. C., and Pritchard, M. P. (2006). Sport publicity: Commitment's moderation of message effects. *Journal of Business Research*, 59, 613–21.

Gantz, W., Wang, Z., Paul, B., and Potter, R. F. (2006). Sports versus all comers: Comparing TV sports fans with fans of other programming genres. *Journal of Broadcasting and Electronic Media*, 50, 95–118.

Gray, J. A. (1990). Brain systems that mediate both emotion and cognition. *Cognition and Emotion*, 4, 269–88.

Hammervold, R., and Solberg, H. A. (2006). TV sport programs – Who is willing to pay to watch? *Journal of Media Economics*, 19, 147–62.

Heider, F. (1958). *The psychology of interpersonal relations*. New York: Wiley.

Hirt, E. R., Zillmann, D., Erickson, G. A., and Kennedy, C. (1992). Costs and benefits of allegiance: Changes in fans' self-ascribed competencies after team victory versus defeat. *Journal of Personality and Social Psychology*, 63, 724–38.

Jacks, J. Z., and Cameron, K. A. (2003). Strategies for resisting persuasion. *Basic and Applied Social Psychology*, 25 (2), 145–61.

Jacks, J. Z., and Devine, P. G. (2000). Attitude importance, forewarning of message content, and resistance to persuasion. *Basic and Applied Social Psychology*, 22, 19–29.

Kim, J., Yoon, H. J., and Lee, S.Y. (2010). Integrating advertising and publicity: A theoretical examination of the effects of exposure sequence, publicity valence, and product attribute consistency. *Journal of Advertising*, 39 (1), 97–113.

Knobloch, S., and Zillmann, D. (2002). Mood management via the digital jukebox. *Journal of Communication*, 52 (2): 351–66.
Knowles, E. S., and Linn, J. A. (2004). *Resistance and persuasion*. Mahwah, NJ: Lawrence Erlbaum.
Kwak, D. H., and Kim, Y. K., and Hirt, E. R. (2011). Exploring the role of emotions on sport consumers' behavioral and cognitive responses to marketing stimuli. *European Sport Management Quarterly*, 11 (3), 225–50.
Kwak, D. H., Kim, Y. K., and Zimmerman (2010). User- versus mainstream-media-generated content: Media source, message valence, and team identification and sport consumers' response. *International Journal of Sport Communication*, 3, 402–21.
Kwak, D. H., Lim, C. H., and Kwon, Y. (2012). *Heuristic cues and perceived product value: Effects of priming, team-brand cue and product category*. Presented at the annual conference of North American Society for Sport Management, Seattle, WA, May.
L'Etang, J. (2006). Public relations and sport in promotional culture. *Public Relations Review*, 32, 386–94.
Madrigal, R., and Dalakas, V. (2008). Consumer psychology of sport: More than just a game. In C. P. Haugtvedt, P. M. Herr, and F. R. Kardes (Eds.), *Handbook of Consumer Psychology* (pp. 857–76). New York: Taylor and Francis.
Petty, R. E., and Krosnick, J. A. (1995). *Attitude strength: Antecedents and consequences*. Mahwah, NJ: Lawrence Erlbaum.
Ries, A., and Ries, L. (2002). *The fall of advertising and the rise of PR*. New York: Harper Business.
Snyder, C. R., Lassegard, M., and Ford, C. E. (1986). Distancing after group successes and failure: Basking in reflected glory and cutting off reflected failure. *Journal of Personality and Social Psychology*, 51, 382–8.
Tajfel, H., and Turner, J. C. (1979). An integrative theory of intergroup conflict. In W. G. Austin and S. Worchel. (Eds.), *The social psychology of intergroup relations* (pp. 94–109). Monterey, CA: Brooks-Cole.
Tormala, Z. L., and Petty, R. E. (2004). Resisting persuasion and attitude certainty: A metacognitive analysis. In E. S. Knowles and J. A. Linn (Eds.), *Resistance and persuasion* (pp. 65–82). Mahwah, NJ: Lawrence Erlbaum.
Wann, D. L., and Branscombe, N. R. (1992). Emotional responses to the sports page. *Journal of Sport and Social Issues*, 16, 49–64.
Zillmann, D. (1996). The psychology of suspense in dramatic exposition. In P. Vorderer, H. J. Wulff, and M. Friedrichsen (Eds.), *Suspense: Conceptualizations, theoretical analyses, and empirical explorations* (pp. 199–231). Mahwah, NJ: Lawrence Erlbaum.
Zuwerink, J. R., and Devine, P. G. (1996). Attitude importance and resistance to persuasion: It's not just the thought that counts. *Journal of Personality and Social Psychology*, 70, 931–44.

19

TELEVISION BROADCAST RIGHTS

Still the golden goose

John A. Fortunato

Broadcast rights contracts signed by professional sports leagues and teams, the NCAA for its men's basketball tournament, and collegiate conferences that extend into the decade of the 2020's, clearly indicate that television networks continue to provide a very lucrative revenue source. The money from television networks to purchase the right to broadcast games is the foundation of the economic sports business model and the largest revenue source for a popular sports league such as the National Football League (NFL) or an organization such as the International Olympic Committee (IOC). For example, the IOC generates 47 percent of its revenue from its broadcast contracts, with sponsorship ranking as the second highest revenue source at 45 percent (International Olympic Committee, 2012).

This chapter focuses on the dynamics of television broadcast rights fees contracts and their impact on the sports business. Parente points out that "once a sport, league, or team has had its 'product' bought by television for use as programming, that entity can seldom exist thereafter, at least in the same style or manner, without the financial support of television" (Parente, 1977, p. 128). It is this revenue stream that influences league or team decisions, such as the ability to sign free agents, the overall competitive balance of the league, and recently movement of a university to another conference.

The broadcast rights fee contract process

Sports leagues and television networks sign a broadcast rights contract where the network agrees to pay the league a certain dollar amount for a certain number of years for the rights to televise that league's games (see, for example, Fortunato, 2001; Wenner, 1989). The system of sports leagues selling broadcast rights to television networks was legally established in the Sports Broadcasting Act passed in the US Congress and signed into law by President John F. Kennedy in September of 1961. In what Congress termed as "special interest legislation" for this single industry, the law provides sports leagues with an antitrust exemption that allows them to collectively pool the broadcast rights to all of their teams' games and sell them to the highest bidding television network (see, for example, Fortunato, 2001; Scully, 2004).

Pete Rozelle was commissioner of the NFL from 1960 to 1989. He is largely given credit as the visionary who developed the economic business model for professional sports through the establishment of a league-wide television contract. In the NFL in the early 1960s, each team negotiated its own television contract. Rozelle convinced the NFL owners to change from a system of teams making their own television deals and keeping the money themselves to one of selling the league's television rights as a singular, collective entity to the highest bidding television network.

Rozelle correctly predicted that network television money would be the largest revenue source for the NFL. The NFL is the league that garners the highest television rights fees. In September of 2011, the NFL reached an extension with ESPN that will run through the 2022 season worth an estimated US$1.9 billion per year, a 63 percent increase over the NFL's previous deal with ESPN. In December of 2011, extensions through 2022 were also reached with CBS, Fox, and NBC. Fox will pay the NFL an annual fee of US$1.1 billion, CBS US$1 billion, and NBC US$950 million (SBJ, 2012a).

There are a few variables that can increase the value of a league's television rights. The main variable is the size and demographic of the audience that watches the games. Sports programming attracts the relatively hard-to-reach, male audience between the ages of 18 and 49 that is desirable to advertisers (for example, Wenner, 1989). It is the size and demographic of the audience that will determine the rate that the television network can charge advertisers for commercial time. Viewership data in the form of television ratings are vital because these numbers have such a tremendous impact on the economics of a television network. Webster and Lichty describe ratings as "a fact of life for virtually everyone connected with the electronic media. They are the tools used by advertisers and broadcasters to buy and sell audiences" (Webster and Lichty, 1991, p. 3).

In addition to the audience size and demographic, sports programming has unique characteristics that are valuable to networks. Sports programming tends to provide consistent audience viewership with television ratings for games fluctuating by a small percentage in comparison to other programming. Sports games hold viewers over long periods of time with games lasting three hours. Networks also get to promote their future programming, often doing so during the context of the game when the audience is watching rather than only promoting their shows during commercials when the audience might be more apt to be away from the screen. Lever and Wheeler point out that "astronomical costs (rights fees) can be justified by giving valuable exposure to new series and entertainment specials through promotional spots" (Lever and Wheeler, 1993, p. 135).

Another important audience viewership variable is that fans often watch sports games during the live telecast, not at a later time or another day using a DVR device, making a promotion, a television commercial, or a sponsored portion of the broadcast more relevant because it is viewed at the appropriate time desired by the network or the advertiser. David Levy, president of sales, distribution and sports for Turner Broadcasting System, explained "we know that sports is appointment viewing. We know that five, ten years from now, this might be the only and final appointment-viewing product in the market, other than news. Nobody's watching the Super Bowl on Monday morning" (Ourand, 2011a, p. 17). Levy added:

> you're getting a built-in fan base each time you buy these sports properties. If I buy the Pac-12 or NHL or NFL or NCAA basketball – any of these sports properties have

> automatically built-in fan bases and pretty much a track record of a ratings process you could almost guarantee will be there day in and day out.
>
> *(Ourand, 2011a, p. 17)*

Similarly, Sean McManus, CBS Sports chairman, stated:

> the value of the sports content is increasing as it becomes more and more difficult to get people in front of a set – and a specific demographic in front of a set. Sports is still able to attract that demographic, and it's pretty consistent in terms of the people it brings to the set. That isn't true of a lot of other programming on television.
>
> *(Ourand, 2011a, p. 17)*

A second important variable for a sports league to maximize its revenue from television broadcast is to have multiple networks bidding for the rights to its games. Any time a sports league can get multiple networks competing against each other for its broadcast rights there will surely be an increase in the rights fee paid to the league. The NFL has received substantial right fees because many networks bid to televise that league's games. Cable television networks continue to actively bid on packages of games and provide an astounding level of revenue for sports leagues. The trend of cable television networks acquiring the rights to prominent sporting events is because they have the dual revenue source of advertising income and monthly subscription fees. ESPN is the most expensive cable network. Cable providers pay more than an estimated US$5.00 per month per subscriber to have ESPN as part of the package of channels that they offer to customers (Flint, 2012).

All leagues have cable television networks as part of their broadcast portfolio. In its national television contacts agreed to in 2012 and scheduled to begin with the 2014 season, Fox will pay Major League Baseball (MLB) US$2 billion, ESPN will pay MLB US$5.6 billion, and Turner will pay MLB US$2.6 billion in deals that will run through the 2021 season (Ourand, 2012b). The National Basketball Association (NBA) has broadcast rights contracts with ABC/ESPN and Turner that average US$930 million per year and expire after the 2014 season (*SportsBusiness Journal's Annual Resource Guide and Fact Book* provides a listing of all leagues broadcast rights agreements). The number of networks involved in the bidding process was a factor in MLB receiving an over US$800 million annual increase in its broadcast rights and will be a determinant in the amount of revenue that the NBA will secure in its next television negotiation.

Ourand (2011b) provides an example of how multiple television networks bidding on an event can increase the cost in his description of the negotiations for the rights to the Wimbledon tennis tournament. NBC had been the over-the-air rights holder since 1968 with live coverage of the Men's and Women's Championships. ESPN had been the secondary rights holder providing coverage during the week. NBC was paying US$13 million per year and ESPN was paying US$10 million. The NBC contract expired after the 2011 Wimbledon tournament, with ESPN's contract scheduled to run through 2014.

After preliminary meetings were held with various network officials earlier in 2011, a schedule for presentations by the interested networks was set up by the All England Lawn Tennis and Croquet Club that hosts the Wimbledon championships. Fox made a presentation for why it should be the rights holder on Monday June 27, followed by NBC and ESPN on June 28. Fox indicated that it would use its FX cable channel to televise matches. At the end of its meeting Fox informed the All England Club that it was prepared to sign a ten-year,

US$350 million contract. NBC pledged to show all matches live by also using its cable properties once it acquired all Wimbledon television rights in 2014. NBC did not make a monetary offer in its presentation meeting. ESPN stressed in its meeting that its networks had a larger audience reach than the other networks cable properties. ESPN made a similar monetary bid to that of Fox.

On Wednesday, June 29, the All England Club would contact all the networks. Fox would be informed that it would have to increase its bid to acquire the rights at which time Fox declined and took itself out of contention. NBC would make an offer for an average annual payment in the mid-US$30 million range. ESPN would increase its bid to US$40 million per year. On Saturday, July 2, NBC would make a final bid for a twelve-year contract with an average annual payment in the high-US$30 million range. The All England Club would return to ESPN for a final offer, explaining that if the network increased its US$40 million per year bid from ten years to twelve it would acquire the rights. ESPN agreed and beginning in 2012 for the first time the entire Wimbledon tennis tournament was televised on a cable network.

Another strategy that a sports league can adopt to get more networks involved and increase its rights fees is to take a portion of its games and create another television package that it could sell. In that thinking, again Rozelle would be instrumental in co-creating another television institution: *Monday Night Football*. This prime time package of games would be another product for the networks to bid. In 1985, when the major networks were not looking to greatly increase their rights fees, Rozelle and the NFL developed a package of Sunday night games that would be sold on cable television.

Other sport organizations have used a similar tactic of segmenting their games. For example, MLB created a Sunday afternoon package of games that was purchased by Turner and a Sunday evening game of the week that is the premier attraction of ESPN's contract. The Federation International of Football Association (FIFA) segments it television rights based on language. In 2011, FIFA, signed broadcast contracts worth an estimated US$1.85 billion for the 2018 and 2022 World Cup tournaments, including US$1.2 billion for United States rights from Fox and Spanish-language rights with Telemundo, owned by NBC Universal (SBJ, 2011).

Sports leagues have created two other opportunities for revenue through television. All leagues have partnerships with Direct-TV for satellite subscription packages that provide viewers with the opportunity to watch the league's out-of-market games (a Direct-TV subscription ensures that NFL fans have the ability to see every game of the NFL season). The leagues have also developed their own networks using the cable television business model of the dual revenue stream of subscription fees and advertising. To help increase the audience demand for these channels leagues have put games on their league-owned network. This, in essence, creates another bidder in any rights fees negotiation. In the 2012 season, the NFL Network increased its schedule of games to thirteen. The NFL Network is in 59 million homes and costs cable providers approximately 84 cents per month per subscriber (Ourand, 2012a). In 2012, the MLB Network broadcast playoff games. As part of the agreements between MLB and its broadcast partners, the MLB Network will pay Fox US$30 million per year to acquire the rights to two division series games (Ourand, 2012b).

Finally, the value of broadcast rights and an interest by a network can be increased through the manipulation of the television programming schedule. The signing of a broadcast rights contract creates a partnership between a sports league and a television network where both now have a vested interest in increasing the audience watching the games. In addition to being their greatest revenue source, television networks provide the greatest source of brand exposure (see, for example, Fortunato, 2001). Exposure is ascertained through the league's placement in the television programming schedule (day and time that the game is played) and the selection of the teams playing in those games. The selection of which teams will appear on nationally televised games is in fact the first step in setting up the entire schedule of games for a league (for example, Fortunato, 2001; 2008). This television schedule strategy allows the best teams and best players to receive exposure to the largest possible audience. Fortunato explains that:

> the proper exposure and positioning in the program schedule and offering the best product to viewers in the form of teams, players, and matchups are essential to achieve the best television rating, and subsequently to earn the greatest advertising revenue, which would initially benefit the network – and eventually the league – when negotiating its next broadcast rights contract.
>
> *(Fortunato, 2001, p. 73)*

Leagues and networks work together in making the programming schedule as desirable as possible. For example, the NBA in its broadcast contract with Turner for a package of games on Thursday night, has it so that there are only three games played on that night, with two of them televised by Turner. This eliminates the competition that Turner might receive from NBA games being televised by local channels throughout the country.

The NFL has done multiple programming schedule changes to make its packages more attractive to television networks. First, the NFL bye-week, which gives each team one week off, makes a sixteen-week season of games into a seventeen-week television product. This gives the network an extra week of NFL programming and allows the NFL to ask for higher rights fees. The NFL has also moved its playoff games to later start times which push the games into prime time and larger audience viewership.

In 2006, the NFL adopted a flexible schedule component for its over-the-air, prime-time rights holder, NBC. In flexible scheduling a more attractive game would simply be moved from Sunday afternoon to Sunday evening and televised on NBC. Games that are originally scheduled for Monday, Thursday, or Saturday are not eligible to be shifted. Dick Ebersol, former NBC Sports Chairman, described the process as "we're able to say to the league, 'here is a game we would like to have, and here are reasons why we think this is a compelling game.' And then the league's television department and the commissioner make the final decision" (Stewart, 2006, p. D5). In the "Flexible scheduling procedures" popup window at www.nfl.com/schedules, the NFL described flexible scheduling as a strategy that "ensured quality matchups on Sunday night in those weeks and gave surprise teams a chance to play their way onto primetime" (Stewart, 2006, p. D5, para. 2).

The partnership between a league and a television network in terms of the programming schedule is also seen through developing special games for the network. In 2011, the National Hockey League (NHL) reached a ten-year, US$2 billion agreement with NBC. Each NHL team will earn approximately US$7 million per year from the NBC contract (Vascellaro and Everson, 2011). The NHL and NBC had achieved success in televising the Winter Classic, an outdoor NHL game traditionally played on New Year's Day. In this latest contract agreement, the NHL created a new Thanksgiving Friday afternoon game to be televised on NBC. Overall, NBC agreed to televise 100 regular season games on its over-the-air network and its cable channel, NBC Sports Network.

Local television broadcast rights

For a sports league to thrive, it needs competitive balance, with every team being equipped with the same economic tools, and fans in every city believing that their team, if managed properly, could win a championship. In establishing the system of collectively selling the league's broadcast rights to the highest bidding network, Rozelle believed that competitive balance was linked to the league's distribution of revenues (see, for example, Fortunato, 2006; Lewis, 1998). The revenue generated from the television contracts would need to be shared equally among all teams. This equal sharing of national television money remains the standard revenue distribution model for all major sports leagues.

It must be noted that the NFL is different from other sports in terms of television revenue sharing because each NFL game is televised by a national broadcast network. In MLB, the NBA, and the NHL for the games that are not broadcast on national television, the rights revert back to the teams. For these leagues the majority of games are sold by the teams to local networks and the revenue is not shared equally.

Understanding local cable broadcasts as a potentially huge revenue source in the mid-1980s, George Steinbrenner, former owner of the New York Yankees, was the first owner to sell most of the team's local broadcast rights to a local cable operator, selling the rights at the time to Cablevision's SportsChannel in New York (Fisher, 2010). The Yankees later sold their broadcast rights to the Madison Square Garden (MSG) Network for the 1989 season. In 2001, the MSG Network paid the Yankees US$52 million per year for their broadcast rights.

Recognizing an opportunity to further increase income from cable television by obtaining subscriber fees and advertising revenue led to the creation of team-owned and operated cable television networks. In 2001, the Yankees announced the formation of the Yankees Entertainment and Sports (YES) Network. The primary programming of the regional 24-hour all-sports network would be Yankees baseball beginning in March 2002. One estimate is that the YES Network earned over US$435 million in 2010 (Sandomir, 2011).

Similar to sports leagues with national television networks, on a local level the number of cable networks involved in the bidding process to acquire sports programming can increase the rights fee. The Los Angeles Lakers reached a 20-year, US$3 billion deal with Time Warner as it was set to launch English- and Spanish-language, twenty-four hour sports channels in Los Angeles. With cable networks needing programming Time Warner also signed a deal with the Los Angeles Galaxy of Major League Soccer (MLS) for US$55 million over ten years (Pucin, 2011). In addition to the Time Warner channel, which is planning to seek more than US$3.50 per month, the Los Angeles market has Fox Sports West, which costs subscribers approximately US$2.60 per month, and Prime Ticket, costing US$2.50 per month (Flint, 2012). With the local rights to the Los Angeles Dodgers expiring after the 2013 season, and with the sale of the team to a group led by Magic Johnson for a record US$2.15 billion finalized, the Dodgers can negotiate with any of these networks or start one of its own.

With local television money not being shared equally a large disparity in revenues between teams from larger or smaller markets has the potential to threaten a league's competitive balance. MLB features the greatest disparity in team salaries. The Yankees in 2012 have a payroll of approximately US$200 million while the Oakland A's and the San Diego Padres have total payrolls of only approximately US$55 million (USA Today, 2012). Owing largely to its local television revenue, the Yankees have had the highest payroll every season since 1999 (the Baltimore Orioles had the highest payroll in 1998).

The most notable free agent signings in MLB prior to the 2012 season were largely a result of those teams having recently signed very lucrative local cable television contracts. The Los Angeles Angels reached a ten-year, US$240 million agreement with first baseman Albert Pujols. In December, 2011, the Angels agreed to a 20-year contract with Fox Sports West valued at more than US$3 billion. The Texas Rangers, in August 2010, reached an agreement with Fox Sports Southwest in a deal valued at US$3 billion over 20 years. Prior to 2012, the Rangers spent US$111 million to acquire Japanese pitcher, Yu Darvish. The Detroit Tigers signed first baseman Prince Fielder to a nine-year, US$214 million contract. The Tigers earn US$40 million per year from Fox Sports Detroit with a new broadcast deal to be negotiated before 2018, in the midst of the Fielder contract. Ed Goren, Fox Sports Media Group vice chairman, stated, "the local TV money has changed the entire landscape. There are a lot of other teams that can play with the big boys now and write those big checks" (Nightengale, 2012, p. 1C). Jerry Reinsdorf, Chicago White Sox chairman, commented on the potential impact of local cable television revenue on the competitive balance of baseball, stating, "it does have the potential to hurt competitive balance. The big TV deals are basically a function of market-size and competition. There's no way that Kansas City can get a deal comparable to what the Angels did" (Nightengale, 2012, p. 1C).

National Collegiate Athletic Association

The National Collegiate Athletic Association (NCAA), collegiate conferences, and universities have come to be as reliant on television revenue as professional sports leagues. The most lucrative event for the NCAA is the men's basketball tournament. CBS had been the sole rights holder since 1982. In 2011, however, to continue having some rights to the NCAA tournament CBS was forced to join with Turner and both networks began televising the NCAA men's basketball tournament under a 14-year agreement that will pay the NCAA a total of US$10.8 billion (Ourand and Smith, 2010).

For college football, the NCAA lost control over singularly negotiating television contracts in a 1984 United States Supreme Court decision. At the time the NCAA dictated all television deals, including limiting the number of times a university can appear on television (Hiestand, 2004). In a lawsuit led by the University of Oklahoma and the University of Georgia, collegiate conferences obtained the ability to negotiate their own television deals with the networks. The seven to two Supreme Court decision opened up unprecedented competition for collegiate sports content as conferences presented packages of games for the networks to bid.

Similar to professional sports leagues, collegiate conferences have a primary over-the-air rights holder as well as a cable network rights holder. In football, for example, the SEC has an exclusive contract with CBS as its over-the-air rights holder where the network only shows that league's games every Saturday. The SEC also has a contract with ESPN for prime-time games so once CBS selects the game it will air on its network, ESPN will then select the next two SEC games each week that it will air on ESPN and ESPN 2 on Saturday night.

Recently, conferences have expanded and recruited universities to join their conference to increase their appeal to television networks. In 2011, the Pac-10 Conference had Colorado and Utah join to form the Pacific-12 Conference (Pac-12). This helped the Pac-12 secure a 12-year, US$3 billion contract from ESPN and Fox that extends through the 2022–23 seasons. Universities in the Pac-12 earn approximately US$21 million per year in television revenue. The Big

Ten Conference (Big Ten) provides its schools with similar annual revenue. The Southeastern Conference (SEC) universities earn approximately US$17 million (Smith and Ourand, 2012).

The addition of universities has allowed conferences the opportunity to reopen their broadcast rights agreements. The addition of Pittsburgh and Syracuse to the Atlantic Coast Conference (ACC) led the ACC to renegotiate its agreement with ESPN, increasing each school's annual payment from US$13 million to more than US$17 million (Hiestand, 2012). The Big 12 after adding Texas Christian and West Virginia was able to renegotiate a contract with ABC/ESPN that had an eight-year, US$400 million contract signed in 2007 and due to run through 2016 replaced with a US$1.3 billion, 13-year contract that will run through 2025 (SBJ, 2012b).

In terms of competitive balance within collegiate conferences, it is important to note that each conference can establish its own system of broadcast revenue distribution. The Big Ten, for example, shares all of its broadcast revenue equally. In the past, the Big 12 shared half of the broadcast revenue equally, with the other half being distributed based on appearances on television. As an independent for football, Notre Dame has its own broadcast contract where NBC pays US$9 million per season for all of the Fighting Irish home games and one prime-time neutral site game. For all other sports Notre Dame competes in the ACC and is a part of any rights contracts that the league acquires, most notably for basketball.

Following similar trends in professional sports of developing television assets collegiate conferences have started their own networks. The Big Ten Network was established in 2006. In August of 2012, the Pac-12 launched its own national network and six regional networks devoted solely to the Pac-12 (Pac-12 Enterprises, 2012). The national Pac-12 Network is seeking a reported 80 cents per subscriber per month (Flint, 2012). Universities too have now started their own television networks. In August 2011, the University of Texas launched the Longhorn Network which provides the school US$15 million a year over the next 20 years (Vascellaro and Everson, 2011).

Summary

The monetary increases that the television networks continue to give to sports leagues for the rights to televise their games demonstrate the value of this programming. Investing in sports rights fees remains a viable strategy because of the unique and advantageous characteristics of this programming, most notably the size and demographic of the audience and the fact that games are often watched live. As long as many networks want sports programming on their air and bid for the rights to their games, leagues, teams, and other sport entities will continue receiving high broadcast rights fees. At this point there is no reason to doubt that television revenue is going to remain the foundation of the economic sports business model for the foreseeable future.

References

Fisher, E. (2010, July 19–25). He set the standard. *SportsBusiness Journal*, 13 (1), 1, 32–4.

Flint, J. (2012). Cable bills might take hit: With sports rights fees skyrocketing, cost of Dodgers' record sale could be passed along to viewers. *Los Angeles Times*, March 29, C8.

Fortunato, J. A. (2001). *The ultimate assist: The relationship and broadcast strategies of the NBA and television networks*. Cresskill, NJ: Hampton Press.

Fortunato, J. A. (2006). *Commissioner: The legacy of Pete Rozelle*. Lanham, MD: Taylor Trade.
Fortunato, J. A. (2008). The NFL programming schedule: A study of agenda-setting. *Journal of Sports Media*, 3 (1), 27–49.
Hiestand, M. (2004). 1984 TV ruling led to widening sweep of the college game. *USA Today*, August 20, 2E.
Hiestand, M. (2012). US$3.6 billion in TV money for ACC a good sign for SEC, Big 12. *USA Today*, May 10, 1C.
Lever, J., and Wheeler, S. (1993). Mass media and the experience of sport. *Communication Research*, 20 (1), 125–43.
Lewis, M. (1998). Pete Rozelle: He hooked us on football as show biz and gave Sunday (and Monday) a new kind of religious significance. *Time Magazine*, December 7, 188–90.
Nightengale, B. (2012). Cash flows through MLB cable outlets: Local TV deals add revenue, alter landscape. *USA Today*, February 10, 1C.
Ourand, J. (2011a). How high can rights fees go? More bidders, solid ratings, attractive demos and 'TV Everywhere' fuel a sizzling media rights market, but could the bubble burst? *SportsBusiness Journal*, June 6–12, 14 (8), 1,16–19.
Ourand, J. (2011b). How ESPN captured NBC's turf at Wimbledon. *SportsBusiness Journal*, July 11–17, 14 (12), 4.
Ourand, J. (2012a). No new TV package on the horizon. *SportsBusiness Journal*, February 13–19, 14 (41), 1, 28.
Ourand, J. (2012b). Fox, Turner contribute to $12B rights haul for MLB. *SportsBusiness Journal*, September 24–30, 15 (23), 1, 6.
Ourand, J., and Smith, M. (2010). NCAA's money-making matchup: How CBS, Turner made the numbers work in US$10.8 billion deal. *Sports Business Journal*, April 26–May 2, 13 (2), 1, 27.
Pac-12 Enterprises (2012). About Pac-12 Enterprises. *Pac-12.com*. Retrieved from http://www.pac-12.com/SPORTS/Pac12Networks/Pac12Networks.aspx.
Parente, D. (1977). The interdependence of sports and television. *Journal of Communication*, 27 (3), 128–32.
Pucin, D. (2011). Media titans clash in L.A. sports arena: Time Warner has its eye on Fox's most valuable television asset: The Dodgers. *Los Angeles Times*, December 6, A1.
International Olympic Committee (2012). Revenue Sources and Distribution. *Olympic.org*. Retrieved from http://www.olympic.org/ioc-financing-revenue-sources-distribution?tab=sources.
Sandomir, R. (2011). Regional sports networks show the money. *New York Times*, August 20, D1.
SBJ (2011). FIFA Wraps Up TV Deals. *SportsBusiness Journal*, October 31–November 6 14 (27), 6.
SBJ (2012a). The Season that Was. *SportsBusiness Journal*, January 30–February 5, 14 (39), 22–3.
SBJ (2012b). Current College Television Deals. *SportsBusiness Journal*, March 19–25, 14 (46), 46.
Scully, G. W. (2004). The market structure of sports. In S. R. Rosner and K. L. Shopshire (Eds.), *The business of sports* (pp. 26–33). Sudbury, MA: Jones and Bartlett.
Smith, M., and Ourand, J. (2012). ACC expansion will pay off in new TV deal: $1M to $2M increase annually per school. *SportsBusiness Journal*, February 6–12, 14 (40), 1, 8.
Stewart, L. (2006). Bears-Giants moved under flex schedule. *Los Angeles Times*, October 25, D5.
USA Today. (2012). Salaries databases. Major League Baseball salaries. *USAToday.com*. Retrieved from http://content.usatoday.com/sportsdata/baseball/mlb/salaries/team/.
Vascellaro, J. E., and Everson, D. (2011). TV cash tilts college playing field. *Wall Street Journal*, August 25, B1.
Webster, J. G., and Lichty, L. W. (1991). *Ratings analysis: Theory and practice*. Hillside, NJ: Erlbaum.
Wenner, L. A. (1989). Media, sports, and society: The research agenda. In L. A. Wenner (Ed.), *Media, sports and society* (pp. 13–48). Newbury Park, CA: Sage.

20

DEFINING FITNESS COMMUNICATION

Conceptualizing an emerging segment of the sport industry

Antonio S. Williams

A plethora of academic literature exists on the modes and prescription for exercise (that is, aerobic and anaerobic training). However, little attention has been devoted to the rapid advances in the ways in which fitness organizations, practitioners, and consumers communicate in a fitness-related context. The fitness sector of the sport industry in general has often been overlooked by sport management scholars, despite the vital importance of sport participation to the industry. In the same vein, the communication of fitness is an important component to sport participation and adherence to a healthy lifestyle. The prevalence of obesity and other public health concerns has sparked interest in the development of innovative technologies that communicate fitness services and products to consumers through various mediums. Even the US White House has taken notice of the effectiveness of communicating the benefits of fitness (that is, sport participation) through various mediums with the launching of Michelle Obama's "Let's Move" campaign. Owing to technological advances, connecting consumers with health and fitness information has become easier, more convenient, and less expensive. Fitness organizations and practitioners in the areas of health club administration, television, and new media are constantly evaluating channels of communication to create and deliver brand messages about fitness services and products.

In the US, over 45 million people are health club members, and 15–20 percent of these members engage in personal training (International Health Racquetball and Sports Club Association, 2012). Considering the size and the fact that health clubs are a service driven industry, it is inescapable that members and staff engage in various forms of personal and organizational fitness communication. According to a study conducted on trends in the fitness industry, educated and highly experienced staff and personal training ranked numbers one and seven respectively, which adds to the notion that communication in a fitness setting is of chief importance to health club members (Thompson, 2012). Branded shows such as *Extreme Makeover Weight Loss Edition* target overweight and obese participants to communicate the importance of health and fitness to people around the world (Vogel, 2009). Based on the ratings of fitness-related shows such as *The Biggest Loser*, it is apparent that television provides an essential form of fitness communication. The show had 7.2 million viewers during its 2012 season finale. This volume of exposure is influential as the show provides a plethora of information on fitness and lifestyle management. While traditional media provide beneficial forms of fitness communication, social media is emerging as a common form of communication in various industries (Harris, 2011). More than half of US adults (57 percent) seek health information on the internet and one-fifth use social media to stay abreast on health issues (Fox, 2011). Moreover, as revealed by Fox, 27 percent of internet users have tracked their weight, diet, exercise routine, or other fitness level indicators online.

The work of Pedersen, Miloch, and Laucella (2007) provides the foundation for understanding sport communication. However, to date, no such conceptualization exists for the fitness segment of the sport industry. It is of paramount importance that sport scholars understand the process of communication, as it will allow both scholars and practitioners to see the "big picture" and foster the development of fitness communication as a viable area of scholarly inquiry. Therefore, the ensuing sections examine fitness communication by providing a theoretical definition and presenting a model for understanding its role within the field of sport.

Defining fitness communication

To date, there has only been one attempt to describe fitness communication. Ashton applied a rhetorical approach to defining fitness communication, stating, "fitness communication should persuade people to reflect on the importance of physical activity and motivate them toward positive action" (Ashton, 2004, p. 3). In agreement with the author's notion that fitness communication should be positive and persuade people to live an active lifestyle, it is contended in this chapter that an organic definition of fitness communication should encompass the process and the content of the communication, not just the desired benefits. Therefore, fitness communication is defined as the process by which fitness consumers and practitioners inform, influence, and motivate their constituents about health, sport, and fitness-related matters in a fitness setting (for example, health clubs) through the use of fitness-related products and services (such as mobile applications), and via various mediums (for example, television, the Internet). The context in which the process of fitness communication takes place is personal, organizational, and mediated. Fitness communication is not a concentrated process, but rather practiced in a variety of institutions (that is, sport, retail, and gaming).

Understanding the process of fitness communication requires scholars and practitioners to consider communication perspectives as well as marketing perspectives. Moreover, the proposed definition of fitness communication indicates that it is an exchange of fitness-related and non-fitness-related information. Put another way, consumers may engage in communication about fitness products, services, and exercise tips (that is, communication of fitness). In contrast, they may choose to discuss other aspects of life in a fitness setting (that is, communication in fitness). From a marketing perspective, fitness organizations (for example, Gold's Gym, Nike) may communicate with consumers and potential consumers via advertisements designed to promote their services. On the other hand, corporate brands use fitness-related advertisements to promote non fitness-related products (that is, communication through fitness). Whether it is from the communication or marketing point of view, fitness communication is always a process used to send and receive messages.

Fitness communication is a process

Understanding communication theory and the process of communication is necessary to examine fitness communication. In fitness communication, the theorizing process includes both academic research as well as the practical area of the fitness industry. The communication process allows a sender to relay a message through a channel to a receiver (Thackeray and Neiger, 2009). Fitness communication includes active, interactive, and reactive processes between organizations, texts, and audiences in the public sphere, and can be best described as the process of producing and delivering messages to an audience of one or more persons through an array of mediums. These aspects – adapted from Pedersen, Laucella, Miloch, and Fielding (2007) and applied to the fitness context – allow for a definition and appropriate illustrations of fitness communication. For instance, the fitness communication process, like sport communication, is a process that involves a source, messenger, receiver, and accounts for behavioral and external factors. This is evident in popular exercise videos like Zumba and P90X. The host/instructor gives directions, while images of the exercises are broadcast to the consumer at home. A consumer's response to the messages maybe mediated by the personality of the instructor, background music, video atmosphere, difficulty of exercise, or ability to understand the instruction. Consequently, this may cause the consumer to continue or discontinue using the exercise video.

Fitness communication informs, influences, and motivates

Communication in a fitness setting is essential for motivating customer retention and influencing new clientele. For years, the health club sector of the fitness industry has used price discrimination to influence consumers to buy memberships and products (Williams and Pedersen, 2012). However, the sole focus should not be on the price of the membership or amenities, but rather providing members with knowledge and understanding about the benefits of becoming a member (Williams, 2010). Additionally, quality of service may motivate consumers to purchase products and services offered by health clubs. Previous studies (see, for example, Alexandris, Douka, Papadopoulos, and Kaltsatou, 2008; Kelley and Davis, 1994; Lam, Zhang, and Jensen, 2005) that have examined service quality in the fitness industry may be extended through the conceptualization of fitness communication. Meaning, adopting a strategic approach to communicating with consumers can impact the level of satisfaction consumers have with the organization.

As fitness organizations (that is, health clubs) rely on customer retention and product sales, the Internet offers organizations an opportunity to create and enhance communication that provides a competitive advantage in the marketplace. Previous research has suggested that the Internet has changed the way in which sport and fitness products and services are delivered to consumers (Filo and Funk, 2005; Himel and Munck, 2000). According to Himel and Munck, the Internet is a valuable resource for consumers seeking information, purchasing, communication, and recreation. Moreover, the recent influx of mobile fitness applications allow fitness organization to inform, influence, and motivate consumers in a new way. For example, the mobile application, *MyFitnessPal*, allows users to maintain a diary of their food choices, caloric intake and energy expenditure. The application also allows users to interact with other users and share their progress with friends via message boards. The aforementioned social interactions provide implications for the role of socialization in fitness participation. Previous research on fitness participation suggests that socialization is a key factor in exercise adherence (Drummond and Lenes, 1997; Mullen and Whaley, 2010).

Print media (such as fitness magazines) and TV represent traditional media sources that fitness organizations use to inform, influence, and motivate stakeholders about fitness-related products and services. As part of a niche industry, fitness magazines generally aim to encourage fitness participation and inform consumers about fitness research and trends. Additionally, many magazines have a website that offers differentiated content (Spraul, 2012). *Men's Health*, the fourth most popular male targeted magazine in the world, uses celebrities and athletes as their cover models to influence consumers to purchase their magazine and motivate them to exercise. Fitness magazines also enhance corporate synergy through advertising. That is, promoting other fitness and non-fitness-related businesses and products. Similar to print media, broadcast media offers beneficial information to fitness consumers. Research has suggested that television is a common medium for information and is effective in delivering a message to consumers that is interpretable (Chattopadhyay, Dutta, and Sivani, 2010). Fitness communication can take many forms in an array of contexts. Therefore, it is necessary to develop a comprehensive framework that can be utilized in an academic and practical setting.

The strategic fitness communication model

The strategic fitness communication model (SFCM) – as illustrated in Figure 20.1 – seeks to provide an introduction into the emerging area of fitness communication by using the strategic sport communication model (Pedersen, Miloch, *et al.*, 2007) as a base for the fitness segment of the sport industry. Additionally, the model is developed by synthesizing previous communication and fitness literature. Therefore, this model incorporates personal communication, organizational communication, and the mediated forms of these communications. The SFCM details the scope of the fitness communication process, which includes how fitness communication components – organization and personal communication – are employed to aid communication in fitness, of fitness, and through fitness (see Figure 20.1). These forms of communication may be delivered through the use of various communication channels (such as video gaming, social networks, portable electronics, TV). The underlying principles for the model are defined below and explanations of personal and organization communication – and how they may be mediated – are provided to illustrate their conceptual differences.

Personal fitness communication

Personal fitness communication is best described as interpersonal, or a two-way flow of information between two or more persons (Pedersen, Miloch, *et al.*, 2007). Additionally, interpersonal communication builds knowledge between people as well as creates shared meanings (Wood, 2004). Using this definition, it is proposed here that personal communication occurs whenever individuals in fitness, sharing the roles of sender and receiver, inform, influence, and motivate through personal interactions. The most typical form of personal communication occurs between the fitness professional (for example, personal trainers) and the consumer. Common settings for these interactions are in health clubs where personnel and gym members – or prospects – engage in dialogue about fitness-related topics. Moreover, personal fitness communication depicts the culture of fitness organization, its employees, and their interactions and practices. For instance, much of the day-to-day personal communication may come in the form of personal selling of fitness products, services, and gym memberships. However, personal communication is not limited to these face-to-face interactions and can be mediated via various

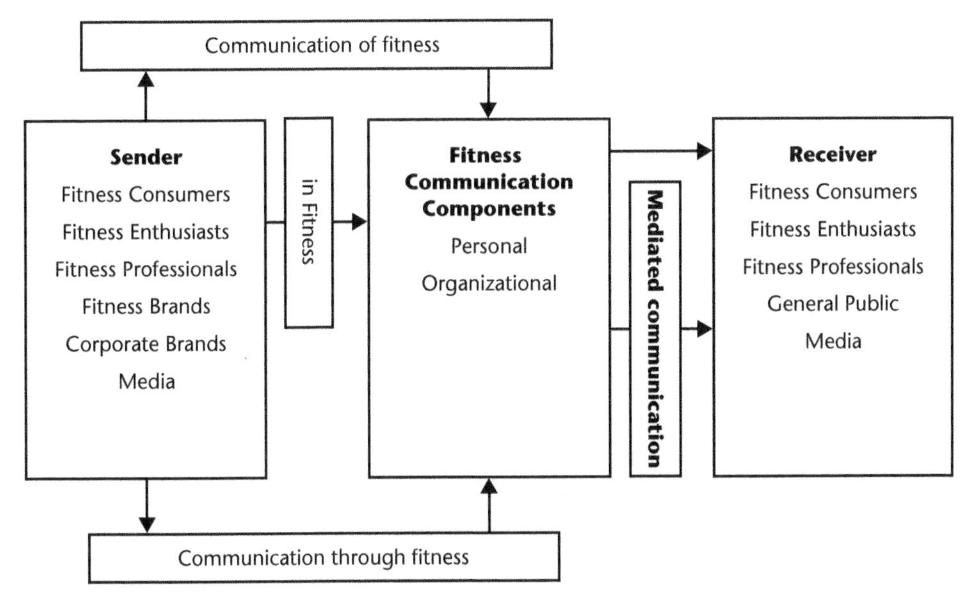

FIGURE 20.1 Strategic fitness communication model. With the above model, personal communication is defined as a two-way flow of information between two or more persons. Organizational communication is defined as communication that takes place within an organization or between the organization and its consumers. Mediated communication occurs when an organizational or personal message is transmitted via a communication channel. Communication *in fitness* means communication occurring in a fitness context or setting. Communication *of fitness* refers to communication of fitness-related messages (e.g., nutritional and exercise information). Communication *through fitness* occurs when fitness-related messages are used to communicate and/or promote non fitness-related products and services

communication channels all with the common goal of informing, influencing, and motivating stakeholders about health, sport, and fitness-related matters.

Mediated personal fitness communication

While the most common form of personal fitness communication is face-to-face, the influence and development of Web 2.0 has provided a new and innovative way to mediate personal fitness communication. For instance, a plethora of fitness celebrities have begun using social media to interact with consumers. Social networking sites allow fitness professionals to deliver their brand message to potential clients without ever meeting them face-to-face or utilizing personal selling techniques. For example, world renowned fitness guru, Tosca Reno, maintains constant interaction with her network of fans by providing fitness tips and recipes via Facebook and Twitter. According to Twitalyzer, Reno has over 23,000 followers on Twitter where she frequently discusses diet, nutrition, fitness, and products (Twitalyzer, 2012). This type of mediated communication allows practitioners to disseminate robust information while providing a dynamic experience for consumers.

Finally, mediated personal communication may occur between fitness consumers. Traditionally, personal fitness communication occurs in fitness settings – like health clubs – where consumers verbally and non-verbally socialize with each other. Research in this area has suggested that socialization in a fitness setting plays a critical role in an individual's attitudinal and behavioral loyalty towards the fitness brand. Similarly, the opinions expressed during these interactions (that is, word of mouth) may have an effect on brand choice (Williams, 2010; Williams and Pedersen, 2012). Moreover, the prevalence of personal gaming consoles, computers, and mobile phone usage has enabled fitness consumers to socialize through mediated communication channels. Fitness consumers are now able to share fitness tips, opinions, reviews, photos, and progress with their social networks instantaneously (Park, Rodgers, and Stemmle, 2011). Popular brands like Nike and Weight Watchers offer mobile-enabled fitness and dieting tools to mediate consumer-to-consumer communication (Dolan, 2012). For example, Nike+ provides mediated fitness communication through social media by allowing users to measure, track, and report their physical fitness progress using social networks (Simonson, 2012). The aforementioned mediated forms of personal communication provide a rich personal experience that was missing from previously technological advances in fitness (for example, exercise videos).

Organizational fitness communication

In contrast to personal communication, organizational communication takes place when one or more organizations – in an effort to inform, influence, and motivate – use fitness to communicate with their constituents. It is important to note that organizational communication may be used by organizations outside of the fitness industry as well. Moreover, it allows companies to use fitness-related brand messages to communicate with consumers. This type of communication has the potential to influence consumers' brand loyalty (Williams, Pedersen, and Walsh, in press), which may explain the influx of co-branding, licensing, and re-branding in the fitness industry.

As previously stated, organizational communication may be applied in the form of co-branding, licensing, and brand extension initiatives, all of which are used to reach a target audience and transfer brand meaning. Co-branding is defined as combining and retaining two or more brands in order to create a single, unique product, service, or message (Leuthesser, Kohli, and Suri, 2002; Pipes, 2012). This type organizational communication offers several benefits to fitness organizations and their associates, such as increased sales and revenue, expanded customer base, and enhanced perceived value (Pipes, 2012). For instance, David Barton Gym and Svedka Vodka used co-branding to promote a "fit people have more fun" brand message to their consumers. Additionally, recent literature has described successful co-branding initiatives between universities and fitness equipment manufacturers targeting future fitness professionals (Kennedy-Armbruster, *et al.*, 2011). While business-to-business endeavors such as co-branding foster organizational fitness communication, licensing also provides an avenue for organizations to communicate with their consumers.

Licensing occurs when one company grants another company the right to use their brand marks in association with a product or service (Kwon, Kim, and Mondello, 2008). For example, a licensing agreement between fitness equipment manufacturer, Matrix, and cancer not-for-profit, Livestrong, targets socially conscious exercisers (Matrix, 2012). Proceeds from the sales of the fitness equipment are donated to charity. In return, the licensed merchandise (treadmills and stationary bikes) display Livestrong's signature black and yellow brand marks.

Likewise, *The Biggest Loser* has licensed its brand to cereal giant Kellogg's to create a line of low-calorie cereals and snacks. As consumers continue to become more health and fitness conscious, fitness organizations will have more opportunities to leverage their brand by partnering with companies from various industries looking to communicate with fitness consumers and enthusiasts.

Manufacturers of sport performance drinks and supplements are no longer alone in communicating fitness to consumers. Corporate brands that have been established in other industries have begun to crossover into the fitness market. Health and nutrient claims promoting the "fitness" of non-fitness-related products is becoming increasingly popular. Given the more recent push to make Americans healthy, companies have rebranded and created new product lines to highlight fitness/nutrition-related attributes. This trend is exemplified with Glacéau, a privately owned subsidiary of Coca Cola, and its line of sport and fitness drinks, Vitamin Water, and Smart Water. The company communicates with its consumers through sport and fitness by using spokespersons like New England Patriots quarterback, Tom Brady, and Boston Red Sox slugger, David Ortiz, to support its sport recovery nutrition claims (Howard, 2007).

Corporate brands, however, should be cautious. The legal community has observed a slew of litigation regarding health, nutrition, and sport performance (that is, fitness) related claims on packaged goods. The Food and Drug Administration (FDA) has strict guidelines qualifying the health and nutrient claims that can be placed on packaged goods. While it may be good business strategy to use fitness-related communication to promote non fitness-related products, misleading advertisements can lead to steep litigation. Using the examples above, in 2009, the Center for Science in Public Interest filed a class-action lawsuit against Coca Cola – the parent company of Vitamin Water – claiming that marketing the drink to the public as a "healthy alternative" is deceptive communication given the 33 grams of sugar in each bottle (Geller and Richwine, 2009).

Mediated organizational fitness communication

Mediated fitness communication can involve organizational communication through a variety of channels, including social media. According to Drell (2012), several fitness brands (such as Zumba, Under Armour) have gained success by engaging consumers through social media. In particular, high end fitness clubs, like Equinox, are realizing the benefits of providing content through their widely popular *Q-Blog*. According to Equinox Chief Marketing Officer, Cie Nicholson, clubs are hiring separate staff to run social media platforms and create "sticky content" on a consistent basis; "there is this whole idea of everyone wants brand new content...it's the new currency" (C. Nicholson, personal communication, March 29, 2012). While social media use is relatively new to the fitness industry, websites are a mainstay for fitness organizations. In contrast to social media, fitness websites typically do not allow user-generated content (Kaplan and Haenlein, 2010). Although websites are not as interactive as other mediums (such as Facebook), they provide a medium for controlled communication between fitness organizations and consumers (Spraul, 2012).

In recent years, fitness gaming has emerged. Literature has suggested that active gaming is more pervasive among younger demographics (Biddiss and Irwin, 2010; Trout and Christie, 2007). Consumers are able to engage in an array of physical activities, track their progress, and interact with other users via the internet connection within gaming consoles (for example, Nintendo Wii, Xbox Kinect). Major gaming corporations such as Nintendo and Microsoft have developed consoles with motion-activated sensors to allow kinesis while playing select fitness inspired video games (Olgethorpe, 2008).

The elements of fitness communication defined and described in this chapter provide a foundation for this emerging field and offer several implications for the sport and fitness industries. Moreover, the final sections of the chapter are devoted to the connection between spectator sport and fitness communication. In particular, how growing concerns about inactivity may change the way we consume sport forever.

The juxtaposition of fitness communication and spectator sport

Fitness is an integral part of the sport landscape. This section explores the role of fitness communication on sport spectatorship. It is evident that nutrition is a vital part of fitness, and food consumption is a huge part of the sport ensemble. The communication and marketing of sport nutrition (that is, sport performance) supplements and the foods synonymous with sport spectatorship at stadiums, sport bars, and homes all across the world are proposed here as a part of fitness communication. With the influx of laws and regulations aimed at fighting obesity, the goal of this section is to provide an understanding of these concepts for sport academicians and practitioners, and detail how the changes in the way organizations communicate fitness (that is, nutrition) will affect the various ways we consume sport.

In the US, Americans receive an estimated one-third of their caloric intake away from home (NY State Restaurant Association, 2007). In 2005, a study found that consumers ate approximately 350 more calories per meal in restaurants than they did in 1990 (Patrick and Nicklas, 2005). Unlike manufacturers of processed and pre-packaged foods and beverages, until recently, restaurants were not required to disclose nutrition information for their products. Without the communication of nutrition information, consumers often have no point of reference for determining the nutrition profile of the products in restaurants and, therefore, do not have the ability to make appropriate choices suitable for their daily calorie and nutritional intake. Spectators of sport are no exception. According to the United States Department of Agriculture (USDA), the Super Bowl is the second largest food consumption day in America. In fact, 32 percent of all Super Bowl commercials are food and drink related (Kim and Cheong, 2011). The need for change in the way organizations communicate fitness (that is, nutrition) will undoubtedly affect the various ways (that is, food consumption at sporting events) that spectators consume sport.

Recently, regulations have been instituted that are forcing sport organizations to communicate fitness on their food product labels. On April 6, 2011, with the authority bestowed to it by Section 4205 of the Patient Protection and Affordable Care Act of 2010 (the "Affordable Care Act"), the FDA issued proposed menu labeling regulations requiring that restaurants and similar retail food establishments (for example, sport bars and grills) with 20 or more locations and substantially the same menu items, provide the calorie content of each menu item be placed on the restaurants' menu board, "drive-thru" menu boards, and individual menu pamphlets. This is based on the theory that calories are considered the most important consideration for weight control and consumers are unable to correctly estimate the calorie content of pre-prepared foods and beverages (Burton, *et al.*, 2006). These regulations have commonly been referred to as the "menu labeling laws." Prior to 2010, menu labeling regulations were only present on a state-by-state basis, resulting in a patchwork of inconsistency throughout the county.

In sport, however, the menu labeling laws will be applied to food establishments (that is, concession stands) within sport arenas, stadiums, and fitness facilities differently from sport bars, restaurants, and grills. The proposed FDA menu labeling regulations define a restaurant or a similar retail food establishment subject to the new legislation as an entity that sells – as its key business endeavor – restaurant or similar-styled food (Compilation of Patient Protection and Affordable Care Act, 2010). Sport bars, restaurants, and grills will be subject to the menu labeling regulations. On the other hand, because sport arenas and stadiums' primary purpose of business is to provide an avenue for sport participation (that is, to spectate and participate in sport) – and likewise, fitness facilities' primary purpose of business is fitness participation – these establishments will not be subjected to the proposed FDA menu labeling regulations. The National Restaurant Association, however, has submitted letters to the FDA arguing that it is well within the intent of Congress to include concession stands in sport arenas, stadiums, and fitness facilities as covered establishments subject to the menu labeling regulations.

Either way, this mandatory communication of fitness (nutrition) on the sport industry will affect the ways spectators consume sport (that is, food consumption while watching sporting events), making fitness an even more essential to the sport landscape. Nutrition is a vital part of fitness and food consumption is a huge part of the sport ensemble. With the influx of laws and regulations aimed at fighting obesity in America, sport spectators will be forced to receive fitness-related messages (nutrition) with the goal of informing and influencing them to make healthier choices.

Conclusion

The purpose of this chapter was to provide researchers and practitioners with a definition of fitness communication and a conceptual model for understanding how fitness industry professionals, consumers, and organizations communicate. First, fitness communication was defined as the process by which fitness consumers and practitioners inform, influence, and motivate their constituents about health, sport, and fitness-related matters in a fitness setting, through the use of fitness-related products and services, and via various mediums. Based on a review of sport communication and fitness industry literature, the SFCM was developed. Based upon the SSCM (Pedersen, Miloch, *et al.*, 2007), the SFCM provides the first conception of fitness communication as a discipline. Lastly, several theoretical implications were offered concerning the future of sport as it relates to fitness communication.

References

Alexandris, K., Douka, S., Papadopoulos, P., and Kaltsatou, A. (2008). Testing the role of service quality on the development of brand associations and brand loyalty. *Managing Service Quality*, 18 (3), 239–54.

Ashton, R. (2004). *Body, mind, spirit: a rhetorical approach to fitness communication*. Master's thesis, Nova Scotia College of Art and Design, Nova Scotia.

Biddiss, E., and Irwin, J. (2010). Active video games to promote physical activity in children and youth: a systematic review. *Archives of Pediatrics and Adolescent Medicine*, 164 (7), 664–72.

Burton, S., Creyer, E. H., Kees, J., and Huggins, K. (2006). Attacking the obesity epidemic: The potential health benefits of providing nutrition information in restaurants. *American Journal of Public Health*, 96 (9), 1669–75.

Chattopadhyay, A., Dutta, R., and Sivani, S. (2010). Media mix elements affecting brand equity: A study of the Indian passenger car market. *IIMB Management Review*, 22 (4), 173–85.

Compilation of Patient Protection and Affordable Care Act. (2010). 42 U.S.C. 300gg-11.

Dolan, B. (2012). Can mobile apps and devices curb obesity? Mobihealthnews.com, January 3. Retrieved from http://mobihealthnews.com/15526/can-mobile-apps-and-devices-curb-obesity/.

Drell, L. (2012). 5 fitness brands kicking butt on social media. *Mashable Lifestyle*, January 6. Retrieved from http://mashable.com/2012/01/06/fitness-brands-social-media/.

Drummond, J., and Lenes, H. (1997). The fitness facility membership questionnaire: A measure of reasons for joining. *Perceptual and Motor Skills*, 85: 907–16.

Filo, K., and Funk, D. (2005). Congruence between attractive product features and virtual content delivery for internet marketing communication. *Sport Marketing Quarterly*, 14, 112–22.

Fox, S. (2011). *The social life of health information, 2011*. Washington DC: Pew Research center. Retrieved from http://pewresearch.org/pubs/1989/health-care-online-social-network-users.

Geller, M., and Richwine, L. (2009). U.S. group sues Coke over Vitamin Water health claims. *Reuters*, January 15. Retrieved from http://www.reuters.com/article/2009/01/15/us-cocacola-vitamin water-idUSTRE50E54L20090115.

Harris, H. (2011). *Employee's perspectives on social media use in organizations as a form of internal communication*. Master's thesis, Gonzaga University, Spokane, WA.

Himel, L., and Munck, P. (2000). Brave new branding – Extending mass-media brand online requires seamless integration. *Digital Marketing*, 1 (6), 18.

Howard, T. (2007). Tom Brady adds some muscle to Glacau water line. *USA Today*, October 31. Retrieved from http://www.usatoday.com/money/industries/food/2007-10-30-brady-water_N.htm.

International Health Racquetball and Sports Club Association (2012). Top Health Club Trends for 2012. *ihrsa.org*. Retrieved from http://www.ihrsa.org/media-center/2012/1/11/top-health-club-trends-for-2012.html.

Kaplan, A.M., and Haenlein, M. (2010). Users of the world, unite! The challenges and opportunities of social media. *Business Horizons*, 53, 59–68.

Kelley, S., and Davis, M. (1994). Antecedents to customer expectations for service recovery. *Journal of the Academy for Marketing Science*, 22 (1), 52–61.

Kennedy-Armbruster, C., Marquette, D., and Williams, A. (2011). Fitness educators and fitness equipment manufacturers working together innovatively. *ACSM's Health and Fitness Journal*, 15 (4), 1–6.

Kim, K., and Cheong, Y. (2011). Creative strategies of Super Bowl commercials 2001–2009: An analysis of message strategies. *International Journal of Sport Marketing and Sponsorship*, 13 (1), 7–21.

Kwon, H., Kim, H., and Mondello, M. (2008). Does a manufacturer matter in co-branding? The influence of a manufacturer brand on sport team licensed apparel. *Sport Marketing Quarterly*, 17, 163–72.

Lam, E., Zhang, J., and Jensen, B. (2005). Service quality assessment scale (SQAS): An instrument for evaluating service quality of health-fitness clubs. *Measurement in Physical Education and Exercise Science*, 9 (2), 79–111.

Leauthesser, L., Kohli, C., and Rajneesh, S. (2002). 2+2=5? A framework for using co-branding to leverage a brand. *Brand Management*, 11 (1), 35–47.

Matrix (2012). Livestrong: Matrix joins the fight against cancer. Retrieved from http://www.matrix-fitness.com/content/about-livestrong.

Mullen, S., and Whaley, D. (2010). Age, gender, and fitness club membership: Factors related to initial involvement and sustained participation. *International Journal of Sport and Exercise Psychology*, 8 (1), 24–35.

N.Y. State Restaurant Association v. N.Y. City Board of Health (NYSRA I), 509 F. Supp. 2d 351,353 (S.D.N.Y. 2007).

Olgethorpe, A. (2008). Get fit with Nintendo's Wii Fit. *Fitness*, June. Retrieved from http://www.fitness-magazine.com/workout/gear/reviews/get-fit-with-nintendos-wii-fit/.

Park, H., Rodgers, S., and Stemmle, J. (2011). Health organizations use of Facebook for health advertising and promotion. *Journal of Interactive Advertising*, 12 (1), 62–77.

Patrick, H., and Nicklas, T. (2005). A review of family and social determinants of children's eating patterns and diet quality. *Journal of the American College of Nutrition*, 24 (2), 83–92.

Pedersen, P. M., Laucella, P., Miloch, K., and Fielding, L. (2007). The juxtaposition of sport and communication: Defining the field of sport communication. *International Journal of Sport Management and Marketing*, 2 (3), 193–207.

Pedersen, P. M., Miloch, K. S., and Laucella, P. C. (2007). *Strategic sport communication*. Champaign, IL: Human Kinetics.

Pipes, K. (2012).Co-branding offers the best of both worlds. *Franchising.com*. Retrieved from http://www.franchising.com/howtofranchiseguide/cobranding_offers_the_best_of_both_worlds.html.

Simonson, M. (2012) Nike+ Connects Fitness to Social Media. *Swish Digital Marketing Agency*, March 9. Retrieved from http://www.micrositezdigital.com/blog/nike-social-media/.

Spraul, M. (2012). Social media + old-school marketing = success. *IDEA Fit Tips*, 10 (4). Retrieved from http://www.ideafit.com/fitness-library/social-media-old-school-marketing-success.

Thackeray, R., and Neiger, B. (2009). A multidirectional communication model: Implications for social marketing practice. *Health Promotion Practice*, 10 (2), 171–75.

Thompson, W. (2012). Worldwide survey of fitness trends. *ACSM Health and Fitness Journal*, 15 (6), 9–18.

Trout, J., and Christie, B. (2007). Interactive video games in physical education. *Journal of Physical Education, Recreation, and Dance*, 78 (5), 29–34.

Twitalyzer. (2012). Retrieved from http://www.twitalyzer.com/profile.asp?u=toscarenoandelapsed=36andtc=andem=andrl=143.

Vogel, A. (2009). Weighing in on the biggest loser. *IDEA Fitness Journal*, 6 (9). Retrieved from http://www.ideafit.com/fitness-library/weighing-in-on-the-biggest-loser.

Williams, A. (2010). Examining the role of brand associations in multipurpose fitness facilities: The relationship between service quality, exercise commitment, brand associations, and brand loyalty (Doctoral dissertation). Available from ProQuest Dissertations and Theses database. (UMI No. 3439606).

Williams, A., and Pedersen, P. (2012). Investigating antecedents of brand equity in the fitness segment of the sport industry: An exploratory study of the role that direct experiences have on the development of brand associations. *International Journal of Sport Management*, 13 (1), 104–14.

Williams, A. S., Pedersen, P. M., and Walsh, P. (in press). Brand associations in the fitness segment of the sport industry in the United States: Extending sport branding conceptualizations and dimensions to participatory sport. *International Journal of Sports Marketing and Sponsorship*.

Wood, J. (2004). *Interpersonal communication: Everyday encounters* (4th ed.). Belmont, CA: Wadsworth/Thomson.

SECTION III

Sport communication and new and emerging media

21

THE NEW WORLD OF SOCIAL MEDIA AND BROADCAST SPORTS REPORTING

Mary Lou Sheffer and Brad Schultz

The Information Age is very much a new world, and in many ways it is defined by the social media, which have become a ubiquitous cultural phenomenon. In 2012, Facebook reported 845 million users (Moire, 2012) while Twitter, the social-networking site that lets people share 140-character messages, is now used by 13 percent of all online adults in the US. Use of Twitter by people in the 25–34 age group has more than doubled since 2010 (Womack and Pulley, 2011). This growth in the social media has had a profound impact on the way sports are created, delivered and consumed. Media audiences are now fully interactive, and extremely demanding in terms of what they want from content providers. "The way people experience sports media has changed," said sports broadcaster Reggie Rivers, speaking on a conference panel presentation. The former National Football League (NFL) player added, "They can tailor it to the way they receive information; the way they follow certain teams" (*Ahead of the curve*, 2010). The migration of athletes and fans to the social media has corresponding changes for how broadcasters interact with both groups. This chapter examines how the rise of social media has influenced and changed the news routines of broadcast sports reporters, while examining the challenges these reporters now face in a world of social media reporting.

Social media

The term "social media" refers to the interactive media technologies that allow consumers to create and disseminate their own content, connect with media outlets and other network users, and voice their opinions on any number of topics. Schorr, Schenk, and Campbell (2003) define new media as communication platforms/devices that facilitate user-to-user interactivity and interactivity between user and information. This new media includes platforms such as websites, blogs, Facebook, Twitter, and LinkedIn. According to a report by the Pew Research Center (Lenhart, 2009) the number of adults using social media jumped from a mere eight percent in 2005 to nearly fifty percent by 2009. More than two billion people, roughly one of every three on the planet, are now using the Internet (Miniwatts Marketing Group, 2011), and social media usage has exploded. According to a 2011 report, the US has more Facebook (155 million) and LinkedIn (46.7 million) users than any other county

(Carmichael, 2011). Over 110 billion online minutes, or 22 percent of all time online in the US, are spent on social networks.

Goffman's (1959) theory of self-presentation helps explain the growing popularity of the social media. Goffman defines self-presentation as the desire to control impressions people form through social interactions. Self-presentations can often lend way to the self-disclosure in that people wish to express various levels of details about daily life to win over friends or followers. According to Kaplan and Haenlein (2010), social media users follow Goffman's description. In other words, in an attempt to increase followers or the number of fans online, social media users consciously determine their level of self-disclosure on social media. Much of the attraction of social media is that they give sports audiences an outlet for personal interaction and a media platform to favorably promote and manage self-image through these interactions (Mehdizadeh, 2010).

Examining this topic first from an audience perspective, social media seem especially relevant in the sports world, where fans and audiences often use the mediated experience to build strong attachments to their favorite players and teams (Wann, 1997). Because of this, Gregory notes that Twitter and other new social media technologies have the potential to "change the athlete/fan interaction forever" (Gregory, 2009, para. 6). As of 2012, there were 3.8 million people following the National Basketball Association (NBA) Twitter site, while 3.4 million were following the Real Madrid soccer team. The NFL had 2.8 million followers (Twitaholic, 2012). Social media are the new measurement of sports visibility and popularity, and athletes are now viewed by how many fans are tracking them on Twitter or reading their blog sites. Sometimes this volume can have staggering consequences, such as the emergence of NBA player Jeremy Lin in 2012. Lin rose from obscure bench player to superstar and fan favorite in less than a week. In that time, his Twitter followers rose from 70,000 to 200,000, the price of his team's tickets jumped 27 percent and attendance at games in which he played increased dramatically (Lopresti, 2012). But audiences are not simply using the social media to consume content; they are creating and distributing their own sports-related material. Sporting events such as the Super Bowl, World Cup, and the Olympic Games have some of the highest TPS (tweets per second) numbers for all of social media. Some fan offerings, including blogs such as Bleacher Report, have become widely used. Thus, the social media are playing an increasingly important role in bringing sports content to audiences, and even creating new audiences to consume sports. There is research to suggest that the social media are reaching previously underserved sports audiences, particularly women and older consumers (Schultz and Sheffer, 2011).

In examining the topic from an athlete's perspective, it is quite clear that athletes have begun to understand the power of the social media to determine their self-presentation to audiences. "We're hitting (Twitter) hard," said NBA player Chris Bosh. "You can put up what you're doing. Or if you have a question, you'd be surprised how much people know. You can be, like, 'I need directions to this spot. People will tell you'" (Feschuk, 2009, para. 5). As of 2012, Bosh had more than half a million Twitter followers, which sounds like a lot, but actually pales in comparison to Spanish soccer star Kaka (8.3 million followers), soccer player Cristiano Ronaldo (6.3 million) and NBA player LeBron James (3.4 million) (Tweeting-Athletes, 2012). In the past, athletes were subject solely to sports critics who filtered accounts of their performances on/off the field. Through personal social media, however, athletes can now publicize their own story. Furthermore, individual athletes, who were shielded from the media and groomed to be cogs in the overall "team," now have a direct communication line to his/her fans. Social media gives rise to the accessible athlete. In this new world, fans no longer have to solely rely on sports reporters to bring them the story. Professional athletes worldwide increasingly have some sort of social media presence, in which they use to tell "their" story.

Twitter, Facebook, and blogging allow athletes to bypass the mainstream media and present themselves unfiltered to audiences. When former Major League Baseball (MLB) star Barry Bonds was under federal investigation related to possible steroid use, he never talked to sports reporters and communicated to fans only through his blog. Shaquille O'Neal has been especially proactive in the social media, managing his image through the help of social media advisor Amy Jo Martin. When O'Neal announced his retirement from the NBA in 2011, the social media allowed him to break the news without going through traditional media channels. "He had full control of when, where and how he wanted to make that announcement," said Martin. "No press releases needed. It was about him using this influence he had built to communicate directly with his fans" (Ortiz, 2011a, para. 20).

However, social media use can create problems for athletes, many of who are unaware of the repercussions of unfiltered communication. Dozens of athletes have been fined, reprimanded, suspended, or come under public ridicule for material they posted in the social media. Rashard Mendenhall of the NFL's Pittsburgh Steelers tweeted after the death of Osama Bin Ladin, "What kind of person celebrates death?" That cost him his endorsement with Champion, and resulted in the Steelers organization issuing a statement of support for all military personnel (Granderson, 2011). Outspoken former NFL player Chad Johnson was fined US$25,000 for tweeting before a game (violating the league's ban on using social media less than 90 minutes before kickoff), and NFL player Antonio Cromartie got a US$2,500 fine for tweeting about his dislike of the food at training camp (Berman, 2010). According to Strutin, "The unguarded remarks of millions who publish their thoughts, criticisms, and gossip on personal profiles are made under an assumed veil of privacy" (Strutin, 2011, p. 248). Barnes (2006) suggests that the boundaries of social media are particularly unclear to younger users, which is reinforced in findings that suggest only 23 percent of social media users believe that the things they post in their own name are available to other viewers on the Internet (Madden and Smith, 2010).

Athletes and sport organizations have also begun to use social media as a branding tool (Pegoraro, 2010) and as a means for fan engagement (Ortiz, 2011b). Social media, with its emphasis on interaction and creating online/mobile relationships, may be helping individual athletes create their own brand that supersedes that of the team while bypassing sports journalists.

The broadcast perspective

All of this makes the job of the sports journalist and broadcaster much more difficult and demanding. While on a panel presentation, the *Denver Post*'s Benjamin Hochman – borrowing from Tom Wolfe – referred to this challenging job as the "new journalism" (*Ahead of the curve*, 2010). As one reporter noted, "Twitter and social media represent a new, powerful platform to broadcast news, crowd source leads and stories, and expand the media's role and earned relevance in the new age of media" (Solis, 2009, para. 46). Gillmor added that the, "collision of journalism and technology is having major consequences for three constituencies: journalists, newsmakers and the audience" (Gillmor, 2004, para. 6). Initially, reporters distrusted social media (especially blogs and Twitter) and thought it would negatively influence their credibility (Schultz and Sheffer, 2008). Those early journalists who embraced social media, however, treated it as an extension of their normal reporting routines. Studies (Daniels and Hollifield, 2002; Giles, 1995; Sheffer and Schultz, 2009; Singer, 2004) show that reporters are reluctant to abandon accepted journalistic practices such as objective reporting while using social media. Unlike citizen journalists, as noted by Sheffer and Schultz (2009), sports journalists maintain high levels of transparency and attribution in their social media posts. Weaver, Beam, Brownlee, Voakes, and Wilhoit (2006) also concluded that modern journalists still put a great deal of importance on factual reporting.

There is evidence, however, that sports broadcasters and journalists are increasingly using social media in non-traditional ways. Furthermore, younger news audiences are consistently turning away from traditional media and toward online news sources, including social media. Research suggests that while television remains the number one source for news, almost all audiences access online news on a daily basis. Integraters, those who get news from both traditional and online sources, "are a more engaged, sophisticated and demographically sought-after audience than those who rely on mostly traditional news sources" (Pew Research Center, 2009, para. 2). Because social media have reduced the sports/news cycle to mere seconds rather than minutes or hours, one of the primary functions of how broadcasters use the social media seems to be breaking news. Research (Sheffer and Schultz, 2010) has shown that sports reporters, especially those under 39 years of age, use Twitter most often to report breaking news. "Twitter has completely changed our beats," noted Lindsey Jones, during an academic panel presentation. The sportswriter added, "I can't remember what the job was like before it. The whole mentality has changed. Who cares when you get it on the website? Twitter is what matters" (*Ahead of the curve*, 2010).

Media outlets are also using the social media for self-promotion and cross-promotion of their work on other platforms (Wenger, 2011). A study conducted by the Project for Excellence in Journalism showed that 93 percent of reporters' tweets linked back to their traditional news outlet, while only three percent of the tweets solicited information from the audience (Holcomb, Gross, and Mitchell, 2011). In 2009, ESPN enacted new rules for its employees that "prohibits tweeting info unless it serves ESPN" (Hiestand, 2009, p. 3C). Hiestand also noted that, "Companies like the idea of their tweeting to hype company stuff" (p. 3C). Broadcasters are also using the social media to interact with fans, allowing them to express opinions and contribute content. "Simply making information available is not enough for today's public," stated Harper, adding that, "Today's audiences expect to be able to choose what they [consume] and most believe they should be able to contribute content and opinions, too" (Harper, 2010, p. 1). A contributing factor to the growth of Bleacher Report is its emphasis on the social media "because sports are inherently a social experience. Bleacher Report is leveraging social media, social networks and social recognition to compete on a shoe string budget" (Fidelman, 2011, p. 1).

Sport has the ability to engage the audience, which is a specific quality that news directors and management value in social media. In terms of engagement and connecting with the audience, it seems broadcast sports reporters prefer Facebook, however, Twitter runs a close second. Research indicates that print sports reporters use social media more for promotion than broadcast reporters. In essence, broadcast sports reporters value the social media more as a stand-alone platform, while print sports reporters see it mainly as complimentary (Sheffer and Schultz, 2010).

Impact and consequences

There is no doubt that the social media have fundamentally changed the way sports broadcasters and journalists do their jobs. In many ways, these changes have been positive. Sports reporters are more attuned to audiences, interact with them more, and provide more content across a variety of platforms. But there are also several unintended negative consequences. For instance, sports broadcasters used to have specific job responsibilities that included defined deadlines. These deadlines occurred when the sports content was delivered, such as in the case of a live game production or the local sports segment on the 11 p.m. news. Social media have added multiple layers of responsibility, requiring sports journalists to report before, during and after their traditional deadlines. Reporters now scour the social media sites of athletes, coaches, and other media looking for stories. They may use that information in their own social media platforms, which they update constantly throughout a work-day. Graham Watson, who spent time as a blogger for ESPN, observed during a panel presentation that, "You wake up at 7 a.m. and put your face into the computer until 10 p.m. It's a grueling, demanding job and burnout is a real danger," (*Ahead of the curve*, 2010).

Many sports reporters and broadcasters are not doing these additional jobs willingly, especially because these new responsibilities often come with no additional pay (Schultz and Sheffer, 2007). Studies (for example, Sheffer and Schultz, 2009; Singer, 2004; Daniels and Hollifield, 2002; Giles, 1995) also show that reporters are reluctant to abandon accepted journalistic practices that may compromise objective reporting. "We're losing the vetting process and a degree of journalistic integrity," said Rivers about the increasing use of social media. He added during his panel presentation that, "There's no time to consider or edit anything" (*Ahead of the curve*, 2010).

Thus, there is a concern among reporters that the social media negatively influence credibility (Schultz and Sheffer, 2008). In an attempt to "test the accuracy of social media reporting" (Benoit, 2010, para. 6), *Washington Post* sports columnist Mike Wise purposely tweeted false information about NFL quarterback Ben Roethlisberger. The tweet quickly circulated through the social media, and many reporters passed it on to audiences without bothering to verify it. The result was a major embarrassment for the *Post*, which suspended Wise for a month. In regard to his suspension, Wise tweeted: "Probably not the best way to go about the experiment" (para. 6). He added, "But in the end, it proved two things: I was right about nobody checking facts or sourcing, and I'm an idiot. Apologies to all involved" (Benoit, 2010, para. 10). To address these issues, several outlets have begun creating social media policies. The *Washington Post* has mandatory social media training for both reporters and editors, which requires employees to establish Twitter and Facebook accounts along with other social media tools to report the news (Pexton, 2001). The Associated Press social media policy requires reporters to post a disclaimer when re-tweeting for fear the public might misconstrued the tweet as an endorsement (Ingram, 2011). ESPN treats social media as an extension to its traditional broadcast platform and states in its guidelines, "[we] expect to hold all talent who participate in social networking to the same standards we hold for interaction with our audiences across TV, radio and digital platforms" (Van Grove, 2011, p. 1). This ESPN policy applies to all staff (for example, anchors, analysts, commentators, reporters, writers) who participate on social media where sports content is involved.

Leagues and organizations have also created their own social media policies, some of which make it much more difficult for sports journalists and broadcasters. In Denver, for example, the

NFL's Broncos instituted a policy that, during training camp, journalists could tweet only from the media room, not the practice field. Thus, when breaking news happens during practice, such as a player getting hurt, journalists have to rush back to the media facility to tweet the information. Since fans watching from the stands have no such restrictions, their tweets often get the information out much earlier. Some of the social media policies, however, are meant to benefit sports journalists. For instance, NBA players are not allowed to text 45 minutes before tipoff, during games, and 45 minutes after games, the National Hockey League (NHL) bans social media use by players two hours before faceoff and until media interviews are complete, the NFL bans social media use by players 90 minutes prior to kickoff and after traditional media interviews conclude, and MLB's social media policy does not apply to players – rather players abide by the electronic equipment rule which prohibits the use of cell phones 30 minutes before games, while on the bench/bullpen/or on the field after batting practice has begun and last until the end of the game (Ortiz, 2011b). In the NBA, NHL, and NFL, players must first "satisfy their obligations to the media" before they're allowed to tweet (Berman, 2010, para. 4).

With the social media dominated by news of celebrities, entertainers and self-promoters (Twitaholic, 2012), sports journalists have often been dragged into the chase to find the latest off-field news about athletes. According to Sanderson, "This increasing demand for sports consumption has promoted many mass media outlets to expand their coverage of professional athletes by devoting attention to athlete's activity away from the playing field" (Sanderson, 2010, p. 1). Hochman, during his comments while sitting on an academic panel, added that, "The way you approach the workday is completely different than just a few years ago. If Carmelo Anthony sneezes, people want to know. A lot of people care" (*Ahead of the curve*, 2010).

Future challenges

There does seem to be an emerging sports journalism hybrid of which Twitter and social media are a part – an instantaneous, interactive, inter-media conglomeration that seems to be continually redefining itself. Among other things, it is part traditional reporting, part blog, part Twitter, part Facebook, part YouTube, and part text messaging. Sports journalists seem to be reacting to this hybrid in different ways. While not necessarily critical or resistant of new technologies like Twitter, older journalists and those at print media outlets seem more tied to the past. They prefer old school journalism – report, write and then repeat the next day. By contrast, it appears that younger sports journalists and those who work at broadcast outlets were more likely to accept and assimilate social media as part of the natural evolution of the profession (Sheffer and Schultz, 2010).

The onset of social media may signal an important sports reporting paradigm shift. Breed (1955) saw a newsroom in which older journalists handed down beliefs and practices to newer generations. Today, the older generation seems to have somewhat distanced itself and left the younger generation to figure out things on its own. Katz (1997) would suggest that the younger generation of journalists is perfectly capable of using new technologies such as Twitter to redefine journalism and communication, arguing that "no other social group is as poised to dominate culture and politics in the 21st century" (Katz, 1997, p. 186). The emerging hybrid of journalism – whatever it may be – should be more conducive to sports broadcast journalists if for no other reason than it will certainly include the electronic elements (video, sound, and so on) of which they are so familiar. These elements are also well known to younger journalists who have been exposed to them in some form or fashion most of their lives. The increase demand for sport content has resulted in news outlets requiring reporters to "stay connected" 24 hours a day. Before a story ever "makes air," a reporter has tweeted about, referenced it on Facebook, and has included a station link on LinkedIn.

New technologies such as blogging and microblogging (for example, Twitter) have also opened up demand for more serious broadcast sports reporting. The new media environment of multiple channels, content options, and fragmented audiences has not only forced more competition between media companies, it has created more content outlets. In theory, competition should improve the quality of broadcast sports journalism, although it could be argued that it has only resulted in more sensationalism and pandering. However, there are more channels available for broadcast sports reporting, and several outlets have used the opportunity to expand their investigative reporting. Social media are simply tools or outlets at the disposal of broadcast sports reporters. Whether these new media assist in sports reporting is up to the reporter.

References

Ahead of the curve: Multimedia and the future of sports journalism. (2010). Panel presentation at the nation convention of the Association for Education in Mass Communication and Journalism, Denver, CO, August 5.

Barnes, S. (2006). A privacy paradox: Social networking in the United States. *First Monday*, September 4, 11 (9). Retrieved from http://firstmonday.org/htbin/cgiwrap/bin/ojs/index.php/fm/article/view/1394/1312.

Benoit, A. (2010). Mike Wise admits Roethlisberger lie. *CBSSports.com*, August 30. Retrieved from http://www.cbssports.com/mcc/blogs/entry/22475988/24211952.

Berman, L. (2010). When social media gets athletes in trouble. *Mashable Social Media*, January 10. Retrieved from http://mashable.com/2010/01/04/social-media-athletes/.

Breed, W. (1955). Social control in the newsroom: A functional analysis. *Social Forces*, 33, 326–35.

Carmichael, M. (2011). The demographics of social media: Ad age looks at the users of the major social sites. *Advertising Age*, May 16. Retrieved from http://adage.com/article/adagestat/demographics-facebook-linkedin-myspace-twitter/227569/.

Daniels, G. L., and Hollifield, C. A. (2002). Times of turmoil: Short-and long-term effects of organizational change on newsroom employees. *Journalism and Mass Communication Quarterly*, 79 (3), 661–80.

Feschuk, D. (2009). Bosh, NBA all a-Twitter over latest blogging fad. *Toronto Star*, February 17. Retrieved from http://www.thestar.com/Sports/NBA/article/588483.

Fidelman, M. (2011). Why BleacherReport.com is killing ESPN.com by leveraging social media. *Business Insider*, March 8. Retrieved from http://www.businessinsider.com/why-bleacherreportcom-is-trouncing-espncom-by-using-social-business-principles-2011-3.

Giles, R. (1995). *Newsroom management: A guide to theory and practice.* Detroit, MI: Media Management.

Gillmor, D. (2004). *We the media: Grassroots journalism by the people for the people.* New York: O'Reilly Media. Retrieved from http://www.authorama.com/we-the-media-13.html.

Goffman, E. (1959). *The presentation of self in everyday life.* New York: Doubleday Anchor.

Granderson, L. (2011). Don't blame Twitter: Athletes have been offending people for a long time through a variety of media. *ESPN*, May 6. Retrieved from http://sports.espn.go.com/espn/commentary/news/story?id=6493234.

Gregory, S. (2009). Twitter craze is rapidly changing the face of sports. *Sports Illustrated*, June 5. Retrieved from http://sportsillustrated.cnn.com/2009/writers/the_bonus/06/05/twitter.sports/2.html.

Harper, R. (2010). The social media revolution: Exploring the impact on journalism and new media organizations. *Student Pulse*, March 11, 2 (3): 7. Retrieved from http://www.studentpulse.com/

articles/202/7/the-social-media-revolution-exploring-the-impact-on-journalism-and-news-media-organizations.
Hiestand, M. (2009). ESPN atwitter about employees' tweeting. *USA Today*, August 6: 3C.
Holcomb, J., Gross, K., and Mitchell, A. (2011). How mainstream media outlets use Twitter. Pew Research Center's Project for Excellence in Journalism. *Journalism.org*, November 14. Retrieved from http://www.journalism.org/analysis_report/how_mainstream_media_outlets_use_twitter.
Ingram, M. (2011). Twitter and journalism: It shouldn't be that complicated. *GigaOm.com*, November 8. Retrieved from http://gigaom.com/2011/11/08/twitter-and-journalism-it-shouldnt-be-that-complicated/.
Kaplan, A., and Haenlein, M. (2010). Users of the world, unite! The challenges and opportunities of social media. *Business Horizons*, 53, 59–68.
Katz, J. (1997). Birth of a digital nation, *Wired*, 5 (4), 184–91.
Lenhart, A. (2009). Adults and social network websites. *Pew Internet and American Life Project*, January 14. Retrieved from http://www.pewinternet.org/Reports/2009/Adults-and-Social-NetworkWebsites.aspx.
Lopresti, M. (2012). New York Knicks guard creating an international Lin-sation. *USA Today*, February 12. Retrieved from http://www.usatoday.com/sports/basketball/nba/knicks/story/2012-02-12/jeremy-lin-cover/53063880/1.
Madden, M., and Smith, A. (2010). Reputation management and social media. Pew Research Center. *Pew Internet and American Life Project*, May 26. Retrieved from http://pewinternet.org/Reports/2010/Reputation-Management.aspx.
Mehdizadeh, S. (2010). Self-Presentation 2.0: Narcissism and Self-Esteem on Facebook. *Cyberpsychology, Behavior and Social Networking*, 13 (4), 357–64.
Miniwatts Marketing Group (2011). *Internet usage statistics. World internet users and population statistics, December 31, 2011*. Internet World Stats. Retrieved from http://www.internetworldstats.com/stats.htm.
Moire, J. (2012). Facebook's 845 million members may not all visit the site. *All Facebook*, February 7. Retrieved from http://www.allfacebook.com/facebook-users_b76790.
Ortiz, M. B. (2011a). Amy Jo Martin blazes trials with Shaq. *ESPN Page 2*, June 27. Retrieved from http://sports.espn.go.com/espn/page2/story?page=burnsortiz-110627_amy_jo_martinand sportCat=nba.
Ortiz, M. B. (2011b). Guide to leagues' social media policies. *ESPN Page 2*, September 27. Retrieved from http://espn.go.com/espn/page2/story/_/id/7026246.
Pegoraro, A. (2010). Look who's talking – Athletes on Twitter: A case study. *International Journal of Sport Communication*, 3, 501–14.
Pew Research Center (2008) Key new audiences now blend online and traditional sources. *Pew Research Center for People and the Press*, August 17. Retrieved from http://people-press.org/2008/08/17/key-news-audiences-now-blend-online-and-traditional-sources/.
Pexton, P. (2001). At the Post, reporters get socialized to social media. *Washington Post*, July 1. Retrieved from http://www.washingtonpost.com/opinions/at-the-post-reporters-get-socialized-to-socialmedia/2011/07/01/AG3I0CuH_story.html.
Sanderson, J. (2010). The nation stands behind you: Mobilizing social support on 38pitches.com. *Communication Quarterly*, 58 (2), 188–206.
Schorr, A., Schenk, M., and Campbell, W. (2003). *Communication research and media science in Europe*. Berlin: Mouton de Gruyter.
Schultz, B., and Sheffer, M. L. (2007). Sports journalists who blog cling to traditional values. *Newspaper Research Journal*, 28 (4), 62–76.
Schultz, B., and Sheffer, M. L. (2008). Left behind: Bloggers, local mass media and the community of sport. *Western Journal of Communication*, 72 (2), 180–95.
Schultz, B., and Sheffer, M. L. (2011). Factors influencing sports consumption in an era of new media. *Web Journal of Mass Communication Research*, 37, October. Retrieved from http://www.scripps.ohiou.edu/wjmcr/vol37/.

Sheffer, M. L., and Schultz, B. (2009). Are blogs changing the news values of newspaper reporters? *Web Journal of Mass Communication Research*, July, 16. Retrieved from http://www.scripps.ohiou.edu/wjmcr/vol16/16-b.html.

Sheffer, M. L., and Schultz, B. (2010). Paradigm shifts or passing fad? Twitter and sports journalism. *International Journal of Sport Communication*, 3, 472–84.

Singer, J. (2004). More than ink-stained wretches: The resocialization of print journalism in converged newsrooms. *Journalism and Mass Communication Quarterly*, 81 (4), 838–56.

Solis, B. (2009). Is Twitter the CNN of the new generation? *TechCrunch*, June 17. Retrieved from http://www.techcrunch.com/2009/06/17/is-twitter-the-cnn-of-the-new-media-generation/.

Strutin, K. (2011). Social media and the vanishing points of ethical and constitutional boundaries. *Social Networking and the Law*, 31 (1), 228–90.

Tweeting-Athletes (2012). Top 10 Twitter athletes. *Tweeting-athletes.com*, January 31. Retrieved from http://www.tweeting-athletes.com/TopAthletes.cfm.

Twitaholic (2012). Top 100 Twitaholics based on followers. *Twitaholic.com*, January 31. Retrieved from http://twitaholic.com/.

Van Grove, J. (2009). ESPN responds to criticism and publishes social media policy. *Mashable Social Media*, August 4. Retrieved from http://mashable.com/2009/08/04/espn-social-media/.

Wann, D. L. (1997). Aggression among highly identified spectators as a function of their need to maintain positive social identity. *Journal of Sport and Social Issues*, 17, 134–42.

Weaver, D. H., Beam, R. A., Brownlee, B. J., Voakes, P. S., and Wilhoit, G. C. (2006). *The American journalist in the 21st century: U.S. news people at the dawn of a new millennium*. Mahwah, NJ: Lawrence Erlbaum.

Wenger, D. (2011). Twitter use in mainstream media. *Advancing the Story*, November 17. Retrieved from http://www.advancingthestory.com/2011/11/17/twitter-use-in-mainstream-media/.

Womack, B., and Pulley, B. (2011). Twitter use climbs to 13% of U.S. adults online, boosted by older Americans. *Bloomberg*, June 1. Retrieved from http://www.bloomberg.com/news/2011-06-01/twitter-use-increases-to-13-of-adults-online-as-mobile-tweets-lead-growth.html.

22

TURNING THE PAGE WITH NEWSPAPERS

Influence of the Internet on sports coverage

Bryan Butler, Matthew H. Zimmerman, and Sharon Hutton

In the past 20 years, the rise of the Internet as a source for news has greatly affected newspaper sports departments across the country by changing the way news is delivered to consumers. This fundamental shift has led to profound changes. Newspaper circulation numbers have dropped dramatically. Sports fans have more options – and more voice – in the sports news marketplace. Technology allows consumers to access sports news in new and different ways. For the newspaper journalist, these changes have changed the nature of the business. Reporters and editors have had to adapt to changing technology and news consumption patterns. They have worked to change the ways they cover sports, and they have had to perform their jobs with fewer resources. The result is that newspapers' sports departments are constantly moving to meet the demands of the sports consumer while working with shrinking budgets. And while some may have predicted the end of the industry, newspapers are looking to dig in and hang on as they figure out their next steps. This chapter outlines the challenges sports print journalists face as they look into an uncertain future.

Information delivery

A little over a decade into the 21st century, newspaper sports sections remain a daily source of sports news for millions of Americans. For those in the newspaper industry, however, recent studies offer sobering news. US respondents to a 2010 Pew Research Center study indicated the Internet to be a more popular news source than newspapers or radio, with the worldwide web trailing only local and national television news broadcasts, which led the way with 78 percent of all usage (Sanger, 2010). The Internet was the third-most popular source for news with 61 percent of consumers using the Web. In the same poll, Sanger notes that only 17 percent of respondents said they read a national newspaper, while many indicated that social media was becoming important to their news consumption and discussion.

Newspapers once represented a means of delivering news in a timely manner, but with cutting-edge media and its ever-changing platforms of delivery, the scope of sport communication has changed. Information freely available at the click of a mouse makes for an appealing option when readers search for a story. Sports journalism also has expanded rapidly since the onset of Web 2.0, a term used to describe the development of websites from static screens to interconnected and interactive networks. The shift has provided an economically friendly form of user interaction. Fans can communicate directly with sports organizations, sports journalists, and perhaps most importantly, with each other. Fans and readers now have the option to move into the online realm and be generators, not just receivers, of information. Newspapers' own story choices have been affected by an increase in competition. With online news sources, news consumers can "choose their own adventure," (Scherer, 2008, para. 1), meaning that instead of only having the opportunity to read what is pre-packaged in newspaper form, readers can seek out and find other non-traditional media outlets to fill their needs.

This has led to changes for the traditional print journalist, who has had to adapt to new technology (Deuze, 2005). Robert J. Samuelson (2007) of *Newsweek* indicated, when he started in print journalism in 1969, that the news industry was not considered a business, and it required two skills – reporting and writing. That is not the case today. The sports reporter who once faced a single deadline for copy in print is now beholden to multiple deadlines and tasked with producing multiple versions of the same story, as the sports department is forced to meet the increasing demands of consumers in a world of blogging, streaming, and live chats. In fact, print reporters often find themselves focused on the online products first (Grabowicz, 2012).

The newspaper's purpose in providing information has not changed. Rather, the options for distribution have. For the editor, this means the job becomes more complex, as it now necessitates juggling various forms of copy across a string of platforms to reach a diverse population. Community-based journalism, often consisting of sports fans producing their own reports, now competes with the traditional sports journalist. With reputable, established media sources no longer always being the first and only source of information in a sports-obsessed society, the newsroom has become a place of decision-making and compromise.

Considering the high level of competition, it is more imperative than ever for newspapers to find a way to stand out from the clutter (Scherer, 2008). Choosing which stories were worthy to be included in the print edition might have been the most important decision of the night in the past, but choosing the platform on which to distribute is also key in a newsroom in the information age. Sports editors are finding that online journalism is not simply a matter of putting the printed product online, with more space available for articles and text. In order to engage sports consumers, journalists must also decide the manner in which they will tell each story. The choices with the move to online include video, opportunities for reader interactivity (such as graphics, podcasts), and the use of hypertext to link to information that can be found elsewhere on the Web (Deuze, 2001). Print space must still be filled, but online is the future and a must for sport communication. Breaking stories do not wait 24 hours – and neither do sports consumers.

Primarily, the move to an online medium has affected the most conventional mode of journalism: the written word. The ability to repeatedly edit and update stories, as well as the unlimited space available, are all factors contributing to the success of online journalism. Even two decades after the first American newspaper went online, how to differentiate the newer online journalism from the traditional print predecessor is an ongoing question (Steensen, 2009). Some differences in content between newspapers' websites and print editions have become apparent. Breaking news and live information on statistics, box scores, injury reports, and even fantasy sports are reported nearly instantaneously online, while print is becoming home to features, sidebars, and other supplemental material, perhaps related to a breaking or ongoing story, where the time element is less critical (English, 2011). With the never-ending foray of sporting events making for a continuous news cycle, and the increasing amount of competition, the newspaper in hard copy is second in line for content from that of online distribution and is often a day, or even more, behind to a story. The web is the automatic go-to for overnight happenings, those that will be read before the paper will hit the driveway. The late, and final, print edition for most East Coast papers goes to press before West Coast sporting events such as late night National Basketball Association (NBA) games end, by default making the Internet the venue of choice for such events. The Olympic Games, which seldom occur on a traditional media timeline, reinforce the importance of this new media in sports communication. In this digital-first approach, immediacy is the guiding factor in a society filled with competition. If one news group doesn't get the story out, somebody else will. The *New York Times* and the *Washington Post* have news desks equipped to handle news 24 hours a day, seven days a week (Grabowicz, 2012).

Modern news organizations must deal not only with competition from each other, but from a once unlikely source: the web. However, certain principles apply to both print and online journalism. Nichol (2011) pointed out that writers seeking to gain the interest of online readers should be cognizant of the idea that readers will seek out hooks (for example, headlines, subheadings, captions) that interest them. Keeping this in mind, slight alterations of the original newspaper text may be necessary to engage the online reader. In addition, standard newspaper principles such as understanding the audience, designing content in a way that is pleasing to the eye and user-friendly, and utilizing the inverted pyramid style still retain their importance in an online journalism world (Nichol, 2011). This is not to mean that the longer, narrative style should be completely avoided online. When writing is part of a multimedia package, more detailed and feature-type writing might be ideal. Wise, Bolls, Myers, and Sternadori (2009) found that news consumers' ability to retain details from an online video increased when the accompanying story was written in a narrative form as opposed to an inverted pyramid style.

New technology

The continued development and integration of new technology (for example, blogging, video production, social media) into sports journalism has prompted the need for individual journalists to frequently update their skills; a must to remain in touch with the competition. However, enthusiasm for the use of newer media can be divided along generational lines. Younger journalists, with most of their life experiences including the evolution of new technologies, are quicker to embrace new ideas. Veteran journalists, on the other hand, might see newer technology as a burden they must adapt to (Schultz and Sheffer, 2010). The newspaper industry's constant challenge is finding ways to make money through online distribution of content (Harper, 2010). However, that has not prevented newsroom leadership and employees from recognizing the necessity of attempting to find ways to best utilize technology (Belena, 2010; Deuze, 2005).

Technological advancements have made a significant impact throughout the history of journalism (Belena, 2010). In the past, creating and distributing the hard copy newspaper product was made more efficient as technology improved. Journalists' own jobs became easier as computers replaced typewriters, and the paste-up table yielded to design programs and digital publishing. Stacks of media guides have been supplanted by official team websites.

While just a dozen years ago a newspaper reporter's typical tools included a notebook, a tape recorder, and a computer, a newspaper's online operation now includes many story options. Among the tools reporters now require to account for different means of storytelling are a digital recorder, a real-time video application (such as Ustream), a video editing suite, and a blogging application (Ferenstein, 2010). Some journalists who might have been strictly print- or broadcast-focused in previous generations will now be charged with writing a story, shooting supplemental video, and posting the complete story package online (Ehrlich, 2009). Those who do this multi-tasking in the online age have often been referred to as "mobile journalists" and the new type of news content producers have been described as "backpack journalists" (Gentile, 2010; Stevens, 2002). As stated by Stevens, this meant that a reporter's tools included a tape recorder, a video camera, and a laptop computer on which to write the story, edit the video, and post the entire package online. In an illustration of just how quickly technology can change journalism and the approach to it, Stevens noted that just after the turn of the century it was thought that backpack journalism would become the norm.

While the idea of backpack journalism remains prominent (Gentile, 2010), the tools have changed greatly in the last decade. More recent advances in electronic media have created a situation in which journalists – and average citizens – only need to carry small devices. Smartphones capable of gathering textual information, as well as images and video and audio recordings, allow reporters and editors to remain in constant contact while also giving the reporter the ability to collect and disseminate information quickly (Belena, 2010).

Breaking news can now be reported in real time, as individual citizens have the tools to post video reports on the Internet, and give eyewitness accounts as news occurs. The low costs inherent with new technology have redistributed the power of the press among the citizenry. Where in recent decades it would have taken a news van with a dish mounted on the roof to report occurrences with live video from the scene, now the smartphone allows individuals to report on events as they occur, with whatever medium they choose (Ferenstein, 2010).

At the same time, the rise of the Internet has allowed reporters to access more information, at a lower cost in both time and money, than ever before. As Garrison (2001) pointed out, more and more journalists will use the web as a place to gather information as journalists adapt to and master new technologies. Stories and perspectives once only accessible through hard-copy archives are now freely available online (Krotoski, 2011). Public records, previously the domain of journalists and Freedom of Information Act requests, are now available online for anyone with a modem to find (Pavlik, 2000). As the web has become more ubiquitous in the newsroom, the role of the news researcher has been virtually eliminated. As noted by Garrison, reporters have access to information quickly and efficiently, negating the need for such specialized personnel.

Social media

Social media is another factor that has changed the way journalists go about the business of reporting (Harper, 2010). While the current popular social media platforms (like Twitter, Facebook) may ultimately yield to future outlets, journalists must continue to adapt to changes in technology (Sheffer and Schultz, 2010). Print journalists might not embrace the idea of social media, owing to an affection for old-school methods (such as report, write, repeat). However, broadcast journalists' affinity for new technologies might make them more amenable (Schultz and Sheffer, 2010). Advances in technology have changed the way news is both created and consumed, as well as affecting content itself, as the news organizations and their publics form a more symbiotic relationship (Pavlik, 2000). As Harper (2010) noted, traditional media's shift to incorporating online elements does not only include news production and distribution. In addition, reporters seeking to engage audiences must now utilize the new social media comprising Web 2.0. The need to utilize Facebook and Twitter posts to update sports consumers has added to the regular duties of a beat reporter. For print journalists, the use of social media is an opportunity to promote their work (Schultz and Sheffer, 2010) as well as post real-time updates.

As one journalist interviewed by Krotoski (2011) pointed out, social media is also a good way for journalists to find stories. The economics editor on BBC2's *Newsnight* said that following the online postings of prominent economists can help tip news producers regarding trends and possible stories. News presentation was formerly hands-off, with journalists choosing which information to disseminate to news consumers. The use of social media has made news more interactive, with more choices in the hands of the reader (Ehrlich, 2009). However, using social media as a way to source stories can be potentially disastrous for reputable news organizations. News outlets which mentioned supposed terrorist ties involving the 2009 Fort Hood shooter based on Twitter reports had been fooled by falsehoods on the microblogging site (Krotoski, 2011).

For this reason, reporters must be engaged in the use of social media, both for news gathering (Belena, 2010) and for distribution of information. With increased – and free – citizen access to producing and consuming media, editors at traditional news outlets no longer enjoy their former gatekeeper role. Information has become freely available, with consumers just as likely to seek news from their favorite blogger as someone who has been a journalist for an old, respected source (Krotoski, 2011). Harper (2010) pointed out that the social media "revolution" does not necessarily mean the end of journalism as it has been understood. Rather, as noted by Harper, the increase in media options, and the ability to choose the media they consume and interact with, potentially allows users the opportunity to interact with and understand the media process.

Utilizing social media, the sports audience has turned the tables and has itself become another source of information and competition. Fans are writing and posting to their own sites, as well as Tweeting and blogging. Twitter is used by sports entities and fans, as well as sports journalists. Blogging allows for round-the-clock publication, available to anybody with Internet access. These open forums leave the door propped for fans-turned-journalists, giving them an opportunity to report. Many do, often posting breaking news online before the sports journalist has time to get the story to an editor. These citizen-produced stories are often uncensored, with live pictures and other details that will not be viewed on the page of a reputable news organization.

There is concern that newspapers' embracing of blogs and other online forms of communication may lead to a decline in journalism standards (Kinsley, 2006). Multimedia journalism is potentially not just a merger of print and broadcast content, but also of hard and soft news as well as marketing and editorial principles. These usually divergent attitudes can cause journalists to approach multimedia warily, even while understanding the need to master such techniques (Deuze, 2005). In addition, the idea of what is newsworthy may differ from a print to an online medium. Cassidy surveyed 655 print and online newspaper journalists and found that traditional print journalists rated the investigative and interpretive roles more highly than online newspaper journalists (Cassidy, 2005). Finally, the speed and ease of newer technology has also caused some journalists to wonder whether accuracy and thoroughness will remain important tenets of their craft (Schultz and Sheffer, 2010).

Financial concerns

Any discussion of the newspaper's role in sport in the 21st century, must include a look at the medium's decline, particularly as the Internet has become a larger source of sports news for the average sports news consumer. And, while sports departments put together print sections every day, reporters and editors are also called upon to do more in other media. To a degree, the newspaper's hope to stay competitive in the industry is reliant on its online savvy. Newspapers have changed their emphasis in an effort to keep up with the competition. Prominent newspaper owner and *USA Today* parent company Gannett has restructured the organization to keep up with what has been known among media giants for some time – that sports is a revenue producer, and must receive a high level of focus in the once newspaper-dominated media world. In 2011, the company brought in a new executive team to oversee *USA Today* Sports Media Group (Lefton, 2011), with its intent to bolster the online version of the publication, which has carried the tag "The Nation's Newspaper" since its beginning in 1982.

A common belief is that the Internet is responsible for the decline of the newspaper industry, but a closer look shows that newspapers have been losing readers and revenue since the 1950s because of changes in tax laws that favored corporate ownership over private ownership, shifts in advertising trends, and a population move from city centers to the suburbs (Anderson, 2009). From 1950 to 1990, the number of daily newspapers dropped from 1,772 to 1,611, a nine percent decline (Newspaper Association of America, 2012). Many cities and towns experienced a reduction from multiple daily newspapers to one daily newspaper well before the Internet became a common source of news. In Texas, for example, the state's three largest cities – Dallas, Houston, and San Antonio – each had lost competing major metro daily newspapers to essentially become one-newspaper towns by 1995. A similar situation occurred in Los Angeles, where the *Herald-Examiner*'s demise in the early 1990s left the *Los Angeles Times* with a stranglehold on the market. By 2009, according to the Newspaper Association of America, there were only 1,397 daily newspapers, a 21 percent decline from 1950.

The decline in circulation and the decline in revenue are linked. Newspapers have been losing financial resources for more than a decade (Meyer, 2008). Newspapers generate the majority of their revenue from advertising sales; the rate a business pays for an ad is often linked to the number of readers that could be exposed to the ad. A reduction in readership means less exposure for the ad and leads to a reduction in ad prices or sales — and less revenue for the newspaper. Changes in society and technology have led to just such reductions in print media, forcing newspapers (and magazines) to take action or close their doors. Many have seen their advertising revenues decline, lost to websites like *Craigslist* (Kinsley, 2006), while still trying to provide content for free online. Many newspapers have met these challenges with a two-pronged approach: cutting costs and creating new revenue streams. Both of these responses have been felt in sports departments across the country.

Newspaper sports departments are seeking to be more cost efficient to keep up with the changing times; Reductions in the size of the paper itself have occurred, as are reductions in workforce and compensation numbers. Free distribution provided by the Internet can be contrasted with the print product's costs for paper, ink, and transport of the product to its readership. Paper acquisition is one of the main expenses of newspaper production, second only to salaries (Rosenberg, 2010). By reducing the dimensions of the newspaper page as well as the size of the average section, newspapers have cut operating costs (Hau, 2008). Circulation departments, which control newspaper delivery, have also reduced their geographical circulation range to reduce the cost of delivering newspapers to areas with few readers, or where the cost to transport papers is too high.

Smaller sports sections increase the pressure on reporters and editors to find ways to keep providing complete coverage for the teams in their area despite having less space to work with. Reporters accustomed to having room for a long feature or an extended analysis of a game or issue find themselves forced to re-think the way they write. Some reporters excel at finding alternate ways to tell stories, such as with charts or photos, but many are frustrated at seeing their stories get smaller and smaller in print. Copy editors, who are responsible for editing stories and make sure they fit in their allocated spaces, find that their jobs may take more time, not less. Taking long stories and whittling them down to smaller stories or brief items can be a time-consuming process. And even when exacting care is taken by reporters and editors to ensure a quality product, readers still notice that their money buys them less. Readers who decide that reduced coverage of their favorite teams isn't worth the price they pay could cancel their subscriptions, creating a cycle of decline (Perez-Pena, 2008).

The other way of cutting costs, by managing compensation costs and staff size, also has taken a toll on sports departments. Layoffs have become a common occurrence at newspapers large and small (Mitchell and Rosenstiel, 2012). Even newsroom unions have been unable to stop the cuts in personnel as newspapers look to reduce operating costs. For the staffers who remain, many have seen raises disappear and cuts to salaries and benefits have become more common. Many of those who kept their jobs after layoffs felt the future was still uncertain, and many looked for other opportunities outside the newspaper business.

Those who remain are left to pick up the slack of those who have left (Mitchell and Rosenstiel, 2012). Many papers institute hiring freezes following layoffs, limiting resources for sports editors, keeping them from filling open positions that have been left vacant for various reasons, leaving their departments that much more short-handed and under-staffed. Reporters are asked to cover more games or beats or are pulled from beats to work as general assignment reporters who can be used to plug the gaps. Editors are given more stories to edit – often with multiple stories from late sporting events. Both are left feeling overworked and under-appreciated, especially taking into account the lack of raises and benefits cuts, as noted above.

In addition to cutting costs, newspapers have also looked for new revenue streams as the old ones dry up. One option is to create special sections to generate revenue. In sports, that often means capitalizing on the success of a team or looking for ways to entice readers and advertisers outside the regular sports coverage. For example, the *Houston Chronicle* printed a special section in 2011 dedicated to the Houston Texans after they reached the playoffs for the first time in franchise history. Special sections are not new – sections for winning team or for seasonal sports with high local interest, such as golf, have been staples of sports coverage. As newspapers have sought new revenue streams, however, special sections have gained more interest as ways to reach advertisers who would not normally buy ads in a newspaper.

Newspapers have also looked to the electronic media for revenue and readers, but with varying success. The Internet, tablets, and mobile devices have been described as the delivery platforms of the future, but so far they have not delivered – particularly as a source of revenue

(Mitchell and Rosenstiel, 2012; Nichols and McChesney, 2009). As sports departments have attempted to make more frequent use of digital media, the workload has increased for reporters. They are now required to write for online media in addition to their print work, and editors, who often update the websites and apps as well as put together the print edition (Mitchell and Rosenstiel, 2012). Ultimately, for those working in sports departments, doing more with less has become the reality. Whether picking up more work as co-workers are laid off or leave, adding duties related to new media or special sections, or looking to change the way they cover and present stories, sports writers and editors are finding themselves with more tasks with less time and materials available to accomplish them.

Conclusion

For newspapers, the Internet has brought challenges, but it might also bring solutions as the industry looks online for ways to supplement its revenues. In the immediate future, however, sports departments still face uncertainty as newspapers work to balance their budgets. Only once financial goals are met will newspapers be able to settle into more stable circumstances. For the sports journalists themselves, the changes bring problems as well as opportunities. Many have more to do and more to learn than ever before. Smaller staffs work harder and longer to get the job the done. New technology and changes in online news consumption force journalists to adapt. Yet for those willing to diversify or take on more, opportunities to work in sports journalism continue to exist.

References

Anderson, D. (2009). Is the great American newspaper dead? *Neilsenwire*, June 1. Retrieved from http://blog.nielsen.com/nielsenwire/media_entertainment/is-the-great-american-newspaper-dead/.

Belena, R. (2010). How technological changes have impacted the newspaper industry. *Helium*, August 5, updated July 6, 2012. Retrieved from http://www.helium.com/items/1913621-how-technology-changes-newspaper-reporting.

Cassidy, W. P. (2005). Variations on a theme: The professional role conceptions of print and online newspaper journalists. *Journalism and Mass Communication Quarterly*, 82 (2), 264–80.

Deuze, M. (2001). Online journalism: Modelling the first generation of news media on the World Wide Web. *First Monday*, October 1, 6 (10). Retrieved from http://firstmonday.org/htbin/cgiwrap/bin/ojs/index.php/fm/article/view/893/802.

Deuze, M. (2005). What is journalism? Professional identity and ideology of journalists reconsidered. *Journalism: Theory, Practice and Criticism*, 6 (4), 442–64.

Ehrlich, B. (2009). Mashable's social media guide for journalists. *Mashable Social Media*, December 30. Retrieved from http://mashable.com/2009/12/30/social-media-guide-for-journalists/.

English, P. (2011). Online versus print: A comparative analysis of web-first sports coverage in Australia and the United Kingdom. *Sport, Media and Journalism*, 140, 147–56.

Ferenstein, G. (2010). 5 essential tools for the mobile journalist. *Mashable Social Media*, February 1. Retrieved from http://mashable.com/2010/02/01/mobile-journalist-tools/.

Garrison, B. (2001). Diffusion of online information technologies in newspaper newsrooms. *Journalism and New Technologies*, 2 (2), 221–39.

Gentile, B. (2010). Defining backpack journalism – again. August 29. Retrieved from http://billgentile.com/backpackjournalism/defining-backpack-journalism-again.

Grabowicz, P. (2012). The transition to digital journalism: Web first publishing. UC Berkeley School of Journalism, *Knight Digital Media Center*, March 8. Retrieved from http://multimedia.journalism.berkeley.edu/tutorials/digital-transform/web-first-publishing/.

Harper, R. A. (2010). The social media revolution: Exploring the impact on journalism and news media organizations. *Student Pulse*, March 10. Retrieved from http://www.studentpulse.com/articles/202/the-social-media-revolution-exploring-the-impact-on-journalism-and-news-media-organizations.

Hau, L. (2008). Dead trees: The incredible shrinking newspaper. *Forbes*, April 2. Retrieved from http://www.forbes.com/2008/04/02/newspapers-advertising-publishing-biz-media-cx_lh_0402sections.html.

Kinsley, M. (2006). Do newspapers have a future? *Time Magazine*, September 25. Retrieved from http://www.time.com/time/magazine/article/0,9171,1538652,00.html.

Krotoski, A. (2011). What effect has the Internet had on journalism? *The Observer*, February 19. Retrieved from http://www.guardian.co.uk/technology/2011/feb/20/what-effect-internet-on-journalism.

Lefton, T. (2011). *USA Today* beefs up sports. *SportsBusiness Journal*, October, 31. Retrieved from http://www.sportsbusinessdaily.com/Journal/Issues/2011/10/31/Media/USA-Today.aspx?hl=Lefton%20USA%20Today%20beefs%20up%20sportsandsc=0.

Meyer, P. (2008). The elite newspaper of the future. *American Journalism Review*, October/November. Retrieved from http://www.ajr.org/article.asp?id=4605

Newspaper Association of America (2012). Newspaper circulation volume. Retrieved from http://www.naa.org/Trends-and-Numbers/Circulation/Newspaper-Circulation-Volume.aspx.

Nichol, M. (2011). 7 tips for writing for online readers. *Daily Writing Tips*, February 10. Retrieved from http://www.dailywritingtips.com/7-tips-for-writing-for-online-readers/.

Nichols, J., and McChesney, R. W. (2009). The death and life of great American newspapers. *The Nation*, April 6, 12–20.

Pavlik, J. (2000). The impact of technology on journalism. *Journalism Studies*, 1 (2), 229–37.

Perez-Pena, R. (2008). Newspaper circulation continues to decline rapidly. *New York Times*, October 27: B4.

Pew Research Center's Project for Excellence in Journalism (2012). *The state of the news media in 2012: An annual report on American journalism*. Washington DC: Pew Research Center. Retrieved from http://stateofthemedia.org/2006/a-day-in-the-life-of-the-media-intro/newspaper/

Rosenberg, J. (2010). Demand be damned: Still cutting capacity, newsprint producers strive to cover cost in the face of newspapers' chronic decline. *Editor and Publisher*, November, 21–7.

Samuelson, R. J. (2007). Long live the news business. *Newsweek*, May 28, 40.

Sanger, S. (2010). Newspapers are old news, the Internet is taking over. *WorldTVPC.com*, March 1. Retrieved from http://www.worldtvpc.com/blog/newspapers-news-internet/.

Scherer, M. (2008). The Internet effect on news. *Time Magazine*, March 24. Retrieved from http://swampland.time.com/2008/03/24/the_internet_effect_on_news/#ixzz1vfmTn4HW.

Schultz, B. and Sheffer, M. L. (2010). An exploratory study of how Twitter is affecting sports journalism. *International Journal of Sport Communication*, 3, 226–39.

Sheffer, M. L. and Schultz, B. (2010). Paradigm shift or passing fad? Twitter and sports journalism. *International Journal of Sport Communication*, 3, 472–84.

Steensen, Steen (2009). Online feature journalism: A clash of discourses. *Journalism Practice*, 3 (1), 13–29.

Stevens, J. (2002). Backpack journalism is here to stay. *USC Annenberg Online Journalism Review*, April 2. Retrieved from http://www.ojr.org/ojr/workplace/1017771575.php.

Wise, K., Bolls, P., Myers, J., and Sternadori, M. (2009). When worlds collide: How writing style and video intensity affect cognitive processing of online news. *Journal of Broadcasting and Electronic Media*, 53 (4), 532–46.

23

CONTENT, COPYRIGHT, AND CARRIAGE

Issues for sports media rights in the digital age

Stephen W. Dittmore and Tiffany E. Fields

When Pittsburgh radio station KQV positioned paid observers just outside the walls of Forbes Field in the 1930s and retransmitted the play-by-play of games on its airwaves, it changed the way sports viewed media rights. At the time, the Pittsburgh Pirates baseball club was involved in a rights agreement with KDKA radio. The Pirates successfully sued KQV for copyright infringement and KQV was forced to stop the practice. Subsequently, the court's ruling established the club's broadcast right, creating a valuable property right (Wong, 2002). Since that 1938 court decision, the world of media rights in sports has experienced many significant legal challenges, which have evolved as technology has changed from radio to television to streaming to social media. Most of the recent challenges can be synthesized into the areas of content, copyright, and carriage. The purpose of this chapter, therefore, is to review the relevant legal challenges in each of those areas as they have played out in the court system in the past few years, and hypothesize about future legal challenges to digital media rights in sports.

Major League Baseball paves the way

Property owners began to experience the financial rewards, and challenges, associated with the sale of digital streaming rights in the early 2000s. While the sale of streaming rights represented a new revenue source for leagues and governing bodies, the rights signaled a "complicated balance of power between content providers and Web distributors" (Hu, 2004, para. 10). Major League Baseball (MLB) is an excellent example of this shift. That's because MLB formed MLB Advanced Media (MLBAM) following a unanimous vote by the 30 baseball club owners in 2000 with an initial investment totaling US$75 million. Its goal was centralize all of MLB's internet operations by managing the official league site and each of the 30 individual club sites, creating "the most comprehensive Major League Baseball resource on the Internet" (MLB Advanced Media, 2004, para. 10).

In one of the first streaming rights deals, RealNetworks Inc. signed a three-year, US$20 million exclusive contract with MLB, giving RealNetworks audio and video content rights for regular-season games. Consumers could purchase broadcasts directly through real.com for US$4.95 per month for six months, or through *mlb.com* for US$9.95 per season, using

RealNetworks software (Migala, 2001). As a result of the agreement, RealNetworks received US$4 million of its 2003 revenue from the MLB contract (Richman, 2004). However, that relationship soured in March 2004, when MLBAM signed a broader agreement with Microsoft's MSN online division in which paid MSN users received access to live online baseball games (Linn, 2004), worth US$40 million over two years (Adams, 2004). At the same time, MLBAM reached a two-year, US$9 million deal with America Online giving AOL broadband subscribers access to live game audio and video highlights (Adams, 2004). RealNetworks terminated its deal with MLB and sued MLBAM, alleging it violated the two companies' agreement by favoring a rival media player from Microsoft Corp. over Real's music and video player.

A US district court judge denied RealNetworks's motion for a temporary restraining order (Evangelista, 2005). An undercurrent to the debate was the antitrust battle between Microsoft Corp. and RealNetworks, which resulted in Microsoft paying US$761 million to RealNetworks in cash and services (Evangelista, 2005). In 2006, MLB became the first professional league to offer in-house streaming on its platform, MLB.TV.

Content

The unpredictable nature of sports drives consumer demand and delivers consistently high television ratings for broadcasters, particularly in a time when audiences for television programming are getting smaller. As David Carter, a professor of sports business at the University of Southern California, noted (as quoted in Flint and Chmielewski, 2011), "At a time when the media landscape is fragmenting and people are scattered up and down the dial, major events are the one thing that can aggregate those audiences" (para. 12). In the same article, ESPN Executive Vice President John Wildhack agreed with Carter, suggesting the cost of sports programming will not come down any time soon. "It delivers consistently high ratings and it provides value to advertisers," noted the ESPN executive. "The value of sports – to both advertisers and distributers – will continue to be very high" (para. 14).

The value of media rights to broadcasters extends internationally as well, as evidenced by a 1980s case involving the Tour de France (*Broadcasting Rights International Corp. v. Société du Tour de France* [1987]). The Société du Tour de France (STDF) is a company organized under French law that was created to organize and administer the Tour. In the 1970s, BRIC, an American broadcasting company in Florida, took steps to promote the Tour outside of France. They contracted with STDF for the exclusive broadcast rights to the Tour in the US. In 1985, BRIC entered an agreement with CBS granting the American broadcasting rights to the Tour. BRIC owned the right to sell broadcast rights to the Tour to another network in the US. However, STDF went around the agreement with BRIC and dealt directly with CBS, requesting that the payments that were to go to BRIC instead go directly to STDF. STDF eventually changed its statement and said the payments should go to BRIC; however, BRIC still brought a suit for tortious interference. This agreement between BRIC and CBS was worth over a quarter of a million dollars to BRIC. While this case was dismissed, it is of value to research this subject because it proves that while media rights agreements are of value in the US, the value is not solely limited to the US, and is actually a global issue.

High-school athletic associations have begun to notice value in media rights recently and often charge a fee as well. Despite their status as public educations systems, the courts have held that this is a lawful action. In *Oklahoma Sports Properties, Inc. v. Independent School District*

No. 11 of Tulsa County, Okla. (1998), a group sought to broadcast a live, play-by-play radio account of high-school football game sought to enjoin school district from collecting a broadcast rights fee. The broadcasters sought an injunction preventing the school from collecting fees; however, the injunction was denied by the district court, and the corporation appealed. The Court of Civil Appeals, held that: (1) independent school districts have the implied power to charge and collect broadcast rights fees for high school athletic events, as incidental to the powers expressly granted by statute, and (2) imposition of a broadcast rights fee did not infringe upon the rights guaranteed under the First and Fourteenth Amendments to the US Constitution, although fees were not charged to other news gatherers, such as the print media.

In *Wisconsin Interscholastic Athletic Association (WIAA) v. Gannett Co., Inc.* (2011), a high-school athletic association brought an action requesting the court to declare the formation of exclusive licensing agreements constitutional. WIAA had contracted with American HiFi, Inc. for the exclusive right to broadcast and live-stream sporting events. Gannett's position, however, was that this license violated the First Amendment right to a free press and in addition violated the Fourteenth Amendment. The media rights packages for collegiate conferences are similar to this agreement in that they also include the license to live simulcasts online. The three contract provisions that Gannett challenged involved the restriction on taking photographs at a game, restrictions on live streaming games, and restrictions on blogging about a game while the game is in play. Osborne and Batista wrote of the Court's decision, "whether the sport organization is a state actor or a private entity, in either case it may own the exclusive rights to production of events, and these rights may be licensed to third parties for a fee" (Osborne and Batista, 2012, p. 55). The courts have held that there is not a constitutional duty to notify all possible interested parties before an athletic association enters into a business agreement with a broadcasting network.

Each media rights agreement comes with its own intricate provisions. For example, ESPN's contract with the Southeastern Conference (SEC) provides that ESPN not only "has acquired the rights to every SEC home football game," but it will serve as the "exclusive national cable home and the syndication rightsholder for the conference" (SEC Sports, 2008, para. 12). ESPN also has the exclusive right to simulcast live events on broadband as well as on mobile devices. In addition, ESPN retains the sole rights to Spanish language broadcasts of sporting events. In an example from another conference, the Pac-12 has split games between ESPN and Fox, with each earning the right to broadcast 22 football games per season. However, the Pac-12 has reserved the right to broadcast 350 live events each year on Pac-12 Network once it is created. Pac-12 Network will show football and men's basketball games not included in the deals with ESPN and Fox (Rosenblatt 2011).

Restrictions on content

Because content has such high economic value to governing bodies and broadcasters, restrictions are frequently placed on how content can be used and shared through traditional media as well as emerging social media platforms. The SEC faced a firestorm of criticism from the digital world when it announced its social media policy in August 2009, prior to the start of the football season. The conference's initial policy stated fans may not "produce or disseminate . . . any account description, picture, video, audio, reproduction or other information concerning the Event" (Ostrow, 2009a, para. 2). Although the SEC quickly relaxed the too-restrictive policy regarding content, the incident was another example of a sport governing body seeking to protect the rights of its television and media partners, while having the consequence of restricting usage by other organizational stakeholders.

The National Football League (NFL) initiated a similar restriction in 2007, when it imposed a 45-second cap on the amount of video that media websites could use per day (Fry, 2007). The NFL subsequently doubled that amount to 90 seconds per day in 2008. By contrast, MLB restricts news sites to 120 seconds per day of audio or video from league facilities, with game highlights restricted only to rights holders that have a separate rights deal with MLBAM (Fisher, 2008).

Violations of restrictions result in cease-and-desist letters or, in the case of traditional members of the media, expulsion from an event. In 2007, *Louisville Courier-Journal* reporter, Brian Bennett, was kicked out of the press box at an NCAA Super Regional baseball game for "live blogging" in violation of the NCAA's exclusive broadcasting agreement with ESPN and infringing on its copyright of the live television broadcast (Moorman and Dittmore, 2007). As a condition of receiving a media credential to cover the event, Bennett agreed to comply with the NCAA's blogging policy which restricted the number of posts a credentialed member of the media could make. So, in that sense, according to Moorman and Dittmore, the issue was not one of copyright, but more of a contract dispute.

One of the more restrictive sport organizations historically has been the International Olympic Committee (IOC), which issues social media and blogging guidelines to all participants, defined as athletes, media, and anyone else receiving a credential, in its events. These guidelines are four pages long and restrict content to personal postings, free of commercialism, and "conform to the Olympic spirit" (International Olympic Committee, 2011, p. 1). Infringement of these guidelines may result in the withdrawal of accreditations, take-down notices, legal action for damages and other sanctions. It is the identification and enforcement of these restrictions which is difficult. Having 10,000 athletes with individual Twitter accounts in multiple languages, guidelines are not easy to enforce. The IOC established a website (www.olympicgamesmonitoring.com) with the intent that participants "discovering unauthorised content" will report it, but as attorney Brad Shear (as quoted in Merron, 2012) noted, "If Olympian A tweets, factually, that he had a Hershey's bar, another company that has paid to be the official Olympic candy bar can complain that the tweet is harming their brand. What is the IOC going to do about it? They will ask the athlete to remove the tweet, but once it's been retweeted, once it's out there online, it's hard to remove" (Merron, 2012, para. 9).

Copyright

Intellectual property has become one of the most valuable assets a sport organization owns. This is evidenced by the value of the television contracts conferences have negotiated in the last five years. When negotiating the media agreements, conferences are essentially granting licenses for the copyrights to the sporting events. In the US, copyrights are unique because their protection is rooted in the US Constitution, which grants Congress the power to enact legislation to "progress science and promote useful arts." Therefore, copyright receives federal protection in the Copyright Act of 1976. The right to broadcast a sporting event is not specifically laid out in the Copyright Act, however, copyright protection is extended to live sports broadcasts because each sport broadcast is a unique script, with an unknown result. Because there is a provision protecting digital works (such as motion pictures, sound recordings), leagues and governing bodies have the ability to license the rights to their sporting events. When this is done, ownership of the rights remains with the league or governing body rather than with the individual club being broadcast on television or on a live stream online. The ability to purchases licenses can make or break a television network. For example, when Fox first came on the scene, the "big three" US television networks (CBS, ABC, and NBC) believed that Fox would never be a true competitor. However, the ability to purchase a license to the NFL allowed Fox to not only build its network but start another station, Fox Sports Network. This was no doubt partially accomplished through the amount of revenue earned during the broadcast of games (Andrews, 2003).

Being granted the right to be the sole broadcaster of an event that is in high demand allows the broadcaster to generate revenue through advertisement sales, creating a valuable asset, one which the rights holder seeks to protect. Rights holders do this by cracking down on copyright infringement. Basic infringement occurs when there is copying and improper appropriation of a copyrighted work.

Copying is determined if there is substantial similarity and access. While similarity does not necessarily prove access to the original work, but only to the same inspiration, if the similarities are so striking as to preclude the possibility that plaintiff and defendant independently arrived at the same result, then access need not be proven. However, some case law, such as the decision of the circuit judge in *NBA v. Motorola, Inc.* (1997), suggests that websites may be permitted to provide real-time updates without infringing upon copyrights (Wong, 2002). The NFL created a social media policy similar to that of the SEC, one which "focused almost entirely on protecting its lucrative television contracts" (Ostrow, 2009b, para. 6). Both policies attempted to tackle emerging communication channels such as Twitter, which could allow for real-time play-by-play updates. However, those policies seemed destined to be ineffective because, as Roberts noted, "once the promoter has intentionally put the real-time data into the public domain, either by broadcast, the web, or other media, its ability to limit further disseminations is limited" (Roberts, 2004, p. 167).

Illegal streaming of copyrighted events

As evidence of the challenge with streaming video, a high profile copyright battle occurred in 2007 when the English Premier League (EPL) sued Google, Inc., owners of YouTube, for US$1 billion, alleging copyright infringement. The EPL alleged that YouTube aided in the dissemination of copyrightable materials. Google argued it was protected under a "safe harbor" in the Digital Millennium Copyright Act (DMCA) of 1998 (Hutchins and Rowe, 2009). The Citizen Media Law Project, a joint resource affiliated with Harvard Law School's Berkman Center for Internet and Society and the Center for Citizen Media at Arizona State University, has noted that the challenges associated with copyright infringement and fair use provisions in the digital age precipitated the DMCA as a way to protect the interests of copyright owners (Citizen Media Law Project, 2009). Summary judgment was awarded in Google's favor in 2010.

Hutchins and Rowe (2009) also document the difficulty involved in regulating streams which cross not just country borders, but oceans as well. As the scholars noted, the 2007 Australian League Football Grand Final match between Melbourne Victory and Adelaide United was only available in Australia via pay television on FOX Sports which has paid AU$120 million over seven years for the exclusive rights. FOX executives became upset when it learned Football Association officials were aware days in advance of the match that channel-surfing.net (a US-based website) would provide a "pirate" stream, proving the vulnerability of rights purchases. The unauthorized web cast of the A-League Grand Final highlights the problems of the transnational distribution of the internet and its network infrastructure with nationalistic legal systems and jurisdictions as well as longstanding intellectual property systems in the digital age (Hutchins and Rowe, 2009).

Similar analogies were drawn in early 2012 when, days before the Super Bowl, federal prosecutors "seized 16 Web sites that provided access to illegal live streams of copyrighted sporting events and brought criminal charges against a Michigan man who allegedly operated nine of those websites" (Bray, 2012, para. 4). The raid came on the same day that New England Patriots quarterback, Tom Brady, speaking at the pre-Super Bowl press conference, commented that he watched the 2011 Super Bowl while rehabbing in Costa Rica via an illegal streaming site (Bray, 2012).

Fantasy sports

Finally, issues of copyright and the Internet have been found in the area of fantasy sports. For example, CBC Distribution and Marketing, Inc. brought suit against MLBAM to establish its right to use without license the names of statistics of MLB players, while MLBAM counter-claimed CBC's fantasy products violated MLB players' rights of publicity, protected under the 1976 Copyright Act. In 2007, the district court awarded summary judgment to CBC (Kaburakis, 2008).

Carriage

In the area of carriage, legal challenges have arisen in the areas of blackouts and transmission. Despite evolving technologies, sport governing bodies continue to enforce blackout policies which were created 40 years ago. President Richard Nixon signed a law in 1973, banning the NFL from blacking out the telecast of any game in a local market if the game was sold out 72 hours in advance (Smith, 2012). Prior to 1973, all home team games were blacked out in the local markets regardless of number of tickets sold. The law signed by Nixon expired two years later, but the NFL and its owners have continued to enforce a similar rule. In a possible attempt to placate a growing criticism of its blackout rules and possibly stimulate attendance at games, the NFL announced in July 2012 that it had altered blackout rules for the 2012 season. Local broadcasts of NFL games will now be permitted based on a benchmark established by each club, so long as the mark is 85 percent of capacity or higher (Clark, 2012).

One of the earliest legal challenges to blackout rules was *NFL v. McBee and Bruno's Inc.* (1985) in which the defendant, a St. Louis restaurant, used a satellite dish to receive the signal of blacked out St. Louis Cardinals football games and show them to patrons inside the establishment. The Federal Communications Commission (FCC) had passed regulation in 1975 prohibiting cable systems from carrying sports events which were blacked out on local television broadcast. The courts ruled that the defendant in the McBee case had violated the NFL's copyrighted broadcast (Mitten, Davis, Smith and Berry, 2005). Additional carriage disputes have occurred in the area of transmission, with sports networks not being distributed through certain cable outlets. Perhaps the most notable case involved Cablevision, the dominant cable provider in the New York City metro area, refusing to carry the New York

Yankee-owned YES Network throughout the 2002 MLB season (Sandomir, 2003). The decision by Cablevision to not carry the YES Network meant that three million Cablevision customers did not have access to Yankees games in 2002.

Usually, the key issue in carriage disputes is over per-subscriber fees. Cable networks generate revenue from two sources: advertising and subscriber fees, whereas traditional over-the-air networks received revenue only from advertising. As cable and satellite systems proliferated in the 1980s and 1990s, over-the-air networks sought to be compensated by multiple system operators (MSOs), such as Comcast and Time Warner, and multichannel video programming distributors (MVPDs), such as Directv and Verizon Fios, in exchange for agreeing to have the network carried by the MSO or MVPD. Because the Communications Act requires a television station give consent to an MSO or MVPD, many broadcast networks have begun to negotiate "retransmission consent" in the form of subscriber fees for carriage. In the event that an agreement cannot be reached, the MSO or MVPD must stop offering the station to its subscribers (Federal Communications commission, 2012).

Cablevision dropped FOX for more than two weeks in October 2010, during the MLB playoffs, after failing to reach an agreement on retransmission consent. A similar result nearly occurred in January 2012 when Sunbeam Television Corporation took its stations in Boston and Miami off Directv on January 14 in effort to increase retransmission fees. The sides negotiated an agreement on January 27, one week before the New England Patriots played in the Super Bowl. According to Ourand (2010), one of the key takeaways from Cablevision-FOX dispute was the importance of sport content. The writer noted that, "Cablevision did the deal because its subscribers wanted to see the MLB playoffs and NFL regular-season games. If there was any doubt before about the power of sports programming, it was erased during this dispute" (Ourand, 2010, p. 15).

The issue of carriage is made more complicated by the sport governing bodies themselves. Consider the five-year dispute between the Mid-Atlantic Sports Network (MASN) and Time Warner in the state of North Carolina. MASN owns the rights to MLB's Washington Nationals and Baltimore Orioles. According to MLB, the television territory for those teams extends from Pennsylvania to North Carolina. However, Time Warner, the dominant MSO in North Carolina, claims that its subscribers are not fans of either team and wanted to carry MASN on a subscription-only sports tier, rather than the more widely distributed basic tier, which is what MASN desired. As a result of what is known as the "Adelphia Order," MASN sought arbitration in June 2007 over its desire to be carried on Time Warner basic tiers. The "Adelphia Order" was a condition the FCC approved in 2006 following the sale of assets from Adelphia Communications to Time Warner and Comcast. It permitted unaffiliated Regional Sports Networks, such as MASN, unable to reach a carriage agreement with Time Warner or Comcast to seek commercial arbitration (Telecompaper, 2006). Arbitrators and FCC's media bureau ruled in favor of MASN in 2008, but Time Warner appealed to the full FCC which, after two years, found in its favor in 2010. MASN appealed to the US Court of Appeals for the Fourth Circuit, which ruled May 14, 2012 in favor of Time Warner, preventing the network from being carried on a basic tier (Sherfinski, 2012).

The future

Predicting the future of digital rights in sports is a difficult proposition, as technologies continue to evolve at a rapid rate. Nonetheless, the trends observed seem to indicate that certain areas will continue to be contentious issues, as sport governing bodies seek to continue to maximize the value of their rights.

In the area of content, we would expect to see continued convergence between content manufacturers and distributors, much like the NFL has done by placing its content exclusively on its own network, the NFL Network. The proliferation of team- and league-owned television networks (for example, Big Ten Network, YES Network, MLB Network) throughout the last decade suggests an extremely lucrative value chain, if done properly. As it negotiates its next large media rights deal, MLB has announced it is seriously considering placing playoff games on its league-owned MLB Network, a first for major sport governing bodies (Ourand and Fisher, 2012).

In the area of copyright, the continued challenges between new media technologies and piracy will continue, particularly for marquee sports events such as the World Cup, Olympic Games, and Super Bowl. Increased mobile broadband capabilities and portable computers will fuel pirated streams of sporting events, as the demand to watch live sporting events continues to grow.

Finally, the biggest changes may occur in the area of carriage where there is growing sentiment to eliminate blackout rules altogether and the possibility of government intervention in retransmission consent. An advocacy group, Sport Fans Coalition, filed a petition in November 2011 asking the FCC to review blackout rules and received notice in January 2012 that the agency is seeking public comments on sports blackout rules. The last comprehensive FCC review of sports blackouts occurred in 1976 (Frederick, 2012).

In addition, government intervention may occur in retransmission controversies, as Congress continues to review the issue. During a 2010 hearing titled "Television viewers, retransmission consent, and the public interest" held before the Senate Subcommittee on Communications, Technology, and the Internet, Massachusetts Senator John Kerry invoked the Cablevision-Fox dispute in the opening minutes of his opening statement. Senator Kerry commented that "our constituents should not be the pawns in these corporate negotiations" (Senate Subcommittee on Communications, Technology, and the Internet, 2011). The politician added that he was "concerned that, without a better, more transparent process for dealing with impasses in negotiations and adequate FCC oversight, more fights and disruptions of service are what people have to look forward to" (p. 2).

References

Adams, R. (2004). MLB goes 2-for-2 in Web distribution deals. *SportsBusiness Daily*, March 29. Retrieved from http://www.sportsbusinessdaily.com/Journal/Issues/2004/03/20040329/E-Sports/MLB-Goes-2-For-2-In-Web-Distribution-Deals.aspx?hl=realnetworks%20mlbandsc=0.

Andrews, D. L. (2003). Sport and the transnationalizing media corporation. *Journal of Media Economics*, 16 (4), 235–51.

Bray, C. (2012). Black Sunday: US attorney, ICE seize illegal sports sites. *Wall Street Journal*, February 2. Retrieved from http://blogs.wsj.com/law/2012/02/02/black-sunday-us-attorney-ice-seize-illegal-sports-sites/.

Citizen Media Law Project (2009). Copyright claims based on user content. Berkman Center for Internet and Society. *Citizen Media Law Project*, October 29. Retrieved from http://www.citmedia law.org/legal-guide/copyright-claims-based-user-content.

Clark, K. (2012). Game changer: NFL scrambles to fill seats. *Wall Street Journal*, July 2. Retrieved from http://online.wsj.com/article/SB10001424052702303561504577495083707417526.html.

Evangelista, B. (2005). Truce declared: Microsoft settles with RealNetworks, promises to promote its online music. *San Francisco Chronicle*, October 12. Retrieved from http://www.sfgate.com/cgi-bin/article.cgi?f=/c/a/2005/10/12/BUGD6F6TGE1.DTLandao=all.

Federal Communications Commission (2012). Retransmission consent. In *FCC Encyclopedia*, Washington DC. Retrieved from http://www.fcc.gov/encyclopedia/retransmission-consent.

Fisher, E. (2008). MLB imposes restrictions for online content. *SportsBusiness Journal*, February 25. Retrieved from http://www.sportsbusinessdaily.com/Journal/Issues/2008/02/20080225/This-Weeks-News/MLB-Imposes-Restrictions-For-Online-Content.aspx?hl=MLB%20rights%20restrictionsandsc=0.

Flint, J., and Chmielewski, D. C. (2011). How high can fees for sports rights go? *Los Angeles Times*, September 8. Retrieved from http://articles.latimes.com/2011/sep/08/business/la-fi-ct-sports-rights-20110908.

Frederick, B. (2012). Sports fans score huge win with FCC review of blackouts. *Sports Fans Coalition*, January 20. Retrieved from http://sportsfans.org/2012/01/sports-fans-score-huge-win-with-fcc-review-of-blackouts/.

Fry, J. (2007). Papers face NFL's 45-second rule. *Wall Street Journal*, July 16. Retrieved from http://online.wsj.com/public/article_print/SB118348291924156787.html.

Hu, J. (2004). MLB lands Microsoft, America Online deals. *CNET News*, March 22. Retrieved from http://news.cnet.com/2100-1026-5177223.html.

Hutchins, B., and Rowe, D. (2009). From broadcast scarcity to digital plentitude: The changing dynamics of the media sport content economy. *Television and New Media*, 10 (4), 354–70.

International Olympic Committee (2011). *IOC social media, blogging and internet guidelines for participants and other accredited persons at the London 2012 Olympic Games*. August 31. Retrieved from http://www.olympic.org/Documents/Games_London_2012/IOC_Social_Media_Blogging_and_Internet_Guidelines-London.pdf.

Kaburakis, A. (2008). *C.B.C. Distribution and Marketing, Inc., v. Major League Baseball Advanced Media, L.P.*, 505 F.3d 818 (8th Cir. 2007). *International Journal of Sport Communication*, 1, 241–5.

Linn, A. (2004). Microsoft strikes deal with Major League Baseball site. *USA Today*, March 22. Retrieved from http://www.usatoday.com/tech/webguide/internetlife/2004-03-22-ms-mlb-deal_x.htm.

Merron, J. (2012). Olympic social media guidelines muzzle athletes. *ReadWriteWeb*, June 26. Retrieved from http://www.readwriteweb.com/archives/olympic-social-media-guidelines-muzzle-athletes.php.

Migala, D. (2001). MLB offers games as ticket for turning free into fee. *SportsBusiness Journal*, April 2. Retrieved from http://www.sportsbusinessdaily.com/Journal/Issues/2001/04/20010402/No-Topic-Name/MLB-Offers-Games-As-Ticket-For-Turning-Free-Into-Fee.aspx?hl=realnetworks%20mlbandsc=0.

Mitten, M. J., Davis, T., Smith, R. K., and Berry, R. C. (2005). *Sports law and regulation: Cases, materials, and problems*. New York: Aspen.

MLB Advanced Media (2004). America Online announces broad expansion of deal with Major League Baseball Advanced Media. *MLB.com*, March 3. Retrieved from http://www.mlb.com/news/press_releases/press_release.jsp?ymd=20040324andcontent_id=669075andvkey=pr_mlbcomandfext=.jspandc_id=mlbcom.

Moorman, A. M., and Dittmore, S. W. (2007). NCAA loses public sentiment points in blogging issue. *SportsBusiness Journal*, June 25, 10 (11), 29.

Osborne, B., and Batista, P. J. (2012). Time out! Federal court decision clarifies ownership of broadcast rights in high school sports events. *Sport Marketing Quarterly*, 21, 53–5.

Ostrow, A. (2009a). Social media banned from college stadiums. *Mashable Social Media*, August 17. Retrieved from http://mashable.com/2009/08/17/sec-new-media-policy/.

Ostrow, A. (2009b). No fun league: The NFL reveals its social media policy. *Mashable Social Media*, August 31. Retrieved from http://mashable.com/2009/08/31/nfl-social-media-policy/.

Ourand, J. (2010). Four takeaways from the Fox-Cablevision Big Apple brawl. *SportsBusiness Journal*, November 8. Retrieved from http://www.sportsbusinessdaily.com/Journal/Issues/2010/11/20101108/Media/Four-Takeaways-From-The-Fox-Cablevision-Big-Apple-Brawl.aspx?hl=ourandandsc=0.

Ourand, J., and Fisher, E. (2012). Now on deck for next sports rights deal: MLB. *SportsBusiness Journal*, June 4. Retrieved from http://www.sportsbusinessdaily.com/Journal/Issues/2012/06/04/Leagues-and-Governing-Bodies/MLBTV.aspx.

Richman, D. (2004). RealNetworks sues baseball over use of Windows Media. *Seattle Post-Intelligence*, March 9. Retrieved from http://www.seattlepi.com/sports/baseball/article/RealNetworks-sues-baseball-over-use-of-Windows-1139049.php.

Roberts, G. R. (2004). The scope of the exclusive right to control dissemination of real-time sports event information. *Stanford Law and Policy Review*, 15: 167–87.

Rosenblatt, R. (2011). Breaking down the Pac-12's new TV deal with ESPN/Fox and Pac-12 Network. *Bruins Nation*, May 4. Retrieved from http://www.bruinsnation.com/2011/5/4/2153940/breaking-down-the-pac-12s-new-tv-deal-with-espn-fox-pac-12-network.

Sandomir, R. (2003). Cablevision agrees to carry the YES Network. *New York Times*, March 13. Retrieved from http://www.nytimes.com/2003/03/13/sports/baseball-cablevision-agrees-to-carry-the-yes-network.html?pagewanted=allandsrc=pm.

SEC Sports (2008) ESPN, SEC reach unprecedented agreement. *SEC DigitalNetwork.com*, August 26. Retrieved from http://www.secdigitalnetwork.com/NEWS/tabid/473/Article/130328/espn-sec-reach-unprecedented-agreement.aspx.

Senate Subcommittee on Communications, Technology, and the Internet (2011). *Television viewers, retransmission consent, and the public interest. Hearing Before The Subcommittee On Communications, Technology, And The Internet Of The Committee On Commerce, Science, And Transportation United States Senate One Hundred Eleventh Congress Second Session November 17, 2010.* Washington DC: Government Printing Office. Retrieved from http://www.gpo.gov/fdsys/pkg/CHRG-111shrg70970/pdf/CHRG-111shrg70970.pdf.

Sherfinski, D. (2012). Court shuts out Nationals, Orioles' fans viewing in N.C. *Washington Times*, May 28. Retrieved from http://www.washingtontimes.com/news/2012/may/28/court-shuts-out-nationals-orioles-fans-viewing-in-/?page=all.

Smith, M. D. (2012). Recording reveals Nixon's anger with NFL blackouts. *ProFootball Talk, NBC Sports*, February 11. Retrieved from http://profootballtalk.nbcsports.com/2012/02/11/recording-reveals-richard-nixons-anger-over-nfl-blackouts/.

Telecom.paper (2006) FCC approves Adelphia takeover by Time Warner, Comcast. *Telecompaper*, July 14. Retrieved from http://www.telecompaper.com/news/fcc-approves-adelphia-takeover-by-time-warner-comcast.

Wong, G. M. (2002). *Essentials of sports law* (3rd ed.). Westport, CT: Praeger.

24

SUBJECTIVITY IN 140 CHARACTERS

The use of social media by marginalized groups

Erin McNary and Marie Hardin

Can you remember a moment in your life when social media did not exist? For many, social media has become a routine part of life. Consider your favorite athletes or teams and think about the ways they connect and engage with you as a fan. Social media have proven to be important in developing fan interaction, forging connections between teams and leagues and respective fans, selling tickets and merchandise while also driving television viewership (Fisher, 2011). Sutton states that "fan connectivity and greater involvement" can be inspired by social media (Sutton, 2011, p. 12). In their relatively new existence, social media have evolved and changed the landscape of how people receive content about their favorite athletes, sports teams, or leagues.

A variety of meanings exist in discussions of social media. Safko and Brake state that social media are about connecting communities, specifically "activities, practices, and behaviors among communities of people who gather online to share information, knowledge, and opinions using conversational media" (Safko and Brake, 2009, p. 6). Social media sites are web-based with the potential for users to "construct public or semi-public profile within a bounded system" and find others with common interests and connect with these individuals (Boyd and Ellison, 2008, p. 211). Additionally, tools, platforms, and applications that allow for connection, communication, and collaboration categorize social media (Williams and Chinn, 2010). Sources of social media include but are not limited to blogging, forums, content communities, podcasting, and social-networking sites (for example, Facebook, Twitter, YouTube Sports Fan Live, ChatSports, Ballhype). In 2010, three of the world's most popular social media sites included Facebook, YouTube, and Wikipedia, and consumers spent three quarters of their time online on social networking sites and blog sites (Nielsenwire, 2010).

This chapter provides a short summary of the marketing of athletes prior to the rise of social media as well as a brief evolution of social media. Although all athletes have the option of using social media as a marketing strategy, this chapter will specifically focus on how marginalized athletes may use social media as an alternative marketing technique. Historically, researchers have documented ways in which traditional media outlets (such as television, radio, newspaper) have marginalized certain groups of athletes. Such marginalization could persuade these athletes to seek alternative marketing outlets, such as social media. Therefore, the primary goal of this chapter is to explore how marginalized athletes may challenge stereotypical representations and ways in which athletes have used social media to reach a broader audience and, in turn, strengthen their fan base. To highlight this focus, the two following questions are addressed: Can lesser known athletes engage in social media to encourage a wider fan base and increased endorsement negotiations? Can social media help to reinvent traditional portrayals of marginalized groups? Finally, current and future trends and challenges are also examined.

Social media

With the advent of the Internet, specifically Web 2.0, the symbiotic nature of sports and media continues to evolve and grow. Currently, sport consumers are able to interact with their favorite athletes and teams via the Internet in ways that were once not possible. Before social media, a typical sports marketing plan would have included the marketing mix of product, price, place, promotion, and, more recently, public relations. Traditional ways of marketing included word-of-mouth marketing, print and online advertising, and event and email marketing. Now more than ever, the sport industry is tasked with embracing social media marketing. This type of marketing refers to the "process that empowers individuals to promote their websites, products, or services through online social channels and to communicate with and tap into a much larger community that may have not been available via traditional advertising channels" (Weinberg, 2009, p. 4).

Although traditional types of marketing have been used, social media has the ability to enhance traditionally used approaches. Social media are fairly new (Twitter was established in 2006 and Facebook in 2004), so athletes and marketers may grapple with finding a formula that is effective. Dustin Godsey, director of marketing at the Wells Fargo Center, home to the Philadelphia Wings (National Lacrosse League), reported that social media are becoming more prominent in marketing plans (Olenski, 2012). The Wings were the first team to allow the Twitter names of athletes on the back of jerseys. Because of the increase in popularity of social media, the Federal Trade Commission (FTC) has created a guide outlining how to leverage social media to promote brands that abide by the legal and policy requirements for promotions in more traditional media. Bloggers "must disclose material connections they share with the seller of the product or service" (Federal Trade Commission, 2009, para. 4). Because of the FTC's guidelines, athletes and agents need to be aware of these parameters and be as honest as possible to avoid legal action (McKelvey and Masteralexis, 2011).

Social media use by athletes and fans

A number of reasons exist as to why athletes find social media important. Some main reasons include the ability of the athlete to manage the content, promote brands and the sport, and interact with fans. The literature focusing on social media is limited in comparison to traditional ways of marketing previously mentioned. More research is necessary to fully understand the impact social media have on the sporting culture.

Social media tools have allowed athletes to dictate coverage on their own terms so they are able to control the message (Tucker Center, 2009). This alternative has great potential for athletes and fans to select content about their accomplishments, respective sport, and other areas of interest. Athletes managing content can also be verified in research on blogging. In their study of blogs, Kwak, Kim, and Zimmerman (2010) found that user-generated content could prove to be an effective communication tool and that the messages were deemed "trustworthy and reliable" just as if the message were communicated in a mainstream source (Kwak, *et al.*, 2010, p. 417). This suggests that fans may be more satisfied with receiving information about their favorite athletes directly from the athlete versus from a secondary source.

Athletes may turn to social media for branding and promotional purposes. Amy Martin, founder of Digital Royalty, a digital branding agency, said that social media strategies are important in strengthening and positioning a brand (Ballouli and Hutchinson, 2010). However, there is a current challenge in the valuation of social media and the return on investment for brands. Martin defines an old measurement system as cold metrics referring to frequency, page views, and impressions, which have been replaced by the more intangible warm metrics. These encompass engagement levels, viral factors, community conversations, and sentiment analysis (Martin, 2011). The experience of athletes may suggest that social media have the ability to provide exposure to their brand but also to a lesser-known sport. Sanderson's (2011) study supports that athletes competing in less notable sports may benefit from social media.

In an attempt to take a more organic approach to building a fan base, many athletes have selected social media as a marketing technique to better connect with their fans. Furthermore, social media sites allow fans to interact and thus contribute to the marketing of the athletes. Such mutual contributions can be exemplified in the number of tweets, blogs, and posts fans make to various social media sites. For example the record for number of tweets (7,196 tweets per minute) during a sporting event occurred during the 2011 Women's World Cup match between the United States and Japan (Fisher, 2011). Fans also act as gatekeepers (see next section) or gatewatchers (Bruns, 2003), selecting articles of interest and filtering media information for one another, as McCarthy (2011) observed in a study involving fans and gymnasts. Pegoraro (2010) studied the Twitter accounts of twenty athletes representing a variety of sports and leagues, and most athletes' activity revolved around responding to fan posts. In addition, sporting organizations such as the 2012 London Olympics and Paralympic Organizing Committees encouraged athletes blogging and tweeting during the games, with an admonition that they "conform to the Olympic spirit and fundamental principles of Olympism as contained in the Olympic Charter" (International Olympic Committee, 2011, p. 1). These examples again illustrate how self-generating marketing from fans and athletes alike can enhance interaction and engagement, and that sports organizations recognize the benefits of this potential.

Traditional media coverage of athletes and sports

Traditionally, editors of mainstream media have framed selected content in a certain and predictable way, one that relies on their understanding of sports and of their audience or readership base (Hardin, 2005; Lowes, 1999). Research indicates, for instance, that sports coverage is organized by beats, guaranteeing routine coverage of the planned events (such as games and press conferences) around most (able-bodied) men's, big-market, professional sports and college teams (Pew Research Center's Project for Excellence in Journalism, 2005; Lowes, 1999). A study by the Project for Excellence in Journalism determined that sports coverage patterns have changed very little over the decades and speculated that "the familiar, perhaps even ritual, nature of the sections is part of their allure" (Pew Research Center's Project for Excellence in Journalism, 2005, p. 3).

Media scholars often rely on the theoretical concepts of gatekeeping and framing to understand the ways media present sports and athletes. Gatekeeping is a concept that has been used extensively in the analysis of journalistic decision-making. Shoemaker and Vos (2009, p. i) suggest that gatekeeping "determines not only which information is selected [for media messages], but also what the content and nature of the messages, such as news, will be". Gatekeeping can be used to understand the choices of media producers on story selection, publication and placement; for instance, why coverage of a boys' soccer match may appear on the home page of a local news website while a local co-ed bowling tournament goes unmentioned. As Shoemaker and Vos explain, a cluster of key factors influences gatekeeping decisions. The scholars note that these factors include journalistic norms and routines; organizational factors such as ownership and corporate culture; social institutional influences such as the impact of advertisers and sponsors on decision making; and the individual characteristics of decision-makers, such as their gender and social roles.

According to Entman, framing refers to selection and salience whereby a frame is to "select some aspects of a perceived reality and make them more salient in a communicating text, in such a way as to promote a particular problem definition, causal interpretation, moral evaluation, and/or treatment recommendation for the item described" (Entman, 1993, p. 52). Most scholars agree that frames "induce us to view issues and situations in a certain way" (D'Angelo, 2010, p. 300). News accounts of events and issues can use several different – and sometimes competing – frames. For instance, an examination of newspaper coverage of subsidies for sports stadiums in the US found that articles used economic development and civic status as lenses through which to present the issues (Buist and Mason, 2010).

Scholars argue that the gatekeeping and framing behind the traditional media coverage of sports are a result of hegemonic ideology related to cultural understandings of bodies and gender, which privilege able, male bodies (Duncan, 2006; Hardin, 2005; Shoemaker and Vos, 2009; Vincent, 2004). For instance, Shoemaker and Vos suggest that an influence on gatekeeping decisions is at the social-system level, which involves the (generally invisible yet powerful) influence of body-ideal ideology on media producers' decisions. Masculine hegemony in sport has been scrutinized by many scholars (for example, Kane and Lenskyj, 1998; Messner, 2002). Although most of the focus has been on the marginalization of women, a handful of scholars have pointed out that hegemonic ideology idealizes able bodies, promoting ableism (Davis, 1999). "No one would dispute that women, gays, subalterns, people of color and so on have been marginalized...But the case of people with disabilities is somewhat different," noted Davis. The scholar added that, "Indeed, one of the most egregious acts of omission committed in the 20th century by progressives and radicals has been the almost complete ignoring of issues surrounding people with disabilities...An ableist cultural hegemony is clearly the rule" (Davis, 1999, p. 1).

The media and marginalized athletes

It is no surprise, based on hegemonic ideology as it relates to sport, that scholars have placed a great deal of focus on the marginalized, stereotypical coverage of female athletes and athletes with a disability. As other chapters in this handbook focus on coverage of female athletes (see Chapter 32 and Chapter 35), only a short summary of that coverage will be presented here:

Sports coverage has been indicted as presenting events and athletes in such a way that it "privileges men and disadvantages women" (Duncan, 2006, p. 231). Dozens of studies examining coverage have confirmed the obvious: female athletes are routinely marginalized in all types of outlets, from magazines to television to newspapers and the web (for example, Eagleman, Pedersen, and Wharton, 2009; Messner and Cooky, 2010; Reichart Smith, 2011; Vincent, 2004). Gatekeeping and framing have both been used to explain journalists' decision making in relationship to the lack of coverage of women's sports and in the stereotyping of women as athletically inferior to men (Hardin, 2005; Lasorsa, 2012; Wanta and Leggett, 1989).

Scholars have paid far less attention to the marginalization of athletes with disabilities in sports coverage, although enough research exists to understand media accounts as problematic in quantity and quality (DePauw, 1997; Hardin, 2006; Schantz and Gilbert, 2001; British Library Sport and Society, 2012; Thomas and Smith, 2009). Reporters often focus primarily on the "disabled" instead of the "athlete"; athletes with disabilities are usually covered as feature stories instead of sports stories (Hardin, 2006; Schantz and Gilbert, 2001). The Paralympics, one of the largest international sporting events in the world, receives very little coverage in the US and less in other countries compared to its counterpart, the Olympics (Hardin, 2006; British Library Sport and Society, 2012). When they are covered, the media's "patronising implications of portraying the Paralympic Games as intrinsically more noble, honest, and more 'family' centered than its Olympic counterpart have angered Paralympians who wish to be regarded simply as athletes" (British Library Sport and Society, 2012, para. 8).

Disability sports advocates and scholars suggest that journalists' framing of disabled athletes as "supercrips" is also problematic (Schantz and Gilbert, 2001). The supercrip stereotype focuses on the courageous character of individuals overcoming a handicap rather than the athletic accomplishment of athletes, and it supports hegemonic ideology in that it rests on the assumption that disability is an individual condition, one for which the larger society has no obligation for accommodation. Thus, media use of the supercrip model assumes that people with disabilities are pitiful (and useless), until they "overcome" their disabilities through rugged individualism (Hardin, 2005; Thomas and Smith, 2009). For example, Jim Abbott, former Major League Baseball (MLB) player for ten seasons, felt frustration with CBS News for focusing on his lack of a right hand rather than his athletic accomplishments (Johnson, 1989). A recent trend pointed out by Thomas and Smith (2009) is to also present disabled athletes as aspiring to able-bodiedness and ignoring their impairments and impact of disability on their lives. Thomas and Smith suggest that, although such representations may be seen as positive, they may also perpetuate "the view that an impairment…is not central to a disabled person's life experiences and self-identity" (Thomas and Smith, 2009, p. 144).

Interview research with competitive wheelchair athletes, including Paralympians, captures their frustration with the lack of coverage and use of stereotypes by journalists (Hardin and Hardin, 2004; Hargreaves and Hardin, 2009). However, athletes also expressed a belief that although they resented stereotypes such as the "supercrip," they did not want the alternative, which might be complete invisibility.

Marginalized groups and social media

The radically altered landscape for mediated communication around sport – driven by technology and the emergence of social media platforms – has opened up a space for marginalized athletes to control and direct alternatives to traditional media coverage (or non-coverage, more accurately). As outlined at the beginning of this chapter, commentary on the sport-social media relationship has focused on ways that sports fans and athletes have been able to bypass traditional media outlets to connect (Ballard, 2006; Glaser, 2010). For instance, Sanderson's (2010) study of the framing of Tiger Woods' sex scandal in the press and on his Facebook page found that athletes can effectively use social media to counteract negative coverage with their fans.

Female athletes

In recent years, the women's sports movement has moved aggressively into the social-media sphere, using multiple platforms to build fan communities, assist in marketing and branding, and publicize events. One example is the blog collective Women Talk Sports, an aggregator of news and commentary about women's sports from a large, eclectic assortment of blogs written by current and former athletes, activists and scholars, and freelance journalists. The collective was launched in 2009 with a goal of promoting female athletes and sports participation.

Female athletes and advocacy organizations also use other platforms. In a 2012 article on the *espnW* website, journalist Jane McManus (2012) described athletes using the 140-character tool to "keep in touch with fans, add sponsors and promote games that don't get the same kind of coverage that those of their male peers enjoy" (McManus, 2012, para. 5). She also described the ways in which female athletes used the platform for marketing and branding in the absence of traditional coverage, adding the advice from US Olympic soccer player Julie Foudy to young female athletes: "[Y]ou need a social media presence to cover the gap between your fans and the mainstream media's coverage" (McManus, 2012, para. 11). Athletes such as tennis player Serena Williams, volleyball player Kerri Walsh, and auto racer Danica Patrick had large Twitter followings in 2012.

Athletes with a disability

The disabled sports movement, a much smaller and less visible arena than that of women's sports and without the protections and opportunities afforded by Title IX in the US, has also moved into the social media sphere (See Box 24.1). Predictably, however – given the deeply entrenched stereotypes about disability that have generally gone unchallenged – the social-media presence for Paralympians and the adapted-sports movement in general has grown more slowly. In 2012, the presence of blogs focusing on disability and sport on the Internet was scant; the Twitter feeds of key adapted-sport organizations in the US, such as BlazeSports America and Disabled Sports USA, did not have a large number of followers, and many athletes did not have a social media presence. Another reason for the smaller presence of disabled athletes on social media platforms could be the technological challenges they face if the platforms are not properly adapted for various impairments (such as blindness).

Conclusion

Although social media are relatively new in comparison to their print and broadcast counterparts, they allow for disintegration of the one-to-many model of mass communication in favor of a much more inclusive, participatory model. Athletes and sports organizations have used it to build communities and expand their fan base, making them more visible and

BOX 24.1 Using social media to amplify disability sports

In February 2012, a YouTube video of Canadian alpine skier Josh Dueck (Canadian Paralympic Committee 2009) went viral, drawing hundreds of thousands of views. Dueck, a freestyle skier for many years, had transitioned to Paralympic competition after he was paralyzed while landing a ski jump in 2004. The short video showed him perform the first-ever back flip on snow in a Sit Ski. When longtime disability sports advocate Eli Wolff saw the video, he decided to promote it to a more traditional venue with an even bigger reach: The Ellen DeGeneres Show, one of the highest-rated daytime talk shows in the US, with a viewership of millions. His choice of promotional tools: Twitter and Facebook, two social media applications that allow users to connect, amplify their messages, and build communities. Wolff said he does not know how many others also tweeted or sent a Facebook message about the Dueck video, but show producers noticed. Dueck was interviewed by host Ellen DeGeneres later that month in a segment that was publicized by sports-media giant ESPN. Dueck's big-time media exposure had its roots in three popular social-media tools: YouTube, Twitter, and Facebook. Wolff believes these applications have the potential to raise awareness and support for accomplished athletes who otherwise do not receive much media attention. Social media "can get good stories out there and get people to mobilize," noted Wolff, in an interview with one of the chapter authors. "That's part of the opportunity for disability sport – in telling good stories."

Disabled athletes and advocacy organizations can also share those stories in their own voices – without a filter that may insert stereotypes or minimize their athleticism. Wolff points to triathlete Sarah Reinertsen as one example of an athlete who has used social media to build a community of thousands of colleagues and fans who follow her training and competition. Other examples include Dueck, Paralympic sprinter Oscar Pistorius, and organizations that promote disabled athletes, such as the US Paralympic Team. College programs, such as Illinois Wheelchair Athletics, use a variety of social-media tools to build their fan base. Wolff regularly uses his own Facebook group to point followers and fans toward mainstream media outlets that are covering disabled sports and to other resources. An important feature of social media is their ability to contextualize and to educate, according to Wolff, because many sports fans may not understand adapted sport.

Of course, that is changing as the sports and their athletes get more media exposure and, as Wolff contends, disability is more culturally visible now than ever. He points to popular television shows such as "Glee," which features a character who uses a wheelchair, and to the higher visibility of people with a disability in advertisements, as evidence. In the world of sports, ESPN recognizes a male and female athlete with a disability each year with one of its coveted "ESPY" awards; athletes such as Oscar Pistorius, a double-amputee who runs with artificial legs – and with world-class times that compete with able-bodied runners – continue to raise the profile for adapted sport (Sokolove, 2012). Wolff believes that social media will play an important role in a concerted, focused, and mobilized effort by disability sports advocates to raise awareness and support. "We're starting to see a shift happening," said Wolff, who traveled to London for the Paralympics, updating his community of Facebook and Twitter fans along the way. "Social media is having an effect. It's worth the effort."

potentially more valuable to marketers (McManus, 2012). Little research has been completed to assess the material impact of social media on the marketing, branding, and publicity potential of social media in sports. Such research would be fruitful, especially as it relates to marginalized groups in sports. These groups may be able to use existing and yet-to-emerge social media platforms to counter hegemonic ideology that has historically kept them on the margins. Without a doubt, social media have changed the landscape of sports coverage. Users of social media (for example, athletes, fans, students, scholars, sport industry professionals) must be aware of the lack of coverage as well as the marginalized, stereotypical coverage of female athletes and athletes with a disability. Users of social media produce and consume content and have the responsibility and ability to provide content that counters stereotypical coverage, creates awareness, and supports marginalized athletes. Next time you blog, post, or tweet, keep this in mind.

References

Ballard, C. (2006). Writing up a storm. *Sports Illustrated*, March 27. Retrieved from http://sportsillustrated.cnn.com/vault/article/magazine/MAG1110302/index.htm

Ballouli, K., and Hutchinson, M. (2010). Digital branding and social media strategies for professional athletes, sports teams, and leagues: An interview with Digital Royalty's Amy Martin. *International Journal of Sport Communication*, 3, 395–401.

Boyd, D. M., and Ellison, N. B. (2008). Social network sites: Definition, history, and scholarship. *Journal of Computer-Mediated Communication*, 13, 210–30.

British Library Sport and Society (2012). The media and the Paralympics. Retrieved from http://www.bl.uk/sportandsociety/exploresocsci/sportsoc/media/articles/paramedia.html.

Bruns, A. (2003). Gatewatching, not gatekeeping: Collaborative online news. *Media International Australia Incorporating Culture and Policy*, 107, 31–44. Retrieved from http://eprints.qut.edu.au/189/.

Buist, E. A., and Mason, D. S. (2010). Newspaper framing and stadium subsidization. *American Behavioral Scientist*, 53 (10), 1492–510.

Canadian Paralympic Committee (2009). Josh Dueck: profile. Retrieved from http://www.paralympic.ca/en/detail/42611.html?id=42378andprofileid=42378andview=detail.

Davis, L. J. (1999). J'Accuse! Cultural imperialism-ableist style. *Social Alternatives*, 18 (1), 1–5.

D'Angelo, P. (2010). Conclusion: Arriving at the horizons of news framing analysis. In P. D'Angelo and J. A. Kuypers (Eds.), *Doing news framing analysis: Empirical and theoretical perspectives* (pp. 356–68). New York: Taylor and Francis.

DePauw, K. (1997). The (in)visibility of disability: Cultural contexts and 'sporting bodies.' *Quest*, 49, 416–30.

Duncan, M.C. (2006). Gender warriors in sport: Women and the media. In A. A. Raney and J. Bryant (Eds.), *Handbook of sports and media* (pp. 231–52). Mahwah, NJ: Lawrence Erlbaum.

Eagleman A. N., Pedersen, P. M., and Wharton, R. (2009). The coverage of gender in *ESPN The Magazine*: An examination of articles and photographs. *International Journal of Sport Management*, 10 (2), 226–42.

Entman, R. M. (1993). Framing: Toward clarification of a fractured paradigm. *Journal of Communication*, 43, 51–8.

Federal Trade Commission. (2009). FTC publishes final guides governing endorsements, testimonials: Changes affect testimonial advertisements, bloggers, celebrity endorsements. Retrieved from http://www.ftc.gov/opa/2009/10/endortest.shtm.

Fisher, E. (2011). 20 great uses of social media in sports. *SportsBusiness Journal*, August 1. Retrieved from http://www.sportsbusinessdaily.com/Journal/Issues/2011/08/01/In-Depth/Social-media.aspx.

Glaser, M. (2010). 5Across: Athletes on social media. *Mediashift*, May 12. Retrieved from http://www.pbs.org/mediashift/2010/05/5across-athletes-on-social-media132.html.

Hardin, M. (2005). Stopped at the gate: Women's sports, "reader interest," and decision making by editors. *Journalism and Mass Communication Quarterly*, 82 (1), 62–77.

Hardin, M. (2006). Disability and sport: (Non)Coverage an athletic paradox. In A. A. Raney and J. Bryant (Eds.), *Handbook of sports and media* (pp. 625–35). Mahwah, NJ: Lawrence Erlbaum.

Hardin, M., and Hardin, B. (2004). The Supercrip in sport media: Wheelchair athletes discuss hegemony's disabled hero. *Sociology of Sport Online*, June, 7 (1). Retrieved from http://physed.otago.ac.nz/sosol/v7i1/v7i1_1.html.

Hargreaves, J. A., and Hardin, B. (2009). Women wheelchair athletes: Competing against media stereotypes. *Disabilities Studies Quarterly*, 29 (2). Retrieved from http://dsq-sds.org/article/view/920/1095.

International Olympic Committee. (2011). IOC social media, blogging and internet guidelines for participants and other accredited persons at the London 2012 Olympic Games. Retrieved from http://www.olympic.org/Documents/Games_London_2012/IOC_Social_Media_Blogging_and_Internet_Guidelines-London.pdf.

Johnson, M. (1989). The "super-crip" stereotype: Press victimization of disabled people. *Fineline: The Newsletter on Journalism Ethics*, 1 (4), 2.

Kane, M. J., and Lenskyj, H. (1998). Media treatment of female athletes: Issues of gender and sexuality. In L. Wenner (Ed.), *MediaSport* (pp. 186–201). London: Routledge.

Kwak, D. H., Kim, Y. K., and Zimmerman, M. (2010). User- versus mainstream-media-generated content: Media source, message valence, and team identification and sport consumers' response. *International Journal of Sport Communication*, 3, 402–21.

Lasorsa, D. (2012). Transparency and other journalistic norms on Twitter: The role of gender. *Journalism Studies*, 13 (3), 402–17.

Lowes, M. (1999). *Inside the sports pages: Work routines, professional ideologies, and the manufacture of sports news*. Toronto: University of Toronto Press.

Martin, A. (2011). How brands can turn the art of social media scientific. *SportsBusiness Journal*, October 31, 14. Retrieved from http://www.sportsbusinessdaily.com/Journal/Issues/2011/10/31/Opinion/Amy-Martin.aspx.

McCarthy, B. (2011). From Shanfan to Gymnastike: How online fan texts are affecting access to gymnastics media coverage. *International Journal of Sport Communication*, 4, 265–83.

McKelvey, S., and Masteralexis, J. T. (2011). This tweet sponsored by...The application of new FTC Guides to the social media world of professional athletes. *Virginia Sports and Entertainment Law Journal*, 11 (1), 222–46.

McManus, J. (2012). Female athletes connect with Twitter. *espnW*, March 23. Retrieved from http://espn.go.com/espnw/more-sports/7727869/female-athletes-connect-twitter.

Messner, M. A. (2002). *Taking the field: Women, men, and sports*. Minneapolis, MN: University of Minnesota Press.

Messner, M. A., and Cooky, C. (2010) *Gender in televised sports: News and highlights shows, 1989–2009*. Los Angeles: USC Center for Feminist Research, University of Southern California. [https://dornsifecms.usc.edu/assets/sites/80/docs/tvsports.pdf.

Nielsenwire. (2010). Social networks/blogs now account for one in every four and a half minutes online. *Neilsenwire*, June 15. Retrieved from http://blog.nielsen.com/nielsenwire/global/social-media-accounts-for-22-percent-of-time-online/.

Olenski, S. (2012). The lines between social media and sports continue to blur. *Forbes*, February 13. Retrieved from http://www.forbes.com/sites/marketshare/2012/02/13/the-lines-between-social-media-and-sports-continue-to-blur/.

Pegoraro, A. (2010). Look who's talking-Athletes on twitter. *International Journal of Sport Communication*, 3, 501–14.

Pew Research Center's Project for Excellence in Journalism (2005). Box scores and bylines: A snapshot of the newspaper sports page. *Journalism.org*, August 22. [www.journalism.org/node/50/.

Reichart Smith, L. (2011). The less you say: An initial study of gender coverage in sports of Twitter. In A. Billings (Ed.), *Sports media: Transformation, integration, consumption* (pp. 146–61). New York: Routledge.

Safko, L., and Brake, D. K. (2009). *The social media bible: Tactics, tools, and strategies for business success*. Hoboken, NJ: John Wiley and Sons.
Sanderson, J. (2010). Framing Tiger's troubles: Comparing traditional and social media. *International Journal of Sport Communication*, 3, 438–53.
Sanderson, J. (2011). To tweet or not to tweet: Exploring division I athletic departments' social-media policies. *International Journal of Sport Communication*, 4, 492–513.
Schantz. O. J., and Gilbert, K. (2001). An ideal misconstrued: Newspaper coverage of the Atlanta Paralympic games in France and Germany. *Sociology of Sport Journal*, 18 (1), 69–94.
Shoemaker P. J., and Vos, T. P. (2009) *Gatekeeping theory*. New York: Routledge.
Sokolove, M. (2012). The fast life of Oscar Pistorius. *New York Times*, January 18. Retrieved from http://www.nytimes.com/2012/01/22/magazine/oscar-pistorius.html?pagewanted=all.
Sutton, B. (2011). Social media at the heart of strategy to achieve fan connectivity. *SportsBusiness Journal*, March 14. Retrieved from http://www.sportsbusinessdaily.com/Journal/Issues/2011/03/Mar-14/Opinion/Sutton-Impact.aspx.
Thomas, N., and Smith, A. (2009). *Disability, sport and society: An introduction*. New York: Routledge.
Tucker Center (2009). Social media: What is it and why it matters to women's sports. *Tucker Center*, September 21. Retrieved from http://tuckercenter.wordpress.com/2009/09/21/social-media-what-it-is-and-why-it-matters-to-women%E2%80%99s-sports/.
Vincent, J. (2004). Game, sex, and match: the construction of gender in British newspaper coverage of the 2000 Wimbledon Championships. *Sociology of Sport Journal*, 21 (4), 435–56.
Wanta, W., and Leggett, D. (1989). Gender stereotypes in wire service sports photos. *Newspaper Research Journal*, 10 (3), 105–14.
Weinberg, T. (2009). *The new community rules: Marketing on the social web*. Sebastopol, CA: O'Reilly Media.
Williams, J., and Chinn, S. J. (2010). Meeting relationship-marketing goals through social media: A conceptual model for sport marketers. *International Journal of Sport Communication*, 3, 422–37.

25
SPORT FANDOM IN THE DIGITAL WORLD

Ann Pegoraro

Sport spectatorship is one of the largest forms of leisure behavior in the world today (James and Ridinger, 2002). Large numbers of individuals attend sporting events and refer to themselves as sports fans, and their consumption of sport is increasingly shifting to online platforms. Sports fans are consuming news and other content via social media and mobile devices more than ever, with 26 percent of sports fans using social media to follow leagues, teams, and players in 2012, compared with just 15 percent the previous year (Laird, 2012). Further evidence of the growth in the use of new media by sports fans is the surging usage of mobile platforms to both consume and convey sports content. Fans do not need to attend the game or even congregate with other fans to share the experience. With changes to media, fans can tweet, text, blog, and Facebook, all while watching the game, providing a new and enriched fandom experience. Because media, like fans, are constantly changing, sport media researchers need to be constantly observing and recording these changes. This chapter provides insight into how fans, teams, athletes, and other stakeholders interact and engage in fandom in the digital world. The chapter commences with an examination of how one becomes a sport fan. It then moves on to how sport fandom manifests itself in the new digital world, including uses and gratification of fans and the increasing potential for fan – athlete interaction. The chapter concludes with a discussion on the role of sport fans as content creators and the challenges and opportunities this presents.

How we become sport fans

There is perhaps no one accepted universal measure for fanship mainly owing to the complexity of the concept and how it is manifested. Perhaps the best example to illustrate this is the sport of football. Fans of American football are very different than fans of traditional football (or, as it is known in North America, soccer) given the different origins of each sport and its place in respective societies. Yet each set of fans might exhibit similar attachment to favorite teams and similar sport fan behavior even though the sport they attach to is vastly different. Studies of fans in each of the versions of football will no doubt produce different results relating to online sport fandom activities given the nature of the two sports, the historic routes to fandom, and geographic differences. Fanship, therefore, is not a universal concept and cannot be captured easily (Gantz, 2011).

There has been more of a consensus on how we become fans. In his seminal work on the topic, Wann (1995, 1997) identified eight common motivations for becoming a sport fan: group affiliation, family, aesthetic, self-esteem, entertainment, escape, economic, and eustress. Many of these motivations are exactly as they appear; an individual becomes a sport fan through the desire to spend more time with his or her family (Gantz, 1981; Gantz and Wenner, 1995; Raney, 2006; Wann, 1995, 1997; Wenner and Gantz, 1989), or to become part of a larger group and share the experience with something larger than themselves such as other fans, a community or their nation (Branscombe and Wann, 1991; Gantz and Wenner, 1995; Melnick, 1993; Sloan, 1989; Wann, 1995, 1997). Others simply enjoy either the aesthetic aspects of sport (Sloan, 1989; Wann, 1995, 1997) or the entertainment value of sport (Gantz, 1981; Gantz and Wenner, 1995; Sloan, 1989; Wann, 1995, 1997; Zillmann, Bryant, and Sapolsky, 1989). Escape can also be a motivator, where fans who are bored or dissatisfied with their life use sport fandom to temporarily forget (Sloan, 1989; Wann, 1995, 1997). Another motive for sport fandom is economics, where sport fans seek to financially gain from the opportunities to gamble on sport (Frey, 1992; Gantz and Wenner, 1995; Wann, 1995, 1997). Many sport fans seek out sport as a way to increase their self-esteem – your team wins – you win (Branscombe and Wann, 1994; Gantz, 1981; Sloan, 1989; Wann, 1995, 1997). And the last motivation for sport fandom is eustress, a positive form of stress that can stimulate and energize a sport fan through the anxiety involved from worrying whether your team will win or not (Branscombe and Wann, 1994; Gantz and Wenner, 1995; Raney, 2006; Sloan; Wenner and Gantz, 1989; Wann, 1995, 1997).

While not all of the eight motivations are present in sport fans at any given time, group affiliation and self-esteem are almost always in play and can form the core explanation for fan behavior (King, 2004). Historically, most fans have consumed sport in group settings and have used sport fandom to build positive connections with other fans, thereby increasing self-esteem. In the past, stadiums, arenas, bars and office water coolers have provided vast stretches of common ground for sport fans to gather in groups and form connections. This physical common ground or community is now greatly augmented by the boundless non-physical community provided by the Internet; fans can now gather in virtual groups to express their fandom.

Fandom in the digital world

With the growth of the Internet, sport fans have experienced an increased opportunity to interact with other fans, with teams, and with athletes. The various avenues (for example, message boards, social networking sites) available on the Internet allow fans choose different environments to connect in and engage in fandom related activities. So where do fans go? And for what purpose? To answer these questions, researchers first looked to how sport fans used the Internet for fandom and what they sought from these activities.

Early research on sport fan behavior in the digital world has focused on uses and gratifications theory to help to explain the extensive growth in sport fan use of Internet platforms. Researchers, focusing on non-sport related online behavior, have identified various traditional motivations behind online consumption. These motives include accessing information and technical knowledge (Raacke and Bonds-Raacke, 2008; Ruggiero, 2000), communicating with like-minded individuals (Raacke and Bonds-Raacke, 2008), and finding entertainment and diversion (Ruggiero, 2000). As Ruggiero noted, unique to online consumption is the motive of developing personal identities and keeping in touch with the global world. In applying the same theory to digital sport world, researchers found many parallel motives for sport fans use of the Internet. The motives of gathering information and technical knowledge, together with receiving entertainment and diversion were found when examining digital media use from a sport perspective (Hur, Ko, and Valacich, 2007; Seo and Green, 2008). Researchers such as Hur and colleagues and Seo and Green found that fans use the Internet to learn about teams and athletes and express team support.

Some of the first work on uses and gratifications theory applied to sport fan media use focused on message boards or online forums. Clavio (2008a) found that nonsubscribers used message boards primarily to gather information on their favorite teams and to interact with other fans while subscribers, who are more vested fans, also used message boards to gather information, but they spent more time on the message boards, and made more posts on message boards than nonsubscribers. Clavio (2008b) also delved into more detail on this online fan behavior. This study revealed four dimensions that explained fan behavior. The first, interactivity comprised fans giving input and opinions, participating in discussions, communicating with fellow fans, and sharing information, explained the largest portion of fan-reported behavior. The second dimension involved fans gathering information on the message boards which was posted by other fans. The third dimension encompassed a variety of uses of message boards that could be categorized as diversionary; for example, talking about other topics (politics, religion), and keeping in touch with college friends and their alma mater. Argumentation, the fourth dimension, included activities such as fans engaging in trash talk and arguing with other users on the forums.

The second part of applying uses and gratifications theory involves gratifications or what enjoyment the sport fan is looking for from using the Internet. Again, Clavio (2008b) found three key dimensions to gratifications with the acquisition, quality, and uniqueness of content available or premium information dimension being the first. Secondly, sport fans were interested in the quality of the communal aspects of interactions with other users, and the premium quality of those users. The third dimension included the motivation to support one's school or the company running the sites, or patronage motivation.

In applying uses and gratifications theory to one of the newest and fastest growing digital media platforms, Twitter, has also produced some similar results. Clavio and Kian (2010) found that the majority of Twitter followers on an athlete's Twitter feed were participating because of their affinity for the athlete and not just because of their affinity for Twitter. Other individuals followed the athlete because of their perceived celebrity or importance. A third factor that explained why fans were following the athlete was interaction, both with the athlete as well as with the larger Twitter community. The study found that the most salient uses of the Twitter feed for respondents dealt primarily with personal affinity for the athlete, perhaps illustrating the unique ability of Twitter to provide that inside look at an athlete's lives. Pegoraro (2010) and Hambrick, Simmons, Greenhalgh, and Greenwell (2010) studied athletes' use of Twitter, and both studies found that the majority of tweets were interacting with other users, including fans, which is in line with Ruggerio (2000) who asserted that individuals use the Internet to interact with other users and keep in touch with the larger world.

Early research into why and how fans use the Internet for their fandom activities, therefore, indicates that, to gather in-depth knowledge about their favorite team and related activities, fans are more likely to go to fan-driven message boards, team websites, and online forums. To find out what their favorite athlete is up to, fans are more likely to turn to social networking sites (such as Twitter, Facebook). These early studies also illustrate that Twitter represents yet another forum in which fans can associate with teams and interact with their favorite players, providing fans what they crave: information and interactivity.

Online transference of offline sport fandom

As noted in Wann (1995, 1997), sport fans all follow similar pathways to becoming a sport fan. Included in the motivations for sport fandom are self-esteem and group affiliation, two factors that can lead to becoming a highly identified fan. But what happens when your team loses – how does a fan ensure this loss does not affect his or her self-esteem? Over time, all fans have developed self-preservation strategies to deal with losses. Cialdini, *et al.* (1976) first introduced the notions of fans *basking in reflected glory* (BIRG). The authors noticed that after football games where their university won, students were more likely to wear school branded merchandise and would refer to themselves as part of the team – "We won!" Conversely, when a team lost, fans show a tendency to put distance between the team and themselves so as to not be identified as a loser. This is referred to as *cutting off reflected failure* or CORFing (Wann and Branscombe, 1990; Wann, Hamlet, Wilson, and Hodges, 1995). CORFing behavior allows the highly identified fan to maintain self-esteem after a loss and Wann and Branscombe labeled BIRGing and CORFing tendencies as a means for fans to demonstrate strategic self-preservation. A second type of self-preservation strategy was identified by Wann, *et al.* (1995) and labeled as *cutting off future failure* (COFF) where fans of successful teams keep their celebrations moderate, to preserve their ego in the future should their teams fail in upcoming games. Research also suggested that sport fans may use a fourth strategy to restore a positive social identity following a team defeat – *blasting* – which involves deriding the opponent, and more specifically their fans (Branscombe and Wann, 1994; Cialdini and Richardson, 1980).

Sports fans express their affiliations with sport teams in several ways, including public displays of their fandom on personal websites, fan forums, and blogs (End, 2001), wearing team clothing (Cialdini, *et al.*, 1976; Madrigal, 2000), and following games fanatically throughout the season. Research into sport fan behavior in the digital era suggests that fans increasingly use the various platforms provided by the Internet to engage in traditional offline fan behavior, including BIRGing, CORFing, COFFing and Blasting. Sheldon (1999) found that subscribers to a newsgroup for the Green Bay Packers were highly identified with the team and that they were less likely to BIRG or CORF but rather would use the newsgroup as a way to share the traditional values of being a Packer fan. Joinson (2000) studied soccer fans and found that these fans are more likely to access their team's web site following a win than after a loss thereby exhibiting traditional BIRGing behavior. In studying fans for the National Football League (NFL), End (2001) found that these fans use online message boards to BIRG and blast opponents; specifically, they will post more messages following a win by their team than after a loss. Interestingly, a greater proportion of blasting messages were posted after victories rather than losses, suggesting that, in some respects, fans were using blasting as an extended form of BIRGing.

In two studies of soccer fans BIRGing, CORFing and blasting behavior was identified. Boen, Vanbeselaere, and Feys (2002) used registered traffic from websites of respective soccer teams following championship game outcomes to measure tendencies for BIRGing and CORFing. As expected, the authors found the team websites had significantly more visitors after a win than after a loss. The second study by Bernache-Assollant, Lacassagne, and Braddock (2007) investigated the online behavior of highly identified soccer fans on fan-based internet communities found traditional BIRGing behavior, but these fans failed to engage in traditional blasting behavior, such as overly criticizing other teams or fans.

Berg and Harthcock (2008) investigated fan behavior in the online forum for men's basketball at *CSTV.com* during an NCAA Men's Basketball Tournament ("March Madness"). Their findings indicated that, as offline fans do, online fans engaged in behaviors such as blasting and BIRGing. Online blasting and BIRGing behavior was principally evident in the screen names chosen by fans the forum. These behaviors were also evident in the signature lines of fan postings. In another study, Porter, Wood, and Benigni (2011) monitored the traffic and analyzed the content of fan-based internet communities to document BIRGing, CORFing or COFFing in blogs, posts or other types of messages displayed by identifiable fans. Fans posts, when analyzed, were found to be 29 percent positive, 31 percent negative and 40 percent neutral. The authors found that fans spend more time on fan-based internet communities in blasting opposing teams' coaches or players than those on their own team. Also, in a second study related to NFL fans, Spinda (2011) examined the self-reported BIRGing and CORFing strategies of these fans, including online behavior. Results indicated that fans demonstrated online support or BIRGing by posting messages online to show support for their teams and chat with other fans online following a win. These same fans demonstrated CORFing behavior by failing to post a message online after a loss and reporting that they are less likely to chat online following a loss.

Gantz, Fingerhut, and Nadorff (2012) investigated the viewing habits of sport fans focusing on whether they used new digital platforms to augment their television sport viewing. Fans who participated in the study indicated that, for some games: 47 percent said that they simultaneously followed the game online; 53 percent said that they called other people during the game; 67 percent said that they texted other people; and 47 percent said that they used social media sites to talk about the game. Even if fans are watching the game on television alone, they are still connected to other fans through new technology. In the study, fans indicated there were four main ways in which the social uses of technology and digital platforms made the game more meaningful or interesting. First, fans liked to immediately share their reactions or feelings related to the game, and secondly, they liked to use the technology to gather information on the reactions of other fans. Thirdly, fans used these technologies to engage in trash talking and gloating behavior when their team won, and finally fans felt these technologies allowed them to feel more connected, providing a sense of community that viewing the game alone does not provide. Fans in the study also engaged in BIRGing and CORFing behavior – when their favorite team won, fans spent almost twice as much time following up using media then they did when their team lost. When their team won, fans also spent twice as much time texting with friends about the game.

Therefore, it would appear that research has been able to demonstrate that sport fans are indeed using new media to engage in typical sport fandom behavior and have taking some traditional sport fan strategies directing into the digital world. Also, new media has allowed sport fans to stay connected even while watching a sporting event alone.

Fan–athlete interactions in the digital world

As fans use of digital media for fandom related activities increases, researchers have also noted the potential of platforms, such as blogs and Twitter, to become the new mechanism for parasocial interactions between fans and athletes (Sanderson and Kassing, 2011). Parasocial interactions involve fans interacting with a media figure as if he/she was an actual acquaintance, resulting in contact that resembles actual social interactions (Giles, 2002). New media, and in particular, Twitter suggests the possibility of interaction is now real. In their work, Marwick and boyd (2011) studied the practice of celebrity, through appearance and 'backstage' access, documenting how celebrity practitioners used Twitter for this purpose. Their study revealed that celebrity practitioners reveal what appears to be personal information on Twitter to create a sense of intimacy with fans. As noted by Marwick and boyd, these practitioners also "publicly acknowledge fans and use language and cultural references to create affiliations with followers" (Marwick and boyd, 2011, p. 139). Further, the tweeting of interactions with other celebrities and personalities give fans the impression they are getting a candid and uncensored look at the lives of these individuals, perhaps revealing the person behind the celebrity.

These concepts have also been studied in a sport context given that many athletes today enjoy a celebrity status in society. Social media has become the predominant choice for athletes and fans to engage in parasocial interactions. In some of the first work in this area, Sanderson (2008) investigated incidents of parasocial interaction occurring on the blog of National Basketball Association (NBA) owner, Mark Cuban, during the time period he spent competing on the popular celebrity-based television dancing show. The research illustrated that fans were highly vested in Cuban's performances on the show, procrastinating over work and family responsibilities to ensure they could watch him live. Fans went as far as to initiating campaigns to increase fan voting for Cuban to remain on the show. Kassing and Sanderson (2009) investigated fan postings on a blog run by cyclist Floyd Landis for his comeback bid during the 2006 Tour de France. Again in this work, fans were found to contribute posts reflective of typical parasocial interactions – posting encouragement, praise, providing congratulations and actively giving advice to the athlete.

In addition to studying blogs, sport communication scholars have also studied Twitter, owing to the greater opportunity for fan–athlete interaction on this micro-blogging platform. Twitter has let fans feel closer to athletes and more involved in their day-to-day lives. Kassing and Sanderson (2010) studied fan–athlete interaction during the Giro d'Italia and found that cyclists in the race were directly interacting with fans via Twitter. The cyclists would invite fans to participate in merchandise giveaways and take their suggestions for warm-up music. The cyclists also provided a behind the scenes look at what it is like to ride a major tour including riding at high speeds and through dangerous conditions. Furthermore, two early studies on athletes' use of Twitter by Pegoraro (2010) and Hambrick, *et al.* (2010) indicated that athletes were primarily using Twitter as a mechanism to respond to fans and talk about their personal lives more so than for formal marketing purposes, leading Pegoraro to suggest the potential important role of Twitter to increase fan–athlete interactions. Thomas (2011) also confirmed the emotional importance of Twitter for athletes to share aspects of their personal life such as pictures or important announcements, to share their thoughts, or send inspirational messages to their fans. The findings of these early studies on fan–athlete parasocial interactions through social media further support that the findings of Marwick and boyd (2011) are applicable to sport as well.

Sport fans as content creators

How sports fans express their fandom through words and actions has changed dramatically with the growth in the Internet and social networking sites. Digital media and associated technology now provide a more direct link between fans and their favorite teams, athletes and other fans and allowing new relationships and interactions that were not possible before. Sport fans used to physically gather in locations like pubs, stadiums, restaurants, private homes to engage in fandom related activities such as debating sport topics, arguing whose favorite team/athlete was better and watching the game together. Now, these same fans can meet online to engage in these same activities, providing for both an enriched sport fandom experience, as well as unpredictable group dynamics, as the gathering of fans online can be much larger than physical gatherings and cross regional and national boundaries (Hutchins and Rowe, 2012).

According to scholars, online groups or crowds of sport fans are not homogenous groups and can represent, "by turns or in combination, a source of harsh criticism, an exploitable and profitable source of free labour, and an economic force that claims ownership of sport" (Hutchins and Rowe, 2012, p. 101). Traditionally, sport fans have been non-influential in the production of sport-related content, acting as consumers of content and are uninvolved in how content gets shaped and presented (Sanderson and Kassing, 2011). As noted by Clavio (2008b), the unique characteristics of online message boards that allow for users to participate both as the creators and the consumers of content should be seen as a new area for scholars to investigate. The challenge, therefore, is how to deal with sports fans that are large producers of sport related content in the digital world but are also virtually impossible to control and who demonstrate minimal regard for the norms of practice in the sport media world.

The content produced by sport fans is referred to as user-generated content and is defined as "to media content created or produced by the general public rather than by paid professionals and primarily distributed on the Internet" (Daugherty, Eastin, and Bright 2008, p. 16). User-generated content exists in a variety of forms, including content uploaded to social networking sites (such as Facebook, LinkedIn), online forums (such as myfootballforum.com); blogs (such as SB Nation); micro-blogs (such as Twitter); photographs and videos uploaded to file-sharing sites (such as YouTube, Flickr); and information uploaded to wikis (for example, Wikipedia) (Glickman and Fingerhut, 2011). Today, sport media production is increasingly driven less by formal publishers and more by sports fans or the general public. The growth in user-generated content is mind-boggling, with predictions indicating that by 2013 there will be nearly 135 million consumers of such content in the US alone, and more than 114 million user-generated content creators, accounting for almost 52 percent of all US internet users (Verna, 2009). Both of these numbers are expected to significantly increase over the coming years.

Understanding this phenomenon and the inability to control fans and user-generated content, some sport organizations have embraced it. While many factors may contribute to a sport organization's growth in followers, the authenticity of having fans talk to fans definitely has a role to play. In Watts' study on the Florida Gator Nation online, the scholar found that fans' discussions on team focused websites "allow them to become active participants in reporting team related news, express their opinions, and even become activists for causes in this online town hall" (Watts, 2008, p. 243). Indeed, the rise of digital media means that fans can now be reporters right alongside those with official press passes, and in fact increasingly sport websites' writers are being granted the same official credentials as members of traditional media. Fans can sometimes take the role of *reporter* very seriously, creating trouble for athletes, especially when it turns to these fans reporting of an athlete's behavior. For example, Sanderson (2009) examined how fans alerted organizations to the conduct of professional athlete's that took place on personal time and at times in what the athlete considered a private space. Fans are likely to engage in such reporting behaviors owing to their identification with a specific team, and their perception that an athlete's behavior can be detrimental to the team would prompt them to publically report it (Sanderson and Kassing, 2011).

Conclusion

Research has found that online media have the greatest effect on the association between fan-identification and self-esteem, followed by broadcast, mobile phones, and print media (Phua, 2010). The Internet has risen to prominence over more traditional media because of its numerous advantages: the ability to disregard both time and geography constraints, thereby making it truly global media, and the infinite bandwidth which puts no foreseeable limits on its growth (Boase and Wellman, 2006). These features of the Internet are especially useful for sports fans because they can access unlimited information about their favorite sport, team, athlete, regardless of time, and they can interact with like-minded fans from around the world (Phua, 2010). Now, sport fans can also watch live streaming of games online, as well as access online versions of sport related print media.

The Internet is home to numerous types of websites focused on sport fans and their fandom activities. Sports leagues and teams maintain websites that provide up-to-date statistics, game schedules, and news. Sport broadcast networks maintain online sites where fans can stream live video and view instant replays. YouTube has allowed any athlete or team to create highlight videos for fan consumption. Online fan forums and message boards allow sport fans to publicly meet other fans, display their team loyalty and employ self-esteem maintenance strategies such as BIRGing and CORFing. On Facebook, Twitter, and blogs, sport fans can get almost instantaneous news on athletes, teams, and leagues. On these same sites, fans can become content creators and even assume the role as reporter. It is important for sport organizations to know what drives individuals to participate and create content, what types of content sport fans are producing and how is this changing the world of online sport fandom. Globally, sport fans in the digital world are making their voices heard by athletes, by teams, and by other fans.

References

Berg, K. A., and Harthcock, A. (2008) "Let the Domination Begin" Sports Fans' Construction of Identity in Online Message Boards. In L. W. Hugenberg, P. M. Haridakis, and A. C. Earnheardt (Eds.), *Sports mania: Essays on fandom and the media in the 21st century* (pp. 203–17). Jefferson, NC: McFarland.

Bernache-Assollant, I., Lacassagne, M. F., and Braddock, J. H., II. (2007). Basking in reflective glory and degradation: Differences in identity-management strategies between two groups of highly identified soccer fans. *Journal of Language and Social Psychology*, 26, 381–8.

Boase, J., and Wellman, B. (2006). Personal relationships: On and off the Internet. In A. L. Vangelisti and D. Perlman (Eds.), *The Cambridge handbook of personal relationships* (pp. 709–23). New York: Cambridge University Press.

Boen, F., Vanbeselaere, N., and Feys, J. (2002). Behavioral consequences of fluctuating group success: An Internet study of soccer-team fans. *Journal of Social Psychology*, 142, 769–81.

Branscombe, N. R., and Wann, D. L. (1991). The positive and self concept consequences of sports team identification. *Journal of Sport and Social Issues*, 15, 115–27.

Branscombe, N. R., and Wann, D. L. (1994). Sport psychology. In F. N. Magill and J. Rodriquez, *Survey of social sciences: Psychology series* (pp. 2363–8). Pasadena, CA: Salem Press.

Cialdini, R. B., and Richardson, K. D. (1980). Two indirect tactics of image management: Basking and blasting. *Journal of Personality and Social Psychology*, 39, 406–15.

Cialdini, R. B., Borden, R. J., Thorne, A., Walker, M. R., Freeman, S., and Sloan, L. R. (1976). Basking in reflected glory: Three (football) field studies. *Journal of Personality and Social Psychology*, 34 (3), 366–75.

Clavio, G. (2008a). Demographics and usage profiles of users of college sport message boards. *International Journal of Sport Communication*, 1, 434–43.

Clavio, G. (2008b). Uses and gratifications of Internet collegiate sport message board users. *Dissertation Abstracts International*, 69 (08). [ProQuest Digital Dissertations database (Publication No. AAT 3319833).

Clavio, G., and Kian, T. (2010). Uses and gratifications of a retired female athlete's Twitter followers. *International Journal of Sport Communication*, 3, 485–500.

Daugherty, T., Eastin, M. S., and Bright, L. (2008). Exploring consumer motivations for creating user-generated content. *Journal of Interactive Advertising*, 8 (2), 16–25.

End, C. M. (2001). An examination of NFL fans' computer mediated BIRGing. *Journal of Sport Behavior*, 24, 162–181.

Frey, J. H. (1992). Gambling on sport: Policy issues. *Journal of Gambling Studies*, 8, 351–60.

Gantz, W. (1981). An exploration of viewing motives and behaviors associated with television sports. *Journal of Broadcasting*, 25, 263–75.

Gantz, W. (2011). Keeping Score: Reflections and suggestions for scholarship in sports and media. In A. Billings (Ed.), *Sports media: Transformation, integration, consumption* (pp. 7–18). New York: Routledge.

Gantz, W., and Wenner, L.A. (1995). Fanship and the television sports viewing experience. *Sociology of Sport Journal*, 12, 56–74.

Gantz, W., Fingerhut, D., and Nadorff, G. (2012). The social dimension of sports fanship. In A. C. Earnheardt, P. M. Haridakis, and W. Hugenberg, (Eds.), *Sports fans, identity, and socialization – Exploring the fandemonium* (pp. 65–75). Lanham, MD: Lexington.

Giles, D. C. (2002). Parasocial interaction: A review of the literature and a model for future research. *Media Psychology* 4 (3), 279–305.

Glickman, L., and Fingerhut, J. (2011). User-generated content: Recent developments in Canada and the U.S. *Internet and E-Commerce Law in Canada*, 12 (6), 49–76.

Hambrick, M. E., Simmons, J. M., Greenhalgh, G. P., and Greenwell, T. C. (2010). Understanding professional athletes' use of Twitter: A content analysis of athlete tweets. *International Journal of Sport Communication*, 3, 454–71.

Hur, Y., Ko, Y. J., and Valacich, J. (2007). Motivation and concerns for online sport consumption. *Journal of Sport Management*, 21, 521–39.

Hutchins, B., and Rowe, D. (2012) *Sport beyond television: The internet, digital media and the rise of networked media sport*. New York: Routledge.

James, J. D., and Ridinger, L. L. (2002). Female and male sport fans: A comparison of sport consumption motives. *Journal of Sport Behavior*, 25, 260–78.

Joinson, A. N. (2000). Information seeking on the Internet: A study of soccer fans on the WWW. *CyberPsychology and Behavior*, 3, 185–90.

Kassing, J. W., and Sanderson, J. (2009). "You're the kind of guy that we all want for a drinking buddy": Expressions of parasocial interaction on Floydlandis.com. *Western Journal of Communication*, 73 (2), 182–203.

Kassing, J. W., and Sanderson, J. (2010). Fan–athlete interaction and Twitter tweeting through the Giro: A case study. *International Journal of Sport Communication*, 3, 113–28.

King, B. (2004). What makes fans tick? *SportsBusiness Journal*, March 1. Retrieved from http://www.sportsbusinessdaily.com/Journal/Issues/2004/03/20040301/SBJ-In-Depth/What-Makes-Fans-Tick.aspx?hl=what%20makes%20fans%20tickandsc=1

Laird, S. (2012). 1 in 4 American fans follow sports via social media. *Mashable Social Media*, June 6. Retrieved from http://mashable.com/2012/06/11/1-in-4-american-fans-follow-sports-via-social-media-study/.

Madrigal, R. (2000). The influence of social alliances with sports teams on intentions to purchase corporate sponsors' products. *Journal of Advertising*, 29 (4), 13–25.

Marwick, A., and boyd, d. (2011). To see and be seen: Celebrity practice on Twitter. *Convergence: The International Journal of Research into New Media Technologies*, 17 (2), 139–58.

Melnick, M. J. (1993). Searching for sociability in the stands: A theory of sports spectating. *Journal of Sport Management*, 7, 44–60.

Pegoraro, A. (2010). Look who's talking – Athletes on Twitter: A case study. *International Journal of Sport Communication*, 3, 501–14.

Phua, J. (2010). Sports fans and media use: Influence on sports fan identification and collective self-esteem. *International Journal of Sport Communication*, 3, 190–206.

Porter, L.V., Wood, C., and Benigni, V. L. (2011). From analysis to aggression: The nature of fan emotion, cognition, and behavior in Internet sports community. In A. C. Billings (Ed.), *Sports media: Transformation, integration, consumption* (pp. 128–45). New York: Routledge.

Raacke, J., and Bonds-Raacke, J. (2008). MySpace and Facebook: Applying the uses and gratifications theory to exploring friend-networking sites. *Cyberpsychology and Behavior*, 11, 169–74.

Raney, A. A. (2006). Why we watch and enjoy sports. In A. A. Raney and J. Bryant (Eds.), *Handbook of sports and media* (pp. 313–30). Mahwah, NJ: Lawrence Erlbaum.

Ruggiero, T. E. (2000). Uses and gratifications theory in the 21st century. *Mass Communication and Society*, 3, 3–37.

Sanderson, J. (2008). Spreading the word: Emphatic interaction displays on BlogMaverick.com. *Journal of Media Psychology: Theories, Methods and Applications*, 20 (4), 157–68.

Sanderson, J. (2009). Professional athletes' shrinking privacy boundaries: Fans, information and communication technologies, and athlete monitoring. *International Journal of Sport Communication*, 2, 240–56.

Sanderson, J., and Kassing, J. W. (2011). Tweets and blogs: Transformative, adversarial and integrative developments in sport media. In A. Billings (Ed.), *Sports media: Transformation, integration, consumption* (pp. 114–27). New York: Routledge.

Seo, W., and Green, B. (2008). Development of the Motivation Scale for Sport Online Consumption. *Journal of Sport Management*, 22, 82–109.

Sheldon, P. S. (1999). Green and gold blood on the information superhighway: An ethnographic log on Into the Green Bay Packer listserver newsgroup. *Advances in Consumer Research*, 26, 652.

Sloan, L. R. (1989). The motives of sports fans. In J. H. Goldstein (Ed.), *Sports, games, and play: Social and psychological viewpoints* (2nd ed., pp. 175–240). Hillsdale, NJ: Lawrence Erlbaum.

Spinda, J. S. (2011). The development of Basking in Reflected Glory (BIRGing) and Cutting off Reflected Failure (CORFing) measures. Journal of Sport Behavior, 34, 392–420.

Thomas, J. A. (2011). Twitter: The sports media rookie. *Journal of Sports Media*, 6, 115–20.

Verna, P. (2009). A spotlight on UGC participants. *eMarketer*, February 19. Retrieved from http://www.emarketer.com/Article.aspx?R=1006914.

Wann, D. L. (1995). Preliminary validation of the sport fan motivation scale. *Journal of Sport and Social Issues*, 19, 377–96.

Wann, D. L. (1997). *Sport psychology*. Upper Saddle River, NJ: Prentice Hall.

Wann, D. L., and Branscombe, N. R. (1990). Die-hard and fair-weather fans: Effects of identification on BIRGing and CORFing tendencies. *Journal of Sport and Social Issues*, 14, 103–17.

Wann, D. L., Hamlet, M. A., Wilson, T., and Hodges, J. A. (1995). Basking in reflected glory, cutting off reflected failure, and cutting off future failure: The importance of identification with a group. *Social Behavior and Personality: An International Journal*, 23: 377–88.

Watts, R. (2008). The Florida Gator Nation Online. In L. W. Hugenberg, P. M. Haridakis, and A. C. Earnheardt (Eds.), *Sports mania: Essays on fandom and the media in the 21st century* (pp. 243–56). Jefferson, NC: McFarland.

Wenner, L.A., and Gantz, W. (1980). The audience experience with sports on television. In. L.A. Wenner (Ed.), *Media, sports and society* (pp. 241–68). Newbury Park, CA: Sage.

Zillmann, D., Bryant, J., and Sapolsky, B. S. (1989). Enjoyment from sports spectatorship. In J. H. Goldstein (Ed.), *Sports, games, and play: Social and psychological viewpoints* (2nd ed., pp. 241–78). Hillsdale, NJ: Lawrence Erlbaum.

26

EMERGING SOCIAL MEDIA AND APPLICATIONS IN SPORT

Galen Clavio

Of all the media present in sport, there is no area which has seen greater change and upheaval than social media over the past decade. Practically unheard of prior to the mass market emergence of the iPhone in 2007, social media has evolved into a powerful yet often misunderstood part of the communication spectrum. Social media have served to give fans and athletes a voice they never possessed before, but they have also engendered fear and concern among sport entities unaccustomed to dealing with media where users control a considerable share of the content flow (Sanderson, 2011). The growth in popularity of social media has been remarkable, with research indicating that worldwide use of social media accounts for 22 percent of all time spent online (Nielsenwire, 2010), a number that is certain to grow as time progresses.

Social media are constantly reinventing themselves, a process which has led to some questioning their viability as either a dedicated communication channel or an appropriate subject of scholarly study. Critics point to the demise of services such as MySpace and Friendster as proof that social media are little more than a flash in the pan. Despite these "failures" (or, more to the point, because of them), social media's viability as a research topic and practical application in the sport industry increases every year. While the brand names associated with particular modes of digital social communication may change or fall by the wayside, the core components of services have sustained and improved, leading to increasing efficiency in the way individuals, athletes, teams, and sponsors interact with one another.

The sport industry has had an uneven relationship with social media, with fans eager to adopt the technologies and sport organizations hesitant to utilize them. An example of this can be found in the collegiate athletic environment, where social media policies for athletes were found to be far more restrictive than encouraging (Sanderson, 2011). Similar restrictions can be found in the professional leagues of the United States. However, with usage continuing to rise among most demographic groups (Smith and Brenner, 2012), social media are here to stay, and it is imperative that both practitioners and scholars understand where social media have come from, and where they are going.

The purpose of this chapter is to identify new and emerging social media in sport, provide an overview of those media, and examine their present and future applications in the sport communication landscape. It is important to keep in mind the ever-changing nature of social media as described in the above paragraphs, and to understand that, in many cases, the specific applications described in this chapter are less important than the concepts and processes which underlie them. Few people in 2006 would have predicted the rise of the mobile phone application in social media, but the concepts of sites such as BlogSpot, Facebook, and Flickr were important harbingers of today's social media environment. To that end, this chapter first focuses on the existent classes of social media in sport, placing applications and processes into broader categories. Following that, the chapter explores new and emerging social media applications in sport, and their utility within that environment. Particular attention is paid to how these applications may be used by fans, the sport media (both traditional and digital), and the entities which comprise sport.

Social media classes

One mistake made by those unfamiliar with social media is to lump the entire online experience into one broad category. In reality, there are many different types of social media, and the individual applications and sites exist in a variety of classes. This section examines three predominant types of social media classes, namely data-rich, streamlined, and locational, and the connections between those classes and existent social media services.

It is within classes that social media should be viewed, rather than within the individual branding of sites or services. This is an important point to remember, because the concepts from the various classes carry over from application to application, as social media's technological basis improves and develops. For instance, the Internet application known as AOL Instant Messenger is no longer a widely used and viable system of communication (Freeburn, 2012), but the concept of speed-focused, media-poor electronic interaction did not disappear with AIM. Instead, it was replaced by the emergence of Twitter and Facebook (Kelly, 2010), as well as with the cell phone text message.

The emergence of the iPhone in 2007 hastened the emergence of social media, by allowing users to connect in a mobile environment, rather than being tied to a laptop or desktop computer. While former Apple chairman Steve Jobs promoted the new iPhone as a combination music player, phone, and mobile communication device (Bonnington, 2012), few could have predicted the emergence of the iPhone's applications as being so important to the development of social media. To that point, social media had been almost entirely browser-based, with sites such as Facebook and MySpace drawing the most traffic. While some smartphones had basic applications for certain social media functions, the iPhone's combination of graphical attractiveness and ease of use made the process both accessible and fun to the average user. The inclusion of a camera interface on the iPhone helped to spur the creation of user-generated content, which became a hallmark of social media content across several platforms.

Data-rich social media

As smartphones became a preferred technological platform for social media, a split in media classes developed. Some applications focused on the richness of media featured in the browser-based environment. These data-rich social-media applications are ideal for the computer screen, but can struggle in the smartphone "app" environment. The advent of data-rich social media predated the current technological environment. As such, data-rich social media retain many of the characteristics of traditional websites, and tend to be multi-purpose and multi-faceted.

The most popular data-rich social medium in today's environment is undoubtedly Facebook. Established in 2004, this service has undergone numerous changes in functionality, while retaining something of its original form. Facebook's primary strength when originally launched was its unique ability to connect technically adept persons to each other in a clean, structured environment that allowed users to do a great many things in a contained space. Facebook's original feature set allowed users to upload and share photos, converse with each other in a virtual space called a "wall", and share personal likes and hobbies in a searchable format. As the service evolved over time, it became more data-rich, allowing users to post and share videos, notes, and links to news articles, while also utilizing third-party applications to do everything from play simplified video games to sharing music playlists and suggestions.

As online interaction continued to evolve, and other social media began to rise to prominence, Facebook often took elements of these new media's core functionality and either integrated them through the usage of in-system applications, or created services which could be used in place of a potential competitor. For example, Facebook's original construction only allowed for limited numbers of profile connections, regardless of whether a profile was owned by an organization or by an individual. This provided services such as Twitter an opportunity to capitalize on business needs for greater connectivity with customers and fans. By 2009, Facebook had revised its profile approach, changing rules to allow for businesses to have their own special page designation (Schonfeld, 2009). Among others, the sport industry has taken advantage of these changes, crafting Facebook pages that accrue fans numbering in the millions in some cases. For instance, as of August 2012, the Facebook page for the Spanish soccer team FC Barcelona had a worldwide following of over 34 million people (SportsFanGraph, 2012).

Despite the trend of social media focusing on mobile application technology to reach users on their smartphones, Facebook has notably lagged behind other services in mobile app quality. One possible explanation is that Facebook's terminal-based advertising revenues are far more lucrative than what the company can generate in a mobile environment, a hypothesis put forth by industry observers as recently as the summer of 2012 (Couts, 2012). Facebook does seem intent on engaging the mobile market, but on its own terms, as it was reported that the company may try to manufacture its own smartphone to compete with Apple and Google (Bilton, 2012). Despite its spotty smartphone integration, Facebook possesses a commanding lead in terms of sport-focused social media market share, as 89 percent of fans who follow sports on social networks say they use Facebook for that purpose, compared to 65 percent for YouTube and 33 percent for Twitter (Laird, 2012b).

There are other data-rich social media which have evolved in more specialized formats. These media do not possess anywhere near the breadth of Facebook's audience, but have managed to create vibrant online communities, often times around the notion of shared content and ratings. Services such as Yelp, UrbanSpoon, and TripAdvisor provide users with a tremendous amount of data, albeit focused on particular business types and the users' interactions with those businesses. Although it is not often considered a social medium, YouTube certainly qualifies, and falls into the data-rich category. YouTube's commenting system forms communities of members who focus on certain video topics, and numerous sports teams have utilized YouTube to create their own virtual channels.

Streamlined social media

Another media class, which we will label "streamlined," developed around the specific technical advantages that smartphones possessed, focusing on data speed rather than breadth of content. The standard-bearer for the streamlined social media class is Twitter, which has risen from obscurity in 2007 to arguably the most talked-about social medium, particularly in the sports media environment.

The mechanics of Twitter are similar to those of blogs, which have their roots in the pre-smartphone era. However, Twitter's focus on speed and asynchroneity separates it from blogs, as well as most other social media. As noted by Clavio and Kian, "Whereas blogging typically involves a dedicated Web site with a main-page focus on expansive content... Twitter uses a much less media-rich interface, where the primary focus is on short burst of content from a large number of users" (Clavio and Kian, 2010, p. 486). Twitter can best be described as a large network of user accounts, with these users able to follow and be followed by other accounts. The primary form of messaging is known as the "tweet", and is limited to 140 characters, with no inline graphics or video. Users can utilize links to external media, but the purpose of the network's mechanics is to keep the data requirements for each message low.

Unlike Facebook, Twitter has a rich history of effective smartphone adaptation, with applications such as HootSuite, TweetDeck, TweetCaster, Echofon, and other competitors offering Twitter network access on a wide variety of phone systems. Many of these applications offer seamless integration with third-party software platforms, allowing for pictures, video, and other dynamic media to be included as links within the user's tweets.

Many athletes have enthusiastically adopted Twitter, although the top levels of professional sports in the US have failed to integrate the service into many of their core operations. The sports media have begun to utilize Twitter consistently in their broadcasts, with ESPN directly quoting athlete tweets on their news programs as reactions to newsworthy events in sports. Twitter and ESPN agreed to partner with each other for branding campaigns surrounding large-scale sporting events, looking to capitalize on smartphone users' tendency to utilize their devices for social media purposes in conjunction with watching live television broadcasts of sporting events (Delo and Del Rey, 2012). Despite these numbers, the total amount of Internet users who utilize Twitter is relatively small, numbering only 15 percent of the total online population as of June 2012, although that number was double what it was the previous year (Smith and Brenner, 2012).

Another example of a streamlined social media application is Instagram, which focuses exclusively on photo sharing. Instagram experienced a rapid growth in popularity, in large part to its ease of use, simple but effective set of built-in picture filters, and fun social engagement features, including the ability to "heart" another user's picture, as well as leave a brief comment on it. The images on Instagram can be posted to existing social media accounts (such as those on Facebook and Twitter), or can be kept on the Instagram network. Sport organizations and athletes have both started utilizing Instagram, finding that users are excited to gain access to behind-the-scenes photographs from their heroes and favorite teams. Whether or not Instagram stays as streamlined is an uncertain question, as the application was purchased by Facebook in 2012.

Locational social media

A third social media class, locational, developed the most recently, and focuses on using smartphone GPS data to allow users to engage in social interaction based on their physical environment. This process combines a virtual meeting space with a tangible one.

The most well-known application that solely focuses on this type of social media is FourSquare, a service which was introduced in 2009 and allows for users to "check in" to locations as part of a point accrual system. Users compete with friends to see who can garner the most points from check-ins, and also attempt to earn online rewards, called badges, for checking in at certain locations. The FourSquare system also allows for users who check in at a location more than others to be proclaimed "mayor" of that location, which places their picture on the location page as a form of recognition. The system allows for businesses, including sports teams, to integrate their own marketing and branding efforts into their FourSquare check-in location, allowing patrons of the location to earn discounts and other specials for checking in.

Other social media have used location-based services as part of their offerings, including Facebook and Google. However, these services are only part of a larger bouquet, whereas with FourSquare, it is the primary focus of the application. Although it is the newest and the least popular among social media users so far, locational-class social media may have the greatest growth potential for sports organizations. Creating a connected environment within a sports team's arena or stadium could allow for a whole new vista of opportunities in terms of sponsorship, branding, marketing, and fan interaction.

Emerging social media in sport

If current trends are any indicator, the future of social media in sport will include two primary types of services. The first will focus on the fan experience inside sports venues, and will encourage users to interact with each other, the organization, media, and sponsors. This type of interaction will likely be marketed by organizations as part of a new digital fan experience, and will allow those organizations to upsell the social media elements to their consumers. For fans, it will likely be seen as a way to more publicly demonstrate fandom, while also potentially providing them with an avenue to interact with athletes, coaches, and media.

The second type of service will likely focus on the fan experience at home while consuming sports through other media types. As has been seen on Facebook and Twitter, the public conversation generated by sporting events on social media is among the largest of any events in the world. For instance, the reactions surrounding the NFL's Super Bowl XLVI generated the second- and third-most tweets-per-second of any event in the service's history (Hernandez, 2012), joining other sporting events, including the 2011 Women's World Cup, in the top ten of that category (Rao, 2011). Given the obvious popularity of interaction surrounding sporting events on social media, the development of applications focusing specifically on these types of interactions is a given.

Owing to the broad nature of the sport marketplace, any examination of emerging social media needs to be separated by industry sector. This section examines new and evolving social media for fans, organizations, and sport media enterprise.

Fans

Many of the emerging sport-focused social media sites are centered on the interaction of fans at home watching games, rather than those at the games themselves. One such service, called FanCake, creates virtual rooms within its application space where fans can interact with one another, while making predictions about various plays within the game they are watching (Laird, 2012a). For instance, if one were to use FanCake to watch a baseball game between the Pittsburgh Pirates and the Cincinnati Reds, one could chat with other fans of those teams who were watching the game, and get the chance to guess whether a particular batter would reach base in a given at-bat. Correct predictions yield points, which users can redeem for discounted merchandise from the site's corporate partners.

Another service, called PlayUp, provides a similar set of controls, but focuses less on the rewards features found in FanCake and more on the interaction. PlayUp allows users to create virtual hangouts, similar to those found on the Google+ service, and interact with fellow fans of teams in real-time.

These types of real-time, crowd-sourced applications are an interesting mixture of data-rich and streamlined application styles, as they tend to be very focused on one topic (sports fandom and interaction) and contain a very small set of features, mostly revolving around chatting and statistics. Several other emergent social media applications, such as SharetheMatch, Chat Sports, and Bantr possess the same mixture of services. However, there are several emergent applications which merge streamlined and locational services. One such service, called Enthuse, combines a FourSquare-like application environment with interactive and rewards-based elements, but focuses purely on sports venues in different cities. This service would allow a network of users to extend beyond a sport organization's proprietary network, and interact with others users in a larger, holistic network of sport consumers and fans.

Organizations

While many sport organizations' first impulse with social media was to create proprietary applications, that approach has proven unsuccessful, as users have demonstrated a desire to carry their identity across application boundaries. By 2012, many sport organizations in the US and elsewhere were starting to regularly utilize broad-based applications such as Facebook (Waters, *et al.*, 2011) and Twitter as well as white-label software, which allowed for individual branding while maintaining a broader online community.

A popular broad-based application which is emerging as a valuable element of sport organization social media use is Tumblr, a service which has actually been around for several years. Similar in structure to a traditional blog, Tumblr differentiates itself by focusing on shorter bursts of activity, serving as a vehicle for pictures, video, and smaller bursts of text. This method of blogging activity focuses on mixed-media content, and can offer far more variety than a blog site, while also providing a far more stimulating visual ensemble than Facebook. Tumblr falls within the data-rich media class, but is considerably more streamlined than Facebook. Sport organizations may prefer to utilize mixed-media methods such as Tumblr in the future, owing to its emphasis on media types other than text.

Another application which has been adopted by sport organizations, somewhat surprisingly, is Pinterest. This application focuses on user interests as represented by "pins", or small board-like elements displayed on a web page. These pins are almost entirely graphical in nature, and businesses utilize the service to display pictures of products and services. Pinterest also falls under the data-rich media class, but like Tumblr is considerably more streamlined than Facebook. One interesting element of Pinterest is the application's demographic profile, which is nearly 70 percent female (Erickson, 2012), providing sport organizations with a rare chance to access that set of media users.

Sport media

Traditional sport journalism outlets, such as newspaper and television, have struggled to adapt to the social media environment. Studies have been conducted which examine the use of new and social media in a professional sports journalism environment (Sheffer and Schultz, 2010; Whiteside, Yu, and Hardin, 2012), with the results indicating that significant differences do exist between both the perceptions of journalists relating to social media and the actions of new media outlets.

In terms of social media applications, the traditional sports media brands have tended to stay on the sidelines. While some of these organizations have produced their own applications, the nature of these applications is almost entirely as a conduit of select information, with the clear implication being that these media would prefer the user to consume the content in other formats, such as traditional media channels or the static website. With that said, a few large sport media organizations have made forays into social media, with ESPN setting the pace. The self-proclaimed "worldwide leader in sports" has attempted to be the social media leader as well, providing content that can be consumed on smartphone and tablet devices. While most of ESPN's offerings on their official applications are aimed at information dissemination and not interactivity, the presentation is far more in line with the current state of sport-focused social media than that of their competitors, and they do offer a large line of applications focusing on smaller, more specialized and/or regional sport elements, such as fantasy baseball, the X Games, and city-specific sites such as ESPN Chicago.

The future of sport media in social media may be through aggregation of existing content, rather than through the creation of proprietary networks. A variety of services exist which connect fans to streaming media sources. Some of these services are free and legal, such as TuneIn Radio, which allows users to listen to live audio from any one of thousands of radio stations across the country. While there are some contractual restrictions placed on these services, the vast majority of content is free, allowing fans to tune in everything from sports talk to play-by-play of games. Other services, such as the now-infamous FirstRowSports, allow individuals to create their own video streams of televised events, and then provide links to those games that are watchable around the world. In many cases, these streams are not allowed under national and international copyright law, and FirstRowSports was actually shut down by the US government for violations of these laws. However, the founders of the site simply moved it to a registered domain in Europe, outside of the reach of such laws, and many fans in the United States continue to utilize the service to watch games that they cannot otherwise get on television.

These types of streaming services, when used in conjunction with conversation-focused media such as Twitter or FanCake, may eventually promote a new kind of online sport media environment, where the video feed of the game is accompanied with a live chat window where users across the globe can interact in real-time. Certain types of programming have already utilized this methodology, both in sports and in news broadcasts, such as those seen on CNN and

Fox News Channel. Additionally, smaller-scale media, including blogs and local newspapers, have created thriving conversational communities surrounding live sporting events.

Theoretical implications of emerging social media

While the above sections have focused primarily on the practical implications of emerging social media in sport, there are quite a few theoretical implications which need to be considered. As the nature of media moves farther away from the mass communication paradigm which dominated the landscape of sport communication for decades, the way in which content is produced and consumed cannot help but change.

Prior studies have utilized the uses and gratifications approach to examine social media implications in sport (Clavio and Kian, 2010; Frederick, Clavio, Burch, and Zimmerman, 2012), owing to the active nature of new media audiences and the plethora of choices at the user's disposal. However, the concept of multi-tasking in sport media consumption is not one which has been explored by scholars, and this concept will become critical as users continue to utilize their devices in tandem. Will a distinction need to be drawn between primary and secondary media source consumption? Do scholars need to investigate augmentation effects of certain types of media on others? These and other questions will need to be addressed, as social media theory gains its own footing.

Another area of theoretical concern involves user networks, and the systems that exist within them. While preliminary examination into social network analysis has been conducted (Hambrick, 2012), very little is known of the nature of these networks, or how users operate across disparate networks; that is, how their behavior on Twitter differs from their behavior on Facebook or Tumblr.

Yet another theoretical implication exists when examining the nature of sport media content itself. Will traditional media brands continue to be regarded as a separate entity from fans, organizations, and non-traditional media on social media platforms? If not, how will that affect the ability of these organizations to utilize agenda setting to steer the focus of conversation among sport fans? In a related matter, how will users react to framing efforts by both traditional media brands and by industry sources such as teams and athletes?

Conclusion

The preceding pages have provided an overview of social media applications in sport, with a particular focus on their evolution and possible future development. Predicting the future of social media in sport is a difficult task, as the direction which technology takes can change, owing to unforeseen innovation or a change in the marketplace. However, the last decade of social media growth has given us a good starting point from which to perform such analysis. If there is one certainty moving forward, it is that sports fans in this era of media will enjoy the greatest level of personal access to players, coaches, team personnel, and sport media that has ever been experienced. This level of access will almost certainly have a significant impact on both the practical and theoretical components of sport communication. It will be incumbent upon both practitioners and scholars to identify these impacts and effectively synthesize them into professional and academic best practices.

References

Bilton, N. (2012). Bits: Facebook tries, tries again on a smartphone. *New York Times*, May 27. Retrieved from http://bits.blogs.nytimes.com/2012/05/27/facebook-tries-tries-again-on-a-smart phone/.

Bonnington, C. (2012). iPhone celebrates 5th birthday – How has it changed? *Wired.com*, January 9. Retrieved from http://www.wired.com/gadgetlab/2012/01/iphone-five-year-anniversary/.

Clavio, G., and Kian, E. M. (2010). Uses and gratifications of a retired female athlete's Twitter followers. *International Journal of Sport Communication*, 3, 485–500.

Couts, A. (2012). Facebook mobile apps: bad on purpose? *Digital Trends*, May 10. Retrieved from http://www.digitaltrends.com/mobile/facebook-mobile-apps-bad-on-purpose/.

Delo, C., and Del Rey, J. (2012). Twitter and ESPN plan branded campaigns around TV sports. *Ad Age*, May 15. Retrieved from http://adage.com/article/media/twitter-espn-plan-branded-campaigns-tv-sports/234761/.

Erickson, C. (2012). 13 'Pinteresting" facts about Pinterest users. *Mashable Social Media*, February 25. Retrieved from http://mashable.com/2012/02/25/pinterest-user-demographics/.

Frederick, E. L., Clavio, G., Burch, L. M., Zimmerman, M. H. (2012). Characteristics of users of a mixed-martial arts blog: A case study of demographics and usage trends. *International Journal of Sport Communication*, 5, 109–25.

Freeburn, C. (2012). A hard fall for AOL's AIM: Instant messaging is declining, with AOL leading the drop. *InvestorPlace*, April 4. Retrieved from http://www.investorplace.com/2012/04/a-hard-fall-for-aols-aim/.

Hambrick, M. E. (2012). Six degrees of information: Using social network analysis to explore the spread of information within sport social networks. *International Journal of Sport Communication*, 5, 16–34.

Hernandez, B. A. (2012). Two Super Bowl moments land in Twitter's record book. *Mashable Social Media*, February 6. Retrieved from http://mashable.com/2012/02/06/super-bowl-tweets-per-second-records-game-madonna/.

Kelly, J. (2010). Instant messaging: This conversation is terminated. *BBC News Magazine*, May 24. Retrieved from http://news.bbc.co.uk/2/hi/uk_news/magazine/8698174.stm.

Laird, S. (2012a). 9 social networks for sports fans. *Mashable Social Media*, April 9. Retrieved from http://mashable.com/2012/04/09/social-networks-for-sports-fans/#578273-FanCake.

Laird, S. (2012b). 1 in 4 American fans follows sports via social media. *Mashable Social Media*, June 12. Retrieved from http://mashable.com/2012/06/11/1-in-4-american-fans-follow-sports-via-social-media-study/.

Nielsenwire. (2010). Social networks/blogs now account for one in every four and a half minutes online. *Nielsenwire*, June 15. Retrieved from http://blog.nielsen.com/nielsenwire/global/social-media-accounts-for-22-percent-of-time-online/.

Rao, L. (2011). Women's World Cup soccer final scores new Twitter record with 7,196 tweets per second. *TechCrunch*, July 17. Retrieved from http://techcrunch.com/2011/07/17/womens-world-cup-soccer-final-scores-new-twitter-record-with-7196-tweets-per-second/.

Sanderson, J. (2011). To tweet or not to tweet: Exploring Division I athletic departments' social-media policies. *International Journal of Sport Communication*, 4, 492–513.

Schonfeld, E. (2009). Facebook's response to Twitter. *TechCrunch*, March 4. Retrieved from http://techcrunch.com/2009/03/04/facebooks-response-to-twitter/.

Sheffer, M. L., and Schultz, B. (2010). Paradigm shift or passing fad? Twitter and sports journalism. *International Journal of Sport Communication*, 3, 472–84.

Smith, A., and Brenner, J. (2012). Twitter use 2012. *Pew Internet*, May 31. Retrieved from http://www.pewinternet.org/Reports/2012/Twitter-Use-2012/Findings.aspx.

Sports Fan Graph (2012). Rankings. *Sports Fan Graph*. Retrieved from http://www.sportsfan graph.com/.

Waters, R. D., Burke, K. A., Jackson, Z. H., and Buning, J. D. (2011). Using stewardship to cultivate fandom online: Comparing how National Football League teams use their web sites and Facebook to engage their fans. *International Journal of Sport Communication*, 4, 163–77.

Whiteside, E., Yu, N., and Hardin, M. (2012). The new toy department? A case study on differences in sports coverage between traditional and new media. *Journal of Sports Media*, 7, 23–38.

27

FOCUS ON FANTASY

An overview of fantasy sport consumption

Brody J. Ruihley and Robin L. Hardin

Fantasy sport is an online activity holding the attention of millions of sport consumers. Industry estimates have fantasy sport being consumed by nearly 35 million US and Canadian participants (Fantasy Sport Trade Association, 2012a). This is an industry quietly becoming a force in the sport communication landscape. Fantasy sport provides consumers with a unique sport encounter aside from traditional ways of consuming sport (that is, viewing, listening, or following a team or sporting event). From statistics to social interaction, there are many factors giving reason as to why people participate in this activity. The fantasy sport user is a unique consumer of sport-based communication and media. These users experience sport beyond team wins, losses, and championships. They become immersed in the minute details and information of sport. They consume statistics as fantasy points, individual players as products, and injury reports as team-altering news. These users view sport through a unique lens. Understanding this type of consumption is important in developing advertising, communication, and marketing campaigns geared towards these consumers. In addition, understanding these consumers provides sport entities with an inside look at what makes this distinct set of consumers unique. The subsequent portions of this chapter provide an overview of the history of fantasy sport and give detail into its consumer motives and consumption.

History of fantasy sport

The history of fantasy sport is a topic of debate within fantasy sport and research communities. Many describe the evolution of fantasy sport as taking place in the early 1980s. The formation of fantasy baseball is popularly attributed to a group of men, headed by Daniel Okrent, meeting at a restaurant called La Rotisserie Française and creating a fantasy baseball league (Davis and Carlisle-Duncan, 2006; Farquhar and Meeds, 2007; Hu, 2003; Roy and Goss, 2007). The professional sports of golf and football also have been recognized as initial sport in fantasy activity as early as the 1950s or 1960s (Shipman, 2001; Vichot, 2009). This chapter uses the history of fantasy baseball as basis for the frontier of fantasy sport.

The meeting described above is a true story; however, according to Walker, it is *not* the beginning of fantasy baseball; it is merely the "live birth" (Walker, 2006, p. 59) of what is generally known as fantasy baseball, specifically rotisserie baseball. Fantasy baseball began in 1960 and was created by a man named Bill Gamson. Gamson, and two friends, utilized an auction-style process to draft Major League Baseball (MLB) players to form a roster of their own. This is similar to what real owners have to do to fill a roster and field a team. The owners in Gamson's fantasy sport "anted up $10, which translated into an imaginary budget of $100,000 to be used to bid on the services of real major leaguers" (Walker, 2006, p. 60). Once the teams were formed, they would then be measured throughout the MLB season by certain "handpicked" statistics (Walker, 2006, p. 60). Simpler than contemporary participants utilizing new sport communication technology, Gamson and his colleagues enjoyed how "the simple act of reading the box scores had become a daily thrill ride" (Walker, 2006, p. 62).

Fantasy baseball's next stage in its growth came in 1962 when Gamson's career moved him to the University of Michigan; his Baseball Seminar followed and quickly grew to 25 teams. Robert Sklar, an Assistant Professor of History, owned one of those teams. One of Sklar's advisees was Okrent. Following graduation and while visiting Okrent, Sklar introduced the Baseball Seminar to Okrent. Okrent created his own version of a fantasy league upon hearing about the Baseball Seminar. This is the timeframe that La Rotisserie Française enters the picture. This restaurant was the meeting place for a group of friends called the "Phillies Appreciation Society" (Walker, 2006, p. 66). The discussion of a fantasy-type league transpired here, however, as noted by Walker, the draft occurred at an apartment. The year was 1979 and the name of the restaurant assisted in forming the name of the league: Rotisserie League Baseball Association.

During the MLB strike of 1981, baseball enthusiasts became even more familiar with Rotisserie Baseball through an article written by Okrent for *Inside Sports*, called, "The year George Foster wasn't worth $36." The article was "well and good" (Walker, 2006, p. 69), but the main piece of information in this article was the rules for the game. As noted by Vichot (2009) and Walker (2006), this caused a myriad of fantasy leagues to form within the sports-writing community. Also adding to the popularity of fantasy sport in the early 1980s was the inaugural edition of *Rotisserie League Baseball*, edited by Okrent, and first published in 1984 (Vichot, 2009).

In one of the first evaluations of fantasy sport consumption in 1990, *USA Today* estimated the industry consumed by 500,000 participants (Vichot, 2009). Years later, in the first half of the 1990s, tremendous growth occurred with an estimated three million people participating (PRWeb, 2008). The 1990s provided a boost for the fantasy sport industry with continued coverage in *USA Today* and by the increased use of the Web. Vichot claims that "the Internet boom of the late 90s...provided a new model for fantasy sports, since the barrier to entry was much lower" (Vichot, 2009, p. 16). The Internet provided the needed platform for fantasy sport and many organizations took advantage and quickly began creating or purchasing websites hosting fantasy sport play. As noted by Vichot, fantasy baseball assisted in this overall fantasy growth in part due to "baseball's fascination with statistics" (Vichot, 2009, p. 11) and also because many statistics experts came to the forefront of the sport world in this time frame. In 2003, the Fantasy Sport Trade Association (FSTA) estimated participation at nearly 15 million FSUs (Farquhar and Meeds, 2007; Hu, 2003; PRWeb, 2008). The fantasy sport industry is currently witnessing rapid growth among North American participants, despite difficult economic times. In 2012, the FSTA estimates that 35 million Americans and Canadians participate in fantasy sport (Fantasy Sport Trade Association, 2012a). Even with this growth, fantasy sport industry professionals do not anticipate a decline or plateau in the near future (Billings and Ruihley, 2012a).

Types of fantasy sport

The most popular fantasy sport is based on competition in the National Football League (NFL). Fantasy football is played by 72 percent of fantasy sport users (Fantasy Sport Trade Association, 2012b). Baseball (based on MLB) is routinely second place to football, with 37 percent of participants playing. The sports following football and baseball are auto racing (24 percent), basketball (20 percent, based on National Basketball Association [NBA]), golf (13 percent, based on the Professional Golfers' Association [PGA]), college football (13 percent), hockey (12 percent, based on the National Hockey Association [NHL]), and soccer (7 percent) (Fantasy Sport Trade Association, 2012b). Non-mainstream fantasy sports revolve around bass fishing, bowling, darts, and tennis. There are several noteworthy non-athletic fantasy leagues. For instance, *Fantasy Congress* is an educational game, choosing both United States' Representatives and Senators to populate rosters. Legislators are "awarded points for introducing bills, having bills pass out of committee, and for getting bills passed in each of the houses of Congress" (Fantasy Congress, 2012, para. 1). The *Umpire Ejection Fantasy League* "objectively tracks and analyzes umpire ejections and their corresponding calls with great regard for the rules and spirit of the game of baseball" (Close Call Sports, 2012, para. 1). There are also fantasy reality shows, where the participants choose contestants on hit reality shows such as *American Idol*, *Bachelor/Bachelorette*, *Big Brother*, and *Survivor*. There is even a fantasy league covering multiple reality shows, with spirited categories focusing on what else: intoxication, fighting, hot tubs, nudity, and crying (Jacoby, 2011). Yet another example is the Celebrity Fantasy League, where *US Weekly* magazine allows a participant to pick 25 celebrities and points are awarded based on photos on or inside the magazine.

Fantasy sport participation

The introduction of this chapter alluded to the idea that fantasy sport users view sport through a different lens. This lens is unique because every play, every scoring drive, and every defensive stop has new meaning. Not only are those plays important in the actual outcome of the game, but each play has different scoring implications to the fantasy sport user. It might be the baseball line drive caught by a great defensive player robbing a fantasy owner of two points for the inevitable double. It could be the blocked field goal attempt awarding a team defense, but stealing three points the kicker would have given the fantasy sport owner. In addition to individual plays skewing the standard sport vision, game results and season results differ as well. For example, a fan of the MLB's Cincinnati Reds may have just witnessed a Reds' win, but his or her fantasy team was defeated with a save by the Reds' closer. Similarly, a Cubs' fan may have experienced a losing season on the field, but the baseball season was not ruined because his or her fantasy team performed very well.

Other areas of new meaning to traditional sport fandom may include aspects of social interaction. In addition to discussing, arguing, or trash-talking someone's hometown or favorite team, now interaction can focus on a person's fantasy team, his or her roster moves, or trade discussion. Understanding why people view sport differently and why they participate in this activity is important for many reasons. Ruihley and Hardin (2011a) argue that content of fantasy sport sites, as well as the promotional aspects of fantasy sport organizations can be heavily impacted by knowing why people participate. Messages can be altered when the information matches the reasons of participation.

So why do people participate in fantasy sport? What is the draw and how does it relate to sport communication? Research has uncovered many possible explanations for why this activity has grown to the magnitude it has. The following list will define and explain some of the key motivations of fantasy sport consumption:

Achievement/self-esteem: Explains the personal sense of achievement when an owner's fantasy team performs well (Spinda and Haridakis, 2008). This can also be reversed, with an owner taking a hit to his or her pride if the team does not perform as expected.

Arousal: This factor revolves around the ever-changing emotions of consuming fantasy sport. Formed from research studying eustress in sport consumption (Wann, 1995), arousal has been described as the stimulation one feels when watching a fantasy team member perform (Billings and Ruihley, 2012b; Ruihley and Hardin, 2011a).

Camaraderie: This factor measures the social side of association with others, being included with others, and staying in touch with people through their participation in this activity. This has been measured in past research under the Social factor umbrella (Seo and Green, 2008; Spinda and Haridakis, 2008), but has been broken down further in subsequent analysis to stand as its own factor (Ruihley and Hardin, 2011a).

Competition: This factor needs no explanation, simply because it is focused on competing with others, winning the competition, or securing the prize fund (Ruihley and Hardin, 2011a).

Escape: Mentally moving away from the daily grind or pressures of work or life is something people frequently do, utilizing some type of mass communication or entertainment outlet. Whether it is a movie, television show, sport, or surfing the Internet, people find ways to forget about pressing issues or thoughts. This factor measures this type of release as it relates to fantasy sport consumption.

Ownership: This motivation was once one of the most highly used marketing factors to encourage people to join a fantasy sport league. This factor focuses on the ownership control and activities of roster moves (Spinda and Haridakis, 2008). The idea behind this factor is that a participant can draft, pick up free agents, perform trades, and manage a roster better than their counterparts trying to do the exact same thing.

Pass time: Stemming from Seo and Green's (2008) work on online sport consumption, this factor gives reason for participation in fantasy sport as a way to alleviate boredom, using free time, or literally just passing the time.

Social sport: This motivation component is another factor that has traditionally been grouped in with camaraderie and simply labeled "social" or "social interaction." The work of Ruihley and Hardin (2011a) separated camaraderie and social sport into distinct factors standing alone. Forming in Hur, Ko, and Valacich's (2007) online sport-consumption work, this factor focuses on actual interaction about sports, sharing opinions, and debating sport-related issues.

Surveillance: This is one of the most intense of the motivating factors of fantasy sport consumption (Hur, *et al.*, 2007; Ruihley and Hardin, 2011a; Seo and Green,

> 2008). Basically, this is information gathering at its finest. Being competitive in a fantasy sport league involves understanding what statistics are important to and will assist in competition. Understanding where to find that essential information is half the battle and with that, participants will survey the landscape to either find information that will help in their preparation or provide the results of their efforts.

The information and activities surrounding sport communication play a pivotal role in many of the fantasy sport motives listed. The following is an example of a typical first two weeks in a fantasy sport season. It will quickly become obvious how interrelated sport communication and fantasy sport are. Most leagues start with a draft. Unless it is a random-selection draft, the owners will prepare and draft each player on the roster. An owner may purchase draft magazines, search the Internet, listen to fantasy-related podcasts or radio, read expert advice, or scour through mounds of statistics to best prepare for the draft. Drafting and utilizing the mentioned mass communication outlets can include motivations of competition, passing time, ownership, self-esteem, and especially, surveillance. Once the draft is complete and the season begins, owners will still use the aforementioned media to follow their teams with the addition of one very important medium: television. Owners will consume loads of programming, both on television and online, to follow their fantasy team players and scout free agents to get the upper hand in their competition. One statistic from ESPN's Department of Integrated Media Research assists in validating the amount of surveillance undertaken by fantasy sport users (ESPN, 2010). Their research claims the standard sport viewer (ages 12 to 64) consumes more than seven hours of ESPN media per week. The fantasy sport user, on the other hand, consumes three times that amount: 22 hours and 40 minutes (Billings and Ruihley, 2012b; ESPN, 2010). If you think that one statistic might change the opinion of this activity in the minds of media executives, you are correct.

Continuing with our hypothetical fantasy scenario, as fantasy sport users are consuming sport information at an immense rate, they are also competing and socializing. This may be direct face-to-face interaction, email communication, social networking, or discussions on message boards. This type of conversation can focus on some of the camaraderie aspects of catching up and discussing general information or it can be specific to the fantasy sport league, competition, or members (social sport). As a week of competition continues, owners may be escaping reality or passing time in their consumption and some owners may even find themselves quite stimulated when watching their baseball closer try to seal a victory for their MLB team and earn ten points for the fantasy owner. Others may have their self-esteem tested when his or her kicker misses two short field goals. Self-esteem is most likely to waiver as the standings update, those that have won feel proud of their work and their team, those that have lost or find themselves moving down in the standings, may feel upset, embarrassed, or even ashamed.

Sport communication and fantasy sport seemingly go hand-in-hand. From the interpersonal aspects to the mass communication avenues, fantasy sport users are consuming and communicating based on the many functions associated with this activity. The major motivating factors play right into the hand of online and traditional media consumption. Knowing this, media companies are able to create, market, and place appropriate content into their programs and products. The following section discusses how media organizations and companies are doing just that; taking advantage of such a devoted and information savvy market.

Media use of fantasy sport users

Media groups are taking advantage of the unique nature of fantasy sport users and using fantasy sport to enhance the sporting experience and to attract consumers to fantasy and non-fantasy products. According to findings from Ruihley and Hardin (in press), in their examination of media use and the fantasy sport experience, media should be taking advantage and paying attention to the fantasy sport users. That research revealed 78.3 percent of fantasy sport users using television as part of their fantasy sport experience. The web was also heavily used, as 65.5 percent of the participants identified, aside from their hosting fantasy sport website, the use of the web. Other media use in fantasy sport showed that 19.9 percent use radio, 41 percent use magazines, and 24.8 percent use newspapers as part of their participation in fantasy sport. This indicates that there is certainly a need for media outlets to be aware of the informational needs of their consumers and how fantasy sport information can be used in marketing to consumers.

The NFL recognized that fans want fantasy sport information, and to that end, mandated all NFL teams display real-time fantasy statistics in their stadiums. This policy began with the 2011 season and was implemented to make attending a game more attractive. NFL spokesperson, Brian McCarthy, said the league recognizes it must do more to keep people attending games and wants to replicate the at-home experience at the stadium (McCarthy, 2011). DirecTV, the exclusive provider of the NFL Sunday Ticket, allows subscribers to watch any NFL game regardless of television market. There are other options available, as well, to access the programming via cellular phones and tablets. Fantasy sport enters the equation as viewers, with Internet capable televisions, can view their fantasy team statistics through NFL.com. Viewers need to be participating in an NFL.com fantasy league, but nonetheless, this melding of television viewership and fantasy sport has created a marketing advantage for DirecTV and NFL.

Television networks are also taking advantage of the growth of fantasy sport to attract viewers, maintain viewers, and create programming. Ruihley and Hardin (in press) discovered that fantasy sport users seek out fantasy-specific information found in programming. One participant in their study said, "ESPN also has their fantasy football experts that give their picks and sits for each week and that can also be used to help you have the best team" and another respondent added "In a typical episode of *SportsCenter* there is almost always a piece on fantasy updates and I use the information presented to expand my knowledge which I base my week to week fantasy decisions." A part of most football preview shows, experts offer advice as to what players could have an impact in fantasy competition, while postgame highlight shows feature fantasy statistics as part of the game recap. The sport that is perhaps the standard for gathering statistical information is baseball. These highlight shows have a myriad of statistics included with the score of the game, and also discuss players standing out from a fantasy perspective. Along with score, winning and losing pitchers, baseball highlight programs will feature the top performing position players regardless of game outcomes. This is done to attract and retain fantasy sport users to the program. These statistics are also part of the rolling scroll bar prevalent during many sporting broadcasts, in particular baseball and football. The NFL's Dallas Cowboys may have won their game but many viewers are interested in how Jason Witten performed because he is the starting tight end for the Cowboys and also for millions of fantasy sport team owners.

Websites have also used fantasy sport as a way to attract users. Many sport governing bodies of professional football, baseball, basketball, hockey, and golf sponsor fantasy sport leagues and host the leagues through their official websites. Media websites, such as

ESPN.com, CBSsportline.com, and SportingNews.com, also offer fantasy sport opportunities through a variety of sports. This is done in hopes to drive traffic to the website and increase users. Once there, site administrators have employed strategies to retain the user. The PGA Tour has split its season into three fantasy segments each consisting of approximately 12 weeks. This allows the user to see a more immediate result rather than having to participate from January through September before the season is complete. The participant has a fresh start if their fantasy team does not perform well during a particular duration of tournaments. People will also have ability to participate even if they choose to join after the PGA Tour season has begun.

Another strategy that can be associated within websites includes the use of message boards. Ruihley and Hardin (2011b) found the use of message boards important in the fantasy sport experience. They provided a platform for participants to interact with one other, ask advice, trash talk, and in general, socialize. The use of message boards creates more of attachment to the host website and allows participants to become more involved. Stemming in work of Li, Browne, and Wetherbe (2006), Ruihley and Hardin applied the concept of stickiness, in that the participant comes to the site and stays, rather than moving on to other sites to seek out more information about fantasy sport.

Another impact fantasy sport has had on media is the creation of a media professional that is a fantasy expert. Websites, newspapers, and television shows have fantasy experts offering advice on fantasy sports. Their advice includes what players should be drafted, should start in a given week, and what players should be benched based on past performance. For instance, a wide receiver may not have overwhelming statistics competing against a team primarily employing man-to-man pass defense as opposed to a team with zone coverage. The fantasy expert studies and refines statistics like this to give fantasy sport users advice on which players to start and sit. Many experts and writers have their own columns, blogs, or Twitter presence to share information pertaining to fantasy performance. Organizations such as Rotworld.com and Rotowire.com are information organizations filled with fantasy experts sharing fantasy-related information. In addition to print and web-based organizations, SiriusXM radio has a channel devoted to fantasy sports that features programming from fantasy experts.

Conclusion

The goal of this chapter was to illustrate just how much the activities of sport communication, marketing, and fantasy sport depend on each other. Fantasy sport is an activity with 35 million consumers seeking out information, utilizing social networking tools, and consuming sport-based media at astonishing rates. Fantasy sport could not exist at its present scale without the technology and communication outlets available. Fantasy sport is, itself, becoming a form of sport communication as it is melding other forms of communication into the entity of the activity.

From a mass communication standpoint, businesses are taking advantage of fantasy sport and it's participants to develop content and programing specifically targeted toward fantasy sport users. DirectTV allows viewers to display their fantasy team members and statistics and many sports news programs provide fantasy statistics to their viewers. There has also been the emergence of a new sport media professional – the fantasy sport expert. Television programming, satellite radio broadcasts, and websites have fantasy experts providing content strictly focused on fantasy sport statistics, content, and other information. Web sites have added fantasy sport sections to allow users to participate in fantasy sport through their site and have added message boards to provide discussion areas strictly for fantasy sport. The aforementioned items have marketing and advertising implications as businesses attempt to reach this demographic.

Many sport marketing texts (Fullerton, 2010; Mullin, Hardy, and Sutton, 2007; Shank, 2009) discuss two ways in which sport and marketing merge. First, there are the activities of marketing sport-related products. Second, organizations and businesses can market non-sport products through sport. This chapter has provided evidence supporting the idea that fantasy sport can be a unique and forceful subset of sport entertainment and can be associated with these two avenues of marketing. Time, effort, money, and media focus have been devoted to marketing fantasy sport products such as website hosts, draft magazines, trophies, television subscriptions, and exclusive analysis and advice. On the other side, fantasy sport is also being used as a vehicle to sell products. Hosting websites utilize banner advertisements and buttons to sell and promote a wide variety of products. In addition to host websites, other fantasy marketing campaigns occur within or around segments on television, information and expert sites such as Rotoworld.com and Rotowire.com, and radio stations (such as SiriusXM Fantasy Sports Radio).

While fantasy sport fits the mold of the two mentioned marketing avenues, it is important to note that fantasy sport can also be considered a marketing tool in a third way; simply standing alone. Organizations can and have used fantasy sport as a vehicle to highlight other products and features. For example, NFL halftime shows encourage viewers to stay tuned for a recap of first-half action complete with statistics, highlights, and fantasy updates. Additionally, host websites will use fantasy sport to attract fantasy sport users to other products and content on the site (that is, expert advice, exclusive access, live scoring, columns, and other sport products). This third marketing avenue is unique because not all sport segments can be used in this way.

The technology explosion during the first part of the 21st century has allowed fantasy sport participation to grow at a rapid pace. The impact on the communication industry has been the development of a different type of content as well as a demand for fantasy sport experts. Fantasy sport has taken the reporting of scores and statistics to a different level, as now, consumers want to know the minute details of games so they can determine how their fantasy team faired. Fantasy sport has also changed the way sport is consumed, in that, it is just not about winning or losing, but also about 100-yard rushing games, free throws made, and on-base percentage. The demand for this information, competition within, and socialization surrounding this activity has created an immense industry leaning on sport communication activities. Scholars and practitioners alike should take note and follow the progress of this niche activity turned sport entertainment enterprise.

References

Billings, A. C., and Ruihley, B. J. (2012a). The Fantasy Sport Trade Association: An inside look into a billion dollar industry. Paper presented at the Fifth Summit on Communication and Sport, Peoria, IL, March 2012.

Billings, A. C., and Ruihley, B. J. (2012b). Why we watch, why we play: Fantasy sports, fanship motivations, and the sport fan 2.0. *Mass Communication and Society*, 15 (6).

Close Call Sports (2012). Umpire Ejection Fantasy League Portal – 2012 MLB season. Retrieved from http://portal.closecallsports.com.

Davis, N. W., and Duncan, M. C. (2006). Sport knowledge is power: Reinforcing masculine privilege through fantasy sport league participation. *Journal of Sport and Social Issues*, 30 (3), 244–64.

ESPN (2010). ESPN top ten list for sport research. *ESPN Integrated Media Research Report*. Broadcast Education Association Research Symposium, Las Vegas, NV, April 15, 2010.

Fantasy Congress (2012). Welcome to Fantasy Congress. Retrieved from http://www.fantasy-congress.net/112/index.php.

Fantasy Sport Trade Association. (2012a). Welcome to the official site of the FSTA [Home page]. Retrieved from http://www.fsta.org.

Fantasy Sport Trade Association. (2012b). *Media kit 2012*. Retrieved from http://www.fsta.org/mk/MediaKit.pdf.

Farquhar, L. K., and Meeds, R. (2007). Types of fantasy sport users and their motivations. *Journal of Computer-Mediated Communication*, 12 (4), article 4. Retrieved from http://jcmc.indiana.edu/vol12/issue4/farquhar.html.

Fullerton, S. (2010). *Sports marketing* (2nd ed.). Boston: McGraw-Hill Irwin.

Hu, J. (2003). Sites see big season for fantasy sports. *ZDNet*, August 8. Retrieved from http://www.zdnet.com/news/sites-see-big-season-for-fantasy-sports/130921.

Hur, Y., Ko, Y. J., and Valacich, J. (2007). Motivation and concerns for online sport consumption. *Journal of Sport Management*, 21, 521–39.

Jacoby, D. (2011). Grantland's Reality TV Fantasy League: The complete rules and draft results. *Grantland*, June 8. Retrieved from http://www.grantland.com/blog/hollywood-prospectus/post/_/id/153/grantlands-reality-tv-fantasy-league-the-complete-rules-and-draft-results.

Li, D., Browne, G. J., and Wetherbe, J. C. (2006). Why do Internet users stick with a specific Web site? A relationship perspective. *International Journal of Electronic Commerce*, 10 (4), 105–41.

McCarthy, M. (2011). NFL orders clubs: Show fantasy stats at stadiums this year. *USA Today Game On*, September 9. Retrieved from http://content.usatoday.com/communities/gameon/post/2011/09/nfl-fantasy-football-stadiums-green-bay-packers-new-orleans-saints/1.

Mullin, B. J., Hardy, S., and Sutton, W. A. (2007). *Sport marketing* (3rd ed.). Champaign, IL: Human Kinetics.

PRWeb (2008). Fantasy sports industry grows to a $800 million industry with 29.9 million players. *PRWeb*, July 10. Retrieved from http://www.prweb.com/releases/2008/07/prweb1084994.htm.

Roy, D. P., and Goss, B. D. (2007). A conceptual framework of influences on fantasy sport consumption. *Marketing Management Journal*, 17 (2), 96–108.

Ruihley, B. J., and Hardin, R. L. (2011a). Beyond touchdowns, homeruns, and 3-pointers: An examination of fantasy sport participation motivation. *International Journal of Sport Management and Marketing*, 10, 232–56.

Ruihley, B. J., and Hardin, R. (2011b). Message board use and the fantasy sport experience. *International Journal of Sport Communication*, 4, 233–52.

Ruihley, B. J., and Hardin, R. (in press). Meeting the informational needs of the fantasy sport user. *Journal of Sports Media*.

Seo, W. J., and Green, B. C. (2008). Development of the motivation scale for sport online consumption. *Journal of Sport Management*, 22, 82–109.

Shank, M. D. (2009). *Sports marketing: A strategic perspective* (4th ed.). Upper Saddle River, NJ: Pearson Prentice Hall.

Shipman III, F. M. (2001). Blending the real and virtual: Activity and spectatorship in fantasy sports. Paper presented at the Fourth Annual Digital Arts and Culture Conference, Providence, RI, April 2001. Retrieved from http://www.csdl.tamu.edu/~shipman/papers/dac01.pdf.

Spinda, J. S. W., and Haridakis, P. M. (2008). Exploring the motives of fantasy sport: A uses-and gratifications approach. In L. W. Hugenberg, P. M. Haridakis, and A. C. Earnheardt (Eds.), *Sport mania: Essays on fandom and the media in the 21st Century* (pp. 187–202). Jefferson, NC: McFarland.

Vichot, R. (2009). History of fantasy sports and its adoption by sports journalists. *News Games*, January 2. Retrieved from http://newsgames.gatech.edu/blog/2009/01/history-of-fantasy sports-and-its-adoption-by-sports-journalists.html.

Walker, S. (2006). *Fantasyland: A sportswriter's bid to win the world's most ruthless fantasy baseball league*. New York: Penguin.

Wann, D. L. (1995). Preliminary validation of the sport fan motivation scale. *Journal of Sport and Social Issues*, 19, 377–96.

28

USING SOCIAL NETWORK ANALYSIS IN SPORT COMMUNICATION RESEARCH

Marion E. Hambrick

The sport industry generates over US$234 billion in revenue annually (Horine, 2011), and comprises organizations such as sports teams, sporting goods manufacturers and retailers, and governing bodies. These entities work extensively with supporting organizations such as hotels and restaurants, advertisers and marketers, and corporate sponsors outside of the industry (Chelladurai, 2009). Within the industry, sport communication represents another important segment, with its public relations organizations, newspaper and magazine outlets, broadcast and network television operators, and social networking sites creating and disseminating sports content to fans and other industry members (Pedersen, Miloch, and Laucella, 2007). Researchers have attempted to quantify the sport industry's numerous activities and interactions but have noted the challenges. Over 49,000 sport organizations, 227 million spectators, and 118 million participants exist, and multiple connections tie them to one another and related entities (Humphreys and Ruseski, 2009).

One analytical approach – social network analysis – may help researchers gain a greater knowledge of the industry with its numerous organizations and individuals plus their myriad of connections and interactions. Organizations, groups, and individuals with the shared relationships among them collectively form social networks, and social network analysis can help researchers understand the networks more fully (Wasserman and Faust, 1994). The sport industry and sport communication segment can be viewed as social networks (Chelladurai, 2009; Thibault and Harvey, 1997), and researchers can use social network analysis to examine the sport industry or individual segments in greater detail. The analytical approach allows researchers to observe which organizations, groups, and individuals exist as network members within a chosen social network, to identify what relationships connect network members together, and to explore how network members use their relationships and the network's structure to share information and other resources. Social network analysis also can help researchers to determine which members assume key roles within the network, plus the consequences of adding members to or subtracting them from the network (Wasserman and Faust, 1994).

This chapter addresses the various possibilities of using social network analysis in sport communication research. The first section provides an overview of sport communication research today and outline why social network analysis can help when examining the industry segment and its body of research. The second section discusses the earliest social network analysis research along with more recent studies. The third section offers information about the social network analysis software packages for researchers. The fourth section concludes with possible sport communication research ideas for future studies.

Sport communication and social network analysis

Sport communication plays a major role within the larger sport industry, with many organizations and individuals helping create or deliver content (Pedersen, *et al.*, 2007). The rising popularity and usage of social media outlets such as Facebook and Twitter have increased the level of communication among sport teams, fans, and others within the industry. These social networking sites along with sports communication providers such as television and cable broadcasters, magazine and newspaper publishers, and public relations agencies combine to provide a wide range of information for the larger sport industry.

The challenge for sport communication researchers is to understand what content is produced and how organizations create and provide the content. Researchers have taken multiple approaches to this examination, whether through quantitative or qualitative analysis or some combination of the two. From a quantitative perspective, Schultz and Sheffer (2010) surveyed journalists to understand how they used the social networking site Twitter to provide news and related content. Qualitatively, Gee and Leberman (2011) conducted semi-structured interviews with television and print media producers to examine how they decided what content to provide for viewers and readers. Cleland (2009) used both methods to explore how football clubs and their fans interacted with media organizations such as newspaper, television, and radio outlets along with fanzines and websites.

Beyond traditional quantitative and qualitative techniques, social network analysis represents another valuable methodological approach for researchers to explore sport communication in more detail. The analytical tools help researchers document and understand social networks such as the sport communication segment or the larger sport industry as social networks. Social network analysis derives from the academic fields of anthropology and sociology, and borrows research techniques from both – observing social network members in their natural settings, defining member roles within the social network, and analyzing and critiquing the network's structure and member relationships. The latter analyses are facilitated through the use of sociograms (Tichy, Tushman, and Fombrun, 1979).

Utilized frequently in social network analysis, sociograms help researchers describe the social network, depicting visually the network members and their shared network relationships (de Nooy, Mrvar, and Batagelj, 2005). Researchers can create sociograms by asking network members to identify other network members and describe their shared interactions, if any, with them. Respondents also may identify the most prominent or influential network members and describe how information and other resources are exchanged among members through their network relationships (Wasserman and Faust, 1994). The collected data then is used to outline the network's structure via sociograms. Each network member is represented in a sociogram by a single point, or node, and a line connecting two nodes shows that two members share a relationship. The collection of nodes and lines form the network's sociogram, which depicts individual members, shared relationships, and relative positions of power within the network. Powerful members are often located at or near the network's center. These members typically have multiple lines, or relationships, linking them to other network members. Conversely, members with fewer connections often reside on the network's outskirts. As noted by de Nooy and colleagues (2005), fewer relationships restrict their ability to access resources available to more centrally positioned members.

Social network analysis research

Social network analysis tools can help researchers to illustrate how information and other resources move among social network members. Mapping the network members and their relationships reveals which members play central roles in the resource-sharing process and how the network's formation facilitates this process (Wasserman and Faust, 1994). The resulting sociograms and data can provide interesting insights, particularly when using them to examine the spread of information and innovations. Some of the first social network analysis studies focused on the diffusion of innovations within social networks, and the researchers used sociograms to explain how network members first learned about new products and how product information spread among them.

Early social network analysis studies

In their seminal study, Ryan and Gross (1943) represented two of the first researchers using sociograms to examine a social network. They used this approach to document the diffusion of a new agricultural product through two local farming communities. The researchers found that accelerated use occurred as more farmers received product information from respected peers. The most informed network members possessed central locations within the network, and they helped spread information quickly to their less-connected and less-informed counterparts (Ryan and Gross, 1943). Similarly, Menzel and Katz (1955) used sociograms to explore medical community interactions as physicians learned about and adopted new pharmaceutical products. Sociograms again were used to map the interactions among physicians as they shared product information. As part of the study, doctors were asked to list colleagues with whom they interacted and from whom they solicited advice. The results revealed that the most frequently named physicians played central roles within the network, as they shared multiple connections with network members. These members provided more advice and exerted more influence on other physicians, persuading other physicians to adopt the new products (Menzel and Katz, 1955).

These early studies illustrate the effective use of social network analysis tools to document the construction of social networks and the diffusion of information and innovations within them. Park (2003) encouraged more researchers to use the analytical approach in other contexts, particularly within the communication industry. He asserted that social network analysis could help researchers better understand how various news organizations work together, creating and disseminating content. Additionally, the approach, as noted by Park, could provide more insights into the information and communication channels developed within the industry's social network, and how organizations and individuals used those channels and network connections to share information.

Within sport communication, researchers can use social network analysis to explore the sport industry segment and its network members in more detail. Sports properties and media outlets form an intricate social network as they rely on their interdependent relationships to create and distribute sports content (Bruce and Tini, 2008). Social network analysis can help researchers to develop a more complete understanding of the sport communication social network, its members and shared relationships, and their combined information and resource exchanges. The analytical approach can reveal potential opportunities to improve various network relationships and the network as a whole (de Nooy, *et al.*, 2005; Wasserman and Faust, 1994).

Recent social network analysis research

Since the first social network analysis studies (Menzel and Katz, 1955; Ryan and Gross, 1943), a multitude of others have emerged. An exploration of research reveals patterns regarding social network analysis application. Studies often fall into one of three categories: exploring (a) knowledge creation and dissemination, (b) organizational structures and relationships, or (c) diffusion of information (de Nooy, *et al.*, 2005; Wasserman and Faust, 1994). Examples of the categories and their use within sport communication research are discussed below.

Knowledge creation and dissemination

Understanding the creation and dissemination of knowledge represents a popular use of social network analysis. Researchers use the approach to explore their academic fields and bodies of research created through scholarly collaborations. For example, Quatman and Chelladurai (2008) examined sport management researchers as a social network. The researchers found multiple collaborations among network members and a tightly knit group of researchers located at the network's center. Together, this smaller group collaborated frequently and published a significant body of research. The researchers shared multiple connections amongst themselves and with other network members. The study's authors concluded that social network analysis can provide important insights about the current sport management research and its evolution, and suggested that more studies employ the analytical approach.

Love and Andrew (2012) followed this work by examining academic relationships connecting sport management research to sociology of sport research. The authors noted that previous studies focused on a single academic field, but their study documented the development of relationships connecting the two fields over time. The results revealed a growing number of collaborations among sport management scholars but not sociology of sport researchers. The authors attributed the difference to more sport management faculty members working in the same departments, leading to convenient collaboration opportunities. Additionally, they observed the presence of key researchers who published repeatedly in both disciplines, and served as important connectors between the two bodies of literature. They recommended more studies use social network analysis, highlighting potential ways to advance sport management and sociology of sport research.

The studies show how social network analysis can help to outline knowledge creation and dissemination via authorship relationships within academic fields – how academic social networks form, plus what they create and disseminate over time. The studies revealed productive groups within the networks and opportunities for additional research exchanges.

Organizational structures and relationships

In addition to knowledge creation and dissemination, researchers have used social network analysis to explore organizations as social networks – how the organizations combine to form a social network, how they create and leverage relationships within the network, and how the network structure facilitates the resource sharing processes. For example, Malinick, Tindall, and Diani (2011) examined a social network formed among media outlets and environmental organizations seeking news coverage of their issues. The researchers used a sociogram to diagram the network containing both organization types and their shared network relationships. The resulting sociogram showed that environmental organizations with more moderate political stances received the most coverage, and they maintained central and powerful positions within the network. These organizations dictated the type and amount of information communicated to the public, and the authors noted that this information exchange could shape public perceptions regarding the environmental issues discussed.

Within sport management, MacLean, Cousens, and Barnes (2011) studied the development of network relationships among community basketball clubs, university athletic departments, and a nonprofit multisport recreation organization. The authors coupled social network analysis with in-depth interviews, and found the community basketball clubs had close relationships with one another, sharing information and related resources. Yet more tenuous relationships existed among the basketball clubs and their counterparts. From the social network analysis results, MacLean and colleagues concluded that a greater opportunity existed for the basketball clubs to strengthen their relationships through better communication and partnerships, thereby improving the level of sport delivery across the community.

Warner, Bowers, and Dixon (2012) used social network analysis to study two college women's basketball teams. The analytical approached helped the researchers outline the many relationships among the teams with their coaches, players, and staff members. The researchers used multiple sociograms to document each team's formation and evolution. The results revealed coaches were located at the center of the social networks at the start of the season, but later moved to less central roles as the season progressed. Of the two teams, the team with a winning record had a more tightly knit network, leading Warner and colleagues to propose that social network analysis can help identify best practices and improvement areas as network members leverage network relationships and resources.

The studies provide pertinent examples of how researchers can employ social network analysis to understand organizational structures and exchanges, including the sharing of information and other network resources. Social network analysis can help reveal key network members participating in such exchanges and identify opportunities to improve the exchanges through the promotion of more conversations and collaborations among network members.

Diffusion of information

Researchers also have used social network analysis to understand how information diffuses from one individual, group, or organization to another, particularly through word-of-mouth communication, within social networks. Many of the studies relied upon interviews and other information collected from network members to outline and explore social networks (Wasserman and Faust, 1994). More recently, social media has greatly facilitated the data collection process by giving researchers readily accessible data obtained independently of network members (Williams, 2006).

Ko, Yin, and Kuo (2008) employed social network analysis to explore the effect of movie reviews shared through blogs on subsequent box office receipts. The study results revealed that blog movie reviews in conjunction with mainstream news stories increased moviegoers' interest in the films. The shared information created a snowball effect, whereby the online movie reviews and news stories increased viewership, resulting in more positive online coverage of the movies. The study also revealed that key individuals within the social networks used the blogs to spread information about the movies to large groups of potential viewers. As noted by Ko and colleagues, this information sharing proved beneficial and lead ultimately to increased box office receipts.

Beyond blogs, numerous social networking sites have surfaced, including more mature applications such as message boards and chat rooms along with newer sites such as Facebook and Twitter. The *SportsBusiness Journal* linked much of Twitter's initial popularity and growth to the sport industry and celebrity athletes such as Lance Armstrong, Tony Hawk, and Shaquille O'Neal (Fisher, 2009), and Bruns and Burgess (2011) urged a greater focus on this social networking site when conducting social network analyses. Twitter and other social media outlets represent a prime opportunity for researchers studying the sport industry as a social network and the accompanying diffusion of information within it. Social networking sites such as Twitter give users the chance to create and spread information, and the authors encouraged more research that identifies and examines popular Twitter users and the information they disseminate. As noted by Bruns and Burgess, the data can help researchers to better understand the diffusion process along with the formation of relationships and smaller social networks within the larger social networking site.

From a sports perspective, Hambrick (2012) collected data from Twitter and used social network analysis to understand how bicycle race organizers used the social networking site for promotional purposes. The researcher examined messages posted by the organizers on the site and their shared relationships with other Twitter users. The resulting sociograms showed that race organizers created smaller social networks within the social media outlet, and used the networks to share information about their events with potential race participants and spectators. Information spread rapidly among network members, leading Hambrick to conclude that social networks formed within social media sites represented an attractive means for sharing information and promoting events.

Clavio, Burch, and Frederick (2012) also examined Twitter usage through social network analysis, looking specifically at the development of a social network within the social media outlet to discuss a Big Ten football team. The study found a network comprising traditional and non-traditional media outlets, the team's athletic department, sports fans, and other Twitter users. The results revealed one main cluster of network members, and this core group contained various users engaged in multiple interactions. The remaining network interactions took place among much smaller groups of fans or media outlets. Clavio and colleagues noted that despite Twitter's emphasis on frequent user interactions, this social network was comprised primarily of small groups engaging in conversations and one-way communication among select network members without more extensive information sharing throughout the larger group.

In a different study, Hambrick and Sanderson (in press) used Twitter to document how sports journalists used the social media outlet to share information about and discuss the Penn

State football scandal. The researchers examined network relationships among the journalists along with messages posted by key sports journalists using Twitter to break news, discuss the latest developments, and provide commentary about the story over time. The study revealed that information spread rapidly among the journalists once the initial news broke. Within the social network, a smaller group of prominent journalists emerged, and these network members served as information hubs, relaying information and dictating commentary about the story to their peers (Hambrick and Sanderson, in press).

The studies reveal the increasing use of social network analysis to examine sport communication with particular focus on social networking sites. Social media outlets such as Twitter provide a prime way for researchers to access historical data from a wide variety of users, explore these interactions, and track the development of social networks over time.

Social network analysis software packages

To facilitate this analysis, numerous social network analysis software packages exist. Pajek and UCINet represent two packages mentioned frequently in the above studies and other academic publications. The software programs can create sociograms and provide descriptive statistics and other social network information.

Researchers can use the software in multiple ways. The tools can help when examining large networks with hundreds or thousands of network members and relationships in scientific and sociological contexts. Researchers also can use the software to outline evolutionary processes, whether the diffusion of innovations or the spread of contagious diseases. Frequent applications of the software include examining large networks or subsets of the networks, developing sociograms to visually depict the networks, and providing quantitative information germane to social network analysis such as network density, closeness centralization, and aggregate constraint values (Batagelj and Mrvar, 2010).

Density

A social network's density reflects the ratio between the actual number of relationships among network members and the maximum number possible within the network. Density values can range from zero to one, where .000 indicates no shared relationships among network members, while 1.000 shows all network members share relationships with their network members. An inverse relationship exists between the number of network members and the network's density. Density tends to decrease when the number of members increases, as network members typically face an upper limit on the number of relationships they can develop and sustain successfully. Higher density values suggest a more efficient flow of resources and information through a network, as members share multiple relationships. Conversely, lower density values indicate a more limited sharing process resulting from fewer relationships within the network (de Nooy, *et al.*, 2005).

Closeness centralization

Closeness centralization quantifies distances among network members at an aggregate level. The values range from zero to one, where higher values indicate smaller distances among network members. Networks with larger closeness centralization values can spread information and other resources more effectively than networks with lower values. Together with density, closeness centralization helps to numerically define the collective network connections and indicate how quickly network members as a whole can reach one another and how easily they can access information and resources (de Nooy, *et al.*, 2005).

Aggregate constraints

Aggregate constraint values are used to quantify a member's relative network power operationalized through network relationships, and these values typically range from zero to one. Values closer to one reveal a network member's heavy dependence on existing network relationships. These members have fewer relationships within the network, and cannot afford to lose a single one without facing partial or complete isolation from other network members. Conversely, members with lower aggregate constraint values have more network relationships and face less network isolation when losing one or more relationships. These network members are often located centrally within the network and play key roles in spreading information and other resources to fellow network members (de Nooy, *et al.*, 2005).

Future research using social network analysis

Software packages can provide extensive network information for researchers, and multiple ways exist to apply social network analysis to sport communication research. Love and Andrew (2012) noted a relatively untapped opportunity to use social network analysis. This section proposes several sport communication research ideas where social network analysis can be applied. For example, following in the footsteps of earlier studies such as Love and Andrew, as well as Quatman and Chelladurai (2008), researchers could focus on the sport communication body of literature and examine where publications such as the *International Journal of Sport Communication* and other communication outlets fit within the larger sport management and communication research. This examination could help document the evolution of sport communication research areas and collaborations. The findings also could help pinpoint potential gaps in the existing literature and the potential for future studies and research partnerships.

Researchers also could use social network analysis to outline the sport communication segment as a social network (Chelladurai, 2009; Thibault and Harvey, 1997), focusing on the segment as a whole or components within it (for example, television and print outlets, public relations organizations, social networking sites). The findings could help researchers and industry leaders to identify strong existing relationships and discuss potential benefits through the creation of new ones. Examining and comparing various industry components could reveal where efficiencies exist and aid in sharing best practices regarding information and resource exchanges.

Studies could employ social network analysis to understand communication channels, whether in online or offline settings. Yoh, Pedersen, and Park (2006) studied the information sources golf consumers used before purchasing new golf clubs. As they found out, consumers relied upon sporting goods salespeople and manufacturer websites; however, they expressed the greatest comfort levels when using information received word-of-mouth from friends and family members. Through in-depth interviews, researchers could further this study. The collected data could help them ascertain how individual consumers gather information, and sociograms could reveal the information diffusion from one consumer or group (for example, sporting goods stores, websites) to another. In a different study, Cleland (2009) examined the interaction among football clubs and their fans with various media outlets, including newspapers, television, radio, fanzines, and websites. The researcher focused on two elements: tracking the evolution of football clubs and fan reliance on various media outlets over time. Social network analysis could extend this study by using a series of sociograms to show transformations in interactions within and among the clubs plus their shifting relationships with traditional and newer media providers.

Social networking sites such as Twitter and Facebook lend themselves naturally to further exploration via social network analysis. Wallace, Wilson, and Miloch (2011) and Waters, Burke, Jackson, and Buning (2011) examined sports organizations and their use of Facebook and organizational websites to interact with fans. Social networking sites allow researchers to see which users like and follow various sports organizations. Similar to the Clavio, *et al.* (2012) study, researchers could use this information to examine social networks developing around a particular sports team or organization and explore how the organizations interact with followers. A variety of potential studies exist to examine sport communication in more detail.

Summary

This chapter has provided an overview of using social network analysis with sport communication research. The academic field has grown rapidly (Pedersen, *et al.*, 2007), and researchers have employed various approaches to understand this area more fully. Social network analysis represents an important tool in the exploration process. Researchers have an opportunity to use this methodological approach as they explore a variety of areas, whether the organizational structures and relationships of sport organizations, the creation and dissemination of sport communication, or how the field itself has grown and evolved over time.

References

Batagelj, V., and Mrvar, A. (2010). *Pajek: Program for analysis and visualization of large networks reference manual.* Ljubljana, Slovenia: University of Ljubljana.

Bruce, T., and Tini, T. (2008). Unique crisis response strategies in sports public relations: Rugby league and the case for diversion. *Public Relations Review*, 34, 108–115.

Bruns, A., and Burgess, J. E. (2011). New methodologies for researching news discussions on Twitter. *The Future of Journalism* 2011, September, 8–9.

Chelladurai, P. (2009). *Managing organizations for sport and physical activity: A systems perspective* (3rd ed.). Scottsdale, AZ: Holcomb Hathaway.

Clavio, G., Burch, L., and Frederick, E. (2012). User characteristics of a Big Ten football Twitter feed: A social network analysis. Presented at the annual conference of the North American Society for Sport Management, Seattle, WA.

Cleland, J. A. (2009). Changing organizational structure of football clubs and their relationship with the external media. *International Journal of Sport Communication*, 2, 417–31.

de Nooy, W., Mrvar, A., and Batagelj, V. (2005). *Exploratory social network analysis with Pajek.* New York: Cambridge University Press.

Fisher, E. (2009). Flight of fancy? *SportsBusiness Journal*, June 1. Retrieved from http://www.sportsbusinessjournal.com/article/62656.

Gee, B. L., and Leberman, S. I. (2011). Sports media decision making in France: How they choose what we get to see and read. *International Journal of Sport Communication*, 4, 321–43.

Hambrick, M. E. (2012). Six degrees of information: Using social network analysis to explore the spread of information within sport social networks. *International Journal of Sport Communication*, 5, 16–34.

Hambrick, M. E., and Sanderson, J. (in press). Gaining primacy in the digital network: Using social network analysis to examine sports journalists' coverage of the Penn State football scandal via Twitter. *Journal of Sports Media*.

Horine, G. (2011). @TEOTD, honing social media skills nothing to LOL about. *SportsBusiness Journal*, April 18. Retrieved from http://www.sportsbusinessdaily.com/Journal/Issues/2011/04/18/Opinion/From-the-Field.aspx?hl=%24213%20billionandsc=1.

Humphreys, B. R., and Ruseski, J. E. (2009). Estimates of the dimensions of the sports market in the U.S. *International Journal of Sport Finance*, 4, 94–113.

Ko, H. C., Yin, C. P., and Kuo, F. Y. (2008). Exploring individual communication power in the blogosphere. *Internet Research*, 18, 541–61.

Love, A., and Andrew, D. P. S. (2012). The intersection of sport management and sociology of sport research: A social network perspective. *Sport Management Review*, 15, 244–56.

MacLean, J., Cousens, L., and Barnes, M. L. (2011) Look who's linked with whom: A case study of one community basketball network. *Journal of Sport Management*, 25, 562–75.

Malinick, T. E., Tindall, D. B., and Diani, M. (2011). Network centrality and social movement media coverage: A two-mode network analytic approach. *Social Networks*, in press, available online 3 December. DOI:10.1016/j.socnet.2011.10.005.

Menzel, H., and Katz, E. (1955). Social relations and innovation in the medical profession: The epidemiology of a new drug. *Public Opinion Quarterly*, 19, 337–52.

Park, H. W. (2003). Hyperlink network analysis: A new method for the study of social structure on the Web. *Connections*, 25, 49–61.

Pedersen, P. M., Miloch, K. S., and Laucella, P. C. (2007). *Strategic sport communication*. Champaign, IL: Human Kinetics.

Quatman, C. C., and Chelladurai, P. (2008). The social construction of knowledge in the field of sport management: A social network perspective. *Journal of Sport Management*, 22, 651–76.

Ryan, B., and Gross, N. C. (1943). The diffusion of hybrid seed corn in two Iowa communities. *Rural Sociology*, 8, 15–24.

Schultz, B., and Sheffer, M. L. (2010). An exploratory study of how Twitter is affecting sports journalism. *International Journal of Sport Communication*, 3, 226–39.

Thibault, L., and Harvey, J. (1997). Fostering interorganizational linkages in the Canadian sport delivery system. *Journal of Sport Management*, 11, 45–68.

Tichy, N. M., Tushman, M. L., and Fombrun, C. (1979). Social network analysis for organizations. *Academy of Management Review*, 4, 507–19.

Wallace, L., Wilson, J., and Miloch, K. (2011). Sporting Facebook: A content analysis of NCAA organizational sport pages and Big 12 Conference athletic department pages. *International Journal of Sport Communication*, 4, 422–44.

Warner, S., Bowers, M., and Dixon, M. A. (2012). Team dynamics: A social network perspective. *Journal of Sport Management*, 26, 53–66.

Waters, R. D., Burke, K. A., Jackson, Z. H., and Buning, J. D. (2011). Using stewardship to cultivate fandom online: Comparing how National Football League teams use their web sites and Facebook to engage their fans. *International Journal of Sport Communication*, 4, 163–77.

Wasserman, S., and Faust, K. (1994). *Social network analysis: Methods and applications*. Cambridge: Cambridge University Press.

Williams, D. (2006). On and off the 'net: Scales for social capital in an online era. *Journal of Computer-Mediated Communication*, 11, 593–628.

Yoh, T., Pedersen, P. M., and Park, M. (2006). Sources of information for purchasing golf clubs: Personal and non-personal references. *International Journal of Sports Marketing and Sponsorship*, 7, 125–35.

29

EVALUATING SPORTS WEBSITES FROM AN INFORMATION MANAGEMENT PERSPECTIVE

Hans Jochen Scholl

Sports on the worldwide web

Nowadays sport organizations, large and small, use the worldwide web as an indispensable platform for connecting internally to members, players, and employees, as well as to external organizations and businesses, the media, fans, and the general public. Web-based channels provide team- and business-related information, foster fandom and team reputation, and expand the commercial side of each organization's business. Complementing the marketing and financial management perspectives, recent studies have analyzed and evaluated the efficacy of sports websites from an information management perspective. In this chapter, a framework is presented which incorporates this particular perspective. Furthermore, within this chapter is an illustration of how web entries of sport organizations can be effectively assessed and compared.

Major-league franchises in North America as well as independent professional sports teams in Europe and other parts of the world routinely use various web-based vehicles such as Facebook, Twitter, YouTube, and their own websites among others to connect to fans and supporters, the media, and the general public (Scholl and Carlson, 2012). For quite some time, professional sport organizations have sold tickets and merchandise online and also published schedules, match reviews and reports, and player and team information (Delpy and Bosetti, 1998). Despite different structures with franchise-based cartel-like major leagues in North America, as opposed to Europe with club-based open leagues, these two distinct business models for professional sport organizations share similar economic histories and success (Cain and Haddock, 2005). Both strands represent multi-billion dollar industries (Hoover's Inc., 2010) and are, as detailed by Scholl and Carlson, leveraging their respective businesses via the web. While today, as noted by Cain and Haddock, the lion's share of revenues is still generated from televised and radio broadcasting of games, franchise and individual team websites seem to have developed into an important lever of public team appearance and an increasingly important instrument of revenue generation. As can be seen in Table 29.1, the North American major-league franchise websites, for example, attract between half and over three million unique visitors every day, and popular open-league teams such as UK soccer sites Manchester United, Chelsea FC, FC

TABLE 29.1 Web traffic of major professional sports sites, June 2012

Site	website unique daily visitors (*n* millions)	Facebook "Likes" (*n* millions)	Twitter followers (millions)	YouTube subscribers (*n*)	YouTube videos (*n*)
MLB.com	3.1	1.3	2.2	394	6,078
NBA.com	2.4	13.6	5.4	661,996	8,516
NFL.com	0.5	5.7	3.5	n/a	n/a
NHL.com	0.6	2.4	1.2	134,897	15,011
Manchester United FC	0.3	25.9	0.3	n/a	n/a
Chelsea FC	0.2	n/a	1.1	95,845	1,162
FC Barcelona	0.1	32.6	5.6	317,111	2,804
Real Madrid	0.1	29.5	5.0	176,994	1,450
FC Bayern Munich	0.1	4.4	0.1	19,401	302

Sources: Google (2012); http://www.facebook.com; http://www.twitter.com; http://www.youtube.com
FC, Football Club; MLB, Major League Baseball; NBL, National Basketball Association; NFL, National Football League; NHL, National Hockey League

Barcelona, Real Madrid, and FC Bayern Munich draw between 90,000 and 280,000 unique visitors every day (Google, 2012). As further detailed in the table, the respective Facebook, Twitter, and YouTube accounts reveal an even more compelling picture. The North American franchises' Facebook pages are liked by up to 14 million National Basketball Association (NBA) members, while the open-league soccer sites are liked by almost 33 million (FC Barcelona) Facebook users. Also, in terms of Twitter followers, huge audiences are attracted by both the North American Franchises (up to 5.4 million for the NBA) and the popular open-league soccer sites in Europe (up to 5.6 million for FC Barcelona).

Via the web, sport organizations, in general, and professional sport organization, in particular, have significantly increased their individual reach, now attracting both local and global audiences, and the share of their web-based revenues might be similar to the seven percent share in general retail (Schonfeld, 2010). As a consequence, web-originated business appears as an increasingly important source of revenue for sport organizations (Shelton, 2003). While, so far, most studies have evaluated sports websites only from a marketing perspective (Brown, 2003; Carlson, Rosenberger, and Muthaly, 2003; Evans and Smith, 2004; Filo and Funk, 2005), a few studies, (for example, Scholl and Carlson, 2012; Scholl, Eisenberg, Dirks, and Carlson, 2011) have incorporated the *information management* perspective (Detlor, 2010), which is a subset of the *information perspective* (Case, 2002; Gleick, 2010; Macdonald, 1995), on this phenomenon (Note: According to Choo [2002, pp. 56-57], information management is concerned with six information processes [identifying information needs, acquiring information, organizing and storing information, developing information products and services, distributing information, and using information] that impact an organization's capacity to learn and adapt). In contrast to other managerial perspectives but also complementing them, the information perspective focuses on both information and information technology from a functionality, content, service, and information-provision angle with special regard to human actors' needs and information behavior (Case, 2002; Gleick, 2010; Macdonald, 1995; Scholl, *et al.*, 2011; Taylor, 1986). On a related note, it should be stated that the information management perspective complements other perspectives, such as the marketing perspective or the finance perspective. These other analytical lenses focus, for example, on phenomena such as market evolution, market shares, communication mixes, bottom-line contributions, or business models providing important insights and results, which complement but cannot replace the information management view.

Employing this perspective in sports aims particularly at assessing and comparing the information artifacts used by sport organizations both internally and externally, for example, their websites, or dedicated sport information systems, including wearable sport information systems, and software applications specifically designed for sports. The Taylor-Eisenberg-Dirks-Scholl framework, or in short, the TEDS framework (Scholl, *et al.*, 2011) is an analytical instrument, which employs the information perspective allowing for the fine-grained analysis of information systems' capabilities and qualities relative to specific human actors' needs and action/interaction scenarios. In this chapter, the TEDS framework is presented, as well as an illustration of its use in evaluating sports websites.

Information artifacts

The term "information artifact" is a summary term referring to sources and pieces of information, as well as information systems and other information technology artifacts. Information artifacts range from papyrus roles, traffic signs, traditional books, newspapers, to modern information systems, electronic note pads, smart phones, and websites and computer programs, which can be accessed via those devices. Information has always come in various forms and formats; however, nowadays, in many cases it can no longer be meaningfully distinguished from its instantiation in technology. As an example, a hypertext document can simultaneously appear as both a piece of information (to an html or xml expert) and as an information system that executes programming code upon activation. While a casual human actor may only understand the effects of the artifact by experiencing its behavior at execution time (including the informational content it may carry), the expert can read the document and envision its run-time behavior with no need to activate the functionality. When human actors, for example, purchase event tickets or pay bills via an information system (the information artifact), they interact with this very information artifact. Its use and the human–artifact interaction can be assessed with regard to how well this use and this interaction serve the specific individual human actor relative to her or his purpose and need. Information system design principles as well as frameworks for assessing information systems in use have been developed for decades (for example, Bevan, 1995; Bødker, 2000; Dahlbom and Mathiassen, 1993; Davis, 1989; Detlor and DeGroote, 2003; Hartmann, Sutcliffe, and Angeli, 2008; Klischewski and Scholl, 2008; Mumford, 1983; Schmidt, Spiessl, and Kern, 2010; Scholl and Carlson, 2012; Shneiderman, 1987; Taylor, 1982, 1986; Venkatesh, 2000; Wixom and Todd, 2005). One of the most comprehensive evaluative frameworks is the so-called Taylor (1986) model of value-added processes in information systems, which was extended and updated under the acronym TEDS for Taylor, Eisenberg, Dirks, and Scholl, who developed the extension/update (Scholl, *et al.*, 2011). In contrast to other evaluative methods, the TEDS framework's orientation is human actor-centric or human actor need-centric rather than system-centric.

Evaluating information artifacts – the TEDS framework

Four major blocks form the TEDS framework, as detailed by Scholl, *et al.* (2011). The first is a model of generic human-actor-centric categories and subcategories of use. The second major block is the case-specific personae representing specific (groups of) human actors and their needs. The third is the case- and persona-specific scenarios of action and interaction. The fourth and final major block is the 13-step TEDS procedure, which systematically guides the evaluation and comparison.

The first building block of the framework, the TEDS model, distinguishes six generic categories of principles and criteria for both designing and evaluating information artifacts (Scholl, *et al.,* 2011). The six categories are ease of use, noise reduction, quality, adaptability, performance, and affection. These generic categories help analytically break down the characteristics of an information artifact, for example, an interactive website of a sports organization. The six generic categories are then divided into 40 subcategories. The categories and subcategories were first detailed by Scholl and colleagues and are presented here in Table 29.2. While these categories and subcategories provide 40 different lenses on the characteristics of an information artifact, they do not define the particular angles of view, which is accomplished by the second and third building blocks.

The second building block of the TEDS framework, the so-called personae, connects the characteristics of the information artifact to the (needs of) specific human actors. Personae are narrative constructs of typified human actors that aim at capturing prevalent traits, interests, beliefs, and values of identifiable groups of specific human actors with similar profiles and needs (Scholl, *et al.*, 2011). Typical elements for forming a persona are gender, income levels, education, affiliations, age group, geographical area, marital status, particular biases, tastes, beliefs, and values among others. Two personae that might play a role in professional sports organizations could be, for example, (1) a supporter or fan in the age group of 25–35, male, US$40k+ annual income, member of a fan organization, urban or suburban environment, unmarried, and season ticket holder, or (2) a supporter in the age group of over 45, male or female, US$50+ annual income, unaffiliated, urban or suburban environment, married, occasional on-site spectator and TV season subscription holder. It is intuitively clear that analyzing the information artifact (for example, the interactive website of a sport organization) through the 40 lenses of the TEDS model produces different results before the backdrop of the two different personae and their different needs. However, even the persona-specific angle of analysis alone would not sufficiently capture the specific needs of the two personae.

For this to happen, the third building block of the TEDS framework (scenarios of action/interaction) helps to analyze the persona's specific actions and interactions with the information artifact. Scenarios are typified ensembles of human action and interaction within a specific context that capture and identify potential problems, choices, and solutions (Scholl, *et al.*, 2011). They are separate from so called "use cases" in traditional information system analysis in that they emphasize a strictly human actor needs-centric perspective. A scenario of action and interaction in TEDS can comprise multiple use cases. For the interactive website of a sport organization exemplary scenarios of action and interaction could include the lookup of player statistics, game schedules, or the purchase of tickets or merchandise among others. For each specific scenario and for each persona, 40 subcategories in the six generic categories are rated (see Table 29.2). Ratings are regularly performed by means of scoring

TABLE 29.2 TEDS categories and subcategories

Ease of Use (1xx)	*Noise Reduction (2xx)*	*Quality (3xx)*	*Adaptability (4xx)*	*Performance (5xx)*	*Affection (6xx)*
Browsing, browsability, searchability (101)	Item identification (201)	Accuracy (301)	Contextuality, closeness to problem (401)	Cost savings (501)	Aesthetics (601)
Formatting, presentation (102)	Subject description, classification, controlled vocabulary (202)	Comprehensiveness (302)	Flexibility (402)	Time savings (502)	Entertainment (602)
Mediation (103)	Subject summary, summarization (203)	Currency (303)	Simplicity (403)	Security (503)	Engagement (603)
Orientation (104)	Linkage/referral (204)	Reliability (304)	Transaction (404)	Safety (504)	Stimulation (604)
Order/ consistency (105)	Precision (relevant retrieved) over (retrieved) (205)	Validity (305)	Trust (405)		Satisfaction, rewarding, incentivizing (605)
Accessibility (106)	Selectivity (206)	Authority (306)	Feedback (406)		
Simplicity (107)	Order (207)		Community, social networking (407)		
	Novelty (208)		Individualization (408)		
			Localization (409)		
			Privacy (410)		

models such as 1-to-5 Likert-type scales. Scores can vary across scenarios and personae for the same information artifact. For example, the scores in one scenario of action and interaction could vary from one persona to another persona depending on the personae' specific needs. As noted by Scholl and colleagues, with TEDS, information artifact evaluations have become highly detailed and fine-grained.

The fourth and last building block of the framework, the TEDS procedure, structures the empirical investigation and consists of 13 steps (Scholl, *et al.*, 2011):

1 Determining the overall goal of the evaluative/comparative study including the research questions.
2 Tentatively identifying personae and scenarios.

3. Validating, verifying, and updating identified personae and scenarios via an adequate procedure interviews, focus groups, etc.
4. Identifying anchors points of reference.
5. Recruiting and training raters.
6. Evaluating one scenario for one persona performed by all trained raters individually.
7. Computing scores, and detecting order-of-magnitude variances.
8. Reconciling inter-rater variances.
9. Assigning study objects to raters: performing evaluations, writing up narratives.
10. Computing scores, and detecting order-of-magnitude variances.
11. Reconcile inter-rater variances.
12. Analyze scores and compare with narratives.
13. Determining and writing up results.

Sport organizations' websites viewed through the TEDS lens

One of the first studies that empirically incorporated the TEDS framework was an evaluation and comparison of the websites of the top-ten UEFA (UEFA10) football (soccer) teams (Scholl and Carlson, 2012). A brief overview of the study's findings is used here to illustrate the application of TEDS for evaluating sports websites.

In Scholl and Carlson's study, the evaluation and comparison was carried out not only within the UEFA10 group but five select Major League (ML5) sites were also used as external references, in order to have a broader perspective and points of reference. Only one persona was chosen for the analysis. The persona was defined by Scholl and Carlson as a female or male between the ages of 16 and 60. The scholars further defined the persona as a "supporter, fan, follower, or flâneur" and someone who was an "average computer literate with unrestricted access to the Internet", was "interested in at least one professional sports team", accessed a professional "sports team websites occasionally to frequently", and purchased "tickets or merchandise never or occasionally to regularly" (Scholl and Carlson, 2012, p. 412). While only a single rather generic persona was chosen for the analysis, a total of eight scenarios of action/interaction was identified: team news, player information, schedules and results, media download, game videos and interviews, leagues and other teams, merchandise/store, and ticketing. Interestingly, despite the differences in the structure of business models, these eight scenarios of action/interaction were equally found across the ML5 websites in North America and the UEFA10 websites in Europe.

Overall UEFA10 website performance

For each of the eight scenarios of action and interaction, at least two raters assessed every UEFA10 and each ML5 reference site. In each scenario, the raters evaluated the website and its functioning and assigned scores in each subcategory within TEDS. For all scenarios and for all categories, totals were computed leading to an aggregate scenario team total (ASTT) and an aggregate category team total (ACTT) for each UEFA10 or ML5 website. Obviously, the two totals add up to the same aggregate score. A second measure of website performance was a weighted average Likert score, which accounted for the unequal number of subcategories in the eight categories. The results reveal the edge that the North American ML5 websites used as a reference held over the European UEFA10 sites. The top three ranks were held by North American ML5 teams: The Red Sox (ASTT = 1308/average Likert score = 3.72), the

Seahawks (1198/3.40), and the NY Giants (1140/3.24) followed by five UEFA10 sites, FC Barcelona (1118/3.18), Manchester United (1120/3.18), Inter Milan (1090/3.10), Real Madrid (1074/3.05), and Arsenal FC (1074/3.05). The two remaining North American ML5 teams followed in ninth (LA Lakers, 1072/3.04) and tenth place (Seattle Sounders, 1041/2.96). Chelsea FC, FC Bayern Munich, Liverpool FC, Juventus Turin, and AC Milan populated the bottom of the ranking table. Furthermore, the score range was far narrower for the reference sites than for the UEFA10 sites. The average score of the North American ML 5 (1152) is higher than the top scorer UEFA10 site, Manchester United (1120). The high average score for ML5 sites indicates a fairly high average quality of the ML5 reference sites compared with the UEFA10 sites (Scholl and Carlson, 2012).

With respect to the scores, the purposefully selected ML5 reference sites outperformed on average their UEFA10 counterparts by 16 percent based on ACTT scores and some 17 percent based on the average Likert score.

Top-scoring UEFA10 and ML5 teams

The two top scorers in the two groups were FC Barcelona (UEFA10) with an average Likert score of 3.18 and the Boston Red Sox (ML5) with and average Likert score of 3.72, which was the highest score for all teams in the sample. The per-team analysis and comparison was performed for (a) the eight scenarios of action and interaction, and (b) for all TEDS sub-categories in the six categories of use across all eight scenarios. While the scores in the scenario perspective indicate the relative performance for this particular scenario of action and interaction, the scores for the categories of use highlight the website's performance relative to a human actor's particular needs, for example, in terms of performance, quality, or ease of use.

In the scenarios of action/interaction, the Red Sox outperformed FC Barcelona based on average Likert scores in five of eight scenarios: game/video/interviews (Red Sox = 3.95 versus FC Barcelona = 1.69), media downloads (3.45 vs. 2.14, player info (3.79 vs. 3.61), schedule and results (3.86 vs. 3.77), and team news (3.77 vs. 3.55), while FC Barcelona had higher scores in three scenarios, league and other teams (FC Barcelona = 3.55 versus Red Sox = 3.47), store and merchandizing (4.00 vs. 3.88), and ticketing (4.05 vs. 3.55). It is an interesting twist that FC Barcelona held the two highest of all scores in the comparison (4.05 and 4.00) and that these scores were earned in the two transaction-oriented (e-commerce) scenarios. One might have assumed a reversed result given the general North American "savviness" in e-commerce matters (such as Amazon.com, E★Trade, eBay).

In terms of categories of use, the superiority of the Red Sox site over FC Barcelona's is more salient. In nine of ten categories, the Red Sox site outperformed their counterpart in terms of average Likert scores, that is, adaptability (Red Sox = 3.56 vs. FC Barcelona = 2.94), ease of use (4.14 vs. 3.50), noise reduction (4.27 vs. 3.46), performance (3.80 vs. 3.21), pleasing (3.85 vs. 3.45), profiling (2.76 vs. 2.13), quality (4.51 vs. 3.86), reviews (2.59 vs. 1.81), and transaction processing (3.13 vs. 2.87). Only in the category of localization, FC Barcelona's site was scored higher (3.10) than the Red Sox site (2.30). Please note that Scholl and Carlson (2012) disaggregated the categories of "adaptability" and "affection" so to separately analyze "localization," "transaction processing" (adaptability) and "reviews" and "profiling" (pleasing/affection). Interestingly, category-wise transaction processing shows a lower performance for the FC Barcelona site than for the Red Sox site despite the higher scoring of the FC Barcelona site in two transactional scenarios (store/merchandizing and ticketing). It must be noted that other scenarios also contain transactional elements so that overall the transactional experience appears to be superior for the Red Sox site.

As is evident from the presentation above, the Red Sox is the top scorer site in the entire sample. With an ACTT score of 1308 its website was rated 26 percent above the sample average score of 1041 and a staggering 33 percent higher than the UEFA10 average. With regard to categories of use, the Red Sox received the highest individual score of any team for quality (4.51) followed by high scores in noise reduction (4.27) and ease of use (4.14). The lowest scores were observed for localization (2.30), reviews (2.59), and profiling (2.79).

While FC Barcelona's ACTT score of 1118 is three percent below the ML5 average of 1152, it is also 13 percent above the UEFA10 average. As reported FC Barcelona's ticketing (4.05) and store merchandising (4.00) are exceptional, even with regard to the Red Sox. FC Barcelona's website also showed some fairly low scores for games/videos/and interviews (1.69) and for media downloads (2.14).

The scenario of action and interaction focus

By and large, the scenarios' rank similarly between ML5 and UEFA10 sites with (1) store and merchandizing on top, with average Likert scores for ML5 = 3.42 and for UEFA10 = 3.46, (2) player information (3.45/3.16), (3) team news (3.39/3.23), (4) schedule and results (3.38/3.08), (5) game video interviews (3.37/2.02), (6) ticketing (3.29/2.85), (7) media downloads (3.07/2.28), and (8) league and other teams (2.79/2.32). Furthermore, with 2.96 on a 1-to-5 scale the average Likert score for all teams and all scenarios is relatively high, suggesting that the visitors generally find what they expect when visiting UEFA10 and ML5 websites. However, for the eight scenarios the ML5 average (3.27) is well above both the overall average (2.96) as well as the UEFA10 average (2.80).

Some scenarios of action and interaction, such as store and merchandizing, team news, player info, schedule and results, and ticketing meet visitors' expectations better, or even far better than others such as media downloads, league and other teams, and game and video interviews. Interestingly, the highest average scenario score (3.46) was found for UEFA10's store/merchandising. Overall, the average scenario scores suggest that the ML5 reference sites more closely meet visitors' expectation than the UEFA10 websites.

The category focus

Unlike the scenario focus, which is action and interaction focused (that is, what human actors want to do), the category focus sheds light on how the information artifact (for example, the website) adds value to serving the human actor in her/his action and interaction. For example, the subcategory of browsing in the ease-of-use category might show across an entire website, or just a single scenario of action and interaction, how easily a human actor can navigate around a website's content and functions. Variances within and across sites, scenarios, and subcategories are detected in a fine-grained fashion.

Again, by and large, the category rank order was found much alike between ML5 and UEFA10. The category of (1) quality held the top rank with ML5 = 4.18 and UEFA10 = 3.57. Next came (2) ease of use (3.62/3.06), (3) noise reduction (3.60/3.04), (4) affection (3.39/2.81), (5) performance (3.38/2.90), (6) adaptability (3.30/2.76), (7) transaction processing (2.72/2.39), (8) reviews (2.42/1.85), (9) profiling (2.28/1.94), and (10) localization (2.00/2.34).

The average Likert score for all teams and all categories is 2.80 on a 1-to-5 scale; that is, visitors largely find sufficient added value in the team websites at least close to what they expect. Once more, the ML5 average (3.09) is higher than both the overall (2.80) and the UEFA10 (2.66) averages. With average scores of 2.23, 2.05, and 2.04, respectively, the categories of localization, profiling, and reviews fall short to meet visitors' expectations. On the other side, the category of quality stands out with an average score of 3.75 followed by the categories of ease of use (3.25), noise reduction (3.22), performance (3.06), affection (3.00), and adaptability (2.94).

The ML5 websites outperform the UEFA10 websites in seven of 11 categories of use meeting or exceeding human actors' use expectations. The ranges of average category scores for both ML 5 (2.18) and UEFA10 (1.72) are relatively large indicating that the websites still do not meet human actors' use expectations in some areas.

Conclusion

The previous sections illustrated the use of the TEDS framework in evaluating websites (and potentially other information artifacts) of prominent professional sport organizations. The framework helps to assess, compare, and rank single organizations' websites, as well as groups of organizations and their websites. The framework provides a fine-grained analysis of what human actors expect to find and what they might want to do with an information artifact such as a website (which refers to the scenarios of action and interaction), as well as how human actors are served by the information artifact (which refers to the categories of use). This type of analysis is conducted from an information perspective, in general, and the information management perspective (Detlor, 2010), in particular, as subsection of the information perspective, which complements, for example, the marketing perspective. However, the two perspectives are not mutually exclusive – on the contrary. Taken together, the two perspectives have the capacity to inform each other and to generate new insights. The information perspective provides insights about and detects changes in human actors' knowledge, human actors' behavioral changes based on information, human actors' information behavior, and organizational and societal changes (see, for example, Meadow and Yuan, 1997) tying it into other management perspectives (Macdonald, 1995). The information (management) perspective helps both information artifact designers and market researchers collect and interpret data on information vehicles, such as information artifacts (such as websites), and provides detailed insights on relative performance and on areas of relative strength and weakness of such information artifacts.

Sport organizations influence public opinion, inform and interact directly with their supporter community, and generate significant revenues from ticketing, media, and merchandise via their own websites and other web-based communication channels like Facebook, Twitter, and YouTube. With ever more bandwidth available over the Internet and smarter terminal devices such as smart phones and smart pads, these media, transports, and devices will become increasingly more important to all commercial organizations including professional sports organizations.

However, the information perspective is not limited to evaluating and comparing information artifacts of sport organizations or to the TEDS framework. For a long time, superior information has become a competitive weapon in competitive sports. Those applications range from collecting and analyzing athletes' health data, competitors' strengths and weaknesses, their strategies and tactics, to devising game plans and set plays to name a few.

Information artifacts play important roles as indispensable carriers and facilitators of actionable information ready to be used in real time by human actors engaged in sports. In all that, the information perspective powerfully complements and connects other perspectives in sports management and communications.

References

Bevan, N. (1995). Measuring usability as quality of use. *Software Quality Journal*, 4 (2), 115–50.

Bødker, S. (2000). Scenarios in user-centred design – setting the stage for reflection and action. *Interacting with Computers*, 13 (1), 61–75.

Brown, M.T. (2003). An analysis of online marketing in the sport industry: User activity, communication objectives, and perceived benefits. *Sport Marketing Quarterly*, 12, 40–7.

Cain, L. P., and Haddock, D. D. (2005). Similar economic histories, different industrial structures: Transatlantic contrasts in the evolution of professional sports leagues. *Journal of Economic History*, 65 (4), 1116–47.

Carlson, J., Rosenberger, P. J., and Muthaly, S. (2003). Nothing but net! A study of the information content in Australian Professional Basketball websites. *Sport Marketing Quarterly*, 12, 184–9.

Case, D. O. (2002). *Looking for information: A survey of research on information seeking, needs, and behavior*. San Diego, CA: Academic Press.

Choo, C.W. (2002). *Information management for the intelligent organization: The art of scanning the environment* (3rd ed.). Medford, NJ: Information Today.

Dahlbom, B., and Mathiassen, L. (1993). *Computers in context: The philosophy and practice of systems design*. Cambridge, MA: NCC Blackwell.

Davis, F. D. (1989). Perceived usefulness, perceived ease of use, and user acceptance of information technology. *MIS Quarterly*, 13 (3), 319–40.

Delpy, L., and Bosetti, H. A. (1998). Sport management and marketing via the World Wide Web. *Sport Marketing Quarterly*, 7, 21–7.

Detlor, B. (2010). Information management. *International Journal of Information Management*, 30 (2), 103–8.

Detlor, B., and DeGroote, M. G. (2003). Internet-based information systems use in organizations: an information studies perspective. *Information Systems Journal*, 13 (2), 113–32.

Evans, D. M., and Smith, A. (2004). The internet and competitive advantage: A study of Australia's four premier professional sporting leagues. *Sport Management Review*, 7 (1), 27–56.

Filo, K., and Funk, D. C. (2005). Congruence between attractive product features and virtual content delivery for internet marketing communication. *Sport Marketing Quarterly*, 14, 112–22.

Gleick, J. (2010). *The information: A history, a theory, a flood*. New York: Pantheon.

Google. (2012). Websites. *Google Trends*. Retrieved from http://trends.google.com/ trends/explore# q=websites.

Hartmann, J., Sutcliffe, A., and Angeli, A. D. (2008). Towards a theory of user judgment of aesthetics and user interface quality. *ACM Transactions on Computer–Human Interaction*, 15 (4), article no. 15, 1–30. DOI: http://doi.acm.org/10.1145/1460355.1460357.

Hoover's Inc. (2010). *Professional sports teams and organizations*. Shorthills, NJ: Hoover's Inc. Retrieved from http://www.hoovers.com/industry/professional-sports-teams-organizations/1449-1.html.

Klischewski, R., and Scholl, H. J. (2008). Information quality as the capstone of e-government integration, interoperation, and information sharing. *Electronic Government, an International Journal*, 5 (2), 203–25.

Macdonald, S. (1995). Learning to change: An information perspective on learning in the organization. *Organization Science*, 6 (5), 557–68.

Meadow, C. T., and Yuan, W. (1997). Measuring the impact of information: Defining the concepts. *Information Processing and Management*, 33 (6), 697–714.

Mumford, E. (1983). *Designing human systems for new technology: The ETHICS method*. Manchester: Manchester Business School.

Schmidt, A., Spiessl, W., and Kern, D. (2010). Driving automotive user interface research. *Pervasive Computing, IEEE*, 9 (1), 85–8.

Scholl, H. J., and Carlson, T. S. (2012). Professional sports teams on the web: A comparative study employing the information management perspective. *European Sport Management Quarterly*, 12 (2), 137–60. DOI: 10.1080/16184742.2012.670254.

Scholl, H. J., Eisenberg, M., Dirks, L., and Carlson, T. S. (2011). The TEDS framework for assessing information systems from a human actors' perspective: Extending and repurposing Taylor's value-added model. *Journal of the American Society for Information Science and Technology*, 62 (4), 789–804. DOI: 10.1002/asi.21500.

Schonfeld, E. (2010). Forrester forecast: Online retail sales will grow to $250 billion by 2014. *TechCrunch*, March 8. Retrieved from http://techcrunch.com/2010/03/08/forrester-forecast-online-retail-sales-will-grow-to-250-billion-by-2014/.

Shelton, T. (2003). Information technology. In T. Reilly and A. M. Williams (Eds.), *Science and soccer* (2nd ed., pp. 276–83). London; New York: Routledge.

Shneiderman, B. (1987). *Designing the user interface: Strategies for effective human–computer interaction*. Reading, MA: Addison-Wesley.

Taylor, R. S. (1982). Value-added processes in the information life cycle. *Journal of the American Society of Information Science*, 33 (5), 341–46. DOI: 10.1002/asi.4630330517.

Taylor, R. S. (1986). *Value-added processes in information systems*. Norwood, NJ: Ablex.

Venkatesh, V. (2000). Determinants of perceived ease of use: Integrating control, intrinsic motivation, and emotion into the Technology Acceptance Model. *Information Systems Research*, 11 (4), 342–65.

Wixom, B. H., and Todd, P. A. (2005). A theoretical integration of user satisfaction and technology acceptance. *Information Systems Research*, 16 (1): 85–102. DOI: 10.1287/isre.1050.0042.

30

COMMUNICATING THROUGH SPORT VIDEO GAMES

Patrick Walsh and Beth A. Cianfrone

Introduction

In the last decade, the video game industry has experienced a tremendous amount of growth. In 2000, sales of computer and video game items in the United States were estimated by the Entertainment Software Association (ESA) at US$5.5 billion (ESA, 2011). Just ten years later that figure has increased to US$15.9 billion, with the total industry estimated to be valued at over US$25 billion (ESA, 2011). The number of households playing video games and the demographic reach of the industry also remains strong. According to the ESA, 72 percent of American households play computer or video games. The average game player is 37 years old, while 18 percent of gamers are under the age of 18, 53 percent between 18 and 49, and 29 percent are above the age of 50.

Within the video game industry, sport video games (SVGs) are one of the most popular genres, represented by 16.3 percent of the total game units sold in 2010 (ESA, 2011). This ranks as the second most popular game genre behind action games (21.7 percent), and ahead of genres such as shooter games (15.9 percent), family entertainment (9.1 percent), and adventure (7.5 percent). In terms of games sold, two of the top ten selling games in 2010 were SVGs: EA SPORTS *Madden NFL 11* and 2K SPORTS *NBA 2K11*.

Owing to the growth of the video game industry and the popularity of SVGs, many corporations are now utilizing SVGs as a communication and promotional tool. Specifically, corporations are engaging in what is commonly referred to as in-game advertising (IGA) by placing their brand names and virtual advertisements within video games. This chapter provides an overview of the practice of IGA. In particular, the characteristics of the SVG consumer are examined, followed by a discussion of the history and growth of IGA and the common types of IGA executions. Practical and applied research are then be reviewed which has examined how effective IGA is in generating brand awareness, and impacting attitudes and purchase intentions of the brands which are advertising within the SVGs.

The SVG consumer and motivation

Prior to engaging in any form of communication effort (such as advertising, promotions, sponsorship) it is important that corporations understand the market which they will be targeting. This is no different for corporations that place IGA within SVGs. This includes understanding the demographic and psychographic characteristics of the sport video gamer and why consumers play SVGs. This information may benefit the communication process in terms of advertising specific game attributes which may drive more gamers to consume, and/or grow the brand of the leagues and those advertising within the games.

While there are some variances in their demographic profile, research has indicated that the SVG player is typically a highly educated male between the age of 18 and 30 who plays SVGs for approximately eight hours per week (Kim, Walsh, and Ross, 2008). In addition, as noted by Kim and colleagues, SVG players tend to be highly identified sport fans that are engaging in other sport consumptive behaviors. Specifically, SVG players are highly likely to watch sports news on TV, read the sports section of the newspaper, talk about sports with others, and watch sports events on TV (Kim, *et al.*, 2008). This is important for companies to understand, as it provides some evidence that IGA in SVGs can be utilized as a communication tool to reach loyal sport fans.

In addition to understanding who the SVG player is, gamer motivation has been studied to determine the psychological factors that drive a gamer to consume an SVG. Kim and Ross (2006) developed the Sport Video Game Motivation Scale (SVGMS) based on the uses and gratifications theory. They determined that there are seven factors that influence gamers: social interaction, fantasy, sport knowledge application, enjoyment, diversion, competition, and identification with the sport. The social element of gaming includes participating to spend time with others (either online or in person). Fantasy represents a gamer's ability to fulfill a role in a fantasy environment, such as simulating being a coach or player. Sport knowledge application describes a gamer's ability to utilize and show off sport knowledge within the game. Others play for the pure entertainment value (the enjoyment factor) or to avoid the daily grind of life (that is, diversion). Competition encompasses the concept of playing against another person or against the game. Finally, gamers can be motivated to play because they identify with a sport (for example, baseball fans who are motivated to play the 2K SPORTS *MLB 2K* series). Cianfrone, Zhang, and Ko (2011) confirmed the original SVGMS and added the factor of team identification as a motive, suggesting some gamers may play because they are highly identified with a team. For example, if someone is highly identified with Real Madrid, s/he may be motivated to play an EA SPORTS FIFA game, to play as her/his favorite team within the game and see different features of her/his team within the game.

Because online gaming is somewhat different than traditional single-player or multi-player gaming, Kim, Ko, and Ross (2007) determined that online gamers have slightly different motives to play and created the Online Sport Video Game Motivation Scale. The motives most salient to online gamers included: socialization, fantasy, entertainment, knowledge application, and competition. Whether considering placing IGA in online or traditional console-based gaming, gaming publishers and advertisers can benefit from knowing the motives of their consumers. Gaming publishers can design game elements to optimize and match the motives of gamers. For instance, for those who play for the competition, games that provide many competitive levels or various modes are more attractive. SVGs with team related aspects, like realistic crowd noises or uniforms, may match a person's interest in identification with her/his favorite team. Advertising campaigns for the games can highlight game attributes that feature the entertainment value or socialization options. IGA can also be matched with specific portions of the games that feature competition or sport knowledge application. For example, advertising during a "player of the game" feature or when statistical highlights are shown during halftime of a football video game may reflect the competitive or sport knowledge application aspect of the game.

In-game advertising

History and growth of in-game advertising

While the use of IGA in sport video games has become commonplace in the last decade (Clavio, Kraft, and Pedersen, 2009), there are some historical examples of companies using video games for their communication and marketing efforts. For instance, in 1978 an advertisement for an upcoming game (*Pirate Adventure*) was placed in another computer game which was called *Adventureland*, and in 1983 Anheuser-Busch placed their brand in a game titled *Tapper* (ESA, 2012). Further examples included licensed games such as one developed for Town and Country Surf Designs (T&C Surf Hawaii, 2010) and more traditional IGA such as Adidas placing a sideline billboard in EA SPORTS *FIFA International* soccer game in 1994 (MobyGames, 2011).

While there were sporadic examples of IGA from the late 1970s to late 1990s, only recently has IGA been viewed as a viable communication tool (Walsh, Kim, and Ross, 2008). This has been fueled by the potential positive business-orientated results which will be discussed later in this chapter, the increase in SVG sales, the ability to reach an engaged audience with desirable demographics (Arrington, 2003; Lefton, 2005), and the increase in corporate spending on IGA. One study has estimated that spending on IGA would reach US$969 million by 2011 (Mermelstein and Fielding, 2007), and Massive Inc., an IGA company, estimates that spending may reach US$1 billion globally by 2014 (ESA, 2012). In addition, with the advances in game technologies, IGA has moved beyond the simple static advertisement into more advanced types of ad placements.

Types of IGA executions

The most common and traditionally used form of IGA is what is known as a static advertisement. In this type of IGA, a brand is placed somewhere within a game and will remain unchanged throughout the game. Such placement typically is found in the form of a billboard, signage in the background of the game, or attached to a game feature (for example,"The Doritos Player of the Game"). For instance, in EA SPORTS *NHL 12* a number of companies ranging from automobile manufacturer Honda to hockey equipment company CCM have placed static advertisements along the dasherboards of the ice rink. These advertisements do not change and are consistent throughout gameplay.

With online gaming came the introduction of dynamic advertising within SVGs. Dynamic advertising is similar to static advertising in that it typically takes place in some sort of signage within the game. However, unlike static advertising, dynamic advertising can change at any time and an advertising agency or game developer is able to alter the advertisements in real time. In other words, the brand that is advertised in a particular point in the game may change from hour-to-hour, day-to-day, and so on. With the development of dynamic advertising companies now have the ability to develop very targeted IGA campaigns down to a specific geographical region or even time of day. For instance, during his 2008 presidential campaign, then presidential candidate Barack Obama placed early voting advertisements within a series of SVGs. Because of the functionality that dynamic advertising provides the campaign was able to place these advertisements only in states that were considered to be swing states for the election, and only during a specified time during the evening hours (Walsh, Clavio, Mullane, and Whisenant, 2009).

Another form of IGA is known as interactive advertising. This occurs when brands place their products within the games and those products are then required for game play. For instance, in the EA SPORTS *Tiger Woods PGA Tour* videogame series, gamers are able to choose what type of golf equipment and apparel they would like their golfer to use within the game. Within the "Pro Shop" feature in the game, one can choose to utilize actual golf clubs from brands such as Calloway, Nike, Cleveland, and Ping. Gamers are also able to choose actual branded products in categories such as hats, polos, shoes, watches, and sunglasses to name a few. This type of interactive IGA provides for a high level of engagement between the gamers and the brands which are utilized in the game in that it provides companies with a way for consumers to utilize their products within a virtual world (Clavio and Walsh, 2009).

Finally, a relatively new IGA advertising execution has taken traditional static advertising and added an additional communication feature. With the traditional form of static advertising, a gamer would simply be exposed to the visual cue of the corporate brands logo in the advertisement. In many instances, those static visual cues are now being accompanied by verbal cues which make mention of the brand name. Examples of IGA featuring verbal cues can be found in EA SPORTS *Madden 11*. Within this particular game, when the scoring drive statistics are shown, a Verizon logo appears on screen. However, as opposed to just having the logo placed on screen the in-game announcer would accompany the logo with the statement "This scoring drive brought to you by Verizon, the official wireless carrier of the NFL." Another example in the game appears when the "Red Zone" statistics are displayed with the Old Spice logo. At this point the announcer says "These Red Zone statistics brought to you by Old Spice; smell like a man, man." The inclusion of verbal cues within IGA provides another way to potentially draw attention to the brand to impact awareness (Walsh, Zimmerman, Clavio, and Williams, 2011). In addition, this is another way to communicate a brand sponsorship with a sport property, such as Verizon did in the example above, or to promote a company's brand messaging as Old Spice does with their "smell like a man" positioning statement within the game.

Effectiveness of in-game advertising

As companies continue to spend more of their promotional budgets on IGA, the need exists to understand the effectiveness of this practice from a business perspective. As such, research has begun to examine the effectiveness of this practice with a focus on the impact of IGA on the key areas of brand awareness, attitude formation and change, and purchase intentions.

Brand awareness

As IGA has increased considerably in recent years (Clavio, *et al.*, 2009), companies have realized the opportunity that exists to increase brand awareness of their brands through IGA

(Lee and Faber, 2007). Awareness of brands that are placed within SVGs is typically measured with either brand recall or brand recognition techniques. In the IGA setting, brand recall is said to occur when an individual can recall a brand name that was advertised within the game without having any cues to assist her/him (Aaker, 1991). On the other hand, brand recognition requires an individual to be able to choose a brand from a list that s/he believes s/he saw in the game (Aaker, 1991).

A variety of studies have examined brand awareness levels within SVGs and found that IGA is successful at generating brand awareness levels generally in the range of 25–40 percent (Cianfrone, Zhang, and Ko, 2008; Nelson, 2002; Walsh, *et al.*, 2008; Yang, Roskos-Ewoldsen, Dinu, and Arpan, 2006). For instance, Nelson (2002) was the first to examine the impact of IGA on brand awareness levels and found that gamers were able to successfully recall 25–30 percent of brands which appeared within a racing game. This study also found that gamers were able to recognize brands which appeared in the game which they had no previous knowledge of prior to playing the game. Similar results were found by Yang, *et al.* (2006) and Cianfrone, *et al.* (2008), both of which found correct awareness levels of IGA to be approximately 40 percent for those that played a soccer game and an *NCAA Football* game, respectively.

While the previous studies examined the awareness levels of brands which just appeared within SVGs, Walsh, *et al.* (2008) compared awareness levels of IGA with traditional advertising within a televised sports contest. They found that recall was higher for brands that were advertised during the traditional communication outlet of the televised sports event, while there were no significant differences in the brand recognition rates between the IGA and the brands during the televised event. Finally, a recent study (Walsh, *et al.*, 2011) also found that the relatively new IGA execution of providing a verbal cue to go along with a static advertisement was successful at generating higher levels of brand awareness than just simply a static advertisement. Specifically, when provided with just a static advertisement with no verbal cue, those that had played the game were able to correctly identify approximately 30 percent of the brands after game play. However, when including a verbal cue to go along with the static advertisement, correct awareness levels rose to a significantly higher level of approximately 70 percent.

The results of these studies provide some evidence that SVGs are effective at generating brand awareness. However, there may be some factors which could influence a gamer's ability to correctly recall or recognize the brands within the game which are worth noting. For instance, a unique benefit to IGA when compared with traditional advertising during sporting events is that a fan may typically watch a sporting event one time, while a gamer will play a SVG on multiple occasions. SVGs then provide advertisers with the ability to have their brand viewed each time the gamer plays the game over a period of days, weeks, months, and so on.

While this is a benefit, the unique aspect of SVGs is that the game itself may not have the total attention of the gamer whereas a televised sports contest might. As opposed to just watching a game on TV, a SVG player must manipulate the game controller to advance within the game, thus using more mental processing, which may take away from the ability to process and recall the IGA. While this effect has not specifically been studied with IGA and SVGs, previous research would suggest that this would limit the gamer's ability to generate brand awareness for the brands which are advertised within the games (Eveland and Dunwoody, 2001; Southwell, 2005; Southwell and Lee, 2004). This would also indicate that more advanced or skilled gamers may have higher levels of awareness for IGAs than those that are not as comfortable with the games or its controls (Boyd and Lalla, 2009). Other factors that may influence awareness of IGA are the placement of the advertisements within the game and how realistic the advertisements are. For instance, a well-placed IGA execution, or one that is in clear view of the gameplay, will be more likely to be noticed (Chang, Yan, Zhang, and Lou, 2010). In addition, research has indicated that IGA is most effective when the advertisement is a fit into the game's environment and would be considered to add some realism to the game (Boyd and Lalla, 2009; Lewis and Porter, 2010). This is a benefit to IGA within SVGs, as an accurate and realistic image of any sporting event will include numerous advertisements throughout a sport venue or during a televised sports contest (Cianfrone, *et al.*, 2008; Cianfrone and Zhang, 2009).

Attitude formation and change

In addition to brand awareness, another factor that companies may wish to gain is the ability to form or change attitudes towards their brands which are advertised in SVGs. Consumers' attitude toward the brand (favorable/unfavorable, like/dislike, and so on) is a common measure of promotional effectiveness because of its relationship with predicting future purchase intention and consumption (Mitchell and Olson, 1981). If a gamer has a favorable attitude toward a brand advertised in an SVG, then the assumption is that s/he is more likely to purchase that brand.

There are many approaches used to explain change in attitude toward a brand. The mere exposure effect suggests the more often a consumer is exposed to an object (in this case, a brand), the more favorable the attitude (Zajonc, 1968). In SVGs, the frequent repetition of IGA may elicit a favorable attitude toward the advertised brand. The image transfer effect is used to explain the merging of an individual's attitudes toward an event and transfers this image to the event sponsor (Gwinner, 1997; Gwinner and Eaton, 1999). IGA may have the same effect, as gamers may feel positively about their favorite video game and subsequently feel the same about the brands that are part of the game. There also may be a good will feeling created if the gamers assume that the branding within an SVG generates revenue for the publisher, thus allowing them to produce better games.

In an effort to study brand attitude, attitude toward advertising is often an initial step (MacKenzie, Lutz, and Belch, 1986). Nelson (2002) found gamers' attitudes toward IGA were relatively positive, especially when the branding enhances the realism of the games (such as in SVGs) and if the ads fit within the game environment. A follow-up study noted that realistic ads with entertainment value were also favorable (Nelson, Keum, and Yaros, 2004). With SVGs visually mimicking televised sports, and the prevalence of advertising within sport, the placement and type of advertising (for example, on the sideboards of the EA SPORTS *FIFA* or *NHL* series or golf equipment in EA SPORTS *Tiger Woods PGA Tour*) seem to add to the realism, rather than intrude on the game. To this point, Lewis and Porter (2010) noted that, when compared with other game genres, gamers believed that IGA was most appropriate and realistic when used in SVGs. Whether the advertisements in SVGs are seen as annoying or viewed as part of the game, making the game more realistic, remains to be studied. However, the ability of IGA to facilitate attitude formation or reiterate brand attitude may be limited. Cianfrone, *et al.* (2008) found that the advertising within SVGs was insignificant in creating positive consumer attitudes when studying gamers who played a SVG with IGA compared with a game without advertisements. The type of products may have influenced the attitude toward brands, further justifying the importance of fit in these types of brand placements.

Purchase intentions

A final goal of communicating a brand through a SVG is influencing purchase intentions or consumption of the advertised brand. Studies on the effectiveness of IGA in prompting purchase intention are somewhat limited in the sport literature. A study on first-person shooter video games found a weak correlation between billboard signage advertisements within the game and purchase intentions (Chaney, Lin, and Chaney, 2004). While assessing awareness and attitudes, Cianfrone, *et al.* (2008) also examined the gamers' purchase intentions of the advertised brands. They found that IGA did not influence gamers' intention to purchase the advertised brands; however, previous attitudes toward the brands may have influenced the gamers' results, as well as the types of brands being advertised.

Further study by Cianfrone and Zhang (2010) examined the hierarchical relationships between gamers' motivation, consumption (game-play), and IGA effectiveness (such as brand awareness, attitudes, purchase intentions). Through a structural model analysis, they found that gamer motivation positively influenced gamer consumption; consumption in turn influenced awareness of the IGA brand; the awareness influenced the gamer attitude toward the brand; and brand attitude influenced purchase intentions of the brand. With this knowledge of the entire consumer behavior effects, practitioners can promote behavior intentions to drive consumption levels of both the games and purchase intentions of the advertised brands, which, in turn, could further benefit IGA effectiveness.

Conclusion

SVGs continue to be a popular form of entertainment and a unique means for companies to reach a coveted and captivated consumer. As with all advertising, the line of how much IGA is too much for sport video gamers remains to be determined, but at the present time gamers are open to IGA as long as it adds some sense of realism to the game. IGA has proven to have an impact on the awareness levels of the brands which are advertised within the games, while the findings on attitude formation, attitude change, and purchase intentions are still somewhat limited in this growing field of inquiry to make a final judgment on those effects. The future of IGA is reliant on maintaining pace with the improvement of technology, as the growth of online and handheld gaming continues and new and advanced forms of IGA are developed which could aid in reaching desired brand effects.

With better metrics available from online gaming, the ability to create cost-effective and targeted IGA campaigns, and a growing interest in the popularity and reach of SVGs, companies will continue to seek out IGA. Video game manufacturers must focus their attention on not only what types of IGA will impact brand awareness, but what may impact brand attitudes and purchase intentions. This will lead to a positive return on investment for their advertising partners, which will ensure that IGA remains a viable communication tool for advertisers and revenue generating option for the game manufacturers.

References

Aaker, D. A. (1991). *Managing brand equity*. New York: The Free Press.

Arrington, D. (2003). From gamers to fans? Video-game enthusiasts of today could morph into real-life devotees of professional leagues tomorrow. *San Diego Union-Tribune*, December 28: C1.

Boyd, G. and Lalla, V. (2009). Emerging issues in in-game advertising. GamaSutra, 11 February. Retrieved from http://www.gamasutra.com/view/feature/3927/emerging_issues_in_ingame_.php.

Chaney, I. M., Lin, K., and Chaney, J. (2004). The effect of billboards within the gaming environment. *Journal of Interactive Advertising*, 5 (1), 54–69.

Chang, Y., Yan, J., Zhang, J. and Luo, J. (2010). Online in-game advertising effect: Examining the influence of a match between games and advertising. *Journal of Interactive Advertising*, 11 (1), 63–73.

Cianfrone, B. A., and Zhang, J. J. (2009). Sport video game sponsorships and in-game advertising. In N. K. L. Pope, K.L. Kuhn, and J. Forster (Eds.), *Digital sport for performance enhancement and competitive evolution: Intelligent gaming technologies* (pp. 286–98). Hershey, PA: IGI Global.

Cianfrone, B. A., and Zhang, J. J. (2010). The influence of motives and consumption of sport video games on sponsorship effectiveness. Presentation conducted at the 8th Annual Sport Marketing Association Conference, New Orleans, LA, October 2010.

Cianfrone, B. A., Zhang, J. J., and Ko, Y. (2011). Dimensions of motivation associated with playing sport video games: Modification and extension of the sport video game motivation scale. *Sport, Business and Management: An International Journal*, 1, 172–89.

Cianfrone, B. A., Zhang, J. J, Trail, G. T., and Lutz, R. L. (2008). Effectiveness of in-game advertisements in sport video games. An experimental inquiry on current games. *International Journal of Sport Communication*, 1, 195–218.

Clavio, G., and Walsh, P. (2009). Tiger doll: An analysis of brand choice in sport video games. Presentation conducted at the 7th Annual Sport Marketing Conference, Cleveland, OH, October 2009.

Clavio, G., Kraft, P., and Pedersen, P. (2009). Communicating with consumers through video games: An analysis of brand development within the video gaming segment of the sports industry. *International Journal of Sports Marketing and Sponsorship*, 10, 143–56.

ESA. (2011). *Essential facts about the computer and video game industry*. Washington, DC: Entertainment Software Association.

ESA. (2012). In-game Advertising. Entertainment Software Association. Retrieved from http://www.theesa.com/games-improving-what-matters/advertising.asp.

Eveland, W. P., and Dunwoody, S. (2001). User control and structural isomorphism or disorientation and cognitive load? Learning from the web versus print. *Communication Research*, 28, 48–78.

Gwinner, K. (1997). A model of image creation and image transfer in event sponsorship. *International Marketing Review*, 14, 145–58.

Gwinner, K. P., and Eaton, J. (1999). Building brand image through event sponsorship: The role of image transfer. *Journal of Advertising*, 28 (4), 47–57.

Kim, Y., and Ross, S.D. (2006). An exploration of motives in sport video gaming. *International Journal of Sport Marketing and Sponsorship*, 8, 34–46.

Kim, Y., Ko, Y., and Ross, S.D. (2007). Online sport video gaming motivations. *International Journal of Human Movement Science*, 1 (1), 45–64.

Kim, Y., Walsh, P., and Ross, S.D. (2008). An examination of the psychological and consumptive behaviors of sport video gamers. *Sport Marketing Quarterly*, 17, 44–53.

Lee, M., and Faber, R. (2007). Effects of product placement in online games on brand memory. *Journal of Advertising*, 36 (4), 75–90.

Lefton, T. (2005). NFL deal has other leagues looking for a video-game score. SportsBusiness Journal, January 24, 7, 1.

Lewis, B., and Porter, L. (2010). In-game advertising effects: Examining player perceptions of advertising schema congruity in a massively multiplayer online role-playing game. *Journal of Interactive Advertising*, 10 (2), 46–60.

MacKenzie, S. B., Lutz, R., and Belch, G. E. (1986). The role of attitude toward the ad as a mediator of advertising effectiveness: A test of competing explanations. *Journal of Marketing Research*, 23, 130–43.

Mermelstein, E., and Fielding, M. (2007). Virtually surrounded by ads. [Graphic depicting eMarketer study of projections of future revenue from In-game advertising]. *Marketing Management*, July/August, 16: 6.

Mitchell, A. A., and Olson, J. C. (1981). Are product attribute beliefs the only mediator of advertising effects on brand attitude? *Journal of Marketing Research*, 18, 318–32.

MobyGames (2011). FIFA International Soccer. [Screenshots depicting 1994 version of EA Sports' FIFA International Soccer]. Retrieved from http://www.mobygames.com/game/fifa-international-soccer/screenshots].

Nelson, M. (2002). Recall of brand placements in computer/video games. *Journal of Advertising Research*, 42, 80–92.

Nelson, M. R., Keum, H., and Yaros, R. A. (2004). Advertainment or adcreep? Game players' attitudes toward advertising and product placements in computer games. *Journal of Interactive Advertising*, 5 (1), 3–21.

Southwell, B. G. (2005). Between messages and people: A multilevel model of memory for television content. *Communication Research*, 32, 112–40.

Southwell, B. G., and Lee, M. (2004). A pitfall of new media? User controls exacerbate editing effects on memory. *Journalism and Mass Communication Quarterly*, 81, 645–56.

T&C Surf Hawaii (2010). TandC Surf Hawaii: Our roots. Town and Country Surf Shop. Retrieved from http://tcsurf.com/roots/roots.aspx.

Walsh, P., Clavio, G., Mullane, S., and Whisenant, W. (2009). The effectiveness of political advertisements in sport video games. Presentation conducted at the North American Society for Sport Management Conference, Columbia, SC, May 2009.

Walsh, P., Kim, Y., and Ross, S.D. (2008). Brand recall and recognition: A comparison of television and sport video games as presentation modes. *Sport Marketing Quarterly*, 17, 201–8.

Walsh, P., Zimmerman, M., Clavio, G., and Williams, A. (2011). Brand awareness of different advertising executions in sport video games. Presentation conducted at the 9th Annual Sport Marketing Conference, Houston, TX, October 2011.

Yang, M., Roskos-Ewoldsen, D. R., Dinu, L. and Arpan, L. (2006). The effectiveness of "In-game" advertising: Comparing college students' explicit and implicit memory for brand names. *Journal of Advertising*, 35 (4), 143–52.

Zajonc, R. B. (1968). Attitudinal effects of mere exposure. *Journal of Personality and Social Psychology*, 9, 1–27.

SECTION IV

Sociological aspects of sport communication

31

ENJOYMENT FROM WATCHING MEDIATED SPORTS

Four conceptual frameworks to understand the enjoyment construct

Kihan Kim and Lira Yun

Enjoyment is perhaps the central reason for people to be tuned in to mediated sports. By mediated sports, we refer to the relays of sport programs via communication media that not only deliver live sport games but also the replays of games to audiences. The communication media involved in the delivery process of sport programs are not limited to the traditional media such as television but also include new media such as personal computers and mobile communication devices, as long as they are capable of delivering moving images and sound to audiences. Sport programs may include those programs that are sport-related but are not necessarily the relays of sport games, such as sport news and documentaries. These non-game sport programs are excluded from the discussion in this chapter, although the theories and concepts presented in this chapter can be applied to understand audiences' enjoyment from watching such non-game sport programs as well.

In this chapter, we provide theoretical frameworks to understand the nature of enjoyment from watching mediated sports. We focus on the nature of the enjoyment construct, rather than explicating the antecedents and consequences of enjoyment. This is because, without a clear conceptual understanding of the enjoyment construct, it is difficult to examine any causal relationship among factors that either predict or are derived from the audiences' enjoyment from watching mediated sports. Yet, there have been few attempts in prior research to provide theoretically sound conceptualization of the enjoyment construct, especially in sport communication literature. We attempt to fill this gap by presenting theoretical frameworks that help readers understand the enjoyment construct in the sport communication context.

We first present a simple classification scheme for different types of sport contests, as prior research suggests that people may enjoy different aspects of mediated sports from different types of sport games, just as varying motivations are associated with different genres of television programs. Next, we present four frameworks, drawn from the literature of entertainment research, that help us conceptualize the enjoyment construct. In the concluding section, an overall discussion of the four theoretical perspectives is presented.

Classifications of mediated sports

People respond in unique ways to different genres of programs (Klimmt and Vorderer, 2009). Entertainment programs, for example, are mostly viewed in pursuit of hedonic benefits, or because of the thrilling experience at the stimulus level, whereas documentaries may be watched for reasons other than seeking fun. Even within the same genre of programs, the processes through which people enjoy the program may differ from one specific type of program to another (Oliver and Bartsch, 2010; Krakowiak and Oliver, 2012). That is, different types of programs are likely to appeal to different aspects of audience enjoyment. Literature in sport communication suggests that not all sport programs are alike (Raney, 2003a). Therefore, although it is true that the most prevalent reason for people to enjoy mediated sport is the attainment of fun and excitement, some specific types of sport programs may lead to enjoyment for reasons other than the hedonic benefits of the program. Thus, to have a fuller understanding of the enjoyment construct, we first need to classify sports into meaningful categories that help to understand various aspects of the enjoyment construct.

Among various approaches to classifying sports, we follow the classification scheme proposed by Sargent, Zillmann, and Weaver (1998). These scholars cluster-analyzed people's perceptions of 25 sports and categorized those sports into three fundamental types of sports on the basis of performance affinities: combative, stylistic, and mechanized sports. Combative sports are characterized by direct physical contact between competitors; stylistic sports are characterized by a striving for perfectionism in terms of form; and mechanized sports are characterized by tool use. Specifically, the combative sports emphasize not only physical strength and domination, but also agility and speed; they also feature confrontations in which one party wins at the expense of an opposing party. The combative sports are further classified by the intensity of contact: violent combative sports (such as football, boxing), and aggressive combative sports (such as basketball, baseball). Stylistic sports are characterized by such attributes as beauty, and elegance of body position and movement, but they also emphasize speed and agility. On the basis of risk and elegance attributions, stylistic sports are further classified into risky stylistic sports (such as gymnastics, skiing), and elegant stylistic sports (such as swimming, aerobics). Mechanized sports are characterized by tool uses for imparting motion to an object (such as golf clubs), moving objects in a gathering fashion (for example, fishing gear), setting performers themselves in motion (such as bicycles), or assisting in locomotion (for example, ropes for rock climbing). Mechanized sports are further classified by risk and activity attributions into non-risky mechanized sports (like fishing), active mechanized sports (like whitewater rafting), and violent mechanized sports (such as auto racing).

After classifying sports into the three types described above (that is, combative, stylistic, and mechanized sports), Sargent, *et al.* (1998) found that males tend to report greater enjoyment for combative sports featuring violence and aggressiveness (for example, football, soccer, boxing), whereas females report greater enjoyment for stylistic sports which highlight the stylistic movement of individual bodies in terms of beauty (for example, gymnastics, figure skating). Similar findings are also reported in other studies such as Zillmann (1995), who found that males tended to favor violent and risky sports more than do females, who preferred artistic sports instead. These findings suggest that different groups of people enjoy different aspects of sport programs. Thus, audience enjoyment from watching mediated sports should be understood from a perspective broader than simply focusing on how people respond to the stimulating media content. The following section presents four perspectives on the enjoyment construct.

Four perspectives to understand enjoyment from mediated sports

The notion that individuals typically enjoy watching mediated sport is so evident (Nabi and Krcmar, 2004) because, if they did not enjoy it, the media coverage of sport would not have become a huge business today (Raney, 2003a). That is, if a person chooses and continues to view some mediated sport programs, it is assumed that, by definition, the person in some way enjoys the viewing experience (Oliver and Nabi, 2004). For this reason, much existing research has treated enjoyment as a "given." And, as a result, the concept of enjoyment itself has received much less scholarly attention (for example, Raney, 2003b) than other aspects of sport communication. Observation of recent literature on entertainment, however, shows a significant development in conceptualizing the enjoyment construct. We attempt to apply these perspectives to expand our understanding of the enjoyment construct in the mediated sport context. Major perspectives on understanding media enjoyment are reviewed according to the following four categories: hedonistic, tripartite, functional, and appraisal perspectives.

Hedonistic perspective

A vast amount of research in media enjoyment has taken a hedonistic model of enjoyment, which assumes that media users are hedonistically oriented agents, seeking cheerfulness or fun in their media usage (Vorderer, Klimmt, and Ritterfeld, 2004; Zillmann, 1988). From this perspective, the experience of and need for hedonic pleasure have been a central component of the enjoyment concept (Tamborini, Bowman, Eden, Grizzard, and Organ, 2010). Accordingly, media enjoyment has been generally understood as a pleasurable affective response to media contents and the experience associated with the media consumption (see, for example, Raney, 2003b; Raney and Bryant, 2002; Tamborini, 2003; Vorderer, *et al.*, 2004).

Similarly, Raney (2003b) conceptualizes enjoyment generally as the sense of pleasure derived from consuming media products, but he is careful to note that the exact nature of enjoyment has yet to be fully determined. This is because there have been various terms used interchangeably with, or as a proxy for, enjoyment, leaving the term enjoyment somewhat vague in academic research. For example, such concepts as liking (Zillmann and Bryant, 1985), attraction (Krcmar and Greene, 1999), appreciation (Oliver and Bartsch, 2010), and preference (Tamborini, Stiff, and Zillmann, 1987) have been used to infer the similar phenomena of enjoyable experiences of media consumption (Vorderer, *et al.*, 2004; Zillmann and Bryant, 1994).

The hedonistic perspective of enjoyment has been well reflected in the measurement scales adopted by various researchers. Enjoyment is often recorded with single-item measures in which respondents are asked to rate how much they enjoyed or liked the media offering (for example, Krcmar and Kean, 2004; Zillmann, 1989). Some researchers use multiple items to measure enjoyment (for example, enjoyable, entertaining, likeable) that then load on a single dimension (see, for example, Gan, Tuggle, Mitrook, Coussement, and Zillman, 1997; Krcmar and Albada, 2000). This approach generally offers greater statistical reliability, but the construct itself is not inherently better understood (Nabi and Krcmar, 2004) because component parts of enjoyment are never recognized or explicated (Tamborini, *et al.*, 2010). For this reason, Tamborini and colleagues noted that the "past research has generally relied on a tautological understanding of enjoyment defined vaguely as pleasure" (Tamborini, *et al.,* 2011, p. 1025).

Nevertheless, experiences of pleasure during and after media consumption experiences are undoubtedly one of the central facets in audience enjoyment from watching mediated sports

(Raney, 2003a). Thus, the criticism of the hedonistic perspective on enjoyment should not be taken as indicating incorrectness of the perspective, but rather as indicating that the hedonistic value alone, even in a mediated sport context, is not enough to capture the fuller aspects of the enjoyment construct.

Tripartite perspective

Despite the prevalence of the hedonistic perspective in understanding audience enjoyment, scholars have begun to take into account both affective and cognitive responses to understand enjoyment from media consumption (Nabi and Krcmar, 2004). According to this line of thought, enjoyable media experiences are considered to be made up of multiple subcomponents, such as affective and cognitive components, rather than to be outcomes of a single monolithic process of pleasure-seeking (Davidson, 2003).

Such an expansion of the concept is due in part to the empirical evidences suggesting the importance of cognitive appraisals for affective responses, as well as the notion that affective and cognitive structures are inter-dependent (Davidson, 2003; Roseman and Evdokas, 2004). In the media consumption context, for example, individuals' identification with fictional characters is considered to be an affective response, while their assessment of the overall themes of the media offering may involve cognitive processing (Raney, 2003b). With such a broad perspective on enjoyment, Nabi and Krcmar (2004) conceptualize enjoyment as attitude toward a media consumption experience, complete with affective, cognitive, and behavioral components – thus proposing a tripartite view of enjoyment, operating at an evaluative and an experiential level toward a program, or a specific element within a program.

It is important to note that Nabi and Krcmar's (2004) enjoyment-as-attitude perspective accounts for both the process of enjoyment (that is, fluctuations in enjoyment during media exposure), as well as more end-state assessments of enjoyment (that is, global assessment of various cognitive, affective, and behavioral responses to the media). As the scholars note, the process of enjoyment focuses on one's point-by-point evaluations of one's experience regarding various affective, cognitive and behavioral reactions to the stimuli during media exposure, whereas the end-state assessment indicates the global perceptions of enjoyment, based on the combined evaluations of the media consumption experience as a whole.

With respect to the end-state assessment of enjoyment perceptions, the three components (that is, cognitive, affective, and behavioral responses to media) could be understood as antecedent factors of the global perceptions of enjoyment, rather than seeing enjoyment as being made up of the three underlying components. Although Nabi and Krcmar (2004) did not articulate the issue of whether the three components are antecedents or subcomponents of enjoyment perceptions, it is clear from the relevant research that media-related enjoyment is a complex construct that includes references to multiple facets of media consumption experiences including affective, cognitive, and behavioral dimensions (Vorderer, *et al.*, 2004).

Functional perspective

The functional theory derives its name from the idea that individuals enjoy their media consumption experience to the extent that the media offering fulfills their underlying needs. Thus, enjoyment is understood as reflecting basic motives of the individuals that "function" in a certain fashion for those individuals. Building on functional theory developed in attitudinal research in the 1950s and 1960s, in the communication literature some recent scholars have attempted to explain media enjoyment as the satisfaction of intrinsic human needs. Specifically, Tamborini, *et al.* (2010) have examined the validity of defining entertainment enjoyment as the satisfaction of intrinsic needs, and have drawn attention to the value of including needs associated with psychological well-being identified in self-determination theory. The psychological well-being, according to self-determination theory (for example, Deci and Ryan, 2000), is related to the satisfaction of three basic intrinsic needs, which are autonomy (that is, feelings of volition when engaging in a behavior), competence (that is, a need for challenge and feelings of effectiveness), and relatedness (that is, a need to feel connected to others). Tamborini, *et al.* posit in their 2010 work that the more these three intrinsic needs are fulfilled by a media consumption experience, the more enjoyment an audience is likely to experience during and after the media consumption. Consistent with this view, the scholars demonstrated a strong association between enjoyment and the satisfaction of intrinsic needs in a video game context. These findings suggest that even the entertainment media such as video games can be enjoyed if the media consumption experience fulfills intrinsic human needs, aside from attaining hedonic benefits.

More recently, Tamborini, *et al.* (2011) applied Vorderer's (2009, as cited in Tamborini, *et al.*, 2010) two-factor model of media enjoyment to incorporate not only the non-hedonic needs, but also the hedonic needs, to explain media enjoyment. According to this view, the concept of enjoyment consists of a lower-order factor labeled enjoyment that focuses primarily on hedonic needs, such as the desire to seek pleasure, and a higher-order factor that centers on the satisfaction of the three intrinsic needs explicated by the self-determination theory above. In addition, Vorderer associated the satisfaction of the higher- and lower-order needs with distinct systems of cognitive and emotional processing, respectively. Consistent with the predictions, Tamborini, *et al.* found that satisfaction of either lower- or higher-order needs (or a combination of both) led to positive valuations of the media consumption experience.

It should be noted that the non-hedonic needs tested by Tamborini, *et al.* (2010, 2011) – the three intrinsic human needs (autonomy, competence, and relatedness) – and the hedonic needs do not represent a comprehensive list of human needs or motivations for watching mediated sports. According to Raney (2006), there are emotional motivations (such as entertainment, eustress, self-esteem, escape), cognitive motivations (such as learning, aesthetic), and behavioral and social motivations (such as release, companionship, group affiliation) for mediated sports consumption. Therefore, all of these motivations could be interpreted within the functional perspective on enjoyment.

Appraisal perspective

Media enjoyment can be understood based on appraisal theories of emotion (for example, Bartsch, Vorderer, Mangold, and Viehoff, 2008). According to these theories, emotional gratifications are the outcomes of cognitive appraisals of events and situations that cause specific reactions in different people (Bartsch, Mangold, Viehoff, and Vorderer, 2006). From this perspective, positive appraisals of a media consumption experience result in the feelings of enjoyment (Bartsch, *et al.*, 2006; Scherer, 2001; Vorderer, *et al.*, 2004).

Mangold, Unz, and Winterhoff-Spurk (2001, as cited in Bartsch, *et al.*, 2006) proposed that media use is a complex situation that allows for multiple appraisals. That is, there are multiple objects of appraisals in the media consumption situations, such as the media content, the reception situation, and the emotions elicited during the media use. Appraisal theorists such as Scherer (2001) and Lazarus (1991) identified various dimensions within which emotion-eliciting appraisals are made. Applying these dimensions of appraisals, Bartsch, *et al.* (2006) suggest that media consumption experiences are appraised at the stimulus level (for example, novelty, pleasantness), the schema level (for example, goal conduciveness), and the symbolic meaning level (for example, individual and social norms).

Accordingly, people appraise a series of evolving media events and situations at those three levels of appraisals, which result in distinct emotional gratifications; these are called the primary emotions because they are the direct outcomes of appraising the media content and experience while consuming the media (Bartsch, *et al.*, 2006). Because multiple appraisals are made during media consumption, primary emotions may conflict with each other, such as when one likes the play of a specific athlete, but the preferred player eventually loses the game. After an exposure to a given media offering is complete, according to Bartsch and colleagues, people then perform a holistic appraisal of the overall media consumption experience. This is done by appraising the various emotions elicited while consuming the media offering. The outcomes of such a holistic appraisal are called meta-emotions, because the object of appraisal is the primary emotions that are formed while consuming the media, with the same set of appraisal criteria that give rise to the primary emotions (Bartsch, *et al.*, 2006). From this perspective, media experience that elicits positive emotions from favorable appraisals of media consumption experiences is considered to be enjoyment (Oliver and Bartsch, 2010).

A careful review of the three levels at which people appraise media consumption experiences (that is, the stimulus, schema, and symbolic meaning levels) indicates that the three perspectives on enjoyment previously discussed (hedonistic, tripartite, and functional perspectives) can be interpreted from the perspective of appraisal theories. Specifically, the stimulus-level appraisal of the media offering essentially indicates that people enjoy the media offering to the extent that it generates pleasant emotions; this is consistent with the hedonistic perspective on enjoyment. Also, the schema-level appraisal is concerned with the goal conduciveness of the media consumption, which is consistent with the functional perspective on enjoyment. Finally, the tripartite perspective on enjoyment can be explained with the appraisal perspective, because the process of appraising media consumption experiences involves cognitive and affective processing, as well as the emotions elicited from the media viewing behaviors, which the tripartite perspective considers as constituting or predicting the enjoyment perceptions. In this sense, the appraisal perspective provides a broader scope of enjoyment construct than the remaining three perspectives (the hedonistic, tripartite, and functional perspectives) on enjoyment.

Discussion

This chapter reviews four different perspectives for understanding the enjoyment from watching mediated sports. The perspectives include the hedonistic, tripartite, functional, and appraisal perspectives. Although each perspective provides somewhat different conceptualizations of the enjoyment construct, they should be considered to be complementing each other, rather than viewing them as competing or conflicting frameworks. This is because media-related enjoyment is a complex construct involving affective and cognitive processing of media stimuli and messages, so that each perspective should be viewed as focusing on or having advantages in explaining a specific facet of the enjoyment construct. For example, the hedonistic perspective is the most efficient approach to understand enjoyment when the media offerings – such as telecasts of football games – primarily possess hedonic features. Likewise, the functional theory is most appropriate when focusing on the motivations behind watching mediated sport; such motivations include the entertainment motive, learning and aesthetic motive, and group affiliation motive, among others (Raney, 2006). The tripartite and appraisal perspectives are well suited to account for the global perceptions of enjoyment, by taking into consideration the meta-level processing of or the combination of affective, cognitive, and behavioral responses to the media consumption experience.

The review of prior conceptualizations of enjoyment suggests that one of the distinguishing features of enjoyment as different from other related terms is that the enjoyment construct not only accounts for individuals' reactions to the media content, but also captures the more experiential nature of the viewing dynamic (Nabi and Krcmar, 2004). That is, as noted by Nabi and Krcmar, there are two underlying sources of valence in the enjoyment construct: the media content and the fuller media experience including situational and contextual elements. As noted above, the experiential nature of enjoyment helps distinguish enjoyment from other related terms such as liking and preference. For example, whereas liking only reflects reactions to media content, enjoyment captures both the reactions to the media content and the viewing experiences. Thus, although it is reasonable to assume that an individual simultaneously likes and enjoys mediated sport consumption, it is possible for one to like media content but not enjoy the experience of viewing it due to, for example, an uncomfortable social context in which one is exposed to the mediated sports (Nabi and Krcmar, 2004). Similarly, preference suggests assessments made prior to, rather than during, the viewing experience (for example, Tamborini, *et al.*, 1987); therefore, preference is distinguished from the enjoyment construct, which as noted by Nabi and Krcmar (2004) accounts for the experiences during the media consumption. As such, one might prefer watching basketball games, but the advantages could be one-sided throughout the game, which may not be enjoyed by the viewer.

Prior research in enjoyment also suggests that it is not a single, fixed object such as a painting or sculpture that people enjoy, but, instead, it is a constantly evolving drama (for example, televised sporting games) and continued experience of a media offering that people enjoy. Therefore, there are point-by-point perceptions of enjoyment as the sport program unfolds, as well as the global or holistic perceptions of enjoyment after the media consumption experience is complete. The point-by-point enjoyment may or may not be consistent with the global perceptions of enjoyment, because the global enjoyment is the result of combining one's point-by-point perceptions of enjoyment, which the appraisal perspective of enjoyment refers to as the meta-processing. Accordingly, the enjoyment construct measured after the completion of media exposure, as found in many enjoyment studies, should be understood as the measures of global perceptions of enjoyment, unless the respondents of the studies are instructed to respond to a specific aspect of the media offerings.

In summary, four approaches (the hedonistic, tripartite, functional, and appraisal perspectives) to understanding the nature of enjoyment from watching mediated sports have been examined in the sections above, with each taking slightly different perspectives to address the enjoyment construct. The review of prior research in enjoyment indicates that the object of enjoyment not only includes the point-by-point perceptions of enjoyment as the media content evolves, but also includes the global perceptions of enjoyment after the completion of media exposure. In addition, it appears that there are multiple sources of enjoyment – the media content and the media consumption experience – which is one of the distinguishing features of the enjoyment construct. All of these indicate the importance of providing a clear operational definition of enjoyment in any empirical study. This chapter provides theoretically driven frameworks that future researchers can apply to conceptualize media enjoyment and to test causal relationships among variables that predict or are derived from the perceptions of enjoyment.

References

Bartsch, A., Mangold, R., Viehoff, R., and Vorderer, P. (2006). Emotional gratifications during media use: An integrative approach. *Communications*, 31 (3), 261–78.

Bartsch, A., Vorderer, P., Mangold, R., and Viehoff, R. (2008). Appraisal of emotions in media use: Toward a process model of meta-emotion and emotion regulation. *Media Psychology*, 11, 7–27.

Davidson, R. J. (2003). Seven sins in the study of emotion: Correctives from affective neuroscience. *Brain and Cognition*, 52 (1), 129–32.

Deci, E. L., and Ryan, R. M. (2000). The "what" and "why" of goal pursuits: Human needs and the self-determination of behavior. *Psychological Inquiry*, 11 (4), 227–68.

Gan, S. L., Tuggle, C. A., Mitrook, M. A., Coussement, S. H., and Zillmann, D. (1997). The thrill of a close game: Who enjoys it and who doesn't? *Journal of Sport and Social Issues*, 21 (1), 53–64.

Klimmt, C., and Vorderer, P. (2009). Media entertainment. In C. R. Berger, M. E. Roloff, and D. Roskos-Ewoldsen (Eds.), *The handbook of communication science* (pp. 345–61). Thousand Oaks, CA: Sage.

Krakowiak, K. M., and Oliver, M. B. (2012). When good characters do bad things: Examining the effect of moral ambiguity on enjoyment, *Journal of Communication*, 62, 117–35.

Krcmar, M., and Albada, K. F. (2000). The effect of an educational/informational rating on children's attraction to and learning from an educational program. *Journal of Broadcasting and Electronic Media*, 44 (4), 674–89.

Krcmar, M., and Greene, K. (1999). Predicting exposure to and uses of television violence. *Journal of Communication*, 49 (3), 24–45.

Krcmar, M., and Kean, L. G. (2004). Uses and gratifications of media violence: Personality correlates of viewing and liking violent genres. *Media Psychology*, 7 (4), 399–420.

Lazarus, R. S. (1991). *Emotion and adaption*. Oxford: Oxford University Press.

Mangold, R., Unz, D., and Winterhoff-Spurk, P. (2001). Zur Erklärung emotionaler Medienwirkungen: Leistungsfähigkeit, empirische Überprüfung und Fortentwicklung theoretischer Ansätze [Explaining emotional media effects: Efficiency, empirical testing, and further development of theoretical approaches. In P. Rössler, U. Hasenbrink, and M. Jäckel (Eds.), *Theoretische Perspektiven der Rezeptionsforschung* [Theoretical perspectives on media reception research.] (pp. 163–80). Munich, Germany: Reinhard Fischer.

Nabi, R. L., and Krcmar, M. (2004). Conceptualizing media enjoyment as attitude: Implications for mass media effects research. *Communication Theory*, 14 (4), 288–310.

Oliver, M. B., and Bartsch, A. (2010). Appreciation as audience response: Exploring entertainment gratifications beyond hedonism. *Journal of Communication*, 36 (1), 53–81.

Oliver, M. B., and Nabi, R. L. (2004). Exploring the concept of media enjoyment: An introduction to the special issue. *Communication Theory*, 14 (4), 285–7.

Raney, A. A. (2003a). Enjoyment of sports spectatorship. In J. Bryant, D. Roskos-Ewoldsen, and J. Cantor (Eds.), *Communication and emotion: Essays in honor of Dolf Zillmann* (pp. 397–416). Mahwah, NJ: Erlbaum.

Raney, A. A. (2003b). Disposition-based theories of enjoyment. In J. Bryant, D. Roskos-Ewoldsen, and J. Cantor (Eds.), *Communication and emotion: Essays in honor of Dolf Zillmann* (pp. 61–84). Mahwah, NJ: Erlbaum.

Raney, A. A. (2006). Why we watch and enjoy mediated sports. In A. A. Raney and J. Bryant (Eds.), *Handbook of sports and media* (pp. 313–30). Mahwah, NJ: Erlbaum.

Raney, A. A., and Bryant, J. (2002). Moral judgment and crime drama: An integrated theory of enjoyment. *Journal of Communication*, 52 (2), 402–15.

Roseman, I., and Evdokas, A. (2004). Appraisals cause experienced emotions: Experimental evidence. *Cognition and Emotion*, 18 (1), 1–28.

Sargent, S. L., Zillmann, D., and Weaver III, J. B. (1998). The gender gap in the enjoyment of televised sports. *Journal of Sport and Social Issue*, 22 (1), 46–64.

Scherer, K. R. (2001). Appraisal considered as a process of multilevel sequential checking. In K. R. Scherer, A. Schorr, and T. Johnstone (Eds.), *Appraisal processes in emotion* (pp. 92–120). New York: Oxford University Press.

Tamborini, R. (2003). Enjoyment and social functions of horror. In J. Bryant, D. R. Roskos-Ewoldsen, and J. Cantor, (Eds.), *Communication and emotion: Essays in honor of Dolf Zillmann* (pp. 417–43). Mahwah, NJ: Erlbaum.

Tamborini, R., Bowman, N. D., Eden, A., Grizzard, M., and Organ, A. (2010). Defining media enjoyment as the satisfaction of intrinsic needs. *Journal of Communication*, 60 (4), 758–77.

Tamborini, R., Grizzard, M., Bowman, N. D., Reinecke, L., Lewis, R. J., and Eden, A. (2011). Media enjoyment as need satisfaction: The contribution of hedonic and nonhedonic needs. *Journal of Communication*, 61 (6), 1025–42.

Tamborini, R., Stiff, J, and Zillmann, D. (1987). Preference for graphic horror featuring male versus female victimization: Individual differences associated with personality characteristics and past film viewing experiences. *Human Communication Research*, 13 (4), 529–52.

Vorderer, P. (2009). What do we want when we want narratives? *New Literacies Collaborative Research Site.* Retrieved from http://sites.google.com/a/newliteracies.co.cc/xin-su-yang-yan-jiu-qun/2009shu-wei-xushi-guo-ji-gong-zuo-fang/1-2-vorderer/What_do_we_want_when_we_want_narratives_v 1.3.doc.

Vorderer, P., Klimmt, C., and Ritterfeld, U. (2004). Enjoyment: At the heart of media entertainment. *Communication Theory*, 14 (4), 388–408.

Zillmann, D. (1988). Mood management through communication choices. *American Behavioral Scientist*, 31 (3), 327–40.

Zillmann, D. (1989). Aggression and sex: Independent and joint operations. In H. Wagner and A. Manstead (Eds.), *Handbook of social psychophysiology* (pp. 229–59). New York: Wiley.

Zillmann, D. (1995). Sport and the media. In J. Mester (Ed.), *Images of sport in the world* (pp. 423–44). Cologne: German Sports University.

Zillmann, D., and Bryant, J. (1985). Affect, mood, and emotion as determinants of selective exposure. In D. Zillmann and J. Bryant (Eds.), *Selective exposure to communication* (pp. 157–90). Hillsdale, NJ: Erlbaum.

Zillmann, D., and Bryant, J. (1994). Entertainment as media effect. In J. Bryant and D. Zillmann (Eds.), *Media effects: Advances in theory and research* (pp. 437–61). Hillsdale, NJ: Erlbaum.

32

GENDER AND SEXUALITIES IN SPORT MEDIA

Alina Bernstein and Edward (Ted) M. Kian

Much of the academic research on sport media over the past 30 years has examined the amount and types of coverage received by female athletes and women's sport when compared with content on men's sport and male athletes. Hundreds of studies have shown that sport media generally devote considerably more space and provide greater emphasis to male athletes regardless of the type of sport, level or age of competitors, form of medium, or host country of the media outlet (for example, Bruce, Hovden, and Markula, 2010; Duncan and Messner, 2000).

A possible reason for the importance placed upon men's sport by the media is a hegemonic masculine cultural and organizational structure that not only permeates most sport organizations and franchises, but is also prevalent within the overall ranks and hierarchy of the sport media outlets that determine which athletes and sports are worthy of coverage in capitalist societies (Knoppers and Elling, 2004; Pedersen, Whisenant, and Schneider, 2003).

Connell (2005) defined hegemonic masculinity as the configuration of gender practices that strengthen societal dominance of men who conform to and exhibit accepted forms of masculinities. The two most ostracized groups from hegemonic masculinity are women and openly gay men (Anderson, 2005). Many scholars have argued that sport and the mass media are two of the main forces helping to preserve hegemonic masculinity in the democratized world, often working in conjunction to uphold the status quo (see, for example, Duncan, 2006; Vincent, Kian, Pedersen, Kuntz, and Hill, 2010). An assumption from this is that only men truly comprehend sport, and thus only masculine, heterosexual men are qualified to work in sport media (Hardin, 2005).

Sport media as a gendered institution

Since its inception, the sport media industry has seemingly never been a hospitable vocation for female journalists. Sadie Kneller Miller may have been the first prominent female sport journalist in the United States, but she felt the need to publish under the byline SKM to disguise her sex (Creedon, 1994). The Associated Press estimated only about 25 women were employed as sports writers at US newspapers in the early 1970s (Creedon, 1994). In the most recent and comprehensive demographic survey of North American sports writers employed at newspapers and mainstream Internet sites, men comprised 94 percent of sports editors, 90 percent of assistant sports editors, 89 percent of reporters, 90 percent of columnists, and 84 percent of copy editors/designers (Lapchick, Moss II, Russell, and Scearce, 2011). Research has shown women make up only seven to ten percent of US television sports journalists (Etling, Young, Faux, and Mitchell, 2011; Sheffer and Schultz, 2007), and more than 80 percent of all sports-talk radio hosts are men (Nylund, 2004). Similarly, women comprised just seven percent of sport journalists in the Netherlands (Claringbould, Knoppers, and Elling, 2004), and 4–33 percent of Italian television sport journalists (Capranica and Aversa, 2002). Moreover, many women in television sport journalism are seemingly hired as sideline reporters largely for their sex appeal (Davis and Krawczyk, 2010). In addition, male dominance of sport journalism extends to the newest medium, as a survey by the John Curley Center for Sports Journalism (2009) revealed at least of nine of ten Internet sport bloggers are men.

Studies in numerous countries (for example, Australia, Canada, Great Britain, New Zealand, Spain, The Netherlands, US) have consistently shown that men author most sport media content regardless of medium (for example, Biscomp and Griggs, 2012; Crolley and Teso, 2007; Kian and Hardin, 2009; King, 2007; Strong and Hannis, 2007; Urquhart and Crossman, 1999). In all media, the percentage of female employees generally drops at the higher ranks of sport journalism, particularly among media gatekeepers or editors, who determine what sports and athletes receive coverage, meaning that a glass-ceiling effect is present for women trying to advance within the sport journalism profession (Hardin, 2005; Pfister, 2010). However, just hiring more female journalists or editors may not equate to more coverage of women's sport. Some researchers found evidence that many female sport journalists adopt masculine practices and tend to imitate their male colleagues' attitudes toward the importance of specific men's and women's sports (Tamir and Bernstein, 2011). As a result, Hardin and Shain concluded that the majority of women in sport journalism "seem to have adopted hegemonic values, making them more willing to accept their marginal status in the field and less likely to facilitate any change for the marginalized status of women's sports coverage" (Hardin and Shain, 2005, p. 804).

Cultivation theory and framing

Underlying the discussions in many of the studies mentioned above is the assumption that contemporary media preserve, transmit, and even create important cultural information. According to Gerbner and colleagues' cultivation theory, the more a viewer watches, the more that viewer will form expectations about reality based on the represented world, rather than the experienced one (Gerbner, Goss, Morgan, and Signorielli, 1994). Thus, the assumption is that how members of society see themselves, and how they are viewed and treated by others, is determined to a great extent by their media representations (Dyer, 1993). Such ways of thinking attribute a great – and in many cases harmful – influence to mass media, although it is now clear to many media researchers that these effects must be studied rather than just assumed to be present.

Also related to the notion that the mass media play an important role in shaping individual and public opinions is framing theory. The terms "frame" and "framing" are used in sociology, psychology, and others disciplines, while also being widely employed in media studies (Chong and Drucknam, 2007; Scheufele, 1999). Put simply, "media frames are principles of selection – codes of emphasis, interpretation and presentation," and "media producers routinely use them to organize media output and discourses, whether verbal or visual" (O'Sullivan, Hartley, Saunders, Montgomery, and Fiske, 1994, p. 122). In fact, these frames play an important, institutionalized part of encoding of media texts, and thus can potentially play a key role in structuring audience decoding.

Gender framing by sport media

The mismatch between femininity and athleticism has been discussed in the literature by many scholars because attributes associated with sport – physical strength, competitiveness, mental toughness, speed, and muscle – are also signifiers of masculinity, so much so that the concept of the *female athlete* can in itself be viewed as an oxymoron (O'Reilly and Cahn, 2007). The roles that the mass media play to uphold these views have been studied extensively over the last 30 years, although it should be noted that most research in this area was produced by scholars from Western societies.

A plethora of research findings overwhelmingly shows that female athletes are framed by media in a different manner than their male counterparts, although explanations as to how exactly this takes place and what can be done to change it differ. As for why this persists, the answer is at least partly provided by the studies noted above that concluded sport media is a gendered institution dominated by men.

The differences found in the ways that male and female athletes – as well as sports and tournaments – are framed by media show that the "the skills and strengths of women athletes are often devalued in comparison to cultural standards linked to dominant standards of male athletic excellence, which emphasize the cultural equivalents of hegemonic masculinity: power, self-control, success, agency, and aggression" (Sabo and Curry Jansen, 1992, p. 176). Indeed, whereas male athletes are "valorized, lionized, and put on cultural pedestals" (p. 174) and referred to as "men" or "young men," female athletes are infantilized through media framing as "girls" or "young ladies" (Koivula, 1999; Wensing and Bruce, 2003). This linguistically acknowledges the men's status as adults, even though the male and female athletes were generally of similar age.

Further gendered practices in sport media content were identified in a variety of studies conducted over the years; they include the "framing of women athletes according to their familial roles, the second-guessing of their emotional and/or psychological states, the selective application of masculine descriptors to successful female athletes" (Daddario and Wigley, 2007, p. 30). In fact, women athletes tend to be framed within traditionally feminine physical and emotional characteristics, namely as being small, weak, emotionally unstable, and dependent upon others, all of which situation them as no threat to the traditional gender order (Wensing and Bruce, 2003), and as emotionally and physically weaker than men (Bernstein, 2002).

In contrast, scholars found that men are regularly framed as active subjects, whereas women were framed as reactive objects (Whannel, 2002). Whereas male athletes tend to be described in terms of strengths and successes, female athletes' physical strengths are often neutralized by ambivalent language (Bernstein and Galily, 2008). Indeed, while the male performance is often linked with power metaphors such as war, the coverage of female athletes is often framed within stereotypes that emphasize their appearance and attractiveness rather than athletic skill (Duncan and Messner, 2000). Overall, the accumulating evidence amounts to the conclusion that sport media trivialize, and therefore undermine women's athletic achievements. This, in turn, constructs female athleticism not only as *other than* but as *less than* male athleticism (Kane and Greendorfer, 1994).

Even as early as the late 1990s, there was already some evidence that within traditional media coverage of major female sporting events, some changes for the better did take place. For example, a study on media coverage of the 1996 Olympic Games found that, for female athletes playing what are regularly constructed as female-appropriate sports, there was a trend in the print media accounts to focus more on describing their performance, namely providing details of what a gymnast does – "as opposed to simply describing how graceful she looked or how she has the personality to make her America's next sweetheart" (Jones, Murrell, and Jackson, 1999, p. 190). This can be explained by the framing technique called ambivalence, which refers to generally more positive media images of women athletes since the last 1990s, but they are (still) juxtaposed with images that undermine and trivialize the women athletes' efforts and successes (see discussion of *The New Rule* in Wensing and Bruce, 2003).

Importantly, the general coverage of sport and the ways in which it is related to gender have to take into account the rise of the Internet as a news source. This could have potentially presented a challenge to the ways in which women athletes and their competitions are framed by the (traditional) media. However, most of the relatively few studies that do exist to date show that there is still no major challenge emerging from the Internet to traditional findings (for example, Cooper, 2008; Kian, Mondello, and Vincent, 2009; Sagas, Cunningham, Wigley, and Ashley, 2000). In this context, the emphasis on appearance and attractiveness in the framing of women athletes seems particularly worthy of future investigation to see what – if any – influences the Internet has on media framing of female athletes.

Appearance and attractiveness

A consistent finding among researchers analyzing media portrayal of women athletes is that coverage is often framed within stereotypes that emphasize non-sport-related aspects of female athletes, including family relationships, personal life, personality, and most notably appearance and attractiveness rather than athletic skill (Clavio and Eagleman, 2010). Moreover, scholars have found that media tend to focus on the female athletes as sexual beings, rather than serious performers, thus helping to preserve hegemonic masculinity (Kane and Greendorfer, 1994; Mikosza and Phillips, 1999). For example, in their study on television coverage of the 1996 Olympic Games, Eastman and Billings found that "although instances of gender stereotyping were located, their presence was not as overwhelming as expected", and yet, even in this case, "as traditional gender stereotyping suggests, the descriptors applied to women athletes contained more commentary about physical appearance than the descriptors applied to men athletes" (Eastman and Billings, 1999, p. 163).

It is difficult to be optimistic regarding any potential challenges that the advent of the Internet might bring to mainstream media framing of female athletes. An interesting example to consider here is Rotas' (2010) analysis of top tennis players' personal websites, in part because media have long framed tennis as a female-appropriate sport (Vincent, 2004). Rotas (2010) found that while the men were framed as tennis players, the women presented themselves as sex objects available for the masculine gaze: pouting, semi-naked, and/or lying down in sexual positions (see also Choi, 2000). These results were also supported on the female athletes' websites through the style of clothing worn, the particular pose adopted, the nature of their gaze at the camera, and the angling of the camera, all of which resulted in a "soft porn" effect. Although these objectifying images are often used by mainstream media,

Rotas' work showed that top tennis players used their official websites to also post provocative photos of themselves, thus actively participating in their own trivialization and objectification.

Coverage and framing of sexuality

Through its content, sport media strengthen heteronormativity, which affirms heterosexuality as natural and desirable, while simultaneously creating an environment where gays and lesbians are not respected as equals (Calhoun, LaVoi, and Johnson, 2011). Sport has always been associated with males and continues to play a major part in defining desirable forms of masculinities – or even hypermasculinity – in most modern societies (Burstyn, 1999; Connell, 1990). Many young boys are indoctrinated into a masculine sporting culture through participation in contact sports, where strong pressure to partake comes from both a masculine peer culture and society as a whole (Anderson, 2002). In contrast, female sport participation on a large scale is a relatively new phenomenon in some Western societies, and still has yet to reach that point in many countries. A primary reason why women have been historically been discouraged from sport participation is an implicit or explicit fear that athletic females are more masculine and/or lesbian (Griffin, 1998).

The internal sport social culture, however, has been much worse for gay male athletes in team sports, which have historically been very intolerant of homosexuality (Messner, 1992). A recent, comprehensive study of Americans' sexual identity and behavior by Indiana University Center for Sexual Health Promotion (2010) found that eight percent of US adult males self-identified as gay. But no gay male athlete has ever publicly revealed his homosexuality while actively playing in any of the four major US professional men's team sport leagues. In fact, only six have announced they were gay after their careers, and none was a household name (Kian and Anderson, 2009). Similar trends are evident in men's team sports throughout the world, as no male player in any of the most popular professional soccer leagues in Europe (such as the English Premier League or La Liga) has ever publicly come out as gay through media during or even after his career.

The majority of prominent, open lesbians in sport competed in individual sports, highlighted by tennis legends, Billie Jean King, Martina Navratilova, and more recently Amélie Mauresmo (Chawansky and Francombe, 2011). In part because so few athletes have publicly revealed that they are gay, traditional Western media have historically ignored gays in sport, including open lesbians (Plymire and Forman, 2000). In doing so, they could simply be trying to avoid agitating some of their target audience, because research has shown that self-identified male sport fans and/or participants are more likely to maintain sexist and anti-gay attitudes than non-sporting men (Knight and Giuliano, 2003). The same differences do not hold true for women, who tend to be more accepting of gays regardless of their sport participation (Gill, Morrow, Collins, Lucey, and Schultz, 2006). And while no published research has yet to examine statistical representation of gays and lesbians within the sport media profession, the only known study that surveyed actual sports journalists' attitudes toward homosexuality showed that the vast majority believed that homophobia was a major problem in men's sport, but the majority of those same print journalists said they were not comfortable writing articles about gay athletes' sexual orientation (Hardin and Whiteside, 2009).

The limited scholarly research on sport media coverage and treatment of lesbian and gay athletes has mostly focused on content of openly gay athletes – particularly lesbians – although a few recent studies have examined the media coverage and reactions to athletes coming out in what has become a far more accepting Western world toward gays and lesbians in recent years (Staurowsky, 2012). Even after female cricketer Denisse Annetts filed a complaint that she was dropped from the Australian national team owing to her lesbianism, newspaper, radio, and television narratives on the story reinforced negative stereotypes and prejudices often used against female athletes (Burroughs, Ashburn, and Seebohm, 1995). In research about newspaper coverage of AIDS (and therefore somewhat about homosexuality, particularly in the 1990s), a textual analysis of content on basketball star Ervin "Magic" Johnson, diver Greg Louganis, and boxer Tommy Morrison found that most of the articles on Johnson and Morrison expressed shock that they contracted the HIV virus, while also explicitly noting that these two athletes proclaimed their heterosexuality (Dworkin and Wachs, 1998). However, as noted by Dworkin and Wachs, no article on the openly gay Louganis in any of the newspapers examined following his announcement noted that he had contracted a virus which, at that time, was associated predominately with gay men.

More recent studies have shown that the content of sport media has been far more positive toward openly gay athletes, although heterosexuality is still framed as the norm for sexual orientation (Butterworth, 2006). A pair of textual analyses on media coverage of former NBA player John Amaechi's revelation that he was gay found that both international and US sport media were very supportive of Amaechi, with prominent newspaper columnists' arguing that it is time for gays to be accepted in sport (Hardin, Kuehn, Jones, Genovese, and Balaji, 2009; Kian and Anderson, 2009). Similarly, Chawansky and Francombe (2011) found that media narratives on the self-outings of lesbian golfer Rosie Jones and bisexual basketball star Sherryl Swoopes were mostly framed in a positive light. The overall research on sport media coverage of gays and lesbians, though, is too limited to make any broad generalizations, although that will likely change in ensuing years.

Conclusion

Sport plays a major role in the development and maintenance of a masculine-dominant culture in most Western societies. In general, media have historically framed men's sports as important and of great significance, whereas women's sports receive minimal or only token media coverage. Moreover, when mainstream media do cover female athletes, content often focuses on their appearance and sex appeal. Men dominate all ranks of the sport journalism profession, which is permeated by a masculine, macho-oriented culture in the workplace. Sport media are a key contributor in attitude formation towards various sport and athletes, and thus media and sport combine to help uphold hegemonic masculinity throughout society. However, a few recent research studies indicate a subtle shift in the amount and type of media coverage given to female athletes, in part owing to more media options and specialization of coverage with the advent of the Internet. Regardless, male athletes still receive the vast majority of coverage and media framing remains stereotypical for male and female athletes. Gays and lesbians in sport have mostly been ignored by sport media, in part because so few have publicly declared their sexual orientation. However, both are expected to change in the future as society becomes more tolerant of homosexuality.

References

Anderson, E. (2002). Openly gay athletes: Contesting hegemonic masculinity in a homophobic environment. *Gender and Society*, 16 (6), 860–77.

Anderson, E. (2005). *In the game: Gay athletes and the cult of masculinity*. New York: State University of New York Press.

Bernstein, A. (2002). Is it time for a victory lap? Changes in the media coverage of women in sport. *International Review for the Sociology of Sport*, 37 (3–4), 415–28.

Bernstein, A., and Galily, Y. (2008). *Games and sets: Women, media and sport in Israel*. Bloomington, IN: Indiana University Press.

Biscomp, K., and Griggs, G. (2012). 'A splendid effort!' Print media reporting of England's women's performance in the 2009 Cricket World Cup. *International Review for the Sociology of Sport*, January 9. Online before print. DOI: 10.1177/1012690211432061.

Bruce, T., Hovden, J., and Markula, P. (2010). *Sportswomen at the Olympics: A global content analysis of newspaper coverage*. Rotterdam: Sense.

Burroughs, A., Ashburn, L., and Seebohm, L. (1995). "Add sex and stir": Homophobic coverage of women's cricket in Australia. *Journal of Sport and Social Issues*, 19 (3), 266–84.

Burstyn, V. (1999). *The rites of men: Manhood, politics, and the culture of sport*. Toronto: University of Toronto Press.

Butterworth, M. L. (2006). Pitchers and catchers: Mike Piazza and the discourse of gay identity in the national pastime. *Journal of Sport and Social Issues*, 30 (2), 138–57.

Calhoun, A. S., LaVoi, N. M., and Johnson, A. (2011). Framing with family: Examining online coaches' biographies for heteronormative and heterosexist narratives. *International Journal of Sport Communication*, 4, 300–16.

Capranica, L., and Aversa, F. (2002). Italian television sport coverage during the 2000 Sydney Olympic Games. *International Review for the Sociology of Sport*, 37 (3–4), 337–49.

Chawansky, M., and Francombe, J.M. (2011). Cruising for Olivia: Lesbian celebrity and the cultural politics of coming out in sport. *Sociology of Sport Journal*, 28, 461–77.

Choi, P.Y. L. (2000). *Femininity and the physically active woman*. London: Routledge.

Chong, D., and Druckman, J. N. (2007). Framing theory. *Annual Review of Political Science*, 10 (1), 103–26.

Claringbould, I., Knoppers, A., and Elling, A. (2004). Exclusionary practices in sport journalism. *Sex Roles*, 51 (11/12), 709–18.

Clavio, G., and Eagleman, A. N. (2011). Gender and sexually suggestive images in sports blogs. *Journal of Sport Management*, 25, 295–304.

Connell, R. W. (1990). An iron man: The body and some contradictions of hegemonic masculinity. In. M.A. Messner and D. F. Sabo (Eds.), *Sport, men, and the gender order: Critical feminist perspectives* (pp. 83–114). Champaign, IL: Human Kinetics.

Connell, R. W. (2005). *Masculinities* (2nd ed.). Berkeley, CA: University of California.

Cooper, C. G. (2008). NCAA website coverage: An analysis of similar sport team gender coverage on athletic department's home Web pages. *Journal of Intercollegiate Sports*, 1 (2), 227–41.

Creedon, P. J. (1994). Women in toyland: A look at women in American newspaper sports journalism. In P. J. Creedon (Ed.), *Women, media and sport: Challenging gender values* (pp. 67–107). Thousand Oaks, CA: Sage.

Crolley, L., and Teso, E. (2007). Gendered narratives in Spain. *International Review for the Sociology of Sport*, 42 (2), 149–66.

Daddario, G., and Wigley, B. J. (2007). Gender marking and racial stereotyping at the 2004 Athens Games. *Journal of Sports Media*, 2 (1), 29–51.

Davis, D. C., and Krawczyk, J. (2010). Female sportscaster credibility. *Journal of Sports Media*, 5 (2), 1–34.

Duncan, M. C. (2006). Gender warriors in sport: Women and the media. In A. A. Raney and J. Bryant (Eds.), *Handbook of sports and media* (pp. 231–52). Mahwah, NJ: Lawrence Erlbaum.

Duncan, M. C., and Messner, M. A. (2000). *Gender in televised sports: 1989, 1993 and 1999*. Los Angeles: Amateur Athletic Foundation of Los Angeles.

Dworkin, S. L., and Wachs, F. L. (1998). "Disciplining the body": HIV-positive male athletes, media surveillance, and the policing of sexuality. *Sociology of Sport Journal*, 15 (1), 1–20.

Dyer, R. (1993). *The matter of images – Essays on representations*. London and New York: Routledge.

Eastman, S. T., and Billings, A. C. (1999). Gender parity in the Olympics: Hyping women athletes, favoring men athletes. *Journal of Sport and Social Issues*, 23 (2), 140–70.

Etling, L. W., Young, R. W., Faux, W. V., and Mitchell, J. C. (2011). Just like one of the guys? Perceptions of male and female sportscaster's voices. *Journal of Sports Media*, 6 (2), 1–21.

Gerbner, G., Gross, L., Morgan, M., and Signorielli, N. (1994) Growing up with television: The cultivation perspective. In J. Bryant and D. Zillmann (Eds.), *Media effects: Advances in theory and research* (pp.17–42). Hillsdale, NJ: Lawrence Erlbaum.

Gill, D. L., Morrow, R. G., Collins, K. E., Lucey, A. B., and Schultz, A. M. (2006). Attitudes and sexual prejudice in sport and physical activity. *Journal of Sport Management*, 20, 554–64.

Griffin, P. (1998). *Strong women, deep closets: Lesbians and homophobia in women's sport*. Champaign, IL: Human Kinetics.

Hardin, M. (2005). Stopped at the gate: Women's sports, 'reader interest,' and decision-making by editors. *Journalism and Mass Communication Quarterly*, 82 (1), 62–77.

Hardin, M., and Shain, S. (2005). Strength in numbers? The experiences and attitudes of women in sports media careers. *Journalism and Mass Communication Quarterly*, 82 (4), 804–19.

Hardin, M., and Whiteside, E. (2009). Sports reporters divided over concerns about Title IX. *Newspaper Research Journal*, 30 (1), 58–80.

Hardin, M., Kuehn, K. M., Jones, H., Genovese, J., and Balaji, M. (2009). 'Have you got game?' Hegemonic masculinity and neo-homophobia in U.S. newspaper sports columns. *Communication, Culture, and Critique*, 2 (2), 182–200.

Indiana University Center for Sexual Health Promotion. (2010). *National survey of sexual health and behavior*. Retrieved from http://www.nationalsexstudy.indiana.edu/.

John Curley Center for Sports Journalism. (2009). *From outside the press box: The identities, attitudes, and values of sports bloggers*. July. Retrieved from http://comm.psu.edu/about/centers/john-curley-center-for-sports-journalism/blogsreport.pdf.

Jones, R., Murrell, A. J., and Jackson, J. (1999). Pretty versus powerful in the sports pages: Print media coverage of U.S. women's Olympic gold medal winning teams. *Journal of Sport and Social Issues*, 23 (2), 183–92.

Kane, M. J., and Greendorfer, S. L. (1994). The media's role in accommodating and resisting stereotyped images of women in sport. In P. J. Creedon (Ed.), *Women, media and sport: Challenging gender values* (pp. 28–44). Thousand Oaks, CA: Sage.

Kian, E. M., and Anderson, E. (2009). John Amaechi: Changing the way reporters examine gay athletes. *Journal of Homosexuality*, 56 (7), 799–818.

Kian, E. M., and Hardin, M. (2009). Framing of sport coverage based on the sex of sports writers: Female journalists counter the traditional gendering of media content. *International Journal of Sport Communication*, 2, 185–204.

Kian, E. M., Mondello, M., and Vincent, J. (2009). ESPN – The women's sports network? A content analysis of Internet coverage of March Madness. *Journal of Broadcasting and Electronic Media*, 53 (3), 477–95.

King, C. (2007). Media portrayals of male and female athletes: A text and picture analysis of British newspaper coverage of the Olympic Games since 1948. *International Review for the Sociology of Sport*, 42 (2), 187–99.

Knight, J., and Giuliano, T. (2003). Blood, sweat, and jeers: The impact of the media's heterosexist portrayals on perceptions of male and female athletes. *Journal of Sport Behavior*, 26 (3), 272–84.

Knoppers, A., and Elling, A. (2004). 'We do not engage in promotional journalism': Discursive strategies used by sports journalists to describe the selection process. *International Review for the Sociology of Sport*, 39 (1): 57–73.

Koivula, N. (1999). Gender stereotyping in televised media sport coverage. *Sex Roles*, 41 (7/8): 589–603.

Lapchick, R., Moss II, A., Russell, C., and Scearce, R. (2011). The 2010–11 Associated Press Sports Editors racial and gender report card. Retrieved from http://www.tidesport.org/RGRC/2011/2011_APSE_RGRC_FINAL.pdf.

Messner, M. A. (1992). *Power at play: Sports and the problem of masculinity.* Boston: Beacon.

Mikosza, J. M., and Phillips, M. G. (1999). Gender, sport and the body politic: Framing femininity in the Golden Girls of Sport Calendar and the Atlanta Dream. *International Review for the Sociology of Sport,* 34 (1), 5–16.

Nylund, D. (2004). When in Rome: Heterosexism, homophobia, and sports talk radio. *Journal of Sport and Social Issues,* 28 (2), 136–68.

O'Reilly, J., and Cahn, S.K. (2007). *Women and sports in the United States: A documentary reader.* Boston: Northeastern University Press.

O'Sullivan, T., Hartley, J., Saunders, D., Montgomery, M., and Fiske, J. (1994). *Key concepts in communication and cultural studies* (2nd ed.). London and New York: Routledge.

Pedersen, P. M., Whisenant, W. A., and Schneider, R. G. (2003). Using a content analysis to examine the gendering of sports newspaper personnel and their coverage. *Journal of Sport Management,* 17, 376–93.

Pfister, G. (2010). Women in sport – Gender relations and future perspectives. *Sport in Society,* 13 (2), 234–48.

Plymire, D. C., and Forman, P. J. (2000). Breaking the silence: Lesbian fans, the Internet, and the sexual politics of women's sport. *International Journal of Sexuality and Gender Studies,* 5 (2), 141–53.

Rotas, A. (2010). Hello boys! Top women tennis players play to the male crowd on their Websites. Paper presented at the IAMCR 2010 annual conference, Brage, Portugal, July 2010.

Sabo, D., and Curry Jansen, S. C. (1992). Images of men in sports media: The social reproduction of gender order. In S. Craig (Ed.), *Men, masculinity, and the media* (pp. 169–84). Newbury Park, CA: Sage.

Sagas, M., Cunningham, G. B., Wigley, B. J., and Ashley, F. B. (2000). Internet coverage of university softball and baseball web sites: The inequity continues. *Sociology of Sport Journal,* 17 (2), 198–205.

Scheufele, D. A. (1999). Framing as a theory of media effects. *Journal of Communication,* 49 (1), 103–22.

Sheffer, M. L., and Schultz, B. (2007). Double standard: Why women have trouble getting jobs in local televised sports. *Journal of Sports Media,* 2 (1), 77–101.

Staurowsky, E. J. (2012). Sexual prejudice and sport media coverage: Exploring an ethical framework for college sports journalists. *Journal of the Study of Sports and Athletes in Education,* 6 (2), 121–40.

Strong, C., and Hannis, J. (2007) The visibility of female journalists at Australian and New Zealand newspapers: The good news and the bad news. *Australian Journalism Review,* 29 (1), 115–25.

Tamir, I., and Bernstein, A. (2011). Battlefield sport: Female sport journalists in Israel. Paper presented at the 2011 IAMCR annual conference. Istanbul, Turkey, July 2011.

Urquhart, J., and Crossman, J. (1999). The Globe and Mail coverage of the winter Olympic Games: A cold place for women athletes. *Journal of Sport and Social Issues,* 23 (2), 193–202.

Vincent, J. (2004). Game, sex, and match: The construction of gender in British newspaper coverage of the 2000 Wimbledon Championships. *Sociology of Sport Journal,* 21 (4), 435–56.

Vincent, J., Kian, E. M., Pedersen, P. M., Kuntz, A., and Hill, J. S. (2010). England expects: English newspapers' narratives about the English soccer team in the 2006 World Cup. *International Review for the Sociology of Sport,* 45 (2), 199–223.

Wensing, E. H., and Bruce, T. (2003). Bending the rules: Media representations of gender during an international sporting event. *International Review for the Sociology of Sport,* 38 (4), 387–96.

Whannel, G. (2002) *Media sports stars: Masculinities and moralities.* London: Routledge.

33

GOING PUBLIC

Communicating a critical perspective on sport

Adam Love

As one of the first major social theorists to take sport as a serious scholarly issue, Bourdieu (1998) suggested that sociologists of sport are "doubly dominated," being "scorned by sociologists" and "despised by sportspersons" (p. 153). They are "scorned by sociologists" because sport is often not viewed as an important area of academic inquiry and "despised by sportspersons" because their research often highlights problems associated with the ways in which sports are organized. Although much of my attention in this chapter will be directed toward sport sociology, I believe that Bourdieu's concerns are relevant to scholars across the fields of sport studies, particularly those who seek to communicate a critical perspective on sport through public and media engagement. Specifically, in this chapter I present Burawoy's (2004a, 2004d, 2005) model of public sociology as a framework for sport scholars to utilize in conceptualizing how to pursue interaction with various sporting publics. First, I provide a general summary of the rationale for public sociology before going on to build a further case for the relevance of public sociology to sport scholars. Next, I provide an overview of Burawoy's division of sociological labor and note some key issues highlighted in the debates surrounding the development of public sociology. Finally, I provide examples of and discuss complications involved in pursuing critical engagement and communication with sporting publics.

A rationale for public sociology

The topic of public sociology received substantial attention during Michael Burawoy's term as president of the American Sociological Association (ASA), as exemplified by the theme of the 2004 ASA meetings – public sociologies – as well as notable discussions, debates, and symposia about the issue in such journals as *Social Forces* (82[4], 2004), *Social Problems* (51[1], 2004), *Critical Sociology* (31[3], 2005), *The American Sociologist* (36[3/4], 2005), and the *British Journal of Sociology* (56[3], 2005). In fact, the "public sociology wars" saw well over 100 papers written on the subject in little more than a four-year span (Burawoy, 2009).

While a comprehensive overview of the historical basis for public sociology is beyond the scope of this chapter, it is important to note that Burawoy (2004a) frames his conception of public sociology by referencing the moral commitment that drove sociological pioneers such as Marx, Weber, Durkheim, DuBois, and Addams, to seek social change through public engagement. However, while most individuals still enter academia with a commitment to issues of social justice, "graduate school seeks to expel that moral moment through a variety of disciplinary techniques – standardized courses, regimented careers, intensive examination, the lonely dissertation, the refereed publication, all captured by the all-powerful CV" (Burawoy, 2004b, p. 104). In light of this state of affairs, public sociology is an attempt to recognize and reflect upon moral commitment rather than seeking to silence and repress it.

Burawoy further justifies his call for public sociology by bringing attention to what he labels the "scissors movement" (Burawoy, 2004a, p. 6). By this, he refers to a gap between sociology and the public in which sociology has moved left and society has moved right. In other words, "the political center of gravity in sociology has moved in a critical direction while the world it studies has moved in the opposite" (p. 6). Burawoy (2004a, 2004d) explains that this scissors movement is particularly concerning because, just as the economy is the distinctive object of economics, civil society is the distinctive object of sociology. However, when civil society disappears, as in the case of Stalin's Soviet Union, Hitler's Germany, or Pinochet's Chile, so too disappears sociology. In other words, sociology's affinity to the public comes from the fact that "sociology is born with civil society and dies with civil society" (Burawoy, 2004d, pp. 1615–16). We should take caution, however, against holding an overly romanticized view of the public, as civil society "is a terrain of many interests and perspectives," and engaging with civil society is made difficult by such forces as "commodification, bureaucratization, privatization, markets, and coercive states" (Burawoy, 2004c, p. 129). In the face of such threats to civil society and its publics, however, Burawoy argues that scholars "can curl up into a professional cocoon" or they can "venture forth to constitute and articulate public voices, thereby sustaining the basis of our existence" (Burawoy, 2004c, p. 129).

Thus, Burawoy's rationale for public sociology is based upon arguments about the roots of sociology involving a moral commitment to the public, the growing division that exists between sociology and the public, and the inextricably linked nature of sociology and civil society. At a basic level, these arguments have relevance across the social sciences, including those dedicated to studying sport, given their connections with the broader field of sociology. However, I suggest that there are additional reasons why public sociology is relevant to scholars of sport, which is where I turn my discussion in the next section.

Public sociology in the context of sport

As a point to begin thinking about how public sociology is relevant to sport scholars, I return to Bourdieu's concern about being "despised by sportspersons." Such a state of affairs would, of course, pose challenges in communicating with sportspersons and limit the ability of scholars to have an impact on actual sporting practice. Specifically, I suggest that this concern applies broadly to all scholars who produce critical work that highlights problems with how sport is organized and carried out in society.

Issues related to public engagement and the desire for research to have a greater impact on sport have long been points of consideration for sport scholars. For example, in an early overview of the field, Lüschen (1980) was critical of the fact that sociology of sport had done little to impact sport and physical education practice or contribute rational insight into sporting policy. Melnick (1980), meanwhile, demonstrated a similar concern, issuing a call for sport sociologists to give specific attention to the issue of application. Notably, he pointed to a growing gap between sport researchers and practitioners, similar to Burawoy's "scissors movement", but he suggested that a "humanistically oriented, applied sociology of sport can help close this gap" (Melnick, 1980, p. 11). Yiannakis (1989) later followed the lead of Melnick, lamenting the fact that sport sociologists had done little, either conceptually or methodologically, to further the previous work concerning application. Yiannakis, however, went beyond these earlier calls by presenting a model for the relationship of theory to application.

Yiannakis' (1989) model elicited a critical response from Ingham and Donnelly (1990), who agreed that direct intervention by sociologists of sport into social processes is necessary, but disagreed with a number of Yiannakis' other points. A key source of their disagreement concerned Yiannakis' use of the term "applied." Ingham and Donnelly argued that distinguishing "applied" research from "basic" research implies a positivistic dualism that suggests the scientific process is devoid of values. Instead, they favored the concept of "practical" knowledge that may be of value to society. Both Yiannakis' (1989) original article as well as the response of Ingham and Donnelly (1990) were included in an anthology edited by Yiannakis and Greendorfer (1992) entitled *Applied Sociology of Sport*. In the publication, which contained articles on topics ranging from broad conceptual issues to specific examples of applied work, Yiannakis and Greendorfer attempted to "articulate a theoretical framework for the conceptual development of an applied sociology of sport" (p. vii). The collection also included an article authored by Yiannakis (1992), in which he sought to extend his earlier theoretical model by outlining four potential roles that could exist in an applied sociology of sport: the applied researcher, the knowledge broker, the change agent, and the consultant. Notably, an important aim of Yiannakis in defining roles of the applied sport sociologist and in outlining a model of applied sociology of sport was to bring greater attention and legitimacy to such activity, similar to Burawoy's goals for public sociology.

More recently, Jones and Armour (2000) published an anthology entitled *Sociology of Sport: Theory and Practice*, in which they attempted to provide rationale for the relevance and importance of sociology for publics such as the sports student and the sports practitioner. Additionally, Yiannakis (2000) contributed a chapter to the anthology in which he again challenged scholars to give more attention to applied work and better demonstrate the value of the field to society and the world of sport. Likewise, Harris (2006), noting that sociology of sport has often been marginalized in sociology and kinesiology, also made a call for directing more attention to conducting applied research. In offering recommendations to address the issue of marginalization, she specifically called for sociologists of sport to give more attention to sport and physical education in local community settings. Overall, given the extent of sport scholars' attention to the question of how research might make a more substantial impact on the way sports are organized and carried out in society, I suggest that engaging with the framework of public sociology may be one way to help improve this impact.

While my discussion thus far has focused on debates largely in sociology of sport, I suggest that these concerns with application have potential relevance for all sport scholars, particularly those who conduct critical work. In the area of sport management, for example, several prominent scholars have issued calls for more critical work to be conducted in the field. Notably, Frisby (2005) urged sport management scholars to embrace critical social science as a lens of inquiry. Reflecting on the fact that she received very few manuscripts operating from a critical stance during her time as editor of the *Journal of Sport Management* (JSM), Frisby wondered if sport management scholars had left critical work to their colleagues in other fields. Further, she questioned how sport management professors can claim to want their students to be strong critical thinkers when they are not themselves engaging with critical social science theory. In a special issue of the JSM dedicated to promoting critical and innovative approaches to the study of sport management, Amis and Silk (2005) echoed many of Frisby's comments. They specifically problematized the fact that when sport management scholars organize their research around the attempt to understand and design effective organizations, they usually fail to consider the question of *for whom* these organizations are effective. Overall, such calls for critical work indicate the potential importance of public sociology for scholars in a range of areas across sport studies. To help further conceptualize the role of public sociology in the fields of sport studies, I next outline Burawoy's division of sociological labor.

Public sociology and a division of sociological labor

In order to conceptualize the role of public sociology in the field, Burawoy has constructed a division of sociological labor as an organizational framework. In this division of labor, he differentiates public sociology (for example, concern for the public image of sociology, presenting findings in an accessible manner, dialogic engagement with various publics) from the areas of policy sociology (such as solving problems as defined by a client), professional sociology (for example, research conducted within research programs that define assumptions, theories, concepts, questions, and puzzles), and critical sociology (such as critical debates of the discipline within and between research programs). The questions of (a) sociology for whom? and (b) sociology for what? are at the center of Burawoy's (2004a) framework. In response to the question of "sociology for whom?" (Lee, 1976) Burawoy distinguishes sociological dialogue for an academic audience from that for an extra-academic audience. In response to the question of "sociology for what?" (Lynd, 1939), he distinguishes instrumental knowledge, which is concerned with means to solve problems, from reflexive knowledge, which is concerned with the ends of society themselves. Public sociology, then, involves public dialogue about the fundamental direction of society, and is distinguished from policy sociology, which involves the solving of problems as defined by a client. Professional sociology, meanwhile, involves the solving of puzzles within academic research programs, while critical sociology involves interrogating the foundations of the research programs of professional sociology. This framework was designed to "replace tired divisions between micro and macro, quantitative and qualitative, pure and applied, positivist and hermeneutic, theoretical and empirical work" (Burawoy, 2009, p. 454). It is important to emphasize that these divisions refer to ideal types, and in the real world the distinctions between these ideal types may often blur and work may straddle or move across multiple areas over time. Further, rather than being separate realms, the four types of sociology are interdependent in that "the flourishing of each type of sociology is a condition for the flourishing of all" (Burawoy, 2004a, p. 4).

During the "public sociology wars," many important issues about Burawoy's division of sociological labor and the concept of public sociology itself have been raised. Despite the fact that I am presenting Burawoy's conception of public sociology as a framework that deserves attention from sport scholars, I do not hold illusions that engaging in public sociology is a simple endeavor that is without challenges, problems, contradictions, and pitfalls. Rather, the practice of scholars engaging with various publics is a complex issue requiring thorough examination. While being able to thoroughly treat all the important points raised in the debates concerning public sociology is not possible in this chapter, I will briefly note some of the major themes that exist in critiques of public sociology.

One set of concerns has come from those who fear that public sociology threatens the integrity or legitimacy of the field. For example, critics have argued that sociology is not ready to go public or that the public is not ready for sociology (see, for example, Brint, 2005; Calhoun, 2005; Tittle, 2004; Turner, 2005). As Tittle (2004, p. 1641) suggested, "what we think we know today may prove contrary to what we learn tomorrow," and as such, "sociologists are as likely to be wrong as right and in the process they can easily cause damage". Or, as Turner (2005) put it, "we will penetrate the public's consciousness and places where important decisions are made when we demonstrate again and again over a period of some decades that we possess an important body of knowledge" (p. 44). Closely tied to these criticisms is a concern with the impact of public sociology on politicizing the discipline (for example, Brint, 2005; Holmwood, 2007; Massey, 2007; Turner, 2005). For instance, Holmwood (2007, p. 62), who feared the "accelerated politicization" of the discipline created by public sociology, argued that political neutrality must be central to sociology because it "creates the space for dialogue and is the condition for any sociology to have a voice" (p. 63). Owing to the energy generated by these debates, public sociology has and likely will continue to grow. For example, its continued development is evidenced by the publication of the *Handbook of Public Sociology* (Jeffries, 2009), which sought to analyze and extend Burawoy's model of sociological practice from a variety of perspectives and in a range of contexts. Sport, however, is currently one context from which this explicit connection to public sociology is lacking.

In addition to the aforementioned concerns, perhaps the greatest obstacle to a flourishing public sociology is the current system of rewards in higher education. For example, while Brady (2004) credited it as an admirable endeavor, he feared that public sociology may fail, owing to the fact there are few rewards for engaging with the public. When most academics have time available outside from responsibilities such as teaching, grading, advising, paperwork, committee work, and other exigencies, their time is justifiably spent on researching and publishing scholarship that will get them tenured and promoted. Brady (2004) suggested that "regardless of whether this incentive system is justifiable, the reality is that faculty are not likely to deviate from this unless new incentives emerge for public sociology" (pp. 1632–3). While such issues will no doubt be key in the continued development of public sociology, it is important to note that Burawoy's call for public sociology is not just a call for scholars to increase their engagement with the public. Rather, it is an attempt to institutionalize public sociology within the academy, define criteria for what is good and bad public sociology, and make it an essential part of the system of rewards. Similarly, my call for increased engagement with public sociology by sport scholars is not just a call for more interaction with sporting publics (work that a number of scholars are already doing), it is also a call for directing increased attention to the concept of public sociology and, in turn, working to make public engagement a more valued part of the system of rewards in sport studies. Thus, sport scholars who already conduct this type of work have even more reason to engage themselves with discussions about public sociology. As a point of stimulating such engagement, I next provide some examples of what public sociology in the context of sport might entail.

Performing public sociology in the context of sport

Having outlined a case for the possible benefits of giving more attention to public engagement and having highlighted key points of Burawoy's public sociology, I now provide readers some further insight related to pursuing public sociology in the context of sport. While my discussion of public engagement initiated by sport scholars is certainly only a small sample of all such work that exists, it is intended as a beginning in making explicit connections between such work and the concept of public sociology.

In this discussion of performing public sociology in the context of sport, I refer to Burawoy's analytical concepts of traditional and organic public sociology. Traditional public sociology includes such activities as writing editorials that appear in newspapers, writing books that are read beyond the academy, and other forms of media engagement. In traditional public sociology, "the publics being addressed are generally invisible in that they cannot be seen, thin in that they do not constitute a movement or organization, and they are usually mainstream" (Burawoy, 2004a, p. 7). Organic public sociology, meanwhile, involves working "in close connection with a visible, thick, active, local and often counter-public" (p. 7). For example, organic public sociology may involve working with labor movements, neighborhood associations, communities of faith, or human rights organizations. Work with such publics involves a dialogue and a "process of mutual education" (p. 8). However, just as the four areas in Burawoy's division of labor are interconnected and complementary, so too are traditional and organic public sociology.

One form of traditional public sociology in which many sport scholars have certainly been involved is media engagement. For example, a scholar may be interviewed by a reporter for a story related to his/her area of research, thus serving as a resource for the journalist. While such engagement can be rewarding and can serve as a valuable way of informing members of the media and public about important issues, such efforts can also entail frustration, particularly when a scholar is engaged in critical work. A major source of such frustration is the fact that in this type of engagement, a scholar's ideas are filtered (that is, transmitted to the public second-hand through the words written or spoken by a reporter). As many scholars have found, a thorough interview with a reporter does not guarantee that the information discussed will be conveyed in the story produced by that media member. For example, a reporter from the TV program *60 Minutes* conducted a two-hour, taped interview with law professor Nancy Hogshead-Makar for a segment the program was airing about a lawsuit filed by opponents of Title IX. Despite Hogshead-Makar's legal credentials, very little of her analysis was included in the final story, which presented a largely one-sided argument supporting the claims of Title IX opponents (Cole, 2003).

In contrast to having their ideas conveyed to a public audience second-hand by a reporter, scholars may seek to directly disseminate their work through other media channels. Activities of this type include writing articles that appear in newspapers, magazines, industry-specific publications (such as *SportsBusiness Journal*), or on websites published by media entities. Another outlet that potentially allows scholars to have a more direct voice is appearing in person as a guest on formats such as television or radio programs. For example, Dave Zirin's weekly radio show, *Edge of Sports Radio*, has frequently featured a segment entitled "Ask a Sports Sociologist." Beyond these traditional forms of media, blogging is perhaps one of the most important opportunities for scholars to disseminate their ideas in a more unfiltered way. Wilson (2007), for example, has argued that a "revolutionary moment" exists, owing to the unprecedented opportunities for engagement created by new forms of communication technology, which can play an important role in helping sport scholars bring their ideas to a broader public audience.

Of course, regardless of the format involved, media engagement is certainly not without its difficulties. For instance, while Burawoy (2004a) emphasizes the dialogic nature of public sociology, Stacey (2004) is somewhat reserved about the prospects of being able to engage in a productive public dialogue, particularly when interacting with members of the media. While stating that she was initially enthusiastic about calls for increased attention to public sociology, Stacey describes having become much more cautious after her experiences with public engagement. Through work as a critical scholar, Stacey (1996) has attempted to question the glorified, celebratory view of marriage and to point out that the family is changing, but not declining. She describes, however, that while working with a group seeking marriage equality, she found herself fortifying a celebratory view of marriage with which her own research took issue. Stacey suggested that, owing to the inability to frame the questions posed or the format of an admissible response, "to perform public sociology from a critical perspective, a sociologist immediately learns that she must agree to play on the home field of an alien team, and by their rules" (Stacey, 2004, p. 134). Such rules often involve subscription to "a positivist belief that social scientific truth is singular, transparent, measurable, and objective," (p. 138) and a belief that research questions and findings are value-free.

Another challenge in pursuing public engagement involves the negative backlash that a scholar may receive from some members of the public. For example, after Bruce (2007) received media coverage for research that she and colleagues (Hurley, Dickie, Hardman, Lardelli, and Bruce, 2006) conducted about a sports comedy show, she faced insulting *ad hominem* attacks both in traditional media and on blog sites. The fact that engaging with the public potentially opens scholars up to such attacks from a wide range of individuals – attacks they would be less likely to face without entering the public arena – presents another important issue for scholars to ponder in pursuing public engagement. Overall, such perspectives about the potentially conservative nature of public engagement and the varied reactions one can receive from the public remind us that public sociology is a complex endeavor with many issues to be considered closely.

Beyond seeking to communicate their ideas to a broader audience through various forms of media, many sport scholars are involved in more organic forms of public engagement. As an example of such work in the area of "sport for peace," Sugden and colleagues (see, for example, Sugden and Wallis, 2007) have sought to use sport as a vehicle to build connections between differing communities, such as with Jewish and Arab children in Israel. Through work with their organization, Sport 4 Peace (www.sport4peace.org), meanwhile, Sarah Hillyer and Ashleigh Huffman have been involved with projects in Iran, Iraq, and Israel, using sport to build cross-cultural connections and impact the lives of girls and women. In another example, Frisby and her colleagues (for example, Frisby, Reid, and Ponic, 2007) have pursued projects seeking to improve access to recreation for low income women.

The Tucker Center for Research on Girls and Women in Sport at the University of Minnesota (www.cehd.umn.edu/tuckercenter), meanwhile, provides an example of an interdisciplinary effort toward exploring how sport and physical activity affect the lives of girls and women in our society and involves work of a public nature. For example, scholars associated with the center have engaged in research projects involving local publics, such as youth sport coaches and young athletes. The center also produces a blog and newsletter, sponsors a lecture series, and makes use of new technology, such as Facebook and Twitter, to disseminate ideas and further connect with various publics. Thus, through both its research efforts and communicative activities, the center provides examples of engagement in both traditional and organic forms of public sociology.

Certainly there are many further examples of sport scholars engaging in work that constitutes public sociology. My intent here is not to give a comprehensive inventory of such work. Rather, I have provided a small sample, which is intended as a beginning in making connections explicit between public work by sport scholars and concepts related to traditional and organic forms of public sociology.

Conclusion

In this chapter, I have outlined a case for increased attention to the concept of public sociology in the context of sport. Certainly, among other limitations, I must raise the issue of biases present in my status as a US scholar. Pointing out that the prominence of public sociology differs greatly based upon national context, Burawoy (2004a) notes that the term "public sociology" is an American invention, as sociology has a strong public presence in, for example, Scandinavian countries and a number of countries in the global South. Similarly, national context is an important factor influencing the conditions under which sport scholars work. For example, engagement with various publics has been a key component of the success of British sport sociologists in being able to institutionalize and legitimate the study of sport within higher education and society at large (Yiannakis, 2000). I believe it is beyond the scope of this chapter for me to attempt to comment at any length about the various forms engagement with sporting publics may take in different national contexts. Rather, as the "public sociology wars" have seen articles published in journals from Finland, Portugal, Italy, France, Hungary, China, Hong Kong, Russia, Brazil, South Africa, Germany, and Iran (Burawoy, 2009), I challenge sport scholars around the globe to engage with the general arguments I present and explore how these issues are relevant to them.

Further, it is important to note that other frameworks for public engagement and communication, such as cultural studies-driven intervention and other activist research, have certainly influenced many scholars in the field. In the broader context of kinesiology, for example, Martinek and Hellison (1997; Martinek, Hellison, and Walsh, 2004) have elaborated the concept of "service-bonded inquiry." My point in this chapter is not to present public sociology as the singular framework through which scholars conducting critical research in sport should pursue public engagement. Rather, I suggest that public sociology is one perspective with which some sport scholars should seek to more explicitly engage in conducting such work. As we move forward, those who have been influenced by other forms of interventionist work may further consider the (dis)connections between their perspectives and the concept of public sociology. Given the variety of difficulties and complexities involved in public engagement, there is good reason for scholars to consider a wide range of perspectives and frameworks in pursuing such work. Public sociology serves as one such framework.

More than two decades ago, Bourdieu (1988) observed that sociologists of sport are "scorned by sociologists" and "despised by sportspersons." In this chapter, I have suggested that the concern of being "despised by sportspersons" (for example, concerns about sport scholarship having a lack of impact on sporting practice and policy) might be improved through increased attention to public sociology. In addition, an explicit engagement with public sociology may also help address Bourdieu's concern about being "scorned by sociologists." For example, if sport scholars seek to explicitly engage with issues raised in the debates about public sociology – a topic that has received substantial consideration in mainstream sociology – they can also bring added attention to important work that may otherwise receive little attention in fields outside of sport studies. Thus, this chapter serves as a call for both increased interaction with the public by scholars in the field as well as a more explicit engagement with the framework of public sociology for those pursuing such work. Doing so can serve as one way in which sport scholars can continue to develop academic legitimacy and respect for the fields of sport studies, while also making a greater impact on the ways in which sports are organized and carried out in society. While the road to expanding public sociologies in the context of sport certainly contains many difficulties, I argue it is a road worthy of further exploration, consideration, and continued development.

References

Amis, J., and Silk, M. (2005). Rupture: Promoting critical and innovative approaches to the study of sport management. *Journal of Sport Management*, 19, 355–66.
Bourdieu, P. (1988). Program for a sociology of sport. *Sociology of Sport Journal*, 5, 153–61.
Brady, D. (2004). Why public sociology may fail. *Social Forces*, 82, 1629–38.
Brint, S. (2005). Guide for the perplexed: On Michael Burawoy's "public sociology." *The American Sociologist*, 36 (3/4), 46–65.
Bruce, T. (2007). The perils of publicly critiquing (male) sport. Paper presented at the annual conference of the North American Society for the Sociology of Sport, Pittsburg, PA, November 2007.
Burawoy, M. (2004a). 2004 American Sociological Association presidential address: For public sociology. *American Sociological Review*, 70, 4–28.
Burawoy, M. (2004b). Introduction. In M. Burawoy, W. Gamson, C. Ryan, S. Pfohl, D. Vaughn, C. Derber, J. Schor. Public sociologies: A symposium from Boston College. *Social Problems*, 51 (1), 103–30.
Burawoy, M. (2004c). Manifesto for public sociologies. In M. Burawoy, W. Gamson, C. Ryan, S. Pfohl, D. Vaughn, C. Derber, J. Schor. Public sociologies: A symposium from Boston College. *Social Problems*, 51 (1), 103–30.
Burawoy, M. (2004d). Public sociologies: Contradictions, dilemmas, and possibilities. *Social Forces*, 82, 1603–18.
Burawoy, M. (2005). Public sociology: Populist fad or path to renewal? *British Journal of Sociology*, 56, 417–32.
Burawoy, M. (2009). The public sociology wars. In V. Jeffries (Ed.), *Handbook of public sociology* (pp. 449–73). Lanham, MD: Rowman and Littlefield.
Calhoun, C. (2005). The promise of public sociology. *British Journal of Sociology*, 56, 355–64.
Cole, C. L. (2003). Playing the quota card. *Journal of Sport and Social Issues*, 27, 87–99.
Frisby, W. (2005). The good, the bad, and the ugly: Critical sport management research. *Journal of Sport Management*, 19, 1–12.
Frisby, W., Reid, C. and Ponic, P. (2007). Leveling the playing field: Promoting the health of poor women through a community development approach to recreation. In P. White and K. Young (Eds.), *Sport and gender in Canada* (pp. 121–36). Don Mills, ON: Oxford University Press.
Harris, J. C. (2006). Sociology of sport: Expanding horizons in the subdiscipline. *Quest*, 58, 71–91.
Holmwood, J. (2007). Sociology as public discourse and professional practice: A critique of Michael Burawoy. *Sociological Theory*, 25, 46–66.
Hurley, B., Dickie, M., Hardman, C., Lardelli, N., and Bruce, T. (2006). Sports comedy shows and new lad culture in New Zealand: The sportscafe guide to Kiwi masculinity. In Refereed Proceedings of the SAA(NZ) Conference: The University of Waikato. *Sportsfreak*, November 29. Retrieved from http://www.sportsfreak.co.nz/wp/?p=456.
Ingham, A. G., and Donnelly, P. (1990). Whose knowledge counts? The production of knowledge and issues of application in the sociology of sport. *Sociology of Sport Journal*, 7: 58–65.
Jeffries, V. (Ed.). (2009). *Handbook of public sociology*. Lanham, MD: Rowman and Littlefield.
Jones, R. L., and Armour, K. M. (Eds.). (2000). *Sociology of sport: Theory and practice*. Harlow, Essex: Pearson Education.
Lee, A. M. (1976). Sociology for whom? *American Sociological Review*, 41, 925–36.
Lüschen, G. (1980). Sociology of sport: Development, present state, and prospects. *Annual Review of Sociology*, 6, 315–47.

Lynd, R. (1939). *Knowledge for what? The place of social sciences in American culture*. Princeton, NJ: Princeton University Press.

Martinek, T., and Hellison, D. (1997). Service-bonded inquiry: The road less traveled. *Journal of Teaching in Physical Education*, 17, 107–21.

Martinek, T., Hellison, D., and Walsh, D. (2004). Service-bonded inquiry revisited: A research model for the community-engaged professor. *Quest*, 56, 397–412.

Massey, D. (2007). The strength of weak politics. In D. Clawson, R. Zussman, J. Misra, N. Gerstel, R. Stokes, D. Anderson, *et al*. (Eds.), *Public sociology: Fifteen eminent sociologists debate politics and the profession in the Twenty-First Century* (pp. 145–57). Berkeley: University of California Press.

Melnick, M. J. (1980). Toward an applied sociology of sport. *Journal of Sport and Social Issues*, 4, 1–12.

Stacey, J. (1996). *In the name of the family: Rethinking family values in the postmodern age*. Boston, MA: Beacon.

Stacey, J. (2004). Marital suitors court social science spin-sters: The unwittingly conservative effects of public sociology. *Social Problems*, 51, 131–45.

Sugden, J., and Wallis, J. (Eds.). (2007). *Football for peace? The challenges of using sport for co-existence in Israel*. New York: Meyer and Meyer Sport.

Tittle, C. R. (2004). The arrogance of public sociology. *Social Forces*, 82, 1639–43.

Turner, J. (2005). Is public sociology such a good idea? *The American Sociologist*, 36 (3/4), 27–45.

Wilson, B. (2007). New media, social movements, and global sport studies: A revolutionary moment and the sociology of sport. *Sociology of Sport Journal*, 24, 457–77.

Yiannakis, A. (1989). Toward an applied sociology of sport: The next generation. *Sociology of Sport Journal*, 6, 1–16.

Yiannakis, A. (1992). Issues and practical suggestions for the applied sport sociologist. In A. Yiannakis and S. L. Greendorfer (Eds.), *Applied sociology of sport* (pp. 265–75). Champaign, IL: Human Kinetics.

Yiannakis, A. (2000). From theory to application in the sociology of sport. In R. L. Jones and K. M. Armour (Eds.), *Sociology of sport: Theory and practice* (pp. 114–33). Harlow, Essex: Pearson Education.

Yiannakis, A., and Greendorfer, S. L. (Eds.). (1992). *Applied sociology of sport*. Champaign, IL: Human Kinetics.

34

THE COMMUNICATIVE COMPLEXITY OF YOUTH SPORT

Maintaining benefits, managing discourses, and challenging identities

Lindsey J. Meân

Sport is widely viewed as a beneficial site for youth development, education, and leisure, and as a healthy family pastime. Sport does offer significant physical, psychological, social, and emotional benefits to young people that extend far beyond sport-specific contexts, but it can also incur severe damage, especially when the values, pressures, and actions of sport communicated to young athletes deploy the overly competitive discourses of professional adult sport. Sport is a significant discourse for families and individuals because it comprises a valued site within and through which parents and children actively communicate and participate as players, supporters, fans, and consumers of sport and sport media. As such, youth sport provides significant relational opportunities for children and parents which can be enhancing or detrimental depending on how these are managed and what discursive values are communicated. Adults comprise especially powerful role models in sport (Jambor, 1999) because it is such a significant site for identity development, particularly for males (Messner, 1988, 2002), given its long association with men and traditional forms of hegemonic heterosexual masculinity. The advantages of sport have led to a substantive and continued growth in youth sports and its increasing pervasiveness as a central aspect of family life. But adults are becoming over-engaged in youth sport problematically shifting its landscape and culture as other identities, interests and values are enacted (put into action and practice). This is of great concern given the values, lessons and identities developed through youth sport and its detrimental consequences and damaging potential.

The shifting discourses of youth sport

Parents, educators, and policy makers typically view youth sport as an unproblematic way to enhance potential and create community. But the growth of youth sport has been accompanied by troublesome shifts in the culture of youth sport, driven by adults, that have led to more young people experiencing its damaging and injurious potential (Abrams, 2012; Brenner, 2007; Fredricks and Eccles, 2005; Malina, 2010; Siegenthaler and Gonzalez, 1997). These shifts can generally be connected to the significance of sport for identities and the increased positioning of sport as an obtainable career or college opportunity. Together these have resulted in problematic adult over-investment in youth sport and the blurring of boundaries between different sport identities, parent-sport identities, and sport contexts (Fredricks and Eccles, 2005; Meân and Kassing, 2008; Siegenthaler and Gonzalez, 1997). Most notable is an erosion of the distinction between professional and youth sports (that is, the professionalization of youth sport) which has resulted in an over-emphasis on competition, early specialization, and over-long seasons (Brenner, 2007; Fredricks and Eccles, 2005; Malina, 2010; Smoll, Cumming, and Smith, 2011; Theokas, 2009). Consequently, many of the traditional benefits, values, and lessons communicated through youth sport have become subsumed, making the uncritical deployment of sport as an educational, developmental, leisure and entertainment site for young people problematic.

In exploring the landscape of youth sport it is important to realize that what is communicated in youth sport, how and by whom are central to whether sport participation is beneficial or detrimental. Sport has powerful cultural and ideological significance for identities (especially for boys), constructions of race, gender and sexuality, and the production and reproduction (that is, re/production) of competition, success and failure (Abrams, 2012; Fredricks and Eccles, 2005; Johnson and Migliaccio, 2009; Lusted, 2009; Meân, 2001; Meân and Kassing, 2008; Messner, 1998, 2002). These are evident in the multiple ways that youth sport is enacted, organized, represented, and so on, by adults, coaches and parents, as they manage the environment and culture, demands, definitions and understandings, life lessons and relationships that comprise sport for young athletes (Abrams, 2012; Brenner, 2007; Siegenthaler and Gonzalez, 1997; Smoll, *et al.*, 2011).

Parameters of youth sport

Youth sport is used to refer to varied populations and activities, but generally refers to children's and adolescents' sport participation and exposure. Young people experience sport formally and informally, directly and indirectly, and in multiple inextricably intersected ways. While there are exceptions, youth sport is most commonly understood and experienced as participation in organized competitive sport, both recreational and elite/select. Because youth sport is considered highly beneficial, parents actively put children into organized sport to explicitly teach valued attitudes and skills (Kremer-Sadlik and Kim, 2007; Strachan, Côté, and Deakin, 2011). But sport also provides a significant leisure, role, and relational dynamic for families and parenting (Fredricks and Eccles, 2005; Jambor, 1999; Kremer-Sadlik and Kim, 2007; Smoll, *et al.*, 2011). However, it is important to note that children also experience sport through media and merchandizing, and typically this is uncensored (because it's "just" sport) despite the problematic content of sport media (see, for example, Meân, 2010; Oates, 2009). Children also typically learn how to be fans, hence how to consume sport and sport media, as part of relational dynamics with other family members or significant adult or older others (Farrell and Fink, 2011; Mewett and Toffoletti, 2011).

The focus of this chapter is primarily participation in organized youth sport, which essentially refers to formally scheduled sport (rather than informal, unscheduled sport), alongside its intersection with other elements of family life, relations, and roles. However, the interconnection across sporting identities and the multiple ways that sport is experienced and learned, especially as media, need to be acknowledged for fully realizing the influence of sport discourses on organized youth sport and family relations; especially because the mediatization and spectacularization of sport (Rowe, 2004) are highly implicated in the professionalization of youth sport and the slippage of identities across sporting contexts.

Organized youth sport

Participation in organized youth sport is growing globally (Smoll, *et al.*, 2011) and sport and childhood are becoming inextricably bound (for example, Theokas, 2009). This increase in part reflects the value placed on the developmental, educational, and life-skills lessons communicated through sport by parents, governments, and world development agencies. In the US, the National Council of Youth Sports (2008) reported a growth in youth participation from 38 million individuals in 2000 to approximately 44 million in 2008 (this rises to over 60 million if multiple sport participation is counted even excluding high school sports). But, according to the National Council, US youth sport remains consistently male dominated, at 66 percent male to 34 percent female. Similar patterns of growth and participation are echoed in many other nations prosperous enough to support substantive organized youth sport, although female participation is substantially lower in countries where women's equality and sport remains even more ideologically contested.

There are many advantages associated with youth sport across multiple areas of functioning including (but not limited to) short-term and long-term physical health, cognitive and motor skill development, identity development and psychological health (for example, self-efficacy, self-esteem, self-concept), social skills and teamwork development, leadership and responsibility, perseverance and social respect, increased academic performance, reduced delinquency. These benefits are not mutually exclusive and linked to wider societal gains given that the greater self-esteem, efficacy, and so on, associated with sport result in lower probabilities of drug-taking, criminal activity, and, for girls, fewer early, unplanned pregnancies (Strachan, Côté, and Deakin, 2011). These benefits are not intrinsic or natural in sport, but subject to the way(s) in which adults organize and manage youth sport (Smoll, *et al.*, 2011). Coaches and parents impact what is communicated through sport; that is, what aspects of sport are put into action and how the lessons of sport are taught, particularly the increased emphasis on unbridled competition and the professionalization that has led to youth sport becoming described as a site of violence, aggression and poor sporting conduct (Abrams, 2012; Siegenthaler and Gonzalez, 1997). Youth athletes widely report observing and experiencing problematic adult behaviors that vary from yelling and verbal abuse to expectations that enable or demand overly aggressive and competitive behaviors from the athletes. In organized sport, the quality, character, and content of communication and relational work (between children and parents, children and coaches, and coaches and parents) is crucial, especially because the impact of adults as role models is high in sport contexts (Jambor, 1999). Yet the adults who regulate and occupy sport are also subject to the wider identities, culture and ideologies of sport, which may not be suitable for youth sport and conflate with other identities, such as parenting, at this site (Fredricks and Eccles, 2005; Meân and Kassing, 2008). Some of these elements are observable in a recent youth sport incident, its media coverage, and posted public responses concerning a mother's intervention in a youth ice hockey game after referees allowed a fight involving blows to the back of the head to continue for minutes (for example, Kindelan, 2012). Noteworthy are the online comments posted, a substantive number suggesting that violence in sport, hence youth sport, is expected and permissible.

Competition and fun, winning and losing

Competition has always been part of both organized and informal youth sport. But competition and competitiveness take multiple forms, and the purpose, content, and significance of competition should change with context, age, skill level, and so on, just as training purposes and coaching practices should change as children grow and develop (Balyi and Hamilton, 2004). Youth, adult, and professional forms of competition and competitiveness should be different (Smoll, *et al.*, 2011; Theokas, 2009), and it should not be assumed that there is shared understanding of sporting aims, notably competition and competitiveness, between children and adults. Indeed, while children are competitive (in certain ways), participation and fun are typically more important to young athletes than winning or losing. Nonetheless, adults are increasingly over-emphasizing winning in youth sport, negatively impacting children's experiences and communicating powerful, problematic lessons about the values of sport (Abrams, 2012; Brenner, 2007; Fredricks and Eccles, 2005; Siegenthaler and Gonzalez, 1997; Smoll, *et al.*, 2011).

Over-competitiveness and an over-emphasis on winning from parents pressures young athletes and focuses on being "best" rather than being a "winner" based on quality of athletic performance, participation, and sporting conduct (that is, sportpersonship). A winning-at-all-costs mentality has become prominent in youth sports and linked to many of the problems plaguing youth sport (Abrams, 2012; Brenner, 2007; Fredricks and Eccles, 2005; Malina, 2011), yet this is questionable even in professional and/or adult sport contexts. Competition is ideological in orientation, hence learned and acquired, and is more embedded in some cultural systems than others. Discourses of increased competitiveness and the discursive emphasis on winning in youth sport has meant its traditional values and developmental benefits have become muted and subsumed by over-training and early specialization (that is, commitment to a specific sport and elite training at an early age). Together these are referred to as the professionalization of youth sport, a shift driven by adults. Over-competitiveness and a heavy focus on winning in youth sport are commonly associated with a lack of fun and enjoyment which, alongside over-training, are identified as key factors in, and indicators of, burnout and drop-out. Burnout is widely defined as physical and psychological exhaustion, reduced sense of accomplishment, and devaluation of sport (Lemyre, Treasure, and Roberts, 2006; Raedeke, Lunney, and Venables, 2002). Even seriously competitive, older elite youth athletes (nearing the transition to adult sport) report these as major causes of burnout and drop-out.

Professional discourses, early specialization, and injuries in youth sport

Despite established evidence that participation in a range of sports up to adolescence is physically, psychologically and emotionally beneficial, discourses that promote the increased competitiveness and professionalization of youth sport (and its growth as an industry for products and services) has pushed a powerful agenda of early specialization into one sport (Malina, 2010). In conjunction with the increased performance and aggression demands of over-competitiveness, early specialization and over-training have, not surprisingly, been accompanied by a large increase in the number and severity of sport related injuries amongst children, including overuse injuries (American Academy of Pediatrics, 2000; DiFiori, 2010; Malina, 2010). While the dangers of concussion have become much more widely recognized and acknowledged in the last decade, serious over-use injuries exacerbated early specialization and over-training are a growing problem (DiFiori, 2010; Malina, 2010).

Subject to the prominent discourses of professionalism, many parents believe there are advantages to early specialization and fear that later specialization may undermine their child's opportunity to be a great athlete or, in America, get a college scholarship (Malina, 2010). Yet evidence consistently shows early specialization is potentially psychologically and physically detrimental, and contributes to burnout (American Academy of Pediatrics, 2000; DiFiori, 2010; Malina, 2010), and no long-term competitive advantages are reported (Capranica and Millard-Stafford, 2011; Côté, Lidor, and Hackfort, 2009). In fact a break from (specific) sport is recommended for young athletes, yet seasons are now longer than ever and coercive practices are widespread that require attendance at off-season training to maintain inclusion (Brenner, 2007).

Communicating life lessons, morals, and ethical sporting conduct

The over-competitiveness of professionalization discourses have also been implicated in the erosion of traditional sporting conduct and the increase in violence, aggression, and cheating (broadly defined) observed in youth sport (Abrams, 2012; Fredricks and Eccles, 2005; Siegenthaler and Gonzalez, 1997; Smoll, *et al.*, 2011). From my personal observations as a youth coach, coaches' teaching and/or condoning dangerous, aggressive, and illegal play are especially problematic with athletes too young to realize the potential costs of their actions. Equally, the valued lessons of learning how to win and lose (psychologically and emotionally), perseverance, and the moral and ethical codes of sporting conduct have been challenged and undermined by adult over-engagement in youth sport. Appropriate conduct and fair play remain core values connected to sport, but these are not natural or intrinsic and need to be explicitly taught and practiced as a consistent, integrated part of youth sport (Abrams, 2012; Barcelona and Young, 2010) by parents, coaches, and officials (for example, umpires/referees) as key role models (Fredricks and Eccles, 2005; Jambor, 1999). Coaches, parents (or parent-coaches), and officials influence children's understandings of sport and fair play in ways that have a long-lasting impact on identities and life skills, in addition to immediate implications for opponents. While policy-based efforts to address these issues are ongoing, the mere provision and application of rules and policies is inadequate to protect the positive values and benefits of youth sport in the face of current trends (Abrams, 2012).

Adults typically urge young athletes to be aggressive without guiding or teaching what constitutes appropriate physical aggression and aggressive action; language choices and instructions are significant in youth sport. Enforcement of key rules and the management of physical challenges, injury, and aggression are considered "teachable moments" (Abrams, 2012, p. 26), without which overly aggressive action can be enabled in place of strong, competitive action. Learning inappropriate physical contact and honing skills by pulling up clumsy, accidental, or simply dangerous play are important aspects of coaching and regulating sport (Abrams, 2012; Barcelona and Young, 2010). Being tough and strong (self-esteem and efficacy), facing a challenge and developing appropriate skills and technique (mastery) are important but, with the focus on winning at all costs, too often inappropriately aggressive actions are taught and rewarded in youth sport.

The failure to capitalize on teachable moments in youth sport is often compounded in recreational sports by an over-reliance on untrained, volunteer parents in coaching and officiating roles. While the voluntary donation of time is valued, many of these adults are problematically unfamiliar with the rules and skill sets of specific sports and are provided little, if any, guidance and training to fulfill their roles effectively and safely (Barcelona and Young, 2010). In fact, in recreational youth sports many volunteer parent-coaches and officials lack the training, experience, insight and knowledge that should be required to coach the vulnerable population of youth athletes. Equally, there is little monitoring of volunteer performance in these positions. This is highly significant given the power and status of coaches, their influence on young people, and the potential benefits and advantages of being trained by a good coach.

Coaches and coaching young athletes

In response to the detrimental shift in youth sport, positive coaching approaches have increasingly emerged that explicitly emphasize communicating and modeling the broader values of sport alongside the constructive management of coach–athlete relations. To combat the over-emphasis on winning and over-competitiveness a number of programs have returned to an explicit focus on the traditional values and lessons of youth sport (for example, trust, respect, honor, courage, leadership). But the powerful influence of individual coaches over young people (rather than programs *per se*) needs to be widely acknowledged. Equally, the coaches' effectiveness in managing their own identities and emotions, as well as managing coach–athlete and coach–parent relations, is crucial. Coaches have a direct impact on athletes' understandings, behaviors, and team functioning, but this is especially the case in youth sport given the vulnerabilities of young athletes and the status of coaches (Jambor, 1999; Strachan, *et al.*, 2011). Research consistently suggests that positive approaches, for example using praise and constructive feedback, alongside a focus on social support and relational aspects increase team cohesion and are associated with higher ratings of athlete self-perceptions and efficacy, motivation, performance, skills, fun, and the like (Strachan, *et al.*, 2011). Indeed, physical drills and skills training are less effective in the absence of a relational focus. Conversely, aggressive communication by coaches has been observed to have detrimental impacts on a wide array of individual and team indicators, including less satisfaction and more unsporting behaviors (Abrams, 2012; Fredricks and Eccles, 2005; Siegenthaler and Gonzalez, 1997; Smoll, *et al.*, 2011; Strachan, *et al.*, 2011).

Coaches also impact behaviors and understandings outside sport in significant ways that are ideal for promoting important long-term health and social messages (for example, sun-block use), making coaches powerful facilitators of behavioral and attitudinal change that extend beyond immediate sport concerns and contexts. But their potential as facilitators of positive social and cultural change should also be recognized, alongside their potential to cause damage and re/produce negative social values such as racism, sexism, and homophobia. Consequently, as role models, teachers, and gate-keepers to sport, coaches' continued use of gendered and racialized sporting stereotypes remains problematic and contentious (Fielding-Lloyd and Meân, 2008; Lusted, 2009).

Communication and discourses at the intersection of family and sport

Sport provides a naturalized and normalized site for families to negotiate and construct shared or disputed identities, understandings, cohesion, emotional bonds, and communicative satisfaction as they watch, play, and talk about sport. Parents also privilege sport as teaching valued cultural lessons and skills, actively using sport to teach and socialize their children (Coakley, 2006; Harrington, 2006; Kremer-Sadlik and Kim, 2007; Wiersma and Fifer, 2008). Organized youth sport has become an increasingly time-consuming and complex aspect of family life, with growing pressure to invest substantive amounts of family time, money, energy, and emotion to their children's sport and at earlier ages than ever before. Managing and negotiating the increasingly overlapping dynamics and demands of (organized) sport and family life is complex given the increased centrality of sport, its growth as entertainment, and the professionalization of youth sport. As noted by the aforementioned scholars, as well as Meân and Kassing (2008), managing the conflation of identities and roles that intersect for parents in youth sport, especially fathers, is challenging (for example, dad, mom, coach, mentor, manager, spectator, fan, supporter, protector, and discipliner).

Parent identities and parent–child communication

Sport provides valuable and memorable shared experiences for bonding and relational work, but increasingly young athletes predominantly recall parental admonishment, harsh criticism and bad parental behavior both during and after their sporting performances (Meân and Kassing, 2008). Parents' involvement and support are crucial elements in encouraging children's initial and continued participation in sport but also in the over-identification and over-training that cause burnout and drop-out (Siegenthaler and Gonzalez, 1997). Instead, positive and unconditional parental interest, support and involvement make an enjoyable, constructive and beneficial experience for young athletes; which is of course challenging for parents given other identities and the desire to help and teach children. But, as noted by Meân and Kassing, it is especially challenging for parents since our identities also appear to be contingent upon managing our children's sporting behaviors, performances, successes, and failures.

Many experts recommend praising specific aspects of skills and performance before any constructive criticism is offered, to enable active listening and avoid the negative emotions associated with over-invested parent-coaching (Fredricks and Eccles, 2005; Siegenthaler and Gonzalez, 1997; Strachan, *et al.*, 2011). While, for some, this is common sense, in practice it can be less easy to achieve and parents need to be aware of the subtle messages they communicate given evidence that parents display discursive affiliation with successful youth athletes, distance from non-succeeding athletes, and emotional pressure to perform for the parent (Brenner, 2007; Meân and Kassing, 2008). Because children's sporting performances, as noted by Meân and Kassing, also serve to perform parents' parental and sporting identities.

Family patterns of sporting inclusion and exclusion

Children's early involvement in and exposure to sport often reflects parental interests, preferences, experiences, hopes, and ambitions. Sport is typically a central activity for cohesion and identity for individuals and families (whether this is playing or watching organized, informal, live, or mediated) shaped by cultural, economic and geographical opportunities (including gender, race and/or ethnicity) that impact actual and perceived opportunities. Yet the opportunity and support to try varied sports of interest *to the child* (not the parent) are considered important aspects of the psychosocial and physical benefits of sport.

Playing sport, either organized or informal, requires families to have resources like time (to take children), money (especially for organized training, facilities, equipment, etc.), and/or *safe* space (such as roads, driveways, fields, parks, courts). This means that sport provision is lowest in poor urban and rural communities, which are disproportionately populated by minorities. In this way, resources create exclusions that account for the lack of racial diversity amongst American-born players in high-cost sports like baseball (Ogden, 2003). These interact further with other patterns of inclusion and exclusion impacted directly by gate-keepers (such as coaches, journalists) and more indirectly through the sport media narratives and representations that influence the self-exclusionary stereotypes in sport (Johnson and Migliaccio, 2009; Lusted, 2009; Ogden and Hilt, 2003). For example, such patterns and practices re/produce racialized stereotypes that encourage collective identities and over-identification within African-American families with specific sports choices for children (especially boys) over other sports or non-sporting options, problematically limiting more realistic long-term economic and educational choices by parents and children (Johnson and Migliaccio, 2009; Ogden and Hilt, 2003); particularly given the increased pressure for early specialization and elite training. Consequently, youth sport remains a site of limited racial diversity, despite being framed as a race-blind site.

But young people are excluded and self-exclude from sport for a variety of physical, economic, ideological and cultural reasons which powerfully resonate within the family according to their own identities, experiences, and understandings of sport as a socio-cultural phenomenon. As such, sport and families are also highly gendered sites in which parents and children re/produce wider patterns of ideological and cultural practices. Consequently it is common for families to privilege and prioritize fathers' and boys sporting knowledge and involvement (Coakley, 2006; Fredricks and Eccles, 2005; Harrington, 2006).

From the earliest moments, many parents make choices of toys, clothes, activities, playmates, room décor, and so on, based on their child's gender. The greater association of sport with masculinity means boys products and activities are frequently sport themed; or rather male sex-type sport themed. Sport-themed products are much less common for girls and likely to be cheerleading, gymnastics or ballet. These patterns mean that boys typically have earlier and more demanding exposure to the skills and activities required to compete effectively in sport. But these patterns also communicate parental and societal expectations about behaviors and interests and boys disinterested in sport, or showing little aptitude, often cause cultural and parental anxiety given the intersecting categorization of sport, masculinity, and heterosexuality. While some parents resist traditional gendered patterns, the gendered (hetero/sexualized and racialized) organization and content of sport cannot easily be countered.

The gendered nature of sport and the privileging of male sport membership and knowledge mean that mothers and fathers often self-select into traditionally gendered action regardless of their past sporting experience (Coakley, 2006; Fredricks and Eccles, 2005; Harrington, 2006). Consequently, as noted by Coakley, sport and athletic skills are generally overseen by fathers as "coaches, managers, agents, mentors, and advocates for their child athletes" (Coakley, 2006, p. 153) possibly irrespective of actual sporting experience and knowledge. In contrast, mothers most often fulfill the role of "team mom", transporting children to practice and perceived as offering little in sport-specific guidance or lessons (such as skills, coaching). Thus, while support of both parents has been shown to be important, notably for progression to elite athletic performance, it is the interest and support of fathers that has been most frequently noted to impact enjoyment and continued participation for both boys and girls.

This has direct implications for parent–child relationships and the long-term lessons and broader benefits of sport. Because of its association with masculinity, sport is an activity (informal and organized) through which fathers can meet the demands of the cultural shift towards their greater involvement in parenting (Coakley, 2006; Harrington, 2006). Indeed, Harrington (2006) notes that mothers are much less likely to take on formal coaching roles in youth sport than fathers, especially in the voluntary recreational coaching positions, regardless of whether they have substantive experience, skills and knowledge to offer (even if they have more than their volunteering husband). In contrast, fathers are likely to volunteer regardless of experience, in accordance with the cultural privileging of men in sport and as the category members of sport (Meân, 2001). Men are also much more likely to introduce children into sport consumption as fans and to masculine sporting discourses (Ben-Porat, 2009; Farrell and Fink, 2011; Mewett and Toffoletti, 2011). This means that both male and female children typically become subject to versions of sport that value and privilege men's sports and fandom over women's (Ben-Porat, 2009; Farrell and Fink, 2011). Consequently, while many women and girls claim identities as serious sports fans (Ben-Porat, 2009; Mewett and Toffoletti, 2011), they often privilege male sport and resist feminized framing of their fandom (Farrell and Fink, 2011; Jones, 2008).

This continued gendered family pattern is unfortunate because youth sport is argued to be an ideal place for girls *and* boys to experience and observe women in coaching and leadership positions (Harrington, 2006). Mothers "stepping up to the plate" to coach obviously offers girls the opportunity to see a female role model in action. But, more than this, women coaches provide girls and especially boys the chance to understand and experience working with a female leader in a male-dominated context. Such early experiences could provide invaluable lessons and experiences that can impact children's future ability to succeed in the increasingly diverse work place and effectively adapt to changing social roles and patterns of family life. The overall traditionally gendered family pattern of inclusions and exclusions, roles and identities, in youth sport means that children's early experiences typically continue to re/produce male sporting privilege, perpetuating the value placed on male athletes, men's sport and sporting practices, and men as the authority on sport (hence privileged as sport fans, journalists, coaches, and so on). It is sad and problematic that women's increased sporting participation has not impacted gendered family patterns of sporting participation, particularly in the US given the recent 40-year anniversary of the Title IX legislation aimed at ensuring equal sporting access in educational settings.

Conclusion

Youth sport remains widely and unquestioningly considered a valued site for education and development, and participation does continue to offer important individual and social advantages. But the increasing prominence of problematic sporting discourses in youth sport has raised serious concerns about the erosion of its core benefits and the dangers of youth sport being communicated and put into action by over-invested adults warrant genuine consideration. In the current professionalization of youth sport, many of the inherent problems are exacerbated by the long-standing ideological and cultural significance of sport in the US, and the prominence of hypermasculine, aggressive competitive sporting forms. This has been further compounded by the increased economic and mediated significance of sport and its supposed potential for young people.

Young people are excluded and quickly learn to self-exclude from sport for a variety of physical, economic, ideological and cultural reasons which are powerfully communicated through organized sport, coaching practices and relationships, media representations, and so forth. These then typically resonate strongly within the family according to familial identities, experiences, and understandings of sport as a sociocultural phenomenon, but especially reflecting parental identities and understandings. These, in turn, typically get re/produced within family communication, sporting activities, and other relational and discursive practices. This is not only evident in racialized patterns and choices, but in other patterns such as gender, sexuality and dis/ability. All of these are powerful and important patterns of inclusion and exclusion, especially given the potential benefits and advantages offered by positive organized sporting participation.

The significance of sport discourses for the construction of identities offers both an account and a rationale for the current discursive and communicative landscape of youth sport. These powerfully impact the ways that adults practice and manage sport as well as the lessons, relationships and identities children develop and experience because positive or negative, constructive or destructive family and coaching relationships are established and maintained in and through sport. Youth sport is a significant and powerful site that requires careful management and regulation, particularly by parents and coaches, given its ideological and cultural, collective and individual potential. Consequently, Malina (2010) echoes many organizations and individuals in advocating to parents and coaches that "youth sport must be kept in perspective" (p. 364) to combat its problematic professionalization and ensure its benefits and advantages are provided for as many young people as possible. To achieve this parents and coaches need to carefully manage their identities to ensure their communicative practices are effectively promoting and enacting the valued lessons and benefits of youth sport, rather than reproducing the traditional discourses associated with wider competitive sporting practices. However, without a greater public acknowledgement of the issues by sporting authorities – such as regulating organizations and sport media, and the raising of awareness via coordinated public strategic communication – the effective management of youth sport is likely to remain problematic.

References

Abrams, D. E. (2012). Player safety in youth sports: Sportsmanship and respect as an injury prevention strategy. *Seton Hall Journal of Sports and Entertainment Law*, 22 (1), 1–27. Retrieved from http://papers.ssrn.com/sol3/papers.cfm?abstract_id=1807404.

American Academy of Pediatrics (2000). Committee of Sports Medicine and Fitness. Intensive training and sports specialization in young athletes. *Pediatrics*, 106, 154–7.

Ben-Porat, A. (2009). Not just for men: Israeli women who fancy football. Soccer and Society, 10, 883–96.

Balyi, I., and Hamilton, A. (2004). *Long-term athletic development: Trainability in childhood and adolescence; windows of opportunity, optimal trainability*. Victoria: National Coaching Institute British Columbia and Advanced Training and Performance Ltd. Retrieved from http://www.athleticsireland.ie/content/wp-content/uploads/2007/03/bayliLTAD2004.pdf.

Barcelona, R. J., and Young, S. J. (2010). The role of municipal park and recreation agencies in enacting coach and parent training in a loosely couples youth sport system. *Managing Leisure*, 15, 181–97.

Brenner, J. S. (2007). Overuse injuries, overtraining and burnout in child and adolescent athletes. *Pediatrics*, 119, 1242–5.

Capranica, L., and Millard-Stafford, M. L. (2011). Youth sport specialization: How to manage competition and training? *International Journal of Sports Physiology and Performance*, 6, 572–9.

Coakley, J. (2006). The good father: Parental expectations and youth sports. *Leisure Studies*, 25, 153–63.

Côté, J., Lidor, R., and Hackfort, D. (2009). ISSP position stand: To sample or to specialize? Seven postulates about youth sport activities that lead to continued participation and elite sport performance. *International Journal of Sport and Exercise Psychology*, 9, 7–17.

DiFiori, J. P. (2010). Evaluations of overuse injuries in children and adolescents. *Current Sports Medicine Reports*, 9, 372–8.

Farrell, A., and Fink, J. (2011). Female fans of men's sport: Does their interest carry over to women's sport? Presentation at the annual conference of the North American Society for Sport Management. London, Ontario, June 2011.

Fielding-Lloyd, B., and Meân, L. J. (2008). Standards and separatism: The discursive construction of gender in English football coach education. *Sex Roles*, 58, 24–39.

Fredricks, J. A., and Eccles, J. S. (2005). Family socialization, gender, and sport motivation and involvement. *Journal of Sport and Exercise Psychology*, 27, 3–31.

Harrington, M. (2006). Sport and leisure as contexts for fathering in Australian families. *Leisure Studies*, 25, 165–83.

Jambor, E. A. (1999). Parents as children's socializing agents in youth soccer. *Journal of Sport Behavior*, 22, 350–61.

Johnson, T., and Migliaccio, T. (2009). The social construction of an athlete: African American boys' experiences in sport. *Western Journal of Black Studies*, 33, 98–109.

Jones, K. W. (2008) Female fandom: Identity, sexism and men's professional football in England. *Sociology of Sport Journal*, 25, 516–37.

Kindelan, K. (2012). Hockey mom reveals why she stormed the ice mid-fight. *ABC News*, June 18. Retrieved from http://gma.yahoo.com/blogs/abc-blogs/hockey-mom-reveals-why-she-stormed-ice-mid-144410831-abc-news-topstories.html.

Kremer-Sadlik, T., and Kim, J. L. (2007). Lessons from sports: Children's socialization to values through family interaction during sports activities. *Discourse and Society*, 18, 35–52.

Lemyre, P. N., Treasure, D. C., and Roberts, G. C. (2006). Influence of variability in motivation and affect on elite athlete burnout susceptibility. *Journal of Sport and Exercise Psychology*, 28, 32–48.

Lusted, J. (2009). Playing games with 'race': Understanding resistance to 'race' equality initiatives in English local football governance. *Soccer and Society*, 10, 722–39.

Malina, R. (2010). Early sport specialization: Roots, effectiveness, risks. *Current Sports Medicine Reports*, 9, 364–71.

Meân, L. J. (2001). Identity and discursive practice: Doing gender on the football pitch. *Discourse and Society*, 12, 789–815.

Meân, L. J. (2010). Making masculinity and framing femininity: FIFA, soccer and World Cup websites. In H. Hundley and A. Billings (Eds.), *Examining identity in sports media* (pp. 65–86). Thousand Oaks: Sage.

Meân, L. J., and Kassing, J. W. (2008). Fan identities at youth sporting events: A critical discourse analysis. *International Journal of Sport Communication*, 1, 42–66.

Messner, M. A. (1988). Sports and male domination: The female athlete as contested ideological terrain. *Sociology of Sport Journal*, 5, 197–211.

Messner, M. A. (2002). *Taking the field. Women, men and sports*. Minneapolis, MN: University of Minnesota Press.

Mewett, P., and Toffoletti, K. (2011) Finding footy: Female fan socialization and Australian rules football. *Sport in Society*, 14, 553–68.

National Council of Youth Sports (2008). *Report on trends and participation in organized youth sports*. Stuart, FL: NCYS. Retrieved from http://www.ncys.org/pdfs/2008/2008-ncys-market-research-report.pdf.

Oates, T. P. (2009). New media and the repackaging of NFL fandom. *Sociology of Sport Journal*, 26, 31–49.

Ogden, D. C. (2003). Baseball and blacks: A loss of affinity, a loss of community. In E. J. Rielly (Ed.), *Baseball and American culture across the diamond* (pp. 87–97). New York: Haworth.

Ogden, D. C., and Hilt, M. (2003). Collective identity and basketball: an explanation for the decreasing number of African Americans on America's baseball diamonds. *Journal of Leisure Research*, 35 (2), 213–27.

Raedeke, T. D., Lunney, K., and Venables, K. (2002). Understanding athlete burnout: Coach perspectives. *Journal of Sport Behavior*, 25, 101–206.

Rowe, D. (2004). *Sport, culture and the media: The unruly trinity*. Maidenhead, UK: Open University Press.

Siegenthaler, K. L., and Gonzalez, G. L. (1997). Youth sports as serious leisure. A critique. *Journal of Sport and Social Issues*, 21, 298–314.

Smoll, F. L., Cumming, S. P., and Smith, R. E. (2011). Enhancing coach–parent relationships in youth sports: Increasing harmony and minimizing hassle. *International Journal of Sports Science and Coaching*, 6, 13–26.

Strachan, L., Côté, J., and Deakin, J. (2011). A new view: Exploring positive youth development in elite sport contexts. *Qualitative Research in Sport, Exercise and Health*, 3, 9–32.

Theokas, C. (2009). Youth sport participation. A view of the issues. *Developmental Psychology*, 45, 303–6.

Wiersma, L. and Fifer, A. M. (2008). It's our turn to speak: The joys, challenges, and recommendations of youth sport parents. *Journal of Leisure Research*, 4, 702–11.

35

THE BABE/BABY FACTOR

Sport, women, and mass media

Barbara Barnett

For female athletes, the playing field can be a minefield. Women have more opportunities to participate in athletic programs than ever before, yet fewer opportunities than men. Women receive credit for their strength and athletic abilities, but they are more popular and more economically successful if they are pretty. Female athletes take home gold medals and championship trophies, but their roles as mothers, sex symbols, and fashionistas are often what make headlines.

Media coverage of sporting events has increased dramatically in the past 20 years, with dedicated sports channels on cable and satellite television, including ESPN 2 (Whannel, 2008), and the advent of the Internet, which allows media organizations to post more detailed accounts of sporting events and permits athletes to promote their sport and themselves through social media. Yet, this media boom has not necessarily translated into more or better coverage of women's sports. Feminist scholars and women's advocates have criticized mass media, both traditional and new media, saying they cover sport primarily as a male enterprise. "Modern sport has clearly been among the most masculine of institutions" (Messner, 2002, p. 66).

Women's sporting events are underreported, and if they are covered at all, women's accomplishments are trivialized through reports that question their skills, highlight their sexuality, or depict their athletic accomplishments in relation to their roles as mothers, wives, or daughters (Dworkin and Messner, 2002; Hall, 2002; Kane and Greendorfer, 1994). While the media marginalize women, sportswomen themselves use mass media to apologize for their successes (Festle, 1996) and assure fans that they can win championships and still bake cookies, raise children, and look sexy. Women play sports, but they don't enjoy a level playing field.

Mom, cutie pie, Wonder Woman

Over the past few decades (and in the United States, since the passage of Title IX), the presence of women in sport has burgeoned, prompting media scholars to question whether coverage adequately – and accurately – reflects this change. Scholars have examined the quantity and quality of coverage and found that women do not appear as often as men in sports broadcasts, in newspapers, or online. When women do appear, they are cast – or cast themselves – as a loving mother, a cute little girl, or a modern-day Wonder Woman (scantily clad but incredibly powerful). "The presence of women athletes in the media appears to represent fundamental social change in that sportswomen have gained widespread social acceptance," noted Kane and Greendorfer. The scholars further explain, however, that "in reality, these 'feminized' images represent a modernized attempt to reinforce traditional stereotypical images of femininity and female sexuality" (Kane and Greendorfer, 1994, p. 28). In examining sports reporting, men dominate in terms of amount of coverage and number of sources (Project for Excellence in Journalism, 2005). Women receive less than ten percent of the sports coverage in US newspapers and on television, although this percentage does increase during major sporting events, such as the Olympics (Markula, 2009). A study of *Sports Illustrated*, spanning 33 years, found that only nine percent of feature stories focused on women (Lumpkin and Williams, 1991), and a study of ESPN TV found that 96 percent of its stories were about male athletes (Adams and Tuggle, 2004). Analyses of the Olympics, an event whose participants are more than 40 percent female, have repeatedly determined that women receive less media attention than men (see, for example, Billings and Angelini, 2007; Billings, 2008; Greer, Hardin, and Homan, 2009). In 1996, US women won more medals than US men, yet media coverage focused primarily on men – more stories, more airtime, more photos. When women did appear, they were presented in stereotypical ways, with the focus on their femininity, not their athleticism (Smith, 2011). Coverage of women increases, however, when they participate in "feminine appropriate" or graceful sports, such as figure skating.

Although most sport media studies have been conducted in the United States, research in other countries shows similar results. A study of Wimbledon tennis found that British newspapers tended to give more coverage and more favorable coverage to women who met the Eurocentric standards for beauty. For example, Anna Kournikova, who is white, blonde, and heterosexual, received positive coverage, while the press largely ignored Amélie Mauresmo, who is openly gay, and referred to Serena and Venus Williams as "black beauties" and "Amazons" (Vincent, 2010). Analysis of daily newspapers in Turkey found that press coverage presented male athletes as "doers" and female athletes as "pleasers" (Yüce and Bari , 2009). In South Africa's *Sports Illustrated*, female athletes were described as sexual objects or marketable products with a focus on physical beauty, ignoring strength and hard work (Brandt and Carstens, 2005). An examination of sports coverage in the German magazine *Süddeutsche Zeitung* found that men's sports dominated (Worsching, 2010), as was the case with media coverage of athletes in China (Wu, 2009). Korean athletes participating in the 2004 Olympics in Athens were described as mother, sisters, or daughters (Koh, 2009).

A fan searching current websites for information about women's sports will have to look long and hard to find women in any roles other than fans, family members, or "babes." From September 2008 through June 2012, ESPN published 96 issues of its magazine. Its online archives show that, during that time, eight women appeared on the cover: soccer goalkeeper Hope Solo, basketball player Diana Taurasi, and tennis champion Serena Williams; all appeared naked on the cover of the magazine's "body issue." Lindsay Vonn appeared fully clothed, but wearing a short white dress and stilettoes, and pregnant Candace Parker, basketball player, appeared with a headline that asked, "How big can Candace Parker get?" Amanda McCarthy, wearing an open shirt and bathing suit, appeared standing behind her husband baseball player Brandon McCarthy, identified only as "this model." Only race car driver Danica Patrick and tennis player Maria Sharapova appeared in athletic clothes.

From January 2008 through June 2012, *Sports Illustrated* published 388 issues, including multiple issues the same week – preview issues for basketball, baseball, and football that often featured different covers for different geographic regions. Fourteen covers featured women; more than one-third were the swimsuit issue. Of the remainder, three pictured a woman with a man: Tennessee women's basketball coach Pat Summitt, who has won more games than any other college coach, with Duke men's basketball coach Mike Krzyzewski; two female and two male Olympic athletes; and golfer Brian Guy with his wife and two daughters. Four covers featured action shots of female athletes: Lindsay Vonn, Hope Solo, Serena Williams, and a group shot of the Tennessee women's basketball team. Danica Patrick posed in her racing uniform, while *Sports Illustrated* featured the text of Title IX on one cover.

Traditional media have been limited by space, time, and money (Smith, 2011), and the Internet was heralded as a new media platform that might allow increased coverage of women's sports. It has, however, fallen short (Hardin, 2011). Smith (2011) found that men's sports on Twitter outpaced women's sports in number of tweets and secondary materials posted – articles, videos, photos, and re-tweets. An analysis of articles posted on ESPN and CBS SportsLine (now CBSSports.com) sites during the U.S. college basketball tournaments found that nearly three-fourths of the articles focused on the men's games (Kian, Mondello, and Vincent, 2009), and a separate analysis of sports sites, which included CBS SportsLine, CNNSI, and ESPN, found that women's sports received less coverage than men's (Kachgal, 2001). Yet, this same study did find one change: Descriptors of female and male athletes were similar; writers did not rely on traditional gender stereotypes to describe strength and physical appearance.

Scholars have argued that women's sports often are presented as a minor branch of men's sports (Cantelon, 2010; Markula, 2009; Nelson, 2010), and this is evident on sports websites. *Sports Illustrated*'s site has links to professional football, baseball, basketball, racing, hockey, boxing, and golf – all of which provide information about men's athletics. There are three specific links to women's sports: One for "women's hoops" under the "college basketball" tab, another link to the Women's Tennis Association, and, under the "more" tab, there are links to women's professional basketball. Obviously, women play sports; *Sports Illustrated* just doesn't cover them.

ESPN's website shows similar neglect. A viewer has to go to the "more" tab, and look past golf, global soccer, martial arts, horse racing, poker, cricket, lacrosse, bass fishing, and rugby, to find the link to women's professional basketball. However, ESPN does have a site dedicated to women's sports, ESPNW. The website, introduced in 2010, has been praised and criticized by women's advocates, who say it foregrounds women's accomplishments but at the same time reinforces traditional gender roles. Laura Gentile, vice president of ESPNW, called the site a place "where we talk about women finding self-esteem in sports and about getting a pedicure" (Thomas, 2010). The she's-as-strong-as-she-is-pretty message played out in a package honoring the 40th anniversary of Title IX in which ESPNW published a list of the top 40 female athletes. More than half the photos depicted women playing their sports. Yet, four depicted women posing, and 13 depicted women celebrating a victory – holding a trophy or waving a flag – reinforcing the notion that it is better to smile than to sweat. The text presents dualistic descriptors of women – as powerful athletes but also in traditional gender roles. "Nobody has been faster than the 45-year-old mother" the website said of Olympic medalist Dara Torres. The late Florence Griffith-Joyner, Olympic track and field medalist, was described as a superior athlete, but the website noted that she retired early because "she had other passions to pursue: motherhood, for one, and also a career in fashion and design."

When women do appear in sports stories, journalists describe their performance differently than men's. For example, Billings (2007) compared descriptors used for male and female Olympic athletes and found that broadcasters' comments about concentration, strength, experience, courage, emotion, and attractiveness were similar for both sexes. However, female swimmers were more likely than men to be characterized as losing a competition because they lost their composure, and women divers were more likely than men to be described as emotional and introverted. Analysis of NCAA and the US Open coverage found that reporters more often described men, not women, as strong (Duncan, Messner, Williams, Jensen, and Wilson, 1994), while a study of the 2006 winter Olympics revealed that men's successes were likely to be attributed to composure and intelligence, while women's successes were attributed to courage; men's failures were attributed to lack of commitment, and women's to lack of strength (Billings, *et al.*, 2008).

Festle (1996) suggested that even when female athletes are successful, they demonstrate "apologetic behavior" in which they assure journalists and fans they are "ladies first, then athletes" (p. 46). Schell and Rodriguez (2000) have observed that women who adopt the apologetic stance may focus on their physical beauty and heterosexuality while downplaying their athletic skills.

In the 1970s, when Chris Evert was winning Wimbledon matches, she told journalists, "I'd rather be known in the end as a woman than a tennis player" (Festle, 1996, p. 153). Today, female athletes continue the apologetic tradition by presenting themselves as superior sportswomen who hold traditional feminine values. Swimmer Dara Torres' home page shows her lying down, peeking out from blonde hair, wearing make-up and jewelry. The website tells viewers that Torres is a five-time Olympic medalist and the oldest swimmer to compete in the Olympics, but that Torres is "far from your average athlete;" she also is a mom and was the first athlete to appear in the *Sports Illustrated* swimsuit issue. Serena Williams' website describes her as an "A-list" celebrity who has "overcome insurmountable odds to win a total of 23 career Grand Slams" but also explains that "off the court, fashion and acting are Serena's passions" and features a link to her line of nail polishes. Golfer Michelle Wie's website reports that one of her hobbies is baking and offers a link to "fairway fashions," with illustrations of the outfits she wore in past tournaments. Misty May-Treanor's website features information about her volleyball career and sports clinics, but also photos of her in a bikini, wrapped in a volleyball net. Her teammate Kerri Walsh's website features a photo of her with her husband and two children and describes her as "six feet of sunshine." And teammate Jennifer Kessy, before going to the 2012 London Olympics, appeared in a CoverGirl lipstick advertisement, saying, "I'm going for the gold and the pink. I'm strong, I'm beautiful. I am a cover girl."

While the notion that women play multiple roles is realistic, and the equation of feminine strength with beauty is a welcome contrast to gender stereotypes of women as passive, it is also important to ask why being strong is not enough? The answer is that sports has become a commercial enterprise as well an athletic one, and the same standards of beauty and perfection that historically have applied in advertisements and entertainment now apply in sports, where athletes promote, not just their sport, but themselves as a brand.

New media, specifically the Internet, while offering the potential space for more women's voices, has also provided more opportunities for sexual objectification. TotalProSports.com honors "the hottest college sports" and claims that "nothing says college like parties, sports, and girls." CheerleaderCentral.com provides pictures, calendars, trading cards and videos, and includes photos of cheerleaders for professional, college, and high school teams. Similarly, the

Internet offers women a chance to objectify men. Femmefan.com promotes itself as a website that covers sports "from the female's unique perspective;" it also and includes "locker room lookers," photos of shirtless male athletes' abs and biceps.

A new form of this apologetic behavior is the soft porn images of female athletes, in which the perfect athletic body becomes the perfect sexual body. Messner (2002) has suggested that mass media blur the athletic and the erotic, and Rowe cites as an example of soft porn the "honey shots" of scantily clad female fans and *Sports Illustrated*'s swimsuit edition, in which women wear "something skimpy that is vaguely associated with sport or leisure" (Rowe, 1999, p. 128). This sexualization, Kane and Greendorfer (1994) argue, diminishes women's accomplishments because they are regarded as bodies, or parts of bodies, not as successful individuals.

Female athletes, including skater Katarina Witt, have appeared on the cover of *Playboy*, and other men's magazines have featured female athletes naked, or nearly naked, posing with sporting equipment while pouting seductively for the camera. Each year, *Esquire* magazine names its 15 sexiest women alive. In 2011, three of the 15 were athletes: Gina Carano, who was pictured lying in a pool of water wearing a black bikini, "for having the guts of a fighter but not the body of one:" soccer player Hope Solo, posing with hand on hip and wearing shorts, an open sweatshirt and bikini top; and Victoria Azarenka, who was not pictured playing tennis but smiling at the camera with her blonde hair draped over one shoulder. *Maxim* magazine also publishes a "Hot 100 List" and the 2012 list includes female wrestlers, soccer players, and tennis players, as well as cheerleaders. Caroline Wozniacki was described on the magazine's website as "yummier than the kind of Danish you'd get at your local bakery," and the site includes a link that takes viewers to "more hot women of tennis." Soccer player Alex Morgan was compared with Mia Hamm "for her speed and nose for the goal. And what a cute lil' nose it is."

Nowhere is the sexualization of female athletes more evident than in the *Sports Illustrated* swimsuit issue, which first appeared in the 1960s as a way to boost sales between football and basketball season. The swimsuit issues now accounts for about one-tenth of the magazine's total annual revenue, and 40 percent of that revenue comes from digital content and marketing events (Ovide, 2009). Numerous female athletes have appeared in the issue, including swimmer Amanda Beard, skier Lindsay Vonn, snowboarder Hannah Teter, and tennis players Serena Williams and Steffi Graff.

Although it doesn't have a swimsuit issue, *ESPN The Magazine* publishes its annual "body issue," which, according to its website, celebrates the "vast potential of the human form" and offers an opportunity to "unapologetically stand in awe of the athletes who've pushed their physiques to profound frontiers." Recent covers have featured naked soccer player Hope Solo, basketball player Diana Taurasi, and tennis champion Serena Williams. The magazine publishes alternate covers, which feature male athletes.

Why would someone who has reached the upper echelons of athletic accomplishment display her sexuality publicly? Wanneberg (2011), in an analysis of Swedish sports media, discussed self-imposed sexualization, which she says was first used by male athletes who presented themselves to the public as sexy and sexually powerful. She links this practice to commercialization of sports, and Rowe (1999) similarly observed that female athletes are often happy to capitalize on their sexual images because they gain commercial advantages. Athletes can use their sexiness to gain media attention, audience approval, and sponsor interest.

Athletes themselves say posing for such photos gives them pleasure and pleases others. Danica Patrick appeared in the 2008 *Sports Illustrated* swimsuit edition, and in the accompanying video, her racing suit below her knees, she explained that "the swimsuit issue . . . I'm just so flattered because it's just such a unique and prestigious, you know, piece to be a part of." Maria Sharapova appeared in 2006 and told *Sports Illustrated* readers/viewers, "I've never been 80 percent bare in a photo shoot...I'm sure the teenage boy fans will like it." Snowboarder Hannah Teter explained: "It's fun to be sexy." Hope Solo, who appeared in *ESPN The Magazine*'s body issue, naked and holding a water hose, said she did so to celebrate the female athlete's body and found it "pretty amazing" that beauty had evolved from stick-thin models to athletic soccer players.

For second-wave feminists, who lobbied for the most basic of rights in Title IX, such displays are viewed as male exploitation of women's bodies. But, for third-wave feminists, these displays are considered empowering. Third-wave feminists allow that women can be strong and sexy, and that women can use their sexuality to gain attention. Yet, this perspective ignores the fact that sport and the larger society value women – and women value themselves – for their physical appearance. After all, there is no men's swimsuit issue. In this context, athletics moves beyond the traditional notion of "spectator" sport; sport becomes about men viewing women, and women understanding there are rewards for be viewed.

Where do women and men go from here?

Sports broadcasts and newspaper pages historically were produced largely by men for a male audience, and even with women's increased athletic participation and the advent of the Internet, sport media remain a masculine enclave. "Men, money, and the media control modern-day sports" (Salter, 1996, p. 10), and this triumvirate has unnecessarily excluded women. Coakley (2009) has argued that because media compete for circulation, advertising revenues, and profits, their goal is to present the most inoffensive messages for the most affluent audiences. Consequently, media play it safe by perpetuating traditional cultural stereotypes, rather than challenging them. In sport media, the gaze is definitely male.

Because of the historical exclusion of women from social institutions, sport has become a gendered contest that pits women's interests against men's, and the media have played a role in fueling this competition. Women are presented with messages that they are less than men, and men are presented with messages that women's participation in sports somehow diminishes their masculinity. Both are incorrect. Journalists, who are supposed to present an accurate representation of events, have failed when they do not report on women's sports. Advertisers, who must constantly court consumers, risk ignoring half the population, and the group that allegedly makes the most decisions about household purchases, when they present sports as a male preserve.

There are multiple feminisms, but two common tenets of feminist thought are that women hold secondary status to men in society and that this needs to change. For some women's advocates, the remedy for inequality is separation – women-only teams and women-centered websites or publications to cover those teams. For others, the perspective is that sport as an institution must change to provide more opportunities for women without compromising or eliminating opportunities for men. And for others, economics is the lever needed. Corporations should refuse to sponsor events that exclude women; corporations should look to sponsor and support female athletes, especially those that equate sport and health; and advertisers should insist that media take a serious look at audiences and craft publications that meet the interests of women *and* men.

For journalism schools, working to train the next generation of sport reporters and editors, professors can look for opportunities to correct or challenge existing patterns of media coverage. They can assign students to report on women's sporting events as well as men's and to consider how they report on male and female athletes. Campus media staffs can refuse ads that sexualize female athletes or equate sex and sports (for example, sports-bar ads that feature bikini-clad waitresses). Finally, journalism schools should require all students to take courses in diversity, to learn think critically about sexual, racial, and other forms of stereotypes. How can journalists report accurately or advertisers understand their audiences if they base their knowledge on sexual stereotypes?

However, these changes will not erase the fact that women – whether they are athletes, politicians, or journalists – are often evaluated on their looks rather than their accomplishments, and women who excel in any field are taught from childhood to downplay their achievements, to attribute them to luck or accident. Women internalize the notion that their value comes from their ability to conform to traditional feminine standards.

Curry (2002) has written that, in contemporary society, masculinity must be proven over and over again, and sport is one arena where this occurs. Women, too, must prove their femininity – prove they are the "right" kind of woman or girl. They must demonstrate that they can be sexy, that they can be maternal, that they can be cute. They must prove femininity so they will not be labeled "lesbian," which is not used as a descriptor for sexual identity (and is irrelevant in any athletic completion) but used as a synonym for "manly," and connotes an outsider invading male territory. Sexism and homophobia are teammates in contemporary media representations of sports.

Women's participation in sports is increasing, and audiences are changing as more women attend and watch games. The media need to catch up and change, too.

References

Adams, T., and Tuggle, C.A. (2004). ESPN's SportsCenter and coverage of women's athletics: "It's a boys' club." *Mass Communication and Society*, 7 (2), 237–48.

Billings, A. C. (2007). From diving boards to pole vaults: Gendered athlete portrayals in the "Big Four" Sports at the 2004 Athens summer Olympics. *Southern Communication Journal*, 72 (4), 329–44.

Billings, A. C. (2008). Clocking gender differences: Televised Olympic clock time in the 1996–2006 summer and winter Olympics. *Television and New Media*, 9 (5), 429–41.

Billings, A. C., and Angelini, J. R. (2007). Packaging the games for viewer consumption: Gender, ethnicity and Nationality in NBC's coverage of the 2004 Summer Olympics. *Communication Quarterly*, 55 (1), 95–111.

Billings, A. C., Brown, C. L., Crout III, J. H., McKenna, K. E., Rice, B. A., Timanus, M. E., Ziegler, J. (2008). The games through the NBC lens: Gender, ethnic, and national equity in the 2006 Torino Winter Olympics. *Journal of Broadcasting and Electronic Media*, June, 215–30.

Brandt, M., and Carstens, A. (2005). The discourse of the male gaze: A critical analysis of the feature section "The beauty of sport" in *SA Sports Illustrated. Southern African Linguistics and Applied Language Studies*, 23 (3), 233–43.

Cantelon, M. (2010). Sex-a-side: Volleyball uniforms and the reproduction of female objectivity. In L. K. Fullteron (Ed.), *Sexual sports rhetoric: Global and universal contexts* (pp. 13–23). New York: Peter Lang.

Coakley, J. (2009). *Sport in society: Issues and controversies.* (10th ed.). New York: McGraw-Hill.

Curry, T. J. (2002). Fraternal bonding in the locker room: A profeminist analysis of talk about competition and women. In S. Scraton and A. Flintoff (Eds.), *Gender and sport: A reader* (pp. 169–87). London: Routledge.

Duncan, M. C., Messner, M. A., Williams, L., Jensen, K., and Wilson, W. (1994). Gender stereotyping in televised sports. In S. Birrell and C. L. Cole (Eds.), *Women, sport, and culture* (pp. 249–72). Champaign, IL: Human Kinetics.

Dworkin, S. L., and Messner, M. A. (2002). Just do ... what? Sport, bodies, and gender. In S. Scraton and A. Flintoff (Eds.), *Gender and sport: A reader* (pp. 17–21). London: Routledge.

Festle, M. J. (1996). *Playing nice: Politics and apologies in women's sports*. New York: Columbia University.

Greer, J. D., Hardin, M., and Homan, C. (2009). "Naturally" less exciting? Visual production of men's and women's track and field coverage during the 2004 Olympics. *Journal of Broadcasting and Electronic Media*, 52 (2), 173–89.

Hall, M. A. (2002). The discourse of gender and sport: From femininity to feminism. In S. Scraton and A. Flintoff (Eds.), *Gender and sport: A reader* (pp. 6 –16). London and New York: Routledge.

Hardin, M. (2011). The power of a fragmented collective: Radical pluralist feminism and technologies of the self in the sports blogosphere. In A. C. Billings (Ed.), *Sport media: Transformation, integration, consumption* (pp. 40–60). New York and London: Routledge.

Kachgal, T. M. (2001). Home court disadvantage? Examining the coverage of female athletes on leading sports websites; a pilot study. Paper presented at the annual conference of Association for Education in Journalism and Mass Communications, Washington, DC, August 2001.

Kane, M. J., and Greendorfer, S. L. (1994). The media's role in accommodating and resisting stereotyped images of women in sport. In P. J. Creedon (Ed.), *Women, media and sport: Challenging gender values* (pp. 28–44). Thousand Oaks, CA: Sage.

Kian, E. M., Mondello, M., and Vincent, J. (2009). ESPN: The women's sports network? A content analysis of Internet coverage of March Madness. *Journal of Broadcasting and Electronic Media*, 53 (3), 477–95.

Koh, E. (2009). Heroes, sisters, and beauties: Korean printed media representations of sport women in the 2004 Olympics. In P. Markula (Ed.), *Olympic women and the media: International perspectives* (pp. 168–84). New York: Palgrave Macmillan.

Lumpkin, A., and Williams, L. (1991). An analysis of *Sports Illustrated* feature articles 1954–1987. *Sociology of Sport Journal*, 8 (1), 16–32.

Markula, P. (2009). Introduction. In P. Markula (Ed.), *Olympic women and the media: International perspectives* (pp. 1–29). New York: Palgrave Macmillan.

Messner, M. (2002). *Taking the field: Women, men, and sports*. Minneapolis: University of Minnesota Press.

Nelson, K. (2010). Watching women: How spectators talk about female athletes. In L. K. Fuller (Ed.), *Sexual sports rhetoric: Global and universal contexts* (pp. 97–106). New York: Peter Lang,.

Ovide, S. (2009). *Sports Illustrated* builds a buzz: Magazine turns promotions for its swimsuit edition into moneymakers. *Wall Street Journal*, February 9. Retrieved from http://online.wsj.com/article/SB1234138723290621.htm.

Project for Excellence in Journalism (2005). Box scores and bylines: A snapshot of the newspaper sports page; gender on the page. Pew Research Center's Project for Excellence in Journalism. *Journalism.org*, August 22. Retrieved from http://www.journalism.org/node/54.

Rowe, D. (1999). *Sport, culture and the media: The unruly trinity*. Buckingham and Philadelphia: Open University.

Salter, D. F. (1996). *Crashing the old boys' network: The tragedies and triumphs of girls and women in sports*. Westport, CT: Praeger.

Schell, L. A., and Rodriguez, S. (2000). Our sporting sisters: How male hegemony stratifies women in sport. *Women in Sport and Physical Activity Journal*, 9 (1), 15–35.

Smith, L. R. (2011). The less you say: An initial study of gender coverage in sports on Twitter. In A. C. Billings (Ed.), *Sport media: Transformation, integration, consumption* (pp. 146–61). New York and London: Routledge.

Thomas, K. (2010). ESPN slowly introducing online brand to women. *New York Times*, October 15. Retrieved from http://www.nytimes.com/2010/10/16/sports/16espnw.html.

Vincent, J. (2010). Sporting Lolitas, Amazons, and freaks: British newspaper portrayal of female tennis players at Wimbledon. In L. K. Fuller (Ed.), *Sexual sports rhetoric: Global and universal contexts* (pp. 173–84). New York: Peter Lang.

Wanneberg, P. L. (2011). The sexualization of sport: A gender analysis of Swedish elite sport from 1967 to the present day. *European Journal of Women's Studies*, 18 (3), 265–78.

Whannel, G. (2008). *Culture, politics and sport: Blowing the whistle, revisited*. London and New York: Routledge.

Worsching, M. (2010). Gender and sport in the German quality press: The global and the domestic in editorial and advertising. In L. K. Fuller (Ed.), *Sexual sports rhetoric: Global and universal contexts* (pp. 201–13). New York: Peter Lang.

Wu, P. (2009). From "Iron Girl" to "sexy goddess:" An analysis of the Chinese media. In P. Markula (Ed.), *Olympic women and the media: International perspectives* (pp. 70–86). New York: Palgrave Macmillan.

Yüce, Ö. D., and Bari , K. (2009). Belles de sport: Représentation des femmes dan les pages sportives des quotidiens turcs. *Ileti-s-im*, 377–391.

36

BEST PRACTICES FOR MEDIA COVERAGE OF ATHLETES WITH DISABILITIES

A person-first language approach

Joshua R. Pate and Robin L. Hardin

Media coverage of athletes with physical disabilities often overemphasizes successes while downplaying failures. The coverage focuses more on disability rather than athletic performance, even when highlighting disability is considered positive publicity for the athlete. For example, media professionals often emphasize the amazing feats an athlete with a disability reaches when he or she "overcomes" disability to perform an athletic accomplishment at an elite level. The common description is that these athletes perform at high levels *in spite of* their disability. While in many cases those accomplishments merit great praise and recognition, patronizing athletes with disabilities simply for competing marginalizes athletic accomplishments and emphasizes disability. This patronization and emphasis on disability is seen through the misuse of language. Media professionals commonly use phrases and labels that are not always preferred by people with disabilities, such as "handicapped", "disabled athlete", or "special". These terms can be offensive and derogatory to some people with disabilities, although there may be no malicious intent by the sender for the message to be interpreted in this way (University of Kansas Research Center on Independent Living, 2008). It is important here to examine and define those terms in relation to how they are misused while offering suggestions for media professionals.

Acceptable and appropriate terminology regarding people with disabilities and the way athletes with disabilities are portrayed in media has transformed much like terminology for ethnicity and race. Terms like "Hispanic", "Latino", "Chicano," and "Mexican" are mistakenly used interchangeably, although their definitions are different. Definitions of sociocultural labels provide a greater example of how meaning and social acceptance evolves over time. For instance, "handicap" has gone from being socially accepted to primarily obsolete among people with disabilities, to the extent that some people with disabilities refuse to say it and reference it as the "H-word" (Bornman, 2004; Haller, Dorries, and Rahn, 2006; Patterson and Witten, 1987; Sigelman, Tuch, and Martin, 2005). "Handicap," which once was used by the World Health Organization (WHO) to classify people with disabilities, is now considered taboo among many people with disabilities because the term has "socially imposed negative connotations" (Bornman, 2004, p. 184). Similarly, there is a movement supported by the Special Olympics and more than 200 other international advocacy groups to end the term "retarded," which has been used to define people with cognitive disabilities, yet has been considered an offensive term. As noted by Haller and colleagues, extinguishing antiquated language is part of the Disability Rights Movement, in an attempt to change the meaning of disability similar to those efforts with race, ethnicity, and even sexual orientation.

Disabling language

When outdated and offensive terms are used in reference to people with disabilities, it is considered to be disabling language. Disabling language is that which, according to Patterson and Witten (1987), "perpetuates myths and stereotypes about persons with disabilities." Furthermore, they note that disability language, "uses nouns instead of adjectives to describe persons with disabilities" and "uses a demeaning or outdated word or phrase in reference to persons with disabilities" (p. 245). Using "handicap," for example, risks reinforcing stereotypes of having little or no ability to perform a task, or emphasizes a medical focus that brings forth connotations of helplessness or non-normal. One scholar argues that disabling language can reinforce perceptions that people with disabilities are a helpless population: "The language of disability indicates that persons with disabilities are usually perceived exclusively in terms of their disabilities, that they are confined to a 'handicapped role' in which they are seen primarily as recipients of medical treatment," notes Longmore (1985), adding that such a role, "includes ascribed traits of helplessness, dependency, abnormality of appearance and mode of functioning, pervasive incapacitation of every aspect of personhood, and ultimately subhumanness" (p. 419). Clearly, disabling language is offensive and should be considered with sensitivity. Yet, disabling language is common, despite the differences in actual definitions of the words.

Disabling language can be the misuse of words, but it can also be misrepresentation of disability that reinforces inaccurate stereotypes. One common example is when media professionals state that an athlete is confined to a wheelchair. In the example, media professionals "misrepresent disability" while simultaneously display their "misunderstanding of the disability experience; [w]heelchair users are not binding or confining but actually increase mobility, speed, and ability" (Haller, *et al.*, 2006, p. 71). The misunderstanding is often simply a journalist resorting to what has been ingrained into his or her perception of disability. In other words, disability means wheelchair, which then means limited.

Still, not all view disabling language as offensive. Some individuals do not like the term "disability" because it presents the notion that one is without ability and may never overcome those barriers. "Handicap," the argument goes, acknowledges that a task is possible, although it may be accomplished at a slower speed (Berkson, 2012). Think of this example in terms of golf, a sport where "handicap" is within its common vernacular. If a golfer has a disability, then he or she does not have the ability to play golf. However, if a golfer has a handicap, then he or she can play but plays at a different level of success than expected. While viewing the terms in this manner may be the minority viewpoint in a debate on proper language use for people with disabilities, it is important to acknowledge that this debate is not exclusive or one-sided. Yet, a clearer picture is presented when these terms are defined.

Defining impairment, disability, and handicap

The term impairment is often used interchangeably with disability and handicap, although defined differently. Impairment should be considered the medical diagnosis and it is used to "characterize a physical, mental, or physiological loss, abnormality, or injury that causes a limitation in one or more major life functions" (ABILITY, 2012, para 4). Bullock, Mahon, and Killingsworth (2010) define impairment as "any loss or abnormality of psychological, physiological, or anatomical structure or function, which might result from a disease, accident, genetic, or other environmental agents" (p. 2). Therefore, impairment refers to a medical diagnosis or physical condition. Regarding the term disability, Coakley's definition refers to the socially constructed constraints placed upon people with impairments when "accommodations in social or physical contexts are not or cannot be made to allow the full participation of people with functional limitations" (Coakley, 2009, p. 50). Furthermore, WHO adopted disability as its term (rather than handicap), defining it as "an umbrella term, covering impairments, activity limitations, and participation restrictions" (Bornman, 2004; World Health Organization, 2012, para. 1). In this sense, these definitions of disability portray it as an individual's limitation owing to impairment. Lastly, handicap is defined as being sometimes offensive in reference to a physical disability and is said to describe a "barrier or problem created by society or the environment (ABILITY, 2012, para. 6). The term handicap is associated with perception. Coakley explains that when a person is handicapped, "others define them as inferior and 'unable' due to perceived disabilities" (Coakley, 2009, p. 51). Such definitions infer that handicap is more of a socially constructed label in which members of society decide what a person with a disability is capable of doing.

Perhaps the way to make sense of all these definitions is best explained through application. *Impairment* is considered the medical condition, as in "The loss of her right arm was only a slight impairment to her ability to drive" (ABILITY, 2012, para. 4). *Disability* refers to the functional constraints within society, such as "Despite his disability, he still was able to maintain employment" (ABILITY, 2012, para 5). *Handicap* is in reference to a barrier created by society: "The stairs leading to the stage were a handicap to him" (ABILITY, 2012, para 6). These specific terms, even when defined and applied to a sport setting, reinforce differences.

In relation to "normal"

The definitions of impairment, disability, and handicap, all send messages of limiting full participation (for example, impairment), lacking the ability to perform normally (for example, disability), and prevention of a normal role (for example, handicap). All three terms measure against what is considered societal norms (Titchkosky, 2001). Similarly, disabling language places the emphasis on disability and how athletes, no matter the sport or the impairment, do not measure to the norm. This separation from normal reinforces exclusion of people with disabilities in sport (DePauw, 1997).

One of the major influences of media is in the reinforcement of existing attitudes and social myths about disability, which are already often constructed indirectly by media professionals (Schantz and Gilbert, 2008; Silva and Howe, 2012). Media representations, in fact, often create binary labeling of abled vs. disabled. Silva and Howe identify this as "othering," where differences are magnified and similarities are undervalued (p. 178). Othering carries a negative connotation similar to "us vs. them" with the outgroup being outcast as different from what is normal. Silva and Howe argue that othering can also enhance differences when an athlete with a disability performs extraordinarily, resulting in "supercrip" stories. Supercrip stories occur when media professionals embellish successes of people with disabilities as heroic and extraordinary, almost as if success was unexpected or original expectations were low (Hardin and Hardin, 2008; International Paralympic Committee, n.d.; Silva and Howe, 2012). On the surface, supercrip stories present inspiring narrative of overcoming adversity against the odds, yet place the person with a disability at odds with all other athletes who may have performed the same task with the same result and been considered ordinary (for example, othering). Supercrip stories are one example of disabling language in traditional media coverage, which includes both inaccurate word choices and embellishment of accomplishments.

Traditional versus progressive media coverage

Media coverage of sport and disability can be divided into two types: traditional and progressive (Schantz and Gilbert, 2008). As noted by Schantz and Gilbert, the traditional model approaches disability from a medical diagnosis perspective, which results in the portrayal of disability as dysfunctional with successes as heroic accomplishments while oftentimes using disabling language. Conversely, the progressive model does not focus on disability and suggests that it is not the individual's fault for being limited in any capacity, but rather society's fault for not adjusting properly. Progressive coverage, particularly in sport, focuses on abilities and competition rather than disability and overcoming adversity.

Examples of traditional and progressive media coverage of athletes with disabilities are media coverage of the Paralympic Games vs. media coverage of the X Games. Newspapers outside of the US trivialized the 1996 Paralympic Games in many ways, referring to the Olympic Games as the "real" games and in some reports focusing on technologically advanced prosthetic equipment (Schantz and Gilbert, 2008, p. 50). Supercrip stories described victories as heroic achievements, yet defeats were described in patronizing perspectives. Symbolism contributed to the traditional coverage with half of the coverage focused on athletes using wheelchairs and a wheelchair icon accompanying Paralympic Games reports, reinforcing the inaccurate stereotype that all athletes with disabilities use a wheelchair (Schantz and Gilbert, 2008). During the 1996 Paralympic Games, few sports were explained to media professionals, many of whom were covering their first Paralympic Games (MacDonald, 2008). Also, the confusing classification system based on ability level, akin to dividing sport competitions by weight class, made it difficult for inexperienced journalists to follow (International Paralympic Committee, n.d.; MacDonald, 2008).

In contrast, the 2000 Sydney Paralympic Games were much improved from a media relations standpoint (MacDonald, 2008). As noted by MacDonald, media professionals were given flash quotes from winners and top performers, competition previews that identified athletes to watch, and competition reviews that recapped how the favorites fared as well as a brief explanation of the event. This approach was an attempt to educate media professionals and ensure journalists were able to convey accurate messages to consumers.

Television coverage of Winter X Games on ESPN is an example of progressive media coverage. As of 2012, there were three events in the Winter X Games designed for athletes with disabilities. The first and most popular was Mono Skier X, a downhill ski race among athletes using mono skies. The event debuted in 2005 and was promoted to a medal event in 2007 (Leibs, 2009). What categorizes ESPN's coverage as progressive is that the television network emphasizes the competitive aspect of the event rather than highlighting the disabilities of the athletes through supercrip stories (Buchanan, 2010; Leibs, 2009). Integration is also a progressive coverage component in that the Mono Skier X final is held on the last day of the Winter X Games in one of the most coveted time slots among other finals in which able-bodied athletes compete. In 2009, the event had a 1.0 Nielsen rating, just short of the all-time ratings high for the X Games of 1.3 which occurred during that evening's telecast (Buchanan, 2010). Overall, while one example is not enough to prove that progressive media coverage improves ratings, acceptance, or popularity among an audience, it does shed light on the differences in athlete portrayals in relation to their preferences.

Athlete versus media preferences

Many athletes prefer the progressive model of media coverage although they fear society would be hesitant to such a shift because of the attractiveness of supercrip stories (Hardin and Hardin, 2008). For example, *People*'s 1999 "50 Most Beautiful People" list included athlete/model Aimee Mullins, who has had a double below-knee amputation. In the introductory text for Mullins, the publication immediately identified her as a person with an impairment, although the text displayed how Mullins does not want to be known only by her disability:

> Aimee Mullins doesn't have any lower legs, but the last thing she wants, she says, is to be viewed as a gimmicky disabled athlete. Triumph over tragedy – how pathetic! I think people are generally freaked out that I'm multifaceted. You don't hear people saying, 'Gwyneth Paltrow won an Oscar – and she's blonde!'
>
> *(People Magazine, 1999, p. 144)*

Mullins clearly sought her identity to be that of an athlete and model, not as an amputee. That is not to say that Mullins deflects her disability; she is known as an advocate for disability rights and disability sport. However, her reaction to any pity showed she desired equal treatment, whether that was athletically, socially, or in a magazine.

Ironically, the magazine in which Mullins appeared failed to recognize the negative connotation made when it immediately identified her impairment of having no legs. Beside a photo of Mullins, the magazine focused its accompanying text on her accomplishments, but Mullins's quote of triumph over tragedy embodies one athlete's rejection of supercrip stories. Other athletes dislike supercrip stories (Hardin and Hardin, 2004), although those feel-good stories are what spark interest. Supercrip stories are often what connect with readers and sell publications (Dummer, 1998; Hardin and Hardin, 2008). A similar concept is also true for other media coverage of athletes beyond the field of competition. Tiger Woods may be better known among greater demographics for his actions away from golf and rebounding from an unsuccessful personal relationship rather than his successes in his sport, and coverage from non-sport publications during his return to competitive play reinforced that (Hopper, 2010).

Other sport stories transform into news headlines, whether they are major events in sport history or daily occurrences. For example, Roger Clemens is known in baseball as one of the fiercest pitchers in history with seven Cy Young Awards and more than 4,000 strikeouts. Yet, Clemens's baseball reputation transformed into a news story when he was accused of steroid use and indicted for lying under oath. Other athletes have made headlines for reasons beyond their sport, both positively and negatively. Reports of professional golfer Rory McIlroy and professional tennis star Caroline Wozniacki holding a romantic relationship in early 2012 took their professional careers into the news reports. Even post-Super Bowl reports after the New York Giants beat the New England Patriots to win the 2012 NFL championship focused on Patriots quarterback Tom Brady's wife, supermodel Gisele Bundchen, chastising hecklers in defense of her husband. Examples such as these show that even the most popular and successful athletes sometimes become known for reasons other than their athletic accomplishments. Therefore, with regard to disability, media professionals are faced with the juxtaposition of selling content versus the preferences of athletes with disabilities to be known for their skillsets.

Ultimately, the best coverage of athletes with disabilities is the same as the best coverage of able-bodied sport: accurate coverage of intense competition and athlete profiles (Dummer, 1998). Recognition of athletic accomplishments of athletes with disabilities rather than reinforcement of disability can enhance the likelihood of athletes achieving success at higher levels (Dummer, 1998; Hargreaves and Hardin, 2009). However, media coverage of athletes with disabilities often can be inappropriate by emphasizing the impact of disability on the individual's life and focusing solely on the negative aspects of disability (Keller, Hallahan, McShane, Crowley, and Blandford, 1990). Even when the intent is positive, not all athletes with disabilities want to be portrayed as an inspirational story (Hardin and Hardin, 2004; Hargreaves and Hardin, 2009).

Framing sport and disability

The effect from use of disabling language can be a form of bias. Language use results in the subject being framed a particular way based on terminology used by the journalist. Media consumers classify, organize, and interpret life experiences to make sense of them, and these interpretations, or frames, enable people to perceive, identify, and label events or information (Goffman, 1974). Framing can be defined as the process of selecting elements of reality and arranging them to highlight their connections; therefore, shaping the reader's interpretations by presenting only a piece of the full representation of an event, issue, or idea (Entman, 2007; Riechert, 1996). Framing can also be viewed as placing information in context as such, so certain elements of the issue would get more attention from a person (Pan and Kosicki, 1993).

The word framing is conceptualized differently, but most researchers reach a consensus that the "word frame means the perspective a person applies to define an event or a problem" (Takeshita, 1997, p. 23). How media professionals frame an issue sets an agenda of attributes and influences public opinion (Entman, 1989; Severin and Tankard, 1992). According to Ghanem, "depending on how an issue is presented or framed in the media, the public will think about that issue in a particular way" (Ghanem, 1997, p. 7). Therefore, how media professionals cover an issue influences how the public thinks about the issue and can have a considerable effect on readers (Auslander and Gold, 1999). For example, extensive focus on an athlete's disability or competing despite such condition would certainly overshadow any athletic accomplishment he or she made, therefore (a) supporting the supercrip attractiveness, (b) falling into the traditional coverage approach of athletes with disabilities, and (c) influencing how the public perceives that particular individual.

Framing is seen in other social issues of sport as well, where media portrayals can reinforce established stereotypes. For example, media framing of HIV-positive athletes Magic Johnson (basketball), Tommy Morrison (boxing), and Greg Louganis (diving) shows a split in coverage based on sexual preference (Dworkin and Wachs, 1998). Coverage of Johnson and Morrison, both self-identified heterosexual men, emphasized the shock that a heterosexual man could contract the virus whereas coverage of Louganis, a self-identified homosexual man, did not mention promiscuity or surprise. This separation of coverage is one example of media professionals shaping how athletes are perceived. Facts of the story may be accurate, but the choice of how those facts are presented is influential and biased. In the example, it also may have been shocking that Louganis contracted HIV, but media portrayals did not emphasize this like they did with Johnson and Morrison.

Media professionals' use of disabling language over person-first language is not the sole factor for establishing or reinforcing negative stereotypes of athletes with disabilities, but it can be one of many factors involved (Auslander and Gold, 1999). Personal experience, use of the media, external events, opinion leaders, and interpersonal communication all influence the effect of media (Baran and Davis, 1995; Lowery and DeFleur, 1995; McQuail, 1994; McQuail and Windahl, 1993; Severin and Tankard, 1992). Regarding disability, print and online media can positively influence reader perception through enhancing knowledge and social awareness, or negatively influence reader perception through misinformation and reinforcement of stereotypes (Keller, *et al.*, 1990). The latter tends to be the most prevalent belief, owing to people with disabilities and their satisfaction of press coverage (Hargreaves and Hardin, 2009; Keller, *et al.*, 1990). Negative influences through media coverage can be reinforced with the use of disabling language. A change from disabling language may work toward redefining stereotypes and language use with regard to athletes with disabilities.

Guidelines for media professionals

Organizations and publications whose target audience is people with disabilities are cognizant of the terminology transformations and maintain style guidelines for writing about people with disabilities. The Paralympic Games is the largest international stage for athletes with disabilities, and the International Paralympic Committee (IPC) publishes a document on how to report on athletes with disabilities. These types of guidelines reinforce person-first language, provide a list of words and phrases to avoid such as "confined to a wheelchair" or "crippled," and suggest reporting on the subject while avoiding a strict focus on the disability (International Paralympic Committee, n.d.). Periodicals such as *ABILITY*, a magazine publication with emphasis on health and disability, publish their own terminology guidelines with similar stipulations as the IPC (ABILITY, 2012). The Research and Training Center on Independent Living also publishes *Guidelines for Reporting and Writing about People with Disabilities* (University of Kansas, 2008) by collecting input from more than 100 national disability organizations, which provides a comprehensive set of guidelines for print and online media professionals to follow. It is clear that if media professionals intend on reporting about athletes with disabilities, guidelines and stylebooks are available, prevalent, and consistent in message. Perhaps more importantly, those guidelines are offered after input from people with disabilities.

Not all style guidelines are as consistent or comprehensive, however. High-circulation sport periodicals, such as *Sports Illustrated*, follow the *Associated Press Stylebook and Briefing on Media Law* with some adaptations that may pertain specifically to the publication (Adam Levine, personal communication, March 2, 2010). Although many publications adhere to the Associated Press guidelines, its stylebook contradicts previously mentioned organizations' suggested guidelines for writing about people with disabilities. The publication discourages the use of "handicap" and "confined to a wheelchair" but does not make clear the differences between other language such as "blind" vs. "visually impaired" or "deaf" vs. "speech impaired". However, it states that if a person's disability is pertinent to a story, "make it clear what the *handicap* is and how much the person's physical or mental performance is affected" (Goldstein,

2000, p. 75; emphasis added). This contradiction gets directly to the heart of the issue: A lack of knowledge on the topic results in inaccurate and inconsistent actions and may reinforce inaccurate stereotypes of people with disabilities.

Media professionals should be knowledgeable of language evolution and definitions in order to use acceptable words or phrases, particularly for athletes with disabilities. The misuse by media professionals, although most likely not purposeful, can be influential on perception of people with disabilities if aired on a television broadcast or published in print or online mediums. It points to a simple lack of knowledge that person-first language is indeed different from disabling language, and a lack of knowledge that people with disabilities may prefer person-first language. Perhaps more noticeable is that media professionals often fail to adhere to a consistent style when referencing athletes with disabilities, which leads the critic to believe there was no attention paid to covering this topic in the first place.

Conclusion

Defining these terms and setting guidelines for proper use can lead to a more accurate portrayal of athletes with disabilities. In turn, those athletes' accomplishments will then no longer be underappreciated through disabling language or overemphasized through supercrip stories. Person-first language is a process that helps people understand disability in a social context, although that understanding has not been an easy process, particularly in disability sport where supercrip stories dominate narrative (Titchkosky, 2001). Rehabilitation professionals have encouraged person-first language, and many individuals prefer this terminology (Lynch, Thuli, and Groombridge, 1994). As noted by Lynch and colleagues, however, a significant portion sees person-first language and disabling language equally or simply disagree with the logic of person-first language. This is perhaps the biggest hurdle in educating media professionals in one common discourse regarding disability sport that may appeal to the preferences of both media and people with disabilities.

It may be impossible for one to fully know all sides of language preference dilemmas such as this one. However, being aware of the evolving acceptance of labels should be treated with the same diligence journalists place on fact-checking and source credibility, two core journalism practices and characteristics that often change over time. The simple reason for such a call to action lies in the persuasion power of rhetoric in media. While this debate may seem like mere semantics to outgroups, risk to the ingroup is inaccurate public perception and stereotype reinforcement in a sport setting that already has trouble accepting athletic success from people with disabilities without relating it back to an inspirational story or medical rehabilitation. Silva and Howe (2012) argue that the "distorted tendency to either undervalue or overvalue achievements whenever disability is present should be denounced" (p. 179). A shift away from disabling language and the dominant supercrip stories may take time, but it is possible through exposure to athlete preferences, awareness of the language and portrayal presented, and knowledge of how to address it. In many cases, athletes with disabilities just want recognition for their athletic accomplishments and no more or no less.

References

ABILITY (2012) Terminology guidelines. *ABILITY Magazine*. Retrieved from http://www.ability-magazine.com/terminology.html.

Auslander, G., and Gold, N. (1999). Disability terminology in the media: A comparison of newspaper reports in Canada and Israel. *Social Sciences and Medicine*, 48 (10), 1395–405.

Baran, S. J., and Davis, D. K. (1995). *Mass communication theory*. Belmont, CA: Wadsworth.

Berkson, M. (2012). Mike Berkson 101: Handicapped vs. disabled. *Handicap this! Productions*, March 20. Retrieved from http://handicapthis.com/2012/03/20/mike-berkson-101-handicapped-vs-disabled/.

Bornman, J. (2004). The World Health Organization's terminology and classification: Application to severe disability. *Disability and Rehabilitation*, 26 (3), 182–8.

Buchanan, E. (2010). Can SnoCross adapt? X Games adaptive events continue to grow with addition of Adaptive SnoCross. *ESPN Action Sports*, January 26. Retrieved from http://espn.go.com/action/xgames/winter/2010/snowmobiling/news/story?page=adaptive-snocross-mike-schultz.

Bullock, C. C., Mahon, M. J., and Killingsworth, C. L. (2010). *Introduction to recreation services for people with disabilities* (3rd ed.). Champaign, IL: Sagamore.

Coakley, J. (2009). *Sports in society: Issues and controversies* (10th ed.). New York: McGraw-Hill.

DePauw, K. (1997). The (in)visibility of disability: Cultural contexts and sporting bodies. *Quest*, 49, 416–30.

Dummer, G. M. (1998). Media coverage of disability sport. *Palaestra*, 14 (4), 56.

Dworkin, S. L., and Wachs, F. L. (1998). "Disciplining the body": HIV-positive male athletes, media surveillance, and the policing of sexuality. *Sociology of Sport Journal*, 15, 1–20.

Entman, R. M. (1989). *Democracy without citizens: Media and the decay of American politics*. New York: Oxford University Press.

Entman, R. M. (2007). Framing bias: Media in the distribution of power. *Journal of Communications*, 57 (1), 163–73.

Ghanem, S. (1997). Filling in the tapestry: The second level of agenda setting. In M. McCombs, D. Shaw, and D. Weaver (Eds.), *Communication and democracy* (pp. 3–14). Mahwah, NJ: Lawrence Erlbaum.

Goffman, E. (1974). *Frame analysis: An essay on the organization of experience*. Cambridge, MA: Harvard University Press.

Goldstein, N. (2000). *The Associated Press stylebook and briefing on media law*. Cambridge, MA: Perseus.

Haller, B., Dorries, B., and Rahn, J. (2006). Media labeling versus the U.S. disability community identity: A study of shifting cultural language. *Disability and Society*, 21 (1), 61–75.

Hardin, M., and Hardin, M. (2004). The 'supercrip; in sport media: Wheelchair athletes discuss hegemony's disabled hero. *Sociology of Sport Online*, 7 (1). Retrieved from http://physed.otago.ac.nz/sosol/v7i1/v7i1_1.html.

Hardin, M., and Hardin, B. (2008). Elite wheelchair athletes relate to sport media. In K. Gilbert, and O. J. Schantz (Eds.), *The Paralympic Games: Empowerment or side show?* (pp. 25–33). Maidenhead, UK: Meyer and Meyer Ltd.

Hargreaves, J. A., and Hardin, B. (2009). Women wheelchair athletes: Competing against media stereotypes. *Disability Studies Quarterly*, 29 (2). Retrieved from http://dsq-sds.org/article/view/920/1095.

Hopper, D. (2010). Tiger Woods masters headline roundup. *VH1 Celebrity*, April 5. Retrieved from http://www.bestweekever.tv/2010-04-05/tiger-woods-masters-headline-roundup/.

International Paralympic Committee. (n.d.). Guidelines: Reporting on persons with a disability. Retrieved from http://www.paralympic.org/sites/default/files/document/120209105414322_2012_02+Reporting+Guidlines.pdf.

Keller, C., Hallahan, D., McShane, E., Crowley, E. P., and Blandford, B. J. (1990). The coverage of persons with disabilities in American newspapers. *Journal of Special Education*, 24 (3), 271–82.

Leibs, A. (2009). Accessible Recreation: Winter X Games Mono Skier X. *Suite 101*, January 17. Retrieved from http://suite101.com/article/winter-x-games-13-mono-skier-x-a90687.

Longmore, P. K. (1985). A note on language and the social identity of disabled people. *American Behavioral Scientist*, 28 (3), 419–23.

Lowery, S. A., and DeFleur, M. L. (1995). *Milestones in mass communication research: Media effects* (3rd ed.). White Plains, NY: Longman.
Lynch, R. T., Thuli, K., and Groombridge, L. (1994). Person-first disability language: A pilot analysis of public perceptions. *Journal of Rehabilitation*, 60 (2), 18–22.
MacDonald, M. (2008). Media and the Paralympic Games. In K. Gilbert and O. J. Schantz (Eds.), *The Paralympic Games: Empowerment or side show?* (pp. 68–78). Maidenhead, UK: Meyer and Meyer.
McQuail, D. (1994). *Mass communication theory* (3rd ed.). London: Sage.
McQuail, D., and Windahl, S. (1993). *Communication models: For the study of mass communication* (2nd ed.). London: Longman.
Pan, Z., and Kosicki, G. M. (1993). Framing analysis: An approach to news discourse. *Political Communication*, 10 (1), 55–75.
Patterson, J. B., and Witten, B. J. (1987). Disabling language and attitudes toward persons with disabilities. *Rehabilitation Psychology*, 32 (4), 245–8.
People Magazine (1999). The 50 most beautiful people in the world. *People*, May 10, 51 (17), 144.
Riechert, B. (1996). Advocacy group and news media framing of public policy issues: Frame mapping the wetlands debates (unpublished doctoral dissertation). University of Tennessee, Knoxville.
Schantz, O. J., and Gilbert, K. (2008). French and German newspaper coverage of the 1996 Atlanta Paralympic Games. In K. Gilbert, and O. J. Schantz (Eds.), *The Paralympic Games: Empowerment or side show?* (pp. 34–56). Maidenhead, UK: Meyer and Meyer.
Severin, W., and Tankard, J. (1992). *Communication theories: Origins, methods, and uses in the mass media* (3rd ed.). White Plains, NY: Longman.
Sigelman, L., Tuch, S. A., and Martin, J. A. (2005). What's in a name! Preferences for 'black' versus 'African-American' among Americans of African descent. *Public Opinion Quarterly*, 69 (3), 429–38.
Silva, C. F., and Howe, P. D. (2012). The (in)validity of supercrip representation of Paralympian athletes. *Journal of Sport and Social Issues*, 36, 174–94.
Takeshita, T. (1997). Exploring the media's role in defining reality: In issues agenda-setting to attribute agenda setting. In M. McCombs, D. Shaw, and D. Weaver (Eds.), *Communication and democracy* (pp. 15–28). Mahwah, NJ: Lawrence Erlbaum.
Titchkosky, T. (2001). Disability: A rose by any other name? People-first language in Canadian society. *Canadian Review of Sociology and Anthropology*, 38 (2), 125–40.
University of Kansas Research and Training Center on Independent Living. (2008). *Guidelines for reporting and writing about people with disabilities* (7th ed.). Lawrence, KS:
World Health Organization. (2012). Health topics: Disabilities. Retrieved from http://www.who.int/topics/disabilities/en/.

37

RACE PORTRAYALS IN SPORT COMMUNICATION

Andrea N. Eagleman and Tywan G. Martin

For as long as media have reported on sports, they have reported on athletes of differing race. Sport communication researchers have examined race portrayals in many forms of media, including print, broadcast, and most recently new media. This chapter provides a detailed historical overview of the ways in which athletes of different races have been portrayed in the media over time. The chapter focuses on portrayals of athletes based on race in print (that is, newspapers and magazines), broadcast (that is, television), and new media. Because the depth of research and information on this topic is so broad, this chapter primarily focuses on US-based media outlets.

One issue cited within such studies of race, sport, and media is the problematic definition of the term 'race'. Bernstein and Blain explained that some scholars believe there is no such thing as race, citing a lack of biological evidence to support such a concept, but the term nevertheless "carries much ideological weight" (Bernstein and Blain, 2002, p. 17). Haslanger (2000) defined the term "race" as a hierarchical social category characterized by "physical features, ancestry, and geographical origins" (p. 51). Using this notion of race as a hierarchical structure with ideological implications, Armstrong explained many of the intricate relationships between race and sport, one of which includes media portrayals. She stated, "Media messages and images help to shape our view of the world, influence our perceptions, and inform our values and the identities we create and seek to create" (Armstrong, 2011, p. 98). Therefore, the way in which race in sport is portrayed by the media can have profound impacts on our own perceptions and interpretations of race.

Because of this potentially deep impact on society, it is important to study portrayals of race in sport media to better understand the ways in which messages about race are conveyed and also the manner in which they are conveyed. The following sections detail the ways in which race has been portrayed in many different forms of sport media, followed by a section on the implications of these portrayals.

Portrayals of race in print media

The most widely studied forms of print media relating to race portrayals are newspapers and magazines. Some scholars have examined race in terms of the amount of coverage given to athletes of differing race, while others examined race in terms of the language used to describe athletes of differing race. This section explores both areas, beginning with the amount of coverage.

Historically, research shows that minority athletes have been underrepresented in print media sport coverage. Early studies focused mostly on coverage differences between white and black athletes, such as several examinations of *Sports Illustrated*, the most widely circulated general interest sport magazine in the US. One study revealed that, from 1960 to 1974, black and white athletes were afforded the same amount of column inches in the magazine, but white athletes were the focus of more in-depth feature articles than black athletes (Condor and Anderson, 1894). Similarly, an analysis of the magazine from 1954 to 1987 showed that black athletes were underrepresented during the entire time period of the study, concluding that the magazine "disproportionately publicizes the sports achievements of whites when compared to those of blacks" (Lumpkin and Williams, 1991, p. 28). Another study on the amount of coverage granted to white and black athletes focused on newspaper coverage of the 1932 Olympic Games. This study also found discrepancies in coverage based on race, with black athletes receiving less coverage and being virtually ignored by the media in the South (Welky, 1997).

More recently, a study by Eagleman and McNary (2011) focused on media coverage of the 2006 Winter Olympics, and examined the amount of newspaper coverage devoted to white, black, Asian, and Latino athletes in five US newspapers. The results revealed that the minority athletes received statistically significant greater coverage than white athletes when measured against the percentage of white, black, Asian, and Latino athletes competing in the Olympics. Additionally, the study found that when minorities were covered in the newspapers, they received more prominent story placement than white athletes. These findings were consistent with previous research on newspaper coverage of the Olympic Games. For example, Hardin, Dodd, Chance, and Walsdorf (2004) found that black athletes were overrepresented in five US newspapers during the 2000 Olympics, while other minorities were underrepresented. The authors suggested that this overrepresentation of black athletes in sports media is done in an effort to "preserve power relations in U.S. society. This finding reflects an 'enlightened racist' view, that is, sport is the (sole) arena where Blacks can excel" (Hardin, *et al.*, 2004, p. 223).

As the quote from Hardin, *et al.* (2004) alludes, the amount of coverage devoted to athletes of a certain race can only tell part of the story. In order to gain a better understanding of how athletes of differing race are portrayed in print media, several researchers have undertaken qualitative studies. While most quantitative studies examined race in terms of black and white, a greater amount of qualitative research has examined multiple races, including Latino and Asian.

A study by Eagleman (2011) focused on all four of the aforementioned racial groups, examining both *Sports Illustrated* and *ESPN The Magazine*, the second most popular general interest sport magazine in the US, to determine what frames and themes were most prominent when describing Major League Baseball (MLB) athletes of differing race from 2000 through 2007. The findings revealed very different portrayals of each race. White athletes were most often portrayed as hard workers, while the most prominent frame for black athletes was overcoming obstacles. Additionally, the articles about black athletes focused much more on the athlete's race than the articles about white athletes. In terms of Latino athletes, the main frame of the articles was one of the athletes having a strong work ethic. Asian athletes were described as the "other", or being different from their non-Asian teammates. This frame was often used in a negative way, as though there was something inherently bad about being different. The study concluded "the themes revealed in this analysis were reflective of some of the predominant themes historically used to portray black, Latino, and Asian athletes" (Eagleman, 2011, p. 164).

Some scholars have undertaken qualitative research focusing on print coverage portrayals of a specific race. For example, Mayeda examined portrayals of two Asian MLB pitchers and found that one was portrayed as a model minority, or "hard working, self-sacrificing, and quiet" (Mayeda, 1999, p. 211). In other words, because of these qualities, this athlete was viewed as the type of minority that Americans revered. In contrast, the other athlete examined in the study was portrayed as an economic threat. His salary was listed in almost every article examined, and he was portrayed as being overpaid. Mayeda said, "There has been an extreme dearth of literature written on Asian athletes in America" (p. 209). The same is true for Latino athletes, whose portrayals have rarely been examined in print media. The following section examines the portrayals of athletes of differing race in broadcast media. Some findings are similar to those of print media, while others differ.

Portrayals of race in broadcast media

Television is the most popular form of broadcast media that researchers have examined under the lens of race portrayals. Similar to researchers' findings regarding print media, minority athletes are also often underrepresented in broadcast coverage of sport. The amount of coverage, as well as the quality of coverage of athletes of differing race on television, is examined below.

One of the most widely studied sporting events in relation to race portrayals is the Olympic Games. Numerous studies have examined portrayals of athletes in the Olympics, an event which brings together a great number of athletes from varying nations and races. Historically, white athletes, specifically white male athletes, have received the most television coverage during the Olympics. Scholars such as Billings and Angelini (2007), Billings and Eastman (2002, 2003), and Real and Mechikoff (1992) examined television coverage of the Olympic Games and found discrepancies in the amount of coverage devoted to athletes of differing race. For example, Billings and Eastman (2002) found that white athletes received over 1,200 more mentions than black athletes during the 2000 Olympic Games. This indicated that the media showed favoritism to white athletes. Billings, *et al.* (2008) examined NBC's broadcast of the 2006 Winter Olympics and concluded that while white athletes received much greater coverage than minorities, the lack of minority athletes competing in the Winter Olympics likely contributed to this finding and thus the coverage was not deemed to underrepresent minority athletes.

A great deal of the research on TV portrayals of athletes of differing race were conducted qualitatively, focusing more on the words, phrases, themes and frames used to describe athletes than on the amount of coverage devoted to each specific race. One of the most comprehensive studies on televisual race portrayals was conducted by Sabo, Jansen, Tate, Duncan, and Leggett (1996), in which 340 hours of coverage from seven international sporting events was analyzed. While previous research found negative stereotypes of black athletes present in TV coverage, this study noted that "Black athletes were significantly less likely than were Asian and White athletes to receive negative evaluations from commentators" (Sabo, *et al.*, 1996, p. 13). The authors concluded that the findings possibly indicated that journalists took notice of previous research findings and adjusted their coverage accordingly. Despite this finding, however, Asian athletes were still depicted in a stereotypical manner and a heavy focus was placed on Latino athletes' physicality.

Some researchers have focused their efforts on examining media portrayals of specific sports or athletes. For example, Giacobbi and DeSensi qualitatively examined TV portrayals of golfer Tiger Woods, who is unique compared with many athletes in that he is multiracial and refers to himself as "Caublinasian" (Giacobbi and DeSensi, 1999, p. 414) owing to his African-American, Caucasian, Native American and Asian heritage. The study found underlying racist, sexist, and classist ideologies in the media portrayals, with negative racial stereotypes reinforced. Another study by Juffer (2002) focused specifically on TV portrayals of Sammy Sosa, a Latino MLB player. This study found that the media largely ignored Sosa during his race with white MLB player Mark McGwire for the single-season home run record in 1998 until it became evident that Sosa would definitely contend for the record. Furthermore, commentary in the coverage seemed to reflect a longing for the sport of baseball to be a truly 'American' game as it was in the past, without the large number of international players who are currently in the MLB.

In one of the few studies to examine TV portrayals of Asian athletes, Daddario and Wigley (2007) found that Asian female athletes competing in the 2004 Olympics were cast as weak, frail and passive, similar to previous research findings. Additionally, the idea of Asians as the model minority was also present, as Asian athletes were portrayed as "hard-working, self-disciplined, and mechanical in the execution of their sport" (Daddario and Wigley, 2007, p. 43). Despite some findings that minority athletes were portrayed less negatively in TV coverage, the majority of literature on this topic shows that racial stereotypes have been reinforced over time and continue to be perpetuated on television. The next section explores the most recent medium, the Internet, to discover whether race portrayals in new media have followed the same patterns as print and broadcast.

Portrayals of race in new media

New media have fundamentally changed and helped sport reach new levels of success in terms of viewership, commercialization, and popularity because of its ability to offer virtual access that is seemingly unlimited to the public (Coakley, 2009). Sports fans make up a substantial amount of Internet users in the US and they spend a considerable amount of time online engaging in fantasy based sports, streaming sport content, shopping for sport merchandise, and participating in fan forums (Sachoff, 2008). While the Internet serves as a powerful medium that has the ability to enhance sport-related products and content and advance the critically important fan interconnectivity with leagues, teams, collegiate sports, and athletes, new media have also proven to portray the race of athletes similarly to the portrayals found in other forms of media. This section covers some of the research examining portrayals of minority groups in new media. As the majority of adults are now utilizing the Internet (Rainie, 2010), it is important to understand how underrepresented groups are portrayed throughout this platform.

Ruddock's (2005) study of an online forum examined comments by fans after West Ham United, a Premier League soccer team, signed a controversial player after he made racist comments directed at the Asian community. In a poll conducted by the online forum, a total of 79 fans voted, with 71 in support of the club's signing of the divisive Lee Bowyer and eight disapproving. Of those fans, 39 commented on the topic. The majority of the data collected from the forum revealed that many of the posts minimized the controversy as inconsequential and felt that the uproar about the player's signing was primarily the fault of the media. In addition, the results revealed that sport was not a viable arena to discuss social issues, as sport was considered a sacred ground where conversations of race should not be held, and minority groups such as Asians and blacks tend to be more racist than their white counterparts. The study found that the commenters felt the primary focus of the media should be on whether or not Bowyer improves the team's success and not his racially charged insults. The findings proposed that the best solution or strategy for dealing with racially insensitive issues is to change the topic and talk about something entirely different. Furthermore, Ruddock determined the study's results from the online forum "illustrate that the discourses and actions of well-meaning people cultivate an environment where bigotry is tolerated, if not encouraged" (Ruddock, 2005, p. 383).

New media research has also expanded into the country's most prominent and popular intercollegiate sport organization, the National Collegiate Athletic Association (NCAA). In 2005, the NCAA enacted a policy aimed at addressing what the association believed to be a denigrating representation by some of its members in regards to the use of racial mascots, logos, and nicknames (*USA Today,* 2005). While the NCAA ruled that it did not have the authority to ban the use of the nicknames and mascots believed to be hostile or abusive, the organization did ban the use of images deemed dehumanizing and racially insensitive from appearing on uniforms or other clothing items during postseason tournament play. The University of North Dakota (UND) was one of the schools affected by the NCAA's decision, owing to the school's nickname, the Fighting Sioux. To measure the impact of the decision, Steinfeldt, *et al.* (2010) examined online forum comments over a two-year period that included the enactment of the NCAA's ban on racially insensitive mascots and logos usage during postseason play and the lawsuit settlement agreement between UND and the NCAA. Steinfeldt, *et al.* examined 1,699 online forum comments, with 1,009 (59 percent) of the coded written content containing information in support of Native-themed mascots. There were only 115 (seven percent) comments that opposed the use of Native-themed nicknames and 575 (34 percent) coded as neutral. The study revealed that several overarching themes emerged from the content on the online forums. Steinfeldt and colleagues concluded that the forum participants evoked elements of *surprise* (for example, What? This is a problem? Why us?), *power and privilege* (for example, we are the victims, reverse racism, political correctness), *trivialization* (for example, minimize the issue, perpetuate misinformation about Indians), and *denigration* (for example, attack credibility and legitimacy of dissenters, punish Indians if nickname/logo removed). From their findings, the researchers suggested that new media allow for inaccurate, erroneous, and negative portrayals of Native Americans to persist through the use of Native-themed mascots.

Other research in this area also examined online forums to determine the reaction of fans to comments made by former National Basketball Association (NBA) star and current Turner Network Television (TNT) basketball analyst, Charles Barkley, about the 2008 hiring of a head football coach at his alma mater, Auburn University (Sanderson, 2010). On ESPN, Barkley publicly criticized Auburn University for selecting a white coach with a losing record, Gene Chizik, over a black coach, Turner Gill, who helped to rebuild the football program at the University of Buffalo. Sanderson (2010) randomly selected comments made after Barkley's critique of his former institution's decision to hire Chizik from more than 9,000 postings on an ESPN.com forum. Similar to the Steinfeldt, *et al.* (2010) study, four major areas emerged from the data. First, *transference* suggested that the lack or underrepresentation of blacks as head coaches at Football Bowl Subdivision (FBS) institutions was the fault of blacks and had little to nothing to do with racism. The second theme that surfaced was *irrelevance*, which dismissed the notion that race played a role in Auburn's hiring decision. The third element dealt with *reverse racism*, which tended to shift the central problem and focus of latent inequalities in hiring practices by FBS institutions to whites experiencing racism. The fourth and final domain, *recognition*, acknowledged the lack of inclusion at FBS institutions regarding to the hiring of qualified minority candidates. While the comments that comprised the latter domain were progressive in nature, Sanderson suggested that the former domains were just the opposite, as they reinforced a delusional stance in American culture that racism is extinct, culpability was levied at those who endure racism, and many of the comments were in line with the belief that whites were the target of racism.

As revealed with other forms of media, negative portrayals of underrepresented communities have continued with the development of new media. Similar to print and broadcast, new media have disseminated stereotypical and misleading content about minority groups. The next section discusses the significance of this information and offer recommendations.

Implications of race portrayals in sport media

Mayeda (1999) said, "sports, as popular and powerful as they are in America, should be used to break down faulty images, not to reinforce them" (p. 214) yet, based on the information presented in this chapter, it is evident that all forms of media portray athletes of differing race in different ways, and minority athletes are often depicted in a stereotypical or negative manner. It is important to understand why this type of coverage persists even today, and also to understand its impact on society. The following paragraphs explain both of these issues.

It has been suggested that the journalists might have subconscious attitudes about race, which are presented in the media through the words, phrases, themes, and frames they use to describe athletes of differing race (Eagleman, 2011). These subconscious feelings about race can become problematic when presented in the media because, as Bruce (2004) explained, "most Americans understand race through media representations" (p. 863). Because media professionals are viewed as being impartial, objective, and neutral, media consumers perceive them as credible. Therefore, if stereotypical or negative portrayals of athletes of differing race are presented in the media, consumers will treat these stereotypes and portrayals as credible information and might develop underlying stereotypes about certain racial groups. As Eagleman (2011) concluded, "When stereotypes based on race or nationality are continually presented in sport media frames, such stereotypes can become part of sport media consumers' personal perceptions of a falsely constructed reality" (p. 166).

Sabo, *et al.* (1996) suggested that fair treatment of all athletes in sport media can be achieved through efforts by media organizations to attempt to appeal to different ethnic and racial groups, and also suggested that media might be forced to treat athletes of all races equally when multicultural audiences voice their displeasure or offense to stereotyped portrayals of race. Eagleman (2011) echoed this sentiment, stating that the racial makeup of the US is rapidly changing, with current minority groups growing quickly. If such racial groups perceive media coverage of athletes of the same race to be stereotypical or derogatory, they will likely choose to not read or view coverage from those particular media outlets. This could impact the media organizations' bottom lines and negatively impact their businesses if they do not change their reporting style to reflect nondiscriminatory representations of all races. Bruce (2004) suggested that changing the way journalists portray athletes might not be so easy, however, stating, "an implicit racial consciousness inflects the working environment" (p. 874) at sport media organizations.

While it will be difficult to change the ways in which decades of sports journalists have become accustomed to writing about athletes of differing races, it is important to work towards such a shift not just for the sake of media organizations' bottom lines, but more importantly because of the serious societal implications that negative and stereotypical coverage can have. Hardin, *et al.* (2004) stated, "When media endorse racial difference, even subtly, they reinforce tendencies toward prejudice by the majority" (p. 213). Likewise, Eagleman (2011) explained that when sport communication professionals use race inappropriately, it could contribute to the creation and reinforcing of a discriminatory culture in media consumers' everyday lives. That is, when the media constantly reinforces racial stereotypes, it is possible for those stereotypes to become consciously or subconsciously embedded into the media consumer's psyche and could carry over to discriminatory behavior in the workplace or other areas of society. Legitimizing all racial groups and discontinuing the oppression of some groups in sport media can result in not only more equal coverage of athletes of all races, but in greater equality in society as well.

Therefore, difficult conversations are needed in sport media to fully utilize sport as a vehicle for social transformation (LaVoi and Kane, 2011). Thorough and honest discussions on the topic of whiteness could help to overcome some of the issues that currently exist in the portrayals of minority groups in sport media. The concept of whiteness specifically deals with vivid images, information, and cultural symbols that normalize and position white dominance, power, and supremacy as the status quo in American culture (McDonald, 2005). McDonald further suggests that whiteness is extremely complicated because of its influence on many American institutions such as sport and the mass media. Regardless of the complexity of the topic, it may benefit society immensely if more honest discussions on the subject were held on a more consistent basis.

For instance, in 2003 when Rush Limbaugh, from his ESPN *Sunday NFL Countdown* seat, commented that the only reason Donovan McNabb garnered any attention was because of the media's obsession with finding a successful black quarterback, it put the issue of race in sport at the top of many conversations throughout the country. According to Hartmann (2007), Limbaugh's comments provided an opportunity to discuss the critical ideology of whiteness in American sport media culture. Unfortunately, the discussion did not happen as Limbaugh resigned and so did the notion of exploring what McDonald (2005) proposed as the institutionalization of whiteness. Very little media coverage was allocated to the Limbaugh–McNabb situation, which suggests that the media had seemingly no interest in leading the conversation for racial equality in its reporting.

The resistance to discussing the topic of whiteness is further supported by the idea that sport serves as a safe haven from societal issues and concerns (Sanderson, 2010). While ideal, this position is flawed. Research has shown that negative sport images of minority groups viewed by young minority students have a psychologically damaging impact on these individuals (Fryberg, Markus, Oyserman, and Stone, 2008). Conversely, young white students that viewed the same negative images experienced higher levels of self-esteem, suggesting individuals have an early understanding of the benefits and privileges afforded to them through the concept of whiteness. Thus, this provides further evidence that meaningful conversations are needed to enhance the quality of life for all of society.

As previous research discovered (Ruddock, 2005; Steinfeldt, *et al.*, 2010), virtual environments (such as online forums) can provide a space where ideas on the topic of sports can be exchanged in the free marketplace and possibly serve as "a more accurate societal barometer of fans' views on the relevance of race in sport" (Sanderson, 2010, p. 314). The issue here is that one of the many areas new media was intended to improve was sport consumers' lives; however, many old stereotypes and inaccuracies regarding some underrepresented groups have been perpetuated via this format. Because of the anonymity that new media provides, it allows for more open discourse than a face-to-face context. While many of the comments found in the previous literature on sport and new media were disturbing, it is this type of candor that may help to dispel the myth that race in sports is a non-issue and move the dialogue towards serious and honest discussions on the topic of racism that continues to plague our world.

References

Armstrong, K. L. (2011). 'Lifting the veils and illuminating the shadows': Furthering the explorations of race and ethnicity in sport management. *Journal of Sport Management*, 25, 95–106.

Bernstein, A., and Blain, N. (2002). Sport and the media: The emergence of a major research field. *Culture, Sport, Society*, 5 (3), 1–31.

Billings, A. C., and Angelini, J. R. (2007). Packaging the games for viewer consumption: Gender, ethnicity, and nationality in NBC's coverage of the 2004 Summer Olympics. *Communication Quarterly*, 55 (1), 95–111.

Billings, A. C., and Eastman, S. T. (2002). Selective representation of gender, ethnicity, and nationality in American television coverage of the 2000 Summer Olympics. *International Review for the Sociology of Sport*, 37 (3/4), 351–70.

Billings, A. C., and Eastman, S. T. (2003). Framing identities: Gender, ethnic, and national parity in network announcing of the 2002 Winter Olympics. *Journal of Communication*, 53 (4), 569–86.

Billings, A. C., Brown, C. L., Crout III, J. H., McKenna K. E., Rice, B. A., Timanus, M. E., and Ziegler, J. (2008). The Games through the NBC lens: Gender, ethnic, and national equity in the 2006 Torino Winter Olympics. *Journal of Broadcasting and Electronic Media*, 52 (2), 215–30.

Bruce, T. (2004). Marking the boundaries of the 'normal' in televised sports: The play-by-play of race. *Media, Culture and Society*, 26 (6), 861–79.

Coakley, J. (2009). *Sports in society* (10th ed.). New York: McGraw-Hill.

Condor, R., and Anderson, D.F. (1984). Longitudinal analysis of coverage accorded black and white athletes in feature articles of *Sports Illustrated* (1960–1980). *Journal of Sport Behavior*, 7 (1), 39–43.

Daddario, G., and Wigley, B.J. (2007). Gender marking and racial stereotyping at the 2004 Athens Games. *Journal of Sports Media*, 2, 29–51.

Eagleman, A. N. (2011). Stereotypes of race and nationality: A qualitative analysis of sport magazine coverage of MLB players. *Journal of Sport Management*, 25, 156–68.

Eagleman, A. N., and McNary, E. L. (2011). Gender, race, and nationality: An examination of print coverage of the 2006 Winter Olympics. In H. Dolles and S. Soderman (Eds.), *Sport as a business: International, professional and commercial aspects* (pp. 99–114). New York: Palgrave MacMillan.

Fryberg, S. A., Markus, H. R., Oyserman, D., and Stone, J. M. (2008). Of warrior chiefs and Indian princesses: The psychological consequences of American Indian mascots. *Basic and Applied Social Psychology*, 30 (3), 208–18.

Giacobbi, P. R., and DeSensi, J. T. (1999). Media portrayals of Tiger Woods: A qualitative deconstructive examination. *QUEST*, 51, 408–17.

Hardin, M., Dodd, J. E., Chance, J., and Walsdorf, K. (2004). Sporting images in black and white: Race in newspaper coverage of the 2000 Olympic Games. *Howard Journal of Communications*, 15, 211–27.

Hartmann, D. (2007). Rush Limbaugh, Donovan McNabb and "A little social concern": Reflections on the problems of whiteness in contemporary American sport. *Journal of Sport and Social Issues*, 31, 45–60.

Haslanger, S. (2000). Gender and race: (What) are they? (What) do we want them to be? *Nous (Detroit, Mich.)*, 34 (1), 31–55.

Juffer, J. (2002). Who's the man? Sammy Sosa, Latinos, and televisual redefinitions of the "American" pastime. *Journal of Sport and Social Issues*, 26, 337–59.

LaVoi, N. M., and Kane, M. J. (2011). Sociological aspects of sports. In P. M. Pedersen, J. B. Parks, J. Quarterman, and L. Thibault (Eds.), *Contemporary sport management* (pp. 372–91). Champaign, IL: Human Kinetics.

Lumpkin, A., and Williams, L.D. (1991). An analysis of *Sports Illustrated* feature articles, 1954–1987. *Sociology of Sport Journal*, 8 (1), 16–32.

Mayeda, D. T. (1999). From model minority to economic threat: Media portrayals of Major League Baseball pitchers Hideo Nomo and Hideki Irabu. *Journal of Sport and Social Issues*, 23, 203–17.

McDonald, M. G. (2005). Mapping whiteness and sport: Introduction to the special issue. *Sociology of Sport Journal*, 22 (3), 245–55.

Rainie, L. (2010). Internet, broadband, and cell phone statistics. *Pew Internet and American Life Project*, January 5. Retrieved from http://www.pewinternet.org/Reports/2010/Internet-broadband-and-cell-phone-statistics.aspx.

Real, M. R., and Mechikoff, R. (1992). Deep fan: Mythic identification, technology, and advertising in spectator sports. *Sociology of Sport Journal*, 9 (4), 323–39.

Ruddock, A. (2005). Let's kick racism out of football – and the lefties too. *Journal of Sport and Social Issues*, 29, 369–85.

Sabo, D., Jansen, S. C., Tate, D., Duncan, M. C., and Leggett, S. (1996). Televising international sport: Race, ethnicity, and nationalistic bias. *Journal of Sport and Social Issues*, 21, 7–21.

Sachoff, M. (2008). Serious sports fans spend more time online. *WebProNews*, July 21. Retrieved from http://www.webpronews.com/serious-sports-fans-spend-more-time-online-2008-07.

Sanderson, J. (2010). Weighing in on the coaching decision: Discussing sports and online. *Journal of Language and Social Psychology*, 23 (3), 301–20.

Steinfeldt, J. A., Foltz, B. D., Kaladow, J. K., Carlson, T. N., Pagano, L. A., Benton, E., and Steinfeldt, M. C. (2010). Racism in the electronic age: Role of online forums in expressing racial attitudes about American Indians. *Cultural Diversity and Ethnic Minority Psychology*, 16, 362–71.

USA Today. (2005) NCAA bans Indian mascots during postseason. *USA Today*, August 5. Retrieved from http://www.usatoday.com/sports/college/2005-08-05-indian-mascots-ruling_x.htm.

Welky, D. (1997). Viking girls, mermaids, and little brown men: U.S. journalism and the 1932 Olympics. *Journal of Sport History*, 24 (1), 24–49.

38

USES OF SPORT COMMUNICATION IN GROUPS

Meaning and effects in public viewing

Thomas Horky

It is not just in stadiums that big sporting occasions pull in large crowds. More and more, big groups of TV viewers come together for live broadcasts of these occasions so that they can enjoy the experience of live sports together. In Europe, the big football contests (such as the World Cup, European Championship) have meanwhile turned into public TV events; televised football has become an event on town squares, in bars, or in arenas. So-called public viewing of live broadcasts of almost all games indicates a new phenomenon in the reception of sports-in-media: the reception does not happen on your own in front of your TV at home but in the company of smaller or larger groups in a variety of social situations.

Up to now, research has mostly focused on the live reception of sport (for example, in a stadium), in comparison to the individual reception of sports-in-media in the private sphere. What we mean by communal reception of sports-in-media is, by contrast, the collective consumption for which a group comes together or respectively engages in deliberately, and this can happen in the private sphere and in public. In fact, groups as a whole go in for public TV presentations only seldom – with, however, one exception: the communal use of sports-in-media. This consumption of sports-in-media has consequences for communication science's research into reception. This chapter presents the social–psychological peculiarities of group reception of sports-in-media.

Research and theoretical approaches

Empirical research into consumption sufficiently demonstrates that users favor different media content or respectively topics according to sociodemographic data like age, gender, and formal education; in this process, individual motives for use are salient, when considered from social-psychological perspectives (Raney, 2006; Schramm and Klimmt, 2003). Large sporting occasions do, however, lead to conceiving of large audiences, and they do display a high news value as a sort of overarching topic or media event respectively, and with that they bring together audiences in dimensions otherwise not observed. Apparently, around 700 million people simultaneously watched the final of the 2010 World Cup between Spain and the Netherlands in South Africa. Geese, Zeughardt, and Gerhard (2006) demonstrate how the

"World Cup as an event spanning whole societies also pulled in 'echelons otherwise distant from football'" (p. 461). In the sense of its collective consumption, the World Cup can, therefore, be designated a media event with a global reach.

Public TV viewing of sports communally first attracted attention in that form during the 1998 World Cup in France and could subsequently be observed in an expanded mode at the 2002 World Cup. In Japan and in Korea, a total of 2,021 so-called "big screens" were set up at 1,868 locations, and in addition, there were other screens organized mostly privately and installed on trucks. For some games, more than four million people reportedly came together in front of the screens in the city centers (Ufer, 2010). Since 2002, the media reception of major football occasions has changed markedly.

This combination of reception of sports-in-media and communal celebrations also dominated the public viewing carefully organized within the FIFA fanfests at the 2006 and 2010 World Cups. This "third quality of viewing" (Geese, *et al.*, 2006, p. 459) at the 2006 World Cup in all 12 German cities used as venues as well as in 13,000 sports bars led to a "communicative staging" (HISPOJO-Forschungsgruppe and Horky 2007, p. 58). Assessing data from the *Media Perspektiven* indicates, above all, the strong growth in out-of-home viewing of major sporting events through viewing shared with friends, followed by communal viewing in bars and cafés, and – above all, at German games – in front of a big screen in the form of public viewing.

As regards public viewing, highest out-of-home consumption (16.93 million) was posted at the 2006 World Cup by the live broadcast of the play-off for third between Germany and Portugal (Geese, *et al.*, 2006). At the 2010 World Cup, gathering data was reorganized: according to one poll, the highest value for public viewing was reached by the play-off for third between Germany and Uruguay with 16.25 million people in front of public big screens in addition to an assessment of 23.67 million viewers in front of their own sets (Gerhard, Kessler, and Gscheidle, 2010). In other European countries, public viewing has meanwhile become widespread: the 2006 final against France was watched by 200,000 Italians on big screens in the ancient Circus Maximus in Rome; in Milan too, 150,000 fans gathered on the Piazza del Duomo (Ufer, 2010) to watch the Italian victory. In the US, public viewing is clearly not a popular phenomenon as yet; people watch the big sporting events like the Super Bowl above all in sports bars and privately in front of their own sets. However, some stadiums do display big screens in their immediate vicinity and charge admission for viewing the events in them; AT&T Park, home of the San Francisco Giants, is well known for doing that.

These descriptions point up a change in the relationship between sports-in-media and the public sphere, or the audience respectively, and this change throws up questions about how the new reception situation affects the recipients. In contrast to motives for consuming sports-in-media from the viewpoint of individual viewers, which has already been variously described (see, for example, Raney, 2006; Whannel, 1998), there is not much data on communal consumption of sports-in-media. What follows, therefore, presents a theoretical premise on three key characteristic levels as the basis for social-psychological peculiarities in the group reception of sports-in-media.

Reception processes in relation to group constellations

Differentiating the group reception of sports-in-media is, above all, meaningful in the social dimension. That is because the appropriation is bound up with (group) constellations, be they on the spot in the stadium or medially in front of big screens, in rather more private groups in front of the television in families and in sports bars. Wöhler talks about "spaces, or respectively territories, of interaction" belonging to people, who "come together over certain issues" (Wöhler, 2000, p. 57). What is crucial is the institutionally and spatially determined, social interactions of a group; the relations between the members of the group can lead to a rather more homogenous or heterogeneous group structure. In this process, we have to separate interactions relating directly to the event from interactions relating to other topics like, for instance, private issues or the specific group situation. As far as sports-in-media goes, American research has investigated reception behavior in individual social situations, like, for instance, in families, with married couples or in various group constellations of friends (for example, Gantz, 1981; Raney, 2006; Rothenbuhler, 1988; Wenner and Gantz, 1989). The social dimension of the public spheres for sports-in-media also becomes clear through various forms of ensuing communication. As a non-committal topic of conversation in public communication, sports can contribute to producing (private) sociability (Melnick, 1993; for sports-in-media: Wenner and Gantz, 1989); that is, for extending interactions within socially differentiated conversational groupings.

There is an emotional differentiation bound up with the social, as sports-in-media is a cognitive and, above all, an affective-emotional experience. The emotionally determined engagement of reception groups can vary by dint of elements like the number and the relationships of participants sharing in the interactivity (group size, sort of group) or the context's situational conditions (public or private reception) (for example, Sapolsky and Zillmann, 1978; Wenner and Gantz, 1989). Affective differentiation displays further effects in addition: the emotional experience of sports-in-media, as a form of what people feel is a community, depends on the event (possibilities for identification, participation, national consciousness, and so on), on the consumers' involvement as well as that of their co-viewers, on the size of the group and the relationships among the co-viewers, and in addition, we can observe the stimulus of recipients' emotional experience increasingly in sports journalism (Schramm, Dohle, and Klimmt, 2004; Horky, 2006a, 2006b).

Relation to spatial situations

A second aspect of collective consumption is the spatial situation of communal reception, which forms the focus of investigations into sports bars, above all (Eastman and Land, 1997). Weed (2006) sees the reason for the increasing consumption of sports-in-media in sports bars in the shift of the live broadcast rights for football to pay TV, as well as the renovation of stadiums, which have consequently lost atmosphere in the eyes of live visitors. In addition, he sees the development also extending onto other sorts of sport, like rugby.

On the spatial level, differentiating the group reception of sports-in-media is governed by the possibilities for access: to experience sport live in a stadium you need a ticket. In the media sense, the spatial dimension is, on the one hand, bound up with various possibilities for following the event on television (such as, big screen, private TV set), and on the other, with the possibilities for access to the TV program (broadcast on free-to-air, rights with pay-TV, and so on). As a process, the group reception of sports-in-media is thus "integrated into society by its specific spatial nature;" we differentiate private (principally closed) and public (principally open) "home and corporeal territories" (Wöhler, 2000, pp. 56–7). This spatialization leads, according to Wöhler (p. 60), to a "fragmentation of the public sphere," which does not, however, means reducing it, as, on the contrary, the larger number of partial public spheres brings an "increase in the overall public sphere" via the various forms of appropriation.

The reception process in relation to the public sphere

The third approach enquires into the influence of various forms of public sphere on the reception process in the communal reception of sports-in-media. Bette and Schimank (1995, pp. 72–4) use systems theory to reflect on the loss of community in modern society and declare that the "communal experience" in consuming sports offers an "important collective assurance of identity." Sports viewers form "public communities," which do, in one respect, "span social distance," but which can also lead to exclusion, above all of socially disadvantaged groups. Further, Lemish defined four general rules for TV public spheres: according to them, the general situation, other viewers, access to the TV program as well as the social interaction about the program is the decisive particular features in watching TV in groups. TV reception in the public sphere is, according to Lemish, "neither an individualistic form of behavior, nor was it a passive one" (Lemish, 1982, p. 781).

Social–psychological features

The particular social–psychological features of the reception of sports-in-media in situations among different social groups has been something sought after in research to date: empirical investigations are an exception and results often derive from participatory observation without putting categories into effect and tend, in part, to be of dubious validity (Weed, 2006, 2007). It is only rarely that we come across valid empirical verifications, and these apply, above all, to the American sphere (Eastman and Land, 1997; Gantz, 1981; Rothenbuhler, 1988; Sapolsky and Zillmann, 1978; Wenner and Gantz, 1989); differentiation is mostly into motivational and behavior-oriented effects of group reception. In what follows, the attempt will be made to undertake a differentiation and collation of those particular social-psychological features in the group reception of sports-in-media which have been sufficiently demonstrated to date and to refer to the theoretical differentiation of the reception processes in social, spatial and public terms.

Personal involvement and identification

Participation or involvement is generally one of the most important motivations in the reception of sports-in-media and is significantly reinforced through a communal reception. In this process, the social cohesion for the group members is decisive for the intensity of the involvement: in families, the involvement is less than in a group of friends (Wenner and Gantz, 1989, 1998); clear indications for this are the reinforced consumption of drinks and snacks in these socially rather more weakly institutionalized groups. Murrell and Dietz (1992) can demonstrate that, in the case of wins, individuals' identification increases with the number of recipients also watching.

In group reception, high values for the motif of "enjoyment of victories of the favoured team" do, on the one hand, actually result for individuals in connection with their involvement and identification, but annoyance over defeats is reinforced (Wenner and Gantz, 1989, pp. 259–60). In addition, there are clear differentiations between the sexes as regards personal involvement, as men are also more strongly involved in groups and tend to behave more like fans (Wenner and Gantz, 1998); for women, the communal reception is, by contrast, much rather the final possibility for passing the time (Gantz, 1981; Wenner and Gantz, 1998). Eastman and Land (1997, p. 161) also use the example of the provision of catering to demonstrate that the communal reception of sports-in-media is, above all, a men's issue; women are in many cases "adjuncts to men" or "outsiders", who are mainly interested in the food and drink on offer instead of the sports on offer on TV. However, personal involvement in communal reception is subject to demonstrable fluctuations among men too. Krotz and Eastman (1999) demonstrate that the overwhelmingly male patrons of sports bars are much rather inclined to talk to other viewers as distinct from the previously declared interest in particular sports broadcasts – by contrast, it is possible to discern increasing interest in the program among women.

As far as the influence of the spatial situation goes, Eastman and Land (1997) describe an indicator of recipients sitting as close as possible to the TV screen to be involved as intensively as possible in the events. Eastman and Riggs (1994) could demonstrate with their observations and questionnaires that many TV recipients create a stadium atmosphere in the group through inviting co-recipients, in order, in turn, to raise the possibility for personal involvement. Participation in a sports event via the media is fundamentally connected with less effort, costs, and negative social side effects (for example, weather, aggressive fans, lack of facilities), and in addition, the quality of the event is that much higher and, in a certain way, more intensive thanks to the media's technical possibilities, like replays, slow motion and various camera perspectives, which are impossible with a direct, live reception. Reception in a group additionally provides the personal involvement in a community, as in a stadium, so that Eastman and Riggs (1994) talk of group reception as "the best seats at the game" (p. 261).

In the sense of the public sphere, different processes of identification generally arise with personal involvement in the group: identification with the group of co-watchers and with the group of imagined co-watchers as well as with the contents in the media, that is, for example, the team or the sportspeople shown. Wirth and Schramm (2007, p. 159) point to how "knowing that you are part of an audience in the millions can be a source of a different class of feelings. Like awe or pride (national pride)." The collective role of an audience might well be, as a rule, only distal and so could only be experienced notionally, that is, in the imagination. However, forms of reception like public viewing would make "hybrid forms" possible, which render the "collective situation of reception...certainly a matter of proximal experience."

Social control and acquisition of knowledge

Communal reception of sports-in-media is conditioned by a balance between personal involvement in the event witnessed and social control by the group of co-recipients. Sapolsky and Zillmann (1978) were able to demonstrate empirically that the number and nature of the social relationship between co-recipients influences the involvement in sports-in-media. In these investigators' experiment, recipients were on their own, with one other person, in small groups (two to four people) or in large groups (5–100 people) as they watched the TV broadcast of a basketball game between the home team, the US, and the then Yugoslavia. The personal involvement in the form of positive reactions to the opponent's successes was significantly more strongly marked, above all in the large group and also in the lone situation. Sapolsky and Zillmann explained the cause as being that pleasure in the opponent scoring too, something otherwise socially incompatible, seemed possible on your own and as a mostly anonymous member of a group of co-watchers, as here you did not have to anticipate any restrictions. As the small groups and the one other co-watcher mainly consisted of friends, people got more annoyed in this situation about the opponent's successes, as the win desired for your own team was reduced. The study's result is hence able to point to social control by the homogenous group as the most important regulatory factor on personal involvement. It should be noted that regarding the effect of social control, the primary cognitive processes of acquiring and understanding media contents will be subsumed, as a motive of group reception is increasing knowledge in order subsequently to be able to shine in the group as an expert and to secure social status in that way (Schramm, *et al.*, 2004).

Belonging to the group and sociability

Alongside social control, belonging to the group of recipients can be shown to be a particular social–psychological feature in the form of sociability as well. During the public viewings at the 2006 World Cup, 84 percent of those asked praised the great atmosphere at communal viewing, and in addition, society's collective self-confidence increased (Aegis Media, 2006). Weed (2007, p. 405) conducted participatory observation in English pubs and describes the "collective enjoyment" and "shared communal experience" as the essential effects of consuming sports-in-media. Eastman and Land (1997, p. 167) nominate "social interaction as unification" as one of the most important effects of group reception of sports-in-media; belonging to a group was manifested above all via conversations and statements on the fan status of those involved, but also (non commercial, non-professional) betting on results was a frequently observed characteristic. As can be found in the work of Eastman and Land, many of the people observed declared they would go to a sports bar for reception of sports-in-media above all for reasons of sociability. This motivation towards group membership is significantly more marked with men and, above all, with fans of sports on TV than with women or with the group of people not so interested in football on TV (Gantz, 1981). Thus, men more often want to have a beer with friends and use the opportunity of communal reception of sports-in-media to do that.

An important precondition of group reception is arranging to meet, the consensus achieved in advance, as it were, and the concomitant interest along with communal reception of sports-in-media, which differentiates the topic of sport from other topics and generates group membership as well as sociability. This sociability as a community integrated at least as regards its interests then leads in many cases to TV itself becoming the topic and what is being shown being transferred onto the situation of the recipients' personal lives (for sports-in-media, see Gantz, 1981; Horky, 2007). In the case of the 1984 Olympics, it was possible to demonstrate that people talk more often to their co-watchers in connection with sports events than with a normal program; in the process, what they said was determined above all by the media contents (broadcasts of the Olympics) (Rothenbuhler, 1988). Even with chance TV viewing in public places (for example, in front of a shop window), the reception of sports-in-media clearly produces spontaneous and unplanned sociability. What seems, however, conceivable is also an opposite effect in the sense of a conscious or unconscious distinction within a group. The group might claim one individual recipient has no expertise and so it can come to processes of exclusion within communal reception. Hartmann and Dohle (2005, p. 298) nominate "social processes of comparison" linked to reception, which can lead to a positive exclusion of the co-watcher thus viewed in a negative light. It is possible to imagine motivations for communal reception of sports-in-media in the sense of a conscious observation of how other recipients pick up sports-in-media.

Behavior changes and rituals

Membership of a group can generate social acceptance and communal support. This sort of belonging is manifested in sports as deliberate public demarcation by clothes and attributes like fans' scarves or similar. As a communal ritual, this self-presentation increases the coherence of the recipient-group and consequently increases the communal experience of sports-in-media (Bette 2004). In addition, when we analyze the production complex of sports-in-media, we can observe that TV techniques like slow motion or other medial alteration of the time structure of sports action do help to construct a ritual space where recipients find space for personal displays and the presentation of group-membership (Eastman and Riggs, 1994). We can go further to specify personal rituals among recipients of sports-in-media too, both as individuals or group members, in the form of repeated patterns of behavior which turn the nature and the form of TV reception subsequently into a ritual, for example, after a win by the home team (Eastman and Riggs, 1994). A particular sign of this more intensive involvement with group-reception is behavioral changes like calling our loud (that is, yelling) or short discussions on players, trainers, or tactical moves. Where groups of friends are strongly institutionalized socially, these changes can be specified significantly more often than, for example, in families or, above all, with solitary reception of sports-in-media (Gantz, 1981; Wenner and Gantz, 1989, 1998).

Communal reception

As a public event, group reception of sports-in-media can display two different manifestations. On the one hand, the communal reception can be framed as a social event by the costuming described above, by provision of catering, by fitting out rooms and similar measures. This form of reception can be designated sports-in-media as experience. Weed (2006, p. 90) describes the sports bar as a "third place", which, in terms of experience, offers an event between the live action in the stadium and your TV at home. "The 'proximity' is to the experience rather than to the game" (Weed, 2006, p. 92). Crabb and Goldstein (1991, p. 363) focus on the US to describe the communal attendance at sports events as a "social occasion". This event is often centered on families and can also be transferred to communal evenings watching sports on TV. In the US, a telephone poll established that, compared to the usual TV schedule, it is precisely sporting events like the Olympic Games that people prefer to watch communally as an event in front of the TV (Rothenbuhler, 1988). On the other hand, communal reception of sports-in-media as event offers this proximity to the experience of the live action without the negatively considered side effects of experiencing it live, such as bad weather, lack of catering, unpleasant co-recipients, bad sanitary facilities, difficult travel there and back, and entrance charges. In this way, the reception of TV is not only considered to be more comfortable but also a more pleasant event overall (Horky, 2007).

Imagined group membership

From the perspective of the public sphere, actually belonging to a group can also be accompanied by imagining that you belong to a still larger group of co-watchers in the reception of sports-in-media. Journalists' commentaries and switching to other communal situations of reception can certainly suggest membership of a larger communal reception group, particularly as, with public viewing, at least a part of what is an audience in the millions is also visible. To date, this imagined group membership has hardly been taken up in academic research. However, Hartmann and Dohle (2005) do set out some cognitive and affective effects of this form of reception as experience. The significance of media content is heightened and social comparison processes arise between recipients and the (imagined) group resulting from the group's different social composition, but, above all, feelings of inclusion in a wider community in the sense of nationalism or patriotism are reinforced, as already noted above. In addition, the authenticity of the experience can be increased, as well as feelings concomitant on embarrassing or comical content in the media.

During the 2002 World Cup, Schramm and Klimmt (2003) conducted a survey and identified the motive of "cheering along with the Germans" as significant and as uniting aspects of motives such as "identification with your favorite team", "being a supporter along with other Germans", "all cheering in front of the TV" and similar. At the start, this motive, in fact, did not feature strongly, but it grew notably in the course of the competition, above all before the final. In the American study by Eastman and Riggs (1994, p. 262), imagined membership of larger audience groups is a "third dimension" which could also heighten the attraction of communal reception of sports-in-media.

Conclusion

Surveying social-psychological effects in the group reception of sports-in-media has demonstrated the strong influence of the number of co-watchers and of the social relations among them, as well as the social and spatial situation and the differing form of public sphere, has on affective and cognitive effects as well as on recipients' behavior during reception. In comparison with the situation of the solitary consumer, the group situation can, on the one hand, strengthen the social-psychological effects of reception of sports-in-media, and, on the other, it exercises social control in various functions. With sports-in-media, intense identification results in effects of communing with the real and/or imagined audience, for example, in the form of nationalism, which can scarcely be conceived with other media content. It is at most in pop music programs (for example, live broadcast of Eurovision Song Contest) that similar social-psychological particularities are discernible. One significant result is that, with communal consumption of sports-in-media, the event of reception is often itself the focus and not the cognitive/affective access to the media contents on offer.

References

Aegis Media (2006). *Carat expert public viewing study FIFA WM 2006*. Wiesbaden: Aegis Media, July. Retrieved from http://www.carat-expert.de.

Bette, K.-H. (2004). Sportbegeisterung und gesellschaft. In C. Kruse and I. Lüsebrink (Eds.), *"Schneller, höher, weiter?" Sportpädagogische theoriebildung auf dem prüfstand* (pp. 46–78). Sankt Augustin: Academia.

Bette, K.-H., and Schimank, U. (1995). *Doping im hochleistungssport: Anpassung durch abweichung*. Frankfurt: Suhrkamp.

Crabb, P. B., and Goldstein, J. H. (1991). The social psychology of watching sports: From ilium to living room. In J. Bryant and D. Zillmann (Eds.), *Responding to the screen: Reception and reaction processes* (pp. 355–71). Hillsdale, NJ: Lawrence Erlbaum.

Eastman, S., and Land, A. (1997). The best of both worlds: Sports fans find good seats at the bar. *Journal of Sport and Social Issues*, 21 (2), 156–78.
Eastman, S. T., and Riggs, K. E. (1994). Televised sports and ritual: Fan experiences. *Sociology of Sport Journal*, 11 (3), 249–74.
Gantz, W. (1981). An exploration of viewing motives and behaviors associated with television sports. *Journal of Broadcasting*, 25 (3), 263–75.
Geese, S., Zeughardt, C., and Gerhard, H. (2006). Die Fußball-Weltmeisterschaft 2006 im Fernsehen. Daten zur Rezeption und Bewertung. *Media Perspektiven*, 9, 454–64.
Gerhard, H. (2006). Die Fußball-WM als Fernsehevent. Analyse der Zuschauerakzeptanz bei Fußball-Weltmeisterschaften 1954 bis 2006. *Media Perspektiven*, 9, 465–74.
Gerhard, H., Kessler, B., and Gscheidle, C. (2010). Die Fußball-Weltmeisterschaft 2010 im Fernsehen. *Media Perspektiven*, 9: 382–9.
Hartmann, T., and Dohle, M. (2005). Publikumsvorstellungen im rezeptionsprozess. *Publizistik*, 50 (3), 287–303.
HISPOJO-Forschungsgruppe, and Horky, T. (2007). Öffentliches Fernsehen in Gemeinschaft – Studie zur geselligen Rezeption der Fußball-WM 2006. In T. Horky (Ed.), *Die Fußball-Weltmeisterschaft 2006: Analysen zum Mediensport* (pp. 38–60). Norderstedt: BoD.
Horky, T. (2006a). Die Inszenierung von Öffentlichkeit. Fußball-WM-Fernsehen hat Mediengeschichte geschrieben. *Fernseh-Informationen*, 7, 12–14.
Horky, T. (2006b). Sport, Medien und neue Öffentlichkeiten. Die Fernseh-Weltmeisterschaften 2006 in kritischer Nachbetrachtung. *Olympisches Feuer*, 26 (5), 30–3.
Horky, T. (2007). Mediensport und Öffentlichkeit. Zur Ausdifferenzierung eines journalistischen Programmbereichs am Beispiel der Fußball-WM 2006. *Leipziger Sportwissenschaftliche Beiträge*, 48 (2), 13–34.
Krotz, F., and Eastman, S. T. (1999). Orientations toward television outside the home. *Journal of Communication*, 49 (1), 5–27.
Lemish, D. (1982). The rules of viewing television in public places. *Journal of Broadcasting*, 26 (4), 757–81.
Melnick, M. J. (1993). Searching for sociability in the stands: A theory of sports spectating. *Journal of Sport Management*, 7, 44–60.
Murrell, A. J., and Dietz, B. (1992). Fan support of sport teams: The effect of a common group identity. *Journal of Sport and Exercise Psychology*, 14 (1), 28–39.
Raney, A. (2006). Why we watch and enjoy mediated sports. In A. Raney and J. Bryant (Eds.), *Handbook of sports and media* (pp. 313–29). Mahwah, NJ: Lawrence Erlbaum.
Rothenbuhler, E. W. (1988). The living room celebration of the Olympic Games. *Journal of Communication*, 38 (4), 61–81.
Sapolsky, B., and Zillmann, D. (1978). Enjoyment of a televised sport contest under different social conditions of viewing. *Perceptual and Motor Skills*, 46 (1), 29–30.
Schramm, H., and Klimmt, C. (2003). Nach dem Spiel ist vor dem Spiel. Die Rezeption der Fußball-Weltmeisterschaft 2002 im Fernsehen: Eine Panel-Studie zur Entwicklung der Rezeptionsmotivation im Turnierverlauf. *Medien and Kommunikationswissenschaft*, 51 (1), 55–81.
Schramm, H., Dohle, M., and Klimmt, C. (2004). Das Erleben von Fußball im Fernsehen. In H. Schramm (Ed.), *Die rezeption des sports in den medien* (pp. 121–42). Köln: Herbert von Halem.
Ufer, B. (2010). Emotionen und erlebnisse beim public viewing. Explorative interdisziplinäre analyse eines gesellschaftlichen phänomens. Dissertation zur Erlangung des sozialwissenschaftlichen Doktorgrades an der Sozialwissenschaftlichen Fakultät der Georg-August-Universität Göttingen. Retrieved from http://webdoc.sub.gwdg.de/diss/2010/ufer/ufer.pdf.
Weed, M. (2006). The story of an ethnography: The experience of watching the 2002 World Cup in the pub. *Soccer and Society*, 7 (1), 76–95.
Weed, M. (2007). The pub as a virtual football fandom venue: An alternative to 'being there'? *Soccer and Society*, 8 (2/3), 399–414.
Wenner, L. A., and Gantz, W. (1989). The audience experience with sports on television. In L. A. Wenner (Ed.), *Media, sports and society* (pp. 241–69). Newbury Park, CA: Sage.

Wenner, L.A., and Gantz, W. (1998). Watching sports on television: Audience experience, gender, fanship, and marriage. In L.A. Wenner (Ed.), *MediaSport* (pp. 233–51). London: Routledge.

Whannel, G. (1998). Reading the sports media audience. In L.A. Wenner (Ed.), *MediaSport* (pp. 221–51). London: Routledge.

Wirth, W., and Schramm, H. (2007). Emotionen, metaemotionen und regulationsstrategien bei der medienrezeption. In W. Wirth, H. J. Stiehler, and C. Wünsch (Eds.), *Dynamisch-transaktional denken: Theorie und empirie der kommunikationswissenschaft* (pp. 153–84). Köln: Herbert von Halem.

Wöhler, K. (2000). Zur verräumlichung von offentlichkeit. In W. Faulstich and K. Hickethier (Eds.), *Öffentlichkeit im wandel: Neue beiträge zur begriffsklärung* (pp. 48–62). Bardowick: Wissenschaftler Verlag.

39

SPORT, CELEBRITY, AND THE MEANING OF STYLE

John Harris

The commercialization and commodification of elite level sport has contributed to an increased focus on the celebrity athlete as a site for examining the ways in which the media frame various narratives. This chapter provides an overview of the subject and considers the development of research concerned with the cultural politics of sporting celebrity. In addition to this overview, the analysis is extended to focus on style as a subject that has received little attention to date. Here, we see the celebrity athlete transcending boundaries and moving beyond the sports pages to become increasingly visible in other areas of popular culture. The complex interplay of a range of identity markers shapes the (re)presentation of these individuals as they become symbols of something much more than their performances as athletes.

Sport is often ranked as a top ten industry in the US (Pedersen, Miloch, and Laucella, 2007) and is a truly global phenomenon in many respects. As the economic significance of sport has developed so too has the recognition and awareness of its main protagonists and some athletes are now global stars. In different sports, and across the various continents, this has led to an increased focus on these athletes and a seemingly unquenchable thirst for information about their lives beyond the sporting arena. This development has occurred alongside the wider *celebrification* of society and what has been described as "the exorbitance of celebrity's contemporary cultural visibility" (Turner, 2004, p. 4). However we look at it, sport is big business and leading athletes are in some instances now amongst the most recognizable figures on the planet. As Smart has noted:

> High incomes and associated extravagant lifestyles plus the media attention they attract, have transported prominent and successful sporting figures onto another plain, an astral plain that testifies to the growing Americanisation of sport culture. Sport stars appear in many respects now to be comparable with celebrities from the worlds of film, television and popular music, although the extent and durability of their appeal may be greater. In terms of global popularity or appeal there are now few, if any, other professions that can begin to compare to sport.
>
> *(Smart, 2005, p. 17)*

This quote clearly highlights the ways in which sporting celebrities have now assumed an increasingly visible role outside of the sporting arena. In newspapers, for example, athletes once featured almost exclusively in the sports pages of a publication but now seem to increasingly occupy significant space outside of this. Before looking at the development of research surrounding sporting celebrity it is important to firstly offer a very brief account of the rise of celebrity and the positioning of the subject as a focus of academic study.

Celebrity

Boorstin's (1961) locution that to be a celebrity is to be well-known for one's well-knownness has achieved a certain prominence in the literature and points to the ways in which such figures may be fabricated to satisfy our expectations of greatness. There are, of course, numerous factors which have contributed to the seemingly inexorable rise of celebrity culture (Cashmore, 2006; Turner, 2004). The inception and widespread adoption of television in households was particularly important and this also played a central role in the development of (post)modern sport and the sport business that we now recognize today (see Smart, 2005; Whannel, 2002). Kurzman, *et al.*'s assertion that "celebrity status is big business, and the academic study of celebrity is itself a growing industry" (Kurzman, *et al.*, 2007, p. 362) points to the ways in which scholars from a range of disciplinary backgrounds have engaged with the subject to map its development. Various texts have clearly shown that in our consumer society celebrity matters and whatever the criticisms of the rise of celebrity culture it is almost impossible to ignore. Rojek (2001) categorized three broad types of celebrity in relation to how celebrity status is earned or attributed. In this he referred to the ascribed, achieved and attributed status of celebrity. The second of these carries particular resonance for sport where athletic competence is viewed as something "truly meritocratic" (Giles, 2000, p. 107). Turner has noted that "The contemporary celebrity will usually have emerged from the sports or entertainment industries; they will be highly visible through the media; and their private lives will attract greater public interest than their professional lives" (Turner, 2004, p. 3).

Here then we see some indication of how sport fits within the broader cultural landscape and the celebrity industry as a whole. This very brief overview does not mean to oversimplify the subject, for there are of course many different ways of looking at and understanding celebrity. There is now a whole host of texts that provide a detailed and nuanced explanation of how and why the celebrity industry has developed to the extent it has (for example, Cashmore, 2006; Giles, 2000; Rojek, 2001; Turner, 2004). Space does not permit a detailed discussion of this, but before examining the significance of style in celebrity narratives it is important to firstly provide a brief introduction to the work on sport celebrity.

Sport and celebrity

A key moment in the academic study of sporting celebrities was the publication of Andrews and Jackson's (2001) edited text, *Sports Stars*. Drawing in large part upon a theoretical lens that we later saw more overtly defined as physical cultural studies, this collection of case studies provided a detailed insight into the ways in which the emergence of celebrity figures changed from being "a haphazard and arbitrary voyage of discovery" (p. 4) to a much more proactive process focusing on cultivating celebrity. Featuring essays on athletes from sports such as football, tennis and basketball the contributors to this collection clearly outlined the dimensions of sports stardom and the positioning and significance of celebrity athletes in a range of cultural contexts.

Ellis Cashmore has also been an important figure in developing the analysis of sporting celebrity. A sociologist who has published widely on a range of topics, it was his work on the football player David Beckham that garnered considerable media attention as Beckham morphed from an athlete into an international fashion icon and very powerful brand (see also, Vincent, Hill, and Lee, 2009; Wahl, 2009). Cashmore's (2002) book, *Beckham*, represented one of the first attempts to provide a detailed analysis of an individual athlete and locate this individual within and around a discussion of the wider social and cultural landscape. Here, Cashmore argued that "there is more than one way to understand somebody" (Cashmore, 2002, p. 5) and that to look outside of an individual and avert the gaze towards the culture of which they have become an important part can provide a useful means of better understanding any celebrity figure. A general treatise of the broader celebrity sphere in *Celebrity/Culture* (Cashmore, 2006) extended the analysis further by detailing the ways in which it is our preoccupation with famous persons and the extravagant value we attach to them that continues to encourage consumption at all levels.

Barry Smart (2005) has also added to this subject with a text that examines the key economic and cultural factors that have contributed to the popularity of sport stars. Here, Smart showed how sporting figures present a rare quality of authenticity in an age of increasingly inauthentic and manufactured representations. In addition to focusing on Beckham, by now a staple component of any discussion of sporting celebrity, the author casts his critical eye on the golfer Tiger Woods, basketball legend Michael Jordan and the tennis player Anna Kournikova, to demonstrate the ways in which certain athletes come to be seen as representatives of particular ideologies and ideals.

Kournikova represents an interesting choice of subject here, for while Jordan and Woods were dominant athletes in their respective sports and would appear on every poll detailing the greatest athletes of all time, Kournikova did not ever win a Grand Slam tournament as a singles player. At the height of her fame, Internet searches for the Russian tennis player were greater than that for Woods and Jordan combined (noting here that these were the two next most searched for athletes). Kournikova, identified some years earlier as "the masculinists transcendent image of the idiosyncratic sportswoman whereby masculinity is maintained through ideological representations of femininity" (Harris and Clayton, 2002, p. 397) remains one of the most well-known female athletes in the world despite having been retired now for some years. Here, in relation to discussions of style, we see quite clearly the overt sexualization of the female athlete and the ways in which appearance and sex appeal are deemed more important than athletic ability. Yet it was not only female athletes who found themselves subject to media coverage focused predominantly on looks rather than performance. In addition to this, we also witnessed the increased sexualization and commodification of the male athlete. Once again, David Beckham is a visible figure in this respect.

Garry Whannel (2002) used an image of Beckham on the front cover of his text, *Media Sport Stars*. This work, based on Whannel's considerable experience researching sport and the media, provided a detailed appraisal of the role of sport in contemporary culture. In charting the rise of sporting celebrity, and documenting some of the key athletes through the ages who have been prominent in serving as focal points for discourses of masculinity and morality, the text provides a valuable resource in tracking the emergence of the sports star in Britain and the US. A growth in the media coverage of sport helped frame a sporting star system as the lives of various athletes became the focus of numerous media narratives. Central to this trajectory was the increasing commercialization of sport and the centrality of the media in cultivating what we now often see referred to as the sport business. As the media mogul Rupert Murdoch found when stating his intention to use sport as a 'battering ram' to break into new markets, sport has a remarkable capacity to transcend boundaries and carries an important symbolic value. As this became more clearly acknowledged, we saw an increasing importance attached to individual athletes whose appeal promised much in commercial terms for interested stakeholders. Cashmore describes this process well and is worth quoting at some length:

> The sports celebrity is a relatively new and unique creature whose natural habitat is as much the *Star* and the *People* as it is the football field, and who is often seen prowling the savannahs of movie premieres and nightclub launches. Up until recently, only rock and movie stars could command the kind of status that guaranteed invitations to gala openings, launches or benefit concerts. Now, it's almost mandatory that such events include sports celebs. This suggests a change, not only in the structure of sport, but in the overall configuration of the entertainment industry of which sport is now part, as well as in the culture that commissions the voracious consumption of people as well as goods.
>
> *(Cashmore, 2002, pp. 38–9)*

In detailing the scholarship on sport celebrity, it is impossible to even scratch the surface in outlining all other works detailing the emergence of this subject. Even in the relatively narrow field of sport sociology a range of research articles published in periodicals such as the *Sociology of Sport Journal*, *International Review for the Sociology of Sport*, and the *Journal of Sport and Social Issues*, clearly shows that interesting and varied work on sporting celebrity is taking place across the globe. The work of scholars in communication studies, marketing, and cultural studies has also contributed a great deal to this area of study.

Harris and Clayton (2007) note that the contemporary sports star is, or is at least portrayed as, an idealized model for one or more cultural connotation, which he/she carries with them through their efforts, achievements and failures as an athlete. Rowe (1999) suggests that the celebrity arose from the culturalization of economics in capitalist society. The media are the arbiters of this celebrity creating in the consumer market a human desire not only for commodity goods, but for an unattainable lifestyle, which becomes framed in a more structured political discourse (Cashmore, 2002; Smart, 2005). The mediatization of sport, together with an increasingly developed and sophisticated understanding of its marketing potential, meant that the positioning of the industry has changed markedly during the last 20 years. Where once there were sporting heroes (and heroines) now there seems to be far more discussion of sport celebrities. As Smart perceptively highlights, it is not the case that we no longer have heroes but that they "are now in the shadow of a new and more vivid species, the celebrity" (Smart, 2005, p. 9). Central to the cult of celebrity is the subject of style. This is an area that has received relatively limited attention to date.

Playing with style

From the field of aesthetics and art, we see style as something incorporating taste, subjective interpretation and points of view. Mueller (1941) observes how style involves the artist speaking not only as an individual but as a representative of a group, class, nation and tradition. Genova (1979) traces a discussion of style from a signature view through to a meaning-expressing model and argues that the vital role style has played in creating and discovering meaning has often been overlooked. Style remains a somewhat slippery and elusive concept in the scholarship on sport and there are many ways of using and understanding the word. In an essay on sport, leisure and style, Alan Tomlinson argues that the ways in which English (and British) sport has changed can be read as "symptomatic of key changes in the social and cultural life of Britain" (Tomlinson, 2001, p. 399). Ewen (1990) suggests that style has three important roles in contemporary culture. In discussing style as self, as society, and as information, Ewen shows us some of the different ways in which style is performed and how this sits within wider consumer culture.

Playing style has been looked at in sports such as rugby and football to describe the ways in which particular teams are seen to embody and portray perceived national characteristics. In rugby union, for example, the Irish are viewed as playing in a fast, aggressive and somewhat chaotic fashion, culminating in a kind of emerald commotion (Maguire and Tuck, 2005; Tuck, 2003). In the wider sporting landscape the (re)presentation of national styles can also be seen as an integral part of a "mapping of the mythical" that tells us much about the ways in which stereotypes are portrayed and promoted in various media outlets across different nations (O'Donnell, 1994). Much of the discussion of national playing styles has centered on the performance of men's national teams. Giulianotti (1999) has contributed much to this area in the study of football (soccer) with an erudite analysis that captures some of the subtleties and idiosyncrasies of tactical formations and development. Of course, as many of the above authors have capably addressed, the discussion and analysis of national playing styles has become ever more complex and multidimensional in an age of intensified globalization and the increased movement of athletes and coaches between nations.

In addition to the collective identities portrayed in narratives concerning national sporting teams, it is also important to consider the ways in which an individual athlete is perceived to embody certain characteristics. As Miller, Lawrence, McKay, and Rowe (2001) have noted, "the sporting body bears triumphant national mythologies in a double way, extending the body to encompass the nation and compressing it to obscure the social divisions that threaten national unity" (p. 31). Here, we see how individual athletes, just like sporting teams, come to represent and embody particular places and narratives of the nation. Outside of representations relating to nation, though, in what other ways then are individual athletes perceived to have style?

Some athletes are celebrated for different aspects of style and it is clear that others are focused on and/or celebrated for their perceived or clearly identified difference. Parker (2009) notes that celebrity figures do not emerge in a social vacuum but "are products of the cultural, political and historical circumstances upon which their very existence depends" (p. 150). Moreover, as Oates and Polumbaum (2004) suggest in their work on the basketball player Yao Ming, "attainment and maintenance of sports celebrity requires elaboration of a character beyond execution of the athletic job" (p. 198). Here then, it is important to offer a point of departure and provide a site for further exploring the discussion of style, and extending the analysis of sporting celebrity. McDonald and Birrell (1999) advocate focusing on an individual athlete as a means of exploring the fluid character of power relations across various identity markers. As a case study to develop some of the themes identified above, I use the example of a Welsh athlete from the contemporary sports world. This may not be an athlete well known to all readers but the Welsh international rugby player Gavin Henson provides an interesting case to consider the interweaving of sport with other areas of popular culture and the cult of celebrity in a wider sense.

Rugby, Wales, and sport celebrity

Rugby union is the national sport of Wales and its leading male players are revered within this small country. A golden age in the 1970s, just as color images of the sport were beamed through television into people's homes, saw many of the star players of the Welsh team become some of the best known athletes in the whole history of the sport. Later, as the national side experienced an era of almost terminal decline in the professional age (post 1995), the search for heroes became more pronounced as nostalgic recollections of a bygone golden age became more prominent. The first "star" of modern Welsh rugby was Barry John, who, in the early 1970s, was frequently compared to the football player George Best. John, described in Wales as "the King," was perhaps the first celebrity figure of the game but played at a time when rugby was an amateur sport and media scrutiny was far less intense. That being said, he retired from the sport at the age of 27 because he was uncomfortable with the attention he received (John, 1973). Gavin Henson was perhaps the first celebrity of postmodern Welsh rugby and he quickly achieved a status and profile that we had not seen before in this particular realm. More than just an athlete, it was his celebrity that catapulted him beyond the writing of the Welsh rugby press to become a staple feature of wider British popular media.

While some athletes attempt to avoid the spotlight, Henson eagerly embraced the attendant rewards of fame and celebrity. For Henson, it was not only being a member of the Welsh national rugby team that afforded him the media spotlight, but as the boyfriend of the singer Charlotte Church. While Ms. Church may not be a figure well-known to an international audience, she has sold millions of records and has been a regular fixture in the Welsh media for many years. Having first found fame as a child star, she has grown up in the public eye and has endured the media gaze over her various relationships and movement into adulthood. In a similar vein to the well-documented case of David Beckham and Victoria Adams, this coming together of two young and attractive people from the entertainment industries garnered considerable interest. Indeed, the 'Welsh Posh and Becks' first came to prominence at a time when the national game of rugby union was witnessing something of a resurgence. On a small scale then, certainly within the relatively narrow discourse of the Welsh press, we saw evidence of what Whannel (2002) has termed *vortexuality* whereby the various media feed off each other and create something of a vortex effect.

Interest in Henson mushroomed by his positioning as "the first metrosexual rugby star" (Harris and Clayton, 2007). This profiling is best shown by the following quote from the *Observer* newspaper:

> Henson is an icon unlike any ever to grace a Welsh rugby pitch. He gels his hair, shaves his legs and wears gold boots. Twenty years ago, when post-match celebrations meant drinking a skinful of beers and probably a bottle of aftershave, too, he would have been mocked. Now he is lionised – the first metrosexual rugby star.
>
> *(Moss and Smith, 2005)*

Here, it is not only about an athlete's performance on the field but the way he looks. As Wales moved towards its first Grand Slam for more than a quarter of a century, the search for a new star of the game gathered pace. Cleary identifiable on the pitch by his gelled hair, shiny boots and fake tan, Henson was the perfect site for the ascription of the metrosexual label. Yet as has been noted elsewhere, we must also question the very concept of metrosexuality and the degree to which it may be considered a cultural–political challenge to traditional rugby masculinities (Harris and Clayton, 2007). From relative obscurity at the start of the 2004–05 season, Henson was, by the end of it, famous enough for an autobiography entitled *My Grand Slam Year* (Henson, 2005). Within this, he wrote about his grooming habits and the need to look good before running out onto the pitch. A big part of celebrity, and portraying a particular style, is about being seen at the right events and mixing with fellow celebrities. Indeed, it was widely acknowledged that the breakdown in the relationship between Sir Alex Ferguson and David Beckham was caused in large part by the presence of the latter at fashion events and the like.

Henson represents an interesting case to consider style and how celebrity narratives are framed. His newly acquired celebrity status attracted scrutiny outside of the sports pages. So while he had achieved far less as a rugby player than many of his touring colleagues, he was the focus of considerable media attention on the 2005 British and Irish Lions tour of New Zealand. The fact that he was not selected for the first test match became a news story (no other omissions represented such attention) and was the lead story in the *Western Mail* (June 21, 2005). A visit from his girlfriend was also a story deemed worthy of being front-page news in the same newspaper (June 16, 2005). Scholars have commented on the authenticity of sport stars which sets them apart from other more explicitly manufactured celebrities (Andrews and Jackson, 2001: Smart, 2005). However, as Turner notes, whilst the process by which they first come to public attention may be different they are "subject to the same mass mediated process of celebritisation" (Turner, 2004, p. 19).

Henson's increased visibility as a celebrity soon led to questions and concerns about his focus and performances as an athlete. A long-term injury, followed by a ban for striking an opponent, and then some substandard performances on his return to the national team, were all further cause for negative representations of him during the 2005–06 season. This meant that characteristics that were once celebrated, focusing particularly on appearance and discourses of celebrity, were now used as the means to criticize the player. The newspaper serialization, and subsequent publication, of his somewhat controversial book also contributed to this.

Redmond and Holmes (2007) have referred to the derogatory use of the term celebrity in a range of discourses within broader debates concerning the shifts in modern-day fame. There continues to be a school of thought that athletes need to concern themselves with training regimes and performance in competitions rather than pursuing sponsorship activities and associated commercial interests. It is widely agreed that Henson has not fully achieved his potential as a rugby player. Following a number of injury problems, he embarked on a sabbatical from the game and after spending a great deal of time with his two children and Church, we saw the emergence of Gavin Henson as a reality television star.

Appearances on television shows *71 Degrees North* and *Strictly Come Dancing* introduced him to an audience that would not have known who he was or perhaps had some vague recognition of him as the boyfriend of Charlotte Church. An article in *The Guardian* noted that "the celebrity lifestyle seemed to hold far more appeal than a game he appeared to have fallen out of love with" (Rees, 2010). As his relationship with Church broke down, and he briefly re-engaged with his rugby career, with the distinct possibility that he would reclaim his international place, it was announced that Henson would appear on the Channel 5 show, *The Bachelor*. Former England International Brian Moore, writing in *The Telegraph*, questioned whether Henson would really be able to justify choosing the celebrity path over an athletic career particularly in something like *The Bachelor*, which he viewed as "an example of dumb-down consumerism at worst" (Moore, 2012).

Conclusion

Celebrity is a central part of the contemporary sports world and the wider cultural landscape more than ever before. As some share more of their private lives through magazine spreads and reality television shows, they are viewed as much more than just athletes. The increased presence of famous figures on social media sites seemingly offer opportunities to engage with celebrities (albeit not in person) in new ways. Yet despite this seemingly greater access, it is also the case that as the rewards become ever larger sport celebrities are in fact more distant than at any other time before. The massive salaries earned by some athletes in sports such as football and basketball means that they have become ever more dislocated and removed from communities and fans. If the athlete is romantically linked with a celebrity from another field of popular culture then this interest may foster an awareness and profile far greater than the sum of the constituent parts. Tomlinson (2001) has noted that sport and the manifestations of modern sport style express two elements central to consumer culture. He suggests that they not only provide opportunities for "the formulation of self and the display of social identity" (p. 411) but also notes that these are continually reshaped by the dominant economic forces of the cultural industries.

Henson's fellow countryman, Joe Calzaghe, is an interesting case to consider here as he was someone who for the duration of his career as a champion boxer, represented a kind of anti-celebrity and consciously stayed clear of much of the peripheral areas beyond the life of an athlete. Yet after retiring from the ring he actively embraced the celebrity circuit and, like Henson, an appearance on *Strictly Come Dancing* raised his profile outside of the sports pages. Despite his phenomenal achievements in the ring, as an undefeated world champion, it was perhaps as a recognizable face from the primetime BBC television show that made him a legitimate target for the now defunct *News of the World* newspaper to run a story detailing his cocaine use. This was the same newspaper that featured the American swimmer Michael Phelps with a bong at a party in South Carolina. Of course any other swimmer would have not been of interest, but the phenomenal accomplishments of Phelps at the 2008 Olympic Games in Beijing made him a news story of some interest. There is a very fine line between being famous enough to be a front-page story and leading a relatively anonymous existence.

Cashmore (2006) has observed that the most basic imperative of celebrity culture is material and centers upon the encouragement of consumption. It appears as though the inexorable rise of sporting celebrity shows little sign of slowing down. To craft and cultivate a particular style to enhance and develop their status and positioning *vis-â-vis* other competitors is a key part of the contemporary sports world. Scholars will continue to track these developments and look at cases that show the different ways in which celebrity impacts upon a variety of areas within contemporary society.

References

Andrews, D., and Jackson, S. (Eds.). (2001). *Sports stars*. London: Routledge.

Boorstin, D. (1961) *The image: A guide to pseudo-events in America*. New York: Vintage.

Cashmore, E. (2002) *Beckham*. Cambridge: Polity.

Cashmore, E. (2006) *Celebrity/Culture*. London: Routledge.

Ewen, S. (1990). Marketing dreams: The political elements of style. In A. Tomlinson (Ed.), *Consumption, identity and style* (pp. 41–56). London: Routledge.

Genova, J. (1979). The significance of style. *Journal of Aesthetics and Art Criticism*, 37 (4), 315–24.

Giles, D. (2000). *Illusions of immortality: A psychology of fame and celebrity*. Basingstoke: Macmillan.

Giulianotti, R. (1999) *Football: A sociology of the global game*. Cambridge: Polity.

Harris, J., and Clayton, B. (2002). Femininity, masculinity, physicality and the English tabloid press: The case of Anna Kournikova. *International Review for the Sociology of Sport*, 35 (3/4), 397–413.

Harris, J., and Clayton, B. (2007). The first metrosexual rugby star: Rugby union, masculinity and celebrity in contemporary Wales. *Sociology of Sport Journal*, 24 (2), 145–64.

Henson, G. (2005). with G. Thomas. *My grand slam year*. Edinburgh: Mainstream.

John, B. (1973). *The Barry John story*. Glasgow: William Collins and Sons.

Kurzman, C., Anderson, C., Key, C., Lee, Y., Moloney, M., Silver, A., and Van Ryn, M. (2007). Celebrity status. *Sociological Theory*, 25 (4), 347–67.

Maguire, J., and Tuck, J. (2005). A world in union? Rugby, globalisation and Irish identity. In J. Maguire (Ed.), *Power and global sport* (pp. 109–29). London: Routledge.

McDonald, M., and Birrell, S. (1999). Reading sport critically: A methodology for interrogating power. *Sociology of Sport Journal*, 16 (4), 283–300.

Miller, T., Lawrence, G., McKay, J., and Rowe, D. (2001). *Globalisation and sport*. London: Sage.

Moore, B. (2012). Gavin Henson's sorry career will be seen as a Shakespearean tragedy about which we no longer wish to hear. *The Telegraph*, April 2. Retrieved from http://www.telegraph.co.uk/sport/rugbyunion/9179280/Gavin-Hensons-sorry-career-will-be-seen-as-a-Shakespearean-tragedy-about-which-we-no-longer-wish-to-hear.html.

Moss, S. and Smith, D. (2005). From chapel to Church... *The Observer*, March 13. Retrieved from http://observer.guardian.co.uk/focus/story/0,,1436529,00.html.

Mueller, G. (1941). Style. *Journal of Aesthetics and Art Criticism*, 1 (2/3), 105–22.

Oates, T., and Polumbaum, J. (2004). Agile big man: The flexible marketing of Yao Ming. *Pacific Affairs*, 77 (2), 187–210.

O'Donnell, H. (1994). Mapping the mythical: A geopolitics of national sporting stereotypes. *Discourse and Society*, 5 (3), 345–80.

Parker, A. (2009). Sport, celebrity and identity: A socio-legal analysis. In J. Harris and A. Parker (Eds.), *Sport and social identities* (pp. 150–67). Basingstoke: Palgrave Macmillan.

Pedersen, P. M., Miloch, K. S., and Laucella, P. C. (2007). *Strategic sport communication*. Champaign, IL: Human Kinetics.

Redmond, S., and Holmes, S. (2007). Introduction: what's in a reader? In S. Redmond and S. Holmes (Eds.), *Stardom and celebrity: A reader* (pp. 1–2). London: Routledge.

Rees, P. (2010). The strange case of the missing centre Gavin Henson. *The Guardian*, January 12. Retrieved from http://www.guardian.co.uk/sport/blog/2010/jan/12/gavin-henson-ospreys-wales.

Rojek, C. (2001). *Celebrity*. London: Reaktion.

Rowe, D. (1999). *Sport, culture and the media*. Buckinghamshire: Open University Press.

Smart, B. (2005). *The sport star*. London: Sage.

Tomlinson, A. (2001). Sport, leisure, and style. In D. Morley and K. Robins (Eds.), *British cultural studies* (pp. 399–415). Oxford: Oxford University Press.

Tuck, J. (2003). Making sense of emerald commotion: Rugby union, national identity and Ireland. *Identities: Global Studies in Culture and Power*, 10, 495–515.

Turner, G. (2004). *Understanding celebrity*. London: Sage.

Vincent, J., Hill, J., and Lee, J. (2009). The multiple brand personalities of David Beckham: A case study of the Beckham brand. *Sport Marketing Quarterly*, 18, 173–80.
Wahl, G. (2009). *The Beckham experiment*. New York: Three Rivers Press.
Whannel, G. (2002). *Media sport stars*. London: Routledge.

40

MEDIA COVERAGE OF INTERNATIONAL SPORT

John Vincent and John S. Hill

Globalization brought the world closer together during the 20th century. With it came global media coverage of major international news and events, included among which were sports such as the Olympic Games and the Fédération Internationale de Football Association (FIFA) World Cup. Both were media successes, as over half of the world's population watched these quadrennial international sporting events. They mesmerized the global public and for a few weeks every four years the symbiotic relationship between sport and the media became intense as both print and electronic media competed to attract readers, viewers, and advertisers. Both competitions highlighted rivalries among nation states that had come of age during the 20th century as decolonization released 140 new countries onto the global landscape (Alesina and Spolaore, 2003). All were eager to affirm their national identities on the global stage.

As the Second World War ended in 1945, the forum of global sport opened up as a conduit for competitions among nations. Coinciding with this, the globalization of media emerged to provide what Rowe, McKay, and Miller (1998) described as the "sport-nationalism-media troika," or the intersection between countries' elite athletes and teams, media, and national audiences. The sport-nationalism-media troika emerged as an arena where ideologies about national cultures and identities were constructed, defined, redefined and contested (Crolley and Hand, 2006).

In this chapter, we examine a microcosm of this relationship, as we investigate how English newspaper coverage used nationalist "us versus them" rhetoric to generate interest and excitement among the "imagined community" as the English national soccer team competed in the World Cup and European Championship tournaments. We then compare these commentaries with the traditionally more subtle and nondescript support provided by the British Broadcasting Corporation's (BBC) broadcasts of the same events along with the National Broadcasting Company's (NBC) sportscasts of United States athletes and teams competing in the Olympic Games.

Sport and national identity

During the 20th century, national identity became important as the number of nations nearly quadrupled to 192 at the close of the century (Alesina and Spolaore, 2003). Under foreign domination for a long time, all sought to establish themselves as a "community, sharing a common culture, attached to a clearly demarcated territory, having a common past and a common project for the future, and claiming the right to rule itself" (Guibernau, 2007, p. 23). As Guibernau notes, nations used many strategies to achieve this: territorial demarcations, new governments, shared histories and common cultures. They emphasized the collective sense of belonging and the distinguishing characteristics and traits inherent in national culture (Guibernau, 2007). von der Lippe (2002) summarized national identity as "how a citizenry sees and thinks about themselves in relation to others" (p. 373).

Collective identity exists in various forms (gender, class, race and ethnicity among them) all of which intersect with national identity (Smith, 1991). Guibernau suggested that national identity allowed individuals to adopt the overarching collective identity and to "regard as their own the accomplishments of their fellow nationals" (Guibernau, 2007, p. 169). This is particularly evident in international sporting contests, where collective identity has been (re)produced through athletes and teams since the Greek Olympic Games (Hill, 1996). Barnier (2001) noted that athletes playing for their country usually represent the popular national identity. In particular, team sports unite nations and promote their national identity. As they do, Elias (1996) reasoned that sport substitutes for war, with athletic teams becoming symbolic warriors defending their nation's honor. As such, national team performance at major international sporting events reawakens the visceral emotions of national identity politics.

The original intents of the World Cup and the Olympic Games were to compete athletically and through competition foster international relations and mutual understanding. They also provide nations with opportunities to demonstrate countries' athletic superiority. Anxious for nations to be seen as strong and vibrant, international competitions provide opportunities for nations to bask in the reflected glory of national successes (Coakley, 2009). Athletic success or failure become symbols of the nation's overall health and wellbeing (Tuck, 2003). For this reason, many nations invest resources to nurture their elite athletes and teams (Cashmore, 1996).

Sport media, globalization, and national identity

FIFA and the International Olympic Committee (IOC), the governing bodies of football and the Olympic Games, respectively, epitomize global sport organizations. Globalization *per se* challenges national cultures and identities, as it erodes differences among countries (Bairner, 2005) through international flows of people, images, and symbols through global capital investments and trade (Aninat, 2002). This allows market forces to dictate flows of technologies to facilitate cross-cultural and social interactions to reduce parochial outlooks and encourage more cosmopolitan, hybrid, and diasporic identities. Satellite television, for example, permits consumption of both local and global sporting events, causing a clash between local and global identities and loyalties, in creating more internationalist cultural perspectives (Hill and Vincent, 2006). However, the role of national media is to create a sense of national belonging among a country's citizens (Harris, 2006). The media 'storytellers' who cover the World Cup and the Olympic Games become transmitters of nationalistic sentiments worldwide through their coverage of international sport as they inject, rarely subtly, elements of national culture and national identity politics (Vincent, Kian, Pedersen, Kuntz, and Hill, 2010).

The sport media, nationalism nexus

Anderson (1983) notes that "nations are distinguished from one another by the stories they tell about themselves" (p. 6). Major event status therefore makes international sports ideal vehicles to examine various cultural identities. In contrast to most local and regional sport, consumption of major international sporting events is predominantly through the media via television broadcasts, Internet live streams, or newspaper accounts. Billings states that international "sports bond societies and cultures in ways that nothing else can" and this is underpinned by the pivotal role of the sports media in creating collective cultural memories (Billings, 2008, p. xi).

Ardent sports fans are one thing, but the power of the media also resides in generating interest among casual sports observers as they participate in the collective experience of powerful moments in national sport (Billings, 2008). Roche (2000) noted how major international sporting events become mega "media events" capable of transcending news and entertainment by making history (p. 167). Billings (2008) described NBC's coverage of the Olympic Games as "the biggest show on television" (p. 1). He also noted how media coverage of the Olympic Games provides "a global perspective by routinely introducing mass audiences to cultures they have never witnessed before" (p. 10). Such was the case as the 2008 Beijing Olympic Games were televised around the world, with a record 4.7 billion viewers watching at least some of the worldwide Olympic broadcasts (Associated Press, 2008). Similarly, the football World Cup attracts television spectators from every continent with nearly half the world's population watching the World Cup final on television (FIFA, 2012).

Imagined communities and invented traditions

In the context of a major international sport, Anderson's (1983) concept about a nation being an "imagined community" becomes salient because of the interface between media narratives and images of teams competing in major international sporting events. Anderson contended that the nation is an imagined community "because the members of even the smallest nations will never know most of their fellow-members, meet them, or even hear of them, yet in the minds of each lives the image of their communion" (p. 6). He articulated how a national sense of connectedness develops through media reports read by thousands of people, each unaware of each other except through similar nationalistic emotions generated by media accounts. Anderson's theory of the imagined community illustrates the pervasive influence that socially constructed media impressions have in evoking deep feelings about national identities.

Hobsbawm (1983) claimed that national identity is ingrained in invented traditions that he defined as, "A set of practices, normally governed by overtly or tacitly accepted rules and of a ritual or symbolic nature, which seek to inculcate certain values and norms of behaviour by repetition, which automatically implies continuity with the past" (p. 1). Hobsbawm noted how historians, politicians, and journalists create the customs, myths, and symbols, which form the national culture. He argued that national identity is both reinforced through the selective construction of idealized versions of national history in mythological accounts as selective celebrations of a nation's past successes becomes part of the collective national consciousness.

Although history is fixed, Anderson (1983) and Hobsbawm (1983) note that national identity is not. It evolves and is reinvented to fit with contemporary culture. Journalists draw on invented traditions to stimulate interest and create a sense of unity and patriotism.

Mediated sport must be understood within its social, cultural, political and historical context (McDonald and Birrell, 1999). Below, we provide two insights into how the sport media national identity nexus plays out in the context of media coverage. The first is the English national men's soccer (football) team competing in the World Cup and European championships. The second deals with NBC's televised coverage of the United States in the Olympic Games.

England and the World Cup

Newspaper narratives about the En-ger-land

England last won the World Cup in 1966. It was part of the 'swinging sixties', a mythical golden age in English popular culture. Coming two decades after the nation's finest hour against Nazi Germany during the Second World War, it heralded a great era in English popular music with the Beatles and the Rolling Stones captivating audiences worldwide and Carnaby Street fashions setting global fashion trends. The 60s era was capped as England won the World Cup in football, a sport they had helped to pioneer. What made it sweeter for the English, as Weight (2002) noted, was winning the final against arch nemesis, West Germany, on home soil. It showed how sporting "cultural achievements had come to act as a compensation for Britain's political decline since the war" (Weight, 2002, p. 461). However, as Allison, noted, "Nationality which is represented by any given expression of sporting nationhood is usually divisive in some way" (Allison, 2000, p. 347). Weight (2002) also recalled the divisive 'us versus them' tensions that permeated the English press the morning before the 1966 World Cup final. He cites the *Daily Mail* report, "If Germany beat us at Wembley this afternoon at our national sport, we can always point out to them that we have recently beaten them twice at theirs" (p. 459). On the opposing side also there was some rancor over English press coverage. Werner Schneider, Germany's football commentator, claimed that for the English "winning at football is treated like victory in a battle" (quoted in Weight, 2002, p. 459). The aftermath reflected those sentiments, with the ensuing 'feel good' patriotic celebrations endemic throughout England as the game took its place in English folklore as an important milestone in England's cultural and national identity (Weight, 2002).

30 years of hurt – football's coming home

Thirty years later, in a series of studies, Maguire and colleagues examined the English television and newspaper coverage of the English national team competing in the 1996 European Championships (Maguire and Poulton, 1999; Maguire, Poulton, and Possami, 1999a; Maguire, Poulton, and Possami, 1999b). It was significant as it was the first major international football tournament to be held on English soil since the triumph of 1966. Newspaper accounts reflected this in their accounts celebrating "football's homecoming." The outpourings of widespread patriotism seemed to work, with the English team reaching the tournament semifinal. The mood of the nation was reflected in the official song of the England football team, "Three Lions" that was played incessantly throughout the tournament. It celebrated football's "coming home" to its modern birthplace, while lamenting the 30-year lull since

England last won the World Cup, along with expressions that England could repeat their 1966 success. Support for "En-ger-land" was elicited in the media as the collective 'we' reflected the nationalistic surge over the course of the tournament.

On the eve of the semifinal game between England and Germany, English "red-top" newspaper accounts were inundated with Second World War metaphors such as the xenophobic "Let's blitz Fritz" and "Achtung Surrender" headlines. Though later criticized by the National Heritage Select Committee, newspaper narratives continuously drew on the nostalgic invented traditions of England's World Cup winning team of 1966 to reflect a nostalgic yearning to return the England's mythical golden age.

"England Expects"

The more things change, the more they remain the same. Every World Cup tournament the English media hype returned with renewed vigor to those 1966 times. At the outset of the 2006 World Cup media optimism reigned supreme, with the hope that the English team could repeat the glory of the *boys of '66*. Forty years on from 1966, Vincent, *et al.* (2010) examined the 2006 English newspaper narratives surrounding Germany's staging of the 2006 World Cup. In stark contrast to the official theme, *a time to make friends*, English newspapers again galvanized support for the English team with us-versus-them discourses. Though not as egregiously xenophobic as in 1996, the English newspaper coverage still drew on negative German stereotypes. Several newspapers mischievously referred to English comic John Cleese's alternative 2006 World Cup anthem, "Don't Mention the War," that played on German sensitivity about the Second World War. Made famous by Cleese's alter ego character, the notoriously bigoted Basil Fawlty in the comedy TV show *Fawlty Towers*, Vincent and colleagues suggested that these discourses reflected the insecurities of declining English power faced with the modern realities of European Union, UK devolution and the underperforming British economy in the global marketplace.

The 2006 newspaper coverage reflected national frustration over declining English fortunes and a yearning to return to the "good old days." On the eve of the tournament, the front page of the *Daily Mail* led with headline of "England expects," Admiral Horatio Nelson's rallying signal to his men before the Battle of Trafalgar in 1805. Other nostalgic references were made to elicit support for the Eng-er-land that drew on Winston Churchill's famous wartime speeches and Shakespearean lines from Henry V's famous victories in France for inspiration. Despite press exhortations, England lost at the quarterfinal stage. National angst was again expressed in the media. Post mortems and recriminations predictably went through their "build-them-up then knock-them-down" cycle. The obvious scapegoat was the English team's Swedish manager, Sven-Goran Eriksson, who became the target of ridicule in narratives replete with negative Swedish stereotypes.

Don't mention the War (or the score)

English media coverage of the 2010 World Cup in South Africa predictably went the same way as all others. Vincent and Hill (2011) examined England's most popular red-top newspaper *The Sun*'s discourses about the English national team and their "army" of supporters. Almost a half-century had passed since England's 1966 triumph but little had changed. Many of the pervasive narrative themes and images found in the 1966 coverage were reproduced 46 years later.

The only change was greater emphasis on the now-more-affluent but still rabid England fans. *The Sun* featured many photographs of English supporters with painted faces and torsos. Some were dressed in Crusader outfits or with facemasks of the British royal family. All were reflections of England's past or its traditions. Hobsbawm noted the emotional appeal and role of supporters in the (re)construction of national identity, thus: "The imagined community of millions seems more real as a team…the individual, even the one who only cheers, becomes a symbol of the nation himself" (Hobsbawm, 1983, p. 147). Predictably, the England–Germany round of sixteen match was celebrated with jingoistic "us versus them" buildups and references to the Battle of Britain and the Second World War. English fans were photographed posing in Royal Air Force uniforms and plastic Tommy helmets, inflatable bomber planes, and Churchill facemasks.

Vincent and Hill (2011) noted how, on the eve of the England versus Germany game, under the rallying headline, "Now do it for Bobby," the *News of the World* drew on images of the invented tradition of the legendary England 1966 World Cup-winning captain, Bobby Moore. This time though, there was an element of realism, as narratives also compared England's inconsistent tournament performances with Germany's tournament consistency and success since 1966. Given that Germany beat England convincingly again in the 2010 match-up, several English journalists lamented that perhaps "don't mention the War" should be rephrased to "don't mention the score," to reflect the post-1966 domination by the Germans.

Television coverage of the En-ger-land team

Tuck (2003) noted how the partisan media coverage of the red-top press and Independent Television Authority (ITV) and BSkyB's stands in contrast to the more impartial and sedate coverage by the BBC and the broadsheet English newspapers. Poulton's (2004) textual analysis of the BBC and ITV's coverage of the English team in EURO '96 confirmed the subtler framing of the BBC coverage. More cosmopolitan, the BBC coverage even used the European Union's anthem, Beethoven's *Ode to Joy*, as its theme music. In contrast, Poulton (2004) noted how ITV signaled its more patriotic intent with a remixed up-tempo version of English anthem, *Jerusalem*.

Similarly, Poulton (2004) contrasted the xenophobic rhetoric found in the red-top English newspapers to the BBC's coverage of the England vs. Germany semi-final, which contained no references to the Second World War. However, Poulton (2004) also reported that the BBC's group matches coverage occasionally deviated from their impartiality with references to famous English military battles between the two "Auld Enemies" at Bannockburn and Culloden (vs. Scotland). Before the England vs. Spain quarterfinal game, images of Sir Francis Drake's famous English victory over the Spanish Armada in 1588 was evoked (Poulton, 2004).

Partisanship differences among media tend to reflect their differing market circumstances. Boyle (2006) noted how English newspapers were given "a license to be partisan" while television broadcasts had always been more impartial. Both however reflect a "tabloidization," or "dumbing down" of English culture generally, with both television and newspaper media accused of sacrificing accuracy for entertainment and sensationalism. Boyle suggested that as competition in sports media and broadcast has intensified, impartial broadcasting has given way to partisan support for the nation's athletes and teams (Boyle, 2006, p. 63).

NBC's Olympic television coverage

Billig (1995) noted that the original intent of major international sporting events was to foster a spirit of internationalism and peace consistent with the ethos of the modern Olympics founder, Baron de Coubertain. Time however, has eroded that ideology. Butterworth (2007) noted how generally the Olympic Games "have been a forum for fervent nationalism" rather than "peaceful competition" (p. 187). Reflecting this, Billings, Angelini, and Wu (2011) noted how, in the build-up to the 2008 Beijing Olympic Games, the Chinese declared their intent to win more medals than any other nation to underscore its emerging superpower status.

Butterworth (2009) outlined how Olympic television broadcasts have been replete with "us vs. them" binaries between "West and East, Democratic and Totalitarian, Christian and Godless, Good and Evil" (p. 137). The original spirit of internationalism has given way to jingoistic displays of national flag-waving and other acts of what Billig termed "banal nationalism." Elias and Dunning (1993) noted how public displays of support for the nation's athletes and teams' competing in major international sporting competitions has become the accepted norm. Quantitative research examining NBC's coverage of the Olympic Games found a profound home-nation bias. Billings (2008) found that between the 1996 Summer and the 2006 Winter Olympic Games, NBC devoted between 57 and 40.2 percent of the athlete mentions to United States' athletes when they won just 11 percent of the medals, and further, that 44 of the 60 most-mentioned athletes represented the US. Non-US mentions he found tended to be US athletes' main medal rivals.

Qualitative analysis also revealed partisan biases. However, there were attempts to neutralize the home-country bias. Billings (2008) revealed that NBC had conducted pre-Olympic workshops to reduce overt home nation cheerleading. Sportscasters were exhorted to avoid using personal pronouns such as "we" or "our" and to avoid "us vs. them" binaries. The exhortations worked, but only partially. Billings' analysis showed that US athletes were more likely to be praised for their commitment, concentration, determination, courage and their composure under intense pressure. Success was often attributed to their athletic ability and experience. This was in contrast to coverage of foreign athletes, whose lack of success was attributed to lack of concentration, commitment and fortitude.

To elicit interest, NBC's Olympic broadcasters were also more likely to provide background information about US athletes' hometown or local environs. Billings *et. al.* (2011) concluded that greater familiarity with home-nation athletes led to a greater depth of personal commentaries. In comparison, non-US athletes were described in non-personal one-dimensional caricatures and portrayed almost as though they were "emotionless cyborgs, whose purpose is to conquer athletic competitions" (Billings, *et al.*, 2011, p. 263). Billings (2008) concluded that NBC's nationalistic bias was driven by mass media ratings and advertising rates. The need for high ratings has increased with the cost of TV broadcast rights. In 1996, NBC paid US$456 million to broadcast the Atlanta Olympic Games. By 2012, this had increased to US$1.2 billion for the London Olympics (Coakley, 2009).

The need for high Nielsen ratings has also led to what Andrews (1998) called the feminizing of Olympic reality. Traditionally, many sport broadcasters have been male and coverage was also male-oriented, with liberal use of power descriptors and sport/war/martial metaphors (Vincent, 2004). This is changing. With women Olympians accounting for approximately half of the United States team, Andrews noted that NBC's 1996 Atlanta broadcasts were feminized to appeal to the "middle America" female demographic, deemed attractive to advertisers (Andrews, 1998, p. 12). Andrews further noted that Dick Ebersol, the President of NBC sport, repackaged NBC's Olympic Games coverage to emphasize sports and events appealing to female audiences. This included extensive pre-taped personal profiles of female US medal contenders. US female athletes were presented as embodiments of the nation and patriots at play for the imagined community. NBC also created additional drama by representing taped events as though they were live during prime time viewing. Ebersol's strategy worked and generated the TV ratings that placed NBC Olympic broadcasts on the profit side of the ledger.

Conclusions

Billings (2008) articulated, "sports media matter because they are the way most of us consume sports" (p. xi). Although the relationship between sport and national identity is both complex and fluid, the media undoubtedly play key roles in attracting national audiences and appealing to each country's distinctive cultural identifiers. Efforts are made to construct and reinforce popular ideologies about how nations perceive themselves. Each country's athletes for a brief moment in time become everyone's hometown hero. All commentaries become familiarized to appeal to the home market audience and to appeal to ever-broader viewers. Boyle and Haynes (2000) noted how the "images and imaginings of a country's past, present and projections of its future, come together to underpin the mediation of sporting discourses" (p. 154).

Media coverage of major international sporting events has all the ingredients for compelling viewing: rituals, symbols, ceremony, competition and winning (Boyle and Haynes, 2000). Although international sports, by their very nature, have a global dimension, they are sold to audiences based on their local appeal. Necessarily, then, this requires nationalistic orientations to capture the public imagination and secure high ratings. Athletes become patriots at play in their quest to bring athletic success to their nation. Efforts are made to heighten the drama, emotions and tensions of each sport and event. Appealing to nationalist sentiments and common cultural beliefs is part of this sales package. Media discourses intentionally block out divisive realties such as political divisions or socioeconomic inequalities that could undermine national unity (Anderson, 1983).

Media accounts of the English football team competing at the World Cup and European Championships illustrate how the team has become a fulcrum of popular English identity since 1966. This popular identity has been (re)constructed, reinforced, and naturalized in media broadcasts and narratives to appeal to the invented traditions of English history. In English and perhaps global minds, the sports arena is still a battleground. It is still us versus them. Only one of us can win. All underpin divisive, even xenophobic binary discourses.

Although the partisan rhetoric is less overt, the success of NBC's Olympic coverage has also been in large part due to the heightened, collective sense of identification, rooting and pride in US athletes. The US is the bastion of individualism, capitalism and ultra-competitive mindsets. Its mainstream sports of gridiron football and baseball are sports that lack any true world competition. But every four years, the nation unifies in its support of US athletes on the Olympic world stage. Making it work for a network profit has been NBC's task. Taking advantage of this unity, NBC has set about appealing to every demographic to offset expensive broadcasting rights fees. The Olympics is all about nations competing against nations on the sports field. Competition is all about partisanship. This is reflected in the commentaries.

References

Alesina, A., and Spolaore, E. (2003). *The size of nations*. Cambridge, MA: MIT Press.
Allison, L. (2000). Sport and nationalism. In J. Coakley and E. Dunning (Eds.), *Handbook of sports studies* (pp. 344–55). London: Sage.
Anderson, B. (1983). *Imagined communities: Reflections on the origin and the spread of nationalism*. London: Verso.
Andrews, D. L. (1998). Feminizing Olympic reality: Preliminary dispatches from Baudrillard's Atlanta. *International Review for the Sociology of Sport*, 33 (1), 5–18.
Aninat (2002). Surmounting the challenges of globalization. *Finance and Development*, 39 (1), 4–7.
Associated Press (2008). Beijing TV coverage drew 4.7 billion viewers worldwide. *ESPN.com*, September 5. Retrieved from http://sports.espn.go.com/oly/news/story?id=3571042.
Bairner, A. (2001). *Sport, nationalism, and globalization: European and North American perspectives*. State University of New York Press: New York.
Bairner, A. (2005). Sport and the nation in the global era. In L. Allison (Ed.), *The global politics of sport: The role of global institutions in sport* (pp. 87–117). Routledge: London.
Billig, M. (1995). *Banal nationalism*. London: Sage.
Billings, A. C. (2008). *Olympic media: Inside the biggest show on television*. London: Routledge.
Billings, A. C., Angelini, J. R., and Wu, D. (2011). Nationalistic notions of the superpowers: Comparative analyses of the American and Chinese telecasts in the 2008 Beijing Olympiad. *Journal of Broadcasting and Electronic Media*, 55 (2), 251–66.
Boyle. R. (2006). *Sports journalism; Context and issues*. London: Sage.
Boyle, R., and Haynes, R. (2000). Games across frontiers: mediated sport and national identity. In R. Boyle and R. Haynes (Eds.), *Power play: Sport, the media and popular culture* (pp. 143–64). London: Longman.
Butterworth, M. L. (2007). The politics of pitch: Claiming and contesting democracy through the Iraqi national soccer team. *Communication and Cultural Studies*, 4 (2), 184–203.
Butterworth, M. L. (2009). Do you believe in nationalism? American patriotism in Miracle. In H. L. Hundley and A. C. Billings (Eds.), *Examining identity in sport media* (pp. 133–52). Thousand Oaks: CA: Sage.
Cashmore, E. (1996). *Making sense of sports* (2nd ed.). London: Routledge.
Coakley, J. (2009). *Sports in society: Issues and controversies* (10th ed.). New York: McGraw Hill.
Crolley, L., and Hand, D. (2006). *Football and European identity: Historical narratives through the press*. Routledge: London.
Elias, N. (1996). *The Germans*. Cambridge: Cambridge: Polity Press.
Elias, N., and Dunning, E. (1993). *Quest for excitement: Sport and leisure in the civilizing process*. Oxford: Blackwell.
FIFA (2012). 2006 FIFA World Cup Germany. *FIFA.com* Retrieved from http://www.fifa.com/worldcup/archive/germany2006/index.html.
Guibernau, M. (2007). *The identity of nations*. Cambridge: Polity.
Harris, J. (2006). (Re)Presenting Wales: National identity and celebrity in the postmodern rugby world. *North American Journal of Welsh Studies*, 6 (2), 1–13.
Hill, C. R. (1996). *Olympic politics: Athens to Atlanta, 1896–1996*. Manchester: Manchester University Press.
Hill, J. S. and Vincent, J. (2006). Globalization and sports branding: The case of Manchester United. *International Journal of Sports Marketing and Sponsorship*, 7 (3), 213–30.
Hobsbawm, E. J. (1983). Introduction: Inventing traditions' and mass producing traditions: Europe 1870–1914 In E. J. Hobsbawm and T. O. Ranger (Eds.), *The invention of tradition* (pp.1–14, 263–307). Cambridge: Cambridge University Press.
Maguire, J., and Poulton. E. (1999). European identity politics in Euro 96: Invented traditions and national habitus codes. *International Review for the Sociology of Sport*, 34 (1), 17–29.
Maguire, J., Poulton, E., and Possamai, C. (1999a). Weltkrieg III? Media coverage of England versus Germany in Euro 96. *Journal of Sport and Social Issues*, 23 (4), 439–54.

Maguire, J., Poulton, E., and Possamai, C. (1999b). The war of words? Identity politics in Anglo-German press coverage of Euro 96. *European Journal of Communication*, 14 (1), 61–89.

McDonald, M. G., and Birrell, S., (1999). Reading sport critically: A methodology for interrogating power. *Sociology of Sport Journal*, 16, 283–300.

Poulton, E. (2004). Mediated patriot games: The construction and representation of national identities in the British television production of Euro '96. *International Review for the Sociology of Sport*, 39 (4), 437–55.

Roche, M. (2000). *Mega-events and modernity: Olympics and expos in the growth of global culture*. Routledge: London.

Rowe, D., McKay, J., and Miller. T. (1998). Come together: Sport, nationalism, and the media image. In L. A. Wenner (Ed.), *MediaSport* (pp. 119–33). London: Routledge.

Smith, A. (1991). *National identity*. London: Penguin.

Tuck, J. (2003). The men in white: reflections on rugby union, the media and Englishness. *International Review for the Sociology of Sport*, 38 (2), 177–99.

Vincent, J. (2004). Game, sex, and match: The construction of gender in British newspaper coverage of the 2000 Wimbledon Championships. *Sociology of Sport Journal*, 21, 435–56.

Vincent, J., and Hill, J. S. (2011). Flying the flag for the En-ger-land: *The Sun*'s (re)construction of English identity during the 2010 World Cup. *Journal of Sport and Tourism*, 16 (3), 187–209.

Vincent, J., Kian, E. M., Pedersen, P., Kuntz, A., and Hill, J.S. (2010). England expects: English newspapers' narratives about the English football team in the 2006 World Cup. *International Review for the Sociology of Sport*, 45 (2), 199–223.

von der Lippe, G. (2002). Media image: Sport, gender and national identities in five European countries. *International Review for the Sociology of Sport*, 37 (3/4), 371–95.

Weight. R. (2002). *Patriots: National identity in Britain 1940–2000*. Basingstoke: Macmillan.

SECTION V

The management of sport communication

41

MEDIA, SPORT, AND CONSUMER CULTURE

The fan as consumer in television commercials

Lawrence A. Wenner

This chapter considers sport communication as an integral part of consumer culture. A basic function of sport communication is that it facilitates sport being consumed and drives marketplace value. Thus, understanding how we communicate *in* and *through* a sport marketplace that is huge and expanding is important both to those who seek leverage in sport management and to scholars who wish to understand how sport exerts social and cultural influence.

In 2011, Plunkett Research estimated the size of the sports industry in the US alone at US$422 billion, with annual company spending of almost US$28 million on sports advertising (Plunkett Research, 2011). Thus, there is much to substantiate Steven Miles' (1998, pp. 126, 140) assessment in his classic treatise *Consumerism* that "[s]port is perhaps the single area of contemporary social life to have been most profoundly altered in recent years by the everyday impact of consumerism as a way of life" and further, that "[t]elevision is probably the single most influential driving force underlying the commodification of sport."

Conversely, sport is perhaps the most important economic engine to television. Indeed, as both spiraling costs of sports broadcast rights and astronomic price tags for mega-event advertising remind us, sports programming is the most important remaining "big tent" for broadcasters. In this light, this chapter examines how understanding consumer culture has become foundational to understanding sport communication. The chapter is framed by a brief introduction to the study of consumer culture, some basic tensions in understanding the consumer and fan, and the importance of the consumer–fanship link in understanding sport communication's promotional role. These considerations provide context for the body of the chapter that summarizes a recent series of studies examining the narrative characterization of consumption and the casting of sport consumer as fan in television advertising.

The study of consumer culture

It is surprising that consumer culture theory (CCT) has not made a bigger imprint on the study of sport and sport communication. When used broadly and strategically, such as in Garry Crawford's (2004) *Consuming sport: Fans, sport and culture* and John Horne's (2006) *Sport in consumer culture*, CCT seems a tailor-made lens to focus understanding of today's media-driven sport marketplace. In digesting 20 years of work that has defined the core disposition of CCT, Arnould and Thompson note that:

> CCT is not a unified, grand theory, nor does it aspire to such nomothetic claims. Rather, it refers to a family of theoretical perspectives that address the dynamic relationships between consumer actions, the marketplace, and cultural meanings...Consumer culture theorists read popular culture texts (advertisements, television programs, films) as lifestyle and identity instructions that convey unadulterated marketplace ideologies (i.e., look like this, act like this, want these things, aspire to this kind of lifestyles) and idealized consumer types...By decoding and deconstructing these mass-mediated marketplace ideologies, consumer culture theorists reveal the ways in which capitalist cultural production systems invite consumers to covet certain identity and lifestyle ideals.
>
> *(Arnould and Thompson, 2005, pp. 868, 875)*

While the research that Arnould and Thompson (2005) reflect upon is broad and there are many landmark works (see, for example, Aldridge, 2003; Cohen, 2004; Lury, 1996; McCracken, 1990; Paterson, 2006; Smart, 2010) that chart the area, no scholar has contributed more to understanding the consumer culture model than Zymunt Bauman. For Bauman, consumer culture "is a *circulum vitiosus*, magic circle with an osmotic circumference—easy entrance, no exit" (quoted in Rojek, 2004, p. 304). He sees a postmodern "liquid modern life" dominated by a "consumer sociality" where pleasure rules and choices abound. Here we act within an obligatory "market-mediated mode of life" with a "consumerist attitude" that views life as challenges to be solved through individual action. Bauman poses that a "collateral casualty" of consumerism has been a "syndrome" with a "masturbatory sociality" focused on individual pleasure and instant gratification that has enabled aesthetics to overtake ethics (Bauman 2007; Blackshaw 2008).

The consumer

Bauman's view of the consumer is complex. He sees individuals as self-reflexive about understandings of their power and its limits within the confines of the consumerist model. Thus, he sees us as active agents, but contained by ground rules that we recognize govern our "market-mediated" lives. Here, our actions are voluntarily shaped by the pleasures we seek, but to obtain them requires an agency relativized by the logic of the marketplace (Bauman, 2007).

The many ways that consumers have been viewed in scholarly and applied work reflect the tensions and contradictions in Bauman's characterization of the modern consumer. As Slater (1997, p. 51) observes, these variances show that study of consumption takes place on contested academic terrain between "the study of formally rational behavior (economics) and the study of its irrational, cultural context (the rest)." In this vein, Gabriel and Lang (1995) characterize nine persistent stereotypic images of consumers driving scholarly work that run the gamut from pejorative to positive. Here, consumers have been divergently viewed as choosers, communicators, explorers, identity-seekers, hedonists/artists, victims, rebels, activists, or citizens.

Such 'imaginings' of the consumer into such discrete categories are, of course, simplistic. Consumption is complex and consumers can be multifaceted. A more useful way to view the tensions and contradictions over the consumer can be seen in Aldridge's (2003, p. 16) typology of the four kinds of consumers seen in "images of the consumer in Western discourse." Aldridge places his types – rational actor, communicator, dupe, and victim – along two axes, a horizontal axis representing "the objective dimension of power, contrasting powerful rational actors and communicators with the dominated victims and dupes" and a vertical axis representing "the subjective dimension of orientations to consumption, contrasting the instrumental rational actors and victims with the expressive communicators and dupes."

The fan

Similarly, cultural understandings of fans run the gamut from cultural dope to empowered. On one hand, fans are seen as obsessive, hysterical, or engaging in psychological compensation. On the other, they are ripe with cultural capital from the richness of engagement, creativity, and even resistance (Sandvoss, 2005). Studying fanship in sport brings unique complications. Thinking of the sports fan as a generic does little to advance understanding. Few are broad-based sport fanatics, following all play with equal interest. Sports fans are discriminating, centered on a sport, team, player, or locale. Further, fanship is variant, running from rabid to casual and features disparate sporting knowledge.

When consumer typologies focus on sport, characterizations anchored in fanship emerge. In a comprehensive review, Stewart, Smith, and Nicholson (2003) note much instability in defining the sport consumer in research and point to competing "dualistic," "tiered," and "multidimensional" fanship typologies as evidence that "sport consumers can be segmented from many perspectives" (p. 212) depending on whether the central focus is behaviors, motivations, or beliefs. Even the best "conceptually based classification" schemes, such as Hunt, Bristol, and Bashaw's (1999) are seemingly reliant on fanship types – temporary, local, devoted, fanatical, and dysfunctional – that overlap while pulling in different directions. More simplistic typological attempts, such as A. T. Kearney, Inc.'s (2003) report on *The new sports consumer* miss much nuance by positioning "sports fanatics" and "sports indifferent" on opposing consumer poles with "club and team loyalists," "star-struck spectators," "social," and "opportunistic" sports viewers in-between.

Yet when media characterize the sport consumer, even such distinctions are lost. Popular media characterizations of sport consumers rely on self-serving characterizations of diehard fanship. Interestingly, this focus on pathologized fanship pervades even in straight-laced social psychological inquiries about sport fans' identities. Here, sports fans BIRG (bask in reflected glory), CORF (cut off reflected failure), COFF (cut off future failure) and blast (derogating disliked opponents) to maintain seemingly odd, fragile equilibriums (Wann, Melnick, Russell, and Pease, 2001). Such cultural preoccupation has resulted in an "imagined community" (Anderson, 1983, p. 6) of animated, colorful sports fans with unbalanced commitment who often seem bizarre and possessed (Wenner, 2011).

The consumer–fanship link

It makes sense that media would want to focus its narratives on the most enthusiastic fans. This helps naturalize the importance of sports and increases the salience of sport-linked consumption. Such reliance on an "imagined" truncation of sports consumers and fans meshes with CCT's focus on "idealized consumer types" (Arnould and Thompson, 2005, p. 875) and Bauman's concerns over "consumer sociality." For Bauman (1998, p. 26), we are now in a new cultural epoch wherein the "primacy of consumption in social relations" is such that "one needs to be a consumer first, before one can think of becoming anything in particular."

Recognizing this, Crawford (2004) concludes that sport fanship must necessarily be studied in the context of consumption. In drawing this conclusion, he relies on Giulianotti's (2002, p. 27) evidence that "hypercommodification" has infused our relations with sport and Kellner's (2001, p. 38) observation that the new norm is sport "spectacle that sells the values of products, celebrities, and institutions of the media and consumer society." Reinforced by Horne's (2005) assessment that the "consumerization" of fanship has been driven by media strategies that naturalize the logics of advertising and sponsorship in sporting contexts, Crawford's (2004, p. 4) conclusion that so much relates "directly or indirectly to acts of consumption" that "being a fan is primarily a consumer act and hence fans can been seen first and foremost as consumers" seems inescapable.

In promotional culture's narrative spaces, we are frequently cast into the sport-fan role and see it performed to *simulate* and *stimulate* carrying it into the marketplace. This is a key dynamic in making the spectacle/performance paradigm of the audience (Abercrombie and Longhurst, 1998) so successful in contemporary advertising. Marshaling this, television commercials attempt to use sport to shape characterizations of "imagined" fanship norms to strategic advantage (Anderson, 1993). By casting sports fans in consumer roles, advertisers naturalize how sport relates to the consumption of other things.

The advertising narrative and imagining the sports fan as consumer

The sections that follow summarize findings from a program of research that examines how the sports fan is characterized in consumer narratives featured in television advertising. Collectively, the studies provide an example of how CCT, with its focus on "idealized consumer types" and the reading of popular culture texts "as lifestyle and identity instructions that convey unadulterated marketplace ideologies" (Arnould and Thompson, 2005, p. 875), can be fruitful in the study of sport communication. While the studies should be taken merely as a starting point to illustrate the promise of such a strategy, they provide insight about how "narrative imaginings" about the contexts of sport consumption and the characterization of men and women in those contexts have been strategically used to connect sport and fanship to consumption.

Imagining contexts of consumption

The lead study (Wenner, 2008) sets the stage by identifying the major narrative settings that use "imagined" fanship to fuel consumer ideals. In a broad survey, five categories of television commercials were found.

The *reflecting sports* category promoted products offered by "institutions of sports" such as leagues or sport programming networks and reflected their brands back enmeshed in stories of pathological diehard fanship and reminders, not only of this as expectation, but that failure to exhibit such passion would be suspect and alien. Reinforcing this, narratives often linked fanship to nationalism with consumption as a derivative "duty" that was shown to apply to all by invoking idyllic themes of multicultural inclusiveness.

The *accessing sports* category told fanship stories for a class of merchandisers such as cable/satellite services, phone providers, and fantasy league organizers/developers that provide linkages to sports. Here, the rabid "super fan" who "lives for sport" as archetypal norm was used in companion with a pervasive "new is better" techno-myth that posed that those who are not techno-engaged super fans and always connected and engaged were losers.

The *wearing sports* category idealized the sport fan buying sports clothing from mega-merchandizers such as Nike and from league and retail stores. These commercials naturalize a contradiction of promotional culture where the "billboard" pays the sponsor for the privilege of displaying the branding message. Sports fanship was cast as active performance that was worthy. Here, fan performance was posed as "hard work" that was demonstrative of loyalty and commitment, and thus worthy of being privileged through brand signage.

The *drinking sports* category idealized the fan in pursuit of quenching thirst through beer and soda. Here a "consumption-squared" equation is posed as natural: righteous consumption as sport spectator entails consumption of branded beverages. This category relied heavily an idyllic painting of a "world of fans" as a community through which even the poor may be uplifted. The "imagined" morality tale polices proper fanship by implying that failure to abide by these standards will violate group norms and result in exclusion.

The *paying sports* category idealized how the fan's tab should be paid by using services and products from one of sports' major underwriters, the credit card industry. By invoking a "you spend, you score" logic, the ideology of conspicuous consumption rides on the coattails of sport. Posing the "right to own" as natural law cements the "buy" with the "sell" of sports. Here, buying gets better when one is buying sports or even "buying through sports."

This initial study identifies the primary contexts where connections between sport fanship, marketplace ideologies, and identity instructions are fashioned. Still, it is notable what is largely missing in this "imagined" world. Conspicuously absent is the woman as sport fan. Here, men are "ex-nominated" (Barthes, 1973) as archetypal fans with women, with few exceptions, "symbolically annihilated" (Sabo and Jansen, 1992).

Imagining male fans in consumption: Part I

The focus on the male fan is in some ways understandable. The male fan floats the boat of sports broadcasting. Here, advertisers have a stable way to reach an elusive and desirable young male demographic with discretionary incomes (Horne, 2005). Men, more than women, are likely to fit the diehard fan archetype. Male fanship is more intertwined with self-esteem and identity investment and men tend to be more engaged in preparing for and viewing sports (James and Ridinger, 2002; Wenner and Gantz, 1998).

Thus, a second study (Wenner, 2009) examined how "real men" are imagined in representative sample of beer commercial narratives that use fanship ideals to drive consumption. Beer, as quintessential male product naturalized in companion to sports spectatorship, is shown in narratives that largely free men from the "civilizing influences" of women and idealize how men's bonding through sport is special.

Naturalized answers about idealized male fanship respond to questions such as "why do I put myself through this?" that is asked in Spanish brewer Mahou's "Insight of a Football Fan" commercial. The answer comes not only from the male camaraderie idealized in bar-room viewing of important football games, but in the characterized jubilation when "your team" wins. "Identity instructions" pose this as an opportunity "to call your dad and your best friend and shout like a kid" because "for a moment…it all makes sense."

Other answers are posed about boys being boys. Here there are tensions, pitting the idealized bonding that men have away from the dreaded influences of women against the inherent distrust and disingenuousness that underlie men's relationships with each other, as they always remain in competition, particularly for women, who they outwardly distrust. This is seen in Bud Light's "Picture Phone" commercial where two buddies at a game learn via photos sent to one that the other's girlfriend is cavorting with another man in his apartment. The resultant mock sympathy and demonization of women is featured also in Budweiser's "Break Up" spot, where, watching a game, one man's sympathy for his friend's being victimized by his girlfriend is revealed as both false and natural as the seemingly sympathetic man looks to make a play on the other's now available girlfriend.

Thus, much of the idealized bonding in this moral community exists only on the veneer of sport. True other respecting care and empathy are marginalized as taboo. Taboo is revealed as well by consistent policing of what it means to be a "real man" in these ads. In Heineken's "Male Bonding Incident," two male friends viewing sports action linger too long in an accidental "magic moment" where they are attracted to each other. That this is seen as a mistake is clear in their discomfort and joking about the need for "more cheerleaders." Imagining that "real men" find sexual difference problematic is further seen as a group of men viewing sports in a bar in Amstel's "Offside" commercial joke over a bet that involves a faux romantic approach that "outs" a man voluptuously dressed as a woman.

Collectively, these idealized narratives of male bonding hinge on sport and are reliant on beer. The "identity instructions" legitimize moral disengagement and glorify buddies gleefully deceiving each other with faux empathy. This "manual on masculinity" (Strate, 1992) permits lying for strategic advantage and discourages showing weakness, particularly in performances of gender that are at odds with heterosexual orthodoxy.

Imagining male fans in consumption: Part II

Building on evidence that a fractured moral world is often used to type the male fan as consumer, a related study (Wenner, 2011) explored other ways the imagined diehard male fan may be used to facilitate marketplace ideologies. Considered is narrative reliance on stereotypes of men as bumblers, slackers, and "himbos" (Patterson, 1996). Seen by some as evidence of a larger "crisis of masculinity" and "misandry" (Nathanson and Young, 2001), "gender sneer" in advertising (Kane, 2005, p. C2) often mixes a "white-guy-as-loser-trope" (Messner and Montez de Oca, 2005, p. 1905) with masked anger towards women (Duncan and Aycock, 2009). From a broad survey of television commercials mocking male sports fans, five types were identified: the (1) nut case, (2) loser, (3) juvenile, (4) relationally deficient, and (5) emasculated.

The *nut case* sport fan was an unhinged "whack job" cast as "certifiably insane." While so committed that he "should be committed," his heckling support of sporting favorites, as seen in league, team, and beer commercials, is condoned and even celebrated. Throughout these ads, ironic valorization suggests this is behaviorally legitimate with such pathological fanship "excused" as "boys being boys."

The *loser* narratives bring a bit more bite. Men here, assaulted by the world, struggle for pleasures, even in their home territory of sport. They are Rodney Dangerfields who just "can't get any respect," clumsy, dim-witted bumblers who are both scorned and laughed at in their fanship roles in beer and sport brand narratives.

In *juvenile* narratives, male privilege becomes deservedly vestigial as sport becomes a last playground for men diminished by their own infantilism. Here, characterized childlike male fans are prone to performing euphoric fanship, re-enacting sports highlights, and severely pouting over losses. These ads rely on an idealized claim – that sport makes men boys – as a positive to aid marketing aims and encourage fanship identification.

The *relationally deficient* male fan archetype blends diminished capacity themes of the juvenile and the loser. These narratives view men's disingenuousness as a foundational moral flaw that underlies their pragmatism in relationships with women. Here, men need to be bribed to sex from sport with beer, fake drunkenness to alienate spouses to watch games in peace, and cannot maintain focus on their wives' pregnancy test results in the face of breaking sports news. Throughout, sport is naturalized as driving men's self-absorption and inability to be genuine in relational lives with women.

The *emasculated* sport fan narratives seemingly draw a moral line where tolerance for men's privilege ends as men are called on their game and put in their place by women. Here, women threaten sport-enamored men by seeing them as "too small" and exercise their powers over a now weakened masculinity where a remaining pleasure, in sports, is always under threat.

Mocking the male sports fan to drive consumption is a complex ideological strategy. Yet in typifying the male consumer as "under siege" for their dedication to sport, sport is heightened as a refuge, from not only from women but the responsibilities and expectations that come with a changed contemporary masculinity. In such humorous exaggeration, men may find some truth as well as sanctuary. That "identity instructions" encourage seeing sport as a "safe harbor" makes merchandising products through sports that much easier.

Imagining female fans in consumption

Diehard women fans, while growing, remain harder to find (Wann, Waddill, and Dunham, 2004). When they are found to be holding comparable levels of sports interest and knowledge, they are much like male fans. Still, women's fanship is often less fully formed, anchored in spectating, learning, and companionship (James and Ridinger, 2002; Wenner and Gantz, 1998). The inchoate women fan as apprentice, transitioning from postulant to novitiate to 'authentic,' is often seen in the narrative space and provides reminders of her "otherness" and "outsider status" when it comes to sports (Gosling, 2007). Nevertheless, women are a growing part of the sport market, and how their fanship is typified in commercials narratives reveals much about how they are seen as consumers in the context of sport.

In the fourth study in this series (Wenner, 2012), two things were notable: (1) there were few commercials featuring the female fan, and (2) female sport was absent from a broad sample of commercials. Thus, "identity instructions" pertain only to female fanship of men's sport. Further, these commercials were pitched to the male gaze, with women fans "imagined" as "babes," hysterical, problematic in romance, and unappreciative of males. Three types of female fans populated this imagined world: (1) tokens, (2) shoppers, and (3) authentics.

The *token* category of female fan provides reminders that a "good" woman fan is hard to find. Indeed, here she is the exception, not the rule, the female face in the mostly male crowd. She is obligatorily included within a broader signing of multiculturalism in a male-dominated fanship backdrop. Whereas men are featured regularly as "rugged individuals" or bonding with buddies in the patriotic swagger of the NFL's "Nation of Football Fans" ad, women fans largely stand in the background amidst a wall of men, unless, as is true in half the representations, they are young girls garnering male approval when they take the stage as enthusiastic cheerleaders. Throughout other commercials featuring the token female fan, she is never seen without at least one man. Women in token roles also bridge the next category linking female fanship to shopping.

The *shopper* category of female fan asserts that women are more at ease with the shopper than fan role, and insinuates further that sport-related shopping underlies fanship. In a Dick's Sporting Goods' "Fan Friday" spot, the notion that an attractive young professional women is an authentic football fan is undercut by her strategic purchase of branded team clothing to garner the attention of a handsome male co-worker. Other spots, such as NBC's "Olympic Shopping," cast women as euphoric expert consumers of branded sport merchandise, while others such as the NFL's "Feminine Touch" reach out to characterized appreciative women with the actress/designer Alyssa Milano's "Touch" collection of "authentic NFL fashion apparel."

The sparsely populated *authentic* female fan category reveals narrative possibilities for an autonomous woman fan. Yet, even in her authenticity, these narratives play to the male. Here, women fans scrub floors, shriek inappropriately in spectatorship, or are knowledgeable but sexy sporting companions. When their authentic fanship is at odds with their man's, they are castigated. Throughout these narrative castings of the female fan, the male is provided reassurance: sport is men's domain and women's approach is odd, even in authenticity.

Imagining male–female relationships in consumption

That men and women fans are painted very differently as "idealized consumer types" (Arnould and Thompson, 2005, p. 875) is clear from this set of studies. Here, men find sanctuary while women remain the "other." Thus, the last (Wenner, 2010) in this series of studies examining constructions of the fan as consumer in television commercials focuses more carefully on how this "myth of difference" where "women are not seen as the fellows of men" (Pronger, 1990, p. 178) is reinforced.

Here, a representative sample of beer commercials that feature both sport and cross-gender interaction with sexual relation implications is examined. Collectively, these commercials provide answers to "how women are" and "what men want" (Sabo and Jansen, 1992). Women are others and men want them to get out of the way in the context of sport. These commercials are ripe with reminders of this dual pairing as idealized truism in the ideological world of the fan as consumer.

When given a choice, in a Heineken commercial, of following a soccer ball down the street or advancing romantic engagement with his beautiful girlfriend, the call of sport – evoking a Pavlovian bell or command for national duty – is advanced as the natural order of being. In a Michelob ad, a woman playing co-ed football is seen by men as out of place, deserving resentment for the special treatment she has demanded. When, in a Bud Light ad, men seeking living-room sanctuary for sports viewing find their territory invaded by one's spouse and her friends, they imagine taking command and putting these women in their place in a fantasy of "What would Carlos do?"

In the imagined sport-centered world of these commercials, women's relation with men inherently raises issues. This is true whether the woman is shown as "more than a man," one-upping a group of men on their own barroom turf, as is the case in a Toohey's "Man vs. Woman vs. Beer" spot for the Australian market or whether the woman is idealized, as is the case in Coors Light's "Beer Babe" where an emasculated and awe-struck young man spills his beer – in symbolic premature ejaculation – at the mere sight of his "dream girl" who is both buxom and knowledgeable about sports.

The ideological sensibilities of such stereotypes about how men and women not only relate, but relate in the context of sport, raise questions. Some of these, seen through the lens of CCT, fuel ethical questions about the construction of "idealized consumer types" and "the ways in which capitalist production systems invite consumers to covet certain identity and lifestyle ideals" (Arnould and Thompson, 2005, p. 875). Other questions, however, are more pragmatic. For the sport manager, persistent reliance on truncated stereotypes of "how women are" and continuing to view them as largely oppositional "others," both in the context of sport and to men, seems at cross-purposes to making a sport-related consumer marketplace, where they can fuel much growth, more welcoming.

Conclusion

This chapter provides an introduction to the study of consumer culture for both scholars and practitioners of sport communication. Scholars and managers share an interest in making the marketplace for sport, and how we communication *in* and *through* that marketplace, more democratic, open, and inclusive. Critically oriented scholars, driven by the concerns of CCT, have an underlying responsibility to reveal "truth," to demystify and demythologize marketplace ideologies. Echoing Bauman's (2007) observations about human agency being delimited in "market-mediated mode of life," Arnould and Thompson (2005, p. 869) note that "consumer culture – and the marketplace ideology it conveys—frames consumers' horizons of conceivable action, feeling, and thought, making certain patterns of behavior and sense-making interpretations more likely than others." CCT has a responsibility to reveal this, and also to comment on whether persistent tendencies in market-driven framing mesh with changes in culture and our collective best interests.

This relates in no uncertain terms to sport managers and marketers and their interests in fashioning a healthy and growing sport marketplace. When the dominant communicative frames that surround sport are needlessly truncated and reliant, as we have seen in the central tendencies of the series of studies reviewed here, on idealizing hackneyed stereotypes of how men and women are imagined as consumers in the sport-related marketplace, a disconnect between thematic reliance and achieving the goal of marketplace growth is revealed.

The summarized studies and their narrative paintings of the sports fan as consumer in television commercials should be taken as a heuristic of the potential of CCT for the study of promotional sport communication. We need to ask further questions about the contexts of sport-related consumption seen in advertising. Have we stretched our sport-anchored affinities too far to garner meaningful synergies in selling clothing, drinks, credit cards, and other products that are tangential to the sport spectator experience? Similarly, we need to look more carefully at castings of the sport fan as a consumer in our narratives. Are our efforts ludicrously anchored in cartoonish paintings of pathological diehard fanship? Is it in our best interests to continue to posit that gender remains the great divide of sport in our narrative efforts to sell through sport? Using the lens of consumer culture theory can help bring useful answers to questions such as these for both practitioners seeking to gain leverage in the sport marketplace and for scholars who wish to understand how sport exerts social and cultural influence.

References

Abercrombie, N., and Longhurst, B. (1998). *Audiences*. London: Sage.
Aldridge, A. (2003). *Consumption*. Cambridge, UK: Polity.
Anderson, B. (1983). *Imagined communities*. London:Verso.

Arnould, E. J., and Thompson, C. J. (2005). Consumer culture theory (CCT): Twenty years of research. *Journal of Consumer Research*, 31, 868–82.
A.T. Kearney Inc. (2003). *The new sports consumer.* Chicago, IL: A.T. Kearney, Inc. Retrieved from http://www.ekospor.com/Sports-Marketing/New%20Sports%20Consumer.pdf.
Barthes, R. (1973). *Mythologies.* London: Paladin.
Bauman, Z. (1998). *Work, consumerism, and the new poor.* Buckingham: Open University Press.
Bauman, Z. (2007). *Consuming life.* Cambridge: Polity.
Blackshaw, T. (2008). Bauman on consumerism: Living the market-mediated life. In M. H. Jacobsen and P. Poder (Eds.), *The sociology of Zygmunt Bauman: Challenges and critiques* (pp. 117–35). London, UK: Routledge.
Cohen, L. (2004). *A consumers' republic: The politics of mass consumption in postwar America.* New York: Random House.
Crawford, G. (2004). *Consuming sport: Fans, sport, and culture.* London: Routledge.
Duncan, M. C., and Aycock, A. (2009). "I laughed until it hurt": Negative humor in Super Bowl ads. In L. A. Wenner and S. J. Jackson (Eds.), *Sport, beer, and gender: Promotional culture and contemporary social life* (pp. 245–59). New York: Peter Lang.
Gabriel, Y. and Lang, T. (1995). *The unmanageable consumer: Contemporary consumption and its fragmentation.* London, UK: Sage.
Giulianotti, R. (2002). Supporters, followers, fans, and flaneurs: A taxonomy of spectator identities in football. *Journal of Sport and Social Issues*, 26, 25–46.
Gosling, V. K. (2007). Girls allowed? The marginalization of female sport fans. In J. Gray, C. Sandvoss, and C. L. Harrington (Eds.), *Fandom: Identities and communities in a mediated world* (pp. 251–60). New York: NYU Press.
Horne, J. (2005). *Sport in consumer culture.* New York: Palgrave Macmillan.
Hunt, K. A., Bristol, T., and Bashaw, R. E (1999). A conceptual approach to classifying sports fans. *Journal of Services Marketing*, 13, 439–52.
James, J. D., and Ridinger, L. L. (2002). Female and male sport fans: A comparison of sport consumption motives. *Journal of Sport Behavior*, 25, 260–78.
Kane, C. (2005). As spots belittling women fade out, men become the target of the seemingly inevitable gender sneer. *New York Times*, January 28, p. C2.
Kellner, D. (2001). The sports spectacle, Michael Jordan, and Nike: Unholy alliance? In D. L. Andrews (Ed.), *Michael Jordan, Inc.: Corporate sport, media culture and late modern America.* New York: SUNY Press.
Lury, C. (1996). *Consumer culture.* New Brunswick, NJ: Rutgers University Press.
McCracken, G. (1990). *Culture and consumption.* Bloomington, IN: Indiana University Press.
Messner, M. A., and Montez de Oca, J. (2005). The male consumer as loser: Beer and liquor ads in mega sports media events. *Signs*, 30, 1879–909.
Miles, S. (1998). *Consumerism: As a way of life.* London, UK: Sage.
Nathanson, P. and Young, K. K. (2001). *Spreading misandry: The teaching of contempt for men in popular culture.* Montreal: McGill-Queens' University Press.
Paterson, M. (2006). *Consumption and everyday life.* London, UK: Routledge.
Patterson, P. (1996). Rambos and himbos: Stereotypical images of men in advertising. In P. M. Lester (Ed.), *Images that injure: Pictorial stereotypes in the media* (pp. 93–6). Westport, CT: Praeger.
Plunkett Research (2011). *Sports industry overview.* Houston, TX: Plunkett Research Ltd. Retrieved from http://www.plunkettresearch.com/sports-recreation-leisure-market-research/industry-statistics.
Pronger, B. (1990). *The arena of masculinity: Sports, homosexuality, and the meaning of sex.* New York: St. Martin's Press.
Rojek, C. (2004). The consumerist syndrome in contemporary society. *Journal of Consumer Culture*, 4, 291–312.
Sabo, D., and Jansen, S. C. (1992). Images of men in sport media: The social reproduction of the gender order. In S. Craig (Ed.), *Men, masculinity, and the media* (pp. 169–84). Newbury Park, CA: Sage.
Sandvoss, C. (2005). *Fans: The mirror of consumption.* Cambridge: Polity.
Slater, D. (1997). *Consumer culture and modernity.* Cambridge, UK: Polity.

Smart, B. (2010). *Consumer society: Critical issues and environmental consequences*. London, UK: Sage.

Stewart, B., Smith, A. C.T., and Nicholson, M. (2003). Sport consumer typologies: A critical review. *Sport Marketing Quarterly*, 12, 206–16.

Strate, L. (1992). Beer commercials: A manual on masculinity. In S. Craig (Ed.), *Men, masculinity, and the media* (pp. 78–92). Newbury Park, CA: Sage.

Wann, D. L., Melnick, M. M., Russell, G. W., and Pease, D. G. (2001). *Sport fans: The psychology and social impact of spectators*. New York: Routledge.

Wann, D. L., Wadell, P. J., and Dunham, M. D. (2004). Using sex and gender role orientation to predict level of sport fandom. *Journal of Sport Behavior*, 27, 366–77.

Wenner, L. A. (2008). Playing dirty: On reading media texts and the sports fan in commercialized settings. In L.W. Hugenberg, A. P. M. Haridakis, and A.C. Earnheardt (Eds.), *Sports mania: Essays on fandom and the media in the 21st century* (pp. 13–32). Jefferson, NC: McFarland and Company.

Wenner, L. A. (2009). Brewing consumption: Sports dirt, mythic masculinity, and the ethos of beer commercials. In L. A. Wenner and S. J. Jackson (Eds.), *Sport, beer, and gender: Promotional culture and contemporary social life* (pp. 121–42). New York: Peter Lang.

Wenner, L. A. (2010). Gendered sports dirt: Interrogating sex and the single beer commercial. In H. Hundley and A. Billings (Eds.), *Examining identity in sports media* (pp. 87–107). Thousand Oaks, CA: Sage.

Wenner, L. A. (2011). Mocking the fan for fun and profit: Sports dirt, fanship identity, and commercial narratives. In A. C. Billings (Ed.), *Sports media: Transformation, integration, consumption* (pp. 61–76). New York: Routledge.

Wenner, L. A. (2012). Reading the commodified female sports fan: Interrogating strategic dirt and characterization in commercial narratives. In K. Toffoletti and P. Mewett (Eds.), *Sport and its female fans* (pp. 135–51). London: Routledge.

Wenner, L. A., and Gantz, W. (1998). Watching sports on television: Audience experience, gender, fanship, and marriage. In L. A. Wenner (Ed.), *MediaSport* (pp. 233–51). London: Routledge.

42

SPORT COMMUNICATION AND SOCIAL RESPONSIBILITY

Maria Hopwood and James Skinner

This chapter describes the concept of corporate social responsibility (CSR) and its application to the business of sport. Increasingly, sport teams and franchises operate as a business, with the inherent responsibilities as a business to stakeholders, such as investors, sponsors, and the community at large. Therefore, there is now, more than ever, an increasing expectation that sport organizations assume greater responsibility for their operation and the impact of their operations on their community, fans, and the physical space in which they operate. The concept of sport social responsibility (SSR) derives from an increasing awareness that the business of sport does not operate within a vacuum where only the team, the spectators and the fan base are affected by the operation of the sport. Environmental concern about the operation of sport, for example, is indicative of wider social concerns about the impact of sport business on the environment at large. This chapter discusses particular issues in relation to SSR and looks at how sport managers can use public relations and communications practices to deal with these issues and the impact this can have on the operation of the sport entity as a business.

Corporate social responsibility

As a concept, CSR is still striving to reach a single definition. A dozen years ago, the World Business Council for Sustainable Development defined CSR as "the continuing commitment by business to behave ethically and contribute to economic development while improving the quality of life of the workforce and their families as well as the local community and society at large" (Holme and Watts, 2000, p. 6). Not all definitions of CSR are as all-encompassing. For instance, Heath and Ryan (1989) found that some companies defined CSR as simply as "performing good deeds" (p. 34), while others believed that creating a code of ethical conduct was essential to achieve an acceptable level of CSR. However, there has emerged a consensus within these definitions that corporations must be accountable not only to shareholders in the form of economic returns, but also to stakeholders (Carroll, 2000; Clarkson, 1995). CSR has also been referred to as the continuing commitment by businesses to meet or exceed stakeholder expectations (Carroll, 2000), and further to take greater account of their social, environmental, and financial footprints (Zadek, 2001). Within these definitions, there is a consensus that corporations must be held accountable, not only to their shareholders in the provision of economic or financial returns, but also to stakeholders (Carroll, 2000; Clarkson, 1995).

The concept of CSR evolved from a more general concept of social responsibility, which can be traced back to the early 20th century and to the philanthropic actions of people such as Carnegie and Ford. These business tycoons believed, like many wealthy Americans, that they had a responsibility to give back a portion of their wealth to improve social conditions. While not a major force throughout the first half of the 20th century, social responsibility and the more defined concept of CSR became more significant in the 1960s and 1970s, with the rise of social or public activism and a greater public awareness of the impact of corporations on society at large. With this increasing awareness, segments of society began to question the actions and responsibilities of corporations and the role they should be playing in social issues (Clark, 2000).

Noted economist Friedman (1962) argued that the primary responsibility of businesses was to ensure economic advantage to their shareholders. Any other expenditure outside the limited ambit of profit maximization could be considered a mismanagement of funds. Friedman's strict stance on the responsibility of business, however, was not unilaterally accepted. Carroll (1979) was instrumental in developing CSR theory with this three-dimensional model of corporate performance. His model was not designed to repudiate or discredit Friedman's theory but rather to detail "the social responsibilities of businesses in a more exhaustive manner" (Carroll, 1979, p. 499). Thus, his model – which identified four categories that he believed formed the basis of CSR – can be conceptualized as a pyramid with economic responsibilities serving as the first level, followed by legal responsibilities and then ethical responsibilities, and ending at the top with discretionary responsibilities. Understandings such as Carroll's have led to contemporary thinking on CSR to denote that corporate business strategies need to be socially responsible and follow the triple bottom line (Wildes, 2008). Elkington's (1999) triple bottom line model states that sustainable development occurs when "people-planet-profit" are aligned to ensure that organizations go beyond financial yields to produce more "win-win-win" outcomes. CSR's increase in prominence is mainly due to the change in social values and norms that govern choices that are worth striving for in society (Blau, 1960), such as the strong anti-globalization, anti-corporate sentiments, and disasters that have taken place recently which has necessitated that companies do "social good" (Wood, 2010).

In response to the changing expectations of consumers regarding ethical and social initiatives of business, organizations are increasingly using internal and external communication aimed at stakeholders (Maignan, Ferrell, and Hult, 1999). While these messages commonly generate a positive reaction, research shows that organizations that exhibit their goals come under close scrutiny and run the risk of "protesting too much" (Ashforth and Gibbs, 1990). More recently, the triple bottom line, sustainability, or CSR reporting has become increasingly popular, but also homogeneous and open to manipulation known as "green washing" or "cherry picked" good news (Laufer, 2003). Consequently, many organizations are focusing their energies on internal CSR orientations for this competitive advantage (Noble, Sinha, and Kumar, 2002). Stakeholder engagement is a key feature of CSR orientation and, as such, the internal stakeholder (that is, employees) take on an even greater significance (Blomback and Axelsson, 2007). Research advocates that engaging employees in CSR is vital and contributes to long-term benefits (Bohdananowicz and Zientara, 2008). To achieve this, Nord and Fuller (2009) recommend an "employee-centred approach" where employees are encouraged at all levels to work for small gains of socially responsible actions, which help to set in place CSR-oriented values. This is essential, as employees carry the burden of responsibility for implementing sustainable behaviors into their roles and successful outcomes are determined by their willingness to collaborate (Collier and Esteban, 2007).

For sport businesses, this means that they need to consider their core capabilities, mission, values, current social performance, and industry characteristics (Smith, 2003). Sports teams and, in particular, sports franchises, like other businesses, must operate at and generate a profit in order to be successful. In most cases, being successful equates to being able to continue operating. This success is to a large extent dependent on community support for the team – be it locally, regionally, or nationally. Sports teams and franchises, however, also have varying management and ownership models – teams in the major US leagues, for example, may be owned by a single individual, a group of partners, or even a multinational corporation. These varying ownership structures may create a differing approach to the issue of who influences CSR within the organization.

Sport social responsibility

The term CSR does not fully apply within the sport context, chiefly because sport has a range of unique characteristics which differentiate it from other business sectors and operations. For this very reason, the concept of SSR has emerged. SSR (Hopwood, Kitchin, and Skinner, 2010) is a new concept which is in the process of development, in an attempt to address the unique requirements of sport business and communications. Its philosophy is firmly grounded in the three distinct but different orientations of corporate social responsibility (CSR_1), corporate social responsiveness (CSR_2), and corporate citizenship, originally articulated by Frederick (1994) and further examined by Walker and Parent (2010) in their research into social involvement in sport. Each of these orientations encompasses specific criteria and characteristics, which are directly relevant to the concept of SSR. According to Walker and Parent, CSR_1 is typically undertaken with the intent to improve an aspect of society or relationships with communities and/or nongovernmental organizations. All sport organizations have a range of stakeholders or publics with whom they need to develop and maintain mutually beneficial relationships to achieve core business objectives. In order to serve these varied stakeholders, organizations implement CSR_1 activities, which range from community enrichment and development programs to environmental initiatives.

As a concept, CSR_2 emerged during the early 1970s as a result of corporations reacting to growing concerns about their role in society. Murphy (1978) suggested that social responsiveness was a more accurate term than social responsibility, as corporations were already recognizing their obligations to society and were now responding to stakeholder demands in increasingly diverse ways. CSR_2 is concerned with the strategic implementation of activities ranging from environmental assessments, stakeholder management, issues management and public relations management. From an important SSR perspective, CSR_2 is much more pragmatically directed and does not have the same moral imperative as CSR_1. An important dimension to CSR_2 activities is that they incorporate the necessary strategic tools for gaining and sustaining competitive advantage as well as facilitating CSR_1, all of which are integral to SSR and contain the vital communications dimension which is integral to sport business but which tends to be overlooked in the literature on CSR in sport.

Corporate citizenship is concerned with the role that organizations play in society, their position with other citizens and members of society and the community in which they are based. The concept of "being a good corporate citizen" resonates with the overarching philosophy of CSR which is concerned with doing good as well as being good. CSR_1 can be seen more as an external orientation and a moral obligation while corporate citizenship has more of a cultural, legal, and global dimension. This is evidenced in the practices of companies such as Nike, which undertake human rights initiatives in the countries in which they base their manufacturing operations. From an SSR perspective, corporate citizenship is regarded as a natural extension of CSR_1 and CSR_2.

Subsuming the basic concepts of CSR, SSR then adapts them to the business of sport in its various interactions in the local, national and global communities. SSR is of increasing importance for sport organizations. As sport becomes a global commodity with an increasing influence across a range of markets, individual teams and franchises are becoming increasingly interdependent on the very consumer/fan base that initially elevated them to this position. The sporting public, as a major subset of the general public, is more socially aware than it has been in the past, with the first decade of the 21st century playing host to a range of corporate misdeeds (Walker, 2007).

Sports franchises differ from traditional business in that revenue forms the basis of their value, as opposed to the cash flow and assets on which traditional business determines its value. Lee and Chun (2002) see the revenue that underpins the value of professional sports teams and franchises generated by the buying and selling of goods (for example, tickets, merchandise, broadcasting rights, advertising), services (for example, the staging of major events, concessions, parking) and labor (for example, players, managers, coaches). Professional sports teams and franchises have different operating structures, and this can affect how the team operates financially. For example, very few teams in major US leagues (for example, NBA, NHL, MLB, NFL) are owned by corporations as most are run by families or small partnership groups (Extejt, 2004). When a single owner or a small group of owners are making decisions on a sports team or franchise's financial future and responsibilities, the decision-making process is substantially different from that of a traditional business operation, which is most likely owned by stockholders and managed by a chief executive officer and board of directors who are responsible to the stockholders for the outcome of any decisions that are made. Extejt further discusses the discretionary power of sports managers/team owners and how they may choose to redirect revenue or even forego revenue in certain circumstances for the good of the team, the franchise or the fans. The discretionary power to determine CSR in these circumstances, says Extejt, is significantly greater than that of a chief executive officer or board of directors of a traditional business, who are still bound by the stricter definition of CSR in relation to business profit making.

Sport, as an important microcosm of society, has witnessed a changing environment of expectations and values. In most instances, the values espoused by the sports team or franchise are clearly representative of their major stakeholders – the fans – and society in general, although at times sports teams and franchises will appear to be playing "catch up" in relation to acceptable player behavior both on and off the field. There are also other instances where sports teams, franchises, and major international organizations such as the International Olympic Committee will take a harder line than that generally expected in society, but in general respected by society – an example being a zero tolerance for performance-enhancing drugs, use of alcohol, and violence against women.

Ethical responsibilities may be hard to define, but it is easy to see when an organization has not been ethical. In today's age of corporate scandals, companies are called to set the standards high or their ethics are often called into question. Sport, as an international business, faces the same scrutiny. Professional baseball in the US (such as MLB), for example, received negative coverage when several of its major players tested positive for using performance-enhancing substances. This forced the league and players association to agree to put a tougher anti-drug policy into place in order to appear more ethically responsible. Another example of ethical responsibility is "green sport business" in which environmental concerns are placed at the core of the business practices of sport organizations. Until recently, sport managers have typically accorded minimal attention to the environmental crisis. This is surprising, as "the right to a clean environment" (Johnson, 1995) is crucial for the realization of international human rights. Johnson further argues that "these rights are important to understand because the environment is the foundation to which all things derive life" (p. 112). The concept of "green sport" recognizes the essential importance of sports teams, franchises, and organizations adopting eco-friendly strategies in the planning, marketing and staging of all levels of sporting events.

Smith and Westerbeek (2007) suggest that environmental sustainability and awareness is not only making sporting events more marketable, but is also attracting corporate sponsors who are keen to leverage public approval to enhance their corporate reputation. They put forward that an increasing global awareness of the essentiality of environmental sustainability for the future of the human race has the potential to work to the financial advantage of sport and sport-related products. By promoting those aspects of the sport or sport-related product that are "green," the sport organization can capitalize on this growing awareness of the dangers of environmental damage (Dingle, 2007).

Philanthropic responsibility is another part of social responsibility, and hence part of CSR/SSR. In general terms, philanthropic responsibility includes making cash donations to causes or non-profit organizations, in-kind donations, such as free tickets, sponsorship of community events, and active employee volunteerism. Along with promoting an eco-friendly profile, this category is one of the most important to sports teams because, to succeed financially, each team is dependent on the local community to purchase tickets and other team goods (Extejt, 2004). Virtually all professional teams participate in some kind of philanthropic activities. In the US, most professional sports leagues themselves strongly encourage their athletes to be involved in the community. Extejt pointed out that each athlete in the NBA, according to a relatively recent collective bargaining agreement, was required to make at least five individual and five team appearances at community functions. In addition to professional franchises, the sports industry also makes contributions through individual player or owner donations. Increasingly then, organizations are seeking a competitive advantage with the ongoing dilemma of allocating limited resources in a fiercely competitive environment. Sport organizations are no different. CSR/SSR can deliver competitive advantage to a sports team, franchise or organization in a number of different ways, most of which concern the ethical and philanthropic applications of CSR/SSR in order to generate positive perceptions of, and support for, sports teams, franchises, and even mega-events. As Juholin (2004) and other scholars have noted, this ultimately leads to a greater demand for products and is achieved by establishing a connection between the team, franchise, or organization and the major stakeholders on an intrinsically ethical and values-based level.

For some sport organizations, seeking a sustainable competitive advantage can be a complex and perilous activity, with most not even sure where to start. Identifying the range of internal and external stakeholder issues are often conflicting and varied when employing CSR strategy (Maon, Lindgreen, and Swaen, 2008). As noted above, a sport organization must consider a range of relevant issues, such as its core capabilities, mission, values, and current social performance as well as the industry's characteristics (Smith, 2003). With this knowledge, a sport organization will develop its own connotation and clarify its motivation that underlies its commitment to CSR (Maon, *et al.*, 2008). Given the intensified expectation on sport businesses to perform in the current competitive marketplace, CSR can be a valuable tool to safeguard corporate reputation; however, for many sport organizations, CSR may be seen as a luxury in which only the most successful businesses invest, or as damage control insurance (Freeman and McVea, 2001). Pinkston and Carroll (1996) agree, that putting funds towards discretionary responsibilities such as CSR may be risky for sport managers given rising costs of sport businesses and increasing legal and social responsibility. The consequences of not doing it, however, may be proven to be greater in the long term. Recently, a conference was held in India in which corporate responsibility in sport was given critical attention. The key findings of the conference fit within the context of this chapter and help in conceptualizing the concept of SSR. For instance, one finding was that a somewhat tarnished "commercial" image has been attached to professional sporting events, which tends to overshadow the potential benefits and power of sport as a catalyst for social development. Another conference finding was that sport programs can offer a bridge across socioeconomic gaps and can be designed to contribute to improving the quality of individual lives, while enhancing community "togetherness" and aspirations and serving as a catalyst for social and economic progress. One final conference finding that should be pointed out is that sport, by itself, helps to build the capacity for leadership and contributes to the development of decision making and communication skills, organizing skills, and teamwork. The above examples were only a few of the many key findings of the conference (FICCI Aditya Birla CSR Centre for Excellence, 2011).

SSR research and case studies

Sport organizations around the globe are intrinsically bound up with their wider community, which means that their corporate citizenship role is constantly scrutinized by their publics and the media. The sport product – wherever in the world it is produced and consumed – together with the actions and behavior of those who produce it, continue to be constant sources of interest to an increasingly global audience meaning that SSR activity is coming increasingly under the spotlight and magnifying glass. Within the context of sport, CSR has only emerged fairly recently (for example, Filizöz and Fine, 2011) as a subject for analysis. At the time of writing, the body of literature in this field is relatively small but is showing continual growth as CSR within sport gains wider recognition.

Much of the research on CSR in sport (for example, Babiak and Wolfe, 2009; Bradish and Cronin, 2009; Godfrey, 2009; Sheth and Babiak, 2010; Walker and Parent, 2010) has been produced by scholars from the US and Canada, which means that the focus is very much on CSR activity in North American sport. However, arguably the seminal article on social responsibility in sport has been written by two Australian authors (Smith and Westerbeek, 2007) who take the view that sport by its unique nature is inherently socially responsible. They considered the following issues to be of specific concern to professional and elite sport and used them as the basis for the creation of the ten unique features of corporate responsibility in sport: performance enhancing drug taking, crowd violence, racial vilification, gender inequalities, sex and alcohol offences, anti-competition legislation regarding the structure of sporting competitions, and general role modeling.

The European football (soccer) industry continues to be a rich source of SSR activity and a number of scholars have produced a range of articles which deal specifically with football social responsibility (see, for example, Breitbarth and Harris, 2008; Walters and Tacon, 2010). In addition, the European governing bodies for football – FIFA and UEFA – have both developed social responsibility strategies and initiatives which feature prominently on their websites and provide good examples of how social responsibility is increasingly gaining prominence in the world of sport. Adding another dimension to the academic interest in sport and CSR, Levermore (2010) considers its potential in furthering social and economic development via the mechanism of sport mega-sports events such as the FIFA World Cup.

Sports entities around the world are engaging in SSR initiatives, many of which go unnoticed and unreported. Such initiatives are important from a sports public relations perspective, as they are an integral element of sports relationship management strategies. The social responsibility activities of a number of international sports entities such as Barcelona FC (http://foundation.fcbarcelona.com) have gained widespread coverage and recognition. Another recently formed organization, the Didier Drogba Foundation, provides an excellent example of SSR through football. Didier Drogba is an internationally recognized football player who, until the end of the 2011/2012 season, played for Chelsea Football Club in the English Premier League. Drogba's country of birth is the Ivory Coast in Africa, and he has represented his country in international football tournaments such as the FIFA World Cup and the African Cup of Nations. Like many other countries in Africa, the Ivory Coast has many social and economic challenges. Drogba's foundation, created in 2007, aims to provide financial and material support in both health and education to the African people, especially in the Ivory Coast. The rationale for the foundation along with its means (for example, Didier's personal funds, book profits, charity ball) and actions (such as hospital construction, Red Cross support, personal care) are detailed on its website: http://www.thedidierdrogbafoundation.com/missions.html. The Didier Drogba Foundation's fundraising is ongoing and the third annual charity ball was held at the Dorchester Hotel in London in 2012. Overall, Drogba's social responsibility ethic has gained him widespread admiration beyond the football pitch resulting in him being awarded the status of United Nations Development Programme Goodwill Ambassador and, in 2011, being named in *Time* magazine's 100 most influential people in recognition for his charity work.

One last case study example – from the McGrath Foundation (http://www.mcgrathfoundation.com.au/) – further illustrates SSR in action. As a result of the personal experience of breast cancer that resulted in the untimely death of his wife Jane in 2008, Australian cricketer Glenn McGrath, together with Jane, launched the McGrath Foundation in 2005, whose mission it is to ensure that every Australian family touched by breast cancer has access to the support of a breast care nurse (Cricket South Africa, 2011). Extensive media coverage in Australia and beyond has helped the McGrath Foundation to achieve the funding of its 75th breast care nurse in 2012. One of the most visible elements of the McGrath Foundation's activities is the annual Vodafone Test Series Pink Test, which takes place at the Sydney Cricket Ground. The third day of this test match is now named Jane McGrath Day, and everyone attending on that day wears pink as a way of showing support for the breast cancer awareness cause. During the 2012 Pink Test, AU$104,388 were raised in support of the McGrath Foundation and the event was covered widely in the media both at home and abroad. In 2011, the Pink Test went global for the first time when South Africa played Australia at the Wanderers ground in Johannesburg (SouthAfrica.info, 2012). It is Glenn McGrath's intention that further future Pink Tests will take place at other international cricket grounds such as at Lord's – the home of cricket – in London, England, thus ensuring that this excellent example of SSR through cricket's message is disseminated to the widest possible audience.

In summary, stakeholders at every level are increasingly demanding that the sport organizations and entities with whom they choose to engage demonstrate proactive CSR/SSR in all their undertakings. For this reason, SSR can justifiably be considered a fundamental element of contemporary sport communication.

References

Ashforth, B., and Gibbs, B. (1990). The double-edge of organizational legitimation. *Organization Science*, 1 (2), 177–94.

Babiak, K., and Wolfe, R. (2009) Determinants of corporate social responsibility in professional sport: Internal and external factors. *Journal of Sport Management*, 23, 717–42.

Blau, P. (1960). Structural effects. *American Sociological Review*, 25 (2), 178–93.

Blomback, A., and Axelsson, B. (2007). The role of corporate brand image in the selection of new subcontractors. *Journal of Business and Industrial Marketing*, 22 (6), 418–30.

Bohdananowicz, P., and Zientara, P. (2008). Hotel companies' contribution to improving the quality of life of local communities and the well-being of their employees. *Tourism and Hospitality Research*, 9 (2), 147–58.

Bradish, C., and Cronin, J. (2009). Corporate social responsibility in sport. *Journal of Sport Management*, 23, 691–97.

Breitbarth, T., and Harris, P. (2008). The role of corporate social responsibility in the football business: Towards the development of a conceptual model. *European Sport Management Quarterly*, 8 (2), 179–206.

Carroll, A. B., (1979). A three dimensional model of corporate performance. *Academy of Management Review*, 4 (4), 497–505.

Carroll, A. B., (2000). Ethical challenges for business in the new millennium: corporate social responsibility and models of management morality. *Business Ethics Quarterly*, 10 (1), 33–42.

Clark, C. E., (2000). Differences between public relations and corporate social responsibility: an analysis. *Public Relations Review*, 26 (13), 363–81.

Clarkson, M., (1995). A stakeholder framework for analyzing and evaluating corporate social performance. *Academy of Management Review*, 20 (1), 92–116.

Collier, J., and Esteban, R. (2007). Corporate social responsibility and employee commitment. *Business Ethics: A European Review*, 16 (1), 19–33.

Cricket South Africa (2011). Pink test goes global. *Facebook*, November 17. Retrieved from http://www.facebook.com/notes/cricket-south-africa/pink-test-goes-global/10150420687882505.

Dingle, G. (2007). Sport in a carbon-constrained twenty-first century. *Bulletin of Sport and Culture. Victoria University Sport and Culture Group*, No. 27, March.

Elkington, J. (1999). *Cannibals with forks: The triple bottom line of 21st century business*. Oxford: Capstone.

Extejt, M. M. (2004). Philanthropy and professional sport teams. *International Journal of Sport Management*, 5 (3), 215–28.

FICCI Aditya Birla CSR Centre for Excellence (2011). Corporate Social Responsibility: Changing Lives through Sports, 14th February 2011, FICCI, New Delhi. Retrieved from http://assets.sportanddev.org/downloads/ficci_csr_conference_summary_report.pdf.

Filizöz, B., and Fi ne, M. (2011). Corporate social responsibility: A study of striking corporate social responsibility practices in sport management. *Procedia Social and Behavioral Sciences*, 25, 1405–17.

Frederick, W. C. (1994). From CSR1 to CSR2: The maturing of business-and-society thought. *Business and Society*, 33, 150–64.
Freeman, R. E., and McVea, J. (2001). *A stakeholder approach to strategic management*. Darden Business School Working Paper, No. 01-02. Social Science Research Network, SSRN eLibrary. DOI: 10.2139/ssrn.263511.
Friedman, M. (1962). *Capitalism and freedom*. Chicago: University of Chicago Press.
Godfrey, P. (2009). Corporate social responsibility in sport: An overview and key issues. *Journal of Sport Management*, 23, 698–716.
Heath, R. L., and Ryan, M. (1989). Public relations' role in defining corporate social responsibility. *Journal of Mass Media Ethics*, 4 (1), 21–38.
Holme, R. and Watts, P. (2000). *Corporate social responsibility: Making good business sense*. Geneva: World Business Council for Sustainable Development. Retrieved from http://www.wbcsd.org/web/publications/csr2000.pdf.
Hopwood, M., Kitchin, P., and Skinner, J. (2010). *Sport public relations and communication*. Oxford: Butterworth-Heinemann.
Johnson, B. (1995). Human rights and the environment. *Human Ecology*, 23, 111–23.
Juholin, E. (2004). For business or the good of all? A Finnish approach to corporate social responsibility. *Corporate Governance*, 4 (3), 20–31.
Laufer, W. (2003). Social accountability and corporate greenwashing. *Journal of Business Ethics*, 43 (3), 253–61.
Lee, S., and Chun, H. (2002). Economic value of professional sport franchises in the United States. *Sport Journal*, 5 (3), 1–10.
Levermore, R. (2010). CSR for development through sport: Examining its potential and limitations. *Third World Quarterly*, 13 (2), 223–41.
Maignan, I., Ferrell, O. C., and Hult, G. T. M. (1999). Corporate citizenship: Cultural antecedents and business benefits. *Journal of the Academy of Marketing Science*, 27 (4), 455–69.
Maon, F., Lindgreen, A., and Swaen, V. (2008). Thinking of the organization as a system: The role of managerial perceptions in developing a corporate social responsibility strategic agenda. *Systems Research and Behavioral Science*, 25 (3), 413–26.
Murphy, P. E. (1978). An evolution: corporate social responsiveness. *University of Michigan Business Review*, November, pp. 20–22.
Noble, C. H., Sinha, R. K., and Kumar, A. (2002). Market orientation and alternative strategic orientations: A longitudinal assessment of performance implications. *Journal of Marketing*, 66 (4), 25–39.
Nord, W., and Fuller, S. (2009). Increasing corporate social responsibility through an employee-centered approach. *Employee Responsibilities and Rights Journal*, 21, 279–90.
Pinkston, T., and Carroll, A. (1996). A retrospective examination of CSR orientations: Have they changed? *Journal of Business Ethics*, 15 (2), 199–206.
Sheth, H., and Babiak, K. M. (2010). Beyond the Game: Perceptions and practices of corporate social responsibility in the professional sport industry. *Journal of Business Ethics*, 91, 433–50.
Smith, A., and Westerbeek, H. (2007). Sport as a vehicle for deploying corporate social responsibility. *Journal of Corporate Citizenship*, 25 (1), 43–54.
Smith, C. (2003). Corporate social responsibility: Whether or how? *California Management Review*, 45 (4), 52–76.
SouthAfrica.info (2012. South Africa: Wanderers Test 'Goes Pink' for Cancer. *AllAfrica*, November 17. AllAfrica. Retrieved from http://allafrica.com/stories/201111180161.html.
Walker, M., and Parent, M. M. (2010). Toward an integrated framework of corporate social responsibility, responsiveness and citizenship in sport. *Sport Management Review*, 13, 198–213.
Walker, M. B. (2007). Assessing the influence of corporate social responsibility on consumer attitudes in the sport industry (Unpublished doctoral dissertation). Florida State University, Tallahassee.
Walters, G., and Tacon, R. (2010). Corporate social responsibility in sport: Stakeholder management in the UK football industry. *Journal of Management and Organization*, 16 (4), 566–86.

White, J. (2012). Didier Drogba is the Chelsea striker who possesses more power than Ivory Coast's president. *The Telegraph*, February 16. Retrieved from http://www.telegraph.co.uk/sport/football/teams/chelsea/9085118/Didier-Drogba-is-the-Chelsea-striker-who-possesses-more-power-than-Ivory-Coasts-president.html#.

Wildes, V. (2008). How can organizational leaders really lead and serve at the same time? *International Journal of Contemporary Hospitality Management*, 20 (1), 67–76.

Wood, J. (2010). Measuring corporate social performance: A review. *International Journal of Management Reviews*, 10 (1), 50–84.

Zadek, S., (2001). *The civil corporation: The new economy of corporate citizenship*. London: Earthscan.

43

FOR THE CURE, THE KIDS, AND THE CAUSE

Practicing advocacy through communication and sport

Jeffrey W. Kassing

Sport and advocacy have a long shared history. Charity football matches in England and Scotland date back to the inception of the modern game (Kay and Wray, 2010). Likewise, the bicycle and bicycling have been used as tools for dissent, protest, and cultural critique for some time (Furness, 2005). A notable high watermark for sport and advocacy was the civil rights protests enacted by American sprinters Tommie Smith and John Carlos at the 1968 Olympic Games in Mexico City. But their protest, which was vilified at the time only to be celebrated decades later, was the culmination of months of advocacy (Hartmann, 1996). The Olympic Project for Human Rights, which formed in the months preceding the Games, organized a boycott of an indoor meet, coordinated protests and meetings on 35 college campuses, and threatened but eventually aborted an effort to stage an alternative 'Third World' Olympics. At the actual Games, several athletes wore black stockings and berets in their early heats and one, winner of the 100 meters, Jimmy Hines, refused to shake the hand of then International Olympic Committee (IOC) President Avery Brundage (Peterson, 2009).

Examining the connection between sport and advocacy involves crisscrossing interdisciplinary boundaries that consider sport as it relates to activism, protest, peace, reconciliation, and development. This chapter gives shape and structure to this broad area of research by illustrating some apparent themes. Figure 43.1 depicts the major areas where sport and advocacy come together. Two main domains occupy the central territory of sport and advocacy – sport participation and the entity of sport. Around sport participation is a constellation of spheres that include advocacy for participation, advocacy enacted by sport participants, and participation as a form of advocacy. The arrows connecting these spheres to sport participation denote the flow of advocacy either into sport or extending outwards from it. The other major domain, the enterprise of sport, is surrounded by a constellation of spheres that include advocacy against sport, advocacy that targets sport, and the commodification of sport for advocacy. The overlap between sport participation and the entity of sport is the realm of sport for development and peace (SDP). It is worth noting that, while treated independently for the sake of this review, there is in reality sizeable overlap between these domains, as they mutually inform one another and contribute to larger socio-cultural agendas.

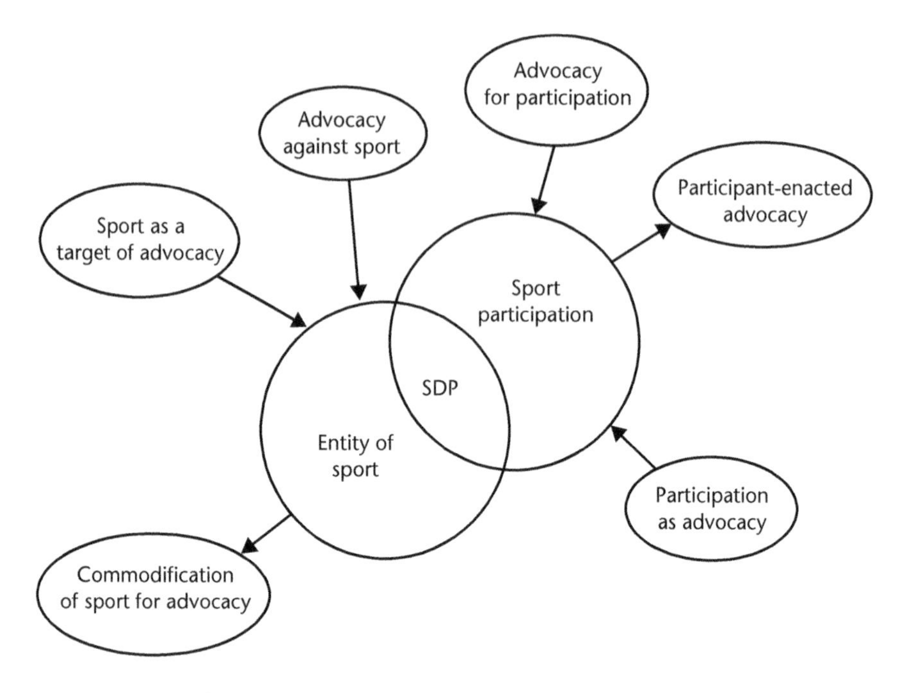

FIGURE 43.1 Domains of sport and advocacy

Advocacy and sport participation

Advocacy for sport participation

While sport arguably has universal appeal, it historically has been exclusionary. For this reason, one sphere of advocacy related to sport simply concerns advocating for involvement with and in sport (Barnett and Hardin, 2010; Stevenson, Rowe, and Markwell, 2005). As noted by Barnett and Hardin, this has been most pronounced, perhaps, with the struggles that women have confronted to achieve equal access and treatment in sport. Women's sports advocacy groups have emerged in many places in response to this ongoing struggle (Comeau and Church, 2010). These groups focus on addressing lower participation rates for women and girls, lack of representation of women in leadership roles, and the image of women in sport. Barnett and Hardin examined press releases related to Title IX that were crafted by the Women's Sports Foundation (WSF), the leading women's sports advocacy group in the US. The WSF framed cooperation and community as keys to ensuring women's access to sport alongside collaboration with a variety of constituents. Their press releases "served as calls to collective action to end discrimination for women wanting to play sports" (Barnett and Hardin, 2010, p. 185) and celebrated distinguished women athletes as influential contributors to society and the sport community. The group also plugged into the capability of sport to be transcendent and transformative for people by improving their social and work lives along with their health. Advocacy groups in the US and Canada also encouraged supporters to lobby government officials, educated citizenry, and promoted sport and physical activity for girls and women (Comeau and Church, 2010).

Advocacy for sport participation can manifest in the staging of alternative sporting events. Stevenson, *et al.* (2005) refer to the International Gay Games, which began in 1982 with the intention of dispelling stereotypes about gay athletes, as cosmopolitan advocacy. It incorporates a layered agenda with substrata that span beyond sheer sport to include "a combination of identity, camaraderie, and the carnivalesque at the expense of competition, winning, or overt political resistance" (Stevenson, *et al.*, 2005, p. 449). Finally, advocacy for sport participation can be seen in extreme circumstances where sport helps promote normalcy (Korr, 2010). This was the case for political prisoners on Robben Island in South Africa. They waged a four-year campaign that resulted in the creation of a football league, perhaps "the most exceptional football league ever organized" (Korr, 2010, p. 34).

Advocacy enacted by sports participants

This section considers how sports participants have used sport as a stage to practice advocacy (Kaufman and Wolf, 2010; Meân, Kassing, and Sanderson, 2010; Power, 2011). Kaufman and Wolf identified and interviewed 21 activist athletes. They uncovered four predominant themes that defined athletes' experiences. First, athlete activists developed a social conscientiousness, recognizing that sport was a potent platform from which to mobilize change. Second, the performance-based reward system inculcated in sport sensitized them to take up causes where meritocracy was not the standard of operation. Third, responsible citizenship grew when athletes embraced sport as a politicized place rather than an apolitical space and when they recognized their capacity to not only be good, but to do good. Fourth, they recognized the role interdependence played when achieving athletic goals that depended on the help of others, teamwork, and connection. In addition, athletes spoke about how endemic athletic characteristics, like discipline and striving for progress, translated well to the arduous and unpublicized acts required of activists.

In some instances advocacy unfolds directly during or as the result of sport performance (Meân, *et al.*, 2010; Muller Myrdahl, 2011). With regard to contested performances, American cyclist and dethroned Tour de France champion Floyd Landis' defense against allegations of doping turned into a full blown advocacy campaign targeted at the inconsistencies and punitive inclination of the doping establishment (Meân, *et al.*, 2010). Landis started the Floyd Fairness Foundation, barnstorming across the US to drum up support and raise money for his defense during the months between his initial guilty verdict and the subsequent hearing of his appeal in front of the Court of Arbitration for Sport. In the interim he often roundly criticized the United States Doping Agency, cycling's governing body the Union Cycliste Internationale, and the French laboratory that produced the positive test for testosterone by posting press releases on his website. His advocacy campaign proved ineffectual, as he ended up stripped of his title and banned from the sport for two years and disingenuous when he admitted several years later to systematic doping during his career.

While Landis ended up sanctioned by the sport's governing body, other athlete advocates have suffered under the weight of public scrutiny. This was certainly true for collegiate basketball player, Toni Smith, who turned her back on the US flag during the playing of the national anthem prior to games. Her on-court expression of dissent displayed to protest US involvement in Iraq became newsworthy and widespread, meeting with disapproval from critics and fans alike. Underlying the criticism was the fundamental premise that athletes should not be political or social activists in sport space (that is, on courts, fields, and pitches) and that sport should remain apolitical. Ironically, this sentiment prevails, despite the fact that sport space is highly nationalized through pre-game rituals that include military flyovers, facing the flag, and singing the national anthem (Muller Myrdahl, 2011).

Sport fans have a history of practicing advocacy alongside their sporting heroes. For example, in January of 2007, fans of Liverpool Football Club attending a home match sang a repeated chorus of "Justice for the Ninety-Six" vociferously for six uninterrupted minutes at the beginning of the game. While Liverpool fans have a strong history of singing a variety of songs during their matches, this was unusual for two reasons. First, it drew people's attention away from the match. Second, it overrode the competitive discourse routinely expressed in songs and chants between supporters of competing clubs. The song was the result of weeks of orchestrated lobbying by Return to the Kop, a group of devoted fans who hoped to restore singing as a key piece of Liverpool fan culture. But there was more to it than that. As a work of advocacy that day, the song was particularly resonant because it publicly and directly contested the BBC's use of Kelvin McKenzie as a panelist and presenter. McKenzie had maligned the Liverpool faithful in a piece he wrote in response to the 1999 Hillsborough disaster that claimed the lives of 96 Liverpool fans due to crushing. Liverpool fans were never implicated in the formal investigation, but McKenzie ran a front-page story that condemned and blamed them for the tragedy (Power, 2011).

Sport participation as advocacy

The enactment of sport participation can serve as a mechanism for advocacy as well (Anderson, 2009; Atkinson, 2009; Lindemann and Cherney, 2008). In these instances, the very act of participation takes shape as a form of advocacy. The Special Olympics and the Paralympic Games emerged from this premise. As noted by Anderson, athletes competing despite physical disabilities benefit from identity development, particularly athletic identity. In addition, participation challenges ableist assumptions about disability, masculinity, and ability (Lindemann and Cherney, 2008). Thus, participation in sport provides a venue that serves to advocate for marginalized, underserved, and disenfranchised people and in doing so challenges societal assumptions of these groups.

Sport and identity are inextricably linked (Meân, 2001). As a consequence, sport can serve as a powerful form of advocacy that promotes social, political, and national identity (Sorek, 2009). For boxers in the 1960s, sport participation served to mute long-standing social differences and protest between Israeli and Palestinian men, while simultaneously constructing a social space where Arab men could rehabilitate their diminished image of masculinity and national pride (Sorek, 2009). Similarly, sport participation can be a vehicle for youth development, particularly in impoverished and underserved communities (Wamucii, 2011). For example, residents of a Nairobi slum who participated in a youth sports outreach program felt a degree of prestige as a result of their affiliation with the organization and took great pride in the soccer team it sponsored, despite the lack of opportunities afforded them in their daily lives (Wamucii, 2011).

Thus, sport participation can advance positive and recuperative identities when positioned as a form of advocacy. It also can foster activist attitudes (Atkinson, 2009). In an ethnography of traceurs (Parkour runners), Atkinson found that participants consider themselves to be modern urban critics – drawing attention to the capitalist dominance of city space and the modalities of movement they implicate. "Urban traceurs illustrate the schism between the natural body, free movement and the environment" (Atkinson, 2009, p. 185) by throwing into contrast what is permissible in urban spaces. As one traceur stated, "basic things like running and jumping [in open public] are weird or against the rules" and another added "It's about not looking at city block as a pre-mapped out space that indicates where you can and cannot go."

Advocacy and the entity of sport

Advocacy against sport

While universally popular, sport is not without its detractors. In fact, there is much to loathe about sport – its capacity to exclude, marginalize, and stereotype to name a few. Thus, it is not surprising that there has been extensive advocacy directed at various aspects of sport. These include but are not limited to concerns about the use of mascots (Davis-Delano, 2007; Miller, 1999), the environmental and cultural impact of sport (Barnes, 2009; Ngonyama, 2010), exclusionary practices (McDonald, 2008), and athlete misbehavior (Dimitrov, 2008; Wilson, 2002). The scope and breadth of these advocacy efforts directed at sport bring into relief the cultural and social significance of sport and the need at times to challenge the seemingly impermeable entrenchment of sport within culture.

The choice and use of Native American mascots has come under fire (Davis-Delano, 2007; Miller, 1999). Davis-Delano reviewed both successful and unsuccessful cases advocating for the removal of offensive Native American mascots. Successful cases of dismissal were marked by strong leadership, word-of-mouth recruitment, knowledge and skills, development of local support, and building Native support for opposition. Miller examined Native American advocacy enacted during the 1995 World Series between the Cleveland Indians and the Atlanta Braves. One tactic involved Native American advocates physically positioning themselves outside Major League Baseball (MLB) parks in both cities to demonstrate how indigenous people were different than their stereotypes. Another tactic entailed drawing attention to the insensitive underpinnings of the practice by dressing in hyperstereotypical attire representing black faced old-timey entertainers, Ku Klux Klansmen, and the Pope. Through these collective efforts American Indians successfully raised conscientiousness about "the bastardization of Native American symbols and rituals by the dominant culture" (Miller, 1999, p. 199).

Another flashpoint for advocacy against sport stems from the choice of locations to host sporting events (Barnes, 2009; Ngonyama, 2010). In these instances, advocates give voice to cultural, societal, and environmental concerns. The first Eco-Challenge race held in southern Utah in 1995 was met with protests from environmentalists who were concerned with the commercial nature of the event and the possibility of overuse and degradation of pristine areas (Barnes, 2009). Similarly, criticism was widespread when the 2010 FIFA World Cup was hosted in South Africa (Ngonyama, 2010). The tournament relied heavily on volunteers in a country strapped with 40 percent unemployment. It required the removal of slums to accommodate development of needed facilities and demanded the redirecting of funds away from the poor and toward staging the event. And it legitimized the payment of insufficient wages to construction workers responsible for building the new facilities. Advocates surfaced in response to all of these apparent miscalculations in the lead up to the World Cup. As a powerful force that brings with it significant social, cultural, economic, and environmental impact, sport carries a sizeable footprint – one that is not lost on advocates who attend to the consequences of hosting major sporting events.

The missteps of professional athletes and those that mirror their behavior are plentiful. Advocacy against sport surfaces when such behavior is particularly egregious and uncontested (Dimitrov, 2008; Wilson, 2002). For example, in Australia, fans started the advocacy organization, Football Fans against Sexual Assault, in response to several high-profile cases of violence against women perpetrated by Australian football and rugby players. In a concerted and ongoing effort the group practiced what Dimitrov called "fan advocacy" – a coordinated public relations strategy that stressed representing and behaving as fans rather than experts. In other cases, advocacy develops out of a desire to address those that emulate superstar athletes (that is, "jocks"). Wilson explored the use of the Internet by advocates of the "anti-jock" movement. Participants combined to provide helpful, proactive, and direct strategies for addressing jocks as well as outlets for maligning them. Together these web destinations promoted an alternative society that refrained from subjecting people to the dominant interests of a jock-infused masculinist sport culture.

A final instance in which advocacy against sport emerges involves advocacy directed at the institutions that govern, promote, and organize sport. McDonald (2008) offered an interesting case that considered the "kiss-in" held by the "Lesbians for Liberty" during a nationally televised game between the New York Liberty and Miami Sol of the Women's National Basketball Association (WNBA). Participants in the protest kissed during every time out in an effort to bring attention to the franchise's failure to recognize and reach out to its sizeable lesbian fan base. As part of a larger effort, the group also posted a list of seven demands on their website and handed out pamphlets at the fan appreciation night that directly and clearly recognized and thanked lesbian fans.

Sport as a target for advocacy

Occasionally, sport ends up being the target of advocacy, a venue in or platform upon which people can advocate for a particular cause (Kay, 2008; MacLean, 2010; Palmer, 2001). This was the case with early suffragettes in Edwardian England. They aimed their militant attacks at various sport venues. Golf courses were attacked initially with slogans like "Votes for women" carved into the greens before the campaign spread to horseracing, cricket, tennis, bowling, football, rowing, swimming, billiards and rugby premises. In their wake, suffragettes destroyed boathouses, grandstands, tennis courts, and cricket pavilions. Though the press coverage of these incidents was limited, damage was extensive throughout the country (Kay, 2008).

Iconic sporting events like the Tour de France provide a global stage for advocates (Palmer, 2001). While many protestors have used the race as a backdrop, the most enduring advocacy performed during the Tour can be attributed to the Basque separatists who worked annually during the 1990s to usurp and upstage the symbol of French national identity. When the race entered the Basque homeland that straddles the French and Spanish border, the region was awash with symbols of Basque nationalism which included pamphlets advocates distributed, buttons and hats emblazoned with patriotic colors, and roads painted with the Basque flag and nationalistic declarations. More aggressive actions included storming stage villages to prevent the race from starting and littering the road with nails and tacks to keep support vehicles from progressing.

The potential for major sporting events to incite advocacy unfolded in 1981 when the South African Springboks rugby team visited New Zealand. Reaction to the rugby tour promoted massive and ongoing anti-apartheid protests. Twice a week for 56 days thousands of New Zealanders faced off against riot police and ended up baton charged, assaulted, and imprisoned. The advocacy campaign began with mass demonstrations 18 months prior to the arrival of the Springboks whereby activists unsuccessfully lobbied to have players refused visas to enter the country. Subsequently, pitch invasions led to the cancellation of two matches, while one-third ended up being played in a barbed wire fortified stadium (MacLean, 2010).

The commodification of sport for advocacy

The proliferation of LIVESTRONG yellow bands and the invasion of pink embellishments in sports uniforms during the month of October (Breast Cancer Awareness Month) signal the clear bond between sport and commodification in the service of advocacy. Clearly, advocacy can leverage the commodification and commercialization of sport. Major sports merchandise corporations like Nike and PUMA have become involved in advocacy endeavors (Cole, 1996; Giardina, 2010). PUMA made a concerted effort to sponsor several African nation football sides, while also providing financial support for activist organizations in the region (Giardina, 2010). Competitor Nike launched the P.L.A.Y. (Participate in the Lives of Youth) campaign in an attempt to promote access to sport for kids. But Nike's altruistic venture has been criticized for promoting the company as patriotic, charitable, and socially responsible while obscuring their global impact and the campaign's simplistic bifurcation of playing sport over joining a gang (Cole, 1996). Other work has examined the transnational advocacy network – a collection of labor, human rights, and religious organizations that confronted the labor practices of Nike. A four-year campaign ended in substantial changes to Nike's labor practices that included minimum age requirements, improved standards for monitoring health and safety, better education programs for workers, and substantial pay increases in certain sectors (Sage, 1999).

Sport for Development and Peace

While sport and advocacy come together for a variety of reasons, they are intentionally and purposefully deployed in concert within the SDP movement (Kidd, 2008; Sugden, 2010). Accordingly, SDP forefronts the capacity of sport to be used to address humanitarian relief, post-war reconciliation, and social development. Early manifestations of sport development included efforts to improve middle and working class in the late nineteenth century and the playground movement of the early twentieth century, but the most recent incarnation differs in that its propagation is agency and organization driven, volunteer-centric, financially backed by major international sports federations, and endorsed by the United Nations (Kidd, 2008). The benefits of SDP can be far reaching, creating a ripple effect that extends from the children involved through significant others like coaches, parents, teachers, and on to local politicians, networked partnerships, policy communities, and political society (Sugden, 2010).

Yet SDP is also a cautionary tale punctuated by corporate, colonial, and governmental overtones (Black, 2010; Darnell and Mayhurst, 2011; Guilianotti, 2004). For example, Guilianotti criticized SDP for treating sport as primarily functional while disregarding its potential to express and intensify nationalism, sexism, racism, and xenophobia. When deployed in this way, sport acts as a neocolonial mechanism. Scholars have responded to these concerns by forwarding suggestions for new research and methodological approaches that enable the decolonization of SDP (Darnell and Mayhurst, 2011) and with suggestions for choosing local sport celebrities that, according to Black, "highlight the resilience and creativity of local communities rather than the benevolence and celebrity of these sporting heroes" (Black, 2010, p. 126).

A recent series of discourse analysis studies provide a glimpse into the internal operations, strategies, and attitudes of those involved with SDP interventions (Darnell 2010; Guilianotti, 2011; Hayhurst, 2009). Interviews with SDP officials from a variety of organizations across several continents revealed that they stressed the development for and not of sport so as to deflect criticism about the marketing and colonization of particular sports. Officials also espoused the value of sport for connecting people in divided and conflict-laden regions or societies, but recognized the need to promote sport first and foremost instead of the peace and community building functions it could possibly serve. Connecting to and keep ties with families, local communities, and area authorities proved important as well (Guilianotti, 2011). Whereas shared objectives and strategies for enacting SDP are clearly operational, policy documents remain quite ambiguous (Hayhurst, 2009). Nonetheless, these same policy documents reflect obvious political agendas as well as the interests of donors, United Nations agencies, and nongovernmental organizations. The tension between policy and practice was captured interestingly enough by interns working in SDP organizations. They understood sport to be a vehicle for overcoming social inequality, facilitating leadership and responsibility, and establishing social mobility. At the same time interns recognized how these factors compounded momentum in the movement that, according to Darnell (2010, p. 69), "precluded a reflexive and critical perspective."

Conclusion

This chapter negotiated the varied terrain of sport and advocacy research. Communication, while not always pronounced in the chapter, certainly underlies the enactment of advocacy in sport contexts – whether that take the form of disabled athletes talking about their experiences in sport, fans singing protests songs at matches, or organizations campaigning for sport inclusion or sport development. Essentially, communication bridges sport and advocacy through discourse, identity, activism, protest, dissent, public relations, and communication campaigns. There are examples of each contained here as well as instances where one can see how these communicative acts intertwine in intricate, complex and layered ways. Thus, seeing sport and advocacy as a product of communication requires attending to both the ebb and flow and the shape shifting nature of it.

We can look to the fluctuation and adaptation of the IOC to illustrate the fluidity of sport and advocacy. In the early decades after its inception, the IOC emphasized sport as a mechanism for benefitting the progress of an international society. In the postwar period, the inclusion of newly independent states and the development of their sporting infrastructures took precedence with a focus on welcoming developing countries and former colonies into the international community. In the years after the collapse of the Soviet Union, the IOC turned its attention to making the games a true representation of global participation. And most recently, the IOC has brought to the fore a grassroots community-centered participatory approach to social change through SDP (Peacock, 2011).

Although riddled with tension and discord, sport is a formidable platform for advocacy that merits the continued attention of sport scholars. We still have much to learn about how advocacy can enlarge the scope of participants in sport and bolster the identity of those traditionally excluded from it. How participants can use sport to promote and campaign for an array of causes. And how sport can benefit from and evolve as a result of being the focus and target of advocacy. Additionally, consideration of how sport commodification and commercialization get affixed to matters of advocacy could prove beneficial. Athletes' foundations, fan support organizations, fundraising efforts that commodify sport performance and achievement, health and wellbeing campaigns endorsed by associations, governing bodies, and leagues, and athletic organizations designed to serve the underprivileged and disabled are all fertile ground for pursuing future research in the area. Sport often is grand and dramatic. And when devoted to advocacy it can become something noble.

References

Anderson, D. (2009). Adolescent girls' involvement in disability sport: Implications for identity development. *Journal of Sport and Social Issues*, 33, 427–49.

Atkinson, M. (2009). Parkour, anarcho-environmentalism, and poiesis. *Journal of Sport and Social Issues*, 33, 169–94.

Barnes, B. A. (2009). "Everybody wants to pioneer something out here": Landscape, adventure, and biopolitics in the American Southwest. *Journal of Sport and Social Issues*, 33, 230–56.

Barnett, B., and Hardin, M. C. (2010). Advocacy from the liberal feminist playbook: The framing of Title IX and women's sports in news releases from the Women's Sports Foundation. *International Journal of Sport Communication*, 3, 178–97.

Black, D. R. (2010). The ambiguities of development: Implications for 'development through sport'. *Sport in Society*, 13 (1), 121–9.

Cole, C. L. (1996). American Jordan: P.L.A.Y., consensus, and punishment. *Sociology of Sport Journal*, 13, 366–97.

Comeau, G. S., and Church, A. G. (2010). A comparative analysis of women's sports advocacy groups in Canada and the United States. *Journal of Sport and Social Issues*, 34, 457–74.

Darnell, S. C. (2010). Power, politics and "Sport for Development and Peace": Investigating the utility of sport for international development. *Sociology of Sport Journal*, 27, 54–75.

Darnell, S. C., and Mayhurst, L. M. C. (2011). Sport for decolonization: Exploring a new praxis of sport for development. *Progress in Development Studies*, 11 (3), 183–96.

Davis-Delano, L. R. (2007). Eliminating Native American mascots: Ingredients for success. *Journal of Sport and Social Issues*, 31, 340–73.

Dimitrov, R. (2008). Gender violence, fan activism and public relations in sport: The case of "Footy Fans against Sexual Assault". *Public Relations Review*, 34, 90–8.

Furness, Z. (2005). Biketivism and technology: Historical reflections and appropriations. *Social Epistemology*, 19 (4), 401–17.

Giardina, M. D. (2010). One day, one goal? PUMA, corporate philanthropy and the cultural politics of brand 'Africa'. *Sport in Society*, 13 (1), 130–42.

Guilianotti, R. (2004). Human rights, globalization and sentimental education: The case of sport. *Sport in Society*, 7 (3), 355–69.

Guilianotti, R. (2011). Sport, transnational peacemaking, and global civil society: Exploring the reflective discourses of "Sport, Development, and Peace" Project officials. *Journal of Sport and Social Issues*, 35, 50–71.

Hartmann, D. (1996). The politics of race and sport: Resistance and domination in the 1968 African American Olympic protest movement. *Ethnic and Racial Studies*, 19 (3), 548–66.

Hayhurst, L. M. C. (2009). The power to shape policy: Charting sport for development and peace policy discourses. *International Journal of Sport Policy*, 1 (2), 203–27.

Kaufman, P., and Wolf, E. A. (2010). Playing and protesting: Sport as a vehicle for social change. *Journal of Sport and Social Issues*, 34, 154–75.

Kay, J. (2008). It wasn't just Emily Davison! Sport, suffrage and society in Edwardian Britain. *International Journal of the History of Sport*, 25 (10), 1338–54.

Kay, J., and Wray, V. (2010). Beyond altruism: British football and charity, 1877–1914. *Soccer and Society*, 11 (3), 181–97.

Kidd, B. (2008). A new social movement: Sport for development and peace. *Sport in Society*, 4, 370–80.

Korr, C. (2010). Tony Suze's reflections on the importance of sport in the struggle to end Apartheid. *Sport in Society*, 13 (1), 32–5.

Lindemann, K., and Cherney, J. L. (2008). Communicating in and through "Murderball": Masculinity and disability in wheelchair rugby. *Western Journal of Communication*, 72, 107–25.

MacLean, M. (2010). Anti-apartheid boycotts and the affective economies of struggle: The case of Aotearoa New Zealand. *Sport in Society*, 13 (1), 72–91.

McDonald, M. G. (2008). Rethinking resistance: The queer play of the Women's National Basketball Association, visibility politics and late capitalism. *Leisure Studies*, 27 (1), 77–93.

Meân, L. (2001). Identity and discursive practice: Doing gender on the football pitch. *Discourse and Society*, 12, 789–815.

Meân, L. J., Kassing, J. W., and Sanderson, J. (2010). The making of an epic (American) hero fighting for justice: Commodification, consumption, and intertextuality in the Floyd Landis defense campaign. *American Behavioral Scientist*, 53, 1590–609.

Miller, J. B. (1999). "Indians," "Braves," and "Redskins": A performative struggle for control of an image. *Quarterly Journal of Speech*, 85, 188–202.

Muller Myrdahl, T. (2011). Politics "out of place"? Making sense of conflict in sport spaces. *Leisure/Loisir*, 35 (2), 153–68.

Ngonyama, P. (2010). The 2010 FIFA World Cup: Critical voices from below. *Soccer and Society*, 11 (1–2), 168–80.

Palmer, C. (2001). Outside the imagined community: Basque terrorism, political activism, and the Tour de France. *Sociology of Sport Journal*, 18, 143–61.

Peacock, B. (2011). 'A secret instinct of social preservation': Legitimacy and the dynamic (re)constitution of Olympic conceptions of the 'good'. *Third World Quarterly*, 32 (3), 477–502.

Peterson, J. (2009). A 'race' for equality: Print media coverage of the 1968 Olympic Protest by Tommie Smith and John Carlos. *American Journalism*, 26 (2), 99–121.

Power, B. (2011). Justice for the ninety-six: Liverpool FC fans and uncommon use of football song. *Soccer and Society*, 12 (1), 96–112.

Sage, G. H. (1999). Just do it! The Nike transnational advocacy network: Organization, collective actions, and outcomes. *Sociology of Sport Journal*, 16, 206–35.

Sorek, T. (2009). The only place where an Arab can hit a Jew and get a medal for it': Boxing and masculine pride among Arab citizens of Israel. *Sport in Society*, 12 (8), 1065–74.

Stevenson, D. S., Rowe, D., and Markwell, K. (2005). Explorations in 'event ecology': The case of the International Gay Games. *Social Identities*, 11 (5), 447–65.

Sugden, J. (2010). Critical left-realism and sport interventions in divided societies. *International Review for the Sociology of Sport*, 45 (3), 258–72.

Wamucii, P. (2011). Walking the extra mile: Navigating slum identities through social activism in Mathare, Kenya. *Howard Journal of Communications*, 22, 183–99.

Wilson, B. (2002). The "anti-jock" movement: Reconsidering youth resistance, masculinity, and sport culture in the age of the Internet. *Sociology of Sport Journal*, 19, 206–33.

44

THE CULTURE OF COMMUNICATION IN ATHLETICS

Frederick L. Battenfield

The last three decades have brought forth massive paradigmatic changes in the methods that professional sport communicators use to communicate in the performance of their job responsibilities, and that has set in motion a change in the culture of communication inside the offices of these individuals. Those engaged in sport communication prior to the mid 1980s used devices that are now housed in museums, like the typewriter, mimeograph machine, or telecopier. The dissemination of information was conducted mainly through hard-wired telephones and traditional postal services. Modern sport communication has evolved rapidly into a succession of electronic technology that has permanently changed the communicative culture into one of the omnipresent email, text, blog, PDF file, tweet, or any other device readily available. However, a scholarly argument could be made that this electronologically fueled development is not necessarily in the best interest of the sport communication industry. This chapter takes a theoretical look at the development of the culture of communication within the sport industry, the methodology for acquiring data, and analysis of the patterns that emerge from a unique sport communication model. But most importantly, a robust description is presented as to why the discovery of the communicative culture inside a sport program has demonstrative value to athletic administrators.

The dawning of the communication age

James Lull, in his 2002 book, *Culture in the Communication Age*, rightly describes the dawning of the communication age, which he noted is the efficient transmission of digitized bits and bytes and signifies the entire communication process for real people. Out of this definition, several stimulating questions must be asked: Has the communicative culture of modern society become engrossed in communicating mainly with technology? Have our symbolic exchanges facilitated by high technology and new networks of complex connectivity (Tomlinson, 1999) become the primary expressions of basic human communication? Has real face-to-face human contact become obsolete and "transmogrified into seamless robotic conversations with databanks somewhere in cyberspace?" (Lull, 2002, p. 1).

Prior to Battenfield's (2004) three-month longitudinal study of the culture of communication inside a Division I-A football playing institution, minimal research had been conducted about the communication patterns existing for the primary purveyor of athletic communications – the sports information director (SID). In addition, any scholarly attempts to study the transition from an old-school communications culture, to today's recognized technological communication age, has been limited. Lull presents the term "communication age" as an umbrella term to "broaden, humanize, and make more accurate a description and interpretation of this exciting era" (Lull, 2002, p. 1). He notes that information technologies have sped up and altered some of the ways human beings communicate. Yet, in his opinion, the motivations behind the practices and actions that people use to construct their social and cultural worlds remain virtually unchanged.

In a sporting context, the statement that information technology has become our dominant mode of human communication must be better defined. Battenfield (2004) utilized an intensive qualitative study, an ethnography of communication, to try to create insight into the highly specific culture which exists among sport communicators. His longitudinal observations, conducted over months of data collection, reveal deep detail about how the electronic has surpassed the verbal as the sport communicator's primary method of communication.

Methods for discovering the culture of sport communication

To facilitate the accrual of new information on communication in college athletics, an ethnographic methodology was employed to obtain answers regarding the culture of the sports information office. A naturalistic, or discovery-oriented phenomenological inquiry, where the research takes place in real-world settings and the researcher does not attempt to manipulate the phenomenon of interest (Dobbert, 1982; Guba, 1978; Hammersley and Atkinson, 1995), is the methodological approach chosen for Battenfield's study. Clifford Geertz' (1973) concept of going native and providing thick description of the observed group was central to the study of the sport communicators. Battenfield observed them in their natural work environment and the intentions, motives, beliefs, rules, and values of the group were collected and evaluated. Denzin (1978) noted that the primary goal of naturalism is to capture the culture from within and understand it. By living close to the culture, the outside observer can acquire a certain objectivity to better interpret the behaviors of the group. The existence of specific communicative cultural patterns within the SID office will be the outcome of the ethnographic research process.

Several communication practices were observed and evaluated in Battenfield's study. The study of language, verbal and non-verbal, spoken and written in this sports context, is one facet. Communicative interactions between the entire SID staff were another primary section of the study. Additionally, the technology used by the SID staff to communicate, leadership issues, and tensions that arose owing to office space limitations, excessive overtime, and stress, were evaluated. The artifacts produced by the staff, ranging from press releases, media guides and website updates, to press passes and photography, were also observed, along with staff rituals and traditions. The goal of Battenfield's study was to observe the daily operations of the sport communications office, watch closely how the staff interacted with each other and attempt to "crack the code" of the group's communication culture. The examination of athletic rituals and traditions practiced by the SID office at this large football playing institution provided rich data on the culture of sports information. At the conclusion of the study, Battenfield discovered particular themes that clarified how communicators actually communicate with each other and with internal and external publics. Following the analysis of the volume of raw data, Battenfield was able to generate insightful recommendations to the communications group that was studied, to other major university SID offices, and to athletic administrators about the effectiveness of the communication patterns utilized by sport communicators.

Toward an understanding of sport culture

Sport administrators and communications professionals frequently ask the question, "Why do I need to know anything about the culture within my organization?" Realistically, a critical evaluation of the culture inside the organization can provide invaluable awareness into the inner dynamics of which the administrator may or may not be aware. By embracing this conceptual idea of the culture of communication, administrators can become more aware of the communication activities inside each functional area within their management domain. The study of culture is the desire to observe and record the behavior patterns, beliefs and traditions deeply rooted in a people (Patton, 2002; Sands, 2002; Spradley, 1980). Spradley further defines culture as the acquired knowledge that people use to interpret experience and generate behavior. When ethnographers study other cultures, they must deal with three fundamental aspects of the human experience: What people do, what people know, and the things people make and use. When members of a group share these, we speak of them as cultural behavior, cultural knowledge, and cultural artifacts.

Sands (2002) stated "sport reflects culture and culture reflects sport" (p. 150). In his book *Sport Ethnography*, Sands argues that sport has become a dominant part of contemporary human society. He posits, "Sport is pervasive and never ceasing, casting giant shadows on other facets of life. For a culture, a world to go crazy over a ball game, a camel race, a lacrosse match, a run, speaks volumes about human behavior" (p. 150). Besides Sands' naturalistic sports ethnographical studies, a large body of popular books, like *From Red Ink to Roses* (Telander, 1994), *Friday Night Lights* (Bissinger, 1990), *Hockey Night in Canada* (Gruneau and Whitson, 1993), and *A Season On The Brink* (Feinstein, 1986) have been written to chronicle sport culture. These are examples of researchers and journalists immersing themselves in the sporting culture and then reporting the ensuing cultural patterns that emerge.

Toward an understanding of communications culture

Communication is highly pervasive in our society, and is an important, yet complex aspect of human life (Littlejohn, 1999). As noted by Littlejohn, communication is central to all human experience; it separates us from other animals because of our ability to communicate at a higher level, and helps to create meaning in our everyday experiences. Because the process of communication is so complex, a precise definition is arguably impossible to put forward. Dance and Larson (1976) listed 126 different definitions of communication in *The Functions of Human Communication: A Theoretical Approach*, and it is one of the most overused terms in the English language (Clevenger, 1991).

Communication is a complex expression that is the focus of many studies in modern society. The addition of modern technological devices such as personal computers, cellular telephones, and the Internet, have made the examination of this subject even more convoluted. Because of society's fanatical interest in sport, a study of the communication behaviors in an SID office could provide answers to the questions relating to the verbal and electronic communication in college athletics. Battenfield's 2004 study of the daily interactions inside a Division I-A communication office was used in this chapter to assess whether the communicative issues of modern society have reached the gatekeepers of access to the inner workings of intercollegiate athletics (for example, the SID).

A unique theoretical framework

The selection of a theoretical framework to examine the culture of communication inside the working domain of the sport communications office is a matter of what Patton (2002) called "methodological appropriateness." Battenfield utilized a phenomenological, naturalistic approach because of his extensive background as a sport communication professional, and a profound interest in discovering a realistic view of the communicative culture of the sports information office. Each culture has its own behaviors, beliefs, values, morals and worldviews, but the overall culture is manifested through the use of symbols, which are understood through the expression of social behavior (Sands, 2002). All social interaction is symbolic, and meaning is derived from the way in which these symbols are constructed and put to use. As noted by Sands, participants involved in the interactions that produce meaning cannot explain how they know the meaning of the behaviors, but they consistently act in ways that others can understand and interpret. The interpretation of culture is trying to understand a culture's way of life (or, its cultural reality, according to Sands). Bronislaw Malinowski, followed by Geertz and others, said that ethnography is an attempt at seeing culture through the "eyes of the native" – and what Geertz (1973) also said, figuring out "what the devil they think they are up to" (p. 58).

The ethnography of communication is the application of ethnographic methods to the communication patterns of a group (Littlejohn, 1999). More simply, the interpreter attempts to make sense of the forms of communication employed by the members of the group or culture. This study of language, verbal and non-verbal, spoken and written in its social context, forms the basis for ethnography of communication. Formed in the traditions of linguistics and anthropology in the 1960s and 1970s by anthropologist Dell Hymes, the ethnography of communication seeks to discover the communicative conduct of a community; this conduct is the unit of analysis in the study. Noted ethnographer Gerry Philipsen (1989) presented four assumptions of the ethnography of communication: 1) participants in a local cultural community create shared meaning, or, they use codes that have some degree of common understanding; 2) communicators in any cultural group must coordinate their actions; there must be some order or system when individuals communicate; 3) meanings and actions are particular to individual cultural groups; and 4) not only are the patterns of behavior and codes different from group to group, but each group also has its own way of understanding certain codes and actions.

Methodology to discover a communications culture

Battenfield's (2004) three-month ethnographic study, still the only work of its kind to date, has provided rich data on precisely how sport communicators communicate. A participant observation methodology, combined with structured and informal interviews to examine the culture, the building of individual relationships, and the symbols, rituals and other icons of the sports public relations business, were central to data collection. Analysis of field notes and audio recordings, divulged much about this distinctive sports culture. The primary focus of the data collection related to what was happening to individuals in a setting and how individuals were affected by the setting (Patton, 2002). Data collection was chronicled in the ethnographic record, which is the compilation of field notes, transcripts of audio recordings, reviews of SID artifacts and documents, and other methods of communication used by the sports information staff. The actual processes in the record (such as participant observation), interviews, and a review of documents, symbols, rituals, and icons, were included.

The methods for data analysis are vital to the discovery of the culture of communication. The goal of the initial phase of data analysis was to organize, catalogue, and code the voluminous amount of raw field notes, interview transcriptions, artifacts, and other observational data. Additionally, ethical concerns such as trustworthiness of the data, the credibility of the researcher, the control of bias, and the maintenance of confidentiality for the study participants, are other components of the Battenfield's ethnographical look at SIDs. The analysis of data from an ethnography of communication is essential to identifying the communications culture of an organization. However, Littlejohn (1999) stated that recognizing that cultures are very different from one another makes generalization difficult. The sports information office is a unique and distinct sporting subculture, so those interested in discovering a particular culture must solely focus their research on the specific culture desired.

The intent of the study was to "crack the code" of communication patterns of sport communicators from a macro perspective, observing all occurrences and incidents to consider all communicative patterns that may occur in the entire athletic department. Battenfield's study was designed to allow a wide-angle look at the interactions of the staff during normal working hours, at home football games (and other selected athletic events), at football operations meetings, athletic staff meetings and the weekly scheduled SID staff meeting. The strategy contained several assumptions, one of which was that the observed events in the SID office occurred in the public domain and were organized and evaluated with respect to the three types of information included in Spradley's (1980) definition of culture. Inferences about the culture of the sports information office were made based on how human behavior was observed, by listening to the oral speech messages, examining the written communications of the SID staff, and by sorting through the artifacts made by the SID office. A second assumption was that the communicative tools used by sports information professionals to interact with each other, with other athletic staffers, and with external publics like news media and fans, were normal tools used in the profession.

The compilation of field notes, transcripts of audio-recorded interviews, reviews of press releases, media guides, promotional materials, website updates, daily emails, official documents, and memorandums, comprised the ethnographic record. This vast body of information resulted in a thorough documentation of what occurred in the sports information office during the study period. Furthermore, qualitative researchers Lincoln and Guba (1985) offer a specific set of criteria that they noted should be used for assessing an ethnographic study. They stated that the research should demonstrate its trustworthiness, and should be linked to credibility, transferability, dependability, and confirmability. Credibility is built by intensive contact in the field, data collected from multiple sources, and by triangulation. Triangulation is a common strategy used by qualitative researchers and it will be employed to affirm the credibility of the data analysis.

Results of the ethnography of communication

Following the analysis of the raw field notes and interview transcripts, in combination with a review of the rituals, traditions, and artifacts of the sports information culture, a series of patterns emerged to define the culture of communication. Overall, there were five dominant communication themes that emerged from this ethnographic study. These included office space, verbal communication, electronic communication, non-verbal communication, and rituals and artifacts.

Office space

Office space was a defining factor in identifying the culture of communication in the SID office. Physical distances between the supervisor's office from the assistants created a culture of separation. The distance between them facilitated an anti-hierarchy culture that festered because of the space issue. Not only did the real space between the offices generate separateness, it also fostered real communication breakdowns.

Verbal communication

From the onset of Battenfield's observations, a pattern of slow responses to phone calls, requests, and other demands on the SID staff were identified as a norm of this culture. The culture of avoidance of real interpersonal communication was a highly problematic finding within this culture. A primary finding was an "over the wall" system of verbal communication. The participants would merely shout over the walls to each other, rather than get up and walk five feet. This unorthodox style to get quick information from each other generated a culture of connectedness between the SIDs. The spatial problem of separated offices was overcome by using this communications technique. Since verbal communication is one of the primary modes of interpersonal communication in the sports information office, this finding became a central finding from the observations. The SIDs explained this away by saying that the fast pace and deadline-driven nature of the business made this form a necessity to make progress on job tasks, but it pointed out a lack of direct interpersonal communication among the group. Another piece of the verbal communication culture was the use of "drive-by" meetings. This was used because of the hurried pace, the vast job load and the pressure of deadlines. Drive-bys are similar to the over-the-wall discussions because of the maximization of interconnectedness between the individual groups during the day.

It should be noted that a culture of surveillance was also identified in Battenfield's observations. This was used by the superior, who mentioned that he used the drive-by meeting to check up on his staff. This practice was upsetting to the staff, as in the interviews they saw the superior's "management by walking around" style as intrusive and distracting, and a culture of avoidance was created, owing to his surveillance style. Furthermore, the repeated use of humor indicated three primary conclusions about SID culture. First, humor was almost unanimously described as a stress buster by the entire staff. Second, humor was revealed as an anti-hierarchy device. Third, a disjointed haphazard degeneration of the communication lines at the end of staff meetings indicated communication problems.

Electronic communication

Lull (2002) believes that electronic communication has become an ever-powerful influence in the shaping of the culture of communication. His description of digitized bits and bytes has become the norm in sport communication. Battenfield's ethnography also discovered that, in the sporting context, electronic communications technology has become a dominant mode of human communication. The contentious shift from a paper culture to electronic technology as the primary method of producing sports information artifacts was a major finding. Thus, an observed key paradigmatic change in SID communications culture was the skirmish along old-school/new-school lines. The confirmation of the PC (personal computer) or PDA (personal digital assistant) as the central communications device in the SID office was a foundational finding of the ethnography. All sport communicators now use it for all tasks within the communication and media relations spectrum; it is a temple, a close companion, and for a major part of the day, a communication device. However, despite the PC/PDA's widespread use, the battle lines of this cultural struggle raged along the lines of old-school SIDs, or those who remained loyal to verbal communication, either face-to-face or via the telephone, deployed against those new-school individuals, a younger, more computer-hip generation who believed in the PC or dataphone as the primary ways to communicate. The old-school/new-school dyad is divided on whether the telephone or the computer is the preferable communications device for SIDs. The old-school staff members were trained during an era when public relations specialists were taught that one-on-one interpersonal communication was the most essential element in good media relations. Their primary tool of choice is the telephone. However, the new-school members clearly eschewed the phone in favor of the PC/PDA.

Non-verbal communication

Two major non-verbal communication findings emerged from the study. The discovery of a technique described as "talk vs. the turn", and the use of body language, facial expressions and eye contact to communicate in specific office situations and other communicative observations, were major discoveries. The talk vs. the turn became a centerpiece element in the culture of sports information. Every member of the SID staff used the talk vs. the turn during the study. The talk occurred when the staff member did not feel like communicating and sent a strong non-verbal message to the interloper to "not bother me right now." The turn was used when the individual was in a more relaxed, communicative mode and would literally turn their entire body toward the questioner to begin a normal human interaction. This machine-gun communications style helped to confirm again that the SIDs communicate on the fly much more than was originally believed. This non-verbal display became part of the culture because they were used as techniques to avoid interpersonal communication. The computer became a shield to avoid human communication by sending this negative non-verbal body message.

Rituals and artifacts

Two predominant rituals materialized from the analysis of the field notes and interviews transcriptions. The first was the conduct of the SIDs during the five high cultural Fall holidays – home football games. The ritual of the home football game fostered a different type of communication between the SIDs. The lack of a written plan to prepare the staff for hosting a large media gathering five times on Saturday led to the conclusion that the communication between the SID staff during the game had indeed become ritual – passed down from superiors and more experienced SIDs to the subordinates through the use of oral tradition. Home football games are a ritual not only for college football fans, but for the SID staff as well. As the definition states, a ritual is a faithfully followed condition characterized by the presence of established procedure or routine. The key words faithfully followed and routine define a key component of SID culture. The oral tradition in preparing the staff for the game, the excitement and subsequent tension that builds up as the game approaches, and the heightened tension during the actual contest are all key components that add to the communicative culture of the sports information director.

The other predominant ritual was the presence and consumption of food in the press box during home games. Food as ritual during home games became important because of the social value importance. It could be surmised that food helps generate enhanced public relations opportunities, and foster better relations with an external public like the news media. Sports information culture was enhanced because the staff was able to interact with each other and the news media over a norm in sports culture.

In terms of artifacts, in sport communication these are objects produced or shaped by human craft, especially those of archaeological or historical interest (Pickett, 2002). The sports information staff spends the majority of its work day (and nights) producing several different types of artifacts – mostly of the printed kind. Press passes, press releases, media guides and game programs, and electronic website documents are the artifacts that consume the SID staff's time. A culture of production, both printed and electronic, is highly evident in this group of sport communicators. A dramatic finding was the importance of press passes as a cultural icon in the SID office. The institution examined in this study spent in excess of US$6,500 to print press passes for five home games. The passes are symbolic of a power mechanism that allows them to control the access and the hierarchy of the press box environment. Press releases are the most frequently produced artifact of the sports information staff. The majority of press releases are disseminated via email and on the department's website. This marked a cultural change away from paper to technological distribution methods fostered by the culture of immediacy derived upon a dependency on the Internet. Media guides and game programs are artifacts where the creativity, resourcefulness, and true production skills of the SID staff are displayed. They spend vast quantities of time, (sitting at the computer), doing layout, updating previous year's statistics, biographical sketches, research, and the most important, time-consuming task – writing. The department website is arguably the most important artifact in the modern SID office. Accessibility and immediacy are now the central tenets for the communicative culture for sport professionals.

Laboring in anonymity

A surprising discovery from this ethnography was the blunt fact that the sport communicators studied labored in virtual anonymity. With the notable exception of home events, the SIDs are immersed in a solitary environment within the walls of either their office or cubicle with the personal computer as their primary companion. The culture that emerged was one of long hours, and a subservient technician's role in the most vital event for the athletic program – a home football game. During home contests, the SIDs remain in shadows, toiling in the background in support of media, athletic administrators and those responsible for running the actual contest.

Communication artifacts are homogeneous products where the writers, designers, and creators are in essence anonymous in the process, and one could argue, meaningless to the actual production. Nameless, faceless people spent countless days, weeks, and months at a keyboard producing a highly anticipated artifact that thousands clamber for each August when the printed version is delivered. Yet, credit for this astonishing piece of journalistic work is limited to a one-inch square box on page one of the guide. Virtual anonymity.

Conclusions

This chapter has been devoted to investigating and providing an analysis of the culture of communication within a major NCAA Division I-A football-playing institution. It should be invaluable to the sport communicator because it may stimulate a different way of observing and evaluating why the culture surrounding sports public relations professionals can reveal more than a perfunctory look would show. As detailed in the sections above, five dominant communicative themes emerged from the ethnographic study: office space; verbal communication; electronic communication; non-verbal communication; and rituals and artifacts. A thorough observational study, detailed field notes, and a complete and reliable analysis of these behavioral patterns, all combine to reveal why studying communications culture is critical. The daily communicative interactions of the study participants, both interpersonal and technological, combined with an assessment of the knowledge they possess and how they acquire it from each other, and a complete appraisal of the rituals they engage in and the artifacts they produce, a much clearer depiction of the culture of communication could be provided. Sport communication professionals work hard to produce the various artifacts required to adequately perform the function of the SID. The artifacts help promote their organization to media, boosters, students, faculty and other internal and external constituents. Yet, the virtual anonymity of the sport communicator, and the various subcultures that were discovered (that is, production, immediacy, separateness, surveillance, and avoidance), show that careful analysis and correct responses to the culture of communication must be exercised by athletic administrators.

The detailed explanation of an ethnography of communication in this chapter may serve as a future research methodology to further study sport communications and perhaps other sport entities. By revealing the communications cultural patterns and themes inherent in a sport culture, a better way to identify how to correct the ubiquitous lack of communication problems can be utilized in the management of sport. Lull may have been correct in his assertion that the communications age is fully embedded into the culture of sport communication, and Battenfield's groundbreaking study on SIDs certainly reaffirmed that statement. Electronic technology has greatly increased the speed at which sport communicators can perform their responsibilities, but there is evidence to indicate that interpersonal communication should not be ignored completely in deference to the gadgets that allow the sport communicator to work solely in the world of the PC/PDA.

References

Battenfield, F. L. (2004). An ethnographic study of the culture of communication in the sports information office at a NCAA Division I-A athletic program. (Unpublished doctoral dissertation). Florida State University, Tallahassee, Florida.

Bissinger, H. G. (1990). *Friday night lights: A town, a team, and a dream*. Reading, MA: Addison-Wesley.

Clevenger, T. (1991). Can one not communicate? A conflict of models. *Communication Studies*, 42, 340–53.

Dance, F. E. X., and Larsen, C. E. (1976). *The functions of human communication: A theoretical approach*. New York: Holt, Rinehart and Winston.

Denzin, N. K. (1978). The logic of naturalistic inquiry. In N. K. Denzin (Ed.), *Sociological methods: A sourcebook* (2nd ed., pp. 6–28). New York: McGraw-Hill.

Dobbert, M. L. (1982). *Ethnographic research*. New York: Praeger.

Feinstein, J. (1986). *A season on the brink: A year with Bob Knight and the Indiana Hoosiers*. New York: Macmillan.

Geertz, C. (Ed.). (1973). *The interpretation of cultures*. New York: Basic.

Gruneau, R. S., and Whitson, D. (1993). *Hockey night in Canada: Sport, identities, and cultural politics*. Toronto: Garamond.

Guba, E. G. (1978). *Toward a methodology of naturalistic inquiry in educational evaluation*. Los Angeles: Center for the Study of Evaluation.

Hammersley, M., and Atkinson, P. (1995). *Ethnography: Principles and practice*. New York: Routledge.

Littlejohn, S. W. (1999). *Theories of human communication*. Belmont, CA: Wadsworth.

Lincoln, Y. S., and Guba, E. (1985). *Naturalistic inquiry*. Beverly Hills, CA: Sage.

Lull, J. (2002). *Culture in the communication age*. London: Routledge.

Patton, M. Q. (2002). *Qualitative research and evaluation methods*. New York: Sage.

Philipsen, G. (1989). An ethnographic approach to communication studies. In B. Dervin, L. Grossberg, B. J. O'Keefe, and E. Wartella, (Eds.). *Rethinking communication: Paradigm exemplars* (pp. 258–69). Newbury Park, CA: Sage.

Pickett, J. P. (2002). *American heritage college dictionary* (4th ed.). Boston: Houghton Mifflin.

Sands, R. R. (2002). *Sport ethnography*. Champaign, IL: Human Kinetics.

Spradley, J. P. (1980). *Participant observation*. New York: Holt, Rinehart and Winston.

Telander. R. (1994). *From red ink to roses*. New York: Simon and Schuster.

Tomlinson, J. (1999). *Globalization and culture*. Cambridge: Polity.

45

STRATEGIC INFLUENCE AND SPORT COMMUNICATION LEADERS

Joe Moore

College sports public relations (PR) directors are the professionals in college athletics charged with publicizing and promoting the department, its student-athletes and coaches. Traditionally referred to as sports information directors (SIDs), they serve as PR specialists, event managers, media liaisons, publications and web professionals, and administrators. As noted in a brochure published by the College Sports Information Directors of America (1993), SIDs "serve as a positive communication link with a variety of the institution's publics, including the staff, media, fans, community members, alumni, student-athletes, parents and prospective students." Because college sports PR directors are connected to these groups more than anyone else, it is imperative that the PR representative be involved in decision-making and leading the athletic department.

Unfortunately, this is not always the case. The members of the College Sports Information Directors of America (CoSIDA) have said they have seen their influence diminish in the last 20 years. Meanwhile, marketing professionals, fundraisers, senior woman administrators, and business managers have surpassed the PR director and claimed the once occupied seat at the decision-making table. CoSIDA's leadership has recognized this and in 2008 initiated a strategic initiative to regain an influential seat at the decision-making table and, as a result, to help practitioners gain more professional stature, including salary and job satisfaction (College Sports Information Directors of America, 2008). They also began to meet with members of the National Association of College Directors of Athletics (NACDA) in an effort to regain some of their lost ground.

Berger and Reber (2006) noted a similar lack of influence as a concern throughout the PR profession. They found that, rather than serving as managers and advisors, PR practitioners in corporations, health care, not-for-profit organizations, and education have been relegated to publicists and "journalists in residence." Through a longitudinal study that included surveys and in-depth interviews, they developed a theory as to why PR directors have lost influence. They learned that two perceptions seemed to prevail as to why PR professionals may suffer from a "power shortage." They suggested the causes are "organizational leaders who just don't get it and professionals who just don't have it" (Berger and Reber, 2006, p. 2). Berger and Reber determined that PR practitioners viewed themselves as too passive, too focused on the technical aspects of their jobs, and lacking in leadership and strategic management skills. As a result, they did not have the influence they desired. These same shortcomings may be found among college sports PR directors who are dissatisfied with their level of strategic influence (Moore, 2011).

As may be expected, for college sports PR directors, experience is vital to gaining more influence. However, experience alone will not suffice. When comparing professional role orientations, leadership personality traits, leadership skills, and leadership styles and their impact on strategic influence, practitioners who have developed their management skills perceive they are considered in higher regard. Assertive directors, those who have strong conceptual leadership skills, and those who are more relationship oriented in their leadership also enjoy more strategic influence. Thus, if college sports PR directors want more strategic influence, and if they want to move from information directors to strategic communicators, it is clear that practitioners need to reconsider how they operate and need to become more progressive as strategists and managers. If college sports PR professionals hope to have a seat at the decision-making table, and if they desire to have their voices heard, they must develop the professional role orientation, personality traits, and leadership skills and style that are conducive to strategic influence.

Of course, it is first important to define what is meant by strategic influence, professional role orientation, leadership personality traits, and leadership skills and style.

Strategic influence

Influence has been defined as the "power to affect others" or "power to produce effects because of wealth, high position, etc." (Agnes, 2003, p. 332). Berger and Reber (2006) further noted that "every individual and group has some power and can exercise influence" (p. 4) and found that power may come from formal authority, access to decision makers, information, problem-solving expertise, experience, and/or relationships. Berger and Reber took much of their definition of power from French and Raven (1960), who developed one of the earliest studies that determined different types of power. They defined five types of power: coercive, reward, legitimate, referent, and expert.

Coercive power is the ability to force someone to do something against his or her will. It may be viewed as negative, but can also be used to keep the peace. Conversely, reward power is based on the positive valence seen as a result of positive action. In short, it is a bonus for completing a task well. The third type of power that French and Raven (1960) defined is legitimate power, or power that is provided those in authority simply by their position within the organization. Police officers, managers and university presidents enjoy legitimate power because they are in high-ranking positions. Referent power deals with attraction between O (the person or group in authority) and P. If P respects O, believes O's values are much the same as P's, and is appreciative of P, then P will have the power to influence O's actions. Finally, expert power is derived from having knowledge or skills that another requires. According to French and Raven, "The strength of expert power of O/P varies with the extent of the knowledge or perception which P attributes to O within a given area" (p. 620).

The goal then is to utilize whatever power is available to gain influence. Of course, it is important to differentiate between strategic influence and technical influence. It may be assumed that PR directors have the authority to develop publicity materials as they see fit; studies conducted by Stoldt, Miller, and Comfort (2001) and Ruihley and Fall (2009) suggested that athletic directors give their PR professionals high marks for the technical aspects of their jobs. Based on Berger and Reber's findings, though, it is a lack of strategic influence – the opportunity to be involved in the planning and direction of the organization – that frustrates practitioners. The scholars determined that "most practitioners equate influence with having a seat and a voice at the decision-making table" (Berger and Reber, 2006, p. 20). In order to find a place at the table, Berger and Reber found that PR practitioners must gain access to the dominant coalition, the powerful collection of professionals within the organization who make the majority of the decisions. Berger and Reber, however, stressed that "being a member of the dominant coalition or inner circle is no guarantee of influence. Being present and being listened to are not the same" (p. 7). They added that "Membership in organizational power circles nevertheless provides some important advantages" (p. 7) because being in the inner circle of management offers a level of authority that provides position and participation power.

Dozier, Grunig, and Grunig (1995) reached a similar conclusion. Leaders (that is, chief executive officers, [CEOs]) and top communicators were asked to indicate "the extent to which the dominant coalition…supported the public relations or communication function in the organization" (p. 78). They found that the least-excellent organizations had less than half the support score from CEOs when compared to the most-excellent organizations. Further, Dozier, *et al.* (1995) learned that, of the organizations with excellence scores in the top ten percent, 76 percent of their top communicators were members of the dominant coalition. They noted that, "After studying the data, we can say that top communicator membership in the dominant coalition is not necessary for communication excellence, but it sure helps" (p. 78).

Another way to gain influence is to demonstrate the worth of the PR arm of any organization, including college athletics. Grunig (1992) proposed that the dominant coalition must be educated as to the value of PR. Practitioners, she said, must present themselves more as managers than as technicians. She also said that PR departments should be at the top of the organizational hierarchy, rather than the middle, stressing that such efforts are essential if PR practitioners want to fully benefit the organization, as "Professionals who want to influence strategic decisions have more effect when they are part of a group than when they act as organizational entrepreneurs" (p. 491).

Professional role orientation

If, as Grunig (1992) suggested, influence and power are tied to the roles played by practitioners, it would seem that a practitioner's professional orientation (managerial or technical) must be considered. CoSIDA explained that SIDs are PR specialists, event managers, media liaisons, publications/web professionals, and administrators (College Sports Information Directors of America, 1993). Technical tasks include recording and reporting statistics, maintaining the department website, designing publications, and producing written materials. Whereas a technically oriented PR director may be more concerned with producing "the stuff" that gets an athletic department noticed, a more managerially oriented director considers the long-term objectives of the athletic department and the best strategies for achieving those outcomes. Managerial assignments like ensuring compliance and regulations, serving on the campus marketing committee, collaborating with athletic marketing and promotions, and developing comprehensive communication plans are more the norm for college sports PR directors focused on the managerial roles related to the job (Broom and Smith, 1979; Grunig, 1992; Stoldt and Narasimhan, 2005; Stoldt, Dittmore, and Branvold, 2006).

John Humenik articulated the desire for college sports PR directors to evolve from technicians to managers. The executive director of CoSIDA stated that, "we not only have to change the way we see ourselves—changing from information directors to communication directors to strategic communications directors—but also have to teach senior leadership; that is how they have to see us and our role within their organizations" (Stoldt, 2008, p. 461). Shortly after Stoldt's interview with Humenik, CoSIDA launched a strategic initiative aimed at changing the focus and image of its members. The strategic plan went so far as to include a revised logo (see Figure 45.1) emphasizing the organization's commitment to advancing the profession. Humenik noted that *information director* implies a professional who collects statistics, writes news releases, and designs publications (Stoldt, 2008). *Strategic communicator*, on the other hand, implies a professional who uses a systematic approach to gather information and communicate a message with long-range departmental goals and objectives in mind, thus providing said professional with more credibility.

FIGURE 45.1 The former (left) and new (right) logos for the College Sports Information directors of America (CoSIDA)
(reproduced with permission from CoSIDA)

After learning that many NCAA Division I SIDs sought more management responsibility, one of Stoldt's (1998) recommendations for future study following his dissertation was to examine how well-prepared college sports PR practitioners are to function in such managerial roles. Broom and Smith (1979) set the standard when addressing such roles. In simplest terms, expert prescriber is an acknowledged expert in communications and PR practices; the communication facilitator is a liaison between management and publics; the problem-solving process facilitator is a consultant to management, helping management think through issues to systematically find a solution; and the technical services provider produces materials needed for publicity purposes.

Studies conducted by Dozier (1992), Dozier and Broom (1995), and Dozier, *et al.* (1995) further examined the roles of PR practitioners. Dozier and Broom determined that "knowledge to enact the manager role was the single most powerful correlate of excellence in public relations and communication management" (p. 4). Further, they determined that practitioners who enact the manager role participate more frequently in management decision making, have higher salaries, and tend to be more satisfied with their jobs. Some of the earliest work in determining PR's place in decision making and its opportunity for influence in organizations came from Grunig (1992) and colleagues. They surveyed PR practitioners in relation to their expertise in communication technician, senior advisor, and media relations roles. Whereas professional orientation looks at where directors focus their attention, expertise refers to the relative skills that PR directors bring to the various aspects of the job. Dozier and colleagues found that "playing advanced organizational roles as communication managers and senior advisers helps top communicators run excellent communication departments" (Dozier, *et al.*, 1995, p. 112).

In his interview with Stoldt, Humenik suggested that the title "sports information director" itself could be part of the problem. He noted:

> In today's collegiate world, and for that matter throughout all areas of PR in our country, the title 'information director' seems to primarily refer to a person who is involved mostly in keeping stats, preparing basic news releases, working on publications, setting up interviews, and managing the press box,
>
> *(Stoldt, 2008)*

He added that:

> The title 'communications director,' however, seems to clearly project a person who has broader, more global studies and who is viewed more in a strategic and visionary capacity...There simply is more 'value' in how others view a person who is an architect and has strategic capacity and interests
>
> *(Stoldt, 2008, p. 460)*

From the research conducted in college sports PR, it would appear that, overall, professionals have not made the move from technician to management. Ottaway (1962) produced one of the earliest research studies focusing on college sports PR professionals. He found that the typical practitioners' primary functions included writing releases and editing brochures and game programs. Almost 40 years later, Stoldt (1998) came up with a similar conclusion: Practitioners view themselves as technicians. Were these professionals content with their positions, seemingly in more technical roles? Apparently not. Stoldt utilized the practitioner's primary roles as defined by Broom and Smith (1979) to determine if significant differences existed between current and ideal primary roles with most practitioners. He learned that practitioners, including those who served in more managerial roles, wanted to engage in management activities more frequently.

Similarly, Helitzer (2000) and Nichols, Moynahan, Hall, and Taylor (2002) listed the college sports PR practitioner's primary responsibilities as developing publications, creating publicity, maintaining statistics, and supervising game management. Based on their findings, it would seem college sports PR directors are still seeking that seat at the decision-making table. And, in 2011, Moore determined that college sports PR directors saw themselves first as media relations professionals, then as technicians in the trade, and finally as managers, thus indicating that college sports PR directors still have work to do in presenting themselves as managers if they hope to become part of the dominant coalition and have more of a decision making voice in the athletic department.

Leadership personality traits

The trait approach to leadership focuses on qualities of effective leaders that are "variously manifest, and the techniques for the cultivation of these qualities" (Christ, 1999, p. 200).

Northouse (2007) added that traits are "innate and largely fixed" (p. 39). Based on this school of thought, a leadership trait may be defined as personal qualities that distinguish one individual from another and that allow a person to lead effectively. Soucie (1994) pointed out that it is difficult to point to a specific trait that allows a leader to have influence, but major leadership traits may be combined into five categories: intelligence, self-confidence, determination, integrity, and sociability. These categories consider a leader's knowledge and expertise, belief in his or her abilities, persistence, honesty, and interpersonal skills. Gilley, McMillan, and Gilley (2009) noted that these traits – along with supervisory ability, need for achievement, decisiveness, and initiative – have been identified as significant when related to leadership and organizational change.

Taking the trait philosophy a step further is the psychodynamic approach to leadership. Whereas the trait approach assumes certain traits are characteristics that are assumed to be important to attaining leadership or performing leadership tasks, the psychodynamic approach suggests that various personality types are better suited to particular leadership positions or situations. Jung (1923, 1993) assumed that human behavior is predictable because people have preferences in how they work and play. He believed that personality could be assessed based on four dimensions. The first involves extroversion and introversion. This relates to how people prefer to obtain information, inspiration, and energy; where people derive their energy. Introverts look inward at their own ideas and do not need external motivation; extroverts enjoy talking and interacting, drawing their energy from those around them. The second consists of sensing and intuition. This considers how people gather information. Sensors gather facts and data by using their senses. They are precise and sequential. Intuitive people are more theoretical and conceptual; they acquire data randomly. The third includes thinking and feeling. This focuses on how people make decisions. Thinkers are rational and desire facts, while feelers are more subjective, use personal feelings, and seek harmony. The fourth involves judging and perceiving. This considers whether people are planners or if they are spontaneous. Judgers seek structure, plans, and resolution of conflicts. Perceivers, on the other hand, are more spontaneous and flexible. Jung said how leaders combine these four dimensions may explain how they interact with subordinates. As such, he believed it is important for leaders to identify and understand their own dominant personality traits, as this may explain why they take particular actions.

Richmond and McCroskey (1990) focused on two distinct personality traits: assertiveness and responsiveness. They argued that these two personality traits "make a substantial contribution to the prediction of communication and other social behavioral patterns" (p. 449). Neupauer (1999) recognized the importance of these two personality traits as leaders examine themselves and their effectiveness. He conducted the first examination of personality traits as it pertains to college sports PR, using four-trait scale measurements to study the communicative personalities of eastern sports PR directors. One instrument he utilized was Richmond and McCroskey's Assertiveness–Responsiveness Measure (ARM), which examines how aggressive or passive individuals are in making their point. Communicators are classified into four groups: noncompetent (low responsiveness, low assertiveness), aggressive (low responsiveness, high assertiveness), submissive (high responsiveness, low assertiveness) and competent (high responsiveness, high assertiveness). Aggressive and competent communicators are more constructive because, while they are more argumentative, they focus on the task at hand, and not on personal attacks (Martin and Anderson, 1996). Based on this assessment, modern college sports PR directors, as a whole, perceive that they are more responsive. This is much to their detriment, as more assertive directors tend to have more influence in their athletic departments.

Leadership skills

Whereas traits are often considered a part of who the leader is, skills are thought to be more attainable through education and training. Leadership skill is the degree to which an individual is able to perform tasks necessary to guide and support others (Katz, 1955; Christ, 1999; Northouse, 2007). Gilley, *et al.* (2009) stressed that leaders' skills strengthen the "linkage between leader behaviors and effectiveness in implementing change" (p. 41) and that lack of change management skills has been shown to impede success. In French and Raven's (1960) definition of power, it is the fifth type of power – expert power – that coincides with the skills approach to leadership, as it assumes the more expertise a leader has in a given area, the more power he or she possesses. Consequently, the more power the leader has, the more influence.

When discussing skills in relation to mass communication (specifically journalism, broadcasting and film, and PR and advertising), Christ (1999) made the distinction between "craft skills" and "intellectual skills." Craft skill is the ability to perform tasks related to the job, such as writing a lead for a newspaper reporter or making an oral presentation for a public speaker. Intellectual skills, meanwhile, relate to activities like designing and conducting research, analyzing data, and engaging in knowledgeable debate.

Taking this idea a step further, Soucie (1994) and Northouse (2007) supported the three-skills approaches to leadership presented by Katz (1955). Katz's three-skills approach to leadership included: technical leadership skills (focusing on the tasks), human leadership skills (with an emphasis on interactions with others), and conceptual leadership skills (centered on things such as goal setting and analysis of research). He pointed out that managers on a supervisory level typically have highly developed technical and human skills, but are less adept at conceptual skills. Middle managers tend to be balanced, while top management usually focused less on technical skills, as human and conceptual skills are more critical.

Professionals in athletics administration (Dohrety, 2004; Kutz, 2008; McDermott, 2008; Platt Meyer, 2002; Skemp-Arlt and Toupence, 2007; Tock, 2009) have agreed with these assessments, noting that effective leaders possess expertise in the field, honesty, and quality communication skills. In addition, they care for the needs and training of others and are visionary, with an ability to develop strategy and plan campaigns. As noted above, CoSIDA has stressed that college sports PR practitioners must be highly skilled in the technical aspects of their job. They also must be effective communicators. However, if they really want to move up and become more involved in strategic management, the ability to develop plans and strategy must be present.

Leadership style

The styles approach to leadership posits that the leader's behavior influences the effectiveness of subordinates (Slack, 1997). Because a focus only on traits seemed to be too limited, researchers at Ohio State University and the University of Michigan analyzed how individuals acted when they were leading groups. They determined that leaders were either relationship-oriented or task-oriented (Northouse, 2007; Slack, 1997). These orientations also may be defined as transformational or transactional leadership. As noted by Northouse, transformational leadership "is a process that changes and transforms people" (p. 175) and "creates a connection that raises the level of motivation and morality in both the leader and the follower" (p. 176). It focuses on emotions, values, ethics, standards, and long-term goals. In contrast, other leadership theories, which Burns (1978) termed transactional, are more concerned with the bottom line and use rewards and punishments in leadership.

As it relates to athletics, Branch (1990) conducted one of the earliest empirical studies related to effective leader behavior. After surveying athletic administrators, he found that effective athletic departments have leaders who are more autocratic and task oriented than relationship oriented. Branch said, "consideration was not a significant contributor to the effectiveness of the organization" (Branch, 1990, pp. 170–1). Soucie, on the other hand, following an in-depth review of leadership literature, found that developing and nurturing "interpersonal relationships with subordinates, peers, superiors, and outsiders" and "maintaining a balanced concern for the needs of the organization and those of people within the organization" (Soucie, 1994, p. 9) is a much more effective means of leading in sports organizations. Further, he learned that effective sports organization leaders believe in people, delegate, and share power. After interviewing leaders who were successful in turning losing professional sports organizations into winners, Frontiera (2009) added that leaders who effectively bring about a culture change recognized focusing on the bottom line rather than people is a sure way to fail. He also found that effective leaders "expressed a genuine interest in the growth of those who worked for them" (p. 25).

One way to see where individual leaders place their focus is to utilize Blake and Mouton's (1985) Managerial Grid. They stressed that, though leadership is a complex process, it has several main elements that are vital to effective leadership: initiative, inquiry, advocacy, conflict resolution, decision-making, and critique. Where others used the terms "transformational" and "transactional" to describe leadership, Blake and Mouton (1985) assumed that all leaders had a central focus, simply stated either on people or on production. They focused on these assumptions, noting that, "There are several different sets of assumptions, and the assumptions a leader acts on may or may not be based on what appears to be sound" (p. 5). They went on to note, "The Grid is useful for helping leaders identify the assumptions they make as they work to get results with and through people" (p. 7). In short, college sports PR directors who desire a more influential role would be advised to examine their dominant leadership style.

Summary

If college sports PR directors are interested in being a part of the dominant coalition, having their voices heard and having influence upon upper administration, they must assume professional roles and possess leadership personality traits, skills and styles that are conducive to strategic management and influence. Studies have shown that PR professionals in all areas, not just college athletics, who serve more as managers are more satisfied with their jobs and are better compensated. Further, PR professionals who seek strategic influence should be assertive, should possess significant conceptual leadership skills, and should focus on the task at hand while still maintaining positive relationships. If they accomplish these goals, college sports PR directors are more likely to enjoy active roles in the decision-making processes in their respective athletic departments.

References

Agnes, M. (Ed.). (2003). *Webster's new world dictionary*. New York: Random House.

Berger, B. K., and Reber, B. H. (2006). *Gaining influence in public relations: The role of resistance in practice*. Mahwah, NJ: Lawrence Erlbaum.

Blake, R. R., and Mouton, J. S. (1985). *The managerial grid III*. Houston: Gulf.

Branch, D. (1990). Athletic director leader behavior as a predictor of intercollegiate athletic organizational effectiveness. *Journal of Sport Management*, 4, 161–73.

Broom, G. M., and Smith, G. D. (1979). Testing the practitioner's impact on clients. *Public Relations Review*, 5 (3), 47–59.

Burns, J. M. (1978). *Leadership*. New York: Harper and Row.

Christ, W. G. (1999). *Leadership in times of change: A handbook for communication and media administrators*. Mahwah, NJ: Lawrence Erlbaum.

College Sports Information Directors of America (CoSIDA). (1993). *Sports information and your institution* [Brochure].

College Sports Information Directors of America (CoSIDA). (2008). *Master strategic initiatives plan for CoSIDA*. Retrieved from http://www.cosida.com/documents/2008/7/6/CoSIDA_STRATEGIC_PLAN3.pdf

Dohrety, M. (2004). Defining a leader. *Sporting News*, 228 (3), 44.

Dozier, D. M. (1992). The organizational roles of communications and public relations practitioners. In J. E. Grunig (Ed.), *Excellence in public relations and communication management* (pp. 327–56). Hillsdale, NJ: Lawrence Erlbaum.

Dozier, D. M. and Broom, G. M. (1995). Evolution of the manager role in public relations practice. *Journal of Public Relations Research*, 7 (1), 3–26.

Dozier, D. M., Grunig, L. A., and Grunig, J. E. (1995). *Manager's guide to excellence in public relations and communication management*. Mahwah, NJ: Lawrence Erlbaum.

Freeman, J. (2004). Personality as an indicator of success: A study of NPPA contest winners. *News Photographer*, 59 (4), 18–22.

French, J. P. R. Jr., and Raven, B. (1960). The bases of social power. In D. Cartwright and A. Zanders (Eds.), *Group dynamics* (pp. 607–23). New York: Harper and Row.

Frontiera, J. (2009). Success of culture change reflects how a leader instills value. *SportsBusiness Journal*, 12 (23), 25.

Gilley, A., McMillan, H. S., and Gilley, J. W. (2009). Organizational change and characteristics of leadership effectiveness. *Journal of Leadership and Organizational Studies*, 16 (1), 38–47.

Grunig, L. A. (1992). Power in the public relations department. In J. E. Grunig (Ed.), *Excellence in public relations and communication management* (pp. 483–503). Hillsdale, NJ: Lawrence Erlbaum.

Helitzer, M. (2000). *The dream job: Sports publicity, promotion and marketing* (3rd ed.). Athens, OH: University Sports.

Jung, C. G. (1923). *Psychological types*. New York: Harcourt Brace.

Jung, C. G. (1993). Psychological types. In V. D. Laszlo (Ed.), *The basic writings of C. G. Jung* (pp. 230–357). New York: Modern Library.

Katz, R. L. (1955). Skills of an effective administrator, *Harvard Business Review*, 33 (1), 33–42.

Kutz, M. R. (2008). Leadership factors for athletic trainers. *Athletic Therapy Today*, 13 (4), 15–20.

Martin, M. M., and Anderson, C. M. (1996). Argumentativeness and verbal aggressiveness. *Journal of Social Behavior and Personality*, 11 (3), 547–54.

McDermott, J. (2008). Effective leadership skills for athletics directors. *Athletic Administration*, 43 (7), 38.

Moore, J. (2011). Predictors of strategic influence among college sports public relations directors in college athletic departments: The impact of managerial orientation and leadership personality trait, skill, and style (Unpublished doctoral dissertation). Colorado State University, Fort Collins, CO.

Neupauer, N. C. (1999). A personality traits study of sports information directors at "Big" vs. "Small programs in the East. *Social Science Journal*, 36 (1), 163–72.

Nichols, W., Moynahan, P. L., Hall, A., and Taylor, J. (2002). *Media relations in sport*. Morgantown, WV: Fitness Information Technology.

Northouse, P. G. (2007). *Leadership: Theory and practice* (4th ed.). Thousand Oaks: Sage.

Ottaway, L. M. (1962). The sports information director at a major institution and how he views his function and purpose in relation to the total public relations program of his institution (Unpublished master's thesis). State University of Iowa, Ames, IA.

Platt Meyer, L. S. (2002). Leadership characteristics as significant predictors of clinical-teaching effectiveness. *Athletic Therapy Today*, 7 (5), 34–9.

Richmond, V. P., and McCroskey, J. C. (1990). Reliability and separation of factors on the Assertiveness–Responsiveness Measure. *Psychological Reports*, 67, 449–50.

Ruihley, B. J., and Fall, L. T. (2009). Assessment on and off the field: Examining athletic directors' perceptions of public relations in college athletics. *International Journal of Sport Communication*, 2, 398–410.

Skemp-Arlt, K. M., and Toupence, R. (2007). The administrator's role in employee motivation. *Coach and Athletic Director*, 76 (7), 28–34.

Slack, T. (1997). *Understanding sport organizations: The application of organization theory*. Champaign, IL: Human Kinetics.

Soucie, D. (1994). Effective managerial leadership in sport organizations. *Journal of Sport Management*, 8, 1–13.

Stoldt, G. C. (1998). Current and ideal professional roles of NCAA Division I-A sports information directors: Analysis and implications (Unpublished doctoral dissertation). University of Oklahoma, Norman, OK.

Stoldt, G. C. (2008). Interview with John Humenik, executive director of the College Sports Information Directors of America. *International Journal of Sport Communication*, 1, 458–64.

Stoldt, G. C., and Narasimhan, V. (2005). Self assessments of collegiate sports information professionals regarding their public relations task expertise. *International Journal of Sport Management*, 6, 252–69.

Stoldt, G. C., Dittmore, S. W., and Branvold, S. E. (2006). *Sport public relations: Managing organizational communication*. Champaign, IL: Human Kinetics.

Stoldt, G. C., Miller, L. K., and Comfort, P. G. (2001). Through the eyes of athletic directors: Perceptions of sports information directors, and other public relations issues. *Sport Marketing Quarterly*, 10, 164–72.

Tock, E. (2009). Leadership skills critical now for club executives. *Fitness Business Pro*, 69 (5), 5.

46

COMMUNICATION AND SPORTS OFFICIALS

Peter Simmons and Ian Cunningham

As noted by the Football Federation of Australia:

> There have been many referees who made good decisions but did not have the confidence of the players. Likewise there have been referees, who comparatively speaking made a large number of errors, but were considered by players to be good referees.
>
> *(Football Federation Australia, 2012, p. 8)*

Studies of sports officiating suggest that skilled communication is as important as most officials believe it is, and that it may be most important when it is most difficult (Mascarenhas, Collins, and Mortimer, 2005). Furthermore, organizational research indicates that managers often "make bad times worse" for staff by distancing themselves when they should be explaining and showing respect (Patient and Skarlicki, 2010, p. 556). Sport officiating investigations have focused on the elite levels of competition, with experienced officials who tend to be highly skilled communicators. But most officiating is done at the grassroots level, where only a rope might separate the official from an angry crowd (Simmons, 2006). Officials at all levels of competition make rapid calls on incidents that are frequently ambiguous, in environments renowned for heightened emotions. In grassroots sport there is no replay technology to prove calls right or wrong, and much depends on officials' ability to align their interpretations with the rules, and otherwise persuade compliance and cooperation from those who wish the decisions were different.

This chapter focuses on understanding communication dimensions that are integral to good officiating, such as the display of strong character, adapting to the nuances of different contexts and rivalries, and behaving with sensitivity and assertion when communication is most challenging. It reflects on contributions from previous research on sport officiating, and a mismatch between prevailing *skills* and *decision* conceptualizations of officiating communication, and requirements to be reflexive and adaptable when communication is most challenging. It draws on sport officiating research and work from other professional fields, where communication has been more extensively researched and theorized, to suggest more holistic approaches to conceptualizing and improving communication.

Officiating research

Sports officiating research has focused on the elite or professional level, and has been dominated by studies from the disciplines of sport and exercise sciences, medicine, and psychology. Sport official researchers have noted that officials are under-researched compared with players, coaches, spectators, and other aspects of sport (MacMahon and Plessner, 2008; Mascarenhas, *et al.*, 2005). Mellick, Bull, Laugharne, and Fleming (2005) said that academic and scholarly discourses relating to officials are "few in number and narrow in scope" (p. 43).

Research since 2000 has focused on physical and mental demands of officials, influences on decision making, and the training of elite officials (MacMahon and Plessner, 2008). Searches of scholarly journals conducted for this chapter showed that this remains the case, but the greatest interest is in influences on decision making. Studies have examined many contextual, psychological, and perceptual factors that that may influence or bias officials' decisions. Thus, research into sport officiating has more often focused on the official as receiver of decision information, than the official as the sender of decision information. Similarly, training for sports officials often focuses on rules and their interpretation – making decisions – without clear programs to help officials become more skilled in communication and game management.

The research focus on decision processes at the elite level is understandable, considering the extremely high stakes that are played for in popular sports, and the emergence of microscopic slow motion replays scrutinized by mass TV audiences. The pressure on elite sport officials to make the right decisions has never been greater, but making the decision is often just the beginning of an official's work.

Communication in sports officiating research

Studies of officiating communication and game management have tended to use the opinions of elite officials and concentrate on techniques in the skillful communication of decisions. Cunningham, Mellick, Mascarenhas, and Fleming (2012) focus on self-presentation strategies during decision communication episodes by rugby union referees. Mellick, *et al.* (2005) asked elite soccer and rugby officials to scrutinize recordings of skillful and unskillful referee decision communication. They explain skilled use of the whistle, hand signals, gaze and other body language, and verbally linking incidents to the rules, thus justifying decisions as a consequence of a player's behavior. They articulate techniques for purposeful impression management and message transmission that officials can aspire to and practice, and highlight three characteristics of best practice in decision communication: "to engage the offender's attention and instigate a decision interaction episode; to project confidence in the decision made; and finally to promote perception of the decision as fair and just" (Mellick, *et al.*, 2005, p. 42). According to these scholars, most sport officials acquire their communication training from what has been described as a "hidden curriculum" (p. 45), developing their approach with experience and advice from peers. Although there is a great deal of wisdom in the experience of the sport community, officials can be poorly advised and may develop unhelpful habits. A lack of formal communication training for officials results from a lack of evidence about what strategies and techniques may or may not work, a lack of structured practice exercises designed to improve communication, and belief that communication and player management skills are difficult to teach compared to rules, fitness and positioning (Mascarenhas, *et al.*, 2005).

Some studies have gathered players' perspectives, and highlighted links between officials' communication styles and various emotional and perceptual outcomes for players. Bar-Eli, Levy-Kolker, Pie, and Tenenbaum (1995) studied the influence of referee behaviors on professional basketball, handball, soccer, and water-polo players. They reported that unnecessary words and actions in referee calls amplified negative performance consequences for players, and drew player hostility on themselves. They said that referees should be better informed about the impact that they have on players' psychological states, and should be encouraged to improve their verbal and non-verbal communication skills. Simmons (2010) measured the influence of different officiating communication styles on player perceptions of the fairness of a referee decision awarded against them. He used an experimental vignette method with a large sample of amateur, semi-professional, and professional players from Spain, Australia, and England. He found that when a referee calmly communicated the decision, players rated the fairness of the referee significantly higher than when the referee communicated the same decision angrily. When a referee gave a short explanation for the decision (for example, six words), players rated the fairness of the referee significantly higher than when there was no explanation. Importantly, Simmons noted that players also rated the decision as more *correct* when it was explained. The study provided rare empirical support for what Bar-Eli and colleagues as well as sports officials have long believed, that it is not just the decision that is important, it is the way it is called. Simmons said the findings were consistent with fairness heuristic theory and uncertainty management (Lind and Van den Bos, 2002). People find uncertainty uncomfortable, and consciously and unconsciously use whatever information is available (heuristics or communicative displays) to lessen uncertainty about decision makers and their decisions. As noted by Simmons, "Footballers appear to use certainty about procedure and interactional style (communicative behaviours) to mitigate uncertainty about fairness and correctness in decisions" (Simmons, 2010, p. 90).

Studies to date indicate that whistle, posture, short explanation, and other verbal and non-verbal techniques provide officials with an important toolbox of skills for situation control, message transmission, and impression management. These skills are the focus of much advice and communication training for officials. But decision communication occurs within broader contexts, and a complex set of interpersonal interactions and relationships. Officials need to interpret people and situations very quickly and respond appropriately. Some techniques may achieve order in some situations, but be highly inflammatory in others.

Parallels are sometimes limited by contextual differences, but theory from other fields can be instructive. Communication has been more extensively researched and theorized in the context of doctor and patient interactions, and the emphasis on discreet skills as a main framework for conceptualizing and training for communication is being challenged. It has been argued that good communication is not developed purely through learning skills at the surface level. Salmon and Young (2011) explained that a more holistic conceptualization of communication and training should aim to help professionals become skilled communicators who adapt appropriately to the requirements of each context.

Conceptualizing the skilled communicator

Sport officiating researchers have discussed an aspect of game management that seems to be associated with charisma, communication, or presence, but has to date defied label. As noted by MacMahon and Plessner (2008), "The best officials seem to possess intangible personal judgment and the ability to manage contests without dominating them" (p. 174). In their study of elite rugby referees, Mascarenhas, *et al.* (2005) referred to an X-factor, an ability that combines reading of the nuances of situations and controlling the game with interpersonal ease.

In communication studies generally, research focusing on discreet skills has examined aspects of communication behavior that are "relatively simple, noninteractive tasks" (Greene, 2003, p. 70). Salmon and Young (2011) argue that conceptualization of communication as skills reduces a very complex, interactive phenomenon to a set of discreet, and somewhat rigid, component behaviors that distort the development of skilled communication practice. They say that qualitative research into communication reveals phenomena that do not correspond to skills defined in quantitative research, and that practitioners reflecting on their communication frequently emphasize the importance of intuition and departure from the "rules" over "expert application of previously defined skills" (Salmon and Young, 2011, p. 218).

Burleson's constructivist approach to understanding communication skills argues that skilled communicators adapt their communication to achieve personal or social goals, such as persuasion that secures acceptance, or sensitivity that brings comfort. Central to his argument is that communicators with a more complex perception of social situations and audiences process a more nuanced range of "interpersonal constructs," and produce "person-centred" communication that is more effective because it is tailored more precisely for the audience (Burleson, 2007, p. 112). More sophisticated communicators are able to adapt for the goals of different interactants, and anticipate hidden features of situations. For example, a coach may protest a decision, even after the official has explained the violation, to save face over a tactical blunder, to protect a player, or to intimidate and make the official think twice about making future, similar calls (Rooff-Steffen, 2011).

Clearly there are patterns in the situations that sport officials manage – similar rule transgressions, score lines, personalities, and so on – but it is also important that officials develop the capacity for sensitivity and adaptation to the novel and the inflammatory. Adaptability is sometimes considered a skill in itself. Simmons examined the strategies that elite soccer referees use to prevent and manage player abuse and aggression. He reported that top referees "differentiate their approaches according to the requirements of the situation, and their perceptions of players," and "select from numerous verbal and non-verbal techniques to restore order to the game and player conduct" (Simmons, 2006, p. 8). Hargie (2011) argued that communication skills are identifiable units of behavior, but are interrelated, responsive, and include the ability to communicate appropriately for the situation. Lefroy and McKinley (2011) contended the value of teaching communication skills to doctors as if they were a toolkit, where what matters most is learning how to use the tools appropriately to the requirements of different situations. They assert the centrality of communication as a clinical skill in itself, rather than seeing communication as an adjunct to clinical training.

The same can be said of sports officiating. Communication is often considered separately when it is clearly integral to effective officiating. The chapter authors recently participated in a mentoring program for soccer referees at the grassroots level. In one group exercise, the participants watched DVDs of infractions in small groups. For each infraction there were two questions. First, they judged the level of infraction and the appropriate sanction according to the rules. Second, they wrote down what they would say to the player they were sanctioning. Curiously, in every group the participants' focus was on the first question, the judgment. The chapter authors had to remind the groups to complete the second question. The decision is crucial, but forming the judgment is just the first part of the official's task in a match situation.

A training model that better integrates communication would perhaps ask just one question: How would you communicate your decision to the players?

Salmon and Young noted that there are no specific skills that are effective in all situations; rather, the researcher said that people are likely to be "more concerned with the whole picture – their impression of the practitioner's character and caring – than with specific communication skills" (Salmon and Young, 2011, p. 221). In sports officiating, players are similarly more influenced by characteristics such as integrity and resilience, than they are by specific communication skills. Some sport officiating communication research draws on the extensive body of organizational justice theory to argue that it is important for officials to communicate qualities related to fairness (Simmons, 2010; 2011).

Fairness as a theoretical frame for officiating communication

Fairness is important because it is integral to expectations of sports officials (Pawlenka, 2005), and because people generally react more positively when they perceive fair treatment, and negatively when they perceive unfair treatment (Van den Bos, *et al.*, 2005). Importantly, there is increasing evidence that decision makers can be trained to communicate sensitively and influence perception of fairness (Patient and Skarlicki, 2010). Skarlicki and Latham (2005) noted that training that aims to increase perceptions of fairness should be designed to increase leaders' "understanding of how perceptions are formed" (p. 506).

If players feel that the official is fair, they are more likely to feel that decisions are fair, and to respond cooperatively. The perception of fairness is assumed to be influenced by players' more general impressions of officials, not simply what occurs during decision communication episodes. Because officials frequently interpret and adjudicate on ambiguity, the communication of qualities associated with fairness is desirable. Thus Simmons (2010) said that referees would benefit from understanding the way players form perceptions of fairness.

Simmons (2011) interviewed Australian grassroots and professional soccer players for insights into the ways that they form perceptions of officials and their decisions. He found that players associate visible displays – behaviors, attitudes, interactions, and appearance – with more abstract qualities such as accountability, resilience, and intelligence. Principles of procedural and interactional fairness were used to interpret associations players made between displays and more general qualities. For example, players positively associate an official's athletic physique with competence to keep up with play, and being close to incidents when decisions need to be made. This in turn is consistent with one of Leventhal's (1980) procedural fairness principles, the requirement that information used as the basis for decisions is accurate. Officials enhance perceptions of interactional fairness (Bies and Moag, 1986) with displays of respect for players such as explaining decisions, a personable demeanor, and encouraging play to flow.

Hundreds of players' comments were used to extrapolate competence, dependability, and respectfulness as players' ideal of a fair referee (Simmons, 2011). Players attend to displays that indicate the official is physically competent to keep up with play, and mentally competent to judge and decide well. It's important to players that officials are dependable, that they will make consistent decisions throughout the game and for both teams, and are resilient to pressures on their decisions. Third, players feel that games are mainly for the benefit of players. It is important that officials are respectful to players, that they are personable (without being over friendly), and accountable to players for their decisions.

Individual referees have different styles, skills, and backgrounds. Competent, dependable, and respectful provide a frame intended to be flexible to officials matching their individual officiating personalities with the qualities players expect in officials.

Experience, practice and a 'feel for the game'

In officiating, the ability to judge context and communicate effectively is generally assumed to improve with experience (Mascarenhas, *et al.*, 2005). But can the development that appears to occur with experience be accelerated? One way to understand the contribution of practice and experience to the development of skilled communication involves procedural memories. "Procedural memories are recollections about how to do something; they are the building blocks of complex actions, like messages," noted Burleson (2007). "Each procedural memory connects recollections about an action, outcomes of that action, and situations in which that action has been used in the past" (p. 116).

The idea behind this conceptualization of communication practice is that when a situation arises requiring a response, we scan our procedural memories for a situation that involved similar goals, constraints or other features. We then use the memories that are available to us in formulating our message or response. According to Burleson, "people who get lots of practice with a particular communicative goal," such as teaching or selling, are likely to develop a larger bank, containing memories that are closely aligned to the demands of each new situation (Burlson, 2007, p. 116). Burleson noted that much human communication is routine and unpressured, and that we can communicate largely without purposeful fine tuning for audience. With a larger bank of memories of strategies and consequences to activate, we can speculate that experienced sport officials are better able to review different communicative options for achieving a range of goals, and to accommodate various perspectives and features of novel situations. For example, the famous Italian soccer referee Pierluigi Collina described a very rare situation where he felt compelled to reverse his own incorrect decision to award a goal. With decades of accumulated memories as an official, and a knowledge of personalities involved with the teams, his first step was to go across to the coaching staff of the team who had been awarded the goal, and explain what he was about to do. In front of many thousands of volatile spectators, his memories helped him to create an effective strategy for a unique situation (Collina, 2003).

The sports arena is known to be a forum for volatility and heightened physical and emotional stressors (Folkesson, Nyberg, Archer, and Norlander, 2002). The notions of cognitive complexity in the perception of situations and the development or person-centered messages may be particularly valuable for understanding sports official communication. Burleson (2007) lamented the paucity of proven strategies to help train adults to become more skilled communicators. But based on evidence from experimental and childhood studies of complexity in communication, he posited several suggestions that hold promise for the development of sports official communication. In particular, he argued for training that openly engages with the internal feelings, thoughts, and motives of other parties. According to Burleson, discussion of situations, emotions, and reactions, will help people to become more familiar with aspects of interactions that are not visible. Such discussions may help sports officials to develop more complex perceptions of interactions, and to produce messages that address different perspectives.

In contemplating the development in communication that occurs with experience of sport officiating, it may be instructive to reflect on the development of sport players. Noble and

Watkins (2003) remind us that sport players take time and practice to develop mastery and a "feel for the game" (p. 527). Masterful players spend much more time in practice than in playing their sport, and the "feel for the game" involves a feel for all aspects of the game including the equipment, the clothing, the pitch, the spectators and the occasion of play. They describe "training" as a "pedagogy in which recalibration of the body occurs through the presentation of good technique and the 'correction' of poor technique" (p. 527), and argue that the development of mastery involves both "doing-practice and theoretical practice" (p. 528). The mind–body process they describe involves the unconscious bodily development that occurs with familiarity and repetition, leading to automatic performance, such as that which occurs in driving a car or balancing on a bicycle. Importantly, they insist that the development of performance leading to effective, "automatic reactions in the environment in which they are to be executed" (p. 535) is not just bodily and unconscious, but is necessarily consciously calibrated and adjusted during repeated actions.

If this mind–body process approximates the development of a feel for sports officiating – and concomitant attitudes and qualities, including Salmon and Young's (2011) notion of skilled communication – there are implications for designing sports officiating training. Borrowing from Noble and Watkins (2003), we adapt their ideas for players to speculate officials' development of a feel for the game. Officials develop a feel for the various dimensions of the game, and become more fluent in their execution, both consciously and unconsciously, through the experience of practice. Along the developmental way, they benefit from theoretical input and conscious reflection. Early on they receive instruction in techniques and discreet skills. Techniques are consciously dissected and performed repeatedly to develop mastery. Performance of skills is integrated or synthesized with other actions. With practice, and reflection on practice, the skills become more rhythmic and automatic, the conscious becomes more unconscious, and they can "concentrate on the result of the action rather than the action itself" (Noble and Watkins, 2003, p. 535). The importance of conscious reflection and habituated technique is emphasized. As competence is developed in the different aspects of performance, officials can reflect on strategies for greater success, and refinement of techniques for efficiency.

For many important aspects of officiating, practice is more difficult to simulate outside real match experience than it is for playing. And a mastery model may demand greater time than many amateur officials are willing or able to commit. However, the principles for developing a feel for the game provide a framework for understanding and supporting a feel for officiating that will be accompanied by skilled communication.

Discussion

We support a conceptualization of officiating that makes communication more integral, and a conceptualization of officiating communication that is more holistic than is implied by an emphasis on skills and techniques. Officials at all levels of competition constantly interpret ambiguous situations in environments of heightened emotion, read and defuse conflict, and align interpretations and judgments with the rules. Although communication is integral to sport officiating, it has largely been sidelined in officiating research and training.

Research on sports officials' communication and game management has focused on the process of communicating decisions, especially techniques for promoting acceptance of decisions by players. It has been argued here that it is very important for officials to learn consistent, purposeful techniques that help to clarify messages, avoid unintended reactions, and manage impressions. Officials need to practice a toolbox of skills that they can learn to draw on with ease. But the most challenging communication is essentially adaptive, reflexive, and dynamic. The ability to read people and respond to the nuances of context is not acquired through rote learning of techniques for delivering decisions. And players' general conduct and reactions to specific incidents are likely to be more profoundly influenced by players' feelings about their perceptions of qualities such as fairness and integrity.

The rulebook is essential, but it is not enough on its own. And we cannot hope to provide a specific set of instructions for interactive human communication. We should aim to support and prepare officials for both the routine and the unexpected in their work. Drawing from the preceding review of sports officiating and approaches to communication development, we suggest the following:

Authorities should continue to help officials to develop a toolbox of techniques and skills that they call on for decision communication and rule implementation, for the many predictable tasks of officiating. Repetition in training and practice helps to smooth the performance of techniques, and eventually make the selection and execution automatic.

Training should help officials aspire to qualities and characteristics most appropriate to officiating. Awareness and understanding build capacity and a sense of control and purpose. Simmons' (2011) tripartite – *competence*, *dependability*, and *respectfulness* – provide a framework within which officials can develop their own officiating personality, and develop strategies for impression management.

Authorities should prioritize opportunities for purposeful reflection through mentoring, group work, and other forums for discussion. This is particularly important and requires innovation and constant renewal in the design of training. To develop a feel for the game and their role, officials benefit from immersion in the environment, feedback, and engaging with the experienced. Reflection helps to build a confidence that comes with insight, understanding, and purpose. Officials can consciously recalibrate techniques to align with rule implementation and other goals (such as safety, order, fairness, prevention, proportion), and review aspects of context and interpersonal interactions that complicate or support the attainment of these goals. Reflection should help to familiarize officials with subtleties of context, and should deliberately make explicit what is often hidden in exchanges with players and coaches, including motives, deception, and feelings.

At all levels of sport, there are increasing expectations of accountability and sophistication in communication and game management. We propose that future researchers could adapt the model above – prioritizing and integrating a toolbox of skills, impression management, and strategies for developing a feel for the game – to design programs of training for sports officials in grassroots programs. With the collaboration of sporting bodies and officials, such an approach could be developed as a case study or as action research, informed by ideas and constructs from constructivist communication and reflection in practice literature. Evaluation of the programs would focus on the notion of the skilled communicator, from a range of stakeholder perspectives.

References

Bar-Eli, M., Levy-Kolker, L., Pie, J. S., and Tenenbaum, G. (1995). A crisis-related analysis of perceived referees' behavior in competition. *Journal of Applied Sport Psychology*, 7, 63–80.

Bies, R. J., and Moag, J. F. (1986). Interactional justice: Communication criteria of fairness. *Research on Negotiations in Organizations*, 1, 43–55.

Burleson, B. R. (2007). Constructivism: A general theory of communication skill. In B. B. Whaley and W. Samter (Eds.), *Explaining communication: Contemporary theories and exemplars* (pp. 105–28). Mahwah, NJ: Lawrence Erlbaum Associates.

Collina, P. (2003). *The rules of the game*. Macmillan: London.

Cunningham, I., Mellick, M., Mascarenhas, D., and Fleming, S. (2012). Decision making and decision communications in elite rugby union referees: An inductive investigation. *Sport and Exercise Psychology Review*, 8 (2), 19–30.

Football Federation Australia. (2012). *Laws of the game* (Reprinted from Fédération Internationale de Football Association). Sydney, NSW: FFA.

Folkesson, P., Nyberg, C., Archer, T., and Norlander, T. (2002). Soccer referees' experiences of threat and aggression: Effects of age, experience, and life orientation on outcome of coping strategy. *Aggressive Behavior*, 4, 317–27.

Greene, J. O. (2003). Models of adult communication skill acquisition: Practice and the course of performance improvement. In J. O. Greene and B. R. Burleson (Eds.), *Handbook of communication and social interaction skills* (pp. 51–87). Mahwah, NJ: Lawrence Erlbaum Associates.

Hargie, O. (2011). *Skilled interpersonal communication: Research, theory and practice*. New York: Routledge.

Lefroy, J., and McKinley, R. K. (2011). Skilled communication: Comments further to 'Creativity in clinical communication: From communication skills to skilled communication'. *Medical Education*, 45, 958.

Leventhal, G. S. (1980). What should be done with equity theory? New approaches to the study of fairness in social relationship. In K. Gergen, M. Greenberg, and R. Willis (Eds.), *Social exchange: Advances in theory and research* (pp. 27–55). New York: Plenum.

Lind, E. A., and Van den Bos, K. (2002). When fairness works: Toward a general theory of uncertainty management. In B. M. Staw and R. M. Kramer (Eds.), *Research in organizational behaviour* (pp. 181–223). Greenwich, CT: JAI.

MacMahon, C., and Plessner, H. (2008). The sport official in research and practice. In D. Farrow, J. Baker, and C. MacMahon (Eds.), *Developing sport expertise: Researchers and coaches put theory into practice* (pp. 172–92). Abingdon, UK: Routledge.

Mascarenhas, D., Collins, D., and Mortimer, P. (2005). Elite refereeing performance: Developing a model for sport science support. *The Sport Psychologist*, 19, 364–79.

Mellick, M. C., Bull, P. E., Laugharne, E. J., and Fleming, S. (2005). Identifying best practice for referee decision communication in Association and Rugby Union Football: A microanalytic approach. *Football Studies*, 8, 42–57.

Noble, G., and Watkins, M. (2003). So, how did Bordieu learn to play tennis? Habitus, consciousness, and habituation. *Cultural Studies*, 17, 520–38.

Patient D., and Skarlicki, D. P. (2010). Increasing interpersonal and informational justice when communicating negative news: The role of the manager's empathic concern and moral development. *Journal of Management*, 36, 555–78.

Pawlenka, C. (2005). The idea of fairness: A general ethical concept or one particular to sports ethics. *Journal of the Philosophy of Sport*, 32, 49–64.

Rooff-Steffen, K. (2011). Communication skills. In *Successful sports officiating: American sport education program* (2nd ed., pp. 57–68). Champaign, IL: Human Kinetics.

Salmon, P., and Young, B. (2011). Creativity in clinical communication: From communication skills to skilled communication. *Medical Education*, 45, 217–26.

Simmons, P. (2006). Tackling abuse of officials: Attitudes and communication skills of experienced football referees. Paper presented at the Australia and New Zealand Communication Association Conference, Adelaide, SA, July. Retrieved from http://www.adelaide.edu.au/anzca2006/conf_proceedings/simmons_peter_tackling_abuse_football_referees.pdf.

Simmons, P. (2010). Communicative displays as fairness heuristics: Strategic football referee communication. *Australian Journal of Communication*, 37, 75–94.

Simmons, P. (2011). Competent, dependable and respectful: Football refereeing as a model for communicating fairness. Ethical Space: *International Journal of Communication Ethics*, 8, 33–42.

Skarlicki, D. P., and Latham, G. P. (2005). Can leaders be trained to be fair? In J. Greenberg and J. Colquitt (Eds.), *Handbook of organizational justice* (pp. 499–524). Mahwah, NJ: Lawrence Erlbaum and Associates.

Van den Bos, K., Burrows, J. W., Unphress, E., Folger, R., Lavelle, J. J., Eaglestone, J., and Gee, J. (2005). Prior experiences as temporal frames of reference in social justice: The influence of previous fairness experiences on reactions to new and old supervisors. *Social Justice Research*, 18, 99–120.

47

RAPIDLY ADVANCING TECHNOLOGY AND POLICY CHOICES

Transforming the economic landscape of the sport media

Joel G. Maxcy

The communication and media industries are in the midst of innovative change that promises great significance for the economic landscape surrounding the entire sports enterprise. Advancements in technology, particularly over the last two decades, have greatly increased the number and types of new media firms that are able to deliver sports content to consumers. Principally, the development of digital technology, and the distribution of media products over the Internet through high-speed broadband networks, has greatly increased the amount of sport broadcast channels. Consequently, the demand for the rights to sports broadcasting content has significantly increased and this has caused substantial increases in total sports media revenues. While media revenues grow as a proportion of total sport revenues, the business model for sports, clubs, leagues, and organizations, is likewise affected. Depending on the magnitude and distribution of these transformed revenue streams, sport consumers may expect changes in, not only in how they receive, and what price they pay to consume, their products, but perhaps transformations of the sports competitions themselves as the incentives of leagues and club owners are altered.

The innovation of broadcast technologies continues to expand. Delivery of internet services to most consumers was initially limited to existing telephone (DSL) and cable lines where bandwidth intensive applications, such as the streaming of movies, television programs and live broadcasts, are limited, and during high use periods are subject to bottlenecks, which greatly diminish quality, as the number of simultaneous users on a system increases. However, internet suppliers – often also the providers of cable television (CATV) systems – are continually expanding the infrastructure to increase bandwidth for their consumers and expand the reach of their networks. New technologies, including high-speed fiber-optic lines are increasingly available for the home delivery of Internet services and this is motivating the development and delivery of more and more bandwidth intensive services, particularly high-definition video products, which have become manifestly preferred as the delivery option for live sports broadcasts. Moreover, wireless telecommunications services, notably Wi-Fi, are able to deliver TV and other video entertainment to mobile personal computers, smartphones, and other portable electronic devices (for example, tablets such as the Apple iPad). Technological advancements continually provide consumers with additional content choices and new reception device products that increase their options as to both when and where they can consume the media products. For example, over-the-top (OTT) technology permits consumers to access voice, video, and data products on their TVs by connecting directly to the public internet without necessarily going through the CATV systems. This phenomenon is already significantly altering the way much programming content, traditionally reserved for TV broadcasts, is delivered, and the effect on the value of live sports programming is substantial.

Communication policy is crucial to the outcomes for sports media consumers. Traditionally, the broadcasting sector of national economies has been heavily regulated, which has resulted in restricted supplies and higher than competitive market prices for consumers. The Telecommunications Act of 1996 accelerated an easing of broadcast regulation toward policies favoring less government intervention, particularly of the Internet, and has to date offered sport media consumers more, though not necessarily less expensive, choices. Notwithstanding, deregulation can bring about a progression of different monopoly and market power issues. We can expect that technology will continue to advance, but a primary question is how will the developing regulatory environment affect sport media consumers? Communication technology at once represents the public good and market failure issues that warrant regulation and government intervention. Because communication resources have always been scarce, once the available frequencies along the radio spectrum and now Internet bandwidth, the government's role in both the allocation and creation of infrastructure resources through intervention and regulatory policy is critical. If allocation policies are too restrictive, or if infrastructure costs are prohibitive, excessive monopolization and the market failure of higher prices and fewer choices for consumers is the consequence.

Historically, sports content programming has played an important role in both broadcast technology and broadcast policy. The market forces advancing sports toward its audience have fostered technological innovation and sports content providers, clubs, leagues, and governing bodies, have been front and center with their demands to governments, and decisively shaped the regulatory environment. This chapter proceeds as follows. The next section comprises a cursory review of the history leading up to current state of communications technology as it applies to the sports industry. This is followed by a section that reviews regulatory issues as they apply to the sport media and suggests the imminent regulatory challenges of the developing technology. The chapter concludes with a discussion of the causes and effects of the new revenue streams on the sports product, the possible transformations of the games and competitions themselves, and reviews the regulatory and judicial choices needed to bring about and maintain an equitable environment for sports consumers and the producers and conduits of sports media.

Sports and the development of broadcast technology

Three broadcasting eras, defined by significant shifts in technology, can be identified. The first is the period extending roughly from World War II to 1980, when TV for most consumers was limited to the free-to-air (FTA) broadcast networks. The airways were dominated by the three national broadcast networks, ABC, CBS, and NBC, each of which distributed its programming to local affiliate stations around the country. Sports broadcasts provided a significant amount of programming content throughout this era. The networks purchased broadcast rights from the major professional sports leagues, the NCAA, and obtained the rights to televise event sports such as championship boxing, Triple Crown horse races, major golf tournaments, and the Olympic Games. The networks also created popular programs comprising collections of unique sport events on shows such as ABC's *Wide World of Sports*. Larger TV markets also included non-network affiliated independent stations, which often secured broadcast rights for the local professional team's Major League Baseball (MLB), National Basketball Association (NBA), and National Hockey League (NHL) games, and other local sport events. Because competition was limited to the few networks, broadcast rights fees paid to sports teams and leagues were relatively modest throughout this period (Noll, 2007).

Cable or subscription based TV eclipsed free-to-air broadcasting for all types of programming in the 1980s and remains, as of 2012, as the primary delivery source for televised programs including sports broadcasts. Digital technology has permitted a significant increase in the number of channels available to consumers. New broadcaster entrants in to the market coveted sports content to attract viewers and competition for sports broadcast rights intensified. The consequence was an increase not only the total annual hours of sports broadcasts, but also in the value of rights fees, particularly for the major sports leagues and other high-demand events traditionally covered by FTA television. The 21st century reveals a new era as TV programs, including live sports broadcasts, are available to consumers via the Internet. All of the US major professional sports leagues, and ESPN, have packages available for subscription purchase via the Internet. Web-based delivery is able to provide consumers with more sports programming content (for example, live/archived broadcasts) than conventional TV.

According to Blain (2010), the demand for sport programming played a significant role in the initial technological development of TV, was a catalyst as CATV began moving toward prevalence in the 1970s, and may again drive the innovation of technologies integral to internet broadcast delivery. Sports programming was prominent in driving the initial demand for TVs. Early NBC sports director Harry Coyle was quoted as follows "Television got off the ground because of sports...when we (NBC) put on the World Series in 1947, heavyweight fights, the Army-Navy football game, the sales of television sets just spurted" (Barron, 2012, para. 1). Likewise sport programming was instrumental in the growth of CATV. Notable independent broadcasters, WGN in Chicago and WTBS in Atlanta, made their programming available via satellite to cable systems nationwide, and transformed themselves into national CATV "superstations." The purchase of sports franchises provided a major programming source for both networks. In 1976, the small, local UHF Atlanta-based WTCG (owned by Ted Turner) began distributing its signal at no charge to local cable providers nationally by satellite. That same year, Turner bought the MLB's Atlanta Braves and the NBA's Atlanta Hawks, to provide programming for WTCG and used "superstation" status to make the Braves' games available to throughout North America. He renamed the station WTBS in 1979 (Encyclopaedia Britannica, 2012). WGN which began distributing its signal by satellite to cable providers in 1978 purchased the MLB's Chicago Cubs, whose broadcast rights it already owned, in 1981. Networks devoted to specific content areas began to appear and accumulate on cable menus by the early 1980s (such as CNN, MTV).

ESPN, the first cable channel exclusively devoted to sports programming, began operations in 1979. Wood and Benigni (2006), among others, detail ESPN's development in their history of sports on CATV. Sport programming is now a staple of the CATV industry. The total number of available cable channels has increased exponentially and the upper bound is established not by technological limits, but only economic constraints. Although cable service providers may, and sometimes do, serve only a single community, the industry has consolidated into several large companies known as multi-system operators (MSOs), many of which serve numerous cities and communities nationwide. Examples of MSOs include Comcast Corporation and Time Warner Cable, Inc., the two largest MSOs in the US, with a combined 35 million subscribers (National Cable and Telecommunications Association, 2012).

By the early1990s, digital cable technology began to substitute for analog delivery. This allows cable providers to compress video channels so that they take up much less frequency space. Cable providers can install as many as twelve standard-definition, and three high-definition, digital channels on a single analog channel frequency (Broadband DSL Reports, 2009). The business model of cable service providers entails that channels are bundled together and sold as selected fixed packages, or tiers offering successively more channels, to their subscribers at set prices for each level. Because they reach national markets, and their net revenues are determined by total subscriber numbers, MSOs are willing to provide their customers with access to a wide variety of networks and channels, some of which are of interest only to small niche markets. This combination of technology and industrial organization has enabled and incentivized MSOs to offer an ever increasing number channels to their subscribers, and sports channels are well represented in that growth.

Technology has now developed to facilitate live broadcasts of sporting events over the worldwide web. Since it arrival as a fundamental expediter of commerce in the mid-1990s, the Internet has rapidly and radically transformed the music, publishing, and newspaper industries. Yet, its influence on broadcasting communications has thus far been more restrained and less severe. Doubtless, broadcast TV is the enduring mainstay of the old media industry, the one that has made only a limited transition to the Internet; the reasons for this are twofold, but steadily eroding. Technological development is one part of the explanation as the infrastructure needed to provide sufficient bandwidth for the consistent delivery of video content over the Internet is much greater than that needed to download text, digital photos, and digital audio tracks. Meanwhile, the development and demand for new video products continues to pressure existing bandwidth capacities. Live steaming is greatly compromised when broadband speeds are insufficient because the viewer cannot simply wait for the download to complete and then enjoy the content later. Sufficiently high-speed capability for live feeds and high-definition video downloads have only recently become extensively and consistently available. DSL telephone landlines are inadequate for high-speed delivery of video content and the existing copper cable lines suffer because they are oversubscribed, and thus the necessary speed is often deficient for the delivery of video applications during peak load periods. MSOs, in particular have rushed to upgrade infrastructure and facilitate delivery for its customer base. Innovations and more production of wireless and fiber optic technologies continue to lessen the claims on traditional cable delivery, but technologies that increase the demand for bandwidth, such as high definition TV and 3-D video transmissions, particularly popular for sports content, also continue to increase in usage, perhaps at a faster rate than the increase in bandwidth capacities.

Secondly, the move toward internet broadcasting is curbed because the CATV industry and the MSOs are the primary gatekeepers to the Internet. The same digital technology that has enabled cable operators to offer more TV channels along their systems has also facilitated the capacity to make them the best equipped conduits for high speed Internet and other two-way digital interactive communication services. By the early 2000s, MSOs were primary in the delivery of web-based services to consumers' homes and they now largely control of much of the development of Internet infrastructure.

CATV operators are of course motivated to preserve revenue streams that may be altered if the delivery of programming moves to the Internet. At present, CATV regulation leaves MSOs with little competition for broadcasting within local markets and technological advantages over other potential Internet providers let them control access and infrastructure development, and with that MSOs maintain considerable monopoly power. This underscores the importance of regulation, and the effect of that regulation, on both the demand and supply sides of the broadcasting market. Sports fans as consumers, and clubs and leagues as content providers, factor significantly into this equation. Sports programming is becoming increasingly valuable in the new paradigm. In fact, it is argued by some that live sports are the only programs now sustaining the cable companies (Backus, 2011). In addition to the management of competition, intellectual property issues are paramount to telecommunications regulation. The better access to two-way digital interactive communication services facilitates file sharing and the capacity to circumvent the primary content providers and content distributers. As with the music and publishing industries, this issue presents a regulatory challenge, and content producers are adamant in their demands for the protection of intellectual property. However, the uncertainty surrounding resolution of these regulatory issues makes live broadcasts, which are less likely to be appropriated, even more valuable to the CATV industry.

Regulation and sports broadcasting

Noll (2007) put forth that regulation has, and will continue to have, greater consequences than technological developments in terms of delivering sports broadcasts to consumers. Regulation presents the task of balancing competing interests up and down the delivery chain, fostering innovation, and protecting consumer interests; none of these factors is mutually exclusive. Regulation presents a challenge because it is not a zero-sum game, that policy which benefits consumers' interests may also foster innovation, but the opposite may likewise be true. On the one hand, it can be argued that competition fosters innovation that benefits consumers with more choices and lower prices and thus the focus of regulation should be to curtail monopoly power. The counter position is that natural monopolies offer lower production costs, which can be passed on to consumers in the form of lower prices, and natural monopolies should be protected, but with prices regulated for maximized social welfare. Moreover, it is claimed that it is a right to profit from the production of intellectual property which motivates innovation. During at least the first 50 years of its existence, Federal Communications Commission (FCC) policy noticeably reflected the latter view; they promoted monopoly outcomes and thwarted both the development of communications technology and consumer access to broadcast media services (for example, Cave and Crandall, 2006). Notwithstanding, modern FCC policy denotes a turnabout. The agency's focus on promoting rather than restraining competition in communications markets is upshot from two factors. First, the settlement of the US Department of Justice's antitrust case which broke up the telecommunications monopoly of AT&T in 1984, quickly motivated innovation and lowered consumer costs in the telephone industry. The event provided empirical evidence on the costs of monopoly and benefits of increased competition for consumers. Second, the Telecommunications Act of 1996 represented a significant overhaul over the original Communications Act, and its intent was specifically the further deregulation of the communications industry (Federal Communications Commission, 2011). In regard to the delivery of the Internet and related products, existing broadband providers, particularly MSOs, have very few competitors and thus consumers are susceptible to imposition of monopoly prices and product restrictions.

A second aspect of broadcast regulation, and one that is more specific in its relevance to sports, concerns rules in regard to the property rights to sport content and the transfer of broadcast rights from the content providers to the broadcast networks. The answer to the question as to who initially owns the broadcast right to a team-sport contest is not clear cut (Jeanrenaud and Késenne, 2006). A major controversy involves whether the sales of rights by the league acting as a cartel, as opposed to sales by individual clubs only, should be permitted. Cartelized sales become more valuable the more effectively the league is able to reduce the total number of available broadcasts. Due to a successful petition of Congress by the NFL, professional sports leagues in the U.S. are granted permission since 1962 to collectively package and sell the broadcast rights of league games to TV networks through the Sports Broadcasting Act (SBA). The law provides no explicit extension to CATV channels. Zimbalist (2006) suggests that the extension should be challenged and that collective sales to cable networks are harmful to consumers. However contractual arrangements between leagues and networks suggest this is implied and it has not been challenged. Collective sales by amateur sport organizations may be exposed to antitrust review, as determined by the 1984 US Supreme Court ruling in *NCAA v. Oklahoma Board of Regents*, which proscribed the NCAA from controlling the sale of broadcast rights collectively for all college football games (FindLaw, 2012). Empirical evidence reveals that centralized sales certainly reduce the total number of broadcasts and raise their prices. The number of NFL TV broadcasts declined considerably in the immediate wake of the SBA and likewise the number of college football telecasts increased multifold after NCAA was banned from the centralized sale of football broadcast rights. In both cases, the per-unit of broadcast price received by the central collector was dramatically higher under cartel sales (Noll, 2007).

Under the SBA, leagues may choose to control the rights to all, or only some portion, of the available games, leaving the rights to games left over available for sale by the individual clubs. In US sports leagues, only the NFL controls all TV broadcast rights at the league level. In part because the broadcast revenues are shared equally by all member clubs and are thus assumed to enhance competitive balance, it is claimed that centralized sales are fundamental to the league's economic success. The law does not impose a revenue-sharing formula, as that is the league's choice. The equal sharing of centrally collected broadcast revenues is actually unique to US professional sports. Notwithstanding, the effect of equally shared broadcast revenue by sports leagues on competitive balance is ambiguous both in theory and when subject to empirical tests.

Economists have mixed views on centralized sales and consumer interests. Gerrard (2006) argues convincingly that decentralized sales harm the sports consumer because competitive balance deteriorates. Conversely, Noll (2007) states that although the allowance of centralized sales can result in a more even distribution of broadcast revenues across clubs, the practice is inefficient as a league-wide revenue-maximizing strategy, and viewing opportunities are restricted by such arrangements. Consumers are further harmed by blackout polices, which are encompassed by the SBA. Blackout rules allow leagues to block broadcast signals, and the policies typically target local markets. The rules are intended to alleviate the perceived negative affect of TV viewing on in-person game attendance. Pustis and Sen's (2000) study of the NFL's policy reveals that league revenue gains from increased attendance are more than offset by the welfare losses to broadcast consumers resulting in a net social welfare loss.

There is of course nothing in the SBA that explicitly recognizes league policy in regard to internet delivery of sport programs. However the MLB, the NBA, and the NHL have assumed full centralized control, not only for the broadcasting of games over the Internet, but each of these leagues, and the NFL also control all member club websites. Investment in Internet-based delivery has proven particularly lucrative for MLB, the foremost league in providing web-based distribution of its sports content (Toms, 2012). The NBA and NHL followed MLB's lead and each offer similar full-service websites that include live broadcasts to subscribers for out-of-market games. The NFL, ever cautious and always effective at limiting consumer viewing access for profit, lags behind when it comes to steaming live games over the Internet. The league has left live steaming options to its contracted broadcast networks, who collectively pay the league substantive rights fees (over US$20 billion in 2011–12 and nearly doubling to US$40 billion per year beginning in 2014) far and away the highest in sports. For example, ESPN is able to live steam *Monday Night Football*, but will do so only for its cable subscribers (Wilson, 2012). General access to the live steaming of games over the Internet is controlled by the NFL's satellite TV partner DIRECTV; access has been limited to those homes where its services are not available or, as of 2011, to those only with specifically listed mobile devices. However live streaming is available universally to all computer devices for the first time for the 2012 championship season at a subscription price of US$300 (DIRECTV, 2012).

Despite the apparent success, not all are happy with the practice of league-centered Internet control. The NHL has already faced and survived an antitrust challenge, as the New York Rangers objected to league control of the club's website (Huntowski, 2009). More important, however, are two unresolved (as of 2012) challenges to the standard practice of restrictions on the delivery of local games in their home markets. The TV and Internet blackout policies of MLB and the NHL are subject to class action antitrust lawsuits filed in May and March of 2012, respectively. The complaints *Laumann v. NHL* and *Garber v. MLB* were both filed in the Southern District of New York. Two of the three named plaintiffs in the NHL case are among the four named plaintiffs in the MLB lawsuit. The plaintiffs allege that each league has violated the Sherman Antitrust Act by unfairly restricting its fans' opportunities to watch local broadcasts via the Internet. The complaints each charge two anticompetitive practices. First, the leagues bundle local and non-local games and require consumers to purchase a package that includes all out-of-market broadcasts. Second, Internet broadcasts are blacked out on all local market games that are broadcast by regional sports networks. Customers cannot use their Internet feeds to watch their local team play, but must instead purchase a cable subscription to watch the games on TV exclusively through their regional sports network. The complaint charges that the exclusive broadcasting policies enable the regional sports networks to charge monopoly prices for their much-sought-after sports programming and this raises the subscription fees for cable consumers. The judicial opinions that resolve these lawsuits are likely critical, not just in regard to the access to and costs of sport programming consumers, but also to the business models of sports clubs and leagues.

Implications from the new media frontier

The most dramatic effect of the new media on sports business is a substantial surge in the broadcast values of live sports programming. By late 2010, OTT technology had become widespread and was increasingly able to provide TV programming through streaming services like Netflix, Hulu, and Amazon.com. Web-ready TVs and other devices, for example SlingBox and Xbox, which could bring Internet streamed content to TVs, became readily available and relatively inexpensive. This situation posed a threat to the cable industry as, for the first time, consumers could bring a wide variety of video applications, movies, and TV programs to their TVs while sidestepping the local cable system and its fees. Customers still often pay MSOs for their internet access, but are less inclined to purchase the bundled offering that includes cable and Internet along with telephone services. Sports programming, and live broadcasts of sports events in particular, remains so far an exception, and one major type of content not easily available through OTT. It is apparent that cable networks believe that live sports programming is the offering that can differentiate them from the OTT alternatives; sports broadcasts are the "last bastion of appointment television" (Van Riper, 2012a, para. 3). Toms (2012) and Van Riper (2012b) provide examples of several commentaries where the authors report on discussions with sports media advisor and investor, Chis Bevilacqua. Cable networks, particularly regional sports networks, have been poised to capitalize, as they are the gatekeepers for live sports broadcasts. Starting in 2010, regional sports networks began offering MLB teams what would have been considered incredible contracts just two or three years earlier, in terms of annual payouts, total value, and contract lengths. *Forbes*, which reports annually on the finances of each major professional sports league, revealed that, in 2010, the Texas Rangers entered into a 20-year contract with RSN Fox Sports Southwest that will pay an average of US$80 million per year; the contract succeeded a deal that paid US$30 million annually (Van Riper, 2012b). In 2011, the California Angels entered into a 17-year contract with Fox Sports West that has an average payout of US$95 million per year replacing a contract that retuned US$46 million annually, and in early 2012 the Los Angeles Dodgers negotiated a US$100 per year annual payout, the highest rate ever for an MLB club, over 20 years with the RSN Prime Ticket. The Yankees, whose US$95 million annual transfer from their YES network, which once so dwarfed all other media deals that there was concern it would ruin competitive balance in baseball, was the previous standard. The Houston Astros and San Diego Padres have also signed lucrative rights deals with FSNs since 2011and several other deals are on the horizon as existing contracts expire.

Likewise in college sports, the Big 12 Conference, Atlantic Coast Conference, and Pac 12 Conference have each negotiated similarly lucrative broadcast rights packages since 2011 (Dosh, 2012). These contracts return to each member school more per-year than was earned by their entire conferences less than ten years ago. While MLB clubs and college sports conferences have so far been the most visible beneficiaries of new contracts, NHL and NBA clubs, and other sports organizations stand to benefit as well as rights contracts expire and new contracts are negotiated. For example, the NBA's Los Angeles Lakers have already entered into a 20-year agreement with TWC that will pay them an average of US$150 million per year (Flint, 2011).

Two immediately identifiable matters are the effects of the evolving broadcast rights landscape on player compensation and franchise values. To start with the latter, in the wake of their new broadcast rights deal the Dodgers were acquired by a new ownership group for a price of US$2.15 billion. That amount, which surprised industry analysts, more than doubled the previous record for the sales price of any American sports franchise. Additionally, the small-market Padres, with their rights deal in hand, were sold for an announced US$800 million in August 2012. Nearly double the value that *Forbes* had placed on the club, only US$485million, in March of that year (Ozanian, 2012). The consequences of escalating franchise values cannot be predicted exactly if this becomes a trend, but the impact of the new media environment on the sports team values appears to be substantial.

As for the former issue, in the wake of their new broadcast rights contract the Angels in 2012 signed star Albert Pujols to a ten-year, US$240 million contact, and, in anticipation of negotiating their new rights deal, the Detroit Tigers locked up free agent slugger Prince Fielder for US$214 million over nine years starting in 2012. The Dodgers agreed to pay their star, Matt Kemp, US$20 million per year over eight years (Van Riper, 2012b). In all three cases, the length and total value of the contracts represent significant escalations in MLB player compensation. MLB's competitive balance (luxury) tax has doubtless checked the annual payments, but the contract lengths are noteworthy. There is some concern this trend may harm competitive balance, as the value of the new rights deals is determined by market size, which is disparate in MLB, and also the NBA and NHL. However, each of these leagues has in place mechanisms (luxury taxes on payrolls and salary caps) which have been effective in reducing payroll disparity across each league (see, for example, Maxcy, 2011). However, we may see the NHL and MLB follow the NBA lead and attempt to impose maximum contract lengths in their next collective bargaining negotiations. More important to the games is perhaps the possible changes to owners' incentives as media revenues supplant gate and stadium revenues largest source of a sports club's revenue. Attendance and therefore stadium revenues are directly correlated with winning, but broadcast contracts with guaranteed payouts over 15 and 20 years are not. This means that there is less financial incentive to win games in any particular season. The weak TV ratings of a loser will not lower the subscriber fees the RSN collects or lower their payments to the clubs. Fans must hope their owners derive other benefits from winning, those which extend beyond the direct annual bottom line, so that the incentive to build the best possible teams will remain intact.

Finally, sport consumers, without some regulatory relief, should expect to pay more to view sports broadcasts. The MSO-RSN-sports league combination represents a three-headed consortium, which bestows on all three parties considerable market power. The escalation of broadcast rights fees is based on the expectations of consumers' willingness to pay and the consortium's ability to extract that full value. Relief may come by way of FCC and Department of Justice intolerance toward mergers and acquisitions in the industry. Consumers should be wary of disproportionate integration within the consortium. For example in addition to ownership of the NBC Sports Network, MSO Comcast also holds the NHL's Philadelphia Flyers. Moreover, favorable rulings for the plaintiffs in either one or both of the two afore mentioned antitrust suits are crucial and represent a far more serious issue than simply whether NFL fans are given only the option of viewing an out-of-market game when they would prefer to see their local team on TV.

The blackouts policies of the NHL and MLB Internet streaming services represent the expected restrictions on broadcasts when centralized cartel sales are permitted. In each case, the blackouts are not protecting clubs from lost gate revenue, but rather the RSN monopolies. Conceivably this is a much more acute problem, and one that has potentially much more severe consequences in terms of the cost to consumers, than NFL blackouts. The blackout policies help facilitate the afore mentioned consortium's market power and that affects not just consumers of sports programming, but potentially all consumers of products delivered via cable and the Internet. How the courts will rule cannot be predicted. There has been more recent questioning of blackout policies. In February 2012, the FCC began a review of the rule permitting blackouts and five US Senators wrote a letter to the FCC urging an end to NFL's blackout policies. However, with the exception of labor issues, league defenses of cartel behavior have fared well in antitrust cases (Huntowski, 2009). Furthermore, baseball's antitrust exemption will be invoked in defense.

Who wins or loses as the evolution of the sports media progresses remains ambiguous. Consumers will have greater options as to when and where they can watch sports programming, but at what cost? The escalating fees and long-term contracts for sports broadcast rights indicate that sports programming is expected to remain highly valuable and whoever controls the property rights to that programming can expect to extract those values. Likewise, as the importance of stadium-based revenues shrinks in relative magnitude, changes in owners' incentives and may adversely affect their willingness to build winning teams, and overall competitive balance. Exactly how sports consumers fare will depend on the regulatory position of the FCC and antitrust interpretations by the courts; much of which may be revealed very soon.

References

Backus, J. (2011). The future of television. *HuffPost Tech*, December 2. Retrieved from http://www.huffingtonpost.com/john-backus/the-future-of-television_b_1125889.html.

Blain, E. (2010). Sports over IP: Dynamics and perspectives (Unpublished master's thesis). Massachusetts Institute of Technology, Cambridge, MA.

Barron, S. J. (2012). Sports and television. Museum of Broadcast Communications. Retrieved from http://www.museum.tv/eotvsection.php?entrycode=sportsandte.

Broadband DSL Reports (2009). Comcast Cable TV FAQ: Why does x area have more HD channels than my area? *DSLReports.com*, May 22. Retrieved from http://www.dslreports.com/faq/comcasttv/Frequently_Asked_Questions.

Cave, M., and Crandall, R.W. (2001). Sports rights and the broadcast industry. *Economic Journal*, 111, 4–26.

DIRECTV (2012). NFL Sunday Ticket. Retrieved from http://www.directv.com/DTVAPP/content/sports/nfl.

Dosh K. (2012). College TV rights deals undergo makeovers. *ESPN Playbook*, May 10. Retrieved from http://espn.go.com/blog/playbook/dollars/post/_/id/705/.

Federal Communications Commission (2011). About the FCC. November 28. Retrieved from http://transition.fcc.gov/aboutus.html.

FindLaw (2012. U.S. Supreme Court. *NCAA v. Board of Regents of Univ. of Okla.*, 468 U.S. 85 (1984). Retrieved from http://caselaw.lp.findlaw.com/scripts/getcase.pl?court=usandvol=468andinvol=85.

Flint, J. (2011). Time Warner Cable, Lakers strike 20-year TV deal. *Los Angeles Times*, February 14. Retrieved from http://articles.latimes.com/2011/feb/14/sports/la-sp-0215-lakers-time-warner-20110215.

Gerrard, B. (2006). Competitive balance and the sports media rights market: What are the real issues? In C. Jeanrenaud and S. Késenne (Eds.), *The economics of sport in the media* (pp. 26–36). Cheltenham, UK: Edward Elgar.

Huntowski, M. (2009). Blades of steal: The fight for control of sports clubs' websites and media rights in Madison Square Garden, L.P. v. National Hockey League. *Villanova Sports and Entertainment Law Journal*, 16, 123–62.

Jeanrenaud, C., and Késenne, S. (2006). Sport and the media: An overview. In C. Jeanrenaud and S. Késenne (Eds.), *The economics of sport in the media* (pp. 1–25). Cheltenham, UK: Edward Elgar.

Maxcy, J. G. (2011). The effect on player transfers of a luxury tax on club payrolls: The case of Major League Baseball. In W. Andreff (Ed.), *Contemporary issues in sports economics: Participation and professional team sports* (pp. 80–92). Cheltenham, UK and Northampton, MA: Edward Elgar.

National Cable and Telecommunications Association (2012). Cable: Top 25 Multichannel Video Programming Distributors. Retrieved from http://www.ncta.com/Stats/TopMSOs.aspx.

Noll, R. G. (2007). Broadcasting and team sports. *Scottish Journal of Political Economy*, 54 (3), 400–21.
Ozanian, M. (2012). Moores wants $800 million for Padres. *Forbes*, May 29. Retrieved from http://www.forbes.com/sites/mikeozanian/2012/05/29/moores-wants-800-million-for-padres/.
Pustis, W. P., and Sen, S. K. (2000). Should NFL blackouts be banned? *Applied Economics*, 32 (12), 1495–507.
Toms, P. (2012). Last week in Bizball: MLB teams are media companies. *Biz of Baseball*, February 7. Retrieved from http://www.bizofbaseball.com/index.php?option=com_contentandview=article andid=5591:last-week-in-bizball-mlb-teams-are-media-companiesandcatid=67:pete-toms andItemid=155.
Encyclopaedia Britannica (2012). Ted Turner. Retrieved from http://www.britannica.com/EBchecked/topic/610307/Ted-Turner.
Van Riper, T. (2012a). TV money is a game changer for baseball and the Dodgers. *Forbes*, March 21(*Forbes Magazine* dated April 9, 2012). Retrieved from http://www.forbes.com/sites/tomvanriper/2012/03/21/the-new-moneyball/.
Van Riper, T. (2012b). The new moneyball. *Forbes*, March 21 (*Forbes Magazine* dated April 9, 2012). Retrieved from http://www.forbes.com/forbes/2012/0409/baseball-valuations-12-mccourt-multibillion-dollar-deals-new-moneyball.html.
Wilson, M. (2012). Super Bowl streaming: Will live sports online ever get better? *Popular Mechanics*, February 2. Retrieved from http://www.popularmechanics.com/technology/how-to/tv/super-bowl-streaming-will-live-sports-online-ever-get-better-6650668.
Wood, C., and Benigni, V. (2006). The coverage of sports on Cable TV. In A. A. Raney and J. Bryant (Eds.), *Handbook of sports and media* (pp. 147–70). London, UK: Taylor and Francis.
Zimbalist, A. (2006). Economic perspectives on market power. In C. Jeanrenaud and S. Késenne (Eds.), *The economics of sport in the media* (pp. 160–78). Cheltenham, UK: Edward Elgar.

48

COLLEGE ATHLETICS COMMUNICATIONS

Evolution of the field

G. Clayton (Clay) Stoldt

More than 2,700 sport communicators work in college athletics in the US and Canada (CoSIDA, 2012a). Working in units designated as "sports information," "media relations," or "athletics communications," they serve as the public relations (PR) person or staff for their institution's athletics department (Miloch and Pedersen, 2006). They have also been described as the "primary gatekeepers in the PR process inside college athletics, the portals through which vital information on multi-million dollar teams flows to the sport media and public at large" (Battenfield and Kent, 2007, p. 237). This chapter provides an overview of the field of college athletics communications. It begins with a brief history of the profession, which includes information on the establishment of the College Sports Information Directors of America (CoSIDA). This leads to a discussion of the job responsibilities professionals (for example, sports information directors) in the field typically assume and the related benefits and challenges commonly associated with such work. The chapter then moves to a discussion of how the field has changed in recent years. Topics include the impact of social media and the changing roles of practitioners as CoSIDA rebrands the profession as being comprised of "strategic communicators for college athletics."

History of the profession

College athletics programs were mostly administered by students until the early 1900s (Covell and Barr, 2010). Yale was the first university to hire professional coaches in the late 1800s (Covell and Barr, 2010), and faculty athletics committees began forming soon thereafter to address concerns regarding athletics programs (Barr, 1998). Universities then began hiring directors of physical education, positions that would eventually evolve into the jobs held by athletics directors today (Barr, 2010). Enter Arch Ward, named as the first sports publicity director in 1919 by Notre Dame (Littlewood, 1990). Ward, a former sports writer whose work also involved the promotion of wrestling and other sport stories, was hired for the position by Knute Rockne. As noted by Littlewood, the legendary football coach hoped to secure national publicity for his program but realized he did not have the resources to hire a professional press agent. In exchange for joining Rockne's staff, Ward was admitted as a non-degree student at Notre Dame and likely received free room and board (Littlewood, 1990).

Ward's responsibilities included writing program stories for area newspapers and producing stories for other newspapers around the country when requested. Littlewood (1990) observed that Ward assumed the Notre Dame position "with little exposure to the concept of objective, independent reporting from a detached point of view. Of course, few press agents ever had a more ambitious or publicity-conscious client than the Notre Dame head coach" (p. 26). Ward's work as Notre Dame football's "official news correspondent" (p. 26) lasted just two years; however, his impact on the profession extended beyond his time with Rockne. Later in his career, Ward became the sports editor of the *Chicago Tribune* and originated the first-ever Major League Baseball All-Star Game in 1933 and the College All-Star football game in 1934 (CoSIDA, 2012b; Littlewood, 1990).

As college athletics grew in popularity, other institutions hired staff members to serve in similar roles to Ward's. By 1931, the profession had a critical mass sufficient to comprise a Sports Section of the American College Public Relations of America (Vista, 2007). Commonly known as sports publicity directors until the 1950s, professionals in the field typically worked in one-person offices with no or limited staff support (Vista, 2007). Offices were sparse and resources limited, but despite those limitations, "[sports information directors] prospered during that time and built strong relationships with media members" (Vista, 2007, para. 11). During this period, professionals in the field utilized a range of tactics to promote their institutions and college athletics on the whole. For instance, Lester Jordan, who served at Southern Methodist University from 1942 to 1980, established the Academic All-America program in 1952 (Vista, 2007).

A major event in the development of the field was the establishment of CoSIDA in 1955–56. The organization had 102 charter members (CoSIDA, 2012b; Vista, 2007) and, in 1957, it held its first conference in Chicago. In addition to an annual meeting for professional development, CoSIDA began producing a newsletter that was the forerunner to today's monthly publication, the *CoSIDA Digest*. In the 50-plus years since its founding, CoSIDA membership has grown to more than 2,700 (CoSIDA, 2012a). CoSIDA's growth is reflective of the advancement of the field. The majority of US colleges and universities now have at least one staff member working in athletics communications, sports information or media relations, all common titles in the profession (Ruihley and Fall, 2009). Many institutions now have large athletics communication staffs (Hardin and McClung, 2002). For instance, Ohio State University's media relations staff is comprised of 12 full-time staff members, an intern, and ten students working on a part-time basis (Stoldt, Dittmore, and Branvold, 2012). The basic function of today's athletics communications professionals is essentially the same as Ward's – promote their institutions, programs, and personnel. The next section addresses the more specific responsibilities of those in the field and the associated benefits and challenges resulting from their work.

Responsibilities, benefits, and challenges

In 1984, Grunig developed a typology of PR practice featuring four models (Grunig and Hunt, 1984). The most basic was the press agentry/publicity model, and the authors observed that sport was one of the settings in which it was most commonly practiced. The model describes a form of PR activity in which practitioners seek to deliver persuasive communication in support of their organization's objectives. The model focuses exclusively on one-way communication, outbound from the organization to the public via the mass media, and it recognizes that the attention-seeking tactics individuals and organizations sometimes employ sometimes violate the values of truth and honesty. Though there is no indication that Ward and other pioneers in college athletics communications engaged in the shadier practices sometimes associated with the press agentry model, the model seems to be an appropriate description of the basic intent and approach they took to their work. For example, Harold Keith, a legendary sports publicist at Oklahoma, wrote that when he first assumed his position in 1930, the institution's football team was in the midst of a decade-long downturn. In an effort to generate ticket sales, Keith crafted an innovative promotional tactic, promoting the program's successful teams and players of the more distant past (Keith, 1948). When practitioners creatively find ways to keep their programs in the public eye, they are working in a manner consistent with the press agentry model.

Grunig and Hunt (1984) observed that as the PR profession developed, a more advanced model of practice emerged – the public information model. Practitioners employing the public information model work to support media coverage of their organization and as a result, generate favorable publicity. Sometimes described as "journalists in residence" (Grunig and Hunt, 1984, p. 22), these practitioners adhere to established journalistic values such as truthfulness and fairness when sharing information with publics, and accordingly, they can serve as valuable resources to members of the sport media. Research by a number of scholars indicates that college athletics communicators have traditionally employed both the press agentry and public information models in the course of their work (Jackowski, 2007). Overall, five areas of primary responsibility were identified in multiple analyses of the field.

The first area of primary responsibility is generating positive publicity for their sports programs (Favorito, 2007; Helitzer, 2000; Neupauer, 1997; Stoldt, *et al.*, 2012). Two of the most commonly used tactics in publicity efforts are news releases and news conferences. McCleneghan's (1995) survey of NCAA sports information directors working at a range of competitive levels (for example, NCAA-I, NCAA-II) found that practitioners spent roughly ten percent of their time writing press releases. Stoldt and Narasimhan's (2005) survey of the CoSIDA membership found that respondents indicated writing press releases was both one of the most important tasks they assumed and one of the areas in which they were most skilled. An additional dimension to this responsibility is promoting coaches and student-athletes for various athletic and academic awards. When representatives of the sport programs receive honors, positive publicity often follows, benefiting the institution and the award recipients. Dealing with negative publicity is also sometimes a part of the job as college athletics programs have proven highly susceptible to crisis situations. Crises ranging from NCAA violations to misconduct by coaches or student-athletes to fan misbehavior often result in considerable media coverage and significant demands on college athletics communicators.

Providing services to the media is the second area of primary responsibility (Favorito, 2007; Helitzer, 2000; Neupauer, 1997; Stoldt, *et al.*, 2012). Practitioners have indicated that they spend approximately ten percent of their time addressing this responsibility (McCleneghan, 1995), and this type of work involves multiple activities. One is responding to media requests for interviews and information about the athletics department and its sports programs. Another is tracking team and individual statistics and maintaining historical records (Favorito, 2007; Helitzer, 2000; Schultz, Caskey, and Esherick, 2010; Stoldt, *et al.*, 2012). A third is managing media services at games and events (Favorito, 2007; Helitzer, 2000; Schultz, *et al.*, 2010; Stoldt, *et al.*, 2012). Administering credential requests, providing workspace and required amenities (for example, Internet access), and delivering event-specific information are all a part of the media services function.

Working with coaches and athletes is the third primary responsibility associated with college athletics communications work (Favorito, 2007; Heltizer, 2000; Schultz, *et al.*, 2010). Practitioners have estimated that 15 percent of their time is devoted to this responsibility (McCleneghan, 1995). A key aspect of this work is assisting coaches and athletes in developing media skills so they are able to best represent both themselves and their institutions. Another dimension to this task is coordinating schedules so that coaches and athletes can maintain an appropriate level of availability to the media without having media commitments overwhelm their schedules to the detriment of their athletic and academic responsibilities.

A fourth primary responsibility is producing legacy media such as media guides and game programs (Favorito, 2007; Heltizer, 2000; Schultz, *et al.*, 2010; Stoldt, *et al.*, 2012). Media guides are significant endeavors because many programs produce separate guides for each of the sports their college sponsors. And although NCAA legislation has limited the size of such guides to 208 pages after an "arm's race" in which some schools were producing publications of more than 600 pages for revenue sports such as football, the task of creating these publications continues to be highly involved. Further, because additional NCAA legislation now prohibits the sending of printed media guides to recruits and the printing of traditional media guides is quite costly, many institutions have opted for online media guides with streaming audio and video features that make them appealing to multiple audiences, including recruits.

Creating content for new and social media is the fifth primary responsibility of college athletics communicators (Favorito, 2007; Stoldt, *et al.*, 2012). This area, far more than the previous four, has changed dramatically in recent years. As far back as 2002, however, Hardin and McClung observed that while certain fundamental skills such as the ability to write effectively still served as the foundation of the profession, technological convergence was resulting in new skills such as the ability to utilize html code becoming valued in the field. In 2003, professionals in the field indicated that maintaining their organization's website was their single most important task (Stoldt and Narasimhan, 2005). Furthermore, as determined through a 2012 survey conducted by the chapter author, when the survey of the CoSIDA members asked how much time they spent working with blogs and social media, the most frequent response (41 percent of respondents) was 11 percent to 25 percent of their time.

The five areas of primary responsibility do not necessarily cover the full breadth of tasks assumed by college athletics communicators. The overall range of responsibilities has led scholars to observe that the work of sports information personnel was different from that of other PR professionals (Neupauer, 1997) and other athletics department personnel (Heltizer, 2000). Practitioners have indicated that as much as 55 percent of their time is consumed with general administrative duties (McCleneghan, 1995). Neupauer observed that sports information professionals often assumed secondary responsibilities such as booster club activities and placing advertising buys. The chapter author's 2012 survey of CoSIDA members indicated that many practitioners also spent at least a moderate amount of time planning and making recommendations regarding PR problems their programs may be facing.

Benefits

College athletics programs have received a number of benefits as a result of the work of their athletics communication professionals. Miloch and Pedersen (2007) surveyed sports information directors in a mid-level NCAA conference and reported that respondents indicated their relationships with members of the media were both positive and mutually beneficial. Respondents also indicated their relationships with members of the media impacted the type of news coverage given to their athletics programs. Such coverage, the respondents indicated, contributed to the marketability of their department's programs (Miloch and Pedersen, 2007).

In 2000, a survey of NCAA athletic directors found more than 80 percent of respondents citing six benefits being realized by their departments (Stoldt, Miller and Comfort, 2001). The frequently cited benefits were (1) positive relationship with the community, (2) favorable publicity, (3) positive relationships with student-athletes, (4) positive relationships with student-athletes' parents, (5) positive relationships with members of the mass media, and (6) positive relationships with university faculty/staff. Further, the mean return on investment (ROI) reported for their department's PR efforts was 732 percent (Stoldt, *et al.*, 2001). The ROI figure is particularly notable because scholars conducting a global study identifying factors associated with excellence in PR reported that the estimated ROI identified by chief executive officers for the top ten percent of organizations studied was 266 percent (Dozier, Grunig, and Grunig, 1995).

Challenges

Despite the recognized benefits associated with the work of college athletics communicators, practitioners and scholars have long recognized two challenges facing the field. The first – lack of respect for college athletics communicators – is somewhat limited in scope in that it is function specific, limited in impact to those working in the profession. The second – an inability to maximize professional contributions to their organizations – is broader in scope because it affects their athletics departments, their universities, and the key publics with whom they interact.

Nearly 20 years ago, McCleneghan (1995) observed that lack of respect was the most common response practitioners offered to describe the challenges they faced on the job. "The SID business today is not practicing what PR wants all its practitioners to do – advise and counsel management" (p. 29). Hardin and McClung (2002) reported that when sports information professionals were asked what advice they had for students, one of the themes in their responses was that prospective practitioners should expect an interesting and fun career, but one that received little appreciation. The scholars noted the profession was dealing with credibility issues, and "(t)his field is apparently still maturing and struggling for recognition and equality outside its own confines" (p. 39).

Following their ethnographic study of the communication culture in a NCAA Division I-A sports information office, Battenfield and Kent (2007) observed that staff members worked in "a culture of virtual anonymity" (p. 249). Staff members were likened to "factory workers" (p. 249) in that their primary function was to produce things such as media guides and news releases. "Anonymity is a major part of being a SID," noted Battenfield and Kent. "The SIDs commented that they are servants to the media, coaches and staff, and the primary researcher firmly can conclude that this production mentality does lead to other negative manifestations" (p. 249). The negative outcomes, according to Battenfield and Kent, included anger, frustration, cynicism, burnout and even turnover.

The related but broader concern facing the field is that based on the professional roles of college athletics communicators and models of PR most commonly employed in the profession, many athletics departments are not maximizing the potential contributions of their communication specialists. Using Broom's PR roles typology (Broom and Smith, 1979; Broom 1982) as the theoretical background for his study, Stoldt (2000) examined the current and ideal professional roles of SIDs at NCAA I-A (now NCAA FBS) institutions. The vast majority of respondents (92 percent) reported that their current primary role was that of communication technicians, practitioners skilled in tactical responsibilities such as writing news releases and designing graphics. Even among those practitioners with senior-level titles, such as assistant athletics director or sports information director, the predominant professional role was communication technician (Stoldt, 2000). When asked about the frequency in which they would ideally engage in various role-related tasks, respondents indicated they would like to assume numerous managerial-related tasks with more frequency (Stoldt, 2000). These tasks included activities such as keeping senior management informed of public reactions to organizational policies and actions and pointing out the need to follow a systematic PR planning process.

Organizations whose top PR official serves primarily in the technician role are likely to employ one-way models of PR practice (Grunig and Grunig, 1989). Both the press agentry and public information models of practice utilize one-way flow of communication, outbound from the organization to its publics (Grunig and Hunt, 1984). Two more advanced models of practices are predicated on two-way communication patterns, exchanges between the organization and its key publics. One is a two-way asymmetric model that is utilized when an organization's goal is "scientific persuasion" (Grunig and Hunt, 1984, p. 22). The other is a two-way symmetric model employed when an organization is seeking "mutual understanding" between itself and key publics (p. 22). Both of the more advanced models are based on the notion that organizations must both listen as well as be heard in order to insure communication effectiveness. The determination of which model to employ in a given situation is driven not only by organizational goals, but by assessments of the environment, including the amount of uncertainty that exists as well as the ability of key publics to constrain the organization (Grunig, 1984; Grunig and Grunig, 1989).

Jackowski (2007) observed that as the environments in which college athletics departments exist have become more complex and challenging, one-way models of pubic relations are no longer appropriate as the primary ways of conducting PR. The PR function must, according to Jackowski, "keep pace" with changes in environment. Failure to do so "may even detract from the building of relationships with key stakeholders" (para. 59). The author recommended employment of the two-way symmetric communication model in order to address difficult PR issues before they rise to the level of public advocacy and regulatory issues for governing bodies.

Changes in the field

College athletics communication professionals are seeing their field evolve in two important ways. As previously mentioned, practitioners now devote significant efforts to new and social media. In addition, professionals in the field, and CoSIDA in particular, are working to address the challenges described in the previous section by recasting the role of the college athletics communicator as being managerial in nature and strategic in its contributions to athletics departments and their institutions. The following sections address both of these topics.

Social media

Advances in communication technologies have fundamentally impacted the field of college athletics (Cooper, 2011; Favorito, 2007; Sanderson, 2011). While traditional mainstream media continue to be powerful communication platforms, new media such as organizational social media sites now provide powerful new communication options. Clavio observed, "In an age of ever-tightening athletic budgets and increasing diffusion of traditional media audiences, social media provides a comparatively inexpensive personal connection with fans, through services already offered by third parties, such as... Facebook, Twitter, and others" (Clavio, 2011, p. 310).

A 2012 survey – conducted by the chapter author – of the CoSIDA membership found that 88 percent of respondents agreed or strongly agreed with the statement that the emergence of social media has impacted the way their organization handled external communications. Besides providing a mechanism for directly sharing organizational messages with large numbers of people, social media applications provide channels for organizations to interact with and receive feedback from members of key publics (Clavio and Kian, 2010; Pedersen, Miloch, and Laucella, 2007; Sanderson, 2011; Schultz, *et al.*, 2010; Wallace, Wilson, and Miloch, 2011). Such ability makes social media a valuable tool for organizations wanting to enact two-way advanced models of PR practice.

Evolution of the field

CoSIDA has taken important steps in recent years to address the challenges facing the profession. After years of being administered by practitioners in volunteer leadership roles, the organization hired John Humenik as its first executive director in 2008 (CoSIDA, 2012c). Humenik, a former sports information director at Princeton, Michigan, and Florida, promptly led the organization in developing a strategic plan designed to "enhance the collegiate sports public relations profession" (CoSIDA, 2012d, p. 2). The plan featured seven guiding principles to support that goal. The guiding principles included advancing the profession, practitioners in the field, and the organization, as well as image building with internal and external constituents (CoSIDA, 2012d). The organization also began the process of rebranding itself as "strategic communicators for college athletics."

Humenik said that a lack of understanding on the part of senior-level leadership in college athletics and the resultant lack of respect for professionals in the field prompted the organization's actions (Athletic Management, 2008). In an interview with Stoldt (2008), Humenik also noted the critical importance of the organization's activities at the time. "It is my sense that most decision makers want, and in many cases are now demanding, their communications staff to go about their jobs in a different way, a more strategic way," stated Humenik:

> If the senior staff is more 'old school' in their approach to PR and communications, then I feel it is up to the communications staff to be proactive and clearly demonstrate what has to take place in the current state of communications for the athletics department to be successful.
>
> *(Stoldt, 2008)*

Humenik further noted that:

> If either group (senior management staff or communications staff) or both groups sit on the sidelines with regard to this issue of changing from being 'information directors' to 'strategic communicators,' they will be left behind in a host of matters as they relate to college sports.
>
> *(Stoldt, 2008)*

The CoSIDA leader added that:

> We have to understand that we not only have to change the way we see ourselves – changing from information directors to communication directors to strategic communications directors—but also have to teach senior leadership; that is how they have to see us and our role within their organizations.
>
> *(Stoldt, 2008, p. 461)*

The organization has taken important steps to realize its new vision. For example, CoSIDA has provided new services in regard to professional development, such as weekly updates on the latest information available in the field and online webinars. It has modified its organizational structure (Athletic Management, 2008; Stoldt, 2008), and it has enhanced relationships with other professional organizations in the field (for example, the National Association of Collegiate Directors of Athletics).

In 2012, CoSIDA initiated a yearlong strategic branding review, led by an external consultant, to assist the organization in defining necessary next steps as the field evolves (T. Di Camillo, personal communication, June 14, 2012). In announcing the project to the membership, Tom Di Camillo, the 2012 CoSIDA president, wrote, "Everything – and I mean everything – is on the proverbial table for discussion and change. Consider this our accreditation review" (personal communication, June 14, 2012).

Research by Ruihley and Fall (2009) indicate the profession is making some progress in regard to its current goals. Their survey of NCAA Division I athletic directors found that most respondents identified a staff member with an identifier such as "media relations," "communication," or "sports information" as their department's top PR official. And when rating their top PR officer's abilities in a variety of PR tasks, Ruihley and Fall found that four of the top six responses were in regard to managerial responsibilities: recommending responses to issues, advising on PR issues, managing PR issues, and evaluating PR issues. Further, the scholars found that athletic directors' responses indicated that the most frequently enacted professional role by their department's top PR official was the problem-solving process facilitator. Noting that this finding represented a change from previous studies that found the communication technician role to be most prevalent, the authors observed that "With high expectations of not only the fan base but also among athletic administrators, it is easy for issues to quickly escalate and for rumors to quickly get out of hand." They added that, "This is when having an officer devoted specifically to PR management is very useful" (Ruihley and Fall, 2009, p. 408). Such a comment alludes to the changes in communication dynamics the field has experienced, as well as the advanced role college athletics communicators have begun assuming with greater frequency. These changes are of seismic nature, and moving forward, it seems fair to expect additional, and possibly major, changes for practitioners in this evolving field.

References

Athletic Management (2008). Meet CoSIDA's new executive director. *Athletic Management*, March 21. Retrieved from http://www.athleticmanagement.com/2008/03/21/meet_cosidas_new_executive_director/index.php.

Barr, C. (1998). Collegiate sport. In L. P. Masteralexis, C. A. Barr, and M. A. Hums. *Principles and practice of sport management* (pp. 166–94). Gaithersburg, MD: Aspen.

Battenfield, F. L., and Kent. A. (2007). The culture of communication among intercollegiate sport information professionals. *International Journal of Sport Management and Marketing*, 2, 236–51.

Broom, G. M. (1982). A comparison of sex roles in public relations. *Public Relations Review*, 8 (3), 17–22.

Broom, G. M., and Smith, G. D. (1979). Testing the practitioner's impact on clients. *Public Relations Review*, 5 (3), 47–59.

Clavio, G. (2011). Social media and the college football audience. *Journal of Issues in Intercollegiate Athletics*, 4, 309–25.

Clavio, G., and Kian, E. M. (2010). Uses and gratifications of a retired female athlete's Twitter followers. *International Journal of Sport Communication*, 3, 485–500.

Cooper, C. G. (2011). The pursuit of innovative communication in college athletics. *International Journal of Sport Communication*, 4, 401–2.

CoSIDA (2012a). General info: What is CoSIDA? College Sports Information Directors of America. Retrieved from http://www.cosida.com/about/general.aspx.

CoSIDA (2012b). Arch Ward Award. College Sports Information Directors of America. Retrieved from http://www.cosida.com/Awards/archaward.aspx.

CoSIDA (2012c). John Humenik. College Sports Information Directors of America. Retrieved from http://www.cosida.com/jhumenik.aspx.

CoSIDA (2012d). CoSIDA strategic plan. College Sports Information Directors of America. Retrieved from http://www.cosida.com/CoSIDAStrategicPlan/csp_index.aspx.

Covell, D., and Barr, C. A. (2010). *Managing intercollegiate athletics*. Scottsdale, AZ: Holcomb Hathaway.

Dozier, D. M, Grunig, L. A. and Grunig, J. E. (1995). *Manager's guide to excellence in public relations and communication management*. Mahwah, NJ: Lawrence Erlbaum.

Favorito, J. (2007). *Sports publicity: A practical approach*. Burlington, MA: Elsevier.

Grunig, J. E. (1984). Organizations, environments, and models of public relations. *Public Relations Research and Education*, 1 (4), 6–29.

Grunig, J. E., and Grunig, L. A. (1989). Toward a theory of the public relations behavior of organizations: Review of a program of research. In J. E. Grunig and L. A. Grunig (Eds.), *Public relations research annual* (Vol. 1; pp. 27–63). Hillsdale, NJ; Lawrence Erlbaum.

Grunig, J. E., and Hunt, T. (1984). *Managing public relations*. New York: Holt, Rinehart and Winston.

Hardin, R., and McClung, S. (2002). Collegiate sports information: Profile of the profession. *Public Relations Quarterly*, 47 (2), 35–9.

Helitzer, M. (2000). *The dream job: $port$ publicity, promotion and marketing* (3rd ed.). Athens, OH: University Sports Press.

Jackowski, M. (2007). Conceptualizing an improved PR strategy: A case for stakeholder relationship marketing in Division I-A intercollegiate athletics. *Journal of Business and Public Affairs*, 1 (1). [www.scientificjournals.org/journals2007/articles/1016.htm.

Keith, H. (1948). *Oklahoma kickoff*. Austin, TX: Eakin.

Littlewood, T. B. (1990). *Arch: A promoter, not a poet*. Ames, IA: Iowa State University Press.

McCleneghan, J. S. (1995). The sports information director – no attention, no respect and a PR practitioner in trouble. *Public Relations Quarterly*, 40 (2), 28–32.

Miloch, K. S., and Pedersen, P. M. (2006). Sports information directors and the media: An analysis of highly symbiotic and professional relationship. *Journal of Contemporary Athletics*, 2 (1), 91–103.

Neupauer, N. (1997). Sports information: The most coveted, ignored profession. *Public Relations Strategist*, 3 (3), 35–7.

Pedersen, P. M., Miloch, K. S., and Laucella, P. C. (2007). *Strategic sport communication*. Champaign, IL: Human Kinetics.

Ruihley, B. J., and Fall, L. T. (2009). Assessment on and off the field: Examining athletic directors' perceptions of public relations in college athletics. *International Journal of Sport Communication*, 2, 398–410.

Sanderson, J. (2011). *It's a whole new ballgame: How social media is changing sports*. New York: Hampton.

Schultz, B., Caskey, P. H., and Esherick, C. (2010). *Media relations in sport* (3rd ed.). Morgantown, WV: Fitness Information Technology.

Stoldt, G. C. (2000). Current and ideal organizational roles of NCAA Division I-A sports information professionals. *Cyber-Journal of Sport Marketing*, 4 (1). Retrieved from http://pandora.nla.gov.au/nph-wb/20000501130000/http://www.cjsm.com/vol4/stoldt41.htm.

Stoldt, G. C. (2008). Interview with John Humenik, executive director of the College Sports Information Directors of America. *International Journal of Sport Communication*, 1, 458–64.

Stoldt, G. C., and Narasimhan, V. (2005). Self assessments of collegiate sports information professionals regarding their public relations task expertise. *International Journal of Sport Management*, 6 (3), 252–69.

Stoldt, G. C., Miller, L. K., and Comfort, P. G. (2001). Through the eyes of ADs: Perceptions of sports information directors, and other PR issues. *Sport Marketing Quarterly*, 10 (2), 164–72.

Stoldt, G. C., Dittmore, S. W., and Branvold, S. E. (2012). *Sport public relations: Managing stakeholder communication* (2nd ed.). Champaign, IL: Human Kinetics.

Vista, B. (2007). CoSIDA looking golden at 50. *Athletic Management*, June 22. Retrieved from http://www.athleticmanagement.com/2007/06/22/cosida_looking_golden_at_50/index.php.

Wallace, L., Wilson, J., and Miloch, K. (2011). Sporting Facebook: A content analysis of NCAA organizational sport pages and Big 12 conference athletic department pages. *International Journal of Sport Communication*, 4, 422–44.

49

DANGEROUS CURRENTS

How public relations and advertising influence sports reporting and cause ethical problems

Thomas Schierl and Christoph Bertling

Media corporations of a Western model have two overriding goals: as social institutions the mass media are expected to create a space for public discourse and transparency through critical observation of society. Besides this they are to act as a socializing agent and ensure quality content (for example, by concentrating on values like rationality, freedom, and accountability). As a free-market enterprise, certain specifications and goals are to be met in terms of broad coverage, reach and advertising revenue. The pursuit of these two goals creates great tensions in editorial departments, because the pursuit of one goal often obstructs the attainment of the other.

These tensions, which we can boldly title self-contradictory, are increasingly apparent in sports newsrooms. This certainly seems to be related to the comparatively notable influence of public relations (PR) and advertising in sports reporting as compared to other departments. This appears to be most apparent in TV sports journalism, which this contribution will focus on. This development can be considered dangerous insofar as diverse difficulties arise for business ethics and media law that demand solutions, while these become ever more elusive. Therefore, this chapter shows a) why television reporting is at particular risk of being exploited economically by the advertising industry; b) which influences are already apparent on a number of levels in TV production of sports reporting, and c) which ethical problem areas have emerged in TV sports journalism, which must be tackled in the future.

On the schizophrenia of sports reporting

Why does TV sports reporting run a particularly high risk of being economically exploited by the advertising industry? This is chiefly the result of the extraordinary mass interest that this journalistic field holds, making it very attractive from not only a media standpoint, but also from a marketing perspective. Major sporting events like the Olympic Games, the Super Bowl, or the Rugby World Cup have a particularly high level of quantitative efficiency, meaning that a low supply level is tied to a high demand. One measure of the huge worldwide demand for major sporting events is the periodically executed *viewer track*. This international study analyzes TV coverage in the 55 most important global markets, which combined constitute over 90 percent of the global national product and advertising spending. According to the *viewer track* study, the final of the 2006 Soccer World Cup had a net reach of 254 million TV viewers; the 2010 World Cup final's net reach was even 329 million viewers. In Europe alone, 71 percent of the population in the five core markets of Germany, England, Spain, Italy, and France have a high interest in soccer, which corresponds to around 175 million Europeans (SportFive, 2009).

The continuously high demand for televised sports is clear from a look at the most viewed TV programs in the year 2009 in various countries. This was a year without any major events like the Soccer World Cup or Olympic Games and yet various sporting events were among the most viewed TV broadcasts. For instance, according to *Television 2009 International Key Facts* (IP Network, 2010), the top five programs in Russia were the New Year's Address (Genre: special event; rating: 20.4 percent; share: 42.5 percent), Russia and Germany in World Cup qualifying (sports; 17.1 percent; 44.1 percent), the New Year's Blue Lantern (variety show; 15.6 percent; 36 percent), The Mold (documentary; 15.4 percent; 34.2 percent), and Russia and Slovenia in World Cup Qualifying (sports; 14.9 percent; 49.5 percent). The top five programs in the United Kingdom were Eastenders (genre: daily soap; rating: 11 percent; share: 25.8 percent), Top Gear/Special (documentary; 8.8 percent; 18.2 percent), France and Wales in Rugby Six Nations (sports; 8.1 percent; 18 percent), Victoria Wood: Seen on TV (documentary; 7.8 percent; 16.1 percent), and Michael Jackson: Memorial Service (special events; 7.6 percent; 19 percent). Lastly, in the US, the top five programs in 2009 were Super Bowl XLIV (genre: sports; rating: 35.7 percent; share: 74 percent), the Super Bowl XLIV Report (magazine-sports; 27.1 percent; 58 percent), the Super Bowl XLIV Pre-Report (magazine-sports; 21.2 percent; 57 percent), the NFC Championship Game between Minnesota and New Orleans (Sports; 20.5 percent; 49 percent), and the NFC Championship Game Report (magazine-sports; 17.1 percent; 40 percent).

TV sports broadcasts that attract such masses can be very lucrative for commercial enterprises, particularly for manufacturers of mass-market products, because they are presented with an opportunity to reach a great number of people with their advertisements. Because professional sports embody values like success, dynamism, and performance, companies can expect a positive image transfer to their products/brand beyond receiving attention and recognition. There is seemingly no better communication platform for advertising to the buying public, with its positive connotations, transcendence of environment, and culture as well as regular, planned appearance (Schierl and Schaaf, 2007). Furthermore, commercial enterprises have a significant interest in exercising as strong an influence as possible over certain aspects of TV sports reporting, since this can optimize the effectiveness of their ads. Interestingly, the success of such influence has increased particularly strongly in recent years.

This is most significantly related to two key areas. First, there has been a loss of quality in TV journalism (including TV sports journalism). Though a global phenomenon, it is apparent that many media enterprises in Western media markets particularly have suffered financially since the financial and economic crisis of recent years (Russ-Mohl, 2009). It is becoming ever more difficult to develop high-quality programming under these conditions. Second, there has been a rise in the price of broadcasting rights to sporting events. Not only the general economic situation of media concerns, but the budgets of sports departments particularly, have been under extreme pressure in recent years. This is related to the steep rise in costs for TV broadcasting rights of many premium sports. As an example of the rise in expense of broadcasting rights to high profile sports over the last decades, we can consider the development of the cost of TV rights for the Summer Olympic Games. For instance, according to Lamprecht and Stamm (2002), the cost of television broadcasting rights for this event has risen worldwide (for example, with estimates of US$1 million for the 1960 Rome Games to US$1.7 billion for the 2008 Beijing Games), in the US (for example, with estimates of US$394,000 in 1960 up to US$894 million in 2008), and in Europe (for example, with estimates of US$274,000 in 1960 up to US$443 million in 2008). If the rise in costs is calculated on the basis of the available figures, there is a global cost increase of around 330 percent between the 1980 Olympic Games in Moscow and the 1984 Olympic Games in Los Angeles, the figures were approximately 310 percent and 390 percent for the US and Europe, respectively. Calculating the price increase for TV rights between 1980 and 2008 gives a global increase of around 1900 percent, around 1200 percent in the US and around 7700 percent in Europe. Similar developments have occurred for soccer. The prices of sports rights for the German Soccer League increased by approximately 2757 percent between 1982 and 2000 and those for the Soccer European Cup went up by around 4275 percent. The price of Soccer World Cup rights even went up by 6781 percent in the same period (see Heinrich, 1999; Schellhaass and Fritsch, 2007). This is particularly problematic since although the expense of TV broadcasts has risen sharply, the number of TV viewers has hardly increased in most countries (on this, see Bertling 2009; Bertling 2011; Gratton and Solberg 2007).

The consequence of these two developments is that purchases of TV sports rights are becoming increasingly risky investments. The increased expense of the input factor has already increased so far that direct refinancing through advertising is almost impossible despite increased reach and market shares. Moreover, there are always numerous risks tied to TV sports broadcasting rights. Over the course of events one never knows how the home team will perform in a championship. Will the national team even qualify? In terms of viewer interest, the question is whether a sports star will attract more viewers. When it comes to the image of the individual sport one must ask how much exclusive coverage fosters the media company's image. In terms of the advertising market, the questions are whether lucrative advertisers can be found for the commercial break/presenter/sponsors and how the advertising market will develop in the meantime.

We can therefore conclude that it has become increasingly difficult to refinance expenditure on the purchase market through income from the advertising and public market. Owing to an ever-growing divide between reach and the price of rights, TV broadcasters must lay out their sports reporting in a way that will give them the best chances of refinancing them. As a result of these developments on the sport, media, and sports rights market, there is increasing (necessary) economic oversubscription of journalistic methodology. TV sports editors then become very susceptible to the influences of commercial companies. Within this context we must ask the extent to which the sports organizer, businessperson, and advertiser influence TV sports reporting.

Economic influences on sports journalism

It can actually be observed that sport organizers, the advertising industry, and commercial enterprises try very hard to exploit sports reporting to their own ends. How strong this influence over sports reporting has already become in many countries is clear when one takes a closer look at procurement and production in TV sport. The strong dependencies of the procurement sector are particularly clear when it comes to TV base signal creation. Numerous sport associations/organizers and sports rights agencies produce the image base signal – as in the case of Formula 1 reporting. Journalists are then only able to comment on the live feed, often without the capacity of altering it, even subtly. Since 2006 the image production firms Olympic Broadcasting Services (OBS), T.E.A.M., and Formula One Management Limited (FOM) have produced the TV images of the Olympic Games, Soccer World Championships, and Formula 1 racing. This has taken most of the journalistic control over the live images out of the hands of TV sports journalists in the editing room. In addition, there are ever more tenuous partnerships between sports organizations and TV broadcasters globally. During rights purchasing, numerous television stations are committing themselves to broadcasting only image enhancing materials. The European Broadcasting Union (EBU), for example, committed itself to broadcasting an IOC PR report at least three times on the channel that covered the 2008 Olympic Games. It is stipulated within the contract that the 52-minute film must be shown without commercial break. It was produced by the IOC and deals with the IOC and the Olympic movement (Schraven, 2009).

The described production of the TV base signal by the organizer leads to further difficulties. When it comes to program arrangement, we are confronted with the problem of promotional images being produced by the sports organizer. Rather than containing journalistic content, strategic product content increasingly takes the foreground in programming. The fact that this methodology has been allowed into image creation is particularly apparent from the globally broadcast live feeds of Formula 1 races. The directors are instructed to maintain certain camera positions so that the advertising banners will be clearly visible. These guidelines are usually complied with, despite the reduction in production values (for example, drama, dynamism). In Formula 1, this results in certain cuts being postponed, even though the racing cars are no longer visible. This is done to make the advertising more memorable to the recipient (Bertling, 2011). Furthermore, it must be noted that there is already a mingling of advertising and programming in the so-called naming rights of stadiums/leagues and in the interviews conducted in front of sponsor walls, shirt and perimeter advertising as well as use of the split screen system during sports broadcasts. They increasingly make use of thematic and musical placements and virtual advertising. References to the programs' promotional nature are near to invisible in TV sports reporting.

One of the core tasks of program production is the actual realization of the planning, management, and execution of the production. This includes a large proportion of brandcasting measures. The word is a composite of broadcasting and brand and describes the link between editorial content and advertising cooperation. A typical example of brandcasting was the 13-part sporting goods soap opera *The Road to Sydney*, ordered by the sporting goods manufacturer Adidas for the 2000 Sydney Olympics, in which the Adidas brand was positioned strategically. There was no explicit mention of Adidas's involvement in the production. In the US, Nike built on Adidas' example and produced the documentary film *Road to Paris*. Viewers watch as the cyclist Lance Armstrong prepares for the Tour de France. Nike succeeded in selling the one-hour production to the US broadcast network CBS. Nike used this opportunity to learn something about its consumers: whoever visited the www.roadtoparis.com website, automatically entered into a dialogue with the sporting goods brand in which they were expected to share personal information. Ross Sleight of the London ad agency HHCL sees this direct dialogue with the customer as a successful extension of brandcasting (Latein and Littger, 2012).

The described influence in the production chain of TV sport shows that economic influences are at times very apparent in TV sports productions. Most of these measures are very unlikely to be noticed by the viewers. This makes a clear distinction between advertising goals and journalistic content impossible. But in the everyday working routines of sports journalists such a separation of advertising and programming is just as impossible in many ways, since the integration of sports, media and economics is already so tightly woven. How strongly the actions of sports journalists are already limited in many media companies is apparent from developments in media enterprises. It is becoming ever more apparent that media companies have no wish to report on independent sporting events, but attempt to use integration strategies to incorporate important sporting events into their portfolios. Critical reporting is naturally unwelcome, since the object of reporting is seen as the broadcaster's own product, to be marketed in the most advantageous way. Consideration of national and international developments in sports news production shows that over the last few years numerous strategies have been developed to introduce so-called TV-sports branding, with the result that the line between journalistic and product related action becomes ever less clear. The following examples support this observation:

- product related use of sports news;
- image transfer and creation through long-term broadcasting concepts;
- brand building and creation of exclusivity through vertical integration;
- sports news as a vehicle for audience flows;
- special media formats/designs for product recognition.

Product related use of sports news

The German independent broadcaster RTL choses to broadcast a few popular sports, which are intended to bolster its image. Formula 1 has been covered extensively since the channel's introduction in an attempt to reach a young audience with purchasing power. In order to raise Formula 1's profile it is tied into news broadcasts to a great extent. Extensive news analysis shows that Formula 1 reporting is embedded into the RTL news format to a very great extent, quantitatively speaking. The strong differences indicate some extent of entrepreneurially motivated news placement and rule out chance as an explanation. Similar tendencies can be seen in various US channels (see Raney and Bryant, 2006).

Image transfer and creation through long-term broadcasting concepts

Sports are adapted ever more to the broadcaster profile. The broadcasting of particular popular sports is expected to contribute significantly to the creation of a specific image around the TV broadcaster. Often it is not the coverage, but the product fit with the broadcaster that stands in the foreground. Such strategies have been very apparent since the 1980s in the case of RTL's use of Formula 1 and boxing as well as on many of Rupert Murdoch's channels (for example, on his TV channel BSkyB and its reporting on the English premier league).

Brand building and creation of exclusivity through vertical integration

TV broadcasters seek ever more exclusive coverage of sporting events in order to place their rivals in disadvantageous positions. Many vertical integrations result from this. A few years ago ESPN-Star Sports attempted to install the Premier Hockey League (PHL) in India. This new hockey league was to develop international stars, through whom ESPN was to extend their market share on the Indian media market. Organizing developments in the U.S. show the degree to which federations and associations are already tied to the entertainment and media industry. In recent years the U.S. companies with the biggest turnover have developed their portfolios in the media and entertainment sector by the addition of athletes and sporting events. Numerous integrations of this kind have increased quickly in recent decades.

Sports news as a vehicle for audience flows

Lately, ever-greater attention is paid to anchoring sports to which the exclusive broadcasting rights are held between the various departments in order to market them as fully as possible. In news as well as in entertainment magazines, stars and events are almost always covered positively. Not only private, but also public service broadcasters take part in these practices, especially when it comes to sports with particularly expensive broadcast rights, which therefore take great investment. Public service broadcasting operators are especially interested in attracting a young target audience to their channel.

Special media formats/designs for product recognition

Besides Rupert Murdoch and his News Corporation, his Australian competitor, Gerry Packer, has spent recent years attempting to design sporting events to be compatible with the broadcasting channel. A legendary example of this is the introduction of a cartoon duck to cricket broadcasts. The duck breaks into tears when the batsman is eliminated. Commentators repeatedly use the phrase "What a duck" and cultivate this cricketing term. The duck is also used as a lucrative merchandising product, bringing in more economic gains. The cricket broadcasts were not simply reports, but popularized a corporate identity by giving it mass appeal.

These examples show how easily a variety of tools and methods of integration can be identified which aid in TV-sports branding.

TV-sports journalists are faced with an ever-greater dilemma: on the one hand, as a journalistic area of activity, TV-sports reporting should be neutral and objective. On the other, the news must increasingly be structured for the greatest affect. This results in an ever more difficult balancing act between journalistic and product-oriented behavior.

Economic primacy – at the expense of (journalistic) quality?

Sports journalism has become closely entangled with the media's economic interests as well as those of commercial enterprises. These entanglements are often taken for granted, but they are not without their societal problems. In democracies after the Western model, the media have an obligation to create public access and transparency. They are expected to observe society and its components (of which the societal domain of sport is one) critically and to comment upon this. Their task is also to provide a corrective to the planned and stage-managed communications of businesses, such as advertising, PR, or publicity work. Advertising, legitimately and with the knowledge of the recipient/consumer, takes a one-sided perspective (generally in favor of the advertiser), seeks sympathy and tries to be persuasive. Journalism on the other hand should be neutral and independent, consider things factually and inform critically, to orient the recipient/consumer and create transparency in a complex world. And this provision of information is what the recipients of the media expect.

Insofar as sports journalism is increasingly subordinated to economic interests, even steered by these or at least modulated by them, it will no longer be capable of fulfilling its actual social function. Even if the sport itself and the reporting on it are primarily consumed as entertainment, sport – beyond the individual sporting event – holds great importance for society in the form of political, economic and cultural relations. Sport is, particularly in its ties to other social areas, far more than entertainment. It is an important area of social reality when it comes to politics, economics and culture. It is of great value to a society to be informed of these things professionally and accurately.

It is also a legitimate and really necessary demand that sport journalism a) contains balanced, impartial, and critical reporting and b) references economic interests and conflicts between the subjects of reports or between the parties involved and the subjects of reports. The clear distinction between this ideal and reality and the complete lack of transparency in sports reporting, including its orientation towards (economic) interests, can likely be explained best by an observable principal–agent problem. In the "principal–agent problem" or "agency dilemma," *principal* refers to the contracting body and *agent* to the contractor (Eisenhardt, 1989). There are a number of principal–agent relationships in the present area of inquiry (see Figure 49.1). The recipient/consumer is the principal to various agents, namely commerce (for example, manufacturers of consumer goods who advertise), the media and the journalists. He or she contracts them and as agents expects certain products from the company; the journalistic media and journalists are expected to provide information, transparency, enlightenment, honesty, relevance, objectivity, and so forth.

But the commercial enterprises and the media are also principles in their own right, contracting other agents: commerce contracts the journalistic media to publicize their ads, PR, and public content and the media contracts journalists to create media content. The contracting of an agent by a principle generally implies an edge on the part of the agent, which is either the reason for the contracting or its result. Either the agent knows more in advance, being a professional, and is hired for this knowledge or the agent gains this knowledge through the intensive and specific assignment to the topic by the principle. This

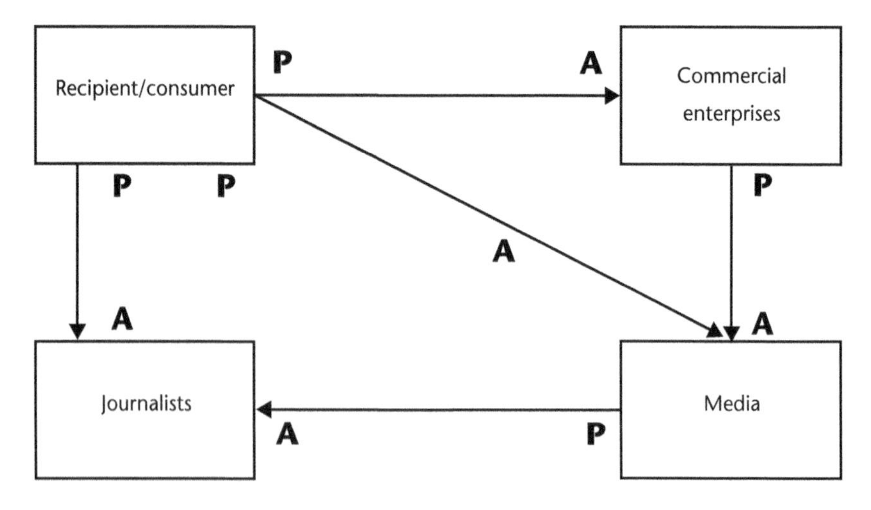

FIGURE 49.1 Principal–agent relationships in sports reporting

asymmetry of knowledge between the principle and the agent can be used to the advantage or disadvantage of the principle. It is, for instance, often used by journalists to create greater transparency for the principle. However, the asymmetry of knowledge can also have negative consequences, the agent's moral hazards for instance. Because the principle is unable to watch the agent entirely or commensurately, the agent may be tempted to act opportunistically – in its own interest, taking account of violations to contracts and norms – in ways that the principle may not approve (Mankiw, 2008). One instance of this is when the agent incorporates the untested assertions of corporations that are intended as PR or advertising, into their editorial offerings and presents this as editorial information, which cannot be checked by the recipient.

Considering the principal–agent relationships in Figure 49.1, one has the impression of several principle–agent relations existing between the four actors depicted that are generally weighted evenly. This impression is, however, misleading to the extent that the economic influences that commercial enterprises can have over the media and that the media can in turn exercise over both free and hired journalists, are disproportionately greater and far more direct than the recipients are able to bring to bear on the various actors. There are direct, process-related structures of communication between the enterprises, media and journalists, through which such influence can be exercised and the success of which can then be tested. The asymmetry of information between recipients and the other three groups of actors is far greater and there is no direct institutionalized structure of communication. Here, influence is only very indirect when it is possible at all. A drawing that is corrected to take account of this weighting of influences would look like Figure 49.2.

We can conclude that, owing to sports reporting, commercial enterprises, media, and journalists each pursuing their own economic ends in practice, sports reporting will be assessed and adapted in the most profitable way. It will only be guided by legal and ethical guidelines where these do not oppose economic goals or when their non-observance may be sanctioned (and is likely to be sanctioned). A show is made of transparency and informing the recipients of those occasions where this does not run counter to the economic interests of the

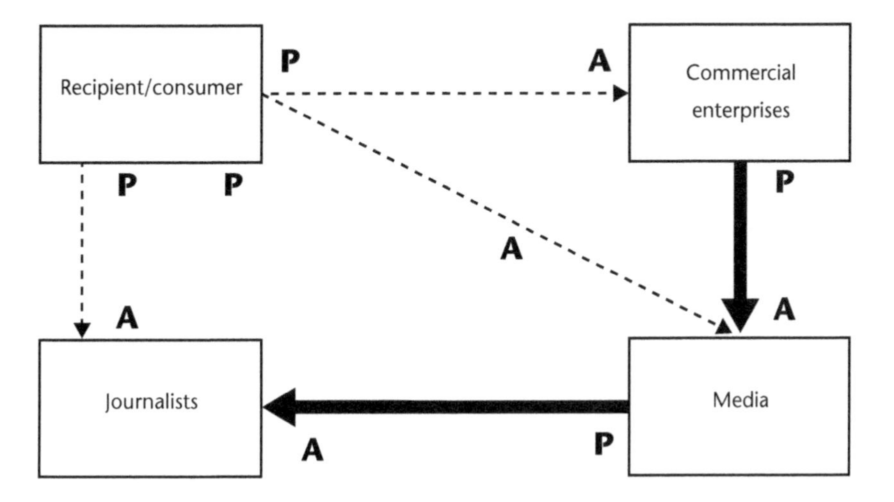

FIGURE 49.2 Principal–agent relationships and their various strengths of influence in sports reporting

various interest groups. PR and advertising interests color reporting very strongly without this becoming apparent to the recipient. Journalism is being replaced by PR contributions that are either directly or indirectly compensated.

Besides the actual social problem of a lack of transparency and information, this leads to an additional economic problem – that is, adverse selection (Akerlof, 1970). Because the market's problem with sports reporting results from the existing asymmetry of information between recipients and the media/journalists, it is not possible for the recipients to differentiate between good and bad quality sports reporting (relating to the criteria of neutrality, balance, critique, and transparency). Insofar as the recipients/consumers tend towards the cheapest offers, which are generally financed through high volumes of open as well as hidden PR and advertising measures. As a consequence products of low quality dominate the market because recipients cannot identify high-quality products. Because the consumer cannot recognize the higher quality, he or she is not prepared to pay more. The quality of the market as a whole inevitably drops despite the fact that recipients would be willing to pay a higher price for better quality.

We must then ask, how can such undesirable developments be avoided, since it cannot be in the interests of a democratic society, the media or the commercial enterprises themselves for the journalistic quality of media to fall continuously. The media must count on the long-term loss of reputation and credibility as well as the collapse of their independent identity. And such loss of reputation and credibility would in turn be a disadvantage to the commercial enterprises, as it leads the advertising effectiveness of the media to suffer. Until now, such developments have been fought, when anything at all has been attempted, using ethical codes and behavioral preambles. These were usually developed by assemblies of sports journalists in order to counter excessive PR and advertising influences. But they imply that individual sports journalists are to be held entirely responsible for the situation. In 1924, at the first international convention of the sports press in Paris, the branch's first ethical code was adopted. Until this day new ethical codes and preambles on responsibility had been passed repeatedly. Yet such an individual approach to questions of ethical responsibility does not appear adequate in the current situation. As we have attempted to show above, sports journalists have forfeited their role as *gatekeepers* to a large extent. Their journalistic contributions are mediated through an opaque mixture of data, information, and communication over which they as individuals have hardly any (to no) influence. The focus should be moved from the individuals to the institutions.

Roughly speaking, two targeted measures can be identified. The first measure is the necessity of turning away from an ethic of individual responsibility on the part of the journalists and media creators and introducing institutional ethics to deal with the questions of the extent and conditions under which institutions act morally. So, in order to defend against a broad loss of quality, the media and commercial enterprises must come to an agreement as to the moral standards they wish to satisfy in which manner. They must commit themselves to formulating accessible ethical codes on specific behavior that puts a stop to the increasing entanglement of reporting and PR/advertising messages. It is not enough to create such ethical codes and make them public, they must also – possibly by means of commissions created for this purpose – be inspected for compliance. Sanctions must be put in place against disregarding of the codes. A second measure towards quality-oriented media resulting from the principal–agent theory is *signaling*. In this case, signaling refers to an action by the knowledgeable party providing private information to an uninformed party (Mankiw, 2008). The media could assign an independent auditor to make a neutral assessment of the reporting quality of the various providers. Such product testing of the media would make recipients able to compare media offerings. Consumers with a greater affinity for quality would then be capable of recognizing those media that meet their standards and be justified in deciding to pay a higher price.

Conclusion

To exaggerate a little, we can ponder whether or not sports journalism is suffering from symptoms of disintegration? Is it being steered significantly by PR and advertising? This chapter shows that these commercial influences are not simply strong, but are to be found on many different levels. There is a real risk of further deterioration in the quality of sports reporting through adverse selection. Owing to a high asymmetry of information, the defense mechanisms that have been developed to date can hardly comprehend, because they follow an ethical conception that is not capable of grasping the relevant ethics. Personal ethical approaches, as formulated by many sports journalists/ federations/ associations, are of scant help in the present situation.

It is far more useful – and besides society, this should also be of interest to the media and commercial enterprises – to stop the loss of reporting quality through established and supervised institutional ethics. The media and enterprise would take this obligation upon themselves (out of long-term economic interests). Similarly, quality media can stop the disintegration of the market for sports reporting by attracting a customer base with an affinity for quality thanks to the signaling of quality. Under present conditions, a strong need is given for the introduction of basic moral and socially recommended behavior and the assistance of sports journalism at (early) signs of disintegration by bringing its focus back to quality and independence.

References

Akerlof, G. A. (1970). The market of "lemons": Quality uncertainty and the market mechanism. *Quarterly Journal of Economics*, 84 (3), 488–500.

Bertling, C. (2011). Zerfahrene Welten. Amerkungen zu ökonomisch-publizistischen Risiken bei exklusiven Free-TV-Sportübertragungen anhand des Fallbeispiels RTL und seiner Formel-1-Berichterstattung. In T. Schierl and D. Schaaf (Eds.), *Sport und Werbung* (pp. 102–19). Köln: Halem-Verlag.

Bertling, C. (2009). *Sportainment*. Köln: Halem-Verlag.

Eisenhardt, K. M. (1989). Agency theory: An assessment and review. *Academy of Management Review*, 14 (1), 57–74.

Gaustad, T. (2000). The economics of sports programming. *Nordicom Review*, 21, 101–13.

Gratton, C., and Solberg, H. A. (2007). *Sports broadcasting*. New York: Routledge.

Heinrich, J. (1999). *Medienökonomie – Hörfunk und Fernsehen* (Vol. 2). Wiesbaden: VS Verlag.

IP Network (2010). *Television 2009: International key facts* (17th ed.). Paris: IP International Marketing.

Lamprecht, M., and Stamm, H. (2002). *Sport zwischen Kultur, Kult und Kommerz*. Zurich: Seismo.

Latein, A., and Littger, P. (2012). Unterschwellige Turnschuhe. *Die Welt*, April, p. 58.

Mankiw, N. G. (2008). *Principles of economics* (5th ed.). Mason, OH: South-Western Cengage Learning.

Pörsken, B., Loosen, W., and Scholl, A. (2008). *Paradoxien des journalismus: Theorie – empirie – praxis*. Wiesbaden: VS Verlag.

Raney, A., and Bryant, J. (Eds.). (2006). *Handbook of sports and media*. Mahwah, NY: Routledge.

Russ-Mohl, S. (2009). *Kreative Zerstörung. Niedergang und Neuerfindung des Zeitungsjournalismus in den USA*. Constance: UKV Universitätsverlag.

Schellhaass, H., Fritsch, C. (2007). Sport im Fernsehen als Grundversorgung. In T. Schierl (Ed.), *Handbuch Medien, Kommunikation und Sport* (pp. 243–55). Schorndorff: Hofmann-Verlag.
Schierl, T., and Schaaf, D. (2007). Der Einsatz von Sportlern als Testimonials in der Werbung. In T. Schierl (Ed.), *Handbuch Medien, Kommunikation und Sport* (pp. 294–309). Schorndorff: Hofmann-Verlag.
Schraven, D. (2009). Skurrile TV-Verträge von ARD und ZDF. *Die Welt*, August 23, p. 32.
SportFive. (2009). *European Football: England, France, Germany, Italy, Spain*. Hamburg: SportFive.

50

CRITICAL PERSPECTIVES IN SPORTS PUBLIC RELATIONS

Jacquie L'Etang

This chapter highlights critical questions that have been raised about sport and its societal impacts and draws out the implications that these may have for public relations (PR) and communications practitioners. The chapter defines sports business in a globalized world and presents a brief overview of scholarship that addresses sports public relations as a way of highlighting functional tendencies and then draws on empirical evidence to reflect upon the role and scope of sports PR practice. This material frames the argumentative substance of this chapter.

The following pages explore ideological discourses and underpinning assumptions that help to shape the sports business industry and sports PR practice, including strategies that seek to idealize and legitimize sports business and its in-built hierarchical and discriminatory aspects. PR academics should not only be concerned about the effectiveness of practice for sport organizations, but should also consider wider issues such as power, politics, exploitation, ethics, children's rights, environmentalism and sustainability, relationships between developed and developing worlds, post-colonial diasporas, cultural imperialism, religion, the promotion and representation of certain body shapes, ageism, gender issues, racism, and the impact of commercialization of sport (L'Etang, in press). To some degree, this chapter considers the ethos of sports business and reflects upon whether the role of PR practice in this context involves the communication of essentially ideological and capitalist discourses. It appears that issues-led and corporate social responsibility-driven approaches to sports PR practice have potential for development and could mitigate the promotional advocacy that appears to dominate.

Sport and sports business

The drama and rituals of sports produce winners and losers, generating emotion and wider meanings in cultural contexts. A key feature of human culture for centuries, the apparent *play* of sport carries wider symbolic significance, for example, nationality, ethnicity, religion, or affiliations of class. Sport operates as a carrier of values, such as those espoused by the Olympic movement and consequently industrialized and capitalized sport opened the way to marketing opportunities and the recasting of sports practice as a repository of brand values.

Sports participation and spectatorship is central to individual and collective identities, and is relevant to societal relations and social change, social movements, diaspora and heritage. Sport is a medium for communication and plays a key role in relational dynamics within societal fabric, as well as being central to the economy. Sports business intersects the creative economy particularly through its digital technology dynamic. The relationship between sport and society is complex, and its location in business and politics has engendered the development of a complicated series of networks, investments and policies. The fact that sport facilitates communication and relationships makes it a natural ally for PR.

Sports business, however, is concerned with sport that can generate capital, and that raises some interesting questions about which sports attract investment and the processes of distinction between the resource-rich and the resource-poor and the consequent influences on society. For example, the greatest rewards in terms of media coverage, sponsorship, and financial rewards are allocated to male sport and inevitably promote a "binary essentialist model of gender norms and differences" (Andrews, 2004, p. 19). Sports business seeks to identify and exploit new opportunities for sports capitalization that will deliver consumers through the branding of sports properties. The sports industry is driven by principles of scientific management, political bureaucracy, positivism realized through the metrics of athletic performance, return on investment, media and marketing statistics (Andrews, 2004). Sports business intersects numerous specialist sectors and is driven by the imperatives of profit and technological determinism, yet is frequently bathed in a glow of idealism and grand claims regarding its societal benefits. The way in which sport and sports business is projected is, or should be, a central question within PR scholarship, in terms of the historical development of the occupation, but also in terms of the extent to which PR uncritically formulates and circulates the discourses of the sports industry, or facilitates reflexive engagement. In short, does PR act as a tool of the sports industry to promote sports ideology or does it work to facilitate exchange and development between sport and society? Furthermore, as representative and spokesperson, it is the PR role that is in the position to make claims about the social legacy of major sports events, yet, the problem of evaluation persists, in common with the PR's industry own professional challenges. "Success in the field of social impact … is still primarily about outputs rather than outcomes," notes Walmsley (2011). Success is "about hosts' ability to deliver programmes aimed at creating community benefits rather than the demonstration of clear linkages between individual events and long-term improvements in health, skills, self-image and the like" (Walmsley, 2011, p. 37).

Sports PR: Scholarship and assumptions

Within PR scholarship, relatively little attention has been given to sport, with some notable exceptions. This may be partly because in the U.S., the heart and soul of professional sport, there is a distinct occupational group referred to as sports directors who appear to encompass PR within their scope (Helitzer, 1999; Irwin, Sutton, and McCarthy, 2002; Johnson, 1996; Neupauer, 2000). Texts for university courses often appear to focus more on media relations and PR tactics (Nichols, Moynahan, Hall, and Taylor, 2002) and articles often focus on specific cases (Anderson, 2006, 2008; Hopwood, 2005). Sports marketers have widened their scope (Beech and Chadwick, 2007; Shank, 2002), but a number of sports management and event management texts do not seem to give PR the attention it deserves (Bowdin, Allen, O'Toole, Harris, and McDonnell, 2006). Unsurprisingly, work from media studies focuses on sports journalism and media sources (Boyle, 2006; Boyle and Haynes, 2000; Haynes, 2005; Lowes, 1997) as has some PR scholarship (Pincus, Rimmer, Rayfield, and Cropp, 1993). The bulk of literature relevant to sports PR focuses on mainstream, commercial and masculine sports; few have considered less capitalized areas such as adventure or extreme sports (L'Etang, 2009; Puchan, 2004).

Contributions to a special issue of *Public Relations Review* on public relations and sport (L'Etang and Hopwood, 2008) largely focused on reputational issues such as those surrounding player transgressions (Wilson, Stavros and Westburg, 2008); crises (Bruce and Tini, 2008; Pfahla and Bates, 2008); reputation and image repair (Fortunato, 2008; Brazeal, 2008); publicity and marketing techniques (Anderson, 2008; Mitrook, Parish and Seltzer, 2008), and online activities (Woo, An, and Cho, 2008). Many of the contributions explored rhetorical strategies and discourses including techniques of apology and diversion (Brazeal, 2008; Jerome, 2008; Pfahle and Bates, 2008). Several authors based their analyses on Benoit's (1995) image repair framework, which comprises strategies such as denial, blame-shifting, minimizing importance, attacking accusers, compensating victims. In their opening chapter, Hopwood, Kitchin, and Skinner (2010) framed sports public relations with the concept of crisis, although contributions to this edited text included corporate social responsibility, marketing, relationship management, fan relations, personal publicity, international communication. However, it is fair to say that this text aligns with the main approach to sports PR by taking a strongly functional approach to sports PR. Few have taken alternative approaches, such as a cultural approach (Curtin and Gaither, 2007; L'Etang, 2006), or the rhetorical analysis of Boyd and Stahey (2008) that explored tensions in a sport organization's rhetoric between corporate and community discourses while attempting to address different audiences. Thus, while much sports PR literature has been rather functional in focus and has drawn in some strategic management perspectives, it is also the case that there has been the tendency to customize the Grunigian paradigm, and to view sports PR from the perspective of the sport organization/client (see, for example, Hopwood, *et al.*, 2010, p. 3). A more critical and questioning approach can garner more diverse and broader societal and stakeholder perspectives that contribute a wider understanding of cultural dynamics and power plays, and challenge common taken-for-granted assumptions, leading to more nuanced insights.

Sports PR: Role and scope

A review of the practitioner publication, *SportBusiness International*, between the years 2005 and 2012 shows that the occupation of PR is not clearly identified as a discreet specialism but embedded in a range of sports marketing activities including brand management, sponsorship (specifically sponsorship activation), event bidding and management, thus exemplifying the challenges of attaining a distinct professional identity and recognition for PR expertise (L'Etang, in press). Business practitioners were much more likely to refer in a general way to communications and networking, with a strong emphasis on business to business. PR activities within the complex, globalized sports industry appears to be subsumed, and in this publication, any explicit reference appears to understand public relations as publicity or media relations.

Despite the silence in this practitioner publication, it is quite clear, from a functional perspective that strategic level public relations work is necessary for the sports business. The sports business faces generic business issues such as: sustainability, corporate social responsibility, financial crisis, intellectual property, diversity, technology; as well as those specific to its operation such as security, event legacy, evaluation (a challenge shared by the rest of the PR industry); as well as well-recognized reputational threats and crises arising from bad behaviour – of athletes, sport organizations, producers in the supply chain. Obvious examples might be sudden death and accidents, drug taking, drunkenness, violence, racism of athletes or fans. Thus, issues and risk management are of central importance in this industry. Sport organizations and corporate bodies clearly have to engage with standard public relations concepts and practice such as: organizational culture, employee communications, organizational symbolism and identity (L'Etang, in press). The widespread use of the term 'sport communication' rather than sports PR tends to promote a technique-orientated occupation rather than a strategic and analytical discipline.

Ideology, discourse, and critique

Popular discourses around sport not only highlight the economic benefits of the sports business industry but also the socio-economic and cultural benefits of healthy lifestyles and the 'feel-good factor' of large sporting events. For example, Thomas Godfrey, commercial director of Sport England, argued that:

> Sport isn't a substitute for other areas of policy and investment. But used effectively there's no doubt it can have a positive impact on everything from urban regeneration to social inclusion. Health, education and economic growth are all potential benefits from participation and events.
>
> *(Fry, 2010, p. 48)*

Sport is promoted as a way of solving a range of social problems including long-standing ethnic conflicts. Furthermore, sport is frequently portrayed as a global good. As the commissioner of the National Football League (NFL), Roger Goodell, noted that, "Sports play such a large role in our world and should play a larger role...It brings everyone together and it is a great thing" (Roberts, 2007b, p. 96). The Monaco-based organization, Peace and Sport, has a corporate social responsibility focus while aiming to build peace-building initiatives in post-conflict areas and attracts business support couched in a particular type of rhetoric exemplified by Mikhail Prokhorov. "I and Onexim's entire senior team deeply believe in sport's massive untapped potential to make the world a better place," noted the President of Onexim Group, one of Russia's largest private investment funds, "by sponsoring Peace and Sport we could have a greater impact because its objective is to leverage sport to improve communication and education in under-privileged areas and regions afflicted by conflict and social unrest." Prokhorov added that, "this is not about return on investment. It is about helping the world to become a better place" (Glendinning, 2008, p. 71).

Furthermore, the ideology of the Olympic movement is also proselytized as an unquestionable force for good. However, even within sports business there can be some cynicism about the predictability of discourses around Olympic bids. "There are some things we can expect from each campaign. Each will develop a narrative that spells out how hosting the Olympics will have beneficial impact not only on the city itself but the host country and its region," noted Roberts in a *SportBusiness International* editorial.

> Each will be at pains to point out how hosting the Olympics will have positive results for sport and the Olympic Movement. There will be talk of a legacy of participation and

> the Games as an engine for social development. Each will find a way of staging a Games in the spirit of Olympism and each will make a film involving children.
>
> *(Roberts, 2011, p. 7)*

The relentless enthusiasm for sport articulated not just by its athletic and business participants and fans but by politicians might distract from the fact that sports business is an industry focused on wealth generation. The ability of sport to present itself as a social good raises interesting questions about the ability to raise critical perspectives about sports practice and the influence of sports business in society. However, the evidence for the claims made on behalf of sports social benefits are less clearly articulated, or indeed evidenced as pointed out by Coalter (2007).

Furthermore, some of the negative features of the sports industry, particularly of its workers – sports practitioners – are less spoken about. Examples include the virtual trafficking of talented sportsmen and women from less-developed countries to the developed world; overwork and burnout including injuries that do not heal owing to the pressure to perform; eating disorders; surgery; extreme training regimens; psychological and moral damage arising from practices such as belittling or hating opponents. "The world of child and youth and professional competitive sport is replete with dubious messages and stories about corruption and nationalistic fervour," noted Watson and White (2007). They added that the transformation of sport into more than a game involves, "fear, anxiety and the potential for experiencing a loss of identity and self-worth through failure in sport. Reports of physical and psychological abuse, especially in child and youth sport, further demonstrate the moral morass that exists" (p. 64). Sport also suffers problems of cheating, corruption, match fixing (international football) challenging the supposed integrity of sport and threatening trust relationships on which hinge its commercial viability.

Sport reflects but also shape societal patterns and flows and here again there are some fundamental issues that are not addressed or seen as largely unproblematic in the sports industry. There are strong gendered and heteronormative assumptions and discourses. The most highly paid professional sports stars are inevitably men, an imbalance that the sports media complex connives in, and justifies on the grounds that male sports are more popular. It is well documented that lesbian, gay and transgender (LGTG) sports people are less well rewarded for their abilities in terms of sponsorship and brand opportunities. It is still the case that in some sports, such as rugby, it may be hard for LGTG players to acknowledge publicly fluid identities. Furthermore, prejudice is still expressed. For example, Anna Rawson was asked by a reporter what women's golf could do to become more popular like women's tennis. The *SportBusiness International* reported:

> Rawson was familiar with the line of questioning. When she's not playing golf she makes a good living as a fashion model so her views on "sexing up" golf have an added frisson. She threw out a few suggestions but said that, on the whole, she felt things were improving. But she didn't just say that. She said that the game was shedding its "dyke" image. Mistake. The interview was quickly relayed to LPGA headquarters in the states where, a few weeks later, the then tour commissioner Caroline Bivens welcome Rawson to the LPGA by making her stand up and apologise for using "the D word.
>
> *(Gillis, 2009, pp. 16–17)*

Processes of commodification dictate that good-looking men and women will generate more income. Sports business practitioners try to talent-spot attractive performers who will be able to generate brand income regardless of their sporting talents. This is particularly the case for female sports stars who are closely assessed on looks and personality, for example, US gymnast Nastia Liukin was dubbed "Queen of Olympics Gymnastics" after winning the Beijing title. The *SportBusiness International* commented:

> Liukin has a bright future…has become the darling of many sponsors and advertisers… presented with a slew of non-sports opportunities, appearing on a variety of TV shows and magazine covers, including a shot with Maria Sharapova in New York…What Liukin has done is place herself in the realm of Mary Lou Retton, the 1984 US gymnasts gold medallist...Liukin seems to possess those same traits [bubbly personality and the gist of veracity] plus the kind of looks that Sharapova has used to attract more sponsors and endorsers than almost any other woman on the planet.
>
> *(SportBusiness International, 2008, p. 17)*

For those at the top of the lucrative sports business, care appears to be taken to promote the idea that individual motivation is nothing to do with money or meeting sports celebrities, but rather a vocation – the most common term employed in *SportBusiness International* is that of "passion" as shown by the following illustrative examples from sport business and marketing practitioners explaining their motivation for work in the sector. For example, Jeff Slack, vice president of Wasserman Media Group, noted that "I wanted to be in a field that had relevance to me and wasn't just a job but a passion" (SportBusiness International, 2006b, p. 50). John Taylor, the chair of Sports Impact, commented that, "It was a passion for sport" (SportBusiness International, 2006c, p. 58). Goodell noted:

> Nobody enjoys NFL football more than I do. I'm as passionate a fan as you'll ever find and I feel so fortunate that I am working in a business where I have a passion – the most satisfaction comes from brining NFL football to more fans. Seeing that passion that fans have makes it the greatest thing we can do.
>
> *(Roberts, 2007b, p. 96)*

Fran Saez, the vice president for Comperio Research was quoted as saying:

> My initial attraction was to the world of research and management and this is where I saw my career progressing, so to have the added bonus of a subject matter I was passionate about – sport – in my working life from day one has given me a great deal of satisfaction.
>
> *(SportBusiness International, 2006a, p. 58)*

Lastly, Mark Thomas, a motorsports executive with D/S2M Group and Vroom Motor Sports Marketing, noted that he was motivated, "purely [by] love of sport and the fact that if you could work in an industry that you have a passion for, sooner or later you will succeed" (SportBusiness International, 2008, p. 58).

While the above quotes highlight the ability to "make profit from passion", another sports business practitioner, Phillippe Blatter, President and CEO of Infront Sports and Media, highlighted the emotional and almost mystical aspects of sport:

> I believe that the business of sport is the most wonderful thing there is. We are in the business of selling dreams to millions of people. We are selling something which appeals directly to emotions and there are not many businesses where that is the case...Sport retains its share of attention and affection because it is about emotions and no matter what happens in life, people will always have emotions. Sports gives us a place where we can express them. It is something outside our everyday lives.
>
> *(Roberts, 2007a, p. 43)*

The discourse of "passion" is connected to the struggle "to capture sport's essence: its capacity for touching us in deep, mysterious and difficult-to-explain ways" (Parry, Robinson, Watson, and Nesti, 2007, p. xi). The notion of sport as a form of practice, that develops life meanings that link to communities and relationships and the expression of values transforms sport into a form of victory cult (Watson and White, 2007, p. 64). Watson and White, writing from a Christian religious perspective argue that where sport is "inflated or substituted for religion then it becomes an idol" (p. 67) and suggest that such analysis should not only take account of the good in sport, but also the evil, focusing specifically on the sin of pride and its connection to power.

Implications for practice and scholarship

Sports PR remains an under-researched area and there is ample room for empirical work including ethnographies, case studies and role and scope type studies, as well as analysis from a PR perspective of source-media relations. PR in sport demands close attention with regard to its discursive role in framing sports business as a social good with regard to conflict resolution, health and fitness, mass participation, development in addition to economic benefits. There is also a need to re-contextualize functional sports PR to take on board strategic and policy level directions of major sport organizations and consultancies, many of which are global in scale, particularly in issues management, engagement programmes and corporate social responsibility. The relationship between policy and communication in this industry and the role that PR plays in lobbying, elite formations and networks in globalized contexts could be usefully delineated as a way of understanding the extent to which PR does solely follow capital rather than ethical principles of professionalism with regard to service to society and the wider public. Those in PR practice and academia should retain a cautiousness about the sports business and not be too easily seduced by its celebrity and glamour. In short, a critical examination of PR practice in a sporting global context may be illustrative of the way in which political and economic power may retain privileged influence over discursive formations, and demonstrate that PR practice is embedded in those processes and far from independent as might be suggested by discourses of professionalism. The sports industry and the various national and international organizations remain idealistic about the power of sport to change the world, just as PR professional bodies claim that PR values can have substantial impacts on institutional and global relationships. Taken together, the rhetoric of sport and PR is ambitious, idealistic and self-justificatory, but must continue to be challenged.

References

Anderson, W. B. (2006). American v. National Football League: Using public relations to "win" a war against a monopoly. *Public Relations Review*, 32 (1), 53–7.

Anderson, W. B. (2008). Pete Rozelle: A historical review of how the NFL commissioner used public relations. *Public Relations Review*, 34 (2), 152–5.

Andrews, D. (2004). Sport in the late capitalist moment. In Slack, T. (Ed.). (2007). *The commercialisation of sport* (pp. 3–28). London: Routledge.

Beech, J., and Chadwick, S. (Eds.). (2007). *The marketing of sport*. Harlow: Pearson Education.

Benoit, W. L. (1995). *Accounts, excesses and apologies: A theory of image restoration strategies*. Albany: State University of New York.

Bowdin, G. A. J., Allen, J., O'Toole, W., Harris, R., and McDonnell, I. (2006). *Events management* (2nd ed.). Oxford: Elsevier Butterworth-Heinemann.

Boyd, J., and Stahey, M. (2008). Communitas/corporatas tensions in organizational rhetoric: Finding a balance in sports public relations. *Journal of Public Relations Research*, 20 (3), 251–70.

Boyle, R. (2006). *Sports journalism*. London: Sage.

Boyle, R., and Haynes, R. (2000). *Power play: Sport, the media and popular culture*. Harlow: Longman.

Brazeal, L. M. (2008). The image repair strategies of Terrell Owens. *Public Relations Review*, 34 (2), 145–50.

Bruce, T., and Tini, T. (2008). Unique crisis response strategies in sports public relations: Rugby league and the case for diversion. *Public Relations Review*, 34 (2), 108–15.

Coalter, F. (2007). *A wider social role for sport: Who's keeping the score?* London: Routledge.

Curtin, P., and Gaither, T. K. (2006). *International public relations: Negotiating culture, identity and power*. Thousand Oaks, CA: Sage.

Fortunato, J. (2008). Restoring a reputation: The Duke University lacrosse scandal. *Public Relations Review*, 34 (2), 116–23.

Fry, A. (2010). The right headlines. *SportBusiness International*, 154, 48.

Gillis, R. (2009). The debate goes on. *SportBusiness International*, 151, 16–17.

Glendinning, M. (2008). Peace and sport: A CSR challenge. *SportBusiness International*, 139, 71.

Haynes, R. (2005). *Media rights and intellectual property*. Edinburgh: Edinburgh University Press.

Helitzer, M. (1999). *The dream job: Sport$ publicity, promotion and marketing* (3rd ed.). Athens, OH: University Sports Press.

Hopwood, M. (2005). Public relations practice in English county cricket. *Corporate Communications: An International Journal*, 10 (3), 201–12.

Hopwood, M., Kitchin, P., and Skinner, J. (2010). *Sports public relations and communication*. Oxford: Butterworth-Heinemann.

Irwin, R. Sutton, W., and McCarthy, L. (2002). *Sport promotion and sales management*. Champaign, IL: Human Kinetics.

Jerome, A. (2008). Toward prescription: Testing the rhetoric of atonement's applicability in the athletic arena. *Public Relations Review*, 34 (2), 124–34.

Johnson, J. (1996). *Promotion for sports directors*. Champaign, IL: Human Kinetics.

L'Etang, J. (2006). Public relations and sport in promotional culture. *Public Relations Review*, 32 (4), 386–94.

L'Etang, J. (2009). Public relations and promotion of adventure sports. In B. Wheaton and J. Ormrod (Eds.), *On the edge: Leisure consumption and the representation of adventure sports* (pp. 43–70). Manchester, UK: Leisure Studies Association.

L'Etang, J. (in press). *Public relations and sport: Theory, practice and critique*. London, Sage.

L'Etang, J., and Hopwood, M. (2008). Editorial: Special issue on public relations and sport. *Public Relations Review*, 34 (2), 87–9.

Lowes, M. D. (1987). Sports pages: Case study in the manufacture of sports news for the daily press. *Sociology of Sport Journal*, 14, 143–59.

Mitrook, M., Parish, N., and Seltzer, T. (2008). From advocacy to accommodation: Case study of the Orlando Magic's public relations efforts to secure a new arena. *Public Relations Review*, 34 (2), 161–8.

Nichols, W., Moynahan, P., Hall, A., and Taylor, J. (2002). *Media relations in sport*. Morgantown, WV: Fitness Information Technology.
Neupauer, N. C. (2000). Sports information directing: A plea for help in an unknown field. In R. Heath (Ed.), *Handbook of public relations* (pp. 551–6). Thousand Oaks, CA: Sage.
Parry, J., Robinson, S., Watson, N., and Nesti, M. (2007). *Sport and spirituality: An introduction*. London: Routledge.
Pfahle, M., and Bates, B. (2008). This is not a race, this is a farce: Formula One and the Indianapolis Motor Speedway tire crisis. *Public Relations Review*, 34 (2), 135–44.
Pincus, J., Rimmer, T., Rayfield, R., and Cropp, E. (1993). Newspapers editors' perceptions of public relations: How business, news and sports editors differ. *Journal of Public Relations Research*, 5, 27–45.
Puchan, H. (2004). Living extreme: Adventure sports, media and commercialisation. *Journal of Communication Management*, 9 (2), 171–8.
Roberts, K. (2007a). Selling the dream. (2007). *SportBusiness International*, 128, 43.
Roberts, K. (2007b). Touchdown man. *Sport Business International*, 128, 96.
Roberts, K. (2011). Editorial. *SportBusiness International*, 171, 7.
Shank, M. (2002) *Sports marketing: A strategic perspective*. Upper Saddle River, NJ: Prentice Hall.
Slack, T. (Ed.). (2007). *The commercialisation of sport*. London: Routledge.
SportBusiness International. (2006a). Expanding horizons. (2006). *SportBusiness International*, 119, 58.
SportBusiness International. (2006b). Slack indulges passion. *SportBusiness International*, 110, 50.
SportBusiness International. (2006c). Taylor made for sport. *SportBusiness International*, 116, 58.
SportBusiness International. (2008a). The queen of gymnastics. *SportBusiness International*, 139, 17.
SportBusiness International. (2008b). Thomas in the driving seat as Chinese sport takes off. *SportBusiness International*, 114, 58.
Walmsley, D. (2011). Long-lasting legacy. *SportBusiness International*, 173, 39.
Watson, N. J., and White, J. (2007). Winning at all costs in modern sport: reflections on pride and humility in the writings of C. S. Lewis. In J. Parry, S. Robinson, N. Watson, and M. Nesti (Eds.), *Sport and spirituality: An introduction* (pp. 61–79). London: Routledge.
Westburg, A., Wilson, B., and Stavros, C. (2008). Player transgression and the management of the sport sponsor relationship. *Public Relations Review*, 34 (2), 99–107.
Woo, C., An, S-K., and Cho, S. (2008). Sports PR in message boards on Major League Baseball websites. *Public Relations Review*, 34 (2), 169–75.

INDEX

Tables are denoted by a 't' e.g. Real Madrid 290t.
Endnotes are denoted by an 'n' followed by the endnote number e.g. Leveson Inquiry 176n5.